FIFTH EDITION

Principles and Practice of
SPORT MANAGEMENT

Edited by

Lisa P. Masteralexis, JD

Department Head and Associate
Professor

Mark H. McCormack Department of
Sport Management

Isenberg School of Management

University of Massachusetts, Amherst

Amherst, Massachusetts

Carol A. Barr, PhD

Vice Provost for Undergraduate
and Continuing Education

University of Massachusetts,
Amherst

Amherst, Massachusetts

Mary A. Hums, PhD

Professor

Department of Health and Sport Sciences

University of Louisville

Louisville, Kentucky

JONES & BARTLETT
LEARNING

World Headquarters
Jones & Bartlett Learning
5 Wall Street
Burlington, MA 01803
978-443-5000
info@jblearning.com
www.jblearning.com

Jones & Bartlett Learning books and products are available through most bookstores and online booksellers. To contact Jones & Bartlett Learning directly, call 800-832-0034, fax 978-443-8000, or visit our website, www.jblearning.com.

Production Credits

Executive Publisher: William Brottmiller	VP, Manufacturing and Inventory Control: Therese Connell
Publisher: Cathy L. Esperti	Cover Design: Michael O'Donnell
Acquisitions Editor: Ryan Angel	Rights & Photo Research Coordinator: Ashley Dos Santos
Associate Editor: Kayla Dos Santos	Composition: Cenveo Publisher Services
Production Editor: Tina Chen	Cover Image: © Zsolt Nyulaszi/ShutterStock, Inc.
Marketing Manager: Andrea DeFronzo	Printing and Binding: Courier Companies
Art Development Editor: Joanna Lundeen	Cover Printing: Courier Companies

To order this product, use ISBN: 978-1-284-03417-2

Library of Congress Cataloging-in-Publication Data
Principles and practice of sport management / edited by Lisa P. Masteralexis, Mark H. McCormack Department of Sport Management, Isenberg School of Management, University of Massachusetts, Amherst, Amherst, Massachusetts, Carol A. Barr, University of Massachusetts, Amherst, Amherst, Massachusetts, Mary A. Hums, Department of Health and Sport Science, University of Louisville, Louisville, Kentucky.—Fifth edition.
       pages cm
   Includes index.
   ISBN 978-1-4496-9195-0
   1. Sports administration. I. Masteralexis, Lisa Pike. II. Barr, Carol A. III. Hums, Mary A.
   GV713.P75 2014
   796.06'9—dc23
                          2014009971

6048
Printed in the United States of America
18 17 16 15 14   10 9 8 7 6 5 4 3 2 1

Contents

Preface   xi
Acknowledgments   xv
Contributors   xvii

Part I: Foundations of Sport Management   1

1 History of Sport Management   3
Todd W. Crosset and Mary A. Hums

Introduction   4
The Club System: Sports and Community   5
Leagues   11
Professional Tournament Sports: Mixing Business and Charity   15
Women in Sport Management   18
The Birth of Sport Management as an Academic Field   20
Summary   22
References   23
Sport Management Time Line   24

2 Management Principles Applied to Sport Management   27
Carol A. Barr and Mary A. Hums

Introduction   28
Definition and History of Management Principles   28
Functional Areas   30
Key Skills   34
Current Issues   41
Beyond the Bottom Line   43
Summary   43
References   44

3 Marketing Principles Applied to Sport Management   49
John Clark

Introduction: What Is Sport Marketing?   50
Historical Development of Sport Marketing   50
Key Sport Marketing Concepts   56
Key Skills   62
Current Issues   63

Box 3-1   Social Media's Role in Sport Marketing: The Dick's
Sporting Goods Pittsburgh Marathon   65
Summary   68
References   69

4   Financial and Economic Principles Applied to
Sport Management   73
Neil Longley and Nola Agha

Introduction   74
Key Concepts   76
Key Skills   86
Current Issues   86
Summary   93
References   94

5   Legal Principles Applied to Sport Management   97
Lisa P. Masteralexis and Glenn M. Wong

Introduction   98
History   98
Key Concepts   99
Key Skills   121
Box 5-1   Sample List of Issues to Consider When Purchasing Equipment   122
Box 5-2   Issues to Consider When Implementing a Drug Testing Program   122
Current Issues   123
Summary   125
References   126

6   Ethical Principles Applied to Sport Management   131
Todd W. Crosset and Mary A. Hums

Introduction   132
Ethical Considerations   133
Morality   138
Key Skills   144
Summary   147
References   147

Part II: Amateur Sport Industry   149

7   High School and Youth Sport   151
Dan Covell

Introduction   152
History   153
Governance   156
Career Opportunities   158
Application of Key Principles   159

Case Study 7-1   Boarding Student-Athletes at Cardinal Ruhle Academy   166
Summary   169
Resources   169
References   170

8   Collegiate Sport   173
Carol A. Barr

Introduction   174
History   174
Organizational Structure and Governance   179
Career Opportunities   183
Current Issues   186
Summary   191
Case Study 8-1   The Role of an Athletic Director   191
Resources   193
References   194

9   International Sport   197
Mary A. Hums, Per G. Svensson, Sheranne Fairley, and Mireia Lizandra

Introduction   198
History   200
The Globalization of Sport   202
Sport for Development and Peace   207
The Olympic Movement   209
Career Opportunities   217
Current Issues   220
Summary   223
Case Study 9-1   Growing Australian Rules Football in the United States   224
Resources   225
References   226

Part III: Professional Sport Industry   229

10   Professional Sport   231
Lisa P. Masteralexis

Introduction   232
History   234
Key Concepts   244
Career Opportunities   249
Current Issues   253
Summary   255
Case Study 10-1   Is the NFL Conduct Policy Working?   256
Resources   258
References   260

11 Sports Agency   265
Lisa P. Masteralexis

Introduction   266
History   269
Sports Agency Firms   278
Career Opportunities   282
Current Issues   292
Case Study 11-1   King Sport Management   297
Summary   300
Resources   300
References   302

Part IV: Sport Industry Support Segments   **307**

12 Facility Management   309
Mary A. Hums and Lisa P. Masteralexis

Introduction   310
History   310
Types of Public Assembly Facilities   312
Types of Events   314
Facility Financing   316
Why Cities Subsidize Sports Facilities   319
Facility Ownership and Management Staff   320
Facility Marketing   320
Career Opportunities   324
Current Issues   328
Case Study 12-1   The Booking Process in a University Venue   332
Summary   333
Resources   333
References   334

13 Event Management   337
Carol A. Barr

Introduction   338
History   338
Sport Management/Marketing Agency Functions   339
Types of Sport Management/Marketing Agencies   341
Critical Event Management Functions   341
Career Opportunities   351
Current Issues   352
Case Study 13-1   Planning for a New Event   354
Summary   355
Resources   355
References   357

14 Sport Sales   359
    Stephen McKelvey

    Introduction   360
    History   360
    Sales in the Sport Setting   362
    Sales Strategies and Methods   362
    Key Skills: What Makes a Good Salesperson?   368
    Sales Inventory   369
    Case Study 14-1   The Outsourcing of College Ticket Sales Operations   374
    Summary   377
    Resources   379
    References   379

15 Sport Sponsorship   381
    Stephen McKelvey

    Introduction   382
    A Brief History of Sport Sponsorship   382
    Sales Promotion in Sport Sponsorship   385
    Sponsorship Packages   390
    Sport Sponsorship Platforms   392
    Evaluating Sport Sponsorships   397
    Sponsorship Agencies   398
    Issues in Sport Sponsorship   398
    Case Study 15-1   Introducing . . . The FedEx, I Mean, the
        Discover Orange Bowl!   401
    Summary   404
    Resources   405
    References   406

16 Sport Communications   409
    Gregory Bouris

    Introduction   410
    History of Sport Communication   412
    Key Topics   413
    Preparing for the Interview   422
    Career Opportunities   427
    Current Issues   430
    Case Study 16-1   Communications Strategies for the Cricket League   431
    Summary   432
    Resources   432
    References   433

17 Sport Broadcasting   435
    Jim Noel

    Introduction   436
    History of Sport Broadcasting   436

The Business of Sport Broadcasting   446
International Sport Coverage   452
Current Issues   453
Career Opportunities   455
Case Study 17-1   The Dominance of ESPN   457
Resources   459
References   461

18 The Sporting Goods and Licensed Products Industries   467
    Dan Covell

Introduction   468
History of Sporting Goods and Apparel   470
Industry Structure   473
Career Opportunities   474
Application of Key Principles   476
Summary   482
Case Study 18-1   Less Is More   483
Resources   485
References   486

Part V: Lifestyle Sports   **489**

19 Golf and Club Management   491
    Jo Williams

Introduction   492
History   492
Types of Clubs   494
Club Organizational Structure   497
Golf and Country Club Industry Performance   499
Managing and Leading in a Course Club Setting   503
Professional Staff Positions in a Private Golf Club   506
Strategies for Entering Golf Management and Club Operations   509
Current and Future Issues for Golf and Club Management   510
Box 19-1   Shared Principles on Sustainability   514
Summary   515
Case Study 19-1   To Host or Not to Host?   516
Resources   517
References   518

20 Recreational Sport   521
    Tara Q. Mahoney

Introduction   522
History   522
Trends in Participation   524

Segments of the Recreation Industry   526
Career Opportunities   529
Current Issues   531
Summary   536
Case Study 20-1   Collegiate University Embracing Technology   536
Resources   538
References   539

Part VI: Career Preparation   **543**

21 Strategies for Career Success   545
    Mary A. Hums and Virginia R. Goldsbury

    Introduction   546
    Myths About Careers in Sport Management: A Reality Check   546
    Finding a Job   549
    Informational Interviewing   552
    Marketing Yourself   553
    Summary   562
    References   562

    Glossary   563
    About the Authors   583
    Index   589

Preface

As the sport industry evolves at a dramatic rate, the goal of providing a comprehensive, current, and concise introductory textbook on sport management becomes a challenging task. Yet, we have attempted to do just that, in providing our readers (students, professors, and practitioners alike) with this fifth edition of *Principles and Practice of Sport Management*.

This is a textbook intended for use in introductory sport management courses. The focus of these courses, and this textbook, is to provide an overview of the sport industry and cover basic fundamental knowledge and skill sets of the sport manager, as well as to provide information on sport industry segments for potential job employment and career choices.

Directed toward undergraduate students, the textbook has three distinct sections:

- Part I provides an overview of basic knowledge areas for the successful sport manager, presenting fundamental principles and key skills as well as information on current issues.
- Parts II through V present overviews of major sport-industry segments in which a sport manager could work, followed by case studies intended to spark debate and discussion.
- Part VI provides the reader with the basics of breaking into the highly competitive sport management industry.

Where appropriate, we have included an international perspective to give readers a broad view of sport management in the global context, which they will need as the world grows increasingly "smaller" in the decades to come. We would like to draw special attention to *Chapter 9, International Sport*, which guides the reader through the global "sportscape" by examining the burgeoning sport industry around the world. The chapter makes the point the reader should not confuse "globalization" of sport with the "Americanization" of global sport.

New to this Edition

This *Fifth Edition* is full of current data and information, and offers a mix of contributions from scholars and practitioners. Based on feedback from faculty using the text, each chapter has undergone review and revision, and chapter authors have been attentive to providing new material and updated information, such as:

- Social media's prevalence today and its usage, role, and impact on sport.
- Sport safety concerns, with a focus on the attention concussions are receiving from youth sports to professional sports and the NFL.

- New! Managerial, legal, and ethical implications of the case involving Jerry Sandusky, the former assistant football coach at Penn State University who was convicted of sexual misconduct involving minors. This case is discussed in several chapters as it is important for the student and future sport manager to understand.

Additional updates include the following:

- **Chapter Learning Objectives:** Revised to correspond with Bloom's taxonomy and are now included in the text.
- **Chapter 8, Collegiate Sport:** Reflects a proliferation of changes in conference affiliations within college athletics.
- **Chapter 9, International Sport:** Includes a new section on the emerging area of Sport for Development and Peace whereby managers use sport as a tool to address social issues in communities worldwide.
- **Chapter 12, Facility Management:** Covers information on new standards being applied in the building of sport facilities including LEED (Leadership in Energy and Environmental Design) certification and Universal Design which extends the Americans with Disabilities Act and makes facilities more accessible for all people.
- **Chapter 13, Event Management:** Explores the complexity of event security brought on by the 2013 Boston Marathon bombings.
- **Chapter 16, Sport Communications:** Expanded to include a section on new media including the use of YouTube, Twitter, and Facebook in the sport industry.
- **Chapter 18, The Sporting Goods and Licensed Products Industries:** Includes a case study on New Balance in the sporting goods industry and how it employed a sustainable growth approach.
- **Chapter 19, Golf and Club Management:** Addresses the new challenges that managers face which include declining demand, changes in lifestyles and family expectations, the need for sustainability, and technological advances.
- **Chapter 21, Strategies for Career Success:** Includes a new section on "The Elevator Speech" that provides instruction on how to prepare for meeting potential employers in informal settings in the course of looking for employment.

Overall, this textbook allows the reader to learn both the foundations and the principles on which sport management operates and offers an opportunity to apply those foundations and principles to the sport industry. This textbook offers historical perspectives as well as thoughts about current and future industry issues and trends. For all these reasons, this textbook will prove a valuable resource to those seeking employment in the sport management field, as well as those whose role it is to educate future sport managers.

Resources for Instructors

As with previous editions, this edition offers instructors a wealth of resources to aid in the teaching of this material. These include:

* Expanded Test Banks
* Lecture outlines in PowerPoint format
* Midterm
* Final

Resources for Students

This edition also includes abundant resources for students to practice and self-test their knowledge of the text. These include:

* Interactive Glossary
* Interactive Flashcards
* Web Links
* Case Studies
* Practice Activities
* Interactive eBook

Acknowledgments

We would like to acknowledge the efforts of some individuals without whom this text would not be possible. First and foremost, we express our deep appreciation to our contributing authors. Each author contributed his or her valuable expertise and experience to create a work that provides a wealth of knowledge to the sport management student. Through the editorial process, we have gained from them a greater understanding of the sport industry and our introductory sport management curriculum.

We have made some changes to the chapters and contributing authors since the last edition of this book. You should note we have left some chapter contributors' names from the previous editions to note the significance of the material carried over from those editions to this *Fifth Edition*. We would like to thank those authors who did not participate in this edition, but who contributed to previous editions and whose original work may still be included in this *Fifth Edition*. These contributors over the years and previous editions of this textbook include: Stephen Bromage, William A. Sutton, Dennis R. Howard, Berend Rubingh, Adri Broeke, James M. Gladden, Michael Graney, Kevin Barrett, Mark A. McDonald, Howard M. Davis, Tim Ashwell, William Howland, Laurie Guillion, Virginia R. Goldsbury, Timothy D. DeSchriver, Nancy Beauchamp, Robert Newman, Andrew McGowan, Betsy Goff, Tracy Schoenadel, Troy Flynn, Kevin Filo, Rod Warnick, Sheranne Fairley, and Mireia Lizandra.

Reviewers

We also thank those faculty members who have adopted *Principles and Practice of Sport Management* for their classes and whose feedback we have incorporated into this edition. Specifically, we thank the reviewers of the *Fifth Edition*:

Dr. Ezzeldin R. Aly, Graceland University

Dr. Kevin Ayers, Radford University

Gary M. Bernstein, University of Louisville

Scott Bukstein, University of Central Florida

Willie J. Burden, Ed.D., Georgia Southern University

Dr. Leigh Ann Danzey-Bussell, Ball State University

Terence L. Holmes, Murray State University

Shane Hudson, Texas A&M University

Jaime Orejan, Winston–Salem State University

Nancy C. Price, Alabama A&M University

Kathryn Shea, Springfield College

We also thank everyone at Jones & Bartlett Learning for their efforts in seeing this project through. Their enthusiasm for the text was a wonderful motivation for tackling the *Fifth Edition*. Finally, we thank graduate students Alicia Cintron and Jin Park from the University of Louisville who provided great help through the editorial process.

Contributors

Editors

Lisa P. Masteralexis, JD
Department Head and Associate Professor
Mark H. McCormack Department of Sport
  Management
Isenberg School of Management
University of Massachusetts, Amherst
Amherst, Massachusetts

Carol A. Barr, PhD
Vice Provost for Undergraduate and
  Continuing Education
University of Massachusetts, Amherst
Amherst, Massachusetts

Mary A. Hums, PhD
Professor and Coordinator of the Sport
  Administration PhD Program
Department of Health and Sport Science
University of Louisville
Louisville, Kentucky

Chapter Authors

Nola Agha, PhD
Assistant Professor
Sport Management Program
University of San Francisco
San Francisco, California

Gregory Bouris
Director of Communications
Major League Baseball Players Association
New York, New York

John S. Clark, PhD
Professor and Director of the MBA Program
School of Business
Robert Morris University
Moon Township, Pennsylvania

Dan Covell, PhD
Professor
Sport Management
College of Business
Western New England University
Springfield, Massachusetts

Todd W. Crosset, PhD
Associate Professor and Director of the
  Undergraduate Program
Mark H. McCormack Department of Sport
  Management
Isenberg School of Management
University of Massachusetts, Amherst
Amherst, Massachusetts

Neil Longley, PhD
Professor
Mark H. McCormack Department of Sport
  Management
Isenberg School of Management
University of Massachusetts, Amherst
Amherst, Massachusetts

Tara Q. Mahoney, PhD
Assistant Professor
Sport Management Department
State University of New York College
  at Cortland
Cortland, New York

Stephen M. McKelvey, JD
Associate Professor and Graduate Program
  Director
Mark H. McCormack Department of
  Sport Management
Isenberg School of Management
University of Massachusetts, Amherst
Amherst, Massachusetts

Contributors

Jim Noel, JD
Practicing Attorney

Per G. Svensson
Doctoral Fellow
Department of Health and Sport Sciences
University of Louisville
Louisville, Kentucky

Jo Williams, PhD
Associate Professor and Department Chair
School of Business
University of Southern Maine
Portland, Maine

Glenn M. Wong, JD
Professor
Mark H. McCormack Department of
    Sport Management
Isenberg School of Management
University of Massachusetts, Amherst
Amherst, Massachusetts

Part I

Foundations of Sport Management

Chapter 1   History of Sport Management

Chapter 2   Management Principles Applied to Sport Management

Chapter 3   Marketing Principles Applied to Sport Management

Chapter 4   Financial and Economic Principles Applied to Sport Management

Chapter 5   Legal Principles Applied to Sport Management

Chapter 6   Ethical Principles Applied to Sport Management

Chapter 1

Todd W. Crosset and
Mary A. Hums

History of Sport Management

Learning Objectives

Upon completion of this chapter, students should be able to:

1. Demonstrate knowledge of the roots of our modern sport management structures and how most have grown in response to broader social or sport industry changes.

2. Evaluate the impact of different cultures on sport and the unique contribution of American management to the development of sport.

3. Assess the methods that successful sport managers developed in the late twentieth and early twenty-first century that promoted honesty.

4. Appraise the effect that the many "honesty crises" (e.g., Black Sox scandal or NCAA college basketball gambling scandal of 1951) have had on the sport industry.

5. Assess the historic tension in American sport between democratic ideals and race, class, and gender segregation, and how in the context of American society, these limitations were used to promote social divisions.

6. Estimate the effects of exclusionary practices such age limits, performance criteria, or geographical/citizenship criteria that teams and leagues impose on their membership.

7. Recognize that aristocrats in eighteenth-century England, who held thoroughbred races, formed jockey clubs, and allowed the masses to be spectators can be viewed as precursors to modern sport managers.

8. Identify the reasons why American baseball and the Olympics have their roots in English culture.

9. Compare and contrast the ways in which unique "American" culture resulted in sport structures that differed from European models, and how harness racing, professional baseball, and professional golf tours in the United States developed differently from each other and from European models.

10. Assess the important role that women have had in the growth of the sport industry.

11. Value the need that sport organizations have for trained sport managers, and how this need grew from a cooperative idea between practitioners and academics.

12. Recognize that academic sport management programs exist around the world, and that although these programs may share similar curricular topics (e.g., sport marketing or sport law), each country trains its sport management students in a manner appropriate for its domestic sport industry.

13. Describe the role of NASSM and COSMA in the growth of sport management research and education.

Introduction

The contemporary sport industry is complex and has unique legal, business, and management practices. As a result, many of the ways this industry is organized are unique, too. The organization of sport has developed over the past 150 or so years and continues to evolve. Most recently, for example, sport managers have been tinkering with structures such as conference alignments, drafts, and playoff systems.

This chapter explores the roots of our modern **sport management structures**. The management structures of sport reviewed in this chapter are **clubs**, **leagues**, and **professional tournaments**. These structures help managers organize sport and are the basic building blocks of many of our sports today. The chapter also addresses the development of the sport management academic discipline, which evolved as the need for trained sport management professionals became apparent.

The primary theme of this chapter is that sport management structures grow in response to broad social changes and/or to address specific issues within a segment of the sport industry. The evolution of these structures illustrates that sport managers need to be creative in the ways they run their sport organizations. One "catch-all" management structure will not work for all situations. History suggests that successful sport managers are flexible and adapt to broader changes in society. This chapter also gives a few examples of innovative and successful sport managers.

Many events have shaped the world of sport and the sport industry. While it is nearly impossible to create a time line that hits all the highlights, one is included at the end of this chapter for your reference. The time line includes the founding dates of many sport organizations as well as a number of "firsts" in the sport industry in terms of events. Try thinking about events or people you would add to this time line—it is a good conversation starter!

Two secondary themes run throughout this brief examination of the history of sport management structures: honesty and inclusion. The legitimacy of modern sport demands honest play, or at least the appearance of honest play. Nothing in sport is more reviled than the athlete who does not try. An athlete who does not exert an honest effort is a spoilsport. Players who throw games are sellouts. So critical is the perception of an honest effort that sport managers will ban people from their sport for life if they tarnish the game by the mere possibility they bet on their team to lose (e.g., Pete Rose).

The appearance of an honest effort is one of the most important precepts organizing modern sport. It is more important, for example, than fair play or equality of competition. Although there are structures that level the playing field (e.g., drafts, salary caps), disparities among teams remain, giving some teams advantages over others. The public is much more tolerant of players breaking the rules when trying to win than it is of players throwing games. The public's notion of what ensures an honest effort also changes over time. One issue addressed throughout this chapter is how sport managers have changed or adapted sport to ensure the appearance of honesty as broader structures have changed.

Another issue this chapter explores is the tension between democratic inclusiveness and the regulation of participation. The desire to create a meritocracy is implicit in modern sport—if you are good enough, you should play. This is illustrated nicely by the slogan and campaign, "If you can play…you can play" (You Can Play Project, 2013). But, by necessity, any form of organized sport includes rules limiting who is allowed to participate. For example, most contemporary sports leagues or teams have age and gender requirements. International governing bodies, as well as local leagues, have citizenship and residency requirements.

Athletes who have just moved to a new nation or town are sometimes excluded from participating in sports.

Answering the questions "Who gets to play?", "Who is encouraged to watch?", and "Who is left out?" requires both an understanding of sport-specific issues and broader social issues. When it comes to who gets to play, what seems "fair" at a particular juncture in history often reflects broader social beliefs. For example, not long ago it would have been unthinkable for girls to play little league baseball or for women to compete against men on the Professional Golfers' Association (PGA) tour. Although it is still unusual, women have competed in PGA tournaments. Michelle Wie has played against men in 14 tournaments, including eight PGA TOUR events. Both Wie and Si Re Pak have made the cut in Asian men's competitions as well.

Historically, the groups with the most power in a society define the limits of participation, usually to their benefit. Sport in the first half of the twentieth century, for example, developed along with the eugenics movement, legal racial segregation, and an ideology of white racial superiority in the United States and South Africa. For many generations, mainstream sport structures in the United States and South Africa either excluded or limited participation by people of color. These structures reflected and promoted an ideology of white racial superiority.

Notions of what makes for honest play and who should be allowed to play or watch sport change over time. Sport managers have adapted sport to reflect changes in the broader society.

The Club System: Sports and Community

England is the birthplace of modern sport and sport management (Mandell, 1984). The roots of most Western sports, including track and field,

all the variations of football, and stick-and-ball games such as baseball, field hockey, and cricket, can be traced to England. The broad influence of England's sporting culture is the result of the British Empire's imperial power in the eighteenth and nineteenth centuries. Britain had colonies all over the world and took her sports to all of them.

The continuing influence of the British sports tradition after the empire's demise has as much to do with how the English organized sport as it does with England's political and cultural domination. Even sports that originated outside England, such as basketball, gymnastics, and golf, initially adopted English sport organizational structures.

In the eighteenth century, the English aristocracy, made up of nobles and the landed gentry, began to develop sports clubs. Membership in these clubs was limited to the politically and economically powerful of English society. The earliest clubs simply organized one-time events or annual competitions and brought members together for social events. By the nineteenth century, clubs standardized rules, settled disputes between clubs, and organized seasons of competitions.

Thoroughbred racing was one of the first sports transformed by the club management system. Other English sports, such as cricket, rugby union, and soccer, also adopted a similar club management structure. The focus here is on thoroughbred racing simply because it is the earliest example of club management.

Thoroughbred Racing

Early races were local events, often associated with holidays or horse sales. By the mid-eighteenth century, thoroughbred racing and breeding had established a broad following among the English aristocracy. Local groups of breeders organized races. Horse owners arranged the events, put up purses, and invited participants to show off their best horses and demonstrate their prestige.

At this time horse racing was managed on a local level. The organization was essentially a volunteer system of management, controlled by the same wealthy men who owned the horses and estates. Despite the extreme stratification of eighteenth-century English society, horse races drew a broad and diverse audience. All levels of society attended races. The owners, the elite of the community, in keeping with tradition and meeting their social obligation to entertain the masses, did not charge admission.

Even though horse races were important for demonstrating prestige, they were rarely the primary business interest of the horse owners who controlled the sport. Consequently, seventeenth-century horse racing and sport remained largely separate from the growing capitalist economy. Horse racing existed primarily for the entertainment of wealthy club members and did not have to be an independent, self-supporting financial entity. This system gave horse racing the appearance of honesty. The public believed that the aristocracy—men of breeding, culture, and wealth—would not be tempted by bribes, influenced by petty feuds, or swayed to make unfair decisions.

The local club system governed the sport successfully as long as racing remained local. Soon, however, two factors combined to create a need for more systematic management: (1) the desire of owners to breed and train the fastest horses in England and (2) the increasing complexity of gambling.

As the elite gained prestige for owning the fastest horses, horses were bred for no other purpose than to win races. Speed was appreciated for its own sake, distinct from its religious, military, or economic purpose—a uniquely modern phenomenon (Mandell, 1984). Races usually consisted of a series of 4-mile heats. The ideal horse combined speed with endurance.

By the 1830s rail transportation enabled owners to compete nationally. Local-level management governing area breeders, owners, and jockeys had worked well because of the familiarity among all involved, but national competition meant race organizers now managed participants they did not know very well, if at all. Thus, the management of thoroughbred racing needed to become more systematic.

Gambling on thoroughbred horse races was common among all classes. Much as speed became appreciated for its own merits, betting on thoroughbred races began to be appreciated for its own value. Gambling not only provided exciting entertainment but also provided bettors with tangible evidence of their knowledge of horses and ability to predict who would win (Mandell, 1984).

Gambling also ensured honest competition. The crowd policed the jockeys. At that time, horse racing was a head-to-head competition. Races were a series of 4-mile runs. The winning horse had to win two out of three races. If the crowd suspected a jockey had allowed the other contestant to win, the crowd would punish that jockey, often physically.

By the eighteenth century, innovations to the sport designed to draw larger audiences and enhance the ways spectators could wager also made the gambling system more complex. The English created handicapping, tip sheets, and sweepstakes; used the stopwatch to time races; standardized race distances; and added weights to horses. All of these innovations enhanced the public's interest in the sport. As the influence and importance of gambling grew and the systems of weights and handicapping leveled the playing field, the opportunity for a "fixed" race to go undetected also increased. All the enhancements and innovations made it difficult for the audience to detect when and how races were fixed. As a result, conventional methods could not be counted on to adequately police the sport (Henriches, 1991).

The Jockey Club: The Birth of Club Governance

The roots of the management system in thoroughbred racing can be traced to around 1750, when a group of noble patrons in Newmarket established the **Jockey Club**. This group's responsibilities were to settle disputes, establish rules, determine eligibility, designate officials, regulate breeding, and punish unscrupulous participants. The club organized, sponsored, and promoted local events (Vamplew, 1989). Like other local clubs, members of the Newmarket Jockey Club put up the purse money and restricted entries to thoroughbreds owned by club members.

The effective organization and management of thoroughbred racing in Newmarket made it a national hub for the sport. Local champions faced challenges from owners outside their region. The Jockey Club sponsored prestigious races that attracted horse owners from across England. As the need grew for a strong national governing body to establish rules and standards and to create a mechanism for resolving disputes, the Jockey Club from Newmarket emerged to serve those functions (Henriches, 1991).

Some of the lasting contributions the Jockey Club made to racing included sponsoring a stud book listing the lineage of thoroughbreds, helping ensure the purity of the breed; promoting a series of race schedules; announcing, regulating, and reporting on horse sales; and restricting the people involved with thoroughbred breeding and racing to the English elite. The Jockey Club served as a model for wider sport management practices in England.

Cricket, boxing, and other English sports adopted the management and organizational structures developed in thoroughbred horse racing. In each case, one club emerged as the coordinating and controlling body of the sport, not out of a formal process but by collective prominence. The Marylebone Cricket Club, for example, revised the rules of cricket in 1788 and became the international governing club for the entire sport (Williams, 1989). In 1814, the Pugilist Society was formed by a group of gentlemen to regulate bare-knuckle boxing and guarantee purses. Even sports such as association football (soccer) and rugby, which were organized much later, adopted the club organizational structure (Henriches, 1991).

Club structure depended on the appearance of fairness, loyal support, and volunteer management for its success. The aristocrats who managed and sponsored sport were presumed to be honest and disinterested, giving spectators the sense that competition was fair. Fairness was cultivated through the reputation of sport organizers and their nonprofit motives. Loyalty to specific clubs was cultivated through membership.

The Modern Olympic Games: An International Club Event

The club structure is also the foundation for the **modern Olympic Games**. Indeed, the early Games can be viewed as an international club event. Created at the peak of the club system, the modern Olympic Games resemble international club events much more than they do the ancient Games for which they are named. The ancient Games, at least initially, were part of a larger religious ceremony and were initially only for the viewing of, and participation by, free, able-bodied, male Greek citizens. These Games existed for 1,169 years and over time became an international gathering of athletes. The Games were discontinued in AD 393, although they were held in some form until AD 521 (Ministry of Culture–General Secretariat for Sports, 1998). Almost 15 centuries passed

before the international Olympic Games were revived in another form.

Although 1896 marked the first official staging of the modern Olympic Games, Olympic-like festivals and revivals had been organized on a local level in England much earlier. The most important in the revival of the Games was the annual festival at Much Wenlock, Shropshire, started in 1850 by Dr. William Penny Brookes. As a logical extension of his annual games, Brookes organized the Shropshire Olympian Association in 1861, which led to the founding of the National Olympian Association four years later (Young, 1996).

The current International Olympic Committee's founding conference for the modern Olympic Games was held in 1894. **Pierre de Coubertin**, a young French physical educator who was influenced by Brookes' vision of an international Olympic Games, Professor William Sloane of Princeton University, and Charles Herbert, Secretary of the (British) Amateur Athletics Association, were the initiating forces behind this meeting, which they dubbed an "international athletic congress." More than 70 attendees representing 37 amateur athletic clubs and associations from at least a dozen different nations attended the congress. The primary focus of the congress was the meaning and application of amateurism. De Coubertin, inspired by the English Olympic

revivals, chivalry, Victorian notions of character development through sport, and the notion of an international peace movement, argued for an Olympic-like festival at the meeting. These Games, he suggested, would be held every four years, in rotating sites, and participants would need to be chivalrous athletes—men who competed with grace and for the honor of their club and country. He proposed that the first Games be held in Paris in 1900. So receptive were the attendees that they voted to convene the Olympic Games earlier, in 1896 in Athens, Greece.

The first modern Olympic Games were a nine-day event and drew 311 athletes from 13 nations. The participants were exclusively amateurs. Most entrants were college students or athletic club members, because the concept of national teams had not yet emerged. Clubs such as the Boston Athletic Association, the Amateur Athletic Association, and the German Gymnastics Society sent the largest delegations. Spectators filled the newly built Panathinaiko Stadium to watch the Games, which featured nine sports: cycling, fencing, gymnastics, lawn tennis, shooting, swimming, track and field, weight lifting, and wrestling (Ministry of Culture–General Secretariat for Sports, 1998). For several Olympic Games following (Paris, St. Louis), the event floundered. The Games did not hit solid footing until, not surprisingly, London hosted them in 1908.

The Club Structure Today

Many contemporary sports and events have organizational roots in the club sport system. These include U.S. collegiate athletics and European football. Although the club system for the organization of elite sports is fading in some places, it is still a popular way to organize sport and recreation.

Some clubs remain committed to serving their broad membership and managing an elite sports enterprise. Many European football clubs and the Augusta National Golf Club, host of the Masters Golf Tournament, are examples of contemporary club governance. Larger clubs such as Olympiakos or Panathinaikos in Athens, Greece, provide recreation for members in addition to managing their high-profile teams or events. Clubs often organize youth teams and academies, adult recreational leagues, and social events such as dinners and dances for their members. Some club sports, like association football in Europe, have large built-in memberships and loyal fan bases and consequently rarely have a problem attracting crowds for their matches.

Once the dominant management structure of elite sport, the club system is slowly being replaced by other sport management structures. Clearly, the Olympic Games have changed dramatically from the early days; they now resemble the tournament structure which will be discussed later in this chapter. Probably the most dramatic change was the decision to allow professional athletes to play in the Games. Beginning in the 1970s, amateurism requirements were gradually phased out of the Olympic Charter. After the 1988 Games, the International Olympic Committee (IOC) decided that professional athletes would be eligible to compete at the Olympic Games. Without amateurism, the last remaining vestige of chivalious, fair, and clean sport is the IOC's rigorous drug testing of athletes.

European football, once the prime example of the club system, is changing, too. It looks more and more like the league structure described later in this chapter. A major change occurred in 1995 when the European Court of Justice ruled in favor of Jean-Marc Bosman, a professional player who argued that his Belgian team was restraining free trade when it refused to grant him a transfer to another club. This opened up the market for the movement of talented soccer players. Now elite European club teams such as Manchester United, Real Madrid, and Olympiakos are increasingly controlled by wealthy individuals, pay handsome salaries for the best players, and operate like entertainment/sport businesses (King, 1997).

Clubs are also no longer local in nature. Today's large clubs feature players from all over the world. For example, in the 2010 World Cup, members of the French soccer team played for clubs in a number of different countries, not just clubs in France. A look at the roster of the Real Madrid team lists players from not only Spain but also Brazil, Germany, and Argentina.

The emerging European sport management system has its roots in the U.S. professional sport league system that appeared in the nineteenth century. The league system in the United States developed when the English club system proved poorly suited to the economic and cultural atmosphere of nineteenth-century United States.

Sport Structures in the United States: Sport Clubs Adapt to a Different Culture

Courtesy of Library of Congress Prints and Photographs Division, FSA-OWI Collection [LCUSF34-055212-D DLC]

In the early 1800s, upper-class sports enthusiasts in the United States attempted to develop sports along the lines of the English club system but had only limited success. The wealthy elite formed clubs throughout the nineteenth century, complete with volunteer management, but these clubs were not able to establish a place in U.S. culture the way clubs had in England and throughout Europe.

Whereas European clubs emphasized sport to attract large and broad memberships, the most prestigious clubs in the United States were primarily social clubs that did not sponsor

sporting events. Athletic clubs, such as the New York Athletic Club, did not gain prestige until late in the century when the profit-oriented league system had already established a foothold in the cultural landscape of the United States (Gorn & Goldstein, 1993).

Nineteenth-century thoroughbred horse racing in the United States, although occasionally wildly popular, repeatedly fell on hard times. One obstacle to the club system in the United States was the country's lack of the aristocratic tradition that had given the club system both its means of support and its legitimacy in Europe. Another was the political power of religious fundamentalism, which periodically limited or prohibited gambling.

Out of the shadow of the struggling thoroughbred horse racing scene, a uniquely American sport developed: harness racing. The league structure, which dominates sport in the United States, grew out of the success and failure of harness racing in the 1830s and 1840s. As such, it is worthwhile understanding this transition between clubs and leagues.

Harness Racing: The First National Pastime and Professional Sport

Nineteenth-century harness racing was the sport of the common person, an early precursor of stock car racing. In the 1820s, the horse and buggy was not only commonplace, it was the preferred mode of transportation of a growing middle class. Many early harness races took place on hard-packed city streets, and anyone with a horse and buggy could participate. The sport was more inclusive than thoroughbred horse racing. The horses pulling the buggies were of no particular breeding. It was relatively inexpensive to own and maintain a horse, and horses that worked and pulled wagons by day raced in the evening (Adelman, 1986).

As the popularity of informal harness races grew, enterprising racing enthusiasts staged races on the oval tracks built for thoroughbred racing. Track owners—whose business was suffering—were eager to rent their tracks to harness racers. Promoters began to offer participants purse money raised through modest entry fees and paid track owners rent by charging admission (Adelman, 1986).

The nineteenth-century middle class in the United States, including artisans, shopkeepers, dockworkers, clerks, and the like, was far more likely to participate in this sport than were wealthy merchants. Because harness racing lacked the elitist tradition of horse racing, the public believed the sport was its own and was more willing to pay admission to subsidize the events. Promoters counted on spectator interest, and participation grew. By the 1830s, harness racing surpassed thoroughbred racing as the most popular sport in the United States (Adelman, 1986).

Although harness racing was not always as dramatic as thoroughbred racing, it was a better spectator sport. A traditional horse racing event was a 4-mile race. The races were so grueling that horses raced only once or twice a year. Consequently, it was difficult for individual horses to develop a reputation or following among fans. In contrast, harness racing was a sprint. Horses recovered quickly and could compete almost daily. Promoters offered spectators as many as a dozen races in an afternoon. Horses of any breed could race, ensuring a large field of competitors. These dynamics gave the public more races, excitement, and opportunities to gamble (Adelman, 1986).

The management structure of harness racing was also distinct from thoroughbred racing. Track owners and race promoters managed the sport. Unlike members of Jockey Clubs, these entrepreneurs' livelihood depended on gate revenues, and therefore they catered to spectators. Ideally, promoters tried to match the best horses against each other to build spectator interest.

This desire for intense competition, however, created problems for harness racing promoters. Potential contestants often tried to increase their chances of victory by avoiding races with other highly touted trotters. To ensure a high level of competition and "big name" competitors, innovative promoters began to offer the owners of the best and most famous trotters a percentage of the gate (Adelman, 1986).

Unfortunately, this arrangement led some participants and promoters to fix races in an effort to promote and create demand for future races. Highly regarded trotters traded victories in order to maintain spectator interest. Harness races were sometimes choreographed dramas. This practice violated the notion of honesty critical to a sport's success. Once the word got out that some races were fixed, harness racing lost its appeal with the public. Unlike members of the Jockey Club, harness racing promoters and participants lacked the upright reputation to convince the public that their races were legitimate. Ultimately, spectators lost faith in the integrity of the sport, and the race promoters, no matter how honest, lacked the legitimacy to convince the public otherwise. By the start of the Civil War, harness racing had lost its appeal and its audience (Adelman, 1986).

Leagues

Harness racing's popularity and commercial promise led sport enthusiasts and managers to further refine and develop a sport management system that would work in the United States. The result was the profit-oriented league, which baseball organizers pioneered in the 1870s. Baseball was the first sport to successfully employ the league structure.

William Hulbert's National League

At first, baseball was organized according to the club system. Club leaders organized practices, rented field time, and invited other clubs to meet and play. Loosely organized leagues formed, encouraged parity of competition, and regulated competition between social equals. For example, the famous early team known as the Knickerbockers played games in Hoboken, New Jersey, to ensure they competed only against upper-class teams who could afford the ferry ride over and back from New York.

Only the best teams, such as the Cincinnati Red Stockings of 1869–1870, were able to sustain fan interest. This Cincinnati team of 1869 was the first openly all-professional team. The Red Stockings' road trips to play Eastern teams drew thousands of fans and earned enough to pay the team's travel expenses and player salaries. Then after two seasons of flawless play, the team lost three games at the end of the 1870 season. Despite the Red Stockings' impressive record, they were no longer considered champions, and their popularity fell along with revenue. The team disbanded prior to the next season (Seymour, 1960).

In the late 1860s and early 1870s, a rift developed along social/class lines. Teams that paid their players a salary were in conflict with teams that did not. The business elite in local communities managed both types of clubs, but there were subtle and growing class and ethnic differences among the participants.

In 1871, a group of professional baseball teams formed the **National Association of Professional Baseball Players** and split off from the amateur club system. Any club willing to pay its elite players could join. The league, like other club sports, still depended on the patronage of its well-off members and consequently lacked stability. Members managed and participated in sporting activities haphazardly, and the break-even financial interests of individual clubs carried more authority than any association of clubs. It was common for teams to form, fall apart, and re-form within a season (Adelman, 1986; Leifer, 1995; Seymour, 1960).

In 1876, **William Hulbert** took over management of the National Association and renamed the body the **National League of Professional Baseball Players**. Hulbert became known as the "Czar of Baseball" for his strong leadership of the game and his role as a major figure in the development of sport management in the United States. He believed baseball teams would become stable only if they were owned and run like businesses. Teams, like other firms, should compete against one another and not collude (secretly work together), as was the case in harness racing. Hulbert called the owners of the best baseball clubs in the National Association to a meeting in New York City. When they emerged from the meeting, the groundwork had been laid for the new National League of Professional Baseball Players. The initial members of the league were from Boston, Chicago, Cincinnati, Hartford, Louisville, New York, Philadelphia, and St. Louis (Abrams, 1998).

Hulbert also understood that unless there were strict rules to ensure honest competition, baseball team owners would be tempted by collusion. For the National League to succeed, authority needed to rest with the league, not with a loose association of teams. Hulbert revamped the management of baseball to center on a league structure and created strong rules to enforce teams' allegiance (Leifer, 1995; Seymour, 1960).

Learning from earlier experiences of owners and supporters abandoning a team or season when it began to lose money, Hulbert structured the National League to force team owners to take a financial risk. Previously, teams had simply stopped playing when they began to lose money, much like a Broadway show. Hulbert understood how ending a season early to decrease short-term costs eroded the long-term faith of the public. In Hulbert's league, teams were expected to complete their schedules regardless of profit or loss.

Tying owners to a schedule resulted in costs from fielding a bad team and benefits from having a competitive team. Hulbert understood fans would see that teams were in earnest competition with one another. The public would have faith that owners needing to field a wining team in order to increase their profits would put forth an honest effort.

Hulbert established the league's credibility by strictly enforcing these rules. In the first year of National League play, two struggling teams, Philadelphia and New York, did not play their final series. Even though the games would not have impacted the final standings, Hulbert banned the two teams from the league (Leifer, 1995; Seymour, 1960; Vincent, 1994). The message was clear: The integrity of the league would not be compromised for the short-term financial interests of owners.

Hulbert also understood that the integrity of baseball would become suspect if the public questioned players' honesty. Baseball became popular at the height of the Victorian period in the United States. Large segments of Middle America followed strict cultural conventions. Many followed religious regimes prohibiting gaming and drinking—staples of the sporting subculture. Hulbert needed to create a cultural product that did not offend the sensibilities of the middle and upper classes. To appeal to this large market segment, Hulbert prohibited betting at National League ballparks. He also prohibited playing games on Sunday and selling beer at ballparks. The Cincinnati club objected to the no-liquor rule and was ultimately expelled from the National League (Sportsencyclopedia, 2002). Hulbert tried to clean up the atmosphere at ballparks further by banning "unwholesome groups" and activities from the game. He raised ticket prices to decrease the number of working-class patrons and make the games more appealing to the "better" classes (Abrams, 1998).

Players, many of them working-class immigrants, benefited from the widely held Victorian notion that a strong athletic body signaled an equally strong moral character. The National League owners imposed curfews on their players to maintain a clean image. Hulbert policed the sport with a vengeance. Players caught gambling were banned from the league for life (Leifer, 1995; Seymour, 1960; Vincent, 1994), a rule emphasizing the importance of the appearance of honest effort.

Central to the organization of American Victorian culture were notions of biological distinctions among ethnic and racial groups. The National League, not surprisingly, prohibited African Americans from participating. Although other major and minor leagues had blacks on their rosters in the mid- to late-1880s, by 1888 the ban would extend to all white baseball leagues.

Once the league established a solid structure and the appearance of honest play, Hulbert still needed to create a market for the game. It was relatively easy to attract spectators to championships and other big games between rival clubs, but team owners needed to find a way to attract audiences to regular season games. Hulbert's dilemma was complicated by the fact that many of the independent clubs (not affiliated with his league) fielded superior teams. In the late 1870s, National League teams lost more often than they won in non-League play (Leifer, 1995).

Hulbert's solution was to create the pennant race, a revolutionary idea in 1876. The success of the National League depended on spectators viewing baseball as a series of games and not a single event. A genuine pennant race requires fairly even competition. In other words, for the league to be a successful business, even the best teams had to lose a substantial portion of their games (Leifer, 1995).

League rules were designed to cultivate pennant fever. Hulbert kept his league small by limiting it to eight teams. A team was either in the league or not. Although local rivalries had been important in the past, Hulbert's league limited membership. As such, the National League was small enough to ensure that no team was so far out of first place that winning the pennant seemed impossible.

Other innovations that Hulbert brought to the sport significantly influenced the history and development of sport management. For example, to protect their teams from being raided by other National League teams during the season, owners agreed to respect each other's contracts with players for one year. Other leagues could pay the National League a fee to participate in this "reservation" system and protect themselves from raids by National League teams. The practice not only helped distribute talent more evenly but also kept player salaries down. This practice eventually developed into the "reserve system," which included a "reserve clause" in player contracts and a "reserve list" of protected players on each team roster. These rules also limited the movement of players, enhancing the sense of a local team and, thus, fan loyalty.

The league structure enjoyed a significant boost from newspapers, another rapidly expanding U.S. institution. Although the initial response to the National League by the media was generally unfavorable (Vincent, 1994), newspapers in cities with teams in the League soon warmed to the idea of a pennant race. In the 1870s, most major cities supported a dozen or more newspapers. One effective way to attract readers was to cover local sporting events. Newspapers played up the concept of the hometown team in a pennant race to hold the attention of sports fans between games. Reports on injuries, other teams' records, players' attitudes, and coaching strategies were given considerable coverage before and after games. Presenting baseball in terms of an ongoing

pennant race sold newspapers and underscored Hulbert's desire to promote continuing attention to and attendance at regular season games (White, 1996).

Courtesy of Arthur Rothstein, 1915, Office of War Information, Overseas Picture Division, Library of Congress

The National League also appealed to fans' loyalty and pride in their towns and cities. League rules prohibited placing more than one National League team in or near any current National League city and prohibited teams from playing non-League teams within the same territory as a National League team (Seymour, 1960). The prohibition required discipline on the part of team owners because non-League games, especially against local non-League rivals, generated strong short-term profits. By avoiding "independent" clubs in National League cities, the League promoted the notion that National League teams represented the community exclusively. Independent teams, languishing from this National League prohibition, moved on to non-League cities, and spectators increasingly identified the National League teams with their cities (Leifer, 1995). The notion of a team's "territory" persists in the management of major and minor league baseball as well as in all other league sports (e.g., the National Basketball Association, National Football League, National Hockey League).

National League teams participated in an early form of revenue sharing. Home teams were required to share their gate revenues with the visiting team. This practice allowed even the least talented teams to draw revenue when they played away from home. Gate sharing redistributed wealth around the National League, enabling teams to compete financially for players (Leifer, 1995).

Leagues Today

The National League's successful strategy seems fairly straightforward when compared with the business strategies used by today's professional sports leagues that take into account naming rights, licensing agreements, and league-wide television deals. But successful contemporary commercial sports leagues still depend on consolidated league play with strong centralized control and regulation. League play is in large part designed to encourage the fans' faith that teams operate on an equal footing, both on the field and off, and that owners, managers, and players are putting forth an honest effort.

The audience has changed over time, however. The need to see teams as independent firms has faded. Recent start-up leagues such as the Women's National Basketball Association (WNBA) and Major League Soccer (MLS) have experimented with a single-entity structure, in which each team is owned and operated by the league, although the WNBA has since moved away from this model. The public's perception of locus of honest effort resides more with the players than it does with the ownership structure.

Not all professional sports are organized in the league structure. Sports such as golf or tennis developed and continue to operate today using a different organizational structure. Sometimes referred to as professional tournament sports, the next section chronicles their development.

Professional Tournament Sports: Mixing Business and Charity

Professional tournament sports such as tennis and golf have their roots in the club system. Private clubs sponsored early tournaments for the benefit of their membership. By the turn of the century, professionals—usually club employees who taught club members the game—were often excluded from club tournaments. Without wealthy patrons' sponsorship of tournaments, professional athletes in some sports needed alternative financial support if they were going to compete. This was the case with golf.

Professional Golf

Many early golf professionals were European men brought to the United States by country clubs to help design, build, and care for golf courses and teach the finer points of the game to club members. By its very nature, golf was an exclusive game, one that catered to upper-class white males. Although these golfers were technically professionals, they were much different from the tournament professionals of the contemporary Ladies Professional Golf Association (LPGA) and Professional Golfers' Association (PGA). The early golf professionals were club instructors and caddies. They made extra money by giving exhibitions. Golf manufacturers hired the best-known professionals as representatives to help publicize the game and their brands of clubs at exhibitions and clinics.

Numerous attempts were made to organize golf leagues prior to the 1930s, but professional leagues failed to capture public interest or attract golf professionals. Professionals shunned these risky tournaments in favor of the stability of exhibitions and clinics, and when they competed they vied for prize money they had put up themselves. Professional tournaments did not stabilize until the professionals found someone else—in the form of community and corporate sponsors—to put up the prize money.

One entrepreneurial type of tournament, which ultimately failed, was an attempt to generate a profit from gate revenues for country club owners. In the first half of the twentieth century, spectator attendance was the primary revenue stream for most sports. Following the proven approach of boxing promoters and baseball owners, individual country club owners produced golf events themselves, selling tickets to the events and operating concessions.

The failure of the privately owned tournaments to catch on is the result of how the sport developed in the United States. Individually owned golf courses were rare. Clubs were either member owned or public courses. Even if there were a consortium of course owners, as was the case in baseball, they did not control the athletes. Golfers operated independently. The players did not need teams, managers, or promoters, and therefore they were difficult to control.

Corcoran's Tournaments

Fred Corcoran, the architect of the professional golf tournament, understood the unique qualities of golf. Golf, he wrote, "operates upside down" in comparison to other sports. "The players have to pay to tee off, and they use facilities constructed for the use of the amateur owners who, occasionally, agree to open the gates" to professionals (Corcoran, 1965, p. 246).

To manage this "upside down" sport, Corcoran took his lead from Hollywood and advertising executives. Corcoran used athletes and golf tournaments the same way newspapers used news—to sell advertising space to the public. Corcoran never promoted golf strictly as entertainment. The golf tournament, for Corcoran, was the medium through which a celebrity, a local politician, a manufacturer, a charity, a town, or a product gained exposure.

He sold the event. As a result, the contemporary professional tournament, unlike other sports operating 50 years ago, was less dependent on ticket sales and more dependent on sponsorship from community groups and corporations.

In 1937, a consortium of golf manufacturers hired Fred Corcoran as tournament director for the men's PGA circuit. He served in that capacity for more than a decade, making arrangements with public and private clubs to host professional tournaments. Then, in 1949, the golf equipment manufacturers hired him again to organize the women's tour (Corcoran, 1965; Hicks, 1956). Corcoran organized the players into associations with rules governing play and eligibility. In essence, the players governed themselves.

One of Corcoran's first contributions to the professional golf tour was the creation of the financially self-sufficient tournament. Prior to 1937, the PGA, through entry fees, had guaranteed to pay the players' purse to entice communities to sponsor tournaments. Corcoran, who had spent a decade organizing amateur tournaments in Massachusetts, understood the potential revenue a tournament could produce for a community. Corcoran was able to convince communities to take responsibility for providing the purse by demonstrating how the revenue generated by 70 professional golfers eating in restaurants and sleeping in hotels would be three times greater than the minimum $3,000 purse (Corcoran, 1965).

Corcoran enhanced the tremendous growth in competitive golf by sharing status with celebrities like Bing Crosby. In addition to being a famous movie star and singer, Crosby was a sports entrepreneur associated with horse racing and golf. In 1934, Crosby orchestrated the first celebrity professional and amateur (pro-am) tournament preceding a men's golf tournament to raise money for charity. The combination of a celebrity and a pro playing together on a team in a mock tournament was extremely successful. Amateur golfers, celebrities, and community leaders paid exorbitant fees to participate. Although these funds were directed toward charity, there were also spin-off professional golf benefits. The appearance of celebrities not only enhanced the athletes' status but also increased attendance, thereby increasing the proceeds for charity and the exposure for professional golf. The celebrity pro-am has been the financial core around which most professional golf tournaments have been built (Graffis, 1975).

The financial power of this type of charity event became clear during World War II. During the war, golf was used to raise money for the Red Cross. Using a celebrity pro-am format, Bing Crosby teamed up with movie costar Bob Hope, professional golfers, and various other celebrities, including Fred Corcoran, to raise millions of dollars for the war effort and the Red Cross (Graffis, 1975). At the end of the war, Corcoran stayed with the pro-am tournament format, using civic pride and charities such as hospitals and youth programs to draw crowds.

Tying professional golf to charity was good business in addition to being good for the community. Donations to charitable organizations were fully tax deductible. Local businesspeople not likely to benefit directly from a golf tournament were more easily persuaded to contribute to the tournaments with tax deductions as incentives. In addition, a good charity attracted the hundreds of volunteers and essential in-kind donations needed to run a tournament. Further, a charity with broad reach and many volunteers acted as a promotional vehicle for the tournament. Thus, Corcoran transformed a potentially costly, labor-intensive event into a no-cost operation. By appealing to the altruism of a community to host a tournament, Corcoran obtained a tournament site, capital, and event management for no cost.

A consortium of golf equipment manufacturers paid Corcoran's salary to organize the golfers into an association and to help arrange tournaments. Golf manufacturers understood that the cost of retaining player representatives could be reduced by putting a solid tournament circuit in place. Manufacturers could retain player representatives at a fraction of the cost and increase players' values as marketing tools. The better players earned their salaries through prize money. The cost of sponsoring a player on tour was far less than hiring a player full-time as a representative and paying expenses.

It was clear to Corcoran that if manufacturers could use their association with tournaments to sell golf products, then celebrities could use it to add to their status, and local community groups could use it to raise funds or gain political influence. Tournaments could also be sold as an advertising medium for non-golf-related merchandise. As tournament director of the PGA and the LPGA, Corcoran orchestrated the first non-golf-related corporate sponsorship of professional golf tournaments. Corcoran arranged for Palm Beach Clothing to sponsor men's tournaments. A few years later he orchestrated a transcontinental series of women's tournaments sponsored by Weathervane Ladies Sports Apparel (Corcoran, 1965).

Corcoran's adaptation of Crosby's celebrity tournaments to tournaments funded by advertising for clothing foreshadowed the immense corporate involvement in contemporary professional tournaments. Still, professional golf was not able to take full advantage of corporate interest in athletes until the late 1950s. Until that time, the major media wire services, Associated Press and United Press International, followed a policy of using the name of the city or town to distinguish a tournament. They argued that using the name of the corporate sponsor was a cheap way to avoid paying for newspaper advertising. In the late 1950s, the newspaper industry reversed its policy and agreed to call tournaments by the name of their corporate sponsors. By sponsoring a national sporting event, a corporation gained tax-free exposure to a target market in the name of charity (Graffis, 1975). In the end, professional golf, charities, and corporations all benefited from this arrangement.

Tournaments Today

Variations of the tournament structure just described can be found today in golf, tennis, track and field, and in multisport events such as triathlons and the Olympic and Paralympic Games. Like Corcoran, today's tour promoters do not sell the event solely as entertainment. Instead, they promote tournaments as a medium through which a person, community, or corporation can buy exposure. Gallery seats, pro-am tournaments, and the pre- and post-tournament festivities are the foci of interaction, access to which can be sold. Although communities, politicians, and radio and movie personalities have found tournaments a worthwhile investment, the corporate community has benefited the most handsomely. The golf tournament has evolved into a corporate celebration of itself and its products (Crosset, 1995).

Associations such as the PGA have been viewed as private groups. They set the rules of eligibility. However, challenges to that idea, as seen with Casey Martin's successful attempt to have the PGA accommodate his disability, suggest that these associations cannot be as exclusive as private clubs. In Casey Martin's case, he used the fact that Qualifying School (Q-School) was open to the public as a means of applying the Americans with Disabilities Act public accommodation provisions to force the PGA to allow him to compete using a cart.

In another trend that is pushing tournament management away from nonprofit private associations, today's tournaments are just as likely to be created by marketing agencies or broadcast media as by player associations. For example, the X-Games and the Alli Dew Tour are the products of corporations. The X-Games are owned by ESPN, which is a subsidiary of the Disney Corporation. The Alli Dew Tour is a division of NBC Sports. It is not yet clear how corporate-owned tournaments will affect older associations or if "made-for-TV" tournaments will be able to sustain their legitimacy with the public. However, a decade into the X-Games and Dew Tour type tours, the public still seems willing to follow them.

The first section of this chapter focused mainly on the historical aspects of professional sports, particularly teams and leagues. Most certainly the sport industry includes many more segments other than these two. This fact becomes obvious simply by looking at the broad range of chapters in this introductory text. Many of the basic tenets covered in this chapter are applicable across other segments as well. To learn more about the historical developments in segments such as intercollegiate athletics, high school and youth sport, recreational sport, and many more areas, the reader can turn to the chapters designed to cover those specific industry segments in-depth. Each chapter has a section devoted to the important historical events for that industry segment.

Women in Sport Management

A text such as this brings together information across different sport industry segments so that the reader is exposed to as broad a landscape of the industry as possible. However, as is the case with many disciplines, parts of the history and the names of some important contributors are sometimes overlooked. Female sport managers have contributed to the growth of the sport industry as a whole, yet all too often their contributions as sport leaders are not formally recognized (Hums & Yiamouyiannis, 2007). This section introduces a selection of these women and their contributions.

Perhaps the first female sport managers lived in the time of the ancient Olympic Games. While we know women were not allowed to participate in those early Games, because participation was limited to free, able-bodied, Greek male citizens, this does not mean no competitions for women existed. As a matter of fact, around the same time period of the ancient Olympic Games, a competition was held for women known as the Heraea Games. These Games, which also took place at the grounds of Olympia but not at the same time as the Olympic Games, consisted of footraces for unmarried girls. The event was organized by a group known as the Sixteen Women. These women, who were considered respected elders of their communities, gathered from nearby locations every four years to administer the Games (Hums, 2010). After the Heraea Games were discontinued, centuries passed before women again organized such events.

Effa Manley was one of the first significant modern female sport managers (O'Connor-McDonogh, 2007). As co-owner of the Newark Eagles in the Negro Baseball League, Manley was responsible for the day-to-day operations of the ball club and was active in league management (Berlage, 1994). For her contributions to professional baseball, in 2006 Manley became the first woman elected to the Baseball Hall of Fame in Cooperstown, New York (MacNeil Lehrer Productions, 2006). She most certainly paved the way for women such as Kim Ng, Senior Vice President of Major League Baseball (MLB), the only woman to have interviewed for a General Manager (GM) position with an MLB team. Ng is paving the way for others. Prior to working for MLB, Ng was Assistant General Manager of the Los Angeles Dodgers and also

Assistant General Manager of the New York Yankees. At the Yankees, she was succeeded by Jean Afterman, a former player agent who is now the Yankees' Assistant General Manager and Senior Vice President.

Today other women hold high executive positions in North American professional leagues, including Heidi Ueberroth, the President of NBA International; Rita Benson LeBlanc, owner/Vice Chair of the Board of the New Orleans Saints; and Jeanie Buss, Executive Vice President of the Los Angeles Lakers. As with many men in the sports business, lineage or marriage often plays a role in getting to the top. Five of *Forbes'* top 10 women in sports business were in the business through heritage or marriage (Van Riper, 2009).

No writing on women in sport would be complete without including the contributions made by women's tennis superstar Billie Jean King. While perhaps best remembered for her victory over Bobby Riggs in the 1973 "Battle of the Sexes," King also established the Women's Tennis Association and was a founder of *WomenSports* magazine, World Team Tennis, and the Women's Sports Foundation, which has done a tremendous amount of work to promote leadership and management opportunities for women in sport (Lough, 2007; Women's Sports Foundation, 2011).

A number of women played important roles in the development of intercollegiate athletics, especially Christine Grant and Judy Sweet. Grant, former Women's Athletic Director at the University of Iowa and former President of the Association for Intercollegiate Athletics for Women (AIAW), championed Title IX and gender equity efforts for female athletes. Sweet was one of the first women to serve as the athletics director of a combined men and women's intercollegiate athletics program in the United States (at University of California–San Diego) and was the first female President of the National

Collegiate Athletic Association (NCAA) (Hums & Yiamouyiannis, 2007).

In terms of recreational sport, three women attended the founding meeting of the National Intramural Association (NIA), with Annette Akins being named Vice President. This organization was the forerunner of the National Intramural and Recreational Sport Association (NIRSA), the primary sport organization in campus recreation. Since then, three other women have served as NIRSA presidents, including Mary Daniels from The Ohio State University and Juliette Moore from the University of Arizona. Moore was the first African American woman to hold that post (Bower, 2007). A number of women have followed in the post as president. In international sport, Anita deFrantz has long been recognized as the most powerful woman in the Olympic Movement by virtue of her tenure as an IOC member and vice president. In the Paralympic Movement, three women currently sit on the International Paralympic Committee (IPC) Governing Board: Ann Cody (United States), Rita van Driel (The Netherlands), and Hyang-Sook Jang (South Korea) (IPC, n.d.).

Finally, other women have contributed to the modern history of the sport industry in terms of sport-related businesses. Some of these women are Lesa France Kennedy, CEO of International Speedway Corporation; Stephanie Tolleson, former Senior Corporate Vice President at International Management Group; Buffy Filipell, founder of TeamWork Online; and Becky Heidesch and Mary Lou Youngblood of Women's Sports Services, which operates two online career placement services accessed by WomenSportsJobs.com and WSSExecutiveSearch.com (Lough, 2007).

The list of names of women who contributed to the modern history of sport management is certainly much longer than this abbreviated introduction suggests. What is important to note is that these businesswomen, and many others whose names are not listed here, have influenced the sport industry as we know it today.

The Birth of Sport Management as an Academic Field

It is clear that as the sport industry evolved, it increasingly took on the business characteristics of other industries. The early sport managers discussed in this chapter came to their sport management positions with some background in sport or some background in business. Very few brought a combination of the two to the workplace. However, to be a successful sport manager in today's industry, preparation in both sport and business is a necessity. The academic field of sport management began to develop in response to this need. How did this field come into existence, and what makes it unique?

Sport clubs, leagues, and tournaments are three of the more prevalent structures currently used to manage, govern, and organize sport. Management systems, including amateur bodies such as the NCAA and U.S. Track and Field, or professional organizations such as the World Boxing Association and the NBA, employ some variation of these structures to produce sporting events. But contemporary sport management is far more complex than its historical antecedents. Furthermore, the growing popularity of newer and emerging sports such as mixed martial arts, cyber gaming, and base jumping, as well as the increasing power of global media, particularly social media, are encouraging the evolution of new management structures.

The continuing growth of the sport industry and its importance to numerous sponsors and institutions created demand for the systematic study of sport management practices. Since the late 1960s, the academic field of sport management has focused on the unique issues facing the people who conduct the business of sport.

As the sport management profession began to grow and prosper, it became apparent that although similarities existed between running a general business and running a sport organization, there are also intricacies unique to the sport industry. Early on, sport managers learned from hands-on experiences gained in the industry. As the sport industry became more complex, however, the need to train sport managers in a more formal fashion became apparent. The formal study of sport management emerged from this need.

The concept of a sport management curriculum is generally credited to two people: **James G. Mason**, a physical educator at the University of Miami–Florida, and **Walter O'Malley** of the Brooklyn (now Los Angeles) Dodgers, who discussed the idea in 1957 (Mason, Higgins, & Owen, 1981). The first master's program in sport management was established at **Ohio University** in 1966 and was based on Mason's and O'Malley's ideas (Parkhouse & Pitts, 2001). Shortly after the Ohio University graduate program began, Biscayne College (now St. Thomas University) and St. John's University founded undergraduate sport management programs (Parkhouse & Pitts, 2001). The University of Massachusetts–Amherst started the second master's program in 1971.

The number of colleges and universities in the United States offering sport management majors grew rapidly. By 1985, the National Association for Sport and Physical Education (NASPE) indicated there were more than 40 undergraduate programs, 32 graduate programs, and 11 programs at both levels offering sport management degrees. Today, the total number of sport management programs is around 350 (North American Society for Sport Management, 2010c). Just over a dozen

Canadian universities offer programs as well. The growth of sport management as an academic field was prompted by the sport industry's need for well-trained managers, but it also was influenced by universities' and colleges' need to attract students. Some schools wishing to increase enrollments in a highly competitive market added sport management programs to their curricula in the 1980s.

Given the rapid growth of the academic field, concern developed among sport management educators over what constituted a solid sport management curriculum capable of producing students qualified to work as managers in the sport industry. The first group of scholars to examine this issue formed an organization called the Sport Management Arts and Science Society (SMARTS), which was initiated by the faculty at the University of Massachusetts–Amherst. This group laid the groundwork for the present scholarly organization, the **North American Society for Sport Management (NASSM)** (Parkhouse & Pitts, 2001).

The purpose of NASSM is to promote, stimulate, and encourage study, research, scholarly writing, and professional development in the area of sport management, both in the theoretical and applied aspects (NASSM, 2010a). In the past, NASSM and NASPE monitored sport management curricula through the Sport Management Program Review Council (SMPRC). Currently the movement toward program accreditation is under way via the **Commission on Sport Management Accreditation (COSMA)**. COSMA is "a specialized accrediting body whose purpose is to promote and recognize excellence in sport management education in colleges and universities at the baccalaureate and graduate levels through specialized accreditation" (COSMA, 2009, para. 1). The first programs were accredited in 2010.

Sport management professional organizations also exist in a number of nations outside

North America. The recently formed International Sport Management Alliance includes the European Association of Sport Management (EASM), the Sport Management Association of Australia and New Zealand (SMAANZ), the Asian Association for Sport Management, and the Latin American Organization of Sport Management. In addition, the African Sport Management Association (ASMA) has now been established as well (ASMA, 2013). As sport management becomes more global in nature, universities implementing successful country-specific curricula outside North America are producing successful sport managers as well. Universities in Belgium, England, Germany, Greece, Ireland, Spain, and the Netherlands, for example, are preparing future sport managers (NASSM, 2010b). Programs are also thriving in Japan, and the continent of Africa is beginning to open up as well. As the sport industry evolves, sport management curricula will continue to change to meet the needs of this global industry.

Summary

It is impossible to cover the complex history of sport management thoroughly in one chapter. This chapter discussed the historical origins of three basic sport management structures: clubs, leagues, and tournaments. Sport management structures that developed over the past 150 or so years organized sporting events in different ways to meet the particular needs of participants, spectators, and sponsors at particular points in history. The club structure, the league structure, and the tournament structure each

arose in response to changes in broad social structures and addressed specific issues within a segment of the sport industry. The evolution of each of these three management structures illustrates that managers need to be creative in the ways they manage sports.

Throughout this text there are a number of mentions of some of the innovators and contributors to the management of sport. This includes such historic figures as John Montgomery Ward, Albert Spalding, Judge Kennesaw Mountain Landis, and Marvin Miller in baseball. Other notable sport managers include Peter Ueberroth in the Olympic Games, David Stern in basketball, Pete Rozelle and Paul Tagliabue in football, Gary Bettman in hockey, Roone Arledge in sport broadcasting, and agents C. C. Pyle and Mark McCormack. These people, along with many others, have contributed to making sport one of the most popular forms of entertainment.

The three basic management structures (clubs, leagues, and tournaments) still operate in contemporary sport, but these structures now operate within highly complex organizational systems. As a result, the sport industry demands well-trained managers. Sport management developed as an academic field to meet this demand. To maintain quality control in this fast-emerging field of study, the COSMA curriculum guidelines have been established. As the sport industry continues to evolve globally, the academic field of sport management will evolve as well in order to produce the future leaders in the industry.

Key Terms

clubs, Commission on Sport Management Accreditation (COSMA), Fred Corcoran, Pierre de Coubertin, William Hulbert, Jockey Club, leagues, James G. Mason, modern Olympic Games, National Association of Professional Baseball Players, North American Society for Sport Management (NASSM), National League of Professional Baseball Players, Ohio University, Walter O'Malley, professional tournaments, sport management structures

References

Abrams, R. (1998). *Legal bases: Baseball and the law*. Philadelphia, PA: Temple University Press.

Adelman, M. (1986). *A sporting time: New York City and the rise of modern athletics, 1820–70*. Urbana, IL: University of Illinois Press.

African Sports Management Association. (2013). Welcome. Retrieved from http://www.asma-online.org/

Berlage, G. I. (1994). *Women in baseball: The forgotten history*. Westport, CT: Praeger.

Bower, G. G. (2007). Campus recreation. In M. A. Hums, G. G. Bower, & H. Grappendorf (Eds.), *Women as leaders in sport: Impact and influence* (pp. 115–136). Reston, VA: NAGWS.

Commission on Sport Management Accreditation. (2009). About COSMA. Retrieved from http://cosmaweb.org/aboutCOSMA

Corcoran, F. (1965). *Unplayable lies*. New York, NY: Meredith Press.

Crosset, T. W. (1995). *Outsiders in the clubhouse: The world of women's professional golf*. Albany, NY: SUNY Press.

Gorn, E., & Goldstein, W. (1993). *A brief history of American sport*. New York, NY: Wang and Hill.

Graffis, H. (1975). *The PGA: The official history of the Professional Golfers' Association of America*. New York, NY: Crowell.

Henriches, T. (1991). *Disputed pleasures: Sport and society in preindustrial England*. New York, NY: Greenwood Press.

Hickok Sports. (n.d.). The first major league (1875–1889). Retrieved from http://www.hickoksports.com/history/baseba04.shtml

Hicks, B. (1956). Personal correspondence, LPGA Archives.

Hums, M. A. (2010). Women's leadership in the Olympic Movement. In K. O'Connor (Ed.), *Gender and women's leadership* (pp. 842–850). Thousand Oaks, CA: Sage Publishing.

Hums, M. A., & Yiamouyiannis, A. (2007). Women in sport careers and leadership positions. In M. A. Hums, G. G. Bower, & H. Grappendorf (Eds.), *Women as leaders in sport: Impact and influence* (pp. 1–23). Reston, VA: NAGWS.

International Paralympic Committee. (n.d.). Governing board. Retrieved from http://www.paralympic.org/TheIPC/HWA/GoverningBoard

King, A. (1997). New directors, customers and fans: The transformation of English football in the 1990s. *Sociology of Sport Journal, 14*, 224–240.

Leifer, E.M. (1995). *Making the majors: The transformation of team sports in America*. Cambridge, MA: Harvard University Press.

Lough, N. (2007). Women in sport related business. In M. A. Hums, G. G. Bower, & H. Grappendorf (Eds.), *Women as leaders in sport: Impact and influence* (pp. 191–206). Reston, VA: NAGWS.

MacNeil Lehrer Productions. (2006). First woman in the Hall of Fame. Retrieved from http://www.pbs.org/newshour/bb/entertainment/jan-june06/baseball_2-28.html

Mandell, R. (1984). *Sport: A cultural history*. New York, NY: Columbia University Press.

Mason, J. G., Higgins, C., & Owen, J. (1981, January). Sport administration education 15 years later. *Athletic Purchasing and Facilities*, 44–45.

Ministry of Culture–General Secretariat for Sports. (1998). *Greek athletics: A historical overview*. Athens, Greece: Author.

North American Society for Sport Management. (2010a). NASSM home. Retrieved from http://www.nassm.org

North American Society for Sport Management. (2010b). Sport management programs. Retrieved from http://www.nassm.com/InfoAbout/SportMgmtPrograms

North American Society for Sport Management. (2010c). Sport management programs: United States. Retrieved from http://www.nassm.com/InfoAbout/SportMgmtPrograms/United_States

O'Connor-McDonogh, M. (2007). Professional sport. In M. A. Hums, G. G. Bower, & H.

Grappendorf (Eds.), *Women as leaders in sport: Impact and influence* (pp. 233–250). Reston, VA: NAGWS.

Parkhouse, B. L., & Pitts, B. G. (2001). Definition, evolution, and curriculum. In B. L. Parkhouse (Ed.), *The management of sport: Its foundation and application* (3rd ed., pp. 2–14). New York, NY: McGraw-Hill.

Seymour, H. (1960). *Baseball: The early years.* Oxford, UK: Oxford University Press.

Sportsencyclopedia. (2002). William Hulbert (1877–1882). Retrieved from http://www .sportsecyclopedia.com/mlb/nl/hulbert.html

Vamplew, W. (1989). *Pay up and play the game: Professional sport in Britain, 1875–1914.* Cambridge, UK: Cambridge University Press.

Van Riper, T. (2009, October 14). The most powerful women in sports. *Forbes.* Retrieved from http://www.forbes.com/2009/10/14 /nascar-wwe-football-business-sports-women.html

Vincent, T. (1994). *The rise and fall of American sport.* Lincoln, NE: Nebraska University Press.

White, G. E. (1996). *Creating the national pastime: Baseball transforms itself, 1903–1953.* Princeton, NJ: Princeton University Press.

Williams, J. (1989) Cricket. In T. Mason (Ed.), *Sport in Britain: A social history.* Cambridge, UK: Cambridge University Press.

Women Sport's Foundation. (2011). Billie Jean King. Retrieved from http://www .womenssportsfoundation.org/home /about-us/people/founder

You Can Play Project. (2013). Mission statement. Retrieved from http://youcanplayproject.org /pages/mission-statement

Young, D. (1996). *The Modern Olympics: A struggle for revival.* Baltimore, MD: Johns Hopkins University Press.

SPORT MANAGEMENT TIME LINE

BC 776	First ancient Olympic Games
AD 393	Last ancient Olympic Games
1750	Establishment of Jockey Club in Newmarket
1851	First America's Cup (sailing)
1869	Cincinnati Red Stockings become first professional baseball club
1871	National Association of Professional Baseball Players founded
1875	First running of Kentucky Derby (horse racing)
1876	National League of Professional Baseball Players established
1892	Basketball invented
1894	International Olympic Committee founded
1896	First modern Olympic Games in Athens, Greece
1900	Women first compete in Olympic Games
1903	First Tour de France
1904	Fédération Internationale de Football Association (FIFA) founded
1906	Intercollegiate Athletic Association of the United States issues first constitution/bylaws
1910	Intercollegiate Athletic Association of the United States changes name to National Collegiate Athletic Association (NCAA)

SPORT MANAGEMENT TIME LINE (*continued*)

1911	First Indianapolis 500
1912	International Association of Athletics Federation (IAAF) began
1916	First Professional Golf Association (PGA) Championship
1917	National Hockey League (NHL) established
1920	National Football League (NFL) began/National Federation of State High School Association (NFSHSA) founded
1924	First Winter Olympic Games in Chamonix, France/International Association of Assembly Managers (IAAM) established
1930	First FIFA World Cup (soccer) in Uruguay/First Commonwealth Games
1933	First NFL Championship
1939	First NCAA basketball tournament/Baseball Hall of Fame inducts first class
1943	First women's professional baseball league (All-American Girls Professional Baseball League)
1946	National Basketball Association (NBA) (originally known as Basketball Association of America) established
1947	Jackie Robinson integrates Major League Baseball
1950	First Formula One Championship (F1)/Ladies Professional Golf Association (LPGA) founded/National Intramural-Recreational Sports Association (NIRSA) began
1951	First Asian Games/Bill Veeck sent Eddie Gaedel up to bat
1959	First Daytona 500
1960	First Paralympic Games in Rome, Italy/Arnold Palmer signed as the International Management Group's (IMG) first client
1961	International Olympic Academy officially inaugurated in Olympia, Greece
1966	Marvin Miller appointed Executive Director of Major League Baseball Players Association (MLBPA)
1967	First Super Bowl
1971	Nike Swoosh designed by Carolyn Davidson
1972	Title IX passed
1974	Women's Sports Foundation founded by Billie Jean King
1975	Arbitrator declares MLB players Andy Messersmith and Dave McNally free agents
1976	First Winter Paralympic Games
1978	First Ironman Triathlon
1982	First NCAA women's basketball tournament
1985	North American Society for Sport Management (NASSM) established/First Air Jordan shoes debut at retail/The Olympic Partner (TOP) Program created
1988	The International Olympic Committee (IOC) decided to make all professional athletes eligible for the Olympics, subject to the approval of the International Federations
1990	Americans with Disabilities Act signed into law
1991	First FIFA Women's World Cup (soccer)
1992	NBA players first played in the Summer Olympic Games

SPORT MANAGEMENT TIME LINE (*continued*)

1994	NFL salary cap came into effect
1995	European Court of Justice ruled clubs restrained trade opening the transfer market in European football
1996	Women's National Basketball Association (WNBA) founded
1998	NHL players first competed in the Winter Olympic Games/first Bowl Championship Series (BCS) games played
1999	World Anti-Doping Agency established
2001	Beijing, China awarded Olympic and Paralympic Games for 2008/U.S. Supreme Court ruled golfer Casey Martin allowed to use a cart in PGA events
2003	Nike acquires Converse
2004	William Perez succeeds Phil Knight as President and CEO of Nike/Athens Organizing Committee (ATHOC) becomes first Organizing Committee for the Olympic Games to jointly manage both Summer Olympic and Paralympic Games/Nextel takes over sponsorship of NASCAR's Winston Cup
2005	Adidas acquires Reebok/NHL labor problems cause first postponement of an entire major professional league season/NHL suspends operations for 2004–2005 season/MLB Players Association and owners announce new drug testing agreement including suspensions and release of player names/United Nations designates 2005 as the International Year of Sport and Physical Education
2006	Germany hosts successful World Cup, featuring a "Say No to Racism" campaign
2007	Barry Bonds becomes new MLB home run king amid steroid allegations
2008	Beijing, China hosts the Summer Olympic Games/Arena Football League announces cancellation of 2009 season/Final year for Yankee Stadium
2009	Rio de Janeiro, Brazil awarded 2016 Summer Olympic Games, marking the first time the Games will be held in South America
2010	NCAA conference realignment: Big 10, Big 12, and Pac-10/South Africa hosts first World Cup on African continent
2011	Former Pennsylvania State University Assistant Football Coach Jerry Sandusky child abuse scandal comes to light
2012	London Olympic Games marked the first Games where every competing nation was represented by at least one female athlete/Lance Armstrong's seven Tour de France victories erased amid doping scandal
2014	The IOC and United Nations sign historic agreement aimed at strengthening collaboration between the two organizations on the highest level

Chapter 2

Carol A. Barr and
Mary A. Hums

Management Principles Applied to Sport Management

Learning Objectives

Upon completion of this chapter, students should be able to:

1. Demonstrate how knowledge of basic management skills is critical to the success of a sport organization.

2. Assess the role that people play in the success of a sport organization.

3. Compare and contrast the historical phases of management theory from scientific management to the human relations movement through organizational behavior.

4. Differentiate between the four functional areas of management: Planning, organizing, leading, and evaluating.

5. Demonstrate understanding of the basic management skills needed to be a successful sport manager include communicating verbally and in writing, managing diversity, managing technology, making decisions, understanding organizational politics, managing change, motivating employees, and taking initiative.

6. Develop a plan to stay abreast of trends occurring in the sport industry that are of concern to managers such as workplace diversity, emerging technologies, and issues unique to international sport management.

7. Assess new and emerging theories of management such as empowerment and emotional intelligence.

8. Analyze the role that social responsibility plays in the management of sport organizations.

Introduction

It has been said that sport today is too much of a game to be a business and too much of a business to be a game. The sport industry in the United States is growing at an incredible rate. Current estimates by *Forbes* magazine of the value of individual professional team sport franchises list the average National Football League (NFL) team's value at $1.1 billion (Ozanian, Badenhausen & Settimi, 2012a), the average National Basketball Association (NBA) franchise at $509 million (Badenhausen, Ozanian, & Settimi, 2013), the average Major League Baseball (MLB) franchise at $605 million (Ozanian, Badenhausen, & Settimi, 2012c), and the average National Hockey League (NHL) franchise at $282 million (Ozanian, Badenhausen, & Settimi, 2012b). Total annual licensed-product sales in the United States and Canada for major sport properties were as follows: NFL, $3 billion; MLB, $3.1 billion; NBA, $2 billion; NHL, $887 million; National Association of Stock Car Auto Racing (NASCAR), $887 million; and Major League Soccer (MLS), $394 million (EPM Communications, 2012). College-licensed merchandise for 2011–2012 was estimated at $4.6 billion (Collegiate Licensing Company, 2012). In 2010, the National Collegiate Athletic Association (NCAA) reached a 14-year, nearly $11 billion agreement with CBS and Turner Sports for television rights to the 68-team NCAA men's basketball tournament (an increase of three teams from the previous year's 65-team tournament) (Wieberg & Hiestand, 2010). In 2012, MLB signed a new broadcasting contract with ESPN and TBS for $12.4 billion over 8 years, an average of $52 million each year to all 30 teams (Ozanian et al., 2012b). The U.S. health and sports club industry reported a 2011 total annual dollar volume of $21.4 billion (International Health, Racquet and Sportsclub Association, 2012). As the sport industry has grown, there has been a shift in focus toward a more profit-oriented approach to doing business (Hums, Barr, & Gullion, 1999).

While keeping the financial scope of the sport industry in mind, it is important to note that in whatever segment of the sport industry they work, sport managers need to be able to organize and work with the most important asset in their organization: people. This chapter on management will help the future sport manager recognize how essential utilization of this most important asset is critical to the success of a sport organization. Every sport manager needs to understand the basics of being a manager in the twenty-first century. A manager in a sport organization can go by many different titles: athletic director, general manager, director of marketing, coach, health club manager, ski resort operator, social media manager, and so on. The purpose of this chapter is to introduce the reader to basic management knowledge areas and skills that sport managers can apply in any segment of the industry.

Definition and History of Management Principles

Management has been defined in a number of different ways, but common elements of these various definitions include (1) goals/objectives to be achieved (2) with limited resources and (3) with and through people (Chelladurai, 2009). The goal of managerial work and the role the manager plays within an organization is to get workers to do what the manager wants them to do in an efficient and cost-effective manner. The management process includes knowledge areas such as planning, organizing, leading, and evaluating. These knowledge areas are discussed in the next section of this chapter.

The development of management theory has gone through a number of distinct phases. Two of the earlier phases were scientific management and the human relations movement. Frederick

Taylor was one of the first true pioneers of management theory. The publication of Taylor's 1911 book, *The Principles of Scientific Management*, laid the foundation for the **scientific management** movement (sometimes referred to today as "Taylorism") in the early 1900s (Taylor, 2002). Taylor worked as an industrial engineer at a steel company and was concerned with the way workers performed their jobs. Taylor believed that through scientific study of the specific motions that make up a total job, a more rational and efficient method of performing that job could be developed. In other words, workers should not be doing the same job in different ways because there exists one "best way" to perform a job efficiently. In Taylor's view, the manager could get workers to perform the job this "best way" by enticing them with economic rewards.

The second major phase in management theory is known as the **human relations movement**. From 1927 to 1932, Elton Mayo was part of the team that conducted the Hawthorne studies at Western Electric's Chicago plant. In the Hawthorne studies, the workers' motivations were studied by examining how changes in working conditions affected output. Mayo found that social factors in the workplace were important, and job satisfaction and output depended more on cooperation and a feeling of worth than on physical working conditions (Mayo, 2002). The human relations movement was also popularized by the work and writings of Mary Parker Follett. Follett was a pioneer as a female management consultant in the male-dominated industrial world of the 1920s. Follett saw workers as complex combinations of attitudes, beliefs, and needs. She believed that effective motivational management existed in partnership and cooperation and that the ability to persuade people was far more beneficial to everyone than hierarchical control and competition (Follett, 2002). The human relations

movement was significant in that it transformed the focus of management thinking onto the behavior of people and the human components in the workplace rather than the scientific approach to performing a task.

Today, it is common to view the study of human behavior within organizations as a combination of the scientific management and human relations approaches. **Organizational behavior** is characteristic of the modern approach to management. The field of organizational behavior is involved with the study and application of the human side of management and organizations (Luthans, 2005). Organizations have undergone numerous changes over the past decades, including downsizing to address economic recessions, globalization, installation and use of information technology, and an increasingly diverse workforce. Managers have been preoccupied with restructuring their organizations to improve productivity and meet the competitive challenges created by organizational changes. Through all the organizational changes and evolution of management thought and practices, one thing remains clear: The lasting competitive advantage within organizations comes through human resources and how they are managed (Luthans, 2005). Current management theory stresses the concepts of employee involvement, employee empowerment, and managers' concern with the human component of employees. Topics explored within organizational behavior research include communication, decision making, leadership, and motivation, among others. However, the essence of organizations is productivity, and thus managers need to be concerned with getting the job done.

In looking at the study of management theory, it is evident that the approaches to management have moved from the simple to the complex, from a job orientation to a people (worker) orientation, from the manager as a dictator and giver of orders to the manager as a facilitator and team member. Human beings, though, are complex and sometimes illogical, and therefore no single method of management can guarantee success. Take, for example, successful basketball coaches Bobby Knight and Phil Jackson. Both amassed wins and championships, yet they each used uniquely different management styles! The role of managers can be challenging as they try to assess the needs of their employees and utilize appropriate skills to meet these needs while also getting the job done.

© Jupiterimages/Comstock/Thinkstock

Functional Areas

Sport managers must perform in a number of functional areas and execute various activities in fulfilling the demands of their jobs. Some of the functional areas used to describe what managers do include planning, organizing, leading, and evaluating (Chelladurai, 2009). Although these functional areas may be helpful in providing a general idea about what a manager does, these terms and their descriptions do not provide a comprehensive list. Organizations are constantly evolving, as are managers and the activities they perform. The functional areas emphasized here describe an overall picture of what a manager does, but keep in mind it is impossible to reduce a manager's activities to the level of a robot following a set pattern of activities.

Planning

The **planning** function includes defining organizational goals and determining the appropriate means by which to achieve these desired goals (Gibson, 2006). Planning involves setting a course of action for the sport organization (VanderZwaag, 1998). Based on VanderZwaag's (1984) model, Hums and MacLean (2013) define the planning process as establishing organizational vision statements, mission statements, goals, objectives, tactics, roles, and evaluation. It is important to keep in mind that the planning process is continuous. Organizational plans should change and evolve—they should not be viewed as set in stone. In case of problems or if situations arise that cause organizational goals to change, the sport manager must be ready to adjust or change the organization's plans to make them more appropriate for what the organization is trying to accomplish.

The planning process consists of both short- and long-term planning. Short-term planning involves goals the organization wants to accomplish soon, say within the next couple of months to a year. For example, an athletic shoe company may want to order enough inventory of a particular type of shoe so that its sales representatives can stock the vendors with enough shoes to meet consumer demands for the upcoming year. Long-term planning involves goals the organization may want to try to reach over a longer period of time, perhaps 5 to 10 years into the future. That same shoe company may have long-term goals of becoming the number one athletic shoe company in the nation within 5 years, so the company's long-term planning will include activities the company will participate in to try to reach that goal. Managers must participate in both short- and long-term planning.

The planning process also includes ongoing and unique plans. An example of an ongoing plan would be a parking lot plan for parking at every university home football game. A unique plan might involve use of that same parking lot as a staging area for emergency vehicles if the city were hit by an unexpected natural disaster such as a flood or tornado.

Organizing

After planning, the sport manager next undertakes the **organizing** function. The organizing function is concerned with putting plans into action. As part of the organizing function, the manager determines what types of jobs need to be performed and who will be responsible for doing these jobs.

When determining what types of jobs need to be performed, an organizational chart is developed (**Figure 2-1**). It shows the various positions within an organization as well as the reporting schemes for these positions. In

addition, an organizational chart may contain information about the people filling the various positions. After an organizational chart has been put together, the next step is to develop position descriptions for the various positions within the chart. These descriptions are important in defining the tasks and responsibilities for each position; they also indicate the authority accompanying each position. For example, the position description of the Assistant Athletic Director for Marketing may include soliciting corporate sponsors, promoting teams or special events, overseeing the department's social media program, and selling stadium signage. Finally, position qualifications must be developed. Position qualifications define what is needed in the person filling a particular position. They will depend on the organizational

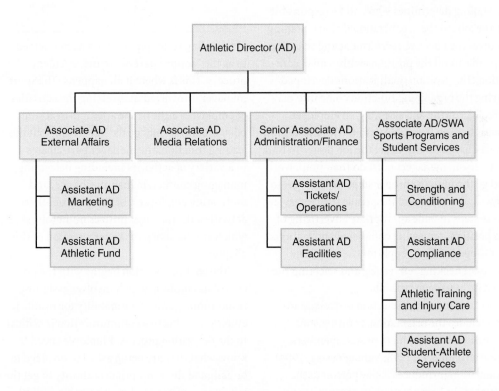

Figure 2-1 Athletic Department Organizational Chart

chart, the responsibilities of a particular position, and the authority given to a particular position. Thus, the position qualifications for the Assistant Athletic Director for Marketing may include a master's degree, 3 to 5 years of athletic department experience, and good written and oral communication skills.

The need for a well-developed and well-communicated organizational chart cannot be overemphasized. On numerous occasions, organizations may find that problems occur because one person does not know what another person in the organization is doing. The organizational chart can be extremely beneficial in showing employees the various positions within the organization, who fills those positions, the responsibilities of each position, and who reports to whom. Once the organizational chart has been developed and the position qualifications established, staffing can take place.

Staffing determines who will be responsible for the jobs in the organizational chart. Staffing involves the effective recruitment and selection of people to fill the positions within an organization. The position qualifications developed during the organizing function come into play here. Recruiting and selecting an employee means finding the right person, with the appropriate qualifications, to get the job done. To find that person, managers must do their homework and go through the proper steps to really get to know and understand the people they interview. These steps include appropriate advertising of the position, reviewing completed applications, choosing qualified people for the interview process, checking references, and selecting the "best fit" person for the job.

In addition to the selection process, staffing includes the orientation, training, and professional development of staff members (Quarterman & Li, 1998; VanderZwaag, 1984). Orientation introduces a new person to the nature of the organization, to organizational goals and policies, and to his or her fellow employees. Training focuses on the actual job and teaching an employee how to do it. For example, new ushers may be involved in a half-day training seminar to learn about seating arrangements, locations of first aid stations and uniformed security, and procedures for checking in and out of work. Professional development involves a commitment to improving employees' knowledge, skills, and attitudes, allowing them the opportunity to grow and become better employees. Sending athletic department employees to a week-long seminar on using social media is one example of how professional development can occur. Unfortunately, many sport managers are so busy trying to do the day-to-day work that they ignore the development of their employees. Professional development can help lead to more efficient and productive workers.

Leading

The **leading** function has often been referred to as the "action" part of the management process. This is where it all happens. The sport manager is involved in directing the activities of employees as he or she attempts to accomplish organizational goals. In carrying out the leading function, the manager participates in a variety of activities including delegating, managing conflict, managing change, and motivating employees. In carrying out these activities, the manager utilizes numerous skills, which are discussed in the next section of this chapter.

The leading function begins with the process of **delegation**, which involves assigning responsibility and accountability for results to employees. Effective communication is critical to the delegation process. Employees need to know what they are being asked to do, need to be assigned the appropriate authority to get the job done, and need to know how they will be evaluated for carrying out the assigned tasks. The importance of delegation cannot be overstated, yet it is one of the most difficult skills for new managers to acquire. One's first inclination is simply to "do it myself" so that a task will get accomplished the way the individual manager wants. Realistically, it is impossible for one person to do everything. Could you imagine if the general manager of an MLB team tried to do everything? In addition to making personnel decisions and negotiating contracts, the person would be broadcasting the game, pulling the tarp, and selling beer! Also, delegation plays an important part in new employees learning to be sport managers. Just as a coach allows substitutes to slowly learn the game plan until they are ready to be starters, so too do sport managers allow their subordinates to hone their managerial skills via delegation.

The leading function also requires the manager to take an active role and manage any differences or changes that may take place within the organization. Ultimately, the manager is responsible for the employees and how they perform their duties. The manager must handle any conflicts, work problems, or communication difficulties so that the employees can achieve their goals. The manager also must be ready to stimulate creativity and motivate the employees if needed. Thus, the manager takes on a very dynamic role in the operations of the organization when performing the leading function.

Evaluating

The manager performs the **evaluating** function by measuring and ensuring progress toward organizational objectives. This progress is accomplished by the employees effectively carrying out their duties. The manager evaluates the workers by establishing reporting systems, developing performance standards, comparing employee performance to set standards, and designing reward systems to acknowledge successful work on the part of the employees. Position descriptions, discussed earlier in this chapter, are important in the evaluating function as well, for they establish the criteria by which employee performance is measured.

The reporting system involves the collection of data and information regarding how a job is being performed. For example, the director of corporate sponsorship for an event would collect information on how many sponsorship packages the local corporate sponsorship representative has sold. This information would be reported to the event director. Developing performance standards sets the conditions or expectations for the employee. In the previous example, the local corporate sponsorship representative, in conjunction with the director, would determine how many local sponsorship packages should be sold. Employee performance can then be evaluated based on how well (or poorly) each employee did in meeting these performance standards. Finally, a reward system should be put in place so employees believe their work is noticed and appreciated. Receiving recognition for good performance and accomplishments helps motivate employees to reach their job expectations. Employees will not be motivated to reach the performance standard placed before them if they believe they will not be rewarded or recognized in some way. There will also be times, however, when employees fail to meet the levels of performance expected of them. Managers must deal with these situations, which may be quite unpleasant. It is necessary to have a plan in place to help employees adjust their work efforts in order to be successful, as well as one to deal with employees who may need to be asked to leave the organization.

Managerial functions involve a manager performing a number of activities requiring various skills. The next section discusses the skills managers use when fulfilling their job responsibilities.

Key Skills

People Skills

As mentioned earlier, the most important resources in any sport organization are the human resources—the people. The sport management industry is a "people-intensive" industry. Sport managers deal with all kinds of people every day. For example, on a given morning a ticket manager for a minor league baseball team may have the task of meeting with chief executive officers or chief financial officers of local businesses to arrange the sale of stadium luxury boxes. That afternoon, he or she may be talking with the local Girl Scouts, arranging a special promotion night. The next morning may bring a meeting with the general manager of the team's MLB affiliate to discuss ticket sales. Before a game, a season ticket holder may call to complain about his or her seats.

Managers in professional sport interact with unique clientele. On the one hand, they deal with athletes making millions of dollars. On the other hand, they deal with the maintenance crew, who may merely be paid minimum wage. The sport manager must be able to respond appropriately to these different constituencies and keep everyone in the organization working as a team. Using interpersonal skills and promoting teamwork are two valuable ways sport

© Dmitriy Shironosov/ShutterStock, Inc.

managers utilize their people skills (Bower, 2009). Without proper **people skills**, the sport manager is destined to fail. Learning to treat all people fairly, ethically, and with respect is essential for the sport manager's success.

Communication Skills: Oral and Written

The importance of mastering both oral and written **communication skills** cannot be overstated (Bower, 2009). Sport managers deal with all kinds of people on a daily basis, and knowing how to say something to a person is equally as important as knowing what to say. Communication may take place one on one with employees or customers, or in a large group setting. When questions arise, people will call wanting help, such as a person with a disability who has questions about parking and stadium access. Sometimes people just need general information, such as when the next home event takes place. To sport managers, these types of questions can begin to seem mundane and repetitive. However, the sport manager must remember that for the person asking the question, this may be the first time he or she asked it, and this instance also may be his or her first personal contact with anyone in the organization. Answering each question professionally and courteously wins a lifelong fan. Being rude or uncooperative only ensures an empty seat in your arena or stadium. Remember: People who have had bad experiences talk to others, which may result in the loss of other existing or potential fans.

Being representatives of their sport organizations, sport managers are often asked to give speeches to community groups, schools, and business leaders. Sport managers need to learn how to give a proper oral presentation to a group. To assess one's readiness to give a presentation, one should consider the following (Hartley & Bruckman, 2002, p. 304):

1. Do you have clear objectives?

2. Do you know your audience?

3. Do you have a clear structure?

4. Is your style of expression right?

5. Can you operate effectively in the setting?

Jacobs and Hyman (2010) offer college students 15 strategies for giving oral presentations. These strategies can be applied later on in your professional career as well. These strategies include:

1. Do your homework.

2. Play the parts (organizing your presentation into a few main parts and telling the audience what these parts are).

3. Do a dry run.

4. Look presentable.

5. Talk, do not read.

6. Take it slow.

7. Use aids (e.g., PowerPoint slides, handouts).

8. Do not bury the crowd (with massive amounts of information that overwhelms them).

9. Be yourself.

10. Play it straight (a little humor may be alright, but not too much).

11. Circle the crowd (make eye contact with people seated in different parts of the room).

12. Appear relaxed.

13. Finish strong.

14. Welcome interruptions (questions are not necessarily a bad thing).

15. Know when to stop lecturing (discussions are great).

No doubt in your sport management classes you will have numerous opportunities to practice and perfect your oral presentation skills!

In addition to oral communication skills, successful sport managers need excellent written communication skills. Sport managers must be able to write in many different styles. For example, a sports information director needs to know how to write press releases, media guides, season ticket information brochures, interoffice memos, and business letters to other professionals, as well as lengthy reports that may be requested by the athletic director or university faculty. Coaches need to be able to write solid practice plans, letters to parents or athletes, and year-end reports on a team's status. A marketing researcher for a footwear company has to write extensive reports on sales, consumer preferences, and product awareness. Remember: Professional writing is *not* the same as writing text messages or posting to Facebook or Twitter. Always write using complete sentences and never include texting abbreviations! Email for business communication purposes needs to follow a succinct, professional approach. According to Stoldt, Dittmore, and Branvold (2012, p. 8), "Although the channels through which the information is carried vary from news releases to publications to blogs, the core competency remains constant—being able to write effectively." Knowing how to communicate facts and information in an organized, readable fashion is truly an art, one a sport manager must master to be successful.

Managing Diversity

Diversity is a fact of life in today's sport workplace and there is a need to include more women, people of color, and people with disabilities at the managerial level in the sport industry. "Diversity—often mistakenly confused with old-style equal opportunities—refers to any differences between individuals, including age, race, gender, sexual orientation, disability, education, and social background. Such differences can affect how people perform and interact with each other in the workplace, hence the need for a diversity management programme" ("Remember Five Things," 2003, p. 31). More recently, Cunningham (2011, p. 6) defined diversity as "the presence of differences among members of a social unit that lead to perceptions of such differences and that impact work outcomes. This definition highlights (a) the presence of differences, (b) the dyadic or group nature of diversity, (c) the manner in which actual differences can influence perceptions of such heterogeneity, and (d) the impact diversity has on subsequent outcomes."

The face of the U.S. workforce is changing rapidly. In 2011, minorities accounted for approximately 35.19% of the workforce (U.S. Equal Employment Opportunity Commission, 2012). Women hold approximately 44.2% of managerial positions in the workforce (U.S. Department of Labor, 2012). Information from the National Organization on Disability indicates that approximately 18% of all Americans (56 million people) have a disability (National Organization on Disability, 2013).

As a part of the greater business community, the sport industry must keep pace with this diversification in the workplace and encourage the inclusion of people of diverse cultures into the management of sport. The latest data in the 2012 Racial and Gender Report Card for college sports (Lapchick, 2012a) revealed that 85% of all head coaches of men's and women's sports in all three divisions were white. In 2012, white athletic directors held 89% of the NCAA Division I positions, with women accounting for 8.3%. All of the conference commissioners (11) at Football Bowl Subdivision (FBS) conferences are white men.

At the senior executive level, 30% of MLB employees were people of color, while women occupied 2.7% of these positions. At the managerial level, 26.7% of employees were people of color, while women occupied 30% of these positions (Lapchick, 2013a). In the NBA, the percentage of people of color who held team professional administration positions increased by 3.1% to 27.6% in 2013, the highest percentage since the 2008–2009 season (Lapchick, 2013b). Unfortunately the percentage of women holding team professional administration positions decreased 4.3% to 35% in 2013 (Lapchick, 2013b).

The Rooney Rule has helped the NFL to double the number of African American head coaches in recent years, from three in 2003 to six in 2012. In 2012, the NFL reached a record high of six African American general managers. The history of NFL teams regarding the hiring of women is poor. Women occupied 20% of senior administrator positions during the 2011 NFL season, while holding only 15% of the team vice president positions (Lapchick, 2012b).

The underrepresentation of women, minorities, and people with disabilities in the sport industry is an important issue for sport managers who value diversity in the workplace.

The employment process, from hiring through retention through the exiting of employees from an organization, has become a much more complex process than in the past. Given the low numbers of women, minorities, and people with disabilities in leadership positions in the sport industry, steps must be taken to increase opportunities for access to the industry. When undertaking to follow ethical considerations for including all qualified individuals in the employment process, each phase of the process should be examined. These stages include recruitment, screening, selection, retention, promotion, and ending employment. The following suggestions offer concrete steps that sport managers can take to successfully manage diversity in the sport industry (Hums, 1996):

- Be knowledgeable about existing labor laws related to discriminatory work practices.
- Be knowledgeable about existing affirmative action guidelines for the employment process.
- Increase knowledge and awareness of multiculturalism.
- Be knowledgeable and supportive on issues of importance to all groups in the workplace.
- Write statements about valuing diversity into the organization's code of ethics.
- Expand personal and professional networks to include those of different races, genders, physical abilities, sexual orientations, and social classes.
- Act as a mentor to people of diverse cultures in one's sport organization.
- Be courageous enough to "buck the system" if necessary. This is indeed a personal challenge and choice. A sport manager who perceives discrimination or discriminatory practices within a sport organization should speak out against these practices.

The North American workforce is rapidly changing and diversifying. Sport leaders must be aware of how this trend will affect their sport organizations. By being proactive and inclusive, sport leaders can ensure that all qualified individuals have an opportunity to work in the sport industry, allowing for the free exchange of new and diverse ideas and viewpoints, resulting in organizational growth and success. Sport leaders advocating this proactive approach will have organizations that are responsive to modern North American society and will be the leaders of the sport industry.

Managing Technology

Technology is evolving more and more rapidly every day, and **managing technology**—that is, being familiar with technology and using it to one's advantage—is something every

manager should strive for. Managers need to be aware of technological advances and the way technology is used in the sport industry. This includes social media, customer data collection and advanced ticketing systems, and video conferencing and multimedia presentations, to name a few. Managers must stay current and be proficient with technology as it is used in the workplace.

The recent explosion in the use of social media has had a major impact on sport managers. Every team in the Big Four (NFL, MLB, NBA, and NHL) uses social media. NASCAR, NCAA schools, and even high school sport teams, in addition to major international events such as the World Cup and Olympic and Paralympic Games, use social media. Individual athletes are active on social media as well. Sport management students should be aware of how sport organizations are using social networking sites such as Facebook and Twitter to promote their athletes, teams, and products (Hambrick, Simmons, Greenhalgh, & Greenwell, 2010).

The Internet has become a pivotal source of information on a variety of subjects. Computerized ticketing systems such as Paciolan and Prologue are used on a daily basis by professional sport teams, major college athletic departments, theme parks, and museums. Paciolan describes itself as follows (2013b, para. 8):

> Founded in 1980, Paciolan is the leader in venue enablement, powering ticketing, fundraising, and marketing technology solutions for leading organizations across North America. Collectively, Paciolan powers over 500 live entertainment organizations who sell over 100 million tickets annually. Primary markets include college athletics, professional sports, performing arts, arenas, and museums. Paciolan is a wholly owned subsidiary of Comcast-Spectacor.

The latest development in ticketing is M-ticketing, which is a barcoded ticket bought over the phone or online that can be sent to a customer's mobile phone for scanning through the turnstiles at a stadium entrance. Also, computerized ticketing systems are encouraging digital marketing and promotions, such as Paciolan's "PACMail," which provide real-time reporting and analyses that measure the performance of client email marketing campaigns. By incorporating marketing and promoting online ticket sales, season renewals, subscriptions, and last-minute incentives, professional organizations and collegiate athletics departments are able to maximize ticket sales (Paciolan, 2013a).

Online surveys are being used for data collection by sport teams and organizations, providing information on fan demographics, purchasing decisions, and brand identity. Numerous sport teams have kiosks in their stadiums or arenas where fans can fill out in-game surveys, providing valuable information about the people attending the game.

In addition, sport managers use technology to access these data via their laptops and transform them into analyzed information for presentation to sponsors. With the explosion of the Internet and other multimedia interactive technologies, sport managers and sport management educators now face new challenges: how to analyze and benefit from the effects of expanding technologies on the sport industry and how to educate future sport managers who are entering into this rapidly evolving high-tech world.

Decision Making

People make decisions every day, ranging from simple to complex. All decisions consist of two basic steps: (1) gathering information and then (2) analyzing that information. For example, when you got up this morning, why did you choose the clothes you have on? Because they matched? Because they were clean? Because they were on the top of the clothes pile? Because of the weather? Because you had a presentation to give in class? Although this is a relatively simple decision (for most people), other decisions are more complex. Think about choosing a college major: What made you decide to major in sport management as opposed to management or accounting or theater management? This choice involves **decision making** on a much deeper level.

Sport managers have to make decisions about how to pursue opportunities or solve problems every day. Sport managers, therefore, need to have a comprehensive understanding of the opportunity or problem and engage in a decision-making process that will lead to an effective decision. The classic model of decision making has four steps (Chelladurai, 2009):

1. *Problem statement/framing the problem.* This first step involves defining the goal to be achieved or the problem that needs to be solved.

2. *Generating alternatives.* The next step involves determining as many courses of action or solutions as possible.

3. *Evaluate alternatives.* The evaluation of each alternative identified takes place in this step. This evaluation may involve cost determination, risk identification, and the effects the alternative will have on employees.

4. *Select the best alternative.* The manager makes and implements the final decision here. Following an organized decision-making process helps ensure consistent decision making throughout the sport organization and ensures that no piece of important information is overlooked.

There is one other consideration for sport managers when making decisions: When is it necessary to include group input and feedback in the decision-making process? **Participative decision making** involves employees or members of the organization in the actual decision-making process. There are benefits as well as drawbacks to using the participative decision-making process within an organization. According to the Holden Leadership Center (2013) at the University of Oregon, the benefits of group decision making include a greater sum total of knowledge and information, a greater number of approaches to a problem, increased acceptance due to participation, better comprehension of decisions, and greater commitment of group members to decisions. Conversely, the potential downfalls of group decision making include social pressure, individual domination, conflicting secondary goals, risk taking, and the time needed when a group is used in the decision-making process (Holden Leadership Center, 2013).

Organizational Politics

What is meant by the term **organizational politics**? Organizational politics are a way of life. The degree of organizational politics varies from one organization to another, but the reality is that all organizations experience some degree of internal political struggle that can rip them apart if not managed appropriately. Dealing with this struggle takes a keen awareness of the landscape, players, and rules of the political game (Bolander, 2011). Although somewhat intangible and hard to measure, politics pervades all sport organizations (Slack & Parent, 2006). Organizational politics and political behavior are met with mixed results. Some people believe that political behavior is demeaning and possibly destructive to an organization. Others view politics as a way of accomplishing goals and objectives. Whatever their beliefs on the subject, sport managers must be aware of the presence of politics within their organization and the different types of political tactics people may use. Four generally accepted types of political tactics used in

organizations are as follows (Slack & Parent, 2006):

1. Building coalitions with others to increase a person's political power

2. Using outside experts to support or legitimize a person's position

3. Building links or creating a network of contacts with people inside and outside the organization

4. Controlling information, thereby influencing decisions and the outcomes of decisions within the organization

What is most important for future sport managers is that they learn to be aware of the political environment around them. Who is truly the most "powerful" person in a sport organization? Sport organizations, like all organizations, have two different types of leaders: formal and informal. The formal leader is a leader because of title, such as athletic director, director of community relations, or store manager. The formal leader may indeed be the person who holds the most power in an organization and is able to influence employees in achieving organizational goals. Informal leaders, by contrast, are leaders because of the power they possess from knowledge, association, or length of time with an organization. Informal leaders may be very influential in terms of what takes place within an organization. For example, if the coaches in an athletic department are trying to convince the athletic director to make some sort of change, they may ask the coach who has been there for many years, knows the ins and outs of the organization, and knows how to persuade the athletic director to speak on their collective behalf. Alternatively, the coaches may ask the coach of the team with the largest budget or one of the higher profile coaches to talk to the athletic director about making this change. Identifying informal leaders can help new sport managers understand the politics of a sport organization.

Managing Change

Sport organizations change on a daily basis. New general managers are hired, teams move into new facilities, league policies and rules change, health clubs purchase new fitness equipment, and environmental use laws affect state or national park recreation areas. Change can be internally driven, such as a professional sport team implementing a new ticket distribution system, or externally driven, such as changes dictated by new government regulations or changes in consumer demand. Life is all about adapting to change and so, too, is the sport industry.

Although most change happens without major resistance, sport managers have to be aware that people tend to resist change for a number of reasons including fear of failure, being creatures of habit, perceiving no obvious need for change, feelings of loss of control, concern about support systems, being closed-minded, unwillingness to learn, a fear that the new way may not be better, a fear of the unknown, and a fear of personal impact (Peter Barron Stark Companies, 2010). For example, a sales representative for a sporting goods company who is assigned to a new geographic area may resist because he or she is scared about getting a new territory (fear of the unknown), may be concerned that the potential for sales and commissions is lower in the new territory (the new way may not be better), may have had friends in the old territory (concern about support system), may now have a territory not as highly regarded in the company (fear of personal impact), may wonder if he or she will be able to establish new contacts (unwillingness to learn), or may just see the change as another hassle (no obvious need for change). Although not all of these reasons may be present, sport managers need to be aware of what employees

may be thinking. Buckley (2013, para. 3) suggests examining five questions to determine if a change can succeed:

1. How is the vision different, better, and more compelling?

2. Are the leaders personally committed to the change?

3. Does the organization have the capacity to make the change?

4. How ingrained is the current culture?

5. Will the change actually deliver the identified outcomes?

How, then, should sport managers effectively implement change in the workplace? When **managing change**, managers should do the following (Douglas, 2010, para. 10):

1. Review the process you want to change and determine exactly what you want to do and why.

2. Carefully consider the risks associated with the change and what affect the risks will have on your employees.

3. If the change appears feasible, consult carefully with your employees and, if relevant, their union.

4. Undertake a careful assessment, based on data and acceptable workloads (through internal and external research) in consultation with your employees.

5. Provide an opportunity for the employees and the union to read the report and comment. If there are criticisms, determine what the particular issues are and consider them carefully.

6. Amend the report, utilizing best knowledge and then, prior to implementation, walk everyone through the proposed changes,

why they are being implemented, and why they are safe.

7. Implement the changes and have legal directions and a set of frequently asked questions and answers available in the event of a dispute.

8. Sport managers need to be keenly tuned into how employees are responding to change so that any resistance can be dealt with fairly and honestly.

Motivation

The ability to motivate employees to strive to achieve organizational goals and objectives as well as their personal goals and objectives is an art form. For example, both a head coach and a player for an NBA team want their team to win. The player also knows, however, that his personal game statistics will determine his salary. As a head coach, how do you motivate a player to be a "team player" (organizational goal) while still allowing him to maximize his personal statistics (personal goal)?

Theories of **motivation** abound, with works including Maslow's hierarchy of needs, Herzberg's two factor ideas, Vroom's expectancy theory, and Adam's equity theory (Luthans, 2005). After reviewing these and other theories, Lipman (2013) points out five practices that can raise the level of employee motivation:

1. Align individual economic interests with company performance.

2. Take a genuine interest in the future path of an employee's career.

3. Take a genuine interest in an employee's work–life balance.

4. Listen.

5. Do unto others as you would have done unto you.

Motivating employees on a daily basis is a constant challenge for any sport manager. For a sport organization to be successful, it is critical for everyone to be on the same page when it comes to working to accomplish organizational goals and objectives.

Taking Initiative

"What else needs to be done?" Sport managers should be ready to ask this important question at any time. When evaluating employees, one of the characteristics an employer in the sport industry looks for is **initiative** (Robinson, Hums, Crow, & Philips, 2001). No doubt, speaker after speaker from the sport industry has visited or will visit your classroom and talk about the importance of taking initiative in his or her sport organization. This will be especially true when you do your internship. When you have the opportunity to help out with an additional task, take advantage of that opportunity. First, it may enable you to learn about a different aspect of the sport organization with which you are working, and learning is a valuable skill in and of itself (Bower, 2009). Second, it may allow you to meet and interact with people outside of the office you work in, thus increasing your network. Finally, it shows your employer your commitment to working in the industry. Working in the sport industry is not always easy. The hours are long, the pay is low, and the work is seemingly endless. People in the organization recognize when someone is willing to do what is necessary to make sure an event happens as it should. Remember, "first impressions last," so leave the impression at your workplace that you are willing to work hard and take initiative.

Current Issues

Diversity in the Workforce

As mentioned in the previous section, the demographics of the North American workforce are ever changing. Sport management professionals need to stay abreast of these changes. Women, racial/ethnic minorities, people with disabilities, people from different nations, people with different sexual orientations, and people with various religious backgrounds all contribute to the sport industry. Sport organizations embracing diversity will be seen as the leaders in the twenty-first century; those who do not will be left behind. Sport managers need to stay on top of the latest legislation and managerial theories in their efforts to help their organizations become truly multicultural. In addition to staying knowledgeable about the current status of diversity in the sport management workforce, it is important for sport managers to be proactive. One suggestion is for sport managers to perform a self-study of their organization to evaluate their effectiveness in terms of recruiting and employing women, racial/ethnic minorities, people with disabilities, people with different sexual orientations, and people from different nations and religious backgrounds. The development and implementation of strategies involving recruitment and employment methods can then take place to encourage diversity in the workplace.

Managing Technology

As mentioned earlier, the technology that sport managers work with is changing every day. Sport managers need to be aware of how these changes affect the segment of the sport industry in which they work and how new technologies can be incorporated into the workplace. It is imperative that sport managers understand how expanding technology will improve customer relations and service. Internet sites such as Universal Sports, ParalympicSport.TV, and ESPN3 are changing how fans consume sport media. Social networks now heavily influence sport organizations, and many sport consumers

are Facebook and Twitter users. Just as the computer replaced the typewriter and email and text messaging are replacing phone calls, the next wave of technology will affect how sport managers run their daily business operations.

International Sport Management

Sport management is not unique to North America. Sport, and with it the field of sport management, continues to grow in popularity throughout the world. For example, Europe has a number of successful major professional soccer and basketball leagues as well as motor sports events. The Olympic Games, the Paralympic Games, the World Cup, and other multinational events are important elements of the sport industry.

In addition, U.S. professional sports leagues are increasingly exporting their products around the world. The NBA has 15 offices around the world, and in 2012 the NBA Finals were broadcast to 215 countries and in 47 different languages (Jessop, 2012). The NFL has broadcast packages for international TV viewers (The Deadline Team, 2013). An NFL regular season game is held at London's Wembley Stadium (NFL London, 2009), and the Jacksonville Jaguars have agreed to play games in London from 2013 to 2016. MLB focuses on worldwide growth and international activities through Major League Baseball International (MLBI) (MLB International, 2013). Opening Day series have been played in Japan, and 2010 saw exhibition games between the Dodgers and Padres in China (Major League Baseball, 2010). The 2014 season opened with a series in Australia (Major League Baseball, 2013). The World Baseball Classic continues to create excitement among fans from many nations. Sport managers from North America working abroad must be aware that they cannot unilaterally impose domestic models of sport governance on other cultures. Differences exist in terms of language, culture, etiquette, management, and communication styles. Sport managers need to learn, understand, and respect these differences when working in the international sport marketplace.

Additional Management Theories

Management theories and approaches to management are constantly changing, with new thoughts and ideas taking hold on a regular basis. Two of the more recent approaches to management are empowerment and emotional intelligence. **Empowerment** refers to encouraging employees to take initiative and make decisions within their area of operations (Luthans, 2005). Workers within the organization are provided with appropriate information and resources in making these decisions. As such, empowerment encourages innovation and accountability on the part of the employee (Luthans, 2005). The idea behind empowerment is that the employee will feel more a part of the organization, be more motivated, and therefore perform more effectively. In his book *Good to Great* (2001), Jim Collins conducted research on those companies that achieved long-term success and superiority. His findings support the empowerment approach to management and identify a culture of discipline common among "great" companies. Collins found that good-to-great companies build a consistent system with clear constraints, but they also give people freedom and responsibility within the framework of that system. They hire self-disciplined people who do not need to be managed and then manage the system, not the people (Collins, 2001).

Emotional intelligence was first defined in the 1980s by John D. Mayer and Peter Salovey but has received more attention with the studies of Daniel Goleman (Goleman, 1997). People at work may experience a variety of different emotions, both positive and negative. These emotions can be detrimental to the work process and organizational work environment. Emotional intelligence refers to the ability of workers to identify and acknowledge these emotions when they occur, and instead of having an immediate emotional response, to take a step back, allowing rational thought to influence their actions (Goleman, 1997).

Beyond the Bottom Line

In the twenty-first century, sport managers are more accountable than ever for looking at how their organizations can act in a socially responsible manner (Babiak & Wolfe, 2009; Bradish & Cronin, 2009; Cortsen, 2013). Sport managers now need to think about how their organizations will contribute to society in relation to issues such as sport and the environment, sport and human rights, and sport for development and peace (Hums, 2010; Hums & Hancock, 2011). These are new skill sets and knowledge areas for managers in the sport industry, but they are becoming more and more essential in the international sport marketplace.

Summary

Sport managers today face rapidly changing environments. One constant, however, is the necessity to successfully manage the sport organization's most valuable resource: its people. The workforce of the twenty-first century will be vastly different from the workforce of even the recent past. The influence of people of different cultures, rapidly changing technologies, and the globalization of the marketplace all make it necessary for tomorrow's sport managers to adapt. The measures of a good sport manager are flexibility and the ability to move with changes so that the sport organization and, more importantly, the people within that sport organization, continue to grow and move forward successfully into the future.

Functional areas of management have been used to explain and prepare managers for the various activities they get involved in as a result of their management role. These functional areas include planning, organizing, leading, and evaluating. In fulfilling these functional activities of management, managers employ a variety of skills essential to their success in this role. The skills discussed within this chapter include people skills, communication skills (oral and written), diversity management skills, technology management, decision-making skills, organizational politics awareness, managing change, motivating employees, and taking initiative.

Sport managers in today's sport organizations need to be aware of constantly evolving management schools of thought and ideas, learn from these theories, and incorporate what works best within their organizations. Sport managers also need to think of their organizations in terms of being good corporate citizens. Management is all about finding the best way to work with employees to get the job done. The fact that there is no one best way to manage underscores the excitement and challenge facing managers today.

Key Terms

communication skills, decision making, delegation, diversity, emotional intelligence, empowerment, evaluating, human relations movement, initiative, leading, managing change, managing technology, motivation, organizational behavior, organizational politics, organizing, participative decision making, people skills, planning, scientific management

References

Babiak, K., & Wolfe, R. (2009). Determinants of corporate social responsibility in professional sport: Internal and external factors. *Journal of Sport Management, 23*(6), 717–742.

Badenhausen, K., Ozanian, M. K., & Settimi, C. (2013). Billion-dollar Knicks and Lakers top list of NBA's most valuable teams. *Forbes.* Retrieved from http://www.forbes.com/sites /kurtbadenhausen/2013/01/23/billion-dollar -knicks-and-lakers-top-list-of-nbas-most -valuable-teams

Bolander, J. (2011). How to deal with organizational politics. Retrieved from http://www.thedailymba.com/2011/02/28 /how-to-deal-with-organizational-politics/

Bower, G. G. (2009). *A guide to field experiences and careers in sport and physical activity.* Deer Park, NY: Linus Publications.

Bradish, C., & Cronin, J. J. (2009). Corporate social responsibility in sport. *Journal of Sport Management, 23*(6), 691–697.

Buckley, P. (2013, May 1). The key to managing change. *Businessweek.* Retrieved from http://www.businessweek.com/articles/2013-05-01 /the-key-to-managing-change

Chelladurai, P. (2009). *Managing organizations for sport and physical activity: A systems perspective* (3d ed.). Scottsdale, AZ: Holcomb Hathaway.

Collegiate Licensing Company (2012, October 8). The collegiate licensing company names top sellers for fiscal year 2011-12. Retrieved from http://www.clc.com/News/Archived -Rankings/Rankings-Annual2012.aspx

Collins, J. (2001). *Good to great.* New York, NY: HarperCollins Publishers Inc.

Cortsen, K. (2013). The application of strategic CSR in the sports industry. Retrieved from http://kennethcortsen.com/sport-economy /the-application-of-strategic-csr-in-the -sports-industry/

Cunningham, G. B. (2011). *Diversity in sport organizations* (2d ed.). Scottsdale, AZ: Holcomb Hathaway Publishers.

Douglas, A. (2010). How to effectively manage change in your workplace. Retrieved from http://www.ohshandbook.com/au/how-to-effectively-manage-change-in-your-workplace/

EPM Communications (2012, June 1). Sports on the rebound: Retail sales of licensed merchandise based on sports properties rises 5.3% in 2011. Retrieved from http://www.epmcom.com/public/Sports_On_The_Rebound_Retail_Sales_Of_Licensed_Merchandise_Based_On_Sports_Properties_Rises_53_in_2011.cfm

Follett, M. P. (2002). In *Business: The ultimate resource* (pp. 988–989). Cambridge, MA: Perseus Publishing.

Gibson, J. L. (2006). *Organizations: Behavior, structure, processes* (12th ed.). Chicago, IL: Richard D. Irwin.

Goleman, D. (1997). *Emotional intelligence*. New York, NY: Bantam Books.

Hambrick, M. E., Simmons, J. M., Greenhalgh, G. P., & Greenwell, T. C. (2010). Examining the use of Twitter in sport: A content analysis of professional athlete tweets. *International Journal of Sport Communication, 3*, 454-471.

Hartley, P., & Bruckman, C. G. (2002). *Business communication*. London, UK: Routledge.

Holden Leadership Center (2013). Group decision making. Retrieved from http://leadership.uoregon.edu/resources/exercises_tips/organization/group_decision_making

Hums, M. A. (1996). Increasing employment opportunities for people with disabilities through sports and adapted physical activity. In *Proceedings from the Second European Conference on Adapted Physical Activity and Sports: Health, well-being and employment*. Leuven, Belgium: ACCO.

Hums, M. A. (2010). The conscience and commerce of sport management: One teacher's perspective. Earle F. Zeigler Lecture. *Journal of Sport Management, 24*(1), 1–9.

Hums, M. A., Barr, C. A., & Gullion, L. (1999). The ethical issues confronting managers in the sport industry. *Journal of Business Ethics, 20*, 51–66.

Hums, M. A., & Hancock, M. G. (2011). Sport management: Bottom lines and higher callings. In A. Gillentine, B. Baker, & J. Cuneen, *Paradigm shift: Major issues facing sport management academia*. Scottsdale, AZ: Holcomb-Hathaway Publishing.

Hums, M. A., & MacLean, J. C. (2013). *Governance and policy in sport organizations* (3d ed.). Scottsdale, AZ: Holcomb Hathaway.

International Health, Racquet and Sportsclub Association. (2012, April 2). 51.4 million Americans are health club members, up 2.4%; club usage at record high, industry revenue up 5%. Retrieved from http://www.ihrsa.org/media-center/2012/4/2/514-million-americans-are-health-club-members-up-24-club-usa.html

Jacobs, L. F., & Hyman, J. S. (2010, Feb. 24). 15 strategies for giving oral presentations. *U.S. News & World Report*. Retrieved from http://www.usnews.com/education/blogs/professors-guide/2010/02/24/15-strategies-for-giving-oral-presentations

Jessop, A. (2012, June 4). The surge of the NBA's international viewership and popularity. *Forbes*. Retrieved from http://www.forbes.com/sites/aliciajessop/2012/06/14/the-surge-of-the-nbas-international-viewership-and-popularity/

Lapchick, R. (2012a). *The 2012 racial and gender report card: College sport*. Orlando, FL: University of Central Florida, Institute for Diversity and Ethics in Sport. Retrieved from http://www.tidesport.org/RGRC/2012/2012_College_RGRC.pdf

Lapchick, R. (2012b). *The 2012 racial and gender report card: National Football League*. Orlando, FL: University of Central Florida, Institute for Diversity and Ethics in Sport. Retrieved from http://www.tidesport.org/RGRC/2012/2012_NFL_RGRC.pdf

Lapchick, R. (2013a, May 21). *The 2013 racial and gender report card: Major League Baseball*.

Orlando, FL: University of Central Florida, Institute for Diversity and Ethics in Sport. Retrieved from http://www.tidesport.org /RGRC/2013/2013_MLB_RGRC_Final _Correction.pdf

Lapchick, R. (2013b, June 25). *The 2013 racial and gender report card: National Basketball Association*. Orlando, FL: University of Central Florida, Institute for Diversity and Ethics in Sport. Retrieved from http://www .tidesport.org/RGRC/2013/2013_NBA _RGRC.pdf

Lipman, V. (2013, March 18). 5 ways to motivate – and demotivate – employees. *Forbes*. Retrieved from http://www.forbes.com/sites /victorlipman/2013/03/18/5-easy-ways-to -motivate-and-demotivate-employees/

Luthans, F. (2005). *Organizational behavior* (10th ed.). Boston, MA: McGraw-Hill.

Major League Baseball. (2010). News and features. Retrieved from http://mlb.mlb .com/mlb/internationalMajor League Baseball (2013). Major League Baseball's 2014 opening series set for Sydney, Australia. Retrieved from http://mlb.mlb.com/news /article.jsp?ymd=20130612&content _id=50461452&vkey=pr_mlb&c_id=mlb

Mayo, E. (2002). In *Business: The ultimate resource* (pp. 1020–1021). Cambridge, MA: Perseus Publishing.

MLB International. (2013). International. Retrieved from http://mlb.mlb.com/mlb /international/mlbi_index.jsp

National Organization on Disability. (2013). About us. Retrieved from http://www.nod .org/about_us

NFL London. (2009, October 5). NFL London 2010. Retrieved from http://www.nfllondon .net

Ozanian, M., Badenhausen, K., & Settimi, C. (2012a, September 5). Dallas Cowboys lead NFL with $2.1 billion valuation. *Forbes*. Retrieved from http://www.forbes.com/sites /mikeozanian/2012/09/05/dallas-cowboys -lead-nfl-with-2-1-billion-valuation/

Ozanian, M., Badenhausen, K., & Settimi, C. (2012b, November 28). Maple Leafs first hockey team worth $1 billion. *Forbes*. Retrieved from http://www.forbes.com/sites /mikeozanian/2012/11/28/nhl-team-values -2012-maple-leafs-first-hockey-team-worth -1-billion/

Ozanian, M., Badenhausen, K., & Settimi, C. (2012c, March 21). The business of baseball 2012. *Forbes*. Retrieved from http://www .forbes.com/sites/mikeozanian/2012/03/21 /the-business-of-baseball-2012/

Paciolan. (2013a). Email marketing. Retrieved from http://paciolan.com/solutions /marketing

Paciolan. (2013b). The University of Oregon renews its 25-year partnership with Paciolan. Retrieved from http://paciolan.com/2011 /hot-topics/the-university-of-oregon-renews -its-25-year-partnership-with-paciolan/

Peter Barron Stark Companies. (2010, January 12). Why employees resist change. Retrieved from http://www.peterstark.com/why-employees -resist-change

Quarterman, J., & Li, M. (1998). Managing sport organizations. In J. B. Parks, B. R. K. Zanger, & J. Quarterman (Eds.), *Contemporary sport management* (pp. 103–118). Champaign, IL: Human Kinetics.

Remember five things. (2003). *Personnel Today*, 31.

Robinson, M., Hums, M. A., Crow, B., & Phillips, D. (2001). *Profiles of sport management professionals: The people who make the games happen*. Gaithersburg, MD: Aspen Publishers.

Slack, T., & Parent, M. (2006). *Understanding sport organizations* (2nd ed.). Champaign, IL: Human Kinetics.

Stoldt, G. C., Ditmore, S. W., & Branvold, S. E. (2012). *Sport public relations: Managing stakeholder communication* (2d ed.). Champaign, IL: Human Kinetics.

Taylor, F. W. (2002). In *Business: The ultimate resource* (pp. 1054–1055). Cambridge, MA: Perseus Publishing.

The Deadline Team. (2013). FOX international channels scores NFL rights for parts of Europe. Retrieved from http://www.deadline.com/2013/09/fox-international-channels-scores-nfl-rights-for-parts-of-europe/

U.S. Department of Labor. (2012). Household data annual averages. Retrieved from http://www.bls.gov/cps/cpsaat39.pdf

U.S. Equal Employment Opportunity Commission. (2012). Job patterns for minorities and women in private industry (EEO-1). Retrieved from http://www1.eeoc.gov/eeoc/statistics/employment/jobpat-eeo1/2012/index.cfm#select_label

VanderZwaag, H. J. (1984). *Sport management in schools and colleges*. New York, NY: John Wiley & Sons.

VanderZwaag, H. J. (1998). *Policy development in sport management* (2nd ed.). Westport, CT: Praeger.

Wieberg, S., & Hiestand, M. (2010, April 22). NCAA reaches 14-year deal with CBS/Turner for men's basketball tournament, which expands to 68 teams for now. *USAToday*. Retrieved from http://content.usatoday.com/communities/campusrivalry/post/2010/04/ncaa-reaches-14-year-deal-with-cbsturner/1

Chapter 3

John Clark

Marketing Principles Applied to Sport Management

Learning Objectives

Upon completion of this chapter, students should be able to:

1. Differentiate between sport marketing and the marketing of traditional goods and services.

2. Assess the historical development of sport marketing, with a particular emphasis on the impact of broadcasting, sponsorship, promotion, and marketing research.

3. Compare and contrast the four P's of the marketing mix: Product, price, place, and promotion.

4. Differentiate between mass marketing and market segmentation, and describe the various demographic, geographic, and psychographic characteristics that can be used to identify specific target markets.

5. Analyze the importance of fostering fan identification and utilizing relationship marketing strategies.

6. Identify the key skills needed to be successful in sport marketing.

7. Illustrate how the rising cost of attending sporting events and the cluttered marketplace present challenges for sport marketers.

8. Evaluate social media's role in sport marketing.

9. Recognize the value of sport marketing research.

10. Assess the importance of developing and cultivating a positive image as part of an individual athlete's or an organization's marketing plan.

Introduction: What Is Sport Marketing?

How does Major League Baseball (MLB) reverse the trend of waning interest among youth? How can the L.A. Sparks of the Women's National Basketball Association (WNBA) sell more tickets? How does your local health club increase its membership? What events, athletes, or teams should Mountain Dew sponsor? How can Major League Soccer (MLS) increase its television ratings? How will conference realignment change the college landscape? How can Australian Rules Football penetrate the American sportscape? These questions and many others fall under the purview of sport marketing.

As defined by Kotler (2003, p. 5), "Marketing is typically seen as the task of creating, promoting, and delivering goods and services to consumers and businesses." Functions such as product development, advertising, public relations, sales promotion, and designing point-of-sale materials are all covered within this definition. However, Kotler (2003) ultimately boils the marketer's job down to one action: creating demand. If the marketer can cause a consumer to want a product, then that marketer has been successful. To accomplish this, marketers must identify customer wants and needs and then identify ways to satisfy them. According to Ries and Trout (1993, p. 106), "Brilliant marketers have the ability to think like a prospect thinks. They put themselves in the shoes of the consumer." Demand for a product will continue only as long as consumers see it as valuable. As such, one of the marketer's greatest challenges is to obtain the best possible understanding of what consumers want.

Sport marketing, therefore, consists of all activities designed to meet the needs and wants of sport consumers. According to this definition, sport marketing includes the marketing of (1) products, such as equipment, apparel, and footwear; (2) services and experiences, such as attendance at a sporting match or participation in sport; (3) entities, such as leagues, teams, or individuals; and (4) the recruitment and retention of volunteers as a relationship marketing exercise. Further, the sport marketer must think outside of their home stadium and consider providing the optimal experience for those who attend away games, events, or tournaments through the development of sport tourism product. Much of this chapter focuses on the marketing of leagues, teams, and individuals. This chapter also focuses on the use of sport promotion to market consumer and industrial products through sponsorships, partnerships, and or/endorsements.

Historical Development of Sport Marketing

Given the multifaceted nature of the definition of sport marketing, there are a variety of significant historical developments relating to key sport marketing concepts. These developments arose to more effectively communicate with **target markets**, the group of consumers to whom a product is marketed. In some cases these concepts were utilized as the result of experimentation, in other cases because of the intuitive nature of the sport marketer, and in still other cases because they were found to be successful in mainstream business marketing. It is a widely held view that Mark McCormack and his agency, International Management Group (IMG), invented sport marketing in the late 1960s. McCormack and IMG created their niche in sport marketing from athlete representation to event management to sponsorship rights fees and television broadcasts. IMG's influence in sports can be felt through its offices in 25 countries and its involvement in sports, entertainment, and media throughout the world. In a 1990 *Sports Illustrated* article, McCormack predicted that Southeast Asia was going to be the center of future sports growth, followed by South America and Africa (Swift, 1990). The 2008 Olympics being held in Beijing, the 2010 World Cup in South Africa, and the 2014 World Cup and 2016 Olympics being awarded to Brazil show that his predictions were correct. The legacy of McCormack, along with the reach, scope, and vertical integration of IMG, continues to impact the industry.

This section examines a number of these key concepts, along with the innovators responsible for these developments. We have separated the developments into four categories: (1) the evolution of sport broadcasting, (2) the growth of sponsorship, (3) the development of promotional strategies, and (4) the birth of research in sport marketing.

The Evolution of Sport Broadcasting

Beyond the actual broadcasting of sporting events, first on the radio, then on television, and now on the Internet and handheld wireless devices, one of the most dynamic changes in sport marketing was the evolution of sport broadcasting from pure, factual reporting aimed at sport fans to sport entertainment aimed at the masses. This was achieved most notably through the efforts of ABC's Monday Night Football television program and an ABC executive named Roone Arledge. Arledge was the first person to recognize that sport televised in prime time had to be more than sport—it also had to be entertainment. He incorporated that philosophy into Monday Night Football through the use of three broadcast personalities: initially sports journalist Howard Cosell; the voice of college football, Keith Jackson (who would be replaced the next year by Frank Gifford); and former National Football League (NFL) star Don Meredith. In doing so, Arledge "was the first executive who refused to let sports owners or leagues approve the announcers" (Bednarski, 2002, p. 41). Arledge also instituted more cameras and more varied camera angles, video highlights of the preceding day's

games, commentary, criticism, humor, and wit. Monday Night Football is now a sports institution.

When asked about his approach and view that sport was entertainment, Arledge responded that his job was "taking the fan to the game, not taking the game to the fan" (Roberts & Olson, 1989, p. 113). Arledge wanted the viewer sitting in his or her living room to see, hear, and experience the game as if he or she were actually in the stadium:

> What we set out to do in our programming (College Football, Monday Night Football, Wide World of Sports, and the Superstars to name a few) was to get the audience involved emotionally. If they didn't give a damn about the game, they might still enjoy the program (Roberts & Olson, 1989, p. 113).

Arledge's innovations—most notably instant replay, multiple cameras, crowd mics, and sideline interviewers—added to the enjoyment of the program.

The manner in which Monday Night Football (and other Arledge creations, such as the Wide World of Sports—a 1970s and 1980s favorite) married sport and entertainment paved the way for the success of other sports in prime time and today represents the norm. Think about it: When was the last time you saw a National Basketball Association (NBA) Finals game or MLB World Series game on during the daytime? This confluence of sport and entertainment is now visible 24 hours a day through ESPN. From the zany nicknames and commentary offered by Chris ("Boomer" or "Swami" depending on the persona) Berman, to the Top Ten List and Pardon the Interruption features on SportsCenter, ESPN has expanded into a global multimedia brand with nine U.S. networks (ESPN, ESPN2, ESPN3, ESPN3D, ESPN Classic, ESPN Mobile TV, ESPNU, ESPN News, Spanish-language ESPN Deportes) and

46 international networks reaching all seven continents, ESPN radio and ESPNDeportes Radio (syndicated in 11 countries), games and shopping (ESPN Shop), and popular websites (ESPN.com, ESPNDeportes.com, TEAM ESPN and market-specific sites) (ESPN, 2013). Today, additional growth is evident in sport-dedicated networks such as the Big Ten Network, Mountain West Network, SEC Network, Versus, and Spike TV. Further, the televised experience has changed substantially in recent times with the introduction of high-definition television and three-dimensional television. The evolution of broadcasting is also international in scope. The World Cup has been televised since 1954. However, the 1970 World Cup broadcast from Mexico in color is largely credited with the growth of international sports television as a whole. During this early time, the growth of international television was also sparked by Olympic and track and field content. Viewers can now follow almost any team, sport, or event live from anywhere in the world through an array of international broadcasting options.

The Acceptance and Growth of Sport Sponsorship

Sponsorship, or "the acquisition of rights to affiliate or directly associate with a product or event for the purpose of deriving benefits related to that affiliation" (Mullin, Hardy, & Sutton, 2007, p. 254), is not a recent phenomenon. The very first collegiate athletic event, an 1852 rowing contest between Harvard and Yale, was held in New Hampshire and sponsored by a railroad company. Coca-Cola has been a sponsor of the Olympic Games since 1928 (Coca-Cola Company, 2006). Sugar (1978) has documented the early roles of such companies as Coca-Cola, Bull Durham Tobacco, Curtiss Candy Company, Chalmers Motor Car Company, Purity Oats, American Tobacco Company, and Gillette in exploiting

the country's interest in sport through sport promotions, contests, advertising, and the use of sport personalities as endorsers. A picture of a professional baseball stadium from the early 1900s shows many signs on the outfield wall. Although the money involved may seem insignificant by today's standards, these early activities set the tone for what is perceived to be acceptable and advantageous in today's marketplace.

There have been, and continue to be, many pioneers in sport sponsorship and corporate involvement related to sport. One of the earliest pioneers was Albert G. Spalding, a former professional baseball player who parlayed his fame into what at one time was one of the largest sporting goods manufacturing companies in the world. Spalding was the first marketer to capitalize on the term "official" as it relates to a sport product, when his baseball became the "official baseball" of the National League in 1880 (Levine, 1985). Having secured the "official" status, Spalding then marketed his baseball as the best because it had been adopted for use in the National League, the highest level of play at that particular time. In the consumer's mind, this translated to the following: "Why choose anything but Spalding? If it is good enough for the National League, it must be superior to any other product in the market." Spalding carried over this theme when he began producing baseball uniforms for the National League in 1882. This type of practice is still prevalent today. Think for a moment—what company makes the highest quality football or basketball? Why is that your perception?

Whereas Spalding had the most profound impact on sport sponsorship in the latter part of the nineteenth century, two forces had a tremendous impact on sport sponsorship in the latter half of the twentieth century. The first was Mark McCormack, who as mentioned built the sport marketing agency IMG from a handshake with legendary golfer Arnold Palmer in 1960 (Bounds & Garrahan, 2003). At the time, Palmer was the most popular professional golfer. McCormack capitalized on this popularity by securing endorsement contracts for Palmer, helping companies promote and sell their products. As a result, Palmer's earnings skyrocketed, paving the way for McCormack to sign other popular golfers, such as Jack Nicklaus and Gary Player. Today, IMG represents thousands of athletes worldwide, including Tiger Woods.

Nike was the second significant force to affect sponsorship in the second half of the twentieth century. From its beginning as Blue Ribbon Sports in 1964 (an American offshoot of the Onitsuka Tiger brand), to its emergence as an independent brand in 1972, to its dominant role in the industry today, Nike has faced numerous challenges and emerged victorious on every front. One of the key elements in the history of Nike and its role in the world today was the packaging of the Nike brand, product, advertising, and athlete into one personality. This was achieved when Nike and Michael Jordan created "Air Jordan" (Strasser & Becklund, 1991). Understanding the impact of an athlete on footwear sales and having experienced disloyalty among some of its past endorsers, Nike sought to create a win–win situation by involving the athlete—in this case, Jordan—in the fortunes of the product. Nike looked at the long term and created a package that provided royalties for Jordan not only for shoes but for apparel and accessories. It was Nike's opinion that if a player had an incentive to promote the product, he or she became a member of the "team." The result of this strategy was the most successful athlete endorsement in history, with more than $100 million of Air Jordan products being sold in a single year (Strasser & Becklund, 1991). More recently, Nike has continued to partner with not only premier athletes but also premier athletes with unique identities. Its successful

endorsement of highly promoted basketball phenomenon LeBron James demonstrates that Nike regularly strives to identify with athletes who personify the best.

Beyond athlete endorsements, Nike has been extremely influential in other aspects of sponsorship. In an attempt to associate with the best college athletic programs, Nike initiated and signed university-wide athletic sponsorship agreements with major athletic programs such as the University of Michigan (now with adidas) and the University of North Carolina (still with Nike). This is a trend that has been followed by Nike competitors Reebok, adidas, and Under Armour. Throughout the 1990s, Nike was also known for the way it increased business while not paying to be "an official sponsor." Perhaps most visibly at the Atlanta Summer Olympic Games in 1996, Nike showed its adeptness with **ambush marketing**—capitalizing on the goodwill associated with an event without becoming an official sponsor. Even though Nike was not an International Olympic Committee (the governing body overseeing the Olympics) sponsor, many people thought it was. To create this impression, Nike employed a variety of strategies. Among them, Nike turned a parking garage in close proximity to the Olympic Village into a "mini-Niketown" experience that included autograph sessions and appearances from Nike athletes such as track star Michael Johnson.

Sponsorship has expanded its look and feel over the past 10 years. Whether they are larger events such as the Olympics and World Cup or a local soccer club, the dynamics of sponsorship have penetrated far beyond field signage and television mentions. The digital era is evolving sponsorship into mobile phone applications. Further, some of the sanctities of sponsorship in the United States are slowly diminishing. For example, naming rights of teams and sponsor logos on team uniforms are no longer off limits as companies such as Red Bull are

branding teams in their image with the creation of the New York Red Bulls. Professional sport leagues in the United States are also following suit. The WNBA allows member franchises to place sponsor logos on player uniforms, and at the beginning of the 2013 season, 7 of the 12 WNBA teams had a jersey sponsorship (Bowman, 2013).

Emphasis on Product Extensions and Development of Promotional Strategies

The emphasis on product extensions and the development of team sport promotional strategies can be attributed to the late Bill Veeck (1914–1986), a sport marketing pioneer in professional baseball for almost 40 years. At various times from the 1940s through the 1970s, Veeck was the owner of the Cleveland Indians, the St. Louis Browns, and the Chicago White Sox (on two different occasions). Prior to Veeck, sporting events were not staged for the masses but rather for the enjoyment of sport fans. Veeck recognized that to operate a successful

and profitable franchise, one could not totally depend upon the success of the team to generate capacity crowds. In other words, Veeck believed that a team must provide reasons other than the game itself for people to attend and support the franchise.

Several philosophies guided much of Veeck's efforts and left a lasting legacy on sport promotion. First, Veeck was firm in his belief that fans came to the ballpark to be entertained (Holtzman, 1986). Veeck's promotional philosophy embraced the goal of "creating the greatest enjoyment for the greatest number of people…not by detracting from the game, but by adding a few moments of fairly simple pleasure" (Veeck & Linn, 1962, p. 119). Promotions and innovations attributed to Veeck include giveaway days like Bat Day, exploding scoreboards, outfield walls that went up and down, fireworks, and the organizing of special theme nights for students, Scouts, and church groups (Veeck & Linn, 1962).

Second, Veeck recognized that to build a loyal fan base, the attending experience had to be pleasurable: "In baseball, you are surprisingly dependent upon repeat business. The average customer comes to the park no more than two or three times a year. If you can put on a good-enough show to get him to come five or six times, he has become a source of pride and a source of revenue" (Veeck & Linn, 1965, p. 20). In addition to being entertaining, part of creating loyal customers entailed ensuring the best possible attending atmosphere. As such, Veeck focused on providing a clean facility and a hospitable environment. He carried out this philosophy by enlarging bathrooms, adding daycare facilities, greeting his "guests," and standing at the exits to thank them for coming.

Finally, Veeck suggested:

> It isn't enough for a promotion to be entertaining or even amusing; it must create conversation. When the fan goes home and talks about what he has seen, he is getting an additional kick out of being able to say he was there. Do not deny him that simple pleasure, especially since he is giving you valuable word-of-mouth advertising to add to the newspaper reports (Veeck & Linn, 1965, p. 13).

In an effort to have people talk about their experience, Veeck devised unique and unorthodox promotions such as "Grandstand Managers" night, in which a section of the audience voted on what a manager should do in a particular situation. While Veeck was often criticized for his practices (and they were quite radical), his legacy is still visible today throughout sport events.

The Birth of Research in Sport Marketing to Improve Performance and Acceptance

Although some early pioneers like Veeck communicated well with their customers through informal contacts, letters, and speaking engagements, Matt Levine is the individual most often credited with formalizing customer research in the sport industry. Like Veeck, Levine was well aware that there were marketing variables other than winning and losing. Employed as a consultant by the Golden State Warriors in 1974 and given the goal of increasing attendance, Levine developed what he termed an "audience audit" to capture **demographic** and **psychographic** information about fans attending games (Hardy, 1996). Levine was also a pioneer in using intercepts (one-on-one onsite interviews) and focus groups (discussion groups involving 8 to 12 individuals with similar characteristics discussing a predetermined agenda) to gather marketing information for professional sport franchises.

The purposes of Levine's research and, for that matter, most research in sport marketing, are as follows:

- To profile the sport consumer demographically, geographically, or psychographically
- To categorize attendance behavior and segment attendance by user groups related to potential ticket packages
- To analyze purchasing behavior as it relates to product extensions such as merchandise, concessions, and so on
- To evaluate operational aspects of the sport product such as parking, customer service, entertainment aspects, and employee courtesy and efficiency
- To measure interest in new concepts that may be under consideration
- To document viewing and listening behavior
- To understand the consumer's information network in order to determine efficient methods of future communication to that consumer and like consumers
- To offer two-way communication with the target market

One of the most successful applications of Levine's market research techniques involved the National Hockey League's (NHL's) San Jose Sharks. Levine used a series of what he calls **"pass-by interviews"** or **intercept interviews**. Pass-by interviews are onsite interviews in heavy traffic areas such as malls. These interviews utilize one or more visual aids and assess the interviewee's reaction to the visual aid. The visual aid is usually a sample or interpretation of a product (style, color, or logo) under consideration. Levine's pass-by interviews were used to determine the reaction of people who had submitted ticket deposits for the expansion of the San Jose Sharks to a series of proposed logo and uniform designs. The results of Levine's research efforts? The color scheme under consideration was eliminated and the graphic logo of the shark was changed. In 1992, the new logo and colors resulted in estimated retail sales of Sharks' merchandise in the United States and Europe of $125 million (Hardy, 1996). As a result of Levine's approach and success with his clients and their acceptance of his methods and findings, market research in the sport industry is increasingly becoming a common practice rather than the exception. Although consumer research continues to be very popular, today's research tends to focus more on sponsorship evaluation such as brand fit, commitment and loyalty, media exposure, digital impact, and one of the toughest concepts, return on investment, or return on objectives.

Key Sport Marketing Concepts

The Sport Marketing Mix

As defined by McCarthy and Perreault (1988), the **marketing mix** refers to the controllable variables the company puts together to satisfy a target group. The marketing mix, then, is the recipe for creating a successful marketing campaign. The elements of the marketing mix most commonly associated with sport are often referred to as the "four Ps": product, price, place, and promotion (Kotler, 2003). In sport marketing, we often refer to the "five Ps," including public relations as its own P (instead of lumping it in with promotion), given the significant role it plays in sport marketing. In comparison with the marketing of a laundry detergent, soup, car, or stereo, there are some unique aspects of marketing the sport product that must be accounted for when discussing the marketing mix. Some of the most important differences are presented in Table 3-1. These differences and their relevance to sport marketers will be discussed throughout the rest of this chapter.

Product

Whereas marketing sporting goods is similar to marketing mainstream products because tangible benefits can be provided, marketing a sporting event (such as a minor league baseball game), a sport service (such as a health club), or even an athlete is different. There has been some debate about what constitutes the "core" product in sport marketing. For example, some posit that the core product is the actual event. On the other hand, if we applied a mainstream marketing definition, the "core" product is the *benefit* that consumers seek from a product, service, or experience, therefore taking the focus off the actual event. Thus, for a Ladies Professional Golf Association (LPGA) event, one side would view the core product as the golfers on the course, whereas the other side would counter that the core product is the benefit that consumers received from attending the event that may or may not be related to what actually happens on the course. Spectators at the event and television viewers cannot touch or taste the product—they merely experience it. Further, spectators and viewers have no idea who is

Table 3-1 Key Differences Between Traditional Marketing and Sport Marketing

Traditional Marketing	Sport Marketing
• The success of any entity may depend on defeating and eliminating the competition.	• In many cases, sport organizations must simultaneously compete and cooperate.
• Very few consumers consider themselves experts and instead rely on trained professionals for information and assistance.	• Due to the preponderance of information and the likelihood of personal experience and strong personal identification, sport consumers often consider themselves experts.
• When a customer purchases a sweater, it is tangible and can be seen and felt and used on more than one occasion.	• The sport product is invariably intangible, subjective, and heavily experiential.
• Customer demand is more predictable because the product is always the same.	• Consumer demand tends to fluctuate widely.
• Mainstream products have an inventory and a shelf life, and supplies can be replenished.	• The sport product (the game) is simultaneously produced and consumed; there is no inventory.
• Although other people can enjoy the purchase of a car, the enjoyment or satisfaction of the purchaser does not depend upon it.	• Sport is generally publicly consumed, and consumer satisfaction is invariably affected by social facilitation.
• Inconsistency and unpredictability are considered unacceptable—for example, if a particular car occasionally went backward when the gear indicated forward, consumers would be up in arms.	• The sport product is inconsistent and unpredictable.
• The mainstream marketer works with research and design to create the perceived perfect product.	• The sport marketer has little or no control over the core product and often has limited control over the product extensions.
• Only religion and politics, which in and of themselves are not viewed as products or services but rather as beliefs, are as widespread as sport.	• Sport has an almost universal appeal and pervades all elements of life.

going to win the event. Such unpredictability is both an advantage and a disadvantage for sport marketers. In one sense, it allows the sport marketer to promote the fact that fans do not want to miss out on a chance to see something spectacular. However, from another perspective, the sport marketer cannot entice people to attend by promising success for a particular athlete or team. In fact, in nearly all cases relating to spectator sport, the sport marketer

has little control over the core product. Again, however, this depends on what one views as the core product. The vice president of marketing for the LPGA cannot orchestrate who will win the LPGA championship. The chief marketing officer for the Dallas Mavericks of the NBA cannot do anything to enhance the chances that the Mavericks will win.

The sport marketer must account for these unique differences relating to the sport product.

For example, because the sport marketer has little control over what happens on the playing surface, he or she must focus on the extensions surrounding the game that can be managed. This is where the works of Veeck, who employed a variety of tactics to enhance the attending experience beyond what happened on the field, are important lessons. For example, if you were to attend almost any NBA game today, you would be entertained during every time-out with on-court performances and the extensive use of interactive video boards that allow fans to text messages and view themselves on the big screen.

© Photos.com

Price

Like any other product, most sport products have an associated price. A variety of products within the sport industry must be priced: tickets, healthclub memberships, satellite television packages, special access areas on sport websites, and so on. When attending an event, there is usually more than one price. For example, beyond the cost of a ticket, the attendee may have to pay to park or to purchase concessions or a souvenir.

Increasingly, the cost of a ticket is separated into the actual ticket price and an additional charge per ticket for access to premium services such as restaurants or waiter/waitress service.

Because the sport product is usually intangible and experiential, its price often depends on the value (or perceived value) provided by the sport product or experience. Consumers can perceive a higher price to mean higher quality. However, the sport marketer needs to be careful to balance perceived value versus perceived quality. Using concessions at a new MLB stadium as an example, just because a Coca-Cola costs $5 does not mean that the consumer will perceive it to be a good value and of high quality. Further, in a time when both ticket prices associated with professional sport and the costs of ancillary items such as concessions have risen dramatically, sport marketers are challenged to provide attendees with more value than ever. A consumer attending an event considers the entire cost of attending when determining the value of the event. This cost includes both the monetary costs (such as the ticket price, concessions, and parking) and the personal cost of attending (which includes the time it takes to travel to a stadium or arena).

Place

The typical mainstream product is made at a manufacturing site and then transferred to a location where it is available for customers to purchase. Further, most products have a shelf life; that is, if they are not bought today, they can still be sold tomorrow. Neither condition is true when examining team sports and events. The place where the product is produced (the stadium or arena) is also the place where the product is consumed. Further, once a game is over, the tickets for that game cannot be sold. What would happen if someone offered to sell you tickets to one of your favorite team's games that had already happened? You would laugh, right? Because of these unique nuances associated with the place at which the sport product is distributed, sport marketers must aggressively pre-sell sporting events.

Although there are some unique differences associated with place in sport marketing, there are also some similarities to mainstream marketing. Location can be very important. People talk about going to Wrigley Field in Chicago for a variety of reasons, including the history and tradition of the facility as well as its location in a popular North Chicago neighborhood. Similarly, the location of a health club can be vitally important to its success. Referring back to Veeck again, facility aesthetics also play an important role. Veeck believed in a clean facility. From 1990 to present, MLB experienced a surge in new ballparks with "retro" features that reminded fans of baseball parks from the early 1900s. Further, the amenities available in new stadiums or health clubs can be a very important part of the place a sport product is sold. Because the sport consumption experience is a social one, most new stadiums and arenas have significant space dedicated to upscale restaurants and bars. One of the newest and most fan-friendly stadiums is AT&T Stadium (previously known as Cowboys Stadium) in Texas. Opened in 2009, it is 3 million square feet and seats 80,000 spectators, but it can comfortably accommodate 100,000 thanks to fan-friendly, standing-room-only spaces among the facility. There are 2,900 television screens (not to mention the largest center video board) throughout the facility, making it virtually impossible to miss a play on the field no matter where a fan is seated. In 2012, the MLB's Miami Marlins opened a new 37,000 seat stadium on the site of the old Orange Bowl. Marlin Park incorporates aspects of Miami and South Florida culture into the entire facility—from colorful art exhibits to aquariums—all designed to make the fans feel connected to the franchise. This type of facility atmosphere and other traditions are a vital part of the fan experience. Vuvuzela horns at the 2010 Fédération Internationale de Football Association (FIFA) World Cup in South Africa, the Pagoda at Indianapolis Motor Speedway, or the Green Monster at Fenway Park are fixtures of the fan experience. As facilities expand, renovate, and/or begin new construction, the fan experience is invoked by the facility. Today, most major sporting facilities offer a tour for interested fans.

Promotion

Promotion typically refers to a variety of functions, including advertising (paid messages conveyed through the media), personal selling (face-to-face presentation in which a seller attempts to persuade a buyer), publicity (media exposure not paid for by the beneficiary), and sales promotion (special activities undertaken to increase sales of a product) (Mullin et al., 2007). In undertaking sport promotion, the unique aspects of sport marketing are important to understand. Sport entities often both compete and cooperate. For example, the Chicago White Sox will probably heavily promote the fact that the New York Yankees are visiting in an effort to increase attendance for the Yankees series, even though they are competing with the Yankees on the field. In fact, in many cases, a sport team's competition may help it draw fans.

In promoting sport, the sport marketer must also take into account the unpredictable and experiential nature of the product. The Seattle Storm of the WNBA would probably promote the chance to have a good time while watching a Storm game instead of promising a Storm win. Staying with the experiential nature of sport, promotion can offer something tangible such as souvenirs or giveaways. A fan who receives a LeBron James bobblehead doll after attending a Miami Heat game is likely to remember that attending experience.

Sponsorships typically try to take advantage of all of the elements of promotion. Consider Coca-Cola's "Bracket Town" ad campaign launched in conjunction with the 2013 NCAA

March Madness Basketball Tournament. As a sponsor of the NCAA, Coca-Cola set up fan interactive zones, or Bracket Towns, in each city hosting regional games. The towns, hyped as the official pre- and post-tournament party sites, had many activities and prizes for fans, as well as celebrities such as basketball announcer Dick Vitale. Coke cross-promoted the Bracket Towns with print, digital, and social media buys to link their brand with the positive emotions people feel toward March Madness. Finally, Coke utilized the Bracket Towns and associated media to allow attendees to test new products and generally promote the sale of its many brands.

Segmentation

As opposed to mass marketing, where an organization markets its products to every possible consumer in the marketplace, **segmentation** entails identifying subgroups of the overall marketplace based on a variety of factors, including age, income level, ethnicity, geography, and lifestyle tendencies. Although the sport product has nearly universal appeal, it would still be foolish of sport marketers to market their product to the entire population. A target market is a segment of the overall market that has certain desirable traits or characteristics and is coveted by the marketer. These traits or characteristics can be (1) demographic, such as age, income, gender, or educational background; (2) geographic, such as a region or a postal code; (3) psychographic, lifestyles, activities, or habits; or (4) product use, such as type of beer they drink, car they drive, or credit card they use most often. Using a women's college basketball program as an example, target markets could include girls aged 8 to 18 (age segmentation) who play organized basketball (psychographic segmentation) within 30 miles of the university campus (geographic segmentation).

Two increasingly popular bases of segmentation are ethnic marketing and generational marketing. As of 2010, 16.3% of the U.S. population was Hispanic (U.S. Census Bureau, 2010). Recognizing that the Hispanic population is a fast-growing and large segment of the U.S. population, sport teams now attempt to market directly to Hispanics through such strategies as producing radio broadcasts and websites in Spanish. For example, ESPN has created ESPN Deportes, a United States–based Spanish-language network targeted to Hispanics (Liberman, 2003). The MLS in particular pays particular attention to the Hispanic market. Almost half of the MLS' league office staff is Latino, it has more Spanish-speaking TV partners than any other U.S. league, and the league hosts SuperLiga, InterLiga, and Mexican national team appearances in the United States.

Sport marketers also are expending significant energies to reach Generation Y (people born between 1977 and 1996). This segment is unlike others in that—in addition to mainstream sports such as football, basketball, and baseball—Generation Y consumers are very interested in "action" sports such as skateboarding and motocross. For sports such as MLB, this presents a challenge in creating future generations of fans.

Another base of segmentation receiving increased attention is product use segmentation as it relates to attendance at sporting events. This tactic assumes that the consumption of people who attend a few games per year can be increased. Teams naturally have information about all people who purchased single-game tickets during a given season. Using these data, the sales force for a given team will call someone after that person has attended a game and inquire about the experience. If the fan had an enjoyable time at the game, then the salesperson will attempt to sell the fan additional games or a partial season ticket package of five or eight games. This strategy is commonly adopted by teams that have excess seats to sell.

© Pamela Moore/iStockphoto

Fan Identification

Fan identification is defined as the sense of oneness with or belongingness to an organization (Bhattarcharya, Rao, & Glynn, 1995). In theory, the more a fan identifies with a team or organization, the greater the likelihood the fan will develop a broad and long-term relationship with that team and attach his or her loyalty to the organization. Sport is unique in the significant fan identification it engenders among its consumers. Think about it: Are you more emotionally connected to your toothpaste or your favorite sports team? Manifestations of fan identification are everywhere. Message boards, painting one's face, and wearing logo apparel are all ways in which sport fans demonstrate their connection to a team. When you talk about your favorite team's games, do you refer to your favorite team as "we" or "they"? Many people refer to their team as "we" (especially after a team wins) even though they have no direct impact on the team's performance. This is an example of high fan identification. Beyond teams, recent research suggests that fans may also identify with an array of elements including coaches, individual players, smaller subgroups of fans, or with sports in general.

Fan identification also is very important for sponsors of sporting events. Ideally, a sponsor will be able to tap into some of the strong emotional connection between a fan and his or her sport team through a sponsorship. For example, it is often thought that sponsors of National Association of Stock Car Auto Racing (NASCAR) drivers earn the business of the drivers' fans through association with the race team. Similarly, it could be argued that a sponsorship with the Dallas Cowboys or New York Yankees, each of which has a large group of vocal and loyal supporters, could result in increased business, at least in part due to the ability to capitalize on the strong identification that exists with each of these teams.

Another method of establishing fan identification is for sport marketers to adopt cause-related marketing into their marketing strategies. Cause-related sport marketing entails a sport organization forming a partnership with a charity or cause in order to market a product or service for mutual benefit (Adkins, 1999). If the sport organization chooses a charity or cause that resonates with its fans or desired target market, fans may develop deeper levels of identification and actively support the cause (Lachowetz & Gladden, 2003).

Relationship Marketing

If marketers adopt relationship marketing strategies, they can help foster identification with sport teams. According to Kotler (2003, p. 13), "**relationship marketing** has the aim of building mutually satisfying long-term relations with key parties—customers, suppliers, distributors—in order to earn and retain their business." Rather than looking at consumers as transactions, relationship marketing suggests that organizations seek to build long-term relationships with their customers, ultimately converting them to or maintaining them as loyal product users (Berry, 1995). Relationship marketing begins with the customer and in essence encourages the organization to integrate the customer into the company; to build a relationship with the customer based upon communication, satisfaction, and service; and to work to continue to expand and broaden the involvement of the customer with the organization. In effect, this integration, communication, service, and satisfaction combine to create a relationship between the consumer and the organization (McKenna, 1991). The implementation of relationship marketing practices is often called **customer relationship management**.

In addition to sport organizations seeking to develop and sustain lasting relationships with sport fans, relationship marketing is also key to the recruitment and retention of a volunteer workforce. Many sport organizations and events rely on the ongoing contributions of volunteers to run and sustain their operations. Therefore, it is critical to develop relationships with these volunteers who provide an ongoing commitment and service to the organization.

Key Skills

Because marketing is a form of communication, the key skills involved in sport marketing are communication based and are in many ways similar to the skills required for sport management. They are as follows:

1. *Oral communication:* The ability to speak in public, speak to large groups, and make persuasive presentations demonstrating knowledge about the product and its potential benefit to the consumer.

2. *Written communication:* The competence to prepare sales presentations, reports, analyses, and general correspondence in a concise and insightful manner.

3. *Data analysis skills:* The use of data to inform the decision-making process. Whether it be projecting the return on investment for a sponsorship program or analyzing a customer database to identify

the organization's best customers, quantitative skills are increasingly in demand in sport organizations.

4. *Computer capabilities:* Beyond basic word processing skills, expertise in all types of software, including databases, spreadsheets, desktop publishing, ticketing systems, webpage design and utilization, and social media tools. In particular, in-depth knowledge of presentation software (such as Microsoft's PowerPoint) is important to the preparation of professional presentations.

5. *Personnel management:* The skills to develop, motivate, and manage a diverse group of people to achieve organizational goals and objectives.

6. *Sales:* The ability to recognize an opportunity in the marketplace and convince potential consumers of the value and benefits of that opportunity. Part of identifying opportunities is understanding the wants and needs of consumers. Therefore, listening is a very important, yet often overlooked, skill for anyone in a sales capacity.

7. *Education:* A minimum of a bachelor's degree in sport management or a bachelor's degree in business with an internship in a sport setting. A master's degree in sport management or a master of business administration degree, although not essential in some positions, is desirable for advancement and promotion.

Finally, the successful marketer must also understand the sport product. It is not essential for the marketer to be a dedicated follower of the sport; however, the marketer must comprehend the sport product, know its unique differences, and know how these differences assist and hinder the marketing of the sport product.

Current Issues

Innovation in sport marketing practices has lagged behind innovation in other service industries, in mainstream marketing, and in business in general because the cultivation of trained sport management professionals is a relatively new phenomenon (only occurring over the past 40 years). However, in recent years, certain approaches and philosophies have begun to be accepted and have become widespread in the sport industry. Yet, as sport moves forward this century, it faces a variety of challenges that will require an increased focus on marketing innovation and sophistication. Some of these challenges, as well as practices being developed to adapt to them, are discussed in this section.

The Rising Cost of Attending a Sporting Event

Table 3-2 depicts the drastic increase in the overall cost of attending an MLB, NBA, NFL, or NHL game from 1991 to 2013. In an era when owners have become more focused on bottom-line performance (in some cases due to teams assuming millions of dollars of debt for new stadiums), ticket prices and the overall cost of attending a major professional event in North America have increased dramatically.

However, there is increasing evidence that sport fans are not able to pay such prices. For example, a 2000 *Sports Illustrated* article reported the results from a research study conducted by the Peter Harris Research Group. One of the findings was that 57% of sport fans cited the total cost of attending as a reason that they are less likely to attend a sporting event (Swift, 2000). These facts suggest that fans either do not have the wherewithal to attend or do not see the value in attending major professional sporting events. This study also suggests that major professional sport teams are increasingly challenged in their efforts to undertake relationship marketing with their fans. In fact,

Table 3-2 Comparison of the Average Ticket Prices and Cost of Attending an MLB, NBA, NFL, and NHL Game in 1991 vs. 2013

	1991		2013			
	League Average Ticket Price	Average Cost of Attending	League Average Ticket Price	Average Cost of Attending	Increase in Ticket Price	Increase in Cost of Attendance
MLB	$9.14	$79.14	$27.48	$207.80	200.66%	162.57%
NBA	$22.52	$141.91	$50.99	$315.66	126.42%	122.44%
NFL	$25.21	$151.33	$73.38	$443.93	191.07%	193.35%
NHL	N/A	N/A	$61.01	$354.82	N/A	N/A

Note: NBA and NHL data for 2012–2013 seasons. NFL data for 2012 season

Data from: Jozsa, F.P, Jr. (2010). *Football fortunes: the business, organization and strategy of the NFL*. Jefferson, NC: McFarland & Company, Inc; Team Marketing Report, Inc. (2009 September). TMR's fan cost index. Retrieved from http://teammarketing.com.ismmedia.com/ISM3/std-content/repos/Top/News/nfl%20fci%202009.pdf; Team Marketing Report, Inc. (2012, November). TMR's NBA fan cost index. Retrieved from http://www .fancostexperience.com/pages/fcx/fci_pdfs/9.pdf; Team Marketing Report, Inc. (2012, September). TMR's NFL fan cost index. Retrieved from http://www.fancostexperience.com/pages/fcx/blog_pdfs/entry0000018_pdf000 .pdf; Team Marketing Report, Inc. (2013, February). TMR's NHL fan cost index. Retrieved from http://www .fancostexperience.com/pages/fcx/blog_pdfs/entry0000020_pdf001.pdf; Team Marketing Report, Inc. (2013, April). TMR's NLB fan cost index. Retrieved from http://news.cincinnati.com/assets/AB20330243.PDF.

sport fans appear to be more skeptical of the motivations of team owners than ever before. This same Harris Research Group study found that "85% of fans believe owners are more interested in making money than in making it possible for Joe Fan to attend games" (Swift, 2000, p. 78).

This circumstance presents a significant challenge for sport marketers. During the time period in which prices and the cost of attending increased so dramatically, a large number of new stadiums and arenas were built and renovated. In many cases, owners of professional teams were responsible for financing at least part of these building projects. As a result, owners today also have to worry about paying off debt associated with stadium development. Increasing ticket prices has clearly been one way that owners have sought to generate revenue. Unfortunately, the aforementioned statistics suggest that sport fans may not be willing to pay much more to attend a sporting event. Some teams, sensing this trend and attempting to repair damaged relationships, have actually decreased ticket prices. But if owners cannot increase ticket prices substantially, they must find additional ways to generate revenue. As such, one of the key challenges for anyone in team sport marketing will be increasing revenues for sport teams.

One way that teams and other sport entities are attempting to enhance relationships while at the same time increase revenue is through database marketing. Database marketing involves creating a database, usually consisting of names, addresses, and other demographic information related to consumers, and then managing that database. Managing the database usually involves developing and delivering integrated marketing programs, including promotions and sales offers, to the database universe or to appropriate segments or target markets of that database. For example, if the

Texas Rangers knew that a season ticket holder purchased extra tickets the last time the Seattle Mariners visited Texas, the Rangers could contact that season ticket holder with a special offer for the Mariners' next visit. In one sense, this would communicate to the season ticket holder that the Rangers cared about serving his or her needs. In another sense, it might help sell several tickets that otherwise might have gone unused for a particular game. Database marketing is often an integral factor in a company's decision to sponsor an event. For example, corporate sponsors often create promotions at events where they offer to give away something special, such as a trip or a valuable product such as a golf driver, if people attending the event will provide their name, address, and other relevant information. The next time you attend an event and a credit card company offers you a T-shirt or floppy hat for your personal information, realize you have just been engaged in database marketing.

Enhanced technology has enabled sport marketers to utilize social media sites to establish and foster relationships with fans. Due to the immediacy social media offers both the marketer and fans, information can be disseminated more effectively and efficiently, problematic issues can be dealt with in a more timely manner, and the personality of the sport organization's brand takes on a new dimension. **Box 3-1** discusses the social media strategy employed by the Dick's Sporting Goods Pittsburgh Marathon marketing team. Despite the need to constantly monitor social media sites, when used properly, they can be an important tool for sport marketers to build and nurture fan relationships.

The Cluttered Marketplace

Competition is fierce for sport organizations and corporations marketing their products through sport. As never before, there are

Box 3-1   Social Media's Role in Sport Marketing: The Dick's Sporting Goods Pittsburgh Marathon

For sport organizations of all types, social media has become a standard part of the marketing toolbox alongside the traditional marketing channels of television, radio, and print. Unlike traditional marketing channels, social media is inexpensive, gives the sport marketer the ability to easily create custom messages, and, most importantly, provides an opportunity for dialogue between the sport organization and the consumer.

One sport organization that does an excellent job employing social media as part of its marketing mix is the Dick's Sporting Goods Pittsburgh Marathon (DSG Pittsburgh Marathon). The original Pittsburgh Marathon was run in 1985, and quickly became one of the top five marathons in the United States (Dee, 2009). Poor regional economic conditions led to the pullout of the marathon's top sponsor, forcing the event to go on hiatus from 2004 to 2008, when a new management team resurrected the event with Dick's Sporting Goods becoming the title sponsor. In the five years since, the new iteration of the marathon has grown from 10,000 to 30,000 participants (Roessner, 2014), with a broad slate of corporate partners. Social media has been instrumental in that growth.

The DSG Pittsburgh Marathon staff takes a three-pronged approach for their social media strategy, which is conducted both prior to and during the race weekend.

1. **Promotional Marketing**

   At least six months prior to an upcoming race weekend, the marathon communications director uses platforms such as Facebook, Twitter, Instagram, and Pinterest to alert runners about registration information, training techniques, the meeting time and place of informal training groups, and nutritional information. This method is also used to market other organizational activities (other races, fundraising events) throughout the year.

2. **Sponsorship Fulfillment**

   Each sponsorship contract the marathon enters into is unique; yet, most include language that deals with the use of social media to promote the sponsors. Taking care not to inundate followers with overt commercials for sponsoring businesses, the marathon staff will only promote a sponsoring brand using social media if the message adds value for the followers. For example, several months before the event day, the marathon staff will use Twitter to notify followers that the official training gear can only be purchased at Dick's Sporting Goods. This tweet includes hash tags for both the marathon and DSG. Additionally, the staff will tag the Facebook page of DSG.

   According to Emily Baum, the Communications Coordinator for the DSG Pittsburgh Marathon, a great deal of attention is paid to managing the Marathon brand as it is

(continues)

Box 3-1   Social Media's Role in Sport Marketing: The Dick's Sporting Goods Pittsburgh Marathon (Continued)

perceived by its customers in relation to sponsored messages. "Our runners are very loyal to the Marathon. We don't send out messages that look like ads. We try to position the sponsors in messages that are valuable to our runners and followers."

An example of this practice can be found in messages (tweets, Facebook postings) sent by the marathon staff on training tips. This content is supplied by the University of Pittsburgh Medical Center (UPMC), an authority in the field and also a marathon sponsor.

3. **Operational Messaging**

   During race week, the marathon staff utilizes social media to inform the public about key race-related information and customer service activities. Staff members on the various full and half-marathon courses monitor traffic and pedestrian activity, and then, using Twitter, text messaging, or a live chat program, convey the problem areas back to the control center, where other staffers can alert the appropriate authorities to deal with the issue. For the 2014 race, the marathon staff created a unique hashtag, #AskPGHMarathon, which fielded questions from race participants, spectators, media, and those local denizens who wished to avoid marathon-related road closures.

   A key component of the DSG Pittsburgh Marathon's social media strategy was the creation of a Social Media Command Center—the first event of its kind in the United States to employ such a strategy. This Center was staffed with 30 volunteers who worked a rotating schedule the two days leading up to the marathon, and the day of the marathon itself. The volunteers were trained as to the type of promotional, operational, and sponsorship-related messages they were to disseminate. Early results indicate a stunning success, with the Center engaging with 93% of its followers (only 10% of whom were registered runners).

   Each sport organization has different marketing objectives that can be achieved in a variety of ways. As described above, traditional marketing channels can be supplemented, or even replaced by the use of social media in order to engage customers and enhance sponsorship agreements.

Data from: Emily Baum, Communications Coordinator, DSG Pittsburgh Marathon (personal communication, May 7, 2014); Dee, R. (2009, February 15). *Return of the Pittsburgh marathon*. Retrieved from http://voices.yahoo.com/return-pittsburgh-marathon-2671704.html; Roessner, B. (2014). Reasons to run the Dick's Sporting Goods Pittsburgh Marathon. Retrieved from http://www.active.com/running/articles/reasons-to-run-the-dick-s-sporting-goods-pittsburgh-marathon.

numerous and greatly varied entertainment options available to a consumer with leisure time. Of particular concern to sport marketers is the next generation of sport fans—children and young adults. Think of the technology options available to a young person today: instant messaging, text messaging, social networking sites, cell phones, DVD and Blu-ray players, video games, the Internet, and so on. There are even new sports that have entered the marketplace with success. Action sports—sports such as skateboarding and motocross—have captured the interest of young kids today. Consider these facts:

- In 2012, 5.4 million people skateboarded and 4.32 million snowboarded (SBRnet, 2012).
- The 2008 Dew Tour drew more than 272,009 people to its five events (Street & Smith's SportsBusiness Daily, 2008).
- Skateboarding legend Tony Hawk's video games have generated $1.1 billion in sales (Hyman, 2006).

With their leisure time absorbed by multiple technology entertainment options and following action sports, do young people have the additional time and resources to participate in mainstream sports? Creative strategies will attempt to answer that question as marketers focus more attention on youths in the future.

A cluttered marketplace is also an issue for sponsors of sporting events and endorsers of athletes. Two factors have contributed to create a sponsorship marketplace that is extremely cluttered:

1. The rise in the sheer number of events and athletes to sponsor. For example, there are now a variety of action sports events, such as the X-Games, Dew Tour, and Vans Triple Crown of Surfing. Similarly, a corporation could sponsor an NFL star or a women's professional basketball star.

2. The focus of sport managers on increasing revenue by identifying as much saleable inventory as possible. Watch the next NASCAR race. Count how many places sponsor logos appear.

Because the sponsorship marketplace is cluttered, it may be increasingly difficult for sponsors to be recognized as such and thus achieve the benefits of sponsorship. In response, sponsors are asking sport teams and events to provide more benefits and are increasing the degree of sophistication with which they measure sponsorship effectiveness. Thus, sporting events in the future will increasingly be challenged to demonstrate how a sponsor will benefit from a sponsorship if they are to attract and retain sponsors.

Image Matters

The development and cultivation of a positive image is becoming increasingly important in sport marketing. This is true for several reasons. First, the cluttered marketplace makes it imperative that corporations identify sports, events, or athletes who have unique images. Second, since the turn of the twenty-first century, corporate ethical scandals, highlighted by the collapse of energy giant Enron, have decreased the amount of trust that consumers have in large companies. Coupled with this perception, reports of athlete arrests may have served to erode the public's positive impression of professional athletes and professional sports.

For these reasons, corporations are more discerning in how they spend their sponsorship and endorsement dollars. One outcome is that corporations are investing more money to sponsor nonprofit organizations (Tatum, 2003). In fact, the International Events Group suggested that $2.7 billion would be spent on cause and arts sponsorships in 2013 (International Events Group, 2013). A corporation may choose to sponsor the activities of a nonprofit organization in an effort to capitalize on the positive image associated with that organization or event.

Image also is important when it comes to athlete endorsements. Although there are still a handful of very large endorsement contracts, such as LeBron James's $90 million deal with Nike ("Nike Foots Bill," 2003), companies are increasingly careful about whom they choose as an endorser. Media accounts of athletes running afoul of the law or breaking the rules of their specific sport are commonplace, even for some athletes who have very positive images. For example, seven-time Tour de France winner Lance Armstrong captivated the world when he won some of the titles after battling testicular cancer and (with the help of Nike) launching the very successful cancer charity, Livestrong. However, in autumn 2012, the U.S. Anti-Doping Agency released a file of incriminating evidence about Armstrong's use of blood-doping throughout his career. As a result, most of Armstrong's sponsors severed ties with him, seven of them in a single day (Shrotenboer, 2012).

One athlete with widespread global appeal is soccer player David Beckham. He has been successful at crafting an image of someone who is fashionable, tolerant, and family oriented (Hale, 2003). Such an image makes him very attractive to corporations as an endorser, and as a result he makes at least $40 million a year from endorsement agreements with such companies as Vodafone (a cellular phone service), adidas, and Armani (Forbes, 2013; Hale, 2003; Rossingh, 2010).

Athletes are besieged with issues associated with steroids, arrests, and infidelity. Today's superstar could be tomorrow's headlines. The increase in social improprieties over the past decade is impacting the sport marketing efforts of leagues, teams, and sponsors. An athlete is recognized not only for his or her performance on the field, but also off the field. Therefore,

many leagues, teams, and sponsors are protecting their brand by strategically placing moral clauses in their rules and contracts. To protect their brand, the NFL's New England Patriots waived tight end Aaron Hernandez on the same day he was charged with murder, and in a further move to distance itself from the player, the Patriots offered to exchange any Hernandez jersey for free at the team store (Rodak, 2013). At a league level, NFL Commissioner Roger Goodell has clamped down on off-field indiscretions by players and other employees by strengthening the league's personal conduct policy and handing out stiffer penalties to offenders in an effort to strengthen the league's brand (Associated Press, 2007).

© Tom Hirtreiter/ShutterStock, Inc.

Summary

The marketing of sport includes unique advantages and disadvantages when compared with the marketing of more traditional products and services. Sport benefits from the immense media coverage afforded the industry, often at no cost, while simultaneously it can suffer from the scrutiny imposed by the same media. Besides sport, there is probably no other industry in which the majority of the consumers consider themselves experts. Finally, the sport marketer's control over the core product offered to the consumer is often significantly less than that of his or her counterparts in other industries.

Sport marketers must not only understand the unique aspects of their own product, but they also must be well informed and knowledgeable about marketing innovations and practices in more traditional business industries and be able to adapt or modify these practices to fit the situations they encounter in sport. In particular, the application of such concepts as the marketing mix, segmentation, fan identification, and relationship marketing is central to the success of a sport marketer. Similarly, recognizing and adapting to current issues such as the rising cost of attending an event, the cluttered nature of the marketplace, and the importance of building a positive image are central to most sport marketers' work. Beyond an understanding of and appreciation for these factors and practices, a sport marketer must have strong interpersonal skills, computer skills, and in many cases the ability to sell a product or concept if he or she is to be successful.

Key Terms

ambush marketing, customer relationship management, demographic, fan identification, intercept interviews, marketing mix, pass-by interviews, psychographic, relationship marketing, segmentation, sponsorships, target markets

References

Adkins, S. (1999). *Cause related marketing: Who cares who wins*. Oxford, UK: Butterworth Heineman.

Associated Press. (2007, April 10). Goodell unveils new conduct policy. *ESPN.com*. Retrieved from http://sports.espn.go.com/nfl/news/story?id=2832098

Bednarski, P. J. (2002, December 9). Applauding Arledge: He invented fresh ways to report sports and news on TV. *Broadcasting & Cable, 132*(50), 41.

Berry, L. L. (1995). Relationship marketing of services—Growing interest, emerging perspectives. *Journal of the Academy of Marketing Sciences, 23*(4), 236–245.

Bhattarcharya, C. B., Rao, H., & Glynn, M. A. (1995). Understanding the bond of identification: An investigation of its correlates among art museum members. *The Journal of Marketing, 59*(4), 46–57.

Bounds, A., & Garrahan, M. (2003, June 26). A question of sport and image: Mark McCormack, the sports marketing pioneer, died in May. *Financial Times*, p. 12.

Bowman, J. (2013). Tulsa Shock pick up jersey sponsorship. SB Nation. Retrieved from http://www.swishappeal.com/2013/1/31/3938278/tulsa-shock-pick-up-jersey-sponsorship

Brown, M. (2009, April 2). Average ticket price up 5.4 percent in MLB. Yankees/Mets skew total. The biz of baseball. Retrieved from http://www.bizofbaseball.com/index.php?option=com_content&view=article&id=3147:average-ticket-price-up-54-percent-in-mlb-yankeesmets-skew-total&catid=56:ticket-watch&Itemid=136

Coca-Cola Company. (2006). The Olympic Games. Retrieved November 10, 2010, from http://www.thecoca-colacompany.com/heritage/olympicgames.html

ESPN. (2013, January 10). ESPN Fact Sheet. Retrieved from http://espnmediazone.com/us/espn-inc-fact-sheet/

Forbes. (2013). The Celebrity 100. David Beckham. Retrieved from http://www.forbes.com/profile/david-beckham/

Greenberg, J. (2008, October 28). 2008–09 NBA fan cost index. Team Marketing Report. Retrieved from http://www.teammarketing.com/blog/index.html?article_id=41

Hale, E. (2003, May 9). He's the most famous athlete in the world (except in the USA). *USA Today*, p. 1A.

Hardy, S. (1996). Matt Levine: The "father" of modern sport marketing. *Sport Marketing Quarterly, 5*, 5–7.

Holtzman, J. (1986, January 3). Barnum of baseball made sure fans were entertained. *Chicago Tribune*, pp. D1, D3.

Hyman, M. (2006, November 13). How Tony Hawk stays aloft. *Business Week*, p. 84.

International Events Group Sponsorship Report. (2013, January 7). 2013 Sponsorship outlook: Spending increase is double-edged sword. Retrieved from http://www.sponsorship.com/iegsr/2013/01/07/2013-Sponsorship-Outlook--Spending-Increase-Is-Dou.aspx

Kotler, P. (2003). *Marketing management*. Upper Saddle River, NJ: Prentice Hall.

Lachowetz, T., & Gladden, J. (2003). A framework for understanding cause-related sport marketing programs. *International Journal of Sports Marketing & Sponsorship, 4*(4), 313–333.

Levine, P. (1985). *A. G. Spalding and the rise of baseball*. New York, NY: Oxford University Press.

Liberman, N. (2003, June 16). Defining Hispanic market challenges teams. *Street & Smith's SportsBusiness Journal*, 20.

McCarthy, E. J., & Perreault, W. D. (1988). *Essentials of marketing*. Homewood, IL: Richard D. Irwin.

McKenna, R. (1991). *Relationship marketing*. Reading, MA: Addison-Wesley Publishers.

Mullin, B., Hardy, S., & Sutton, W.A. (2007). *Sport marketing* (3rd ed.) Champaign, IL: Human Kinetics.

Nike foots bill for James at $90M. (2003, May 23). *The Washington Post*, p. D2.

Ries, A., & Trout, J. (1993). *The 22 immutable laws of marketing*. New York, NY: Harper Business.

Roberts, R., & Olson, J. (1989). *Winning is the only thing: Sports in American society since 1945*. Baltimore, MD: Johns Hopkins University Press.

Rodak, M. (2013, July 6th). Patriot fans flock to jersey trade-in. Retrieved from http://espn.go.com/boston/nfl/story/_/id/9454690/new-england-patriots-fans-line-trade-aaron-hernandez-jerseys

Rossingh, D. (2010). David Beckham's 2009 income from endorsements company fell 9 percent. Retrieved from http://www.bloomberg.com/news/2010-10-07/david-beckham-s-2009-income-from-endorsements-company-fell-9-percent.html

SBRnet. (2009). Skateboarding participation. Retrieved from http://www.sbrnet.com/research.asp?subrid=452.asp?subRID=370

Schrotenboer, B. (2012, October 18). Paying the price: Doping case costs Lance Armstrong. USA Today. Retrieved from http://www.usatoday.com/story/sports/cycling/2012/10/17/lance-armstrong-sponsors-doping-case/1640467/

Strasser, J. B., & Becklund, L. (1991). Swoosh: The unauthorized story of Nike and the men who played there. New York, NY: Harcourt Brace Jovanovich.

Street & Smith's SportsBusiness Daily. (2008, October 30). AST Dew Tour ratings up, attendance down from 2007. Retrieved from http://www.sportsbusinessdaily.com/article/125119

Sugar, B. (1978). Hit the sign and win a free suit of clothes from Harry Finklestein. Chicago, IL: Contemporary Books.

Swift, E. M. (1990, May 21). The most powerful man in sports: Mark McCormack, founder and CEO of International Management Group, rules his empire as both agent and impresario. Retrieved from http://sportsillustrated.cnn.com/vault/article/magazine/MAG1136857/index.htm

Swift, E. M. (2000, May 15). Sit on it! The high cost of attending games is fattening owners' wallets while it drives average fans from arenas, and it may be cooling America's passion for pro sports. *Sports Illustrated*, pp. 71–85.

Tatum, C. (2003, August 8). Companies more hesitant to sponsor splashy sports events. *Denver Post*.

Team Marketing Report, Inc. (2009 September). TMR's fan cost index. Retrieved from http://teammarketing.com.ismmedia.com/ISM3/std-content/repos/Top/News/nfl%20fci%202009.pdf

U.S. Census Bureau. (2010). The Hispanic population 2010. Retrieved from http://www.census.gov/prod/cen2010/briefs/c2010br-04.pdf

Veeck, B., & Linn, E. (1962). Veeck—As in wreck. New York, NY: G.P. Putnam's Sons.

Veeck, B., & Linn, E. (1965). The hustler's handbook. New York, NY: G.P. Putnam's Sons.

Chapter 4

Neil Longley and
Nola Agha

Financial and Economic Principles Applied to Sport Management

Learning Objectives

Upon completion of this chapter, students should be able to:

1. Critically evaluate the various estimates of the economic magnitude of the sport industry.

2. Recognize that, whether large or small, all sport organizations have a need for staff with training in financial management.

3. Identify and define basic financial terms such as revenues, expenses, income statement, balance sheet, assets, liabilities, debt, owner's equity, and return on investment (ROI).

4. Define financial risk and examine some of the factors that affect the risk of sport organizations and how excess risk may lead to default or bankruptcy.

5. Understand how the industrial organization of the spectator sport is fundamentally different from the non-spectator sport industry and the rest of American business.

6. Assess the degree of monopoly power that professional sport leagues enjoy and the effect that it has on teams' ability to earn profits.

7. Judge the challenges that professional and intercollegiate sport organizations will encounter as the industry tries to continue growing revenue in the future.

8. Understand that only a few intercollegiate athletic departments generate an annual surplus and that taken as a whole, college athletics is unprofitable.

9. Define competitive balance and illustrate its importance to leagues and teams.

10. Illustrate how techniques such as salary caps, revenue sharing, reverse-order-of-finish drafts, and luxury taxes may affect the degree of competitive balance within a league.

Introduction

The media are constantly drawing our attention to the financial aspects of the sport world. Some of the numbers that we read and hear can seem staggering to the average person. To get a sense of the magnitude of the dollar values being generated by the industry, consider these statistics:

- The average player salary in the National Basketball Association (NBA) is currently $5.15 million per season (Burke, 2012).
- The 5-year contract that star baseball player Josh Hamilton signed in 2012 pays an average salary of $25 million per year (Associated Press, 2012).
- The cost of the new arena that the NBA's Brooklyn Nets opened in 2012 was $1 billion, and the naming rights to the facility were sold to Barclay's Bank for approximately $10 million per season for 20 years (Russell, 2012).

- Major League Baseball's (MLB's) current 8-year television contract with ESPN calls for the league to be paid $5.6 billion, or about $23 million per team per year (Ourand, 2012).
- The estimated market value of Manchester United is $3 billion, making it the most valuable franchise in the world. The National Football League (NFL) Dallas Cowboys rank second in the world at $2.1 billion (Ozanian, 2013a).

In college sports, the pattern is the same: Participants in college football's Bowl Championship Series (BCS) championship game receive payouts of more than $23 million per team; the National Collegiate Athletic Association's (NCAA's) 14-year contract with CBS and Turner Sports, signed in 2010, to televise the NCAA Men's Basketball Tournament every March will pay the NCAA about $11 billion over the life of

the contract; the budget of the athletic department at the University of Texas was $153 million for fiscal year 2012 (Smith, 2013). The list could go on and on, but one thing is clear—sport is very big business.

The examples given here are from only one segment of the sport industry—the spectator sport segment. The sport industry is much broader than just the spectator side, however. It includes not only a wide range of service businesses related to participatory recreational activities (such as fitness centers, ski resorts, and golf courses) but also the entire sporting goods and related apparel industry.

The sport industry is definitely a major force in North American business, although it is difficult to get an accurate, reliable measure of its true financial magnitude. According to Plunkett Research (2012), the entire U.S. sport industry in 2012 accounted for $435 billion in total spending. Of that, $28.6 billion is sports advertising and $21.4 billion is healthclub spending (Plunkett Research, 2012). In contrast, the U.S. Department of Commerce estimated the combined gross economic output of the sport, recreation, entertainment, and arts categories in the United States combined to be about $231 billion in 2011 (U.S. Department of Commerce, 2012).

Part of the practical problem in measuring the exact size of this industry is deciding what to include. For example, the gambling sector, while not part of the sport sector per se, derives much of its business from betting on spectator sports. So, should gambling be included? Perhaps more importantly, different studies may be measuring different variables. For example, if a golf club manufacturer sold a set of golf clubs to a retailer for $1,000, which in turn sold the clubs to a customer for $1,500, one could naïvely (and incorrectly) add the two together and say the total output of the industry is $2,500. While this might seem like an obvious error—the $1,000 is double-counted, and the true value of

the transactions is $1,500—it is surprising how often errors such as these are made by those conducting impact studies. The point is that unless you know how someone is calculating the magnitude of the industry, you should exercise extreme caution before you put too much faith in the result.

This raises a related issue. There is a difference between an industry's sales and its value added. For example, the golf club manufacturer in the example given earlier may have bought raw materials (e.g., graphite, titanium, rubber) from its suppliers for $300, used these materials to manufacture the clubs, and then sold the clubs to the retailer for $1,000. Although the manufacturer's sale totals $1,000, its value added is only $700 because $300 of the $1,000 sale price was attributable to those outside the industry. When one adjusts for the concept of **value added**, the numbers change considerably. For example, while the Department of Commerce estimates total output for the sport industry in 2011 to be $231 billion, it estimates the value added to be only $148 billion. This $148 billion represents about 0.6% of the U.S. gross domestic product (U.S. Department of Commerce, 2012). The concept of value added is probably the best single measure of an industry's impact.

Despite these practical complexities with actually measuring the size of the industry and the caution one must always take when interpreting the numbers, one thing is certain: Regardless of how one specifically measures it, the sport industry is both significant and growing. Inside sport organizations (whether they are professional or college spectator sports), the recreational service sector, and the sporting goods industry, many managers are now responsible for multimillion-dollar budgets. This financial boom has created a great need in the industry for people with training in finance. Even where the sport organization operates on a more modest scale than the examples given earlier—whether it be a locally owned fitness center, a minor league baseball team, or a Division III athletic department in college sports—the need for sound financial management practices is no less urgent.

This chapter provides an introduction to the fields of finance and economics within a sport context. It examines what finance is and what it is not. It discusses how money flows into and out of a sport organization, and it examines the types of management decisions that must be made to maximize the financial success of an organization. From an economics perspective, this chapter looks at the structure of the sport industry in terms of competition, monopoly, competitive balance, and how those features relate to finance. It also discusses some of the current issues facing various sectors of the industry.

Key Concepts

What Is Finance?

The term *finance* often has quite different meanings to different people. For some individuals not specifically trained in finance, the term is often used very broadly to describe anything related to dollars, money, or numbers. This definition implies that almost everything that occurs in an organization falls under the broad umbrella of "finance," given that almost everything that occurs in an organization has monetary implications.

In fact, those trained in finance tend to define the field somewhat more narrowly. Part of the purpose of this chapter is to illustrate what finance actually is and, just as importantly, what it is not. Because the finance discipline tends to intersect with other managerial disciplines—for example, marketing—it may be unclear to some where the marketing function ends and where the finance function begins.

Perhaps the best way to make this distinction is to consider that what defines finance is not as much the subject matter—it could be ticket sales, merchandise sales, the signing of a free agent, or the construction of a new stadium—as it is the concepts and techniques used to solve problems and make decisions about these issues.

For example, the act of a college athletic department selling a corporate sponsorship has clear financial implications: Sponsorship salespeople must be paid for their services, and the sponsorships they ultimately sell will generate revenues for the department. The act in itself is not about finance, however, but rather it is about sales.

Of course, finance issues could still be embedded within this process. For example, there might be a question about how many salespeople should be allocated to the sponsorship sales department. Might some of the sales staff be more effectively employed in selling season ticket packages instead of selling sponsorships? This question, while not necessarily straightforward, is crucial, and it is an example of a financial allocation decision that a sport organization must make. Allocation decisions such as these tend to occur in the course of the **budgeting** process.

The basic financial "answer" to this question is that the organization should allocate its sales staff based on the magnitude of the financial payoff that each department (tickets and sponsorships) can return for a given salesperson. In essence, the question is this: Would shifting one salesperson from sponsorship sales to ticket sales increase or decrease the overall revenue that flows into the department? In other words, finance is not as much about simply identifying where and how money flows into the organization as it is about how organizations make allocation decisions to ensure the net inflow is maximized.

In summary, the managerial discipline of finance refers to something much more specific than simply anything to do with money or dollars. While there is no single, universally agreed upon definition of finance, *the term* generally refers to two primary activities of an organization: how an organization *generates* the funds that flow into an organization, and how these funds get *allocated* and spent once they are in the organization.

Some Basics: Financial Flows in Sport Organizations

In many ways, the finance function in a sport organization is no different than the finance function in any other organization. The context may be different, but the underlying concepts and principles remain the same. Like any other field, finance is an area that has its own terminology. Being familiar with this terminology is a necessary prerequisite to better understanding the finance function.

This terminology is best introduced by thinking about the process by which funds (i.e., dollars) flow through a sport organization. Let's start with how funds flow into an organization.

The primary business of organizations in the spectator sport sector is to provide entertainment through the staging of athletic contests. The selling associated with these events is the primary way in which sport teams raise funds. These funds are called **revenues**. Revenues may come from a variety of sources including ticket sales, concession and merchandise sales, media contracts, and sponsorship revenues, to name only a few. With sponsorships, other companies try to use the broad appeal of the sport industry to market their own products. For college athletic programs, funds may also come from non-revenue sources, such as budgetary allocations from the university to the athletic department.

Outside of the spectator sport sector, revenues come from the sale of the organization's primary goods and/or service. For example, in a golf country club, revenues might come from a variety of sources, such as yearly memberships, green fees, golf lessons, equipment sales in the pro shop, and food and drink sales at the clubhouse restaurant.

Obviously, money does not just flow into sport organizations; some also flows out. In other words, **expenses** must be incurred to generate revenues. For the golf country club, expenses might include such items as staff salaries, water to irrigate the fairways, electricity to light the clubhouse, and food and beverage items to prepare meals at the clubhouse restaurant. In the spectator sport sector—whether it be college or pro—teams must buy uniforms and equipment (e.g., bats, balls, hockey sticks) for the players; they must pay for player travel, including transportation and hotel accommodation; and so on. Facility-related costs are also incurred. The facility must be staffed on game day with ticket takers, ushers, and concession workers; electricity is used to provide lighting and to run equipment; the facility must be cleaned after an event; and the playing surface must be maintained. For major professional teams, these types of costs are all secondary to the single biggest expenditure item: player salaries.

In a basic sense, the financial success of an organization is ultimately dependent on the difference between revenues and expenses. This difference is called **profits** (sometimes referred to as **income**). Profits can be increased by increasing revenues, by decreasing costs, or both. An organization's revenues, expenses, and profits over a given time period (for example, a year) are usually summarized on a financial statement called an **income statement**.

Another important financial concept is **assets**. Broadly speaking, assets are anything that an organization owns that can be used to generate future revenues. For example, a fitness center's primary assets are its building and exercise equipment; a golf club maker's primary assets are the manufacturing equipment at its production facility. With spectator sports, a team's stadium is an important asset because it provides the team with a venue at which to stage games, which in turn allows the team to earn various types of revenue. As we will see later in the chapter, new stadiums tend to have dramatic and immediate effects on a franchise's revenue stream.

One of the most important assets that major professional sports franchises possess is their membership in the league to which they belong. For example, the NFL's popularity as a league is so high that prospective franchise owners will pay large sums of money simply to join the league. The owners of the NFL's most recent expansion franchise, the Houston Texans, paid the NFL an expansion fee of $700 million (*SportsBusiness Journal,* 2006). This fee was paid just to "join the club" and to enjoy all the future financial benefits that such membership in the NFL may bring; it did not include money for such large-scale expenditures as stadium construction and player salaries.

In essence, all sport organizations, like any other businesses, must spend money up front to generate what they hope will be even greater inflows later on. For example, fitness centers cannot sell memberships until they first buy or lease a building and then stock that building with exercise equipment; golf club manufacturers cannot make and sell any golf clubs until they first purchase the necessary production equipment. In financial terms, any business must make an initial investment in assets to generate future revenues.

One further element can be added to the mix. Assets have to be bought, so where do the dollars come from that are invested in these assets? A new stadium, for example, may cost hundreds of millions of dollars to construct.

For some assets, such as stadiums, professional teams have been very successful in convincing local governments to pay for all or part of the costs of the facility. Of the 121 sports facilities in use in 2010, it is estimated that 78% of all construction costs came from government (i.e., taxpayer) sources (Long, 2013).

This issue aside, professional teams can fund or "finance" assets in a number of ways. First, **owners' equity** (sometimes simply referred to as "equity") can be used to finance assets. Owners' equity is essentially the amount of their own money that owners have invested in the organization. Much of this investment of funds typically occurs when the owners initially purchase (or start up) the entity, but the amount can also increase if the owners reinvest any profits back into it, rather than removing these profits and paying themselves dividends.

In major professional sports, most franchise owners (i.e., the equity holders) tend to be either a sole individual or a small group of individuals. Sometimes, existing owners will sell part of their ownership stake in a team (i.e., sell part of their equity) as a means to inject more cash into the team. For example, in 2012, New York Mets owners Fred Wilpon, Jeff Wilpon, and Saul Katz sold 12 minority shares of the team, each worth $20 million, to infuse much needed cash into the franchise to pay off debts to Major League Baseball (MLB) and Bank of America (Thompson & O'Keeffe, 2012).

A few franchises are owned by corporate conglomerates. **Table 4-1** shows that AEG leads the way with ownership of teams in the National Hockey League (NHL), Major League Soccer (MLS), American Hockey League (AHL), East Coast Hockey League (ECHL), and European hockey and soccer leagues. Corporate ownership can also get very complex. For example, in 2012 Rogers Communications and Bell Canada, two rival telecommunications companies that each own professional teams, joined together to acquire Maple Leaf Sports and Entertainment, which controls teams in the NHL, NBA, MLS, and AHL.

Table 4-1 Examples of Sport Franchises Owned by Corporations

Corporation	Franchise(s) Owned
AEG	Los Angeles Galaxy, Houston Dynamo, Los Angeles Kings, AHL Manchester Monarchs, ECHL Ontario Reign, European hockey and soccer teams
Bell Canada	Montreal Canadians
Comcast-Spectacor	Philadelphia Flyers
The Madison Square Garden Company	New York Rangers, New York Knicks, WNBA New York Liberty, AHL Connecticut Whale
Maple Leaf Sports and Entertainment (owned by Rogers Communications and Bell Canada)	Toronto Maple Leafs, Toronto Raptors, Toronto FC, AHL Toronto Marlies
Rogers Communications	Toronto Blue Jays

There have even been a few occasions where a franchise's shares have been publicly traded on a stock exchange. In these cases, there are literally thousands of owners of a team, most of whom own only a small portion of the franchise. At one time or another in the past 20 years, teams such as the Boston Celtics, Cleveland Indians, Vancouver Canucks, and Toronto Maple Leafs have had publicly traded shares.

In the nonspectator sector, publicly traded shares are much more common than in the spectator sector. Table 4-2 shows some of the sport organizations whose shares are publicly traded. Publicly traded shares give organizations much wider access to investment capital, which potentially allows them to expand more quickly than they otherwise would be able to do.

Besides owners' equity, the other major way that sport organizations raise money to finance their assets is to borrow money. The amount of money that an organization borrows is referred to as its **debt** (also referred to as **liabilities**).

When organizations borrow, they are legally obligated to pay back the original amount they borrowed (the **principal**), plus **interest**. Money might be borrowed from banks, or it might be borrowed from other lenders in financial markets, through, for example, instruments such as **bonds**. Bonds are financial instruments that allow the borrower to both borrow large dollar amounts and to borrow this money for a relatively long period of time (usually 20 or more years). Bonds are normally issued only by relatively large corporate entities and by governments. There is usually a secondary market for

Table 4-2 Examples of Publicly Traded Sport Companies

Name	Type of Business	Stock Exchange
Callaway Golf	Golf products	NYSE
Churchill Downs	Thoroughbred racing	NASDAQ
Electronic Arts	Video games	NASDAQ
Nike	Shoes	NYSE
Vail Resorts	Skiing	NYSE

Abbreviations: NYSE, New York Stock Exchange; NASDAQ, National Association of Securities Dealers Automated Quotations.

Data from: Fried, G., Shapiro, S., & DeSchriver, T. (2008). *Sport finance*. Champaign, IL: Human Kinetics.

bonds, meaning the original buyer (i.e., the lender) can sell the bonds to another buyer any time prior to the bonds "maturing." Bonds are normally purchased by institutional investors, such as mutual funds, insurance companies, and pension funds.

In spectator sports, stadium construction projects are often financed with bonds. In the collegiate setting, Kansas State University issued $50 million in bonds to finance the expansion of its football stadium that opened in 2013 (Kansas State Sports, 2013); at Texas A&M, renovations to Kyle Field will cost over $400 million, financed through a mix of bonds and donations (Hinton, 2013).

While most bond issues in spectator sports are used to finance stadium construction, bonds are occasionally used for other purposes. In 2000, for example, the YankeeNets organization issued $200 million worth of bonds to the market, ostensibly to finance its planned takeover of the New Jersey Devils hockey team (Fried, Shapiro, & DeSchriver, 2008). In 2010, Malcolm Glazer, owner of the Tampa Bay Buccaneers, issued over $800 million in bonds as a way to refinance the debt incurred when he purchased Manchester United (Associated Press, 2010).

The interest rate at which any money is borrowed depends on the lender's perception of the borrower's ability to repay. In turn, this ability to repay depends on a variety of factors: the popularity of the organization's goods or services, the magnitude and stability of the organization's revenue streams, the future prospects for revenue growth, the degree to which costs are controlled and contained, the amount of debt the organization is already carrying, and so forth.

Leagues such as the NFL, NBA, and MLB all maintain "credit facilities," sometimes called loan pools, and they borrow extensively in financial markets to fund these facilities. Individual teams in the league can then borrow

from the credit facilities, rather than borrowing directly in financial markets. Leagues can borrow less expensively than can individual teams, simply because league loans are backed by the collective revenues of all teams in the league, whereas loans to teams are backed only by that individual team's revenues. Companies such as Fitch and Moody's "rate" this debt of major professional leagues, teams, and universities. Generally, the NFL's debt receives the highest credit rating in sports, indicating that the NFL has the lowest credit risk, which allows it to borrow at the lowest possible interest rate. For example, Fitch has rated recent debt issues of the NFL as A+ (Business Wire, 2012); MLB received an A– rating (Business Wire, 2013). On the other hand, in 2013 Fitch and Moody changed the NCAA's credit outlook to negative due to the ongoing *O'Bannon v. NCAA* lawsuit and the threat it poses to amateurism, the potential for damages, and the potential to destabilize the current intercollegiate athletic system (Backman, 2013).

An organization's assets, liabilities, and owners' equity at any given point are shown on a financial statement called a **balance sheet**.

College athletic programs are nonprofit organizations and can have quite different sources of funds. In college athletics, there are no real equity holders—no one "owns" these programs. Typically, outside sources of funds flow into the athletic department through budgetary transfers from the university itself. However, some athletic programs are finding very innovative ways to raise capital. For example, in 2000 Duke University started a Legacy Fund to endow scholarships, salaries, and operational expenses for the men's basketball team. This particular fund, like other venture capital funds, uses the dollars of wealthy individuals (many of whom are Duke alumni) to invest in various start-up companies. The idea is that the fund's earnings from these investments would then be ultimately donated to Duke. In October of 2012, twelve years after the fund was established, it had finally raised enough to permanently endow the men's basketball team (Beaton & Kyle, 2012).

Some college programs, such as the University of Florida, are run through an outside entity that is incorporated by the state (University Athletic Association, 2013). In Florida's case, the Florida Athletic Association seeks revenue through corporate sponsors, media and ticket revenues, and private donors. Funding for expenses, such as student-athlete tuition and expenses, are paid to the university from the athletic association. This structure is common to the Southeastern Conference and is a growing model in collegiate athletics.

Some Typical Financial Decisions

With these basic concepts in mind, let's look at some examples of financial decisions that sport organizations may face. Many of the financial decisions in a sport organization ultimately revolve around the management of assets. For example, in any given season, there may be a variety of investment expenditures that a golf country club could make to increase the value of its assets. Because investment dollars are likely limited, however, choices have to be made about which options will be the most rewarding.

One option might be for the country club to expand its golf facilities by adding another 18-hole course. Another option might be to expand its clubhouse and restaurant. Still another choice might be to upgrade the quality of the existing course by adding a state-of-the-art irrigation system. All of these options will have different initial investment costs, and all will have different revenue potentials.

In the spectator segment, a baseball team might face similar choices. For example, one option might be for the team to go into the free agent market and sign a star player. This move would presumably increase the team's

performance on the field, which in turn might lead to more tickets being sold and/or higher TV ratings. Alternatively, the team could take the money that it would have used to sign the free agent and instead upgrade the luxury suites in the stadium. By making these upgrades, the team could then charge a higher price to its corporate clients to lease the suites. Another option might be to install a state-of-the-art scoreboard in the stadium. This novelty might increase the overall fan experience, making people more likely to attend games. Furthermore, it might provide increased sponsorship and advertising opportunities for the team. Or perhaps the team might want to replace its existing natural grass field with an artificial surface. This change might reduce player injuries, perhaps increasing team performance, and hence ticket revenues, and might also reduce future expenses, in that fewer players will appear on a roster during the season, as fewer replacement players will be needed to take over for injured players. A new artificial surface may also increase revenues in other ways by making the venue usable for a wider range of events.

It is these types of decisions that lie at the heart of finance. Finance-trained people approach these kinds of problems by applying certain concepts and techniques. In this case, one approach is to calculate each alternative's **return on investment (ROI)**. The concept of ROI is very common in finance. It shows the expected dollar value return on each alternative investment, stated as a percentage of the original cost of each investment. For example, an ROI of 9% indicates the team would recover all of its initial investment, plus an additional 9%.

To calculate ROI, the financial analyst needs to estimate two basic things. The first task is to calculate the initial cost of each investment: What will it cost to sign the free agent, or what will the new turf or scoreboard cost? The second, somewhat more difficult task is to estimate the magnitude of the revenues that each alternative will generate. For example, with the free agent, the player's on-field performance should ultimately affect (positively, one hopes) the team's winning percentage, which should in turn affect attendance and media revenues.

© ktasimar/ShutterStock, Inc.

An interesting case study has arisen in recent years that pertains to the ROI of player personnel decisions. The somewhat famous book *Moneyball* (Lewis, 2003) chronicles the processes that Oakland A's general manager (GM) Billy Beane uses to make player selection decisions. Beane contends that many teams in baseball often make systematic player selection errors—"overvaluing" some players while "undervaluing" others. As the GM of a small market team, one of Beane's strategies to more effectively compete with large market teams is to identify and acquire these undervalued players. In essence, an investment in an undervalued player produces a higher ROI than a comparable investment in an overvalued player; undervalued players create more wins per dollar of payroll than do overvalued players, and hence they make a greater contribution to team profits.

When examining free agents, a player's off-field performance must also be evaluated. That is, would he increase merchandise sales? Would she increase the overall visibility of the team?

This raises another key issue. Investments such as these require managers to think about the future. The future is notoriously difficult to predict accurately. For example, no one can know for certain the magnitude of the increased revenues that would result from a golf course expanding in size from 18 holes to 36 holes. Many uncertainties exist: Will golf's popularity, relative to other activities, continue to grow at the rates seen in the past two decades? Will overall economic conditions improve from their recessionary levels of the late 2000s, ensuring consumers continue to have the disposable income necessary to engage in leisure activities such as golf? Will other competing golf courses enter the market, thereby reducing market share for the existing course?

Similarly, in the baseball example, no one can say for certain what value the free agent will actually add to revenues. The player might not perform as expected, adding the player may affect team chemistry in ways not foreseen, the player might be plagued by injuries, and so on.

These difficulties in making accurate predictions about the future relate to the concept of **risk**. Risk is one of the most important concepts in finance. It refers to the fact that the future is uncertain, so that the future benefits of any investment made today cannot ever be known with certainty at the time the investment is made. Of course, some investments inherently carry more risk than others. Financial managers need to take into account these different levels of risk when they evaluate investment projects. For example, investing in upgraded luxury suites may be less risky than investing in a free agent, in the sense that the future revenue payoffs from the former move are more predictable than they are for the latter investment.

Making decisions about which assets to invest in is not the only place where the concept of risk arises in sport finance. As we have seen, there is a whole other class of decisions, called financing decisions, where risk is a crucial factor. These financing decisions revolve around the degree to which financing will occur with equity versus debt. In other words, owners must decide how much of the assets of the franchise they will finance with their own money versus how much they will finance with borrowed money. There are always tradeoffs. Generally, financing with borrowed money is less expensive than equity, but it carries more risk. It is less expensive because lenders do not have any ownership stake in the organization and thus are only entitled to repayment of their original loan, with interest. If the organization's financial performance is better than expected, none of this upside has to be shared with lenders, so it can be retained by the current equity holders.

However, debt carries more risk because the organization is legally obligated to repay the borrowed money, with interest, at a pre-specified date. If the borrower is unable to do so—perhaps because revenues are lower than expected—then the borrower is said to be in **default** on the debt. If a default occurs, the lenders may force the organization into bankruptcy. Such a scenario is not merely hypothetical. It has occurred remarkably often in the NHL, with the Ottawa Senators, Buffalo Sabres, Pittsburgh Penguins, and Phoenix Coyotes. Most recently, in 2012, the New Jersey Devils defaulted on a loan, although the lenders did not opt to force the Devils into bankruptcy (Kaplan & Botta, 2012). MLB teams that have entered into bankruptcy include the Baltimore Orioles, Chicago Cubs, Texas Rangers, and Los Angeles Dodgers.

Similar situations have occurred in the nonspectator sport sector. For example, when the shoe manufacturer Converse filed for bankruptcy in 2001, its spokesperson at the time said, "It's not a lack of business, but our debt structure that made it difficult for the company to survive" (Fried et al., 2008).

The Economics of Sport

What we have discussed up to this point falls within the realm of sport finance. The chapter reviews how managers make decisions about where to raise funds and where to spend those funds. A related area, called sport economics, is also relevant to anyone interested in the financial aspects of sport.

The general field of (micro) economics examines, among many other issues, how an industry organizes itself and how this industry structure affects competition and profits among firms in the industry. In recent years, an entire subfield of economics has developed that examines the peculiar aspects of the spectator sport industry. The focus has been on the spectator sport industry because it is organized so differently from the nonspectator industry and, for that matter, from the rest of American business. In most industries, firms directly compete with each other for market share: General Motors competes with Ford and Toyota, Coca-Cola competes with Pepsi, Sony competes with Toshiba, New Balance competes with Nike, Ping competes with Callaway. There are little or no common interests among the competitors. For example, every set of golf clubs that Ping sells is a set that Callaway did not sell. In fact, all else equal, Callaway would be better off if Ping did not exist, and vice versa.

In the spectator sport industry (whether college or pro), the issue is very different. While teams may compete against each other on the field, they must cooperate off the field. For example, the Boston Red Sox baseball franchise would be less valuable if the New York Yankees did not exist. Thus, the Red Sox and the Yankees are not competitors in the same way that Ping and Callaway are; in a business sense, the Red Sox and Yankees are more like partners. They are both members of the American League, and the existence of one franchise benefits the other franchise.

The other significant feature that differentiates major professional sports leagues from the nonspectator sport sector, and from the rest of American business, is that these sports leagues are considered **monopolies**. That is, these leagues face no direct competition for the products and services they produce. For example, the NBA is currently the only seller of elite-level professional basketball in North America. Fans who enjoy watching the highest caliber of professional basketball must watch the NBA's version of the product because no other league supplies a comparable product. Again, compare this situation to the golf club industry, where a consumer shopping for a new set of clubs has a wide range of manufacturers from which to choose.

Businesses that are a **monopoly**, by definition, face no direct competition. This gives them greater bargaining power when dealing with stakeholders and allows the monopoly to potentially charge a higher price for its product than would be the case if it faced competitors. Thus fans pay higher prices for tickets, media companies pay higher fees for broadcast rights, corporations pay higher amounts to lease luxury suites, and taxpayers pay a large share of stadium construction costs. In short, the monopoly status of sports leagues allows them to earn much higher profits than would otherwise be the case.

North American sports leagues have not always had the luxury of this monopoly status. Until about 25 years ago, many leagues regularly faced competitors. The league that has faced the most competitors over the years is, perhaps somewhat surprisingly, the NFL. Since World War II, the NFL has faced serious competition from the All American Football Conference (AAFC) during the late 1940s, the American Football League (AFL) during the 1960s, the World Football League (WFL) during the mid-1970s, and the United States Football League (USFL) in the mid-1980s. In basketball, the NBA was actually formed in the late 1940s from the merger of two competing leagues—the National Basketball League (NBL) and the Basketball Association of America (BAA)—and then faced competition from the rival American Basketball Association (ABA) from 1967 to 1976. In hockey, the NHL faced competition from the rival World Hockey Association (WHA) during the 1972 to 1979 time span. Only in baseball has there not been a competitor league emerge since World War II.

The presence of these leagues rapidly and dramatically bid up player salaries. In some cases, they also forced a merger with the established league. The AFL was the most successful of all **rival leagues**, gaining a complete merger in 1966, with all eight AFL teams at the time being accepted into the NFL. The ABA and the WHA were also successful in gaining at least partial mergers, with four ABA teams entering the NBA in 1976, and four WHA teams entering the NHL in 1979.

Why have no new rival leagues emerged in more than 25 years? Rival leagues need two elements to be successful. First, they need players, at least some of whom are talented enough to be able to play in the established league, but who have chosen to play in the rival league. Many great players are alumni of rival leagues—Joe Namath and Herschel Walker in football, Julius Erving and Moses Malone in basketball, and Wayne Gretzky and Mark Messier in hockey, to name only a few. Before the emergence of strong players associations, and before the emergence of free agency, players often were "underpaid," generally earning only 20% to 25% of league revenues, compared to the situation today where 55% to 60% is the norm. Thus, players today have much less incentive to jump to a rival league.

In addition to having quality players, a second factor that rival leagues need to be successful is viable cities and markets in which to play. Over the past three decades, the major professional leagues have undergone successive rounds of expansion, to the point where all four currently have 30 or more franchises. This larger geographic footprint forces potential rival leagues either to place franchises in more mid-size, and probably less viable, markets, or to challenge the established league in head-to-head competition in the markets where the established league is already located.

The examination of rival leagues can make for an interesting history lesson, but what relevance does it have to business and finance in today's sport world? It turns out that the monopoly status of sports leagues has a great impact on financial issues. With no real threat of outside competition ever occurring, at least for the foreseeable future, the established sports leagues have large degrees of market power. This, in turn, allows them to have greater bargaining power with players, with broadcasters, with corporate sponsors, and with local governments regarding stadium funding issues. All else equal, it makes the major professional sports leagues much more profitable than they otherwise would be. It also allows them to enact financial policies—such as salary caps and revenue sharing—that would simply not be possible if a league faced direct competition from a rival league.

This level of monopoly power is almost unheard of in any other American business or industry. In fact, some economists argue that major professional sports leagues and their member teams are the only legal monopolies in the United States today. Some economists (Quirk & Fort, 1999) have even called for the federal government to break up the monopoly leagues, similar to the forced breakup of AT&T in 1984. For example, one possibility is that the NFL could be broken into two different leagues, with each league acting completely independent

of the other, thus introducing a measure of competition back into the industry not seen in decades. This competition would benefit—at least theoretically—fans, the media, taxpayers, and players by reducing the bargaining power of the leagues. While this forced breakup is unlikely to occur (the industry simply has too much political power), the industry will no doubt have to continue to occasionally publicly defend its monopoly status from challenges by economists or by certain members of Congress.

Of course, this monopoly position of leagues and teams does not guarantee financial success, nor does it guarantee that every team in every league will enjoy equal financial success. Leagues and teams must still produce a quality product, and they must display sound and innovative business management practices to achieve maximum success. While the monopoly position of the major professional leagues ensures no direct competition in the same sport, teams must still compete for the broader entertainment dollar of consumers. Consumers in many cities have a wide variety of entertainment options, including major professional sports, minor professional sports, college sports, the theater, the symphony, and theme parks.

For example, even though the NFL and the NHL are both monopolies, the former is obviously a much stronger, much more successful business entity. Even within a league, management quality still matters. In the NFL, the New England Patriots went from the lowest valued franchise in 1991 to the second highest valued franchise in 2012, largely, according to some, due to the Kraft family's purchase of the team in 1994 and the subsequent innovative management approaches that were adopted. The market power exercised by the NFL in negotiating their television deals along with the league's revenue-sharing models for media revenues also contribute greatly to the economic success of the NFL as compared to the NHL.

Key Skills

The future will continue to provide many growth opportunities for sport organizations, but it will also present challenges. As sport organizations continue to increase their managerial sophistication, the need for well-trained individuals in finance will become even greater. The specific issues will likely change. The key financial issues facing the industry in 15 years may be quite different than the ones facing the industry today. Thus, managers need to understand underlying financial principles and techniques, rather than just simply being familiar with current issues and facts. The issues will change, but the underlying analytical tools to analyze the issues will not.

No matter what type of sport organization is involved, the finance function is crucial. It is important to remember that finance is not defined as much by the subject matter being analyzed—it could be decisions related to ticket or sponsorship sales, team marketing, stadium operations, or player personnel—as it is by how the issue is analyzed. Finance is a way of thinking about problems that makes use of specific principles, concepts, and techniques to help managers make better decisions. Academic and practical training in finance helps people to think like a "finance person" and to evaluate problems using the fundamental concepts of financial analyses. Specifically, it forces managers to examine problems in terms of the age-old finance concepts of risk and return and to effectively use tools such as ROI to better analyze problems.

While finance people do need to be comfortable working with numbers, this is far from the only skill needed. In addition to formal training in corporate finance, those interested in a career in the area should have a solid grounding in managerial and financial accounting, and in the advanced use of spreadsheets (e.g., Microsoft Excel). For those with aspirations of working in the spectator sport industry, a familiarity with sports economics is also very beneficial.

The specific issues may differ depending on the setting. For example, the issues facing the vice president of finance of a major golf club manufacturer will be different than those faced by an athletic director of a Division III college program, which in turn will be different than those faced by a chief financial officer of a major professional team. However, the common link is that financial decision making in each of these settings should be grounded in the same basic set of principles, techniques, and thought processes.

Current Issues

Can Growth Continue?

In the nonspectator sport sector, a key issue is the extent to which the recreation and leisure market will continue to grow. Much of this sector—from golf to fitness to skiing—is driven by demographics, affluence, and societal values. Over the past 30 years, the U.S. population has aged, our overall affluence has increased, and our societal concerns over health-related issues have grown. The effect has been an explosion in spending on recreational and fitness activities. This large growth in the market has, in turn, propelled the industry to financial heights not seen before.

For individual segments of the nonspectator sport industry, predicting consumer trends also becomes a factor in their growth. For example, will golf remain as "hot" as it has been for the past two decades? Will a new recreational activity emerge that will provide enormous financial potential? These are crucial financial questions because capital investments (e.g., new golf courses, new ski resorts) are made now, but the payoff from these investments does not occur until later. Thus, if our assumptions about the future growth of the industry are incorrect, our ROI calculations will also be incorrect. For

Table 4-3 Average Franchise Values: 1991 and 2012/13 Seasons (in millions of dollars)

	2012/2013 Season	1991	Average Annual Growth Rate
NFL	1,100	132	10.6 %
MLB	744	121	9.0 %
NBA	509	70	9.9 %
NHL	282	44	9.3 %

Data from: Ozanian, M. (2013c). MLB team values. *Forbes*. Retrieved from http://www.forbes.com/mlb-valuations; Ozanian, M. (2012a, November 28). NHL team values. *Forbes*. Retrieved from http://www.forbes.com/nhl -valuations; Ozanian, M. (2013a, January 23). NBA team values. *Forbes*. Retrieved from http://www.forbes.com /nba-valuations; Ozanian, M. (2012b, September 5). NFL team values. *Forbes*. Retrieved from http://www.forbes .com/nfl-valuations; and Quirk, J., & Fort, R. (1997). *Pay dirt: The business of professional team sports*. Princeton, NJ: Princeton University Press.

example, if golf's popularity begins to wane over the next decade, the ROI on any new golf course construction will be lower than it has been in the recent past, and it may even be low enough to cause the investor to not undertake the new project.

Broadly similar questions exist for the spectator side of the sport industry; in particular, can the financial successes of the past continue at their same level into the future? Both the major professional leagues and the major revenue-generating college sports (Division I football and men's basketball) have seen tremendous revenue growth in the past 15 years. Table 4-3 shows how franchise values in the major professional leagues have changed

over this time period. Franchise values capture the future expected profitability (revenues minus expenses) of the franchise and represent the current market price of the franchise. All four leagues have shown significant growth in franchise values over the time period, largely because revenues have risen faster than expenses.

Revenues have also risen in the major revenue-generating college sports. Table 4-4 compares total revenues in 1989 with total revenues in 2011 for football, men's basketball, and women's basketball. All three show healthy yearly revenue growth. Of the three, women's basketball grew the most, showing an 11.7% increase per year over the time period, although

Table 4-4 NCAA Division I-A (Football Bowl Subdivision) Median Total Revenues per School, by Sport: 1989 and 2012 (in thousands of dollars)

	2012	1989	Average Annual Growth Rate
Football	19,593	4,300	6.8 %
Men's Basketball	6,067	1,600	6.0 %
Women's Basketball	690	60	11.2 %

Data from: Fulks, D. (2012). Revenues and expenses 2004–2012 NCAA Division I intercollegiate athletics programs report. Retrieved from http://www.ncaapublications.com/productdownloads/2012RevExp.pdf

this is somewhat offset by the fact that women's basketball started with the lowest base revenue (in 1989) of the three by far. In absolute terms, football continues to lead the revenue parade, with the average Division I-A Football Bowl Subdivision program now earning almost $18 million per year in earned and allocated revenues. While not shown in Table 4-4, the NCAA reports that the highest revenue college football program in 2011–2012, the University of Texas, earned almost $104 million in revenues (Dosh, 2012).

This increased revenue in spectator sports has come from a number of specific areas: gate receipts, broadcast contracts, sponsorship sales, stadium naming rights, and so on. As for gate receipts, ticket prices have increased considerably in all leagues. These increased prices reflect the growing popularity of sport, the increased ability to pay of sport consumers, and the scarcity of tickets in some locations. For example, many universities require a donation to the athletic department for the rights to purchase tickets to games. In 2011, The Ohio State University collected $38.7 million in such donations, followed by Louisiana State University with $38 million, and the University of Texas at Austin with $33.9 million (Eichelberger & Babcock, 2012).

Gate receipts have certainly been enhanced by the preponderance of new (or refurbished) stadiums that now exist. The revenue-generating ability of a stadium depends not only on the quantity of seats, but also on the quality. Teams prefer luxury seating and club seating because these premium seats have much greater revenue potential than the ordinary regular seating. These premium seats allow teams to better target high-income individuals and/or corporate clientele, and they allow teams to capture the increased ability and willingness to pay of these groups. Older stadiums simply do not have configurations that allow for this type

of premium seating. In essence, new stadiums give sport consumers many more ways to spend their money. Many new stadiums have been able to generate even more revenues by selling the naming rights to the stadium. For example, Citigroup purchased the naming rights to the New York Mets new stadium that opened in 2009 for a record $20 million per year (Buxbaum, 2009).

© best images/ShutterStock, Inc.

In addition to these "new" assets, the sport industry has been able to more effectively leverage its popularity and brand through newer media technologies such as the Internet, satellite TV, "on-demand" television, smartphones, and handheld wireless devices. The industry has also been able to better leverage its assets by adopting more sophisticated and professional management techniques, particularly in the areas of marketing and finance.

Media revenues have also continued to grow strongly. For example, a 7-year deal (which began in 1991) between the NCAA and CBS to televise the men's basketball tournament paid the NCAA an average of about $140 million per season. In contrast, the new 14-year agreement signed in 2010 will pay almost $800 million per year. In football, ESPN has signed a 12-year contract for the rights to the college football playoff system that will pay $500 million a year beginning in 2014 (Ourand & Smith, 2012).

These large contracts mean, in turn, lucrative payouts for the teams that reach a BCS game. For example, in 2013 the National Championship Game paid out more than $23 million to Alabama and a smaller $6 million payout to Notre Dame (because it is not part of a conference). Contrast this with the payouts in 1991, when each participating team received only about $2 million.

In professional sports, all four leagues have substantially increased their total TV revenues over the past 20 years. For sports such as baseball and hockey, the growth has been particularly at the local—as opposed to national—level. In the NFL, where almost all TV money is through national contracts, the growth has been the most dramatic. The NFL's contracts with Fox, CBS, NBC, and ESPN collectively will pay an average of $4.95 billion each year from 2014 to 2021, or about $155 million per year in revenues for each NFL team. This is an increase from $100 million per team from 2006 to 2013 and $30 million per team in 1991 (Associated Press, 2011).

© David Lee/ShutterStock, Inc.

Challenges

While revenues have certainly increased over the past 15 years, the cost of doing business has also gone up. In the nonspectator sport sector, increasingly large capital investments are needed to continue to generate revenues. With technological advances and more sophisticated consumer tastes, fitness and recreation businesses are forced to spend even more dollars on their capital assets. For example, many consumers of fitness centers want the newest and most advanced exercise equipment, golfers want to play on challenging well-maintained courses, and skiers want to stay at resorts that offer the latest amenities. Thus, if businesses are to remain competitive, they must always be evaluating the quality of their capital assets, and they must always be prepared to upgrade these assets to counter the competition's moves. As we learned earlier in the chapter, revenues flow from assets. If a firm's assets decline in quality, then its revenues will be negatively affected. Similar concepts apply to the spectator sport industry, where much of the revenue growth is attributable to teams playing in new or refurbished stadiums.

The financial challenge arises because these assets cost money. For example, new stadiums cost hundreds of millions of dollars. While the scale of investment may not be as great for a local fitness club investing in new exercise equipment, it is proportionately no less significant. Usually, these large-scale investments are financed, at least in part, by borrowed money (i.e., debt). However, as discussed earlier, debt is risky, in that interest and a proportion of the principal must be paid back to the lender at regular, prespecified intervals, regardless of whether the business meets its revenue expectations. Failure to meet these loan payments could ultimately result in bankruptcy. This issue is even more critical when one considers that unpredictable events, such as the severe recession that started in 2008, can make future revenue flows much lower than originally expected.

These debt issues have certainly been prominent in the major professional leagues, as teams have often borrowed heavily to finance their portion of stadium costs. Many new team owners have also borrowed heavily to finance the purchase price of the team. In fact, MLB was so concerned with the high debt levels of some of its teams that they included provisions in the collective bargaining agreement (CBA) that limits teams to borrowing up to eight times their cash flow, or 12 times if the borrowing is for stadium construction (Kaplan, 2013).

College sports have faced some unique challenges. The high-profile financial successes of the major revenue-generating sports often overshadow the rest of the college athletics spectrum. In fact, college athletics, taken as a whole, continue to be unprofitable. In 2008, the NCAA began to distinguish between generated revenues (such as ticket sales, sponsorships, media rights, and donations) and allocated revenues (such as student fees, institutional support, and state or local funds). **Table 4-5** shows the breakdown of generated revenues and expenses by division. As the table shows, even Division I schools are, on average, in significant deficit positions with their athletic programs without the external support of allocated revenues. The revenue-generating abilities of football and men's basketball are insufficient

to compensate for the deficits that occur in the other sports. The numbers indicate that Division I-AA, Football Championship Subdivision, schools are unable to generate the revenue of the Division I-A, Football Bowl Subdivision, schools, but they still incur many of the same costs as I-AAA and certainly incur much higher costs than their Division II counterparts.

There is another issue that relates to the financial differences between programs. Even if one focuses on just Division I-A, FBS, programs, there is a very unequal distribution of revenues across programs. For example, the formula used by the NCAA to pay out revenues to conferences from the men's basketball tournament is based, in part, on the success of conference teams in the tournament. Thus, conferences that are traditional powers tend to get the highest payouts, which can help to perpetuate their success while inhibiting the ability of other conferences to increase their success. In football, similar issues exist. For example, payouts from the BCS bowls tend to heavily favor the six BCS conferences, leaving relatively small amounts for other conferences. Schools and conferences that receive greater payouts correspondingly increase their chances of future success: More revenue means schools

Table 4-5 Median Generated Revenues and Expenses per School, Excluding Institutional Support: 2012 (in thousands of dollars)

Division	Median Generated Revenue	Median Expense	Difference
I-A Football Bowl Subdivision	40,581	56,265	−15,684
I-AA Football Championship Subdivision	3,750	14,115	−10,365
I-AAA Without Football	2,206	12,983	−10,777
II With Football (2011)	618	5,057	−4,439
II Without Football (2011)	297	3,645	−3,348

Data from: Fulks, D. (2012). Revenues and expenses 2004–2012 NCAA Division I intercollegiate athletics programs report. Retrieved from http://www.ncaapublications.com/productdownloads/2012RevExp.pdf; Fulks, D. (2011). Revenues and expenses 2004–2011 NCAA Division II intercollegiate athletics programs report. Retrieved from http://www.ncaapublications.com/productdownloads/D22011REVEXP.pdf

can hire better coaches, can build better practice facilities, can do more upgrades to their stadium, and so forth.

This issue of revenue disparities across schools and conferences is part of a larger issue that economists have recently begun to study—namely, the **competitive balance** problem. The competitive balance issue is rooted in the notion that consumers of a spectator sport seek to be entertained by the game itself. Research by economists reveals that this entertainment value is connected to a concept of "uncertainty of outcome": The greater the uncertainty of outcome, the greater the entertainment value for fans. This concept of uncertainty of outcome can be defined for an individual game, for a season, or over a number of seasons.

For an individual game, while local fans may prefer the home team to win, they also value competitiveness. Games that are expected to be a mismatch, where the outcome is largely predetermined, will reduce fan interest. Similarly, if one looks at an entire season rather than an individual game, fans tend to prefer situations where teams in the league are relatively closely bunched in the standings, as opposed to situations where there is a high level of disparity among the teams. In this latter situation, games played later in the season will become much less meaningful because large gaps separate the teams in the standings. Furthermore, one can look at this concept of uncertainty of outcome across seasons. Are the same teams successful year in and year out, or is there considerable change in the standings from year to year? For example, the order of finish in the American League East Division of baseball was exactly the same (New York Yankees, Boston, Toronto, Baltimore, Tampa Bay) for six consecutive seasons, from 1998 to 2003 (and again in 2005). In addition, the New York Yankees and Boston Red Sox finished in the top three of the American League East Division of baseball every season

from 1998 to 2011. Again, the suspicion is that fan interest will be reduced if fans enter each season believing that their favorite team's place in the standings is largely predetermined.

While the concern over competitive balance certainly is relevant to college sports, given the highly differential payouts that tend to favor the already dominant conferences, this issue has received the most attention in professional sports, particularly in baseball. Those who argue that MLB has a competitive balance problem point to the fact that large market teams are still more likely to make the playoffs over the past decade than small market teams. For example, since baseball went to the wild card system in 1995, the New York Yankees have made the playoffs in every season except one, through the 2012 season. The Boston Red Sox, another large market team, have made the playoffs in 10 of those seasons. Contrast this with small market teams such as those in Kansas City and Pittsburgh, who recently made the playoffs in 2013 after a 19-year absence.

This example highlights the economic roots of the competitive balance problem: All else equal, large market teams have greater revenue potential than small market teams and thus will find it more beneficial (in a revenue generation sense) than small market teams to employ higher quality players than will small market teams. To the extent that this higher level of talent ultimately translates into better on-field team performance, large market teams should, over the long run, be able to field consistently better teams than their small market counterparts.

Leagues have long had policies that have attempted to improve the on-field fortunes of poorly performing teams. All leagues use some form of a "reverse-order" draft, whereby those teams with the poorest records during the previous season have the top draft choices for the following season. The NFL also has used the scheduling system to foster competitive balance, by giving teams with poorer records during the previous season "easier" schedules in the following season.

These two mechanisms could be termed "nonfinancial" ways to alter competitive balance. However, neither directly addresses the root of the problem: the fact that differences in market sizes across franchises cause differences in revenue potential, which cause differences in the ability to pay players, which cause differences in team payroll, which cause differences in on-field performance.

In an attempt to better deal with these underlying causal factors, professional leagues have introduced a number of "financial" mechanisms to alter competitive balance. One of these mechanisms is a **salary cap**. Both the NFL and the NHL have "hard" caps, while the NBA has a "soft" cap. With the hard cap, the team payroll limit is an absolute and cannot be violated. A hard cap has been used in the NFL since 1994 and in the NHL since 2005. These hard caps are the result of negotiations between the leagues and their players' associations. The hard cap limit is typically set as a percentage of league revenues, usually between 55% and 60%. The philosophy behind the hard cap is that it will constrain all franchises to spend about the same amount on payroll (hard caps usually include a minimum payroll as well), presumably ensuring that franchises are fielding relatively equally balanced teams on the field. In essence, a hard cap prevents large market teams from using their natural financial advantage to buy the best teams.

With a soft cap, a payroll limit is still set, but teams can exceed this limit through various types of "exclusions." For example, one type of exclusion is situations in which teams sign their own free agents, as opposed to another team's free agents. Given this fairly wide array of exclusions, there is generally a much wider disparity in payrolls across teams with a soft cap than there is with a hard cap. The NBA has had a soft cap since 1984 and made history that year when it was the first league in the modern era of professional sports to implement any type of salary cap.

Revenue sharing is another financial mechanism intended to foster greater competitive balance. With revenue sharing, teams in the league agree to share certain types of revenues among themselves. For example, all four major professional leagues share national television revenues equally. However, the relative significance of this sharing revenues differs across leagues, with the NFL being the only league where national television revenues account for a large portion of total league revenues. In the other three leagues, "local" revenues (such as gate receipts and local television) are much more crucial. These local revenues can vary widely across teams, as mentioned previously, and are directly related to the market size in which the teams play. Thus, unless leagues also have a mechanism to share these revenues, large disparities in total revenues will persist across teams. Historically, there has been little or no sharing of these local revenues, but this has changed significantly in recent years. For example, under the current 2011–2016 CBA, MLB teams share around 34% of their net local revenues, although the actual amounts are determined by a complex formula, and by 2016, the teams in the 15 largest markets will not be eligible to receive any shared revenues. In the NHL, the 2013 CBA increased the amount of shared revenues by over 30% as compared to the amount first implemented in the 2005 CBA.

Most economists have suggested that revenue sharing, in and of itself, will do little to improve competitive balance. The reason is that teams receiving revenue-sharing transfers may have little incentive to use the money to increase payroll. Instead they may be motivated to simply retain the transfer as added profit. In other words, if it were beneficial (in an ROI sense) for small market teams to increase their payroll, they would have already done so, even without the revenue-sharing transfers. This criticism of revenue sharing has frequently been leveled at baseball's revenue-sharing plan, where some small market teams that received significant revenue transfers in recent years do not seem to be noticeably improving their on-field performance (but do seem to be improving their profitability). This is particularly a problem in baseball, because there is no payroll floor to which teams must adhere.

Where revenue sharing may be effective as a tool to improve competitive balance is when it is used in conjunction with a hard salary cap. Hard caps, in addition to having a payroll ceiling, have a payroll floor. For some small market teams, revenues may not be sufficient to meet this floor without revenue-sharing dollars. Thus, the hard cap essentially requires small market teams to use all or part of their revenue-sharing transfers on payroll.

Finally, a **luxury tax** has been used as a mechanism to influence competitive balance. Both the NBA and MLB have a form of a luxury tax. With a luxury tax, a payroll threshold is set prior to a season. Teams that exceed this threshold pay a tax on the excess amount. In baseball, for example, team payroll thresholds under the existing CBA are $178 million in 2012 and 2013 and $189 million from 2014 to 2016 (the last year of the agreement). Teams are taxed at a rate of 17.5% for a first violation of the threshold, 30% for a second violation, 40% for a third violation, and 50% for four or more violations. The luxury tax works somewhat differently than salary caps or revenue sharing, in that it is focused solely on changing the behavior of high-payroll teams, such as the New York Yankees. The Yankees have been the only team to exceed the threshold every season since the tax was introduced in 2003. In 2012, for example, the team paid a luxury tax of almost $19 million and has cumulatively paid $206 million since 2003, while only three other clubs have ever paid the tax (Waldstein, 2013).

Summary

While the recession that started in 2008 temporarily dampened economic growth across all industries, including sport, if one takes a broader perspective, there is no question that the past two decades have proven especially lucrative for all facets of the sport industry. An aging population and growth in the amount of disposable income available to be spent on recreation and entertainment have resulted in skyrocketing revenues in many sectors of the industry.

This financial boom has created a great need in the industry for people with training in finance. The future will continue to provide many growth opportunities for sport organizations but will also present challenges. As sport organizations continue to increase their managerial sophistication, the need for well-trained individuals in finance will become even greater.

The specific issues will likely change. The important financial issues facing the industry in the future may be quite different than the ones facing the industry today. Thus, managers need to understand underlying financial and economic principles and techniques, rather than just simply being familiar with current issues and facts. The issues will change, but the underlying analytical tools to analyze the issues will not.

Key Terms

assets, balance sheet, bonds, budgeting, competitive balance, debt, default, expenses, income, income statement, interest, liabilities, luxury tax, monopoly, owners' equity, principal, profits, return on investment (ROI), revenues, revenue sharing, risk, rival leagues, salary cap, value-added

References

Associated Press. (2010, January 11). Glazers aim to refinance Man. U. debt with bond sale. *The Tampa Tribune*. Retrieved from http://tbo .com/sports/bucs/glazers-aim-to-refinance -man-u-debt-with-bond-sale-56959

Associated Press. (2011, December 14). NFL renews television deals. Retrieved from http:// espn.go.com/nfl/story/_/id/7353238/nfl-re -ups-tv-pacts-expand-thursday-schedule

Associated Press. (2012, December 18). Josh Hamilton's deal valued at $123m. Retrieved from http://espn.go.com /los-angeles/mlb/story/_/id/8758433 /josh-hamilton-los-angeles-angels contract-valued-123-million-mlb

Backman, M. (2013, June 24). Moody's revises NCAA credit outlook to negative. *The Wall Street Journal*. Retrieved from http://online .wsj.com/article/SB1000142412788732418320 4578565862791492832.html

Beaton, A. & Kyle, A. (2012, October 1). Duke basketball completes its Legacy Fund endowment. *Duke Chronicle*. Retrieved from http://www.dukechronicle.com /articles/2012/10/01/duke-basketball -completes-its-legacy-fund-endowment

Burke, M. (2012, December 7). Average player salaries in the four major American sports leagues. Retrieved from http://www.forbes .com/sites/monteburke/2012/12/07/average -playersalaries-in-the-four-major-american -sports-leagues/

Business Wire. (2012). Fitch affirms NFL's league notes at 'A+' & borrowing programs at 'A'. Retrieved from http://www.businesswire .com/news/home/20120523006623/en/Fitch -Affirms-NFLs-League-Notes-Borrowing -Programs

Business Wire. (2013). Fitch affirms MLB club trust securitization sr. secured credit facility and term notes at 'A-'. Retrieved from http://www.businesswire.com/news /home/20130501006470/en/Fitch-Affirms -MLB-Club-Trust-Securitization-Sr

Buxbaum, E. (2009, April 13). Mets and the Citi: $400 million for stadium-naming rights irks some. Retrieved from http://articles.cnn .com/2009-04-13/us/mets.ballpark_1_citi -field-mets-home-stadium-naming?_s=PM:US

Dosh, K. (2012, December 12). Texas tops in football profit, revenue. Retrieved from http:// espn.go.com/blog/playbook/dollars/post /_/id/2556/texas-tops-in-football-profit -revenue

Eichelberger, C. & Babcock, C. R. (2012, October 24). Football-ticket tax break helps colleges get millions. *Bloomberg*. Retrieved from http://www.bloomberg.com/news/2012-10 -25/got-college-football-tickets-take-a-tax -break.html

Fried, G., Shapiro, S., & DeSchriver, T. (2008). *Sport finance*. Champaign, IL: Human Kinetics.

Fulks, D. (2011). Revenues and expenses 2004– 2011 NCAA Division II intercollegiate athletics programs report. Retrieved from http://www.ncaapublications.com /productdownloads/D22011REVEXP.pdf

Fulks, D. (2012). Revenues and expenses 2004–2012 NCAA Division I intercollegiate athletics programs report. Retrieved from: http://www.ncaapublications.com /productdownloads/2012RevExp.pdf

Hinton, M. (2013, February 21). Texas A&M leaks first renderings of Kyle Field renovation. Retrieved from http://www .cbssports.com/collegefootball/blog /eye-on-college-football/21743255

Kansas State Sports. (2013). Project details. Retrieved from http://www.kstatesports.com /weststadiumcenter/projectdetails.html

Kaplan, D. (2013, April 8). MLB will expand loan pool. *SportsBusiness Journal*. Retrieved from http://www.sportsbusinessdaily.com /Journal/Issues/2013/04/08/Finance/MLB -loan-pool.aspx?hl=MLB%20debt&sc=0

Kaplan, D., & Botta, C. (2012, August 13). Deadline near for Devils, but lenders unlikely to act. *SportsBusiness Journal*. Retrieved

from http://www.sportsbusinessdaily.com
/Journal/Issues/2012/08/13/Finance/Devils
.aspx?hl=equity%20stake&sc=0

Lewis, M. (2003). *Moneyball: The art of winning an unfair game.* New York, NY: W.W. Norton.

Long, J. G. (2013). *Public/private partnerships for major league sports facilities.* New York, NY: Routledge.

Ourand, J. (2012, August 28). ESPN secures MLB rights in eight-year, $5.6b deal. *SportsBusiness Journal.* Retrieved from http://www
.sportsbusinessdaily.com/Daily/Morning
-Buzz/2012/08/28/ESPN-MLB.aspx

Ourand, J., & Smith, M. (2012, November 9). ESPN homes in on 12-year BCS package. *SportsBusiness Journal.* Retrieved from http://
www.sportsbusinessdaily.com/Journal
/Issues/2012/11/12/Media/BCS-ESPN
.aspx?hl=ESPN%20BCS%20contract&sc=0

Ozanian, M. (2012a, November 28). NHL team values. *Forbes.* Retrieved from http://www
.forbes.com/nhl-valuations

Ozanian, M. (2012b, September 5). NFL team values. *Forbes.* Retrieved from http://www
.forbes.com/nfl-valuations

Ozanian, M. (2013a, January 23). NBA team values. *Forbes.* Retrieved from http://www
.forbes.com/nba-valuations

Ozanian, M. (2013b, January 27). Manchester United becomes first team valued at $3 billion. *Forbes.* Retrieved from http://www
.forbes.com/sites/mikeozanian/2013/01/27
/manchester-united-becomes-first-team
-valued-at-3-billion/

Ozanian, M. (2013c, March 27). MLB team values. *Forbes.* Retrieved from: http://www.forbes
.com/mlb-valuations

Plunkett Research. (2012). Sports industry overview. Retrieved from http://
www.plunkettresearch.com/sports
-recreation-leisure-market-research
/industry-and-business-data

Quirk, J., & Fort, R. (1997). *Pay dirt: The business of professional team sports.* Princeton, NJ: Princeton University Press.

Quirk, J., & Fort, R. (1999). *Hard ball: The abuse of power in pro team sports.* Princeton, NJ: Princeton University Press.

Russell, J. S. (2012, September 26). Jay-Z concerts to open rusty $1 billion Barclays Center. Retrieved from http://www.bloomberg.com
/news/2012-09-26/jay-z-concerts-to-open
-rusty-1-billion-barclays-center.html

Smith, C. (2013, January 7). The money behind the BCS national championship. *Forbes.* Retrieved from http://www.forbes.com/sites
/chrissmith/2013/01/07/the-money-behind
-the-bcs-national-championship/

SportsBusiness Journal. (2006, July 31). Tagliabue's tenure: The NFL during Paul Tagliabue's reign as commissioner, p. 32.

Thompson, T., & O'Keeffe, M. (2012, March 20). NY Mets close deal to sell 12 minority shares of team, have repaid $25M loan to MLB. *New York Daily News.* Retrieved from http://www
.nydailynews.com/sports/baseball/mets
/ny-mets-close-deal-sell-12-minority-shares
-team-repaid-25m-loan-mlb-article-1.1047096

University Athletic Association. (2013). UAA information. Retrieved from http://www.uaa
.ufl.edu/uaa/info.asp

U.S. Department of Commerce (2012, March 29). Bureau of Economic Analysis. Retrieved from http://www.bea.gov/newsreleases/national
/gdp/2012/gdp4q11_3rd.htm

Waldstein, D. (2013, March 11). Penny-pinching in pinstripes? Yes, the Yanks are reining in pay. *The New York Times.* Retrieved from http://www.nytimes.com/2013/03/12/sports
/baseball/yankees-baseballs-big-spenders
-are-reining-it-in.html

Chapter 5

Lisa P. Masteralexis and
Glenn M. Wong

Legal Principles Applied to Sport Management

Learning Objectives

Upon completion of this chapter, students should be able to:

1. Demonstrate the need for sport managers to have a basic understanding of legal principles to manage risk in their day-to-day activities and know when and how to seek legal assistance.

2. Define risk management and demonstrate how not addressing legal uncertainties can wreak havoc on a sport organization.

3. Develop a risk management program using the D.I.M. Process.

4. Categorize the various reasons why under judicial review courts may overturn the rules of voluntary athletic organizations.

5. Differentiate between the various areas of law that may affect sport organizations, such as tort law, agency law, contract law, constitutional law, antitrust law, labor and employment law, and intellectual property law.

6. Appraise how the federal government enforces Title IX and identify some of the important cases that have shaped the law since its passage in 1972.

7. Understand how the study of law can improve analytical, communication, negotiating, leadership, listening, and ethical reasoning skills.

8. Recognize that the impact of law on sport organizations is likely to increase in the future as the sport business becomes increasingly complex.

Introduction

Sport law refers to the application of law to the sport industry. In a few instances, new **statutes** (laws) have been enacted specifically to regulate the sport industry. The following federal laws are examples: the Sports Agent Responsibility and Trust Act of 2004 (SPARTA regulates sport agents), the Sports Broadcasting Act of 1961 (sport broadcasting antitrust exemption), the Professional and Amateur Sports Protection Act of 1992 (PASPA bans betting on sporting events *except* in states where betting was already legal), and the Ted Stevens Olympic and Amateur Sports Act (regulates Olympic and other amateur sports). At the state level, 42 states plus the District of Columbia and the U.S. Virgin Islands have adopted the 2001 Uniform Athlete Agent Act (Uniform Law Commission, 2013). At least three states have their own laws regulating agents.

Over the past 50 years, the sport industry has evolved into a complex multibillion-dollar global entity. With such growth, there is much at stake for those involved in the business and the participation segments of the industry. When decisions cause disputes, those in sport rely heavily on the legal system for resolution. Thus, sport managers must have a basic understanding of legal principles to manage risk in their daily activities and to know when and how to seek legal assistance.

History

Early sport and recreation cases were tort law cases involving participation in sport and games dating from the early evolution of tort law in the United States and Great Britain. For instance, a treatise published in 1635 in Britain and a landmark 1800s tort case, *Vosburg v. Putney*, both discuss tort liability for participation in games and horseplay (Yasser, McCurdy, Goplerud, & Weston, 1999).

Many of the earliest U.S. lawsuits in the sport industry involved the business of baseball because it hosted the first sport league. Early cases in professional sport involved baseball players challenging the reserve system adopted by owners to prevent players from achieving any form of free agency (*Metropolitan Exhibition Co. v. Ewing*, 1890; *Metropolitan Exhibition Co. v. Ward*, 1890). Interestingly, a player involved in one of these cases, John Montgomery Ward, led the first union efforts in baseball in the late 1800s and went on to become a lawyer (Staudohar, 1996). Throughout the early to mid-twentieth century, most cases in the sport industry were based in contract, antitrust, and labor law.

At the time of these early cases, there was no formally recognized specialty called "sport law." Sport law was first documented in 1972 when Boston College Law School's Professor Robert Berry offered a course focused on legal issues in the professional sport industry (Wong & Masteralexis, 1996). Today numerous law schools and sport management programs include sport law courses in their curricula.

Among the many reasons for the considerable growth in the field over the past five decades is that the legal profession as a whole has moved toward a greater degree of specialization. The amount of litigation and the diversity of cases in the sport industry have increased as more people in our society rely on the courts to resolve disputes. Many athletic associations have adopted their own governance systems with rules, regulations, and procedures that are based on the U.S. legal system. Sport governing bodies operate much like federal and state administrative bodies. **Administrative law** describes the body of law created by rules, regulations, orders, and decisions of administrative bodies. Governance documents of sport organizations resemble state or federal laws, rules, and regulations. For instance, the constitution and bylaws of professional leagues govern the relationship between leagues and their owners and have dispute-resolving mechanisms, internal procedures for resolving disputes. Another example lies in the National Collegiate Athletic Association (NCAA) manual of rules and regulations. The rules and regulations mirror the language of statutes and as a result, when a dispute arises over the interpretation of a rule or regulation, sport lawyers often represent both the governing body and the institution, resolving the dispute through an administrative process established by the NCAA. Because many sport organizations use lawyers to draft their rules and regulations, lawyers can best interpret, challenge, or defend these rules and regulations. Lawyers have developed specialties in the sport industry to address the challenges to governing bodies. Some lawyers now specialize in representing schools and athletes in investigations by and hearings before the NCAA (Haworth, 1996). Other lawyers specialize in representing athletes in crises, representing athletes who have failed drug tests, and representing athletes in front of arbitration panels such as the Court for Arbitration in Sport.

There are three professional associations devoted to sport law in North America, and others around the world in Europe, Australia, and New Zealand. The North American associations are the Sports Lawyers Association, the American Bar Association Forum Committee on Sport and Entertainment Law, and the Sport and Recreation Law Association. These associations publish journals and newsletters, as well as hold conferences. In addition, a number of law schools host sport law institutes. Among them are Loyola (Los Angeles), Marquette, Pennsylvania State, Santa Clara, Tulane, Vermont, Villanova, and the University of New Hampshire.

While possessing a law degree is not a necessity for a sport manager, the skills a legal education provides are beneficial to many in the industry. Legal education teaches written and oral communication, analytical reasoning, critical thinking, problem solving, and negotiating skills. Many in the sport industry possess law degrees but work in sport management rather than practicing law. For instance, in professional sport, National Hockey League (NHL) Commissioner Gary Bettman, and the outgoing and incoming National Basketball Association (NBA) Commissioners David Stern and Adam Silver are lawyers, as were some previous commissioners in Major League Baseball (MLB) (Fay Vincent, Bowie Kuhn, Kennesaw Mountain Landis) and the National Football League (NFL) (Paul Tagliabue). Other positions held by lawyers include league staff, professional team general managers, players association executive directors and staff, NCAA officials, college conference commissioners and staff, athletic directors and compliance staff, International and U.S. Olympic Committee members and staff, national governing body members and staff, player representatives, and facility managers. All of these individuals possess law degrees but do not practice law in the traditional sense. Their knowledge of law guides their decision making and may save organizations the expense of hiring counsel. For example, a facility manager may need to understand local ordinances and codes, tort law, contract law, labor and employment laws, and the Americans with Disabilities Act, just to name a few. A facility manager also may be responsible for negotiating many contracts, including leases with teams, event contracts, concessionaire contracts, sponsorship agreements, employment contracts, collective bargaining agreements with labor unions, and pourage rights for the beverages sold in the facility.

Key Concepts

Legal disputes occur more frequently in the sport industry today as more people turn to the legal system to resolve disputes because there are increased financial interests involved at all levels of high school, collegiate, Olympic, and professional sports. On the high school and intercollegiate side, gender discrimination, constitutional rights violations, recruiting violations, use of ineligible players, and rule violations by athletes, coaches, and educational institutions are all sources of litigation (Wong, 2010). On the professional side, labor disputes, contract issues, misconduct by athletes and owners, health and safety issues (e.g., concussions), and the enforcement of and challenges to rules are the primary sources of litigation. Personal injury and product liability cases filed by recreational sport participants have increased as well. To make legally sound decisions, it is important for sport managers to have a basic understanding of legal principles.

Risk Management

Risk management is an important lesson for a sport manager. Managing risk requires developing a management strategy to maintain greater control over the legal uncertainties that may wreak havoc on a sport business. Whatever the type of sport business, risk management plans contain the same goals: prevention and intervention. Prevention involves keeping problems from arising, whereas intervention involves having a plan of action to follow when problems do occur. Risk management strategy encourages sport managers to develop a plan to prevent legal disputes from occurring and a plan for intervening when a legal problem does arise. Through risk management, sport managers may limit their losses by avoiding becoming defendants in court actions. (Note: a **plaintiff** is a person or organization that initiates a lawsuit, and a **defendant** is the person or organization that allegedly wronged the plaintiff and must respond to the lawsuit.)

The D.I.M. Process is one method used to establish a risk management program. The D.I.M. Process consists of three steps: (1) *developing* the risk management plan, (2) *implementing* the risk management plan, and (3) *managing* the risk management plan (Ammon, 2010). It is important that sport managers follow these

steps to create a risk management program specifically tailored to their organizations. The risk management plan should address all potential legal liability. Many people think of risk management plans only for addressing the potential for tort liability—in particular, **negligence**. Instead, a plan should include the many areas of law discussed throughout this chapter. For example, a risk management philosophy may also keep a sport manager from losing an employment discrimination suit, an arbitration proceeding, or a challenge to an athletic association's rule. A key to a successful risk management strategy is to have all the organization's employees involved in the three stages of the process. This way, employees will have "ownership" in the plan (Ammon 2010). They will know why the plan exists and what its goals are, and they will be more likely to follow it.

Judicial Review

Athletic administrators make decisions regarding athletic rules and regulations daily, about areas such as eligibility or recruiting. As decision makers, athletic administrators must realize that often athletes and coaches will initiate judicial and/or administrative challenges to decisions that are not in their favor. Courts may review their decisions. **Judicial review** occurs when a plaintiff challenges a rule and the court evaluates it to determine whether it should apply. Historically, and as a general rule, courts have declined to overturn rules of voluntary athletic organizations, except where the rule or regulation meets one of the following conditions (Masteralexis & Masteralexis, 2010):

1. The rule violates public policy because it is fraudulent or unreasonable.

2. The rule exceeds the scope of the athletic association's authority.

3. The athletic association breaks one of its own rules.

4. The rule is applied in an arbitrary or capricious manner.

5. The rule violates an individual's constitutional rights.

6. The rule challenged by the plaintiff violates an existing law, such as the Sherman Antitrust Act or the Americans with Disabilities Act.

Courts have the power to grant two types of remedies: monetary damages and equitable relief. Monetary damages compensate a plaintiff or punish a defendant. Money, however, is not always the best remedy. A student ruled ineligible for a tournament simply wants to play. When a plaintiff seeks judicial review, he or she will usually also request an **injunction**, that is, an order from the court to do or not do a particular action. In cases involving a challenge to an athletic association's rule, the plaintiff's interest may be to keep the rule from applying or to force the athletic association to apply it differently in order to play. An injunction is a type of equitable relief that is a better remedy because it provides a court order with the power to do exactly that, which often is to maintain the status quo until there is a full trial on the matter. Injunctions prevent current and future wrongs and can only be used to prevent an irreparable injury. An injury is considered irreparable when it involves the risk of physical harm or death, the loss of a special opportunity, or the deprivation of unique, irreplaceable property (Wong, 2010).

Money does not provide adequate compensation for an irreparable injury such as being barred from participation in sport. For example, assume a high school provided a boys' soccer team but no girls' soccer team. A girl tried out and made the boys' team. Her play impressed the coach, and he gave her a starting position after the first game of the season. Her team went undefeated in the regular season. The night before the first playoff game, the league commissioner called the coach to tell him that the other coaches in the league had launched a complaint against the team for having a girl on its roster when they were competing in a boys' league. The commissioner also stated that if the girl showed up to play in the tournament, the team would have to forfeit those games. In this situation, the coach and the female student-athlete might seek an injunction to compete in the tournament. They are not interested in money. Besides, there is no way to determine how much participating in the soccer game is worth. The girl will argue that she faces irreparable harm by being denied the opportunity to play. She may never have the opportunity to participate in this type of tournament again, and even if she were to have another opportunity, it would not be the same because she has worked hard with this team. Further, the other coaches had all season to complain and they waited until the playoffs in an attempt to damage an undefeated team. No amount of money can compensate her for this lost opportunity. In addition to seeking an injunction, the plaintiff here could file a lawsuit against the league for gender discrimination, seeking damages for the discrimination she faced.

© Photos.com

Tort Liability

A **tort** is an injury or wrong suffered due to another's improper conduct. The goals of tort law are to provide monetary damages to compensate an injured person (plaintiff) and to deter people (defendants and others in society) from engaging in similar conduct in the future. The sport industry is susceptible to tort claims because people participating in sport may hurt themselves or others. Tort law allows people to assess loss and allocate blame.

The defendant's intent while committing the tort helps the court to determine what tort the defendant committed and to assess damages owed to the plaintiff. Intentional torts allow for additional damages, called *punitive damages*, to punish the defendant. Intentional torts occur when one person purposely causes harm to another or engages in an activity that is substantially certain to cause harm. Assault, battery, defamation, intentional infliction of emotional distress, intentional interference with contractual relations, and invasion of privacy are all intentional torts.

Gross negligence falls between negligence (discussed shortly) and an intentional tort. **Gross negligence** occurs when a defendant acts recklessly. Recklessness exists when a person knows that an act is harmful but fails to realize the degree of extreme harm that results (*Hackbart v. Cincinnati Bengals, Inc.*, 1979). This theory is applied routinely in participant versus participant cases, except in Arizona, Nevada, and Wisconsin (*Mark v. Moser*, 2001).

Negligence is an unintentional tort and is the most common tort that sport managers encounter. Therefore, the focus of this introductory chapter is on negligence and not intentional torts.

Sport managers are negligent when they commit an act or omission that causes injury to a person to whom they owe a duty to act with care. To determine whether a sport manager has been negligent, a court will focus on the relationship between the plaintiff (injured) and the defendant (sport manager). Before a sport manager can be found liable for negligence, the plaintiff must show that the sport manager owed the plaintiff a **duty of care**. A legal duty of care is more than simply a moral obligation. According to Van der Smissen (2007), a legal duty arises from one of three origins: (1) from a relationship inherent in a particular situation, (2) from a voluntary assumption of the duty of care, or (3) from a duty mandated by a law.

For example, assume a college track-and-field coach was conducting a private training session with her top athlete. After running 500 meters, the athlete collapsed. Because of her special relationship with the runner, the coach has a duty to provide the athlete with prompt medical assistance. Assume further that a citizen of the community who has no connection to the team is exercising at the facility. The citizen may be under a moral obligation to help the athlete, but the citizen has no relationship to the athlete, and thus no legal duty to render assistance. However, if the citizen ran over to the collapsed athlete to help the coach administer cardiopulmonary resuscitation (CPR), the citizen would then voluntarily assume a duty of care toward the athlete. Finally, the law may impose a duty of care on certain individuals due to their special training or skills. Assume further that the citizen is an off-duty emergency medical technician (EMT) and that the state where the incident occurs requires all certified EMTs to respond to emergencies. Such a law would create a relationship between the collapsed athlete and the EMT who is exercising there. In such a case, if the EMT did not respond, the EMT could be found negligent. To be found negligent, a defendant must also be the actual cause of the injury and the injury must be a reasonable, foreseeable consequence of the defendant's action.

Negligence imposes a duty to refrain from careless acts. A good risk management plan, then, will help a sport manager avoid lawsuits based on negligence. To develop the plan, sport managers must consider potential problems the business may face and contemplate what is reasonable and foreseeable. If the sport manager then implements a plan to avoid reasonable and foreseeable injuries, the risk manager is working to establish an environment free from negligence. This way, the sport manager will also reduce the risk of a successful tort claim.

An issue that arises often is the liability of teams and facilities to spectators injured while attending games. Some courts have adopted a "no duty" or "limited duty" rule to limit negligence cases, particularly in baseball. For example, in *Thurmond v. Prince William Baseball Club, Inc.* (2003), the court held that when an adult spectator of ordinary intelligence and a familiarity with the sport attends a game, he assumes the normal risks of watching a baseball game, such as being hit by a ball when sitting in an unscreened area. Similarly, in *Turner v. Mandalay Sports Entertainment* (2008), a minor league baseball team did not provide a protective screen around its concession area. A patron who was sitting in the concession area was hit in the face with a ball hit from the field of play. The court found that the baseball team had a "limited duty" to the plaintiff and that the plaintiff had been unable to demonstrate that the area in which she was seated constituted an "unduly high risk of injury."

However, in *Crespin v. Albuquerque Baseball Club* (2009), a New Mexico appellate court declined to adopt the limited duty rule, holding that the team and city owed a general duty of reasonable care to all spectators, and determinations regarding whether they breached the duty should depend on the facts and circumstances of each case. The court found no compelling reason to adopt the baseball rule due to the state's comparative negligence statute, under which juries could evaluate risks that spectators accept while attending games. Applying traditional tort law principles, the court found the trial court's granting of summary judgment (due to the limited duty rule) inappropriate, emphasizing that a jury should determine whether the team and city breached their duty to the spectator by failing to screen the picnic area or warn that batting practice was underway. In dismissing the claims against the Houston Astros and the minor league player, the court noted that the player was merely practicing to perform in a manner consistent with the rules of the game, under which his team would be rewarded for home runs.

Contact sports also pose an interesting question for the court to consider, which generally provides immunity from liability for amateurs engaging in that sport. In *Noffke ex. rel Swenson v. Bakke* (2009), the court found that cheerleading should be considered a contact sport and that a male cheerleader's inability to prevent the plaintiff's fall was not an act of negligence. (As noted previously, most courts adopt a gross negligence standard of liability for coparticipant torts.)

Vicarious Liability

Vicarious liability provides a plaintiff with a cause of action to sue a superior for the negligent acts of a subordinate. Often lawsuits arise when an employee commits a tort and a plaintiff seeks to hold the employer responsible because the employer has a greater ability to pay damages. Under vicarious liability, the employer need not be negligent to be liable. The employer is legally responsible provided the employee is in fact an employee and the employee committed a tort while working for the employer. If the employer is also negligent for hiring an unqualified individual or not providing proper training, the employer's negligence may provide an additional legal claim.

Three defenses are available to an employer faced with a vicarious liability claim. First, if the employee was not negligent, the employer cannot be held liable. Second, the employer may argue that the employee was not acting within the scope of employment, as is the case when an employee acts on his or her own. Third, the employer may argue that the employee is an **independent contractor**. An independent contractor is an employee who is not under the employer's supervision and control. Examples of employees who may be independent contractors include freelance sportswriters or photographers, sport officials, part-time instructors or personal trainers at health and fitness centers, and team physicians or athletic trainers.

Agency Law

The law of **agency** affects all businesses, including those in sport. The term *agency* describes "the fiduciary relation which results from the manifestation of consent by one person to another that the other shall act on his behalf and subject to his control and consent," (*Black's Law Dictionary*, 1979, p. 58) One purpose of agency law is to establish the duties that the **principal** and the **agent** owe each other. Although the principal and the agent often have an underlying **contract** to establish the relationship's parameters, agency law is not concerned with promises established by contract (such promises are subject to contract law). **Fiduciary duties** are inherent in the principal–agent relationship and are imposed on the parties in accordance with agency law, regardless of what a contract between the parties specifies. The term *fiduciary* comes from Roman law and means a person holding the character of a trustee. A fiduciary duty obligates a fiduciary to act with trust that one will be loyal and act in the best interest of the other (*Black's Law Dictionary*, 1979). A second purpose of agency law is to hold the principal responsible to others

for actions of the agent, provided the agent is acting under the authority granted to the agent by the principal.

Under agency law, the principal owes the agent three duties:

1. To comply with a contract if one exists

2. To compensate the agent for his or her services

3. To reimburse the agent for any expenses incurred while acting on the principal's behalf

The agent owes the principal five fiduciary duties (Howell, Allison, & Henley, 1987):

1. To obey

2. To remain loyal

3. To exercise reasonable care

4. To notify

5. To account (for information and finances on a reasonable basis)

This list of fiduciary duties is fairly self-explanatory. However, the second duty, to remain loyal by avoiding conflicts of interest, may need some clarification. Because conflicts of interest arise so frequently, an agent can continue representing a principal when a conflict of interest is present, provided the agent fully discloses the conflict to the principal and gives the principal the option to work with a neutral party in the agent's place. For example, assume a player representative has two clients who are all-star catchers and free agents. Both have similar defensive skills and are power hitters. Assume the Atlanta Braves are in need of a top-shelf catcher. The player representative may be in a position of favoring the interest of one free agent over another, as the Braves will need just one of the players. The agent and catchers need not end their relationship. The agent should

disclose the conflict to the catchers and give one the option of finding another negotiator for that contract negotiation.

Another example that occurs quite frequently in the sport industry is when a sport management agency represents both an athlete and the event in which the athlete is competing. For a major event, the athlete may receive an appearance fee that is negotiated by the event division of the agency and the athlete's agent, both of whom work for the same parent company.

Under agency law, a principal will be liable for any torts committed by an agent, provided the agent was acting within the scope of employment, as described in the earlier discussion of vicarious liability. A principal is also liable for any contracts an agent has entered into on the principal's behalf, provided the principal gave the agent authority to enter into contracts.

Agency law is an important component of the sport representation industry. Among other reasons, athletes and coaches hire sport agents to gain a level of parity in negotiations with more experienced negotiators, such as club management or university representatives (Shropshire & Davis, 2003). Sports agent relationships are often based in contract law, but they are also governed by the law of agency and its imposition of fiduciary duties. For this reason, when lawsuits do occur, they may involve claims under contract (*Total Economic Athletic Management of America v. Pickens*, 1995; *Williams v. CWI, Inc.*, 1991; *Zinn v. Parrish*, 1981), tort (*Vick v. Wong*, 2009; *Brown v. Woolf*, 1983), and/or agency law (*Buse v. Vanguard Group*, 1996; *Detroit Lions, Inc. and Sims*

v. Argovitz, 1984; *Hillard v. Black*, 2000; *Jones v. Childers*, 1994).

Contract Law

A **contract** is a written or verbal agreement between two or more parties that creates a legal obligation to fulfill the promises made by the agreement. Every aspect of the sport industry uses contracts. Sport managers use contracts for employing players, officials, and other staff. Contracts are also used for broadcasting deals; licensed property; merchandise, equipment, uniform, and ticket sales; facility leases; sponsorships; concession arrangements; memberships and scholarships; purchasing; scheduling arrangements; and the like. Many sport managers negotiate and enter into contracts regularly. It is essential that sport managers have a basic understanding of contract law to limit their liability and know when to engage a lawyer for help. Sound contract drafting and analysis should be part of a sport manager's risk management plan. **Figure 5-1** depicts the formation of a contract.

A valid contract must have **mutual assent**, which is an offer by one party and an acceptance by another. A contract also requires both parties to give **consideration**. Consideration is something of value, such as money, property, or something intangible. Consideration in a coach's contract will likely include perks received by the coach, such as a car or country club membership (*Rodgers v. Georgia Tech Athletic Assoc.*, 1983).

People entering into contracts must have the **capacity** to understand the nature and effects of their actions. Generally, individuals

Figure 5-1 Contract Formation

older than the age of 18 possess capacity. Under contract law, minors and mentally incompetent individuals may enter contracts but also may **disaffirm** (opt out of) them at any time. Thus, sport managers agreeing to appearances or endorsements with athletes younger than age 18 enter into those contracts at their own risk. They should know that minors may disaffirm the contracts provided they return anything of value that was not earned. The subject matter of a contract must be legal, which means it cannot violate laws or public policy. This concept is known as **legality**.

If a contractual promise is broken, it is considered a **breach**. A full breach occurs when the contract is entirely broken, and a partial breach occurs when one or more, but not all, of the provisions in the contract are broken. The remedy for a breach is usually monetary damages to compensate the injured party, for money will usually enable an individual to fulfill his or her expectations elsewhere. In rare cases, the remedy of an injunction may be used to force a party to comply with a contract. Most often this remedy is available only when the subject matter of the contract is so rare that no amount of money will provide an adequate remedy. For example, if a sports memorabilia collector entered into a contract to purchase the only mint-condition Honus Wagner rookie baseball card in existence and the seller backed out of the deal, then the collector could go to court to obtain a court order to force the seller to comply with the contract.

Waivers and **releases of liability** are contracts that may form an important component of a risk management plan. Through waivers, parties agree contractually to give up their right to sue for negligence. Waivers cannot be used to waive a right to sue for gross negligence or intentional torts. A *waiver* is signed before one participates in the activity for which one is waiving the right to sue. A *release of liability* is similar to a waiver but is a contract that a party signs after an injury occurs by which the injured party gives up the right to sue later, usually in exchange for a financial settlement.

Jurisdictions vary regarding whether a waiver will be upheld against a plaintiff. When using a waiver, a sport manager should be concerned with drafting it carefully so that it will be enforceable. Flawed language in a waiver may lead a court to conclude that the individual signing the waiver did not knowingly and voluntarily agree to waive his or her right to sue. A waiver should be drafted with clear, unambiguous, and precise language that is easily understood by non-lawyers. Waivers should also be printed in large, readable font, preferably 10- or 12-point type. According to Cotten (2010, p. 95), "in at least 43 states, D.C., and the Virgin Islands, a well-written, properly administered waiver, voluntarily signed by an adult, can be used to protect the recreation or sport business from liability for ordinary negligence by the business or its employees." In the past, parental waivers and releases of indemnity were ineffective. More recently, however, courts in the following states have upheld parental waivers in certain circumstances: California, Connecticut, Florida, Georgia, Massachusetts, Minnesota, North Dakota, Ohio, and Wisconsin. Parental indemnity releases have been upheld in California, Florida, Hawaii, Louisiana, Ohio, and New Jersey. Legislatures in Colorado and Alaska have also passed statutes allowing parental waivers. Clearly there is a trend toward greater acceptance of their use in legal transactions.

That said, some courts have ruled waivers invalid as a matter of **public policy**. Generally, a waiver violates public policy if (1) it pertains to a service important to the public, (2) the parties are not of equal bargaining power, (3) there is an employer–employee relationship between the parties entering into the waiver contract, or (4) it attempts to preclude liability for gross negligence or intentional acts (Cotten, 2010).

The mandatory use of waivers to bar negligence claims by high school athletes has been found to violate public policy in Washington (*Wagenblast v. Odessa School District*, 1988). Using waivers for minors produces another important challenge. Because waivers are contracts and minors may disaffirm contracts, it is advisable to have the parents of a minor also sign a waiver. (Cotten, 2010).

© EDHAR/ShutterStock, Inc.

Constitutional Law

Constitutional law is developed from precedents established by courts applying the language of the U.S. Constitution and state constitutions to the actions and policies of governmental entities. State constitutions vary. Some are models of the U.S. Constitution, whereas others grant greater rights to their citizens. The constitutional challenges that tend to arise in the sport industry most frequently are related to due process, equal protection, the right to be free from unreasonable searches and seizures, and invasion of privacy. Occasionally challenges regarding the First Amendment freedoms of religion, speech, and the right to assemble peaceably occur.

State Action

As a rule, the U.S. Constitution and state constitutions do not apply to private entities such as professional teams, athletic associations, private high schools or colleges, or private golf or health

and fitness clubs. However, in some cases it can be argued that the private entity is so enmeshed with the public entity that the two are dependent upon one another. When a private entity meets this standard, it is called a **state actor** and the court may apply the Constitution to that private entity. For example, in *Brentwood Academy v. Tennessee Secondary School Athletic Association (TSSAA)* (2001), the U.S. Supreme Court found state action in the TSSAA's regulatory activity due to the pervasive entwinement of state school officials in the TSSAA's structure. The plaintiff, Brentwood Academy, is a private parochial high school member of the TSSAA.

The TSSAA found that Brentwood violated a rule prohibiting "undue influence" in recruiting athletes when it wrote to incoming students and their parents about spring football practice. The TSSAA placed Brentwood's athletic program on probation for 4 years, declared its football and boys' basketball teams ineligible to compete in playoffs for 2 years, and imposed a $3,000 fine. When the penalties were imposed, all the voting members of the board of control and legislative council were public school administrators. In *Brentwood Academy*, the Court found that the TSSAA's private character was overshadowed by the pervasive entwinement of public institutions and public officials in its structure and activities. Factually, 84% of the TSSAA's members were public schools whose officials acted in their official capacity to provide interscholastic athletics to their students. Without the public school officials, who overwhelmingly determine and perform all but the TSSAA's purely ministerial acts, the TSSAA could not function. In addition, the TSSAA's staff participates in the state retirement system. To complement the entwinement from the bottom up, the state has provided entwinement from the top down: State board members sit *ex officio* on the TSSAA's governing bodies and association. Thus, the Court found constitutional standards applied to the TSSAA.

In a very important case for the NCAA, the U.S. Supreme Court declined to hold the NCAA a state actor. In *NCAA v. Tarkanian* (1988), the Court refused to find state action when the NCAA ordered the University of Nevada, Las Vegas (UNLV) to suspend its basketball coach, Jerry Tarkanian. The difference between the two cases is that the NCAA's policies were shaped not by UNLV alone, but by several hundred member institutions, many of them private and most of them having no connection with UNLV. In *Tarkanian*, the Court did, however, predict in dictum that state action could be found where there is public entwinement in the management or control of an entity whose member public schools are located in a single state (*Id.* at 193).

Due Process

Athletic associations adopt many rules and regulations that they enforce through their own administrative processes. If the athletic association is a state actor, then its administrative process must also provide procedural **due process**. Procedural due process is the right to notice and a hearing before life, liberty, or property may be taken away. Obviously, no athletic association makes decisions to take away a life. Some decisions, however, do affect liberty and property interests protected by the due process clauses in the Fifth and Fourteenth Amendments. Examples of liberty interests include the right to be free from stigma, to be free from damage to one's reputation, and to pursue one's livelihood. Property interests involve the taking away of anything of value. The U.S. Supreme Court has found property interests arise from explicit understandings that can support a claim of entitlement (*Perry v. Sindermann*, 1972). College scholarships have long been held to be property interests (*Gulf South Conference v. Boyd*, 1979), as have tenured positions of employment (*Perry v. Sindermann*, 1972).

Equal Protection

The **equal protection** clause of the Fourteenth Amendment guarantees that no person shall be discriminated against unless a constitutionally permissible reason for the discrimination exists. *Discrimination* occurs when two similarly situated individuals are treated differently on the basis of a status or classification. The equal protection clause often applies in sport when there are allegations of discrimination on the basis of race, gender, or alienage in eligibility or employment decisions. The court employs different standards of review from strict scrutiny to rational basis depending upon the status or classification of the party alleging discrimination to decide whether a rule or regulation in sport discriminates. **Strict scrutiny** applies where one discriminates on the basis of race, religion, or national origin. To withstand a constitutional challenge, a defendant must convince the court it has a compelling need to violate a fundamental right or discriminate. This standard is the most challenging to meet, so defendants usually lose.

The second standard of review applies to discrimination on the basis of gender. A defendant may discriminate on the basis of gender only if a **legitimate interest** for doing so exists. In high school and college athletics, courts have found two legitimate reasons for upholding the use of separate gender teams: (1) to protect the health and safety of the athletes and (2) to avoid existing discrimination or make up for past discrimination.

However, a legitimate reason may not exist to have separate gender practices in the management side of sports. For instance, in 1975, MLB Commissioner Bowie Kuhn enacted a rule that banned female reporters from baseball clubhouses. Despite the contrary wishes of Yankee players, Kuhn insisted that Melissa Ludtke, a female *Sports Illustrated* sportswriter covering the 1977 World Series, be banned from the Yankees' clubhouse (*Ludtke and Time, Inc. v. Kuhn*, 1978). Ludtke challenged the rule because it discriminated against her on the basis of her gender and kept her from pursuing her profession, a liberty protected by the Fourteenth Amendment's equal protection and due process clauses. The court found that MLB's expressed legitimate reason of protecting the privacy of the players and the family image of the game could not withstand judicial scrutiny when it allowed television cameras in clubhouses at the game's end to obtain interviews from scantily clad players.

The third standard of review applies to discrimination based on any other status or classification. Discriminatory actions have been challenged on the basis of economic or social background, sexual orientation, physical or mental disability, or athletic team membership. The court will allow the defendant's actions if it convinces the court there is a **rational basis** for the discriminatory rule. Rational basis standard cases are the easiest for defendants to win.

Unreasonable Search and Seizure

The Fourth Amendment provides that people have the right "to be secure in their persons, houses, papers and effects against **unreasonable searches and seizures**." The act of taking an athlete's urine or blood to test for doping may constitute a seizure and the testing may constitute a search within the meaning of the Fourth Amendment. Such a search may be considered reasonable by a court if the defendant can show a compelling need for it. The U.S. Supreme Court has upheld drug testing of high school athletes on the grounds that schools have a compelling interest in deterring drug use by children to ensure their health and safety and to keep the school environment free from the disciplinary problems created by drug use (*Vernonia School District 47J v. Acton*, 1995). In 2002, the U.S. Supreme Court (in a narrow 5–4 decision) upheld the constitutionality of a

random, mandatory suspicionless test of all students engaged in all competitive extracurricular activities because it was a reasonably effective means of addressing the school district's legitimate concerns in preventing, deterring, and detecting drug use (*Board of Education v. Earls*, 2002). Because the only disciplinary consequence of a positive test for illegal drugs was to limit participation in those activities, the Court allowed the school board to use the testing as a method of deterrence without waiting for a crisis to develop before imposing a testing policy. More recently, the Supreme Court of Washington ruled that a similar random and suspicionless drug testing policy for student athletes violated the State of Washington's Constitution and upheld the parents' appeal (*York v. Wahkiakum School Dist. No. 200*, 2008). The Court agreed with the parents' contention that such a policy violated Washington's State Constitution, which provides "[n]o person shall be disturbed in his private affairs, or his home invaded without authority of law" (*Id.*). On the state level, several courts have also held that the NCAA drug testing program does not violate state constitutional rights (*Brennan v. Board of Trustees*, 1997; *Hill v. National Collegiate Athletic Association*, 1994).

Invasion of Privacy

The U.S. Constitution does not specifically provide a fundamental right to be free from **invasion of privacy**; however, the U.S. Supreme Court has implied one from the constitutional amendments. To bring an action for invasion of privacy, a plaintiff must establish that the invasion is substantial and is in an area for which there is an expectation of privacy. In sports, this most often arises in challenges to drug testing programs. In *Vernonia School District 47J v. Acton* (1995), James Acton challenged Vernonia School District's drug testing program on the basis of invasion of privacy. The Supreme Court found that school children had a reduced expectation of privacy when they entered school and athletes had a lesser expectation of privacy, still. Because athletics subject one to a locker room environment, physical examinations, and the need for medical attention, this lesser expectation of privacy exists. Thus, drug testing of high school athletes was not deemed an invasion of privacy.

It is uncertain if the *Vernonia* ruling applies to collegiate athletes. In the *Vernonia* opinion, Justice Scalia went to great lengths to state that the high school students had a lower expectation of privacy because they were minors under the school's care while away from their parents, and thus, the teachers had to have discipline in the school (*Vernonia School District 47J v. Acton*, 1995). Collegiate athletes are adults under far less supervision. Additionally, just over a year before the *Vernonia* decision, the U.S. Supreme Court refused to hear an appeal of the Supreme Court of Colorado's decision that found that drug testing of football players at the University of Colorado was an invasion of privacy (*University of Colorado v. Derdeyn*, 1993). In *Derdeyn*, the Supreme Court of Colorado held that despite the University of Colorado's interest in protecting the health and welfare of student-athletes and although student-athletes do consent to restrictions on their private lives by participating in collegiate athletics, it is not enough to justify the intrusion on privacy interests of the nature and extent involved in the random, suspicionless testing for drugs.

No constitutional challenge to drug testing in professional sport has been successful because as a general rule, professional sport leagues and teams are not state actors. Drug testing challenges in professional sport are most effectively made through the arbitration process set forth in the league's **collective bargaining agreement** (CBA). The CBA is the contract agreed to by the players association and the owners for all provisions related to hours, wages, and terms and conditions of employment. Drug testing is a term and condition of employment, so drug testing provisions, penalties, and systems of challenging the testing are set forth in the CBA. In leagues where there is no unionization, such as minor league baseball, the rules are set forth by the league and the process for appeal is to the Commissioner of the league.

Title IX of the Educational Amendments of 1972

Title IX, a comprehensive statute enacted to eliminate gender discrimination in educational institutions that receive federal funding, only involves interscholastic and intercollegiate athletics, not professional or Olympic sport.

The U.S. Department of Education's Office of Civil Rights (OCR) establishes policies for applying Title IX to athletic participation. To decide whether a school or college is in compliance, the OCR focuses on three areas. First, the OCR assesses whether an institution's athletic scholarships are awarded on a substantially proportionate basis (male versus female). Second, the OCR assesses the degree to which a school or college has given equal treatment, benefits, and opportunities in specific athletic program areas. The OCR examines areas such as the provision of publicity, promotions, facilities, equipment, and supplies; the opportunity to benefit from quality coaching and support staff; and the scheduling of games and practices. Third, the OCR assesses the degree to which a school or college has equally and effectively accommodated the interests and abilities of male and female students. Most cases have been brought under this third factor, but recently the OCR and potential plaintiffs are placing some attention on examining the treatment of athletes. It has been an area of growing litigation since the U.S. Supreme Court ruled that Title IX did not preclude a plaintiff from receiving compensatory damages and attorneys' fees (*Franklin v. Gwinnett County Public Schools*, 1992). As a result, athletes and attorneys can better afford the cost of pursuing Title IX lawsuits.

© Photos.com

The following decisions highlight the various applications of Title IX. After seven men's and three women's sports at James Madison University (JMU) were cut in 2006 to comply with Title IX requirements, an action group (Equity in Athletics, Inc.) was formed by athletes, coaches, and fans to oppose the move. In *Equity in Athletics, Inc. v. The United States Department of Education* (2008), the plaintiff argued that the defendant university was discriminating against male athletes and thus violating Title IX. The court took a "balance of

hardship" approach to its analysis and noted that students were unfettered in being able to transfer to other schools and would still keep their scholarship entitlements, while JMU would be significantly disadvantaged if it was forced to reconvene any or all sports. The court also denied the plaintiff's argument that equal opportunity should be determined by "expressed interest" rather than "actual participation."

The court applied the triple-pronged test of compliance in *Miller v. University of Cincinnati* (2008), in which the women's rowing team contended the program was inadequately facilitated in terms of resources. It was later eliminated in favor of women's lacrosse. The court found that the university was in compliance with Title IX as 47.5% of the total student population was female and 48.9% of student-athletes were female.

A more recent Title IX class action lawsuit, *Biediger v. Quinnipiac University* (2012), was brought by Quinnipiac University women's volleyball players and their coach (Robin Sparks). In April 2009, Quinnipiac University announced the elimination of its women's volleyball program. The plaintiffs were granted an injunction to prevent Quinnipiac University from dropping the volleyball program (*Biediger v. Quinnipiac University*, 2009). Quinnipiac's plan was to eliminate volleyball and add competitive cheerleading. The plaintiffs argued that Quinnipiac was not in compliance with Title IX because the proportion of male to female students was 38.13% male and 61.87% female. The composition of male to female athletes was 37.73% male to 62.27% female according to the University. However, because the judge found competitive cheerleading was not a recognized NCAA sport, he found Quinnipiac out of compliance. The reasons the cheerleading team was not considered a competitive sport were varied: there was no off-campus recruiting, the season was inconsistent in terms of rules governing competition and the types and quality of opponents, the university did not treat it as a varsity team, and finally, the postseason did not follow the structure of a competitive team. The judge noted he did not mean to belittle the athletic endeavor of the athletes on the cheerleading team, but that at this point the sport was too disorganized and unstructured to be considered a competitive sport for purposes of Quinnipiac's compliance with Title IX (*Biedinger v. Quinnipiac*, 2010). The Second Circuit upheld the district court's decision, also because the court discovered a disparity between the actual participation numbers of female roster spots on the women's teams. In some cases, women were counted more than once, making roster spots "illusory." Once a recalculation was done, 41 athletes were removed from the Quinnipiac calculations (30 cheerleaders and 11 track/cross-country runners counted twice), the participation numbers changed to 58.25% and enrollments were 61.87% female. That 3.62% disparity was considered to be too great a differential, leading to the finding of a Title IX violation. The Second Circuit emphasized a 2% disparity would be acceptable but held that 3.62% was not (Dennie, 2012). When applying Title IX to employment discrimination, courts rely on the standards set forth in Title VII, discussed later in this chapter (*Perdue v. City University of New York*, 1998; *Pitts v. University of Oklahoma*, 1994; *Stanley v. University of Southern California*, 1994).

Antitrust Law

A capitalist economy depends on competition (economic rivalry) between businesses, such that they are engaged in a contest for customers (Howell et al., 1987). To promote competition in the free market, Congress enacted the Sherman Antitrust Act of 1890. The Sherman Act's goal was to break up business trusts and monopolies

and prohibit anticompetitive activity by businesses. It is the nation's primary **antitrust law** covering contracts, combinations, or conspiracies that restrain trade (Section 1) and monopolies (Section 2). Both sections carry a penalty of tripling the damage award. Because professional teams are worth hundreds of millions of dollars and athletes' salaries total millions of dollars, an anticompetitive practice that injures a competitor league, a team owner, or a player's ability to make use of a free market may create a crippling damage award. However, damage awards are seen only rarely in sports antitrust cases because most result in settlements.

Antitrust and Professional Sport

The application of antitrust laws to leagues has left an indelible mark on their structure and the nature of labor–management relations. Antitrust challenges have primarily occurred in professional sport, in which monopolization of the player, product, and geographic markets and restrictive policies are common. Plus, with only one viable major professional league for each sport, their domination of the market for each sport has been challenged by competitors in violation of the Sherman Act (*American Football League v. National Football League*, 1963; *Federal Baseball Club of Baltimore v. National League of Professional Baseball Clubs*, 1922; *Philadelphia World Hockey, Inc. v. Philadelphia Hockey Club, Inc.*, 1972; *United States Football League v. National Football League*, 1986). Restrictive policies are inherent to the operation of professional sports as they strive to maintain competitive balance. Over time, many cases have been brought by players, owners, competitor leagues, prospective cities, and prospective owners challenging the restraints imposed upon them through league rules and policies.

Two recent cases highlight the antitrust issues being litigated. In *American Needle v. National Football League* (2010), the U.S.

Supreme Court reversed the Seventh Circuit Court of Appeals and ruled that the NFL Properties was a not a **single entity** when promoting NFL football by licensing the teams' intellectual property. Relying on *Copperweld Corp. v. Independence Tube Corp.*, 467 U.S. 752, 773, n. 21, the Court reiterated that "'substance, not form, should determine whether a[n] . . . entity is capable of conspiring under section 1.' . . . The key is whether the alleged 'contract, combination, . . . or, conspiracy' is concerted action—that is whether it joins together separate decision makers." The Court found that each of the teams is a substantial, independently owned, and independently managed business and their objectives are not common. More specifically, the Court noted that NFL teams "compete with one another, not only on the playing field, but to attract fans, for gate receipts, and for contracts with managerial and playing personnel" (*Id.* at 9). The Court further explained that NFL teams do compete in the market for intellectual property, a fact directly relevant to the question of whether NFL Properties is a single entity. The Supreme Court remanded *American Needle* back to the district court for a trial consistent with its finding that the NFL Properties was not a single entity. At the time this text went to press, the case remained unresolved. After *American Needle*, it is unlikely that a traditionally created sport league will be considered a single entity, and thus, immune from Section 1 of the Sherman Antitrust Act.

However, a Third Circuit Court of Appeals case upheld the jury's decision in *Deutscher Tennis Bund v. ATP Tour, Inc.* (2010), that the Association of Tennis Professionals (ATP) Tour did not violate antitrust law when it stripped the annual Hamburg event of its Masters Series designation and demoted it to "second-tier" status. The Third Circuit also upheld the jury's finding that the ATP Tour was a single entity immune from Section 1 liability.

Antitrust Exemptions

All unionized professional sport leagues are shielded from antitrust liability by the **labor exemption**, and professional sport labor unions negotiate collectively with MLB. The U.S. Supreme Court has firmly established that during the term of a CBA, terms negotiated in that agreement are exempt from antitrust scrutiny. Provided the defendant proves the plaintiff is, was, or will be a party to the CBA; that the subject being challenged on antitrust grounds is a mandatory subject for bargaining (hours, wages, and other terms and conditions of employment); and that the CBA was achieved through *bona fide* arm's-length bargaining (bargaining that occurs freely, without one party having excessive power or control over the other); the defendant's actions will be exempt from antitrust (*McCourt v. California Sports, Inc.*, 1979; *Reynolds v. National Football League*, 1978; *Wood v. National Basketball Association*, 1987).

Curt Flood Act

All professional sport organizations except MLB are subject to antitrust laws. In 1922, the U.S. Supreme Court found that baseball was not subject to the Sherman Act (*Federal Baseball Club of Baltimore v. National League of Professional Baseball Clubs*, 1922). MLB's antitrust exemption survived two further Supreme Court challenges, and much of it remained intact despite the adoption of the **Curt Flood Act** (*Flood v. Kuhn*, 1972; *Toolson v. New York Yankees*, 1953). The Curt Flood Act granted MLB players, but not minor leaguers, the legal right to sue their employers under the Sherman Act. It also confirmed that the exemption still applies to business areas including the minor leagues; the minor league player reserve clause; the amateur draft; franchise expansion, location, or relocation; franchise ownership issues; marketing and sales of the entertainment product of baseball; and licensed properties.

This protection from antitrust liability sets MLB apart from the other professional sport organizations, whose rules and practices are subject to antitrust scrutiny. In *Los Angeles Memorial Coliseum Commission v. National Football League* (1984), the Ninth Circuit Court of Appeals upheld a jury decision that the NFL's application of its franchise relocation rule was an unreasonable restraint of trade. The threat of prolonged litigation and a potentially large damage award have allowed for unprecedented franchise movement in the NFL and NHL.

The labor exemption continues to protect parties from antitrust scrutiny after a CBA has expired (*Bridgeman v. National Basketball Association*, 1987; *Brown v. Pro Football, Inc.*, 1996; *National Basketball Association v. Williams*, 1995; *Powell v. National Football League*, 1989). In *Brown v. Pro Football*, the U.S. Supreme Court noted that when a bargaining relationship exists between a league and players association, labor policy favors limiting antitrust liability. The Court clarified, however, that it did not intend its holding to "insulate from antitrust liability every joint imposition of terms by employers, for an agreement among employers could be sufficiently distant in time and circumstances from the collective bargaining process that a rule permitting antitrust intervention would not significantly interfere with that process" (*Id.* at 250). The Court did not, however, give an example of such time and circumstance.

The labor exemption eliminates the players association's threat to sue the owners on antitrust grounds provided collective bargaining is occurring. To maintain their negotiating leverage, players opt to disclaim or to decertify their unions, thereby eliminating their bargaining relationship with management and gaining leverage at the bargaining table. This strategy has been employed or threatened in the most recent negotiations in the NBA, NFL, and NHL. A decertification is when the players formally

dissolve the union using the same process with the National Labor Relations Board as when they create a union. A disclaimer of interest is a quicker approach and allows the players to opt out of union representation. Once the players disclaim the union, they are instead represented by legal counsel. Without a formal union representing them, the players maintain the threat of antitrust litigation, providing leverage in negotiations.

Sports Broadcasting Act of 1961

In 1961 Congress passed the Sports Broadcasting Act of 1961 to exempt sport leagues' national television deals from antitrust liability (15 U.S.C. §§ 1291–1294). This statute grants professional teams the right to pool their television rights as a league and increase their bargaining power when negotiating league-wide television packages without the threat of antitrust challenges. It also restricts leagues from defining geographic areas into which the pooled telecasts are broadcast and limits Friday and Saturday telecasts within a 75-mile radius of college and high school football.

Antitrust and College Athletics

As the NCAA has grown into a big business, it has faced more antitrust challenges to its rules from coaches, athletes, alumni, member institutions, and competitors (*Adidas America, Inc. v. National Collegiate Athletic Association*, 1999). Before subjecting association rules and regulations to antitrust scrutiny, the court will decide if the rule regulates a commercial or noncommercial activity. As this text goes to print, the NCAA is facing a federal antitrust suit brought by former UCLA men's basketball player Ed O'Bannon and 20 other plaintiffs charging that the NCAA amateurism rules violate antitrust by not compensating athletes for their images, names, and likenesses. To date, courts have found that eligibility rules, such as those at issue in *O'Bannon v. NCAA*, are noncommercial (*Banks v. National Collegiate Athletic Association*,

1992; *McCormack v. National Collegiate Athletic Association*, 1988) and therefore not subject to antitrust law. However, rules such as those restricting coaches' earnings (*Law v. National Collegiate Athletic Association*, 1995) and limitations on NCAA members' television contracts (*National Collegiate Athletic Association v. Board of Regents of the University of Oklahoma and the University of Georgia Athletic Association*, 1982) have been deemed commercial and therefore subject to antitrust laws.

The two most recent antitrust cases against the NCAA ended in settlement. The first involved a suit by the Metropolitan Intercollegiate Basketball Association (MIBA), the five-university venture that operated the National Invitation Tournament (NIT). In its suit, MIBA alleged that the NCAA's bundle of postseason rules unreasonably limited Division I teams to participation only in the NCAA tournament and thereby eliminated the NIT as a viable competitive postseason basketball event (*Metropolitan Intercollegiate Basketball Association v. NCAA*, 2004). In 2005, in the midst of trial, the NCAA purchased the preseason and postseason NIT from MIBA for $40.5 million and settled with the schools for an additional $16 million. The second case involves a class action antitrust suit by former student-athletes (*White v. NCAA*, 2008) who alleged that NCAA by-laws unlawfully capped the amount of financial aid a student-athlete may receive. The plaintiffs argued that if schools could compete without the cap, they could potentially offer higher amounts of financial aid than the grant-in-aid limits of tuition, fees, room and board, and required books. The plaintiffs alleged and NCAA itself admitted that the grant-in-aid limit was less than the cost of attendance. The suit settled with the NCAA agreeing to an expansion of the Special Assistance and Academic Enhancement Fund, plus an additional $10 million allocated to fund career development and educational reimbursements for former student-athletes.

Labor and Employment Law

The sport industry is people intensive, so sport managers must have a working knowledge of labor and employment laws. There are both state and federal labor and employment laws. This chapter will briefly discuss a few of the federal laws: the National Labor Relations Act, the Equal Pay Act of 1963, Title VII of the Civil Rights Act of 1964, the Age Discrimination in Employment Act, and the Americans with Disabilities Act. There are also many state employment laws, but discussing them exceeds the scope of this chapter.

The National Labor Relations Act

The **National Labor Relations Act** (NLRA) applies to private employers. This law establishes the procedures for union certification and decertification and sets forth the rights and obligations of union and management. The law also created the National Labor Relations Board (NLRB), the federal agency that administers labor laws in the United States. The primary areas of the sport industry in which the NLRA applies are facility management and professional sport. Facility managers may employ various unionized employees, all with different CBAs. Currently, the five major professional sport leagues (MLB, Major League Soccer [MLS], NBA, NFL, and NHL), the Women's National Basketball Association (WNBA), Arena Football League (AFL), the National Lacrosse League (NLL), and minor league hockey players in the ECHL (formerly the East Coast Hockey League), American Hockey League (AHL), and the International Hockey League (IHL) are unionized. State labor laws, not the NLRA, apply to interscholastic coaches, often if they are members of a teachers' union. Staff members in college sports are often unionized under state law. College coaches are not unionized, except in Pennsylvania where 400 coaches are members of the Association of Pennsylvania State College and University Faculty (APSCUF, 2013).

Whether student-athletes are employees for collective bargaining purposes was the subject of a recent NLRB decision. It determined that Northwestern University football players receiving scholarships were employees. The NLRB conducted an election to determine whether the players would choose to be represented by a union, but has yet to release the results. Northwestern is appealing the decision so it will be a while before we know if athletes will unionize. Additionally, there are other hurdles to a national union such as whether public and private university students will be treated identically when it comes to unionization efforts.

Labor relations in professional sport are unique for many reasons, notably the individual bargaining power professional athletes derive from their unique talent. This bargaining power creates leverage for athletes. As a result, professional leagues have adopted restrictive practices for the efficient management of their players (Masteralexis, 2010). Restrictive practices limit a player's ability to make money or move through the free market and include the draft, salary cap or luxury tax, and restrictions on free agency. These practices may violate antitrust laws (*Mackey v. National Football League*, 1976; *Smith v. Pro Football, Inc.*, 1978). As noted previously, practices that normally violate players' antitrust rights that are agreed to through the collective bargaining process may be free from antitrust liability by the labor exemption (*McCourt v. California Sports, Inc.*, 1979; *Zimmerman v. National Football League*, 1986). Therefore, it is in the leagues' best interests to have unions and to negotiate restrictive practices through the collective bargaining process. This approach is unique to sport, because most management groups either prefer not to deal with unions or simply tolerate them. Generally, management in other industries tends to perceive that unions take power and control from them. Players associations differ from unions in other industries. For

one thing, job security is limited. The turnover rate for sport union members is much higher than for other union members because athletes' careers are far shorter than those of employees in other industries. This forces players associations to constantly spread their message to new members. In spreading the message, the players associations also face the logistical challenges of being a bargaining unit with employees on different teams throughout the United States and Canada, not to mention employees from many different countries and cultures. Further, there is a great disparity between players' talent and their need for the union. A player such as LeBron James does not need the services of the union as much as a late-round draft pick or a recently released free agent trying to make his way back onto an NBA roster. When negotiating for the collective interests of the players, unions struggle to keep the superstars and the players on the bench equally satisfied. Without the solidarity of all players, a players association loses its strength (Masteralexis, 2010).

The Equal Pay Act

Enacted in 1963, the **Equal Pay Act** (EPA) prohibits an employer from paying one employee less than another on the basis of gender when the two are performing jobs of equal skill, effort, and responsibility and are working under similar conditions. The EPA only applies to sex-based discrimination on the basis of compensation. To qualify, the plaintiff and comparable employee must be of opposite genders. For instance, the statute would not apply if a man coached a women's team and argued under the EPA that he should be paid a sum equal to the male coach of the men's team. Trivial differences between two jobs will not prevent them from being considered equal in terms of the EPA. Comparable worth is not an issue under the EPA.

Female coaches whose salaries are not equal to those of their male counterparts have filed EPA lawsuits. *Stanley v. University of Southern*

California (1999) involved a complaint by the University of Southern California's women's basketball coach, Marianne Stanley, that she was not paid equally to the male basketball coach, George Raveling. In finding that their jobs were not equal, the court focused on the additional pressure to raise revenue and the responsibility it said Raveling had due to the fact that the men's team had a larger season ticket base and a greater national presence. The court found that such responsibility created more media pressure and a greater time investment in dealing with fans and the media (*Stanley v. University of Southern California*, 1999). Interestingly, the court never considered whether Stanley actually could have had more responsibilities and pressure than Raveling because she constantly labored to get a larger season ticket base and more media attention for her team and herself. The court also focused attention on a comparison of Stanley's and Raveling's skills, qualifications, and work experience. Stanley had 17 years of coaching experience, whereas Raveling had 31. Raveling had a background and prior work experience in marketing that Stanley did not have. Raveling had also worked in the public eye as a television commentator, author, and actor. However, Stanley had done speaking engagements and had won four national championships while also traveling to three other NCAA tournaments. Raveling had coached teams to the NCAA tournaments but had never won a national championship. Despite this last comparative, the court found Raveling's skills and qualifications outpaced Stanley's and justified the pay difference.

If an employee proves the elements of an EPA violation, the four defenses available to the employer are that the disparity in pay is due to the presence of (1) a seniority system, (2) a merit system that is being followed in good faith, (3) a system measuring pay on the basis of quality or quantity of production, or (4) a factor other than gender.

Title VII of the Civil Rights Act of 1964

The Civil Rights Act of 1964 is a federal law prohibiting discrimination in many settings, including housing, education, and public accommodations. **Title VII** covers employers with 15 or more employees. Title VII, however, excludes Native American tribes and "bona fide membership clubs" (such as country clubs) from its definition of an employer. Title VII specifically prohibits any employment decision, practice, or policy that treats individuals unequally due to race, color, national origin, gender, or religion (*Wallace v. Texas Tech University*, 1996).

Although much of the U.S. civil rights movement focused on discrimination against African Americans, Title VII's definition of race is not that limited. It protects all classes of people from dissimilar treatment, including, but not limited to, Hispanics, Native Americans, and Asian Americans. The color focus under Title VII is on skin pigment or the physical characteristics of one's race. Regarding national origin, the court focuses on ancestry. Title VII does not prohibit employment discrimination solely based on a lack of U.S. citizenship; however, the lack of U.S. citizenship may not be used to disguise discrimination that is actually based on race or national origin. In other words, an employer may follow a policy of employing only U.S. citizens but may not give unequal treatment to different noncitizens based on their country of origin. In addition, rules that require communication in "English only" are allowed only if the employer can prove the rule is a business necessity. This may bring to mind the Ladies Professional Golf Association's (LPGA) brief proposal for an English language rule for its players. While many cried foul under Title VII, the LPGA golfers are members, not employees. Nevertheless, under public pressure and criticism from its own members, the LPGA decided not to pursue this proposal (Associated Press, 2008).

As for gender, Title VII is self-explanatory, but it also includes sexual harassment (*Faragher v. Boca Raton*, 1998; *Ortiz-Del Valle v. National Basketball Association*, 1999). Title VII does not provide for remedies against discrimination on the basis of sexual orientation (*Rene v. MGM Grand Hotel*, 2002), although several states prohibit such discrimination under state law.

Title VII prohibits religious discrimination against all well-recognized faiths as well as those considered unorthodox, provided the court is convinced that the belief is sincere and genuinely held and not simply adopted for an ulterior motive. Employers must make reasonable accommodations to religious practices and observances, unless they would place an undue hardship on the employers.

It is not illegal to discriminate based on religion, gender, or national origin if the classification is a **bona fide occupational qualification** (BFOQ). Race and color are never BFOQs. The BFOQ must be reasonably necessary to the normal operation of the business. The BFOQ defense requires the employer to prove that members of the excluded class could not safely and effectively perform essential job duties, and the employer must present a factual basis for this belief. An example of a BFOQ might be as follows: An all-male boarding school makes it a requirement that resident directors in the school's dormitories also be male, justifying the requirement with such reasons as the comfort and security of the male students living in all-male dormitories and the school's desire to establish male role models in the school's social settings.

The Age Discrimination in Employment Act

Enacted in 1967, the **Age Discrimination in Employment Act** (ADEA) prohibits employment discrimination on the basis of age. Currently there is no age limit to protection, but the ADEA exempts several classes of workers, such as public safety personnel and certain top-level managers. It applies to employers who engage in commerce and hire over 20 workers for 20 or more calendar weeks, as well as labor unions and state and federal governments. Proving discrimination under the ADEA is very similar to doing so under Title VII. The ADEA also contains a BFOQ exception that is almost identical to Title VII's. An employer can defend a claim by proving the decision was made due to reasonable factors other than age.

An example of how courts have applied the ADEA to age discrimination cases is *Moore v. University of Notre Dame* (1998). The plaintiff, Joseph Moore, the offensive line coach for Notre Dame, sued the school, alleging age discrimination. In ruling against Notre Dame, a jury found that the school did fire Moore because of his age, a violation of the ADEA. In choosing a suitable remedy, however, the district court refused to grant Moore's request for reinstatement to his former coaching position; reinstatement was not considered an appropriate remedy in this case because it would cause significant friction as well as disruption of the current football program (someone else was currently occupying Moore's position). Although reinstatement is the preferred remedy in ADEA cases, in this case the court granted Moore front pay, which represents the difference between earnings an employee would have received in his old employment and the earnings he can be expected to receive in his present and future employment (Wong, 2010).

The Americans with Disabilities Act

The **Americans with Disabilities Act** (ADA) protects employees with disabilities from discrimination at all stages of the employment relationship. An applicant or employee who is disabled must be able to perform all the essential functions of a position in order to challenge discrimination in employment on the basis of disability. Therefore, an employer must assess the responsibilities required for a position and assess the individual's ability to perform the responsibilities. When interviewing, an employer cannot question an applicant about the specific nature of his or her disability or require medical records or exams as part of the screening process. An employer may, however, prepare a list of essential functions and ask if the applicant can perform those tasks. Although the ADA promotes the removal of barriers, it does not relieve employees with disabilities from carrying out the same job responsibilities as their able-bodied coworkers. If the individual can perform the job with or without a reasonable accommodation, the employer cannot refuse the employee based on disability. An employer must attempt to reasonably accommodate employees with disabilities unless doing so would cause undue hardship to the employer.

The most important ADA court decision related to sport management is *PGA Tour Inc. v. Martin* (2001). The case involved Title III, the public accommodation section, not the employment section. The reason is that Professional Golf Association (PGA) golfers are not employees of the Tour. The case involved Casey Martin, a disabled golfer suffering from a condition that made it very painful and potentially dangerous to walk for long distances. He sued the PGA Tour, alleging that the failure to make a golf cart available to him and the failure to make its golf tournaments accessible to disabled individuals violated Title III of the ADA. In defense, the PGA Tour argued that its walking-only rule was an essential element of professional golf on the PGA and Nike tours, and that waiving the rule would fundamentally alter the nature of the sport. The U.S. Supreme Court affirmed the Oregon District Court and Ninth Circuit Court of Appeals decision in Martin's favor, rejecting the PGA's argument that allowing Martin to use a golf cart would fundamentally

alter the sport and finding that PGA golfers are not a protected class under Title III. The Martin ruling has clarified the application of the ADA to sport participation issues and has led to an increase in filing of ADA sport-related cases (*Kuketz v. MDC Fitness Corp.*, 2001). Recently, the Office of Civil Rights (OCR) issued a clarifying letter that public elementary and secondary schools must provide extracurricular athletic opportunities for disabled students under the Rehabilitation Act of 1973 (OCR, 2013). Where a reasonable modification can be made to the sport, the disabled students will need to be mainstreamed or provided an alternative opportunity for sport and physical education. An example is to provide a visual cue simultaneously to the starting pistol for a hearing impaired runner (OCR, 2013).

The ADA requires public assembly facilities, stadiums, theaters, and health and fitness centers to be barrier free. Sport managers working in facilities that are open to the public must be sure their facilities comply with the ADA regulations for such areas as entrances and exits, seating, walkways, parking, and locker room and bathroom facilities (*Access Now, Inc. v. South Florida Stadium Corp.*, 2001).

Intellectual Property Law

Intellectual property (IP) refers to creations of the mind. IP law governs the right to protect one's inventions, literary and artistic works, and symbols, names, images, and designs used in commerce. This area of law is very important to the commercial growth of sport (World Intellectual Property Organization [WIPO], 2013a). IP protection secures the economic value of sport through patents, trademarks, and broadcasting rights (WIPO, 2013b). A **trademark** is a distinctive sign or "mark" (one or a combination of words, names, numbers, sounds, shapes, vocal sounds, or symbols) used by a specific person or enterprise to help consumers identify and distinguish its goods or services because of its nature and quality, as indicated by its mark (WIPO, 2013c).

Trademarks can be strong, entitled to a wide scope of protection, or weak, entitled to limited protection in only a narrow field (Reed, 1989). Strong trademarks are those that are completely distinguishable, such as Exxon, Polaroid, and Kleenex. Gus Macker (outdoor 3-on-3 basketball tournament) and Rucker Park Street Ball are good examples of fanciful, distinguishable event names. On the other end of the spectrum are the weak names, like Musicfest, Food Fest, and Art Expo, which use common words in their ordinary meanings and would be difficult, although not impossible, to protect (Reed, 1989). Such names may be protected if they possess **"secondary meaning."** Secondary meaning exists if the public distinguishes one product or event from another by the trademark. Reed (1989) uses *World's Fair* as an example. Although the words are common and used in their ordinary meaning, the trademark is descriptive due to the amount of advertising and public exposure it receives. Because there is only one World's Fair, use of this trademark by others without permission may lead consumers to confuse the secondary use with the original trademark.

The **Lanham Act**, which governs trademarks and service marks, gives protection to the owner of a name or logo, keeps others from selling goods as the goods of the original source, and helps to protect against consumer confusion (Anderson, 2007). The law in this area is somewhat complex, and those sport managers involved with licensed products should rely on attorneys who are experts in trademark law to handle registering trademarks and pursuing claims against those who misappropriate them.

Some case examples may help to illustrate the diversity of IP issues. The University of

South Carolina attempted to trademark the letters "S" and "C" that appeared in an interlocked design for use mainly on its baseball team's caps. The University of Southern California formally opposed this trademark application and in 2008, the United States Patent and Trademark Office did in fact find it likely that confusion would occur if the mark was allowed and subsequently denied the application. In *Board of Supervisors for La. State Univ. v. Smack Apparel Co.* (2008), the plaintiff's argument that its university color scheme, when used in concert with specific information pertaining to the school on a t-shirt, even without the University's logo or other marks being present, infringed upon the trademark rights of the school, was upheld. Another interesting case, *Callaway Golf Company v. Acushnet Company* (2008), involved a suit filed by Calloway against the parent company of Titleist alleging that the Pro VI golf ball, the most popular golf ball on the PGA Tour at that time, infringed upon pre-existing Callaway patents. The court's reasoning focused on a person of "ordinary skill" in the golf ball manufacturing industry and whether he or she could have created the Pro VI without Callaway's already patented material. Ultimately the court decided that this would not have been the case and found in favor of Callaway. Finally, the *Keller v. EA Sports* (2009) case was a companion case to *O'Bannon v. NCAA*. Keller's suit was based in the right of publicity and he argued that EA Sports and the NCAA misappropriated his image and likeness for use in its NCAA football games. Keller settled out of court with EA Sports, but if Keller succeeded, college athletes would have won the right to be paid, which would violate current principles of amateurism. The preceding discussion of legal concepts is not all inclusive. It should, however, serve as a place for a sport manager to begin to build a legal knowledge base to manage risk and limit liability.

Key Skills

Rather than focusing on those skills necessary for becoming a practicing sport lawyer, this section examines the skills that a sport manager may acquire from the study of law. The study of law involves a great deal of problem solving. By practicing problem solving, sport managers can improve their logical and analytical reasoning skills. Such skills will make it more likely that a sport manager facing a crisis will resolve it in a logical, thoughtful manner.

For most people, analysis of case and statutory law will lead to more persuasive and clear written and oral communication. The study of law involves studying the language used in cases and statutes and making arguments to apply it to various situations. Practice in this area will help individuals develop the clearly stated written policies and procedures that are an important part of a sound risk management plan. Excellent communication also is a key to good leadership and good relations with staff, peer and superior administrators, the public, and clients. Verbal communication skills can also enhance negotiating skills, and sport managers negotiate on a daily basis, even if they do not realize it. Managers negotiate for everything they need, whether in a formal setting, such as negotiating with a television network to broadcast games, or more informally, such as negotiating with a staff member to cover a shift for a coworker. The study of law, particularly in areas such as negotiation and client interviewing, also focuses on good listening skills. A successful sport manager should be prepared to invest time listening to staff and clients. A good listener will be a better judge of people and will know what it takes to motivate staff and to keep staff and clients satisfied.

Law and ethics are entwined. In setting parameters for acceptable conduct, the law establishes codes of ethical conduct. Studying law may not change a sport manager's behavior, for values may already be instilled, but it may help sport managers to better establish codes of ethical conduct in their workplaces. Sport law also may guide sport managers in how to best resolve disputes and violations of ethical codes without violating individual rights.

Putting Skills to Practice

A sport manager can effectively manage legal problems by knowing and understanding law, specifically sport law. By knowing legal pitfalls, managers can avoid, prevent, or reduce many kinds of problems. A well-written and well-administered risk management plan can help a sport manager avoid legal liability. The challenge for sport managers is to understand the legal implications, if any, of their decisions. Sport managers must know, or know how to obtain, the answers to questions of legal liability, either alone or with the advice of in-house or outside counsel.

For example, a health and fitness club manager may be faced with the option of adding wall-climbing equipment at his or her club. The manager must make this decision based on consumer interest and also financial benefits, costs, and potential legal liability. When contemplating legal liability, a club manager should consider all of the potential problems that may arise with the wall-climbing equipment. This analysis should involve creating a list of issues to consider. See **Box 5-1** for a sample of a list of considerations.

Although the list in Box 5-1 was compiled for a club manager, similar lists can be created for other programmatic and policy decisions made by sport managers in other segments of the industry.

A second example reflects decisions to be made by sport managers at an association, institution, or organization considering the implementation of a drug testing program. **Box 5-2** is an example of a list of important issues to consider (Wong, 2010):

Box 5-1   Sample List of Issues to Consider When Purchasing Equipment

- Who should be allowed to use this equipment?
- Should training be required before use?
- Who is qualified to train users? What additional training will staff need?
- Should participants be required to provide medical approval?
- Should participants be required to sign a waiver of liability?
- Should minors (and their parents) be required to sign a waiver of liability?
- What if someone refuses to sign a waiver of liability?
- If used, how should a waiver of liability be drafted? Is it likely to hold up in court?
- What type of signs or warnings should be posted on or near the equipment?
- What if a physically challenged member wants to participate in the activity?
- What emergency procedures and services are in place if a participant is injured while using equipment?
- Should an individual who became injured while using the equipment be allowed to participate again? When?

Box 5-2   Issues to Consider When Implementing a Drug Testing Program

- Is the drug testing policy clearly defined and in writing?
- Does the organization's drug testing policy conform to conference and association rules and regulations?
- Who will conduct the tests?
- Who will pay for the tests?
- Will the tests be random and mandatory, or only for probable cause or reasonable suspicion?
- What constitutes probable cause or reasonable suspicion?
- How much notice should be given before testing begins?
- What types of drugs (recreational, performance enhancing) will be tested for?
- How frequently will athletes be tested?
- What actions should be taken when an athlete tests positive?
- Will there be an appeal process for a positive test result?
- Is there a method for retesting positive results?
- What confidentiality and constitutional law issues does drug testing raise?
- Do the sanctions to be imposed adhere to federal and/or state constitutional law and statutes?

Sport managers considering drug testing professional athletes must ask many of the same questions, but they must also be cognizant of the player rights negotiated in the CBA. The job of a general manager of a professional sport team once primarily consisted of evaluating talent, drafting amateur players, and making trades. Today a general manager has many other responsibilities, often arising from provisions negotiated in the league's CBA or individual players' contracts that contain complex policies such as luxury taxes, salary caps, and arbitration procedures. In addition, with a global market for talent, there may be a need to understand international laws, plus global sporting rules and regulations. As such, the general manager may find a law degree helpful in doing his or her job. Sport managers who can anticipate potential problems can then reduce risk. For example, the healthclub manager who allows only trained and healthy adults who have signed waivers of liability to participate in an activity has established parameters that reduce the club's risk. People who meet the conditions can then participate in a carefully and adequately supervised activity, with medical procedures in place. (Note that the sport manager has already eliminated some risk by not allowing minors to participate.)

A professional team's general manager may decide against acquiring a particular player because the potential salary of the player, either through salary arbitration or through leverage from free agency, will be too expensive. Or the general manager may take the approach of reducing the risk of this expense by signing a multiyear contract. In the NFL, the general manager can negotiate a "salary cap friendly" contract. For instance, the contract can be negotiated so that the salary cap impact is spread evenly over the years, or it can be structured so that the impact can be made in the early or late years of the contract. Thus, a general manager whose team currently has room under the salary cap can structure the contract so that the salary cap impact is in the early years. This reduces the salary cap cost of the player in later years and gives the club more money and freedom to sign other players.

Current Issues

The impact of the law on sport organizations is more likely to increase than decrease in the future. Sport business is becoming ever more complex. For instance, the most recent NFL CBA is a detailed 318-page document accompanied by several ancillary documents. The NCAA manual also is very detailed and complex. Due to restructuring in 1997–1998, the NCAA now publishes three manuals (one for each division). The 2012–2013 NCAA Division I manual is now 444 pages and has numerous provisions, rules, and regulations that require interpretation, resulting in more legal considerations for sport managers.

Olympic Games

In the Olympic sport industry, there are a growing number of challenges related to the rules and regulations imposed on participants. Sport managers working in the Olympic arena are facing legal challenges resulting from **ambush marketing**, the rights of individual athletes to market themselves, and the imposition of codes of conduct for athletes. Ambush marketing occurs when an organization misappropriates the trademarks, logos, and goodwill of an event or organization (Reed, 1989). For most events of any significance, one brand will pay to become the exclusive and official sponsor of the event in a particular category or categories, and this exclusivity creates a problem for one or more other brands. Often those other brands find ways to promote themselves in connection with the same event, without paying the sponsorship fee but without breaking any laws.

For example, a company that has not paid to be a sponsor but confuses the public by indirectly associating itself with the events or organizations by buying commercial airtime during broadcasts or sponsoring individual athletes or teams at a fraction of the cost is engaging in ambush marketing.

Ambush marketing has been especially prevalent at Olympic events. In early 2010, the U.S. Olympic Committee (USOC) accused Subway of ambush marketing ahead of the Winter Olympic Games in Vancouver. Subway aired a commercial depicting Michael Phelps swimming toward Vancouver. The USOC said that by using Phelps, an Olympic gold medalist, and the words "Vancouver" and "winter" in its commercial, Subway was trying to falsely promote itself as a sponsor of the 2010 Winter Games (Mickle, 2010). In anticipation of the London Olympics of 2012, the United Kingdom took the proactive approach of promulgating specific legislation aimed at preventing ambush marketing (Lowen, 2006). The legislation, The London Olympic Games and Paralympic Games Act of 2006, included the creation of a right known as the "London Olympics association right," which was designed to prevent false representations of sponsorships (London Olympic Games and Paralympic Games Act, 2006). This prevented the use of a combination of a list of words, including "games," "2012," "twenty-twelve," "two thousand and twelve" "gold," "silver," "bronze," "medals," "sponsor" and "summer." While other legal issues beyond ambush marketing exist in the Olympic realm, such as possible unionization of Olympians, drug testing policies, and decisions about which sports are included in the Games, it exceeds the scope of this chapter to go into detail about them.

Collegiate

On the collegiate level, challenges are arising regarding NCAA amateurism rules and the conflict with the commercialism so predominant in Division I football and basketball. This comes at a time when many Division I football and basketball players are questioning NCAA rules that prohibit them from earning revenue from their playing talent and public image while they have remaining eligibility. Thus, problems will continue to arise regarding restrictions on athletes' involvement with sport agents and restrictions on athletes' abilities to market themselves, particularly in men's college basketball, where first- and second-year college players face an opportunity cost in the millions of dollars if they wish to stay in college and graduate with their respective class. Moreover, the pending cases of Ed O'Bannon and Sam Keller illustrate the judicial system's willingness to address the issue of the use of image and likeness of former college players by the NCAA. As noted earlier, both have sued the NCAA, Collegiate Licensing Company, and Electronic Arts (EA) Sports on theories of antitrust law and right of publicity over the use of their names and likenesses in video games. While preventing student-athletes access to the yearly profits it generates from merchandise such as commemorative DVDs and video games, the NCAA claims that the blurring of professionalism and amateurism forms the root of its actions. Despite this, the rights signed away by former student-athletes in aid of the amateur virtue, the basic proprietary rights to their own image and likeness, may be too great to stand up to legal reason (*Keller v. EA Sports*, 2009; *O'Bannon v. NCAA*, 2009).

Gender equity continues to present legal and financial challenges for athletic administrators at the high school and collegiate levels. In addition to participation rate issues, administrators need to be cognizant of how female coaches and administrators are treated in the athletic department. The California State University system provides an example of the how costly litigation can be when this form of risk is not managed. In 2008 and 2009, they settled gender discrimination lawsuits totaling over $17.5 million on behalf of Fresno State and San Diego State Universities' Athletics Departments (Hostetter, 2008; Schrotenboer, 2009).

Professional Sport

For years, the legal issues in professional team sport have focused on whether leagues could maintain labor peace. Currently all professional leagues are in the midst of a period of relative labor peace; however, it came at the cost of some games. During the term of the agreement, the issues facing the league are related to administering the CBA, as well as drug testing challenges, plus addressing health and safety issues such as the long-term impact of concussions.

Legal issues likely to arise in individual professional sports include the implementation and administration of drug testing policies. For instance, the PGA Tour now has a drug testing policy. Men's and women's tennis and cyclists' tours do have testing, but challenges are waged regularly over their test procedures and test results. Another emerging area is the potential for unionization efforts among individual athletes (e.g., Women's Tennis Association and Association of Tennis Professionals Tours, boxers, cyclists, action sports, NASCAR team members) who seek to improve their working conditions. Jockeys are currently unionized in the Jockey's Guild, but the organization has faced serious problems stemming from mismanagement, misconduct of principals, and corruption.

Government Scrutiny

There has been a steady increase in governmental scrutiny and regulation of the sport industry. The Professional and Amateur Sports Protection Act (PASPA) bans betting on sporting events *except* in those states where such betting was legal at the time the law was approved, or in any state that legalized sports betting within a year of that date (American Gaming Association, 2013). In a landmark case being watched closely by other states, New Jersey has appealed, asking permission to offer wagering on professional and college sports. All four major professional leagues and the NCAA are against it (Parmley, 2013). Following governmental scrutiny of performance-enhancing drug use resulting from the BALCO (Bay Area Laboratory Co-Operative) scandal, Congress has called for increased bans on such substances and increased testing of athletes. Congressional hearings have already spurred changes in amateur and professional leagues' drug testing policies, such as in professional baseball where the testing has been a subject of collective bargaining. Other pending congressional actions include rethinking the unrelated business income tax's application to college athletics, commercialization of college athletics, and whether the Bowl Championship Series structure violates antitrust laws. State and federal regulation of player agents has increased over the past decade as well.

Summary

As the sport industry has evolved into a complex multibillion-dollar global entity, law has played an increasingly dominant role in carrying out the management functions of sport organizations. When sport managers make decisions and disagreements arise, those working and participating in sport are relying more heavily on the legal system for resolutions. Thus, knowledge of key aspects of sport law has become increasingly important to the sport manager's ability to manage risk and to know when to seek legal assistance to aid in decision making and dispute resolution.

Key Terms

administrative law, Age Discrimination in Employment Act, agency, agent, Americans with Disabilities Act, ambush marketing, antitrust law, *bona fide* occupational qualification, breach, capacity, collective bargaining agreement, consideration, constitutional law, contract, Curt Flood Act, defendant, disaffirm, due process, duty of care, Equal Pay Act, equal protection, fiduciary duties, gross negligence, independent contractor, injunction, intellectual property, invasion of privacy, judicial review, labor exemption, Lanham Act, legality, legitimate interest, mutual assent, National Labor Relations Act, negligence, plaintiff, principal, public policy, rational basis, release of liability, risk management, secondary meaning, single entity, sport law, state actor, statutes, strict scrutiny, Title VII, Title IX, tort, trademark, unreasonable searches and seizures, vicarious liability, waivers

References

Access Now, Inc. v. South Florida Stadium Corp., 161 F. Supp. 2d 1357 (S.D. Fla. 2001).

Adidas America, Inc. v. National Collegiate Athletic Association, 64 F. Supp. 2d 1097 (D. Kan. 1999).

Age Discrimination in Employment Act of 1990, 29 U.S.C. §§ 621–634 (West 1990).

Ambush marketing is becoming a popular event at Olympic games. (1988, February 8). *The Wall Street Journal*, p. A25.

American Football League v. National Football League, 323 F.2d 124 (4th Cir. 1963).

American Gaming Association. (2013). Governmental scrutiny: Sports betting. Retrieved from http://www.americangaming.org/government-affairs/key-issues/past-issues/sports-betting

American Needle v. National Football League, 130 S. Ct. 2201 (2010).

Americans with Disabilities Act of 1990, 42 U.S.C. §§ 151–169 (West 1990).

Ammon, R. (2010). Risk management process. In D. J. Cotten & J. T. Wolohan (Eds.), *Law for recreation and sport managers* (5th ed., pp. 282–291). Dubuque, IA: Kendall/Hunt Publishers.

Anderson, P.M. (2007). Principles of Trademark Law. In D. J. Cotten & J.T. Wolohan (Eds.), *Law for recreation and sport managers* (4th ed., pp. 608–618). Dubuque, IA: Kendall/Hunt Publishers.

Associated Press. (2008, September 5). LPGA backs down on English only rule. Retrieved from http://www.golf.com/ap-news/lpga-backs-down-english-only-rule

Association of Pennsylvania State College and University Faculty. (2013). APSCUF members: Coaches. Retrieved from http://www.apscuf.org/members/coaches

Banks v. National Collegiate Athletic Association, 977 F.2d 1081 (7th Cir. 1992).

Bensinger, K. (2013, July 9). UCLA contract for coach Steve Alford. Retrieved from http://www.documents.latimes.com/ucla-contract-coach-steve-alford/

Biediger v. Quinnipiac University, 616 F. Supp. 2d 277 (D. Conn 2009).

Biediger v. Quinnipiac University, No. 3:09cv621 (SRU) (D. Ct. 2010). Retrieved from http://courtweb.pamd.uscourts.gov/courtwebsearch/ctxc/KX330R32.pdf

Biediger v. Quinnipiac University, 691 F.3d 85 (2d Cir. 2012).

Black's Law Dictionary, (5th ed.). (1979).

Board of Education v. Earls, 536 U.S. 822 (2002).

Board of Supervisors for La. State Univ. v. Smack Apparel Co., 550 F.3d 465 (5th Cir. 2008).

Brennan v. Board of Trustees for University of Louisiana Systems, 691 So.2d 324 (La. Ct. App. 1st Cir. 1997).

Brentwood Academy v. Tennessee Secondary School Athletic Association, 535 U.S. 971 (2001).

Bridgeman v. National Basketball Association, 675 F. Supp. 960 (D.N.J. 1987).

Brown v. Pro Football, Inc., 518 U.S. 231 (1996).

Brown v. Woolf, 554 F. Supp. 1206 (S.D. Ind. 1983).

Buse v. Vanguard Group of Investment Cos., No. 91-3560, 1996 U.S. Dist. LEXIS 19033 (E.D. Pa. 1996).

Callaway Golf Company v. Acushnet Company, 585 F. Supp. 2d 600 (D. Del. 2008).

Copperweld Corp. v. Independence Tube Corp., 467 U.S. 752, 773, n. 21.

Cotten, D. J. (2010). Waivers and releases. In D. J. Cotten & J. T. Wolohan (Eds.), *Law for recreation and sport managers* (5th ed., pp. 95–106). Dubuque, IA: Kendall/Hunt Publishers.

Crespin v. Albuquerque Baseball Club, LLC, 216 P.3d 827 (N.M. Ct. App. 2009).

Curt Flood Act, 15 U.S.C. § 27 (1998).

Dennie, C. (2012, August 14). Beidiger v. Quinnipiac University: Second circuit affirms and concludes cheerleading is not a sport (yet). Retrieved from http://www .bgsfirm.com/college-sports-law-blog /biediger-v-quinnipiac-university-second -circuit-affirms-and-concludes-cheerleading -is-not-a-sport-yet

Detroit Lions, Inc. and Sims v. Argovitz, 580 F. Supp. 542 (E.D. Mich. 1984).

Deutscher Tennis Bund et al. v. ATP Tour, Inc., 2010 WL 2541172 (C.A.3 (Del.).

Equal Pay Act of 1963, 29 U.S.C. § 206 (d)(1) (West 1990).

Equity in Athletics, Inc. v. The United States Department of Education, 291 Fed. Appx. 517 (2008).

Faragher v. Boca Raton, 524 U.S. 775 (1998).

Federal Baseball Club of Baltimore v. National League of Professional Baseball Clubs, et al., 259 U.S. 200 (1922).

Flood v. Kuhn, 407 U.S. 258 (1972).

Franklin v. Gwinnett County Public Schools, 112 S. Ct. 1028 (1992).

Gulf South Conference v. Boyd, 369 So.2d 553 (Sup. Ct. Ala. 1979).

Hackbart v. Cincinnati Bengals, Inc., 601 F. 2d 516 (10th Cir. 1979).

Haworth, K. (1996, December 20). A cottage industry helps sports programs in trouble. *Chronicle of Higher Education*, A35.

Hill v. National Collegiate Athletic Association, 865 P.2d 633 (Cal. 1994).

Hillard v. Black, 125 F. Supp. 2d 1071 (N.D. Fla. 2000).

Hostetter, G. (2008, July 15). Fresno state settles with softball coach for $605,000. *The Fresno Bee*. Retrieved from http://www.fresnobee .com/2008/07/11/726448/fresno-state-settles -with-softball.html

Howell, R. A., Allison, J. R., & Henley, N. T. (1987). *The legal environment of business* (2nd ed.). New York, NY: Dryden Press.

Jones v. Childers, 18 F.3d 1899 (11th Cir. 1994).

Keller v. EA Sports, No. C 09-1967 CW (ND. Calif. 2009). Order re: Motion to Dismiss. Scribd. Retrieved from http://www.scribd.com/doc/26624013 /Keller-v-NCAA-Order-re-Motion-to-Dismiss

Kuketz v. MDC Fitness Corp., 2001 WL 993565 (Mass. Super. Ct. 2001).

Law v. National Collegiate Athletic Association, 902 F. Supp. 1394 (D. Kan. 1995).

London Olympic Games and Paralympic Games Act 2006. (United Kingdom), s. 33. Retrieved from http://www.opsi.gov.uk/acts/acts2006 /pdf/ukpga_20060012_en.pdf

Los Angeles Memorial Coliseum Commission v. National Football League, 726 F.2d 1381 (1984).

Lowen, D. (2006, March 3). The London Olympic Games and Paralympic Games Act. Retrieved from http://www.couchmansllp .com/documents/news_press/London%20 Olympics%20Act.pdf

Ludtke and Time, Inc. v. Kuhn, 461 F. Supp. 86 (S.D.N.Y. 1978).

Mackey v. National Football League, 543 F.2d 606 (8th Cir. 1976).

Mark v. Moser, 746 N.E.2d 410 (Ind. App. 2001).

Masteralexis, J. T., & Masteralexis, L. P. (2010). Judicial review. In D. J. Cotton & J. T. Wolohan (Eds.), *Law for recreation and sport managers* (5th ed., pp. 418–427). Dubuque, IA: Kendall/Hunt Publishers.

Masteralexis, L. P. (2010). Labor law: Professional sport applications. In D. J. Cotton & J. T. Wolohan (Eds.), *Law for recreation and sport managers* (5th ed., pp. 669–680). Dubuque, IA: Kendall/Hunt Publishers.

McCormack v. National Collegiate Athletic Association, 845 F.2d 1338 (5th Cir. 1988).

McCourt v. California Sports, Inc., 600 F.2d 1193 (6th Cir. 1979).

Metropolitan Exhibition Co. v. Ewing, 42 F. 1989 (S.D.N.Y. 1890).

Metropolitan Exhibition Co. v. Ward, 9 N.Y.S. 779 (Sup. Ct. 1890).

Metropolitan Intercollegiate Basketball Association v. NCAA, 339 F. Supp. 2d 545 (S.D.N.Y. 2004).

Mickle, T. (2010, February 11). Subway campaign 'Crossed the line,' USOC's Baird says. *Street and Smith's SportsBusiness Daily*. Retrieved from http://www.sportsbusinessdaily.com /wintergames/entries

Miller v. University of Cincinnati, 2007 WL 2783674 (S.D. Ohio 2008).

Moore v. University of Notre Dame, 22 F. Supp. 2d 896 (N.D. Ind. 1998).

National Basketball Association v. Williams, 43 F.3d 684 (2nd Cir. 1995).

National Collegiate Athletic Association v. Board of Regents of the University of Oklahoma and the University of Georgia Athletic Association, 468 U.S. 85 (1982).

National Collegiate Athletic Association v. Tarkanian, 488 U.S. 179, 193 (1988).

National Labor Relations Act, 29 U.S.C. §§ 151–69 (West 1990).

Noffke ex. rel Swenson v. Bakke, 760 N.W.2d 156 (Wis. 2009).

O'Bannon v. NCAA, No. C 09-1967 CW (N.D. Calif. 2009). Order re: Motion to Dismiss. Scribd. Retrieved from http://www.scribd .com/doc/26623903/O-Bannon-v-NCAA -Order-re-Motion-to-Dismiss

Office of Civil Rights. (2013, January 25). Dear colleague letter. Retrieved from http:// www2.ed.gov/about/offices/list/ocr/letters /colleague-201301-504.html

Oliver v. NCAA, 2009 Ohio 6587 (2009).

Ortiz-Del Valle v. National Basketball Association, 42 F. Supp. 2d 334 (S.D.N.Y. 1999).

Parmley, S. (2013, June 28). New Jersey makes final appeal for sports betting. *Philadelphia Inquirer*. Retrieved from http://articles.philly .com/2013-06-28/business/40235411_1 _amateur-sports-protection-act-paspa -legalized-sports-wagering

Perdue v. City University of New York, 13 F. Supp. 2d 326 (E.D.N.Y. 1998).

Perry v. Sindermann, 408 U.S. 593 (1972).

PGA Tour Inc. v. Martin, 532 U.S. 661 (2001).

Philadelphia World Hockey, Inc. v. Philadelphia Hockey Club, Inc., 351 F. Supp. 462 (1972).

Pitts v. University of Oklahoma, No. Civ. 93-1341-A (W.D. Okla. 1994).

Powell v. National Football League, 930 F.2d 1293 (8th Cir. 1989).

Reed, M. H. (1989). *IEG legal guide to sponsorship.* Chicago, IL: International Events Group.

Rene v. MGM Grand Hotel, Inc., No. 98-16924 (9th Cir. Sept. 24, 2002).

Reynolds v. National Football League, 584 F.2d 280 (8th Cir. 1978).

Rodgers v. Georgia Tech Athletic Association, 303 S.E.2d 467 (Ga. Ct. App. 1983).

Schrotenboer, B. (2009, October 2). SDSU settles equal pay lawsuit brought by coach. *Sign On San Diego*. Retrieved from http://www .signonsandiego.com/news/2009/oct/02 /sdsu-settles-equal-pay-lawsuit-brought -coach/?sports

Shropshire, K. L., & Davis, T. (2003). *The business of sports agents*. Philadelphia, PA: University of Pennsylvania Press.

Smith v. Pro Football, Inc., 593 F.2d 1173 (D.C. Cir. 1978).

Sport Broadcasting Act, 15 U.S.C. §§ 1291–1294 (1961).

Stanley v. University of Southern California, 13 F.3d 1313 (1994).

Stanley v. University of Southern California, 178 F. 3d 1069 (9th Cir. 1999).

Staudohar, P. D. (1996). *Playing for dollars: Labor relations and the sports business*. Ithaca, NY: Cornell University Press.

Thurmond v. Prince William Professional Baseball Club, Inc., 574 S.E.2d 246 (Va. 2003).

Title IX of the Educational Amendments of 1972, 20 U.S.C. §§ 1681–88 (West 1990).

Toolson v. New York Yankees, 346 U.S. 356 (1953).

Total Economic Athletic Management of America, Inc. v. Pickens, 898 S.W.2d 98 (Mo. App. 1995).

Turner v. Mandalay Sports Entertainment, LLC. 180 P.3d 1172 (Nev. 2008).

Uniform Law Commission. (2013). Athlete agents act. Retrieved from http://www.uniformlaws .org/Act.aspx?title=Athlete%20Agents%20Act

United States Football League v. National Football League, 634 F. Supp. 1155 (S.D.N.Y. 1986).

University of Colorado v. Derdeyn, 863 P.2d 929 (1993).

Van der Smissen, B. (2007). Elements of negligence. In D. J. Cotten & J.T. Wolohan (Eds.), *Law for recreation and sport managers* (4th ed., pp. 36-45). Dubuque, IA: Kendall /Hunt Publishers.

Vernonia School District 47J v. Acton, 115 S. Ct. 2386 (1995).

Vick v. Wong et al., 263 F.R.D. 325 (U.S. Dist. 2009).

Wagenblast v. Odessa School District, 758 P.2d 968 (Wash. Sup. Ct. 1988).

Wallace v. Texas Tech University, 80 F.3d 1042 (5th Cir. 1996).

White v. NCAA, C.D. Cal. Case No. CV 06 0999 VBF.

Williams v. CWI, Inc., 777 F. Supp. 1006 (D.D.C. 1991).

Wong, G. M. (2010). *Essentials of sports law* (4th ed.). Westport, CT: Praeger Publishers.

Wong, G. M., & Masteralexis, L. P. (1996). Legal aspects of sport administration. In F. J. Bridges & L. L. Roquemore (Eds.), *Management for athletic/sport administration: Theory and practice* (2nd ed., pp. 85–132). Decatur, GA: ESM Books.

Wood v. National Basketball Association, 809 F.2d 954 (2nd Cir. 1987).

World Intellectual Property Organization. (2013a). What is intellectual property? Retrieved from http://www.wipo.int /about-ip/en

World Intellectual Property Organization. (2013b). Sport and intellectual property. Retrieved from http://www.wipo.int/ip-sport /en/

World Intellectual Property Organization. (2013c). Trademarks. Retrieved from http:// www.wipo.int/trademarks/en/trademarks .html

Yasser, R., McCurdy, J., Goplerud, P., & Weston, M. (1999). *Sports law* (4th ed.). Cincinnati, OH: Anderson Publishing.

York v. Wahkiakum School Dist. No. 200, 163 Wash.2d 297 (Wash. 2008).

Zimmerman v. National Football League, 632 F. Supp. 398 (D.D.C. 1986).

Zinn v. Parrish, 644 F.2d 360 (7th Cir. 1981).

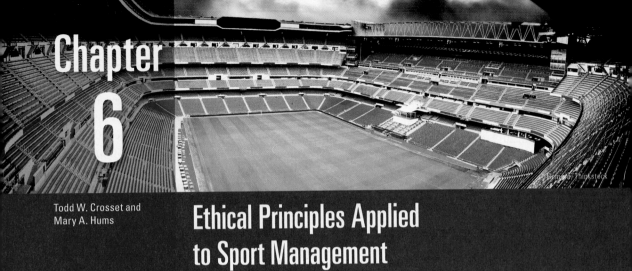

Chapter 6

Todd W. Crosset and
Mary A. Hums

Ethical Principles Applied to Sport Management

Learning Objectives

Upon completion of this chapter, students should be able to:

1. Understand the roles that ethics and morals play in guiding human behavior.

2. Appraise the importance of morality and ethics in the sport workplace.

3. Differentiate between moral and ethical dilemmas.

4. Analyze an ethical dilemma by using an ethical decision-making model.

5. Formulate a code of conduct for a sport organization.

6. Distinguish between *morality* and *legality* and understand how a decision may be legal while at the same time be immoral.

7. Apply moral principles to the workplace through the incorporation of codes of conduct, self-examination, forums for moral discourse, and statements of consequences for ethical violations into organizational documents.

Introduction

Sport managers make tough decisions. Imagine for a moment that you had to decide whether to hold the New York Marathon after Superstorm Sandy in 2012 or stage any professional baseball games following the 2011 tsunami in Japan. Managers around the world were faced with conflicting and equally compelling desires to mourn those who died and to get back to normal. How would you go about making those decisions? What would be your approach? Although these are extreme examples, sport managers frequently face decisions involving ethical dilemmas. What can help guide them with their decision making in complex situations?

Ethics is the systematic study of the values that guide our decision making. The process of making a correct and fair decision is called **ethical reasoning**. Ethical reasoning depends on our values or the values of the organizations for which we work and reflects how we believe people should behave and how we want our world to operate. This chapter provides a framework to help future sport managers think critically and systematically about ethical issues. It discusses two types of ethical issues: ethical dilemmas and morality.

An **ethical dilemma** is a practical conflict involving more or less equally compelling values or social obligations (Solomon, 1992). When to resume play after a community or national tragedy is an example of an ethical dilemma. Ethical dilemmas are solved when we articulate which commonly held values we admire most.

However, ethical values should not be confused with personal preferences. **Ethical decision making** affects other people in a way that personal preferences do not. Ethical dilemmas have social implications. As such, ethics requires decision makers to consider how their actions will affect different groups of people and individuals.

Morality, like ethics, is concerned with the values that guide behavior. Morality deals with a specific type of ethical issue, however. **Morals** are the fundamental baseline values that dictate appropriate behavior within a society (Solomon, 1992). The beliefs that stealing and murder are wrong, for example, are moral values in most societies. Morality is sometimes summarized as a list of those actions people ought to do or refrain from doing. The concept of morality is discussed in further detail later in this chapter. For the moment, however, consider the case of Aaron Hernandez, formerly a player for the New England Patriots in the National Football League (NFL).

Hernandez was accused of murder in 2013. Killing people as a means of solving disputes is considered wrong in our society. If everyone resolved disputes in this manner, society would fall apart, making murder a moral issue. Hernandez's arrest, however, also created ethical issues for the Patriots organization. The main issue was whether the Patriots should release Hernandez immediately or wait for the court to decide guilt or innocence before making a decision. Some of the related ethical questions were: Did the team have a responsibility to support an employee in difficult times or would their support drag the organization down and alienate fans? How should the organization respond to consumers who had purchased an official Aaron Hernandez jersey and were now repulsed by the thought of wearing that shirt? Did the team bear some responsibility for keeping the consumer happy given the special circumstances of Hernandez's fall from grace? There were no clear answers. Although the Patriots' choice of response would not undermine the functioning of society, it remained important because it would affirm the values of the team. The organization's responses to Hernandez's arrest were ethical decisions. The Patriots decision was to release Hernandez immediately and set aside one weekend for fans to exchange their Hernandez jersey for a jersey of another current player.

Ethical Considerations

The world of sport has certainly seen its share of scandals of late, from Hernandez's murder charge to Lance Armstrong's performance-enhancing drug use. Whenever events such as these occur, sport managers need to respond in an ethical manner, making decisions that are guided by strong ethical principles. It is not always easy to do so, as these situations are complex and demanding, but sport managers need to respond to these challenges positively.

Sport managers face ethical dilemmas on a daily basis. Consider the following examples:

- Changing the start time of a contest to accommodate television programming at the expense of class time for college athletes
- Encouraging the use of painkillers by injured athletes to enable them to play hurt
- Helping an athlete with a drug, alcohol, marital, or criminal problem
- Using a team's limited resources to make stadiums accessible for people with disabilities
- Relocating a professional team from a profitable site to another city that promises even more revenue
- Deciding between cutting a less visible, successful nonrevenue sport team or a highly visible football program when facing a budget crisis in a National Collegiate Athletic Association (NCAA) Division I athletic program

How does a sport manager know when he or she is facing such a dilemma? Zinn (1993) suggests managers ask themselves the following questions:

- When talking about the matter at hand, do people use words or expressions such as "right or wrong," "black or white," "bottom line," "conflict," or "values"?
- Will anyone be harmed because of my action/inaction or decision?
- Am I concerned about my decision being equally fair to all parties?
- Do I feel a conflict between my personal values and my professional interest?
- Is there controversy or strong opposition regarding this decision?
- Do I have a feeling something is "just not right" about the situation?
- Will I be hesitant to reveal my decision to others?

If a sport manager answers "yes" to any of these questions, he or she is most likely facing an ethical dilemma.

Few areas of sport management present more difficulty than ethical dilemmas. Sport managers' decision making is complicated because the outcomes of their decisions affect diverse groups of people (e.g., athletes, fans, the community, businesses, the media) whose interests are often in conflict. Plus, sport managers' decisions about ethical dilemmas tend to fall under greater public scrutiny than decisions made by managers in other industries without high-profile employees (professional athletes) or without great media interest, especially in these fast-moving days of social media. At the same moment that managers are weighing decisions regarding the right thing to do, they are also considering financial costs, the effect on a team's and league's reputation, the law, and the impact on winning games. If a sport manager does not approach ethical dilemmas systematically, the complexity of issues and interests involved can easily overwhelm his or her judgment—especially when conflicting options seem to make equally good sense and are being argued emotionally by opposing parties.

To solve an ethical dilemma, decision makers try to make a rational argument. They weigh the pros and cons of two or more seemingly valid choices that reflect equally cherished values. In recreational softball leagues, for example, teams are faced with the decision of whether to play only their best players or to play everyone. The decision is based on the relative value team members place on winning versus the value they place on participation. The argument could be made that the primary purpose of a recreational softball league is for participants to play and have fun. Recreational leagues provide camaraderie and emphasize team spirit that grows out of cheering for each other, playing, and going out together after games. However, an equally compelling argument could be made for competition and winning, which are central to the enjoyment of sport—even on the recreational level. It can be argued that teams should field their best players to make competition more intense and victory more satisfying. Both outlooks make sense; hence, an ethical dilemma exists. In this softball league example, the decision makers have to put themselves in the shoes of both the bench warmers and the starters and consider how both will be affected. They also have to think about what type of values they want to emphasize through their teams.

When sport managers are faced with ethical dilemmas, their decisions are difficult. Ethical decision making does not mean that the sport manager reacts solely based on his or her "gut" feeling. Ethical analysis involves a systematic process of reasoning. It is not a haphazard procedure where one guesses at the best solution (Cooke, 1991). Ethical decision making is similar to the regular decision making process in business situations in that there is a given structure to follow. A model suggested by Zinn (1993) and adapted by Hums and MacLean (2013) outlines the following steps in the ethical decision-making process:

1. Identify the correct problem to be solved.

2. Gather all the pertinent information.

3. Explore codes of conduct relevant to your profession or to this particular dilemma.

4. Examine your own personal values and beliefs.

5. Consult with your peers or other individuals in the industry who may have experience in similar situations.

6. List your options.

7. Look for a "win-win" situation if at all possible.

8. Ask yourself this question: "How would my family feel if my decision and how I arrived at my decision appeared on the Internet tomorrow?"

9. Sleep on it. Do not rush to a decision.

10. Make your best decision, knowing it may not be perfect.

11. Evaluate your decision.

Although this may seem like a complicated process, remember that ethical decisions and dilemmas involve complicated problems, and that often, reasonable people will disagree over what is the "right decision." It is essential for sport managers to fully think through any ethical decisions they must make.

Consider the following case. The 2010 NCAA Men's National Swimming and Diving Championships were scheduled for Thursday through Saturday, March 24–27. On Tuesday, 18 members of the Arizona, Texas, and Stanford teams fell ill. (About one-third of each squad became sick.) All three teams had traveled on the same flight into Columbus, Ohio, and had picked up a viral infection resulting in nausea, vomiting, and diarrhea. On Wednesday, the day prior to the start of the meet, the athletes were being treated at a local hospital. The teams affected were some of the best in the country and each had a chance to win a team trophy. The coaches of these teams are very powerful within the world of swimming. Their athletes, weakened by the stomach bug, would not perform at their best until they could recover. An emergency coaches' meeting was called to discuss the situation. Should the meet proceed as scheduled or be delayed?

The NCAA Crisis Management Team led the effort to resolve the dilemma. Health experts from the Centers for Disease Control and Prevention and from The Ohio State University were consulted. Officials quickly realized that the first issue at hand was the health and safety of all athletes and spectators. The initial decision made by the NCAA Crisis Management Team was to have event managers take special precautions to keep the pool area sanitized as athletes (even the sick ones) were trying to prepare for the meet. Coaches of affected teams were asked to keep their athletes separated from other teams. Whatever the illness was, they did not want it spreading. But the question of what to do about the competition remained.

The NCAA Crisis Management Team prioritized health and safety and then considered the fairest option in light of the health priority. Officials did not want sick athletes on the deck or the pool with other athletes until they were sure they were no longer contagious. Health experts recommended that the sick athletes not compete on Thursday. That meant either barring them from competition for 1 day or delaying the entire meet for 1 day.

Three options were considered. The first option was to start the meet on Thursday as scheduled and leave it up to the medical experts, coaches, and athletes to decide on a case-by-case basis which of the sick athletes could compete. Some coaches thought this was the right thing to do. They argued they had their athletes ready to go for Thursday. Delaying the meet was to their disadvantage. Stick to the original plan, they argued. Athletes get injured all the time.

Let's swim and let the chips fall where they may. If there was a health risk, this contingent argued, affected athletes should not compete (similar to the rule that a player may not participate in a sport if he or she is bleeding). Healthy athletes should not be affected by the sick athletes. Delaying the meet, those opposed to this solution argued, was an unfair burden for the healthy teams to bear. Further, these coaches argued, if a smaller number of athletes from weaker teams had become sick, the emergency meeting would never have been called. The fair thing to do was to treat every situation in a similar fashion. Many of the coaches who made this argument also knew they would gain a competitive advantage by starting the meet on time.

A second suggestion was to start the meet on Friday. This would ensure that the bug did not spread, and it also would give affected athletes an additional day to recover. This, no doubt, was the primary concern of the Arizona, Texas, and Stanford teams. People who made this argument appealed to the notion of least harm. A 1-day delay would not harm healthy athletes and teams as much as asking sick athletes not to compete or to compete in their weakened state on the first day.

Delaying the meet led to another dilemma: how to run the event if it started 1 day later. One suggestion was to run the Thursday and Friday events as timed finals on Friday, compressing the meet into 2 days. This choice ended the meet on Saturday and had the benefit of not disrupting team travel schedules. Another option was to push the entire meet back 1 day and run it as intended, over 3 days, Friday through Sunday.

Most coaches thought running two-thirds of the meet as timed finals on Friday was too great of a modification and quickly rejected the idea of compressing the meet into 2 days. That left two options for the NCAA Crisis Management Team: start the meet on Thursday and make medical decisions on a case-by-case basis, or delay the meet by 1 day. In the end, the NCAA Crisis Management team decided the "fairest" way to proceed was to run the meet in full, beginning on Friday.

That decision seemed the most fair because it allowed all athletes who qualified to compete as intended and had the least disruptive impact on the outcome. Because such a large percentage of top athletes took ill, running the meet without them, even for a single day, would dramatically change the outcome of the championship. It was not clear if the athletes would still be contagious on Thursday. Barring the affected athletes put some teams at a disadvantage for a medical precaution that might not be necessary. However, allowing them to compete in a weakened state might cause medical problems and many of these athletes would not perform up to their capabilities. Pushing the meet back, the NCAA Crisis Management Team reasoned, was medically prudent and had the least adverse impact on the performances of the greatest number of athletes. While not a perfect solution, it meant that athletes would determine the outcome of the meet, not the coaches, officials, and medical staff.

Making ethical decisions is challenging. Managers in any industry need guidelines to help them make decisions and principles to help them assess themselves and their personal values. The Josephson Institute of Ethics (2013) provides an interesting framework for managers to use when making ethical decisions, by offering what it calls the Six Pillars of Character. Table 6-1 illustrates these Six Pillars and some of the subsets within each. Peter Carlisle, the agent for Michael Phelps, refers to values as personal integrity. For Carlisle, integrity is like a keel on a ship. When the going gets tough and the correct choice is not clear, he advises, lean into the keel to help you steer the proper course.

Codes of Conduct

Recall that the third recommendation from the multistep ethical decision-making model described earlier is to consult an organization's **code of conduct** (also called **code of ethics**). The recent rash of corporate scandals in the United States illustrates the need to establish solid ethical climates within corporations. According to Sims (1992), an organization's ethical climate establishes the shared set of understandings that determine correct behavior

Table 6-1 Josephson's Six Pillars of Character

Pillar 1	Trustworthiness
	Includes honesty, integrity, reliability, and loyalty
Pillar 2	Respect
	Includes civility, courtesy, and decency; dignity and autonomy; and tolerance and acceptance
Pillar 3	Responsibility
	Includes accountability, pursuit of excellence, and self-restraint
Pillar 4	Fairness
	Includes process, impartiality, and equity
Pillar 5	Caring
	The "heart" of ethics
Pillar 6	Citizenship
	Includes civic virtues and duties

Source: © 2007 Reprinted with permission of Josephson Institute. www.charactercounts.org

and the manner in which ethical issues will be handled. One way to establish this climate is through codes of conduct or codes of ethics. Codes of conduct are probably the most visible statements of ethical philosophy and beliefs for a company, business, or organization (DeSensi & Rosenberg, 1996). These codes of conduct explicitly outline and explain the principles under which an organization or profession operates. Implicit in any code of conduct are the institutional/organizational values that should help managers and employees resolve ethical dilemmas. Codes of conduct provide employees with guidelines for their behavior.

Codes of conduct and codes of ethics are not twentieth-century inventions. In fact, they are as old as the earliest religious oral traditions and writings, such as the Torah and the Koran. Although the development of modern codes in the United States was initiated in the medical, accounting, and legal professions, these are not the only professional areas to have codes of ethics. The need to address ethical questions and encourage correct actions has led many professions to establish codes of conduct (Jordan et al., 2004). They are found in virtually every type of organization and corporation in the United States. Within the last decade, many corporations have hired ethics officers or created ethics boards to address ethical issues within organizations. For example, the International Olympic Committee (IOC) created its Ethics Commission in 1999 and the Australian Sports Commission undertook an Ethics and Integrity Issues in sport Study in 2010.

In the sport world, codes have been adopted or are being considered by a number of sport organizations. The U.S. Olympic Committee, the IOC, the National Intramural and Recreational Sports Association, the American Camping Association, and USA Hockey are just a few examples of sport organizations with codes of conduct. Numerous youth sport programs, including the Indiana Youth Soccer Association, the U.S. Lacrosse Youth Council, and the National Association for Sport and Physical Education, have adopted codes of conduct as well, often creating separate codes for participants, coaches, and parents. The state of New Jersey passed a code of conduct law that established athletic codes of conduct for players, coaches, officials, and parents (Youth Sports Research Council, 2002).

Codes of conduct are not unique to the sport industry in the United States. The Geelong Cricket Association of Australia has a series of codes for junior cricket players, spectators, and coaches (Geelong Cricket Association, 2013). The Australia Sports Commission has a series of codes of behaviors written for administrators, players, coaches, spectators, officials, parents, and even teachers and the media (Australia Sports Commission, n.d.). England Basketball has an extensive set of codes for administrators, players, coaches, spectators, referees, and parents (England Basketball, 2002). Speed Skating Canada has a code (Speed Skating Canada, 2007), as does British Columbia Athletics (BC Athletics, n.d.).

Periodically, managers are asked to review or create codes of conduct. According to a 2000 Ethics Officer Association survey, 96% of ethics officers had created or rewritten codes of conduct over a 5-year period (Petry, 2001). Codes of conduct should be clear and straightforward. They need not be long or complex and should encourage employees to understand the goals they are trying to accomplish instead of just outlining rules and punishments.

If done well, codes of conduct can help create an ethical climate in an organization. According to Mahony, Geist, Jordan, Greenwell, and Pastore (1999), a number of factors are necessary for a sport organization to possess an effective code of conduct:

- Codes need to avoid being too vague (DeSensi & Rosenberg, 1996).

© Paolo Bona/ShutterStock, Inc.

- Codes should be based on a few overriding principles that can be used to deal with a variety of ethical dilemmas faced by members of the organization (Fraliegh, 1993).
- Codes should clearly state to whom they apply. If codes are to be influential, leadership and membership within the organization must accept and be willing to adhere to the prescribed standards.
- Codes should contain consequences for violations (DeSensi & Rosenberg, 1996).

An example of a code of conduct for a sport organization is given in **Figure 6-1**, which reproduces the International Health, Racquet and Sportsclub Association Associate Members' Code of Conduct (2010).

Codes of conduct are not the be-all and end-all of organizational ethics. If codes of conduct are too long or complex to easily understand, if they try to intimidate employees into acting morally, or if the organization does not demonstrate a commitment to them, codes of conduct may be counterproductive. Further, if codes of ethics are too detailed, they can actually discourage moral reasoning. The NCAA "has become so rule dependent, so comprehensive and so situation specific," sport ethicist Russell Gough argues, "that athletic administrators, coaches and support staff are increasingly not required to make ethical judgments. A myopic emphasis on rule conformity has displaced a more circumspect emphasis on personal integrity and considered ethical judgment" (Gough, 1994, p. 5).

Morality

Not all ethical issues represent choices between equally compelling values. Some ethical dilemmas are about choosing between right and wrong, two opposing choices. When the issue is about doing what is right, it is usually a moral issue. People tend to use the terms morals

The International Health, Racquet & Sportsclub Association is a non-profit trade association serving the athletic, racquet and fitness industry worldwide. As an Associate Member of IHRSA, we consider it our mission to enhance the quality of life through physical fitness and sports. To this end, we endeavor to provide quality products and services. We further strive to instill in those we serve an understanding of the value of physical fitness to their lives.

In order to fulfill our mission, we pledge the following:

- That we produce quality products and services.
- That we deliver on our commitments.
- That we are an equal opportunity employer.
- That we will cooperate with our customers toward the continual expansion of the club and fitness industries.
- That we will utilize our benefits of IHRSA membership solely for the purposes and under the guidelines for which they were established.
- That we agree to conduct our business in a manner which commands the respect of those we serve.
- That customer satisfaction will be the determining factor in all our business dealings.

Figure 6-1 International Health, Racquet and Sportsclub Association
Courtesy of International Health, Racquet and Sportsclub Association, 2010.

and ethics interchangeably; however, morality actually relates to a specific type of ethical issue. As defined earlier, morals are the fundamental baseline values dictating appropriate behavior within a society (Solomon, 1992). A distinctive feature of moral values is their grounding in the practical affairs of social life, whereas other ethical decisions are based on broader abstract principles (DeSensi & Rosenberg, 1996).

In sport, an example of a moral principle is that all athletes give an honest effort whenever they compete. If athletes stopped trying to win, the essence of sport would be threatened. If you ask someone: "Why aren't athletes allowed to throw games [lose on purpose] in exchange for a nice pay check from the highest bidder?", they are likely to say, "Because it is wrong." Pushed further they might say, "Because it would ruin sport."

Similarly, in business, everyone needs to be able to trust that other parties will be honest and deliver the agreed on goods and services. Bernie Madoff, the disgraced financier, played on people's trust to pull off his $50 billion Ponzi scheme. To cultivate and maintain trust, Madoff lied to clients, created fraudulent documents of trades, and—on paper—produced consistent profits. But it was, as he put it, "A big lie." He was simply paying off old clients with new clients' money. When the stock market turned bearish in 2008 and his clients wanted to cash out, he ran out of money. The gig was up and the largest fraud in U.S. history exposed. Madoff was not just being unethical—his actions were immoral.

Our social practices depend on people upholding certain baseline values. When people act morally—according to generally acceptable standards of behavior—they contribute to the maintenance and smooth functioning of society. Shared morality cultivates trust between strangers and enables individuals to function in a society.

Moral values are generally accepted so broadly within a community that they are considered self-evident and largely go unquestioned. Because people perceive moral values as basic and inalienable, it is often assumed these values are derived from a "higher order" or are common sense. If, for example, an athlete is asked why he or she strives to win, a common response would be "Because that's what sports are about." Managers will know they are dealing with a moral issue as opposed to an ethical dilemma if people justify their position with a simple, "Because it is the right thing to do." If pushed, they might refer to a higher principle grounded in their religious convictions or their sense of good sporting conduct. Ethical decisions (e.g., the decision about whether to play everyone or only the best players) may be difficult to make and have serious implications for others, but they do not inherently ruin the game.

Morality Versus the Law

Many moral values in a society are codified in laws. For example, theft is not only considered immoral, it is also against the law. Occasionally, someone may justify distasteful behavior by saying, "It's not against the law, is it?" In sport, doping is one area where this happens. From time to time, performance-enhancing substances are developed or discovered that have not yet been banned. Taking these drugs may not be against the rules, but doing so constitutes an immoral act because they artificially enhance an athlete's performance, violating the principle of fair play. The "It is not against the rules" argument does not justify the behavior. Laws and morality are not the same.

Laws are created and enforced to maintain order and to help society function smoothly. Even so, at times immoral laws are instituted. For much of the twentieth century in the United States, laws in some states prohibited interracial competitive sports. Teams with both white and black players complied with these laws and at times left their black players at home (Adelson, 1999). The long history of legal segregation in this country was clearly immoral, and yet it was protected by law.

Likewise, moral behavior cannot always be legislated, and people cannot be forced to act morally. For example, it is generally accepted that people should try to help others in need or distress, but laws cannot and do not require people to do so. If we see someone who is injured or the victim of a crime, our moral sensibility directs us to come to his or her aid, but in most cases laws do not punish us for failing to do so. Our moral sensibility creates a stronger obligation than the law. There may be cases where some individuals decide that the right thing to do is to break the law (i.e., civil disobedience).

Sometimes people are able to comply with the letter of the law without achieving its spirit or its stated goals. For example, sport teams and events are increasingly adopting charity nonprofit status to gain tax advantages and beneficial bond ratings. They claim that a team or event is a fundraiser for a group in need, or that a new stadium will foster economic development. Meanwhile they hire a private firm, often comprised of the same people who created the nonprofit, to manage the event. Any substantial revenue generation is eaten up by the private management firm and does not go to the group in need. This practice is legal, but it is certainly not moral.

Morality in the Workplace

Sound moral reasoning is the basis of a healthy sport organization. Some **moral principles** are universal and recognized in all aspects of life. Such principles include cooperation, courage, perseverance, foresight, and wisdom. Other moral principles are tied to particular situations. For example, a moral value such as competition is esteemed in business but not in family relations. Honesty is essential in scientific research, but in sport "faking out" an opponent is seen as an acceptable strategy and a way to gain advantage.

Academic discussions of morality often start with a discussion of **absolutism** versus **relativism**. Absolutism argues that moral precepts are universal; that is, they are applicable to all circumstances. Relativism argues that what is moral depends on the situation. Making moral decisions in the practical world of work falls somewhere in between these two extremes. We like to use the expression *situational absolutes* to describe this hybrid approach.

Moral rules prescribing "correct" behavior in one situation can generally be applied to similar situations within similar specific social contexts. For example, people believe it is always wrong for an elite athlete not to give his or her best honest effort. Similarly, it is also wrong for a recreational athlete not to give an honest effort. In the workplace, regardless how large or small the monetary value of a contract, it is always wrong to violate a business agreement made voluntarily in good faith.

According to Jacobs (1992), there are two types of work: commercial and noncommercial. The moral rules guiding each type are distinct. Commercial moral rules have their roots in the rules of the marketplace and guide activities such as sales and marketing. Honesty is a linchpin of commercial trading. Honesty ensures fair trading practices and allows individuals to trust that they will receive agreed upon goods or services. In commercial occupations, insider trading and deceiving customers are forms of dishonesty and are condemned.

Noncommercial moral values guide other occupations, such as accountants, police, and building inspectors. In sport, officials, league commissioners, athletes, and coaches most likely operate according to noncommercial principles. The most important value in noncommercial endeavors is loyalty. These occupations demand loyalty to an oath of office or professional standards to guard against "selling out." Here, loyalty trumps honesty. In these professions it is sometimes all right to withhold information from others for the sake of the overall task (e.g., undercover police work, general managers' discussions of player personnel). Whereas innovation is admired in the commercial realm, tradition is admired in the noncommercial realm. If people holding these noncommercial positions violate moral precepts associated with loyalty, they will be accused of treason, selling out, or failure to uphold an oath.

© Yuri Arcurs/Dreamstime.com

Jacobs (1992) argues that our moral reasoning gets muddled when we do not understand which moral principles our job requires. Take, for example, the role of athlete. The moral order in which athletes operate is generally noncommercial. The expectation is that athletes should be loyal to their team, obedient to and disciplined by the coach, and never compromise the integrity of the game. Within the limits imposed by the rules of the game, athletes are expected to try to win by any means available to them. In fact, many sport strategies depend on forms of deception. Feints and setting up opponents to believe you intend to do one thing when you plan to do another are fundamental sport strategies. However, athletes are trusted not to cheat, gamble, or "sell out" the game. Conversely, if an equipment manager does not send purchase orders out in the marketplace for competitive bid but instead purchases from a loyal friend, he or she could create unnecessary departmental expenses and would be violating the principles of honesty and open competition in the commercial sphere.

Morality and Multiple Roles

Moral decisions are complicated by the fact that moral principles are often applied and valued differently in different social contexts. Decision making is made more difficult by the variety of roles each of us fills. One collection of moral rules does not necessarily apply to all situations, even within the same job.

Some jobs in sport do not actually reside completely within either the commercial or the noncommercial sphere. One example is the position of director of media relations for a college athletic department. To complete the tasks of this job, the director of media relations operates in both moral systems. At one point in the day, this person may be required to be absolutely honest (e.g., producing statistics for coaches and reporters) and at another time may exude loyalty to the point of stretching the truth (e.g., creating recruiting materials for a team). Professional athletes who demonstrate team loyalty throughout the season become commercially minded when renegotiating their contracts. Finally, recall the equipment manager. He or she has a job that is primarily driven by noncommercial precepts that include loyalty to the team, upholding traditions, and so on. But periodically—such as when purchasing

new equipment—he or she enters the commercial sphere. At that point, noncommercial values are set aside and the manager embraces values that are admired within the commercial sphere. Although most jobs fall more or less into one moral order or the other (commercial or noncommercial), it is unrealistic to suggest that any occupation is completely commercial or completely noncommercial.

Consequently, the process of making a moral choice, of deciding what is right and wrong, involves understanding the parameters of acceptable behavior within the context of one's multiple roles in society. This does not mean, however, that people can arbitrarily choose which values will guide their behavior. Specific situations and roles in our society demand specific moral values.

Morality and Corruption

Among the biggest distinctions between moral decision making and other ethical decisions are the extensive ramifications of immoral choices. An immoral decision (e.g., to shave points) can ruin a whole enterprise. One of the most infamous immoral acts in sport occurred at the 1980 Boston Marathon when Rosie Ruiz fooled the world—momentarily at least. Ruiz was crowned the women's champion but actually had jumped out of the crowd and only ran the last half mile to cross the finish line first. Later it was revealed that her qualifying time from the New York City Marathon was a fraud, too. She broke from the race to ride the subway to the finish line. To this day, "pulling a Rosie Ruiz" means skipping out on part of an event only to show up at the end to garner undeserved accolades.

Immoral behavior, such as cheating in sports, violates society's basic assumptions of right and wrong. There are clear cut examples of immoral practices in sport such as Rosie Ruiz's subway run or the Black Sox scandal of 1919 when players cooperated with organized gamblers to lose games in the World Series. Immoral practices can also become institutionalized, which leads to corruption. Corruption may start small, when just a few people act immorally, but can ultimately become a standard operating procedure.

In the world of work, corruption usually occurs when people hop from one set of moral precepts to another when it is inappropriate to do so. For example, the job of stock analysts requires honestly reporting the facts. When a stock analyst works for a large financial firm there is supposed to be a "Chinese Wall" (a reference to the Great Wall of China) between the analysts and the business side of the firm. During the boom years of the late 1990s, however, some companies that received poor reports from stock analysts would sometime threaten to pull business from investment banks. Under this pressure, the wall broke down. Stock analysts employed by investment banks felt pressured to give hyper-positive reports about certain companies in order to help drive up stock prices. In these cases, the analysts became team players, stretching the truth to help their employer, who hoped to gain brokerage fees from investment deals. Actually, they were helping their firm compete by setting aside their core job responsibility, which was the duty to provide clients with fair assessments of a company.

Corruption might start when an employee takes a precept common to his or her profession and applies it in the wrong place. For example, accountants take an oath to be loyal to their profession. They are guardians of business. Morally they have more in common with the medical profession than they do sales and marketing. When an in-house accountant is convinced he or she needs to be loyal to the company and must do so by employing "aggressive accounting" techniques rather than staying loyal to the accounting profession and fulfilling his or her fiduciary duties, immoral behavior is likely to result. In a nutshell, this is what happened in the infamous Enron accounting scandal of 2001. Enron obscured its finances with a complex web of partnerships and questionable accounting practices that fooled debt-rating agencies, Wall Street analysts, and investors. The Enron accountants took their tendency to be loyal (to the accounting profession) and extended it to the company they were supposed to be regulating. In both the financial analysis and accountant examples, little lies eventually became standard operating procedure. When immoral behavior is systemic it is called *corruption*.

When an organization's immoral actions become standard practice, moral reasoning becomes muddled and the rationale for moral behavior unclear. People justify immoral behavior by suggesting that this is how things are done here or that others are doing the same thing and they, too, must act this way to maintain their competitiveness. Consider, for example, the recent doping scandals in Major League Baseball and cycling. In both cases, the incidents and extent of performance-enhancing drug (PED) use initially may have been sporadic, but when regulators and officials turned a blind eye, the use of steroids and human growth hormone spread. Early adopters of these drugs justified their use in a variety of ways: to recover from injury, to be able to stay in the game, to help them recover from long workouts. Eventually some baseball players and cyclists were using PEDs just to keep up with the competition. Little by little, PED use spread, and when cheating became the norm, it no longer seemed so wrong.

Consider also the representation/agency business. Agents now pursue younger and younger athletes. Even though some agents may be hesitant to do this, many have come to believe they have to follow suit to win clients. This same sort of muddled moral thinking can push college coaches to act immorally when recruiting athletes. When one coach offers certain inducements to a recruit such as reduced rates on hotel rooms or merchandise, other coaches may feel compelled to offer similar ones out of fear of losing a potential star recruit.

Corruption spreads little by little through an organization or a sport. Once it becomes systemic, there is usually no way to fix the problem, at least not without some serious consequences. These usually extend far beyond the people who initiated the immoral behavior. The Bernie Madoff investment scandal, discussed earlier, impacted thousands of investors, including many nonprofit foundations and the ownership group of the New York Mets. The Lance Armstrong doping scandal had an impact on the Livestrong Foundation, cancer survivors, and his primary sponsor, Nike. Further, the scandal revealed weaknesses in the governance of the sport and resulted in dramatic changes in the structure and management of professional cycling.

Moral Reasoning and the Changing Nature of Work

Contemporary society is characterized by innovation, which continually presents new ethical dilemmas. Consider, for example, how computer technology forces us to think about privacy and intellectual property in new ways. It was once thought unsportsmanlike for coaches to send in plays from the sideline in football (quarterbacks called the plays). Now coaches call in plays from booths high above the playing field, utilizing technological advances. This changes ideas about the role of the coach.

What we consider to be right or wrong, ethical or unethical, changes as society progresses or changes. Technology, for example, has made it much easier to spy on other teams. Teams

have always tried to steal signs, but in the past, coaches did this with only the naked eye and notation. Knowing this, teams changed up their signs just enough to throw the other teams off. In 2007, Bill Belichick, head coach of the New England Patriots, was fined half a million dollars for stealing the New York Jets' defensive signals with a video camera. In addition, the team was ordered to pay $250,000 and had to give up one draft pick. This may seem like a stiff penalty for doing more efficiently what coaches have been trying to do for decades. Belichick's intent was to review the videotape to learn defensive signs or patterns of signs to decode the Jets' system and use the knowledge in the next game. The use of technology to steal signs pushed what some might argue is unethical behavior into an immoral act. NFL Commissioner Roger Goodell called Belichick's scheme a "calculated and deliberate attempt to avoid long-standing rules designed to encourage fair play and promote honest competition on the playing field" (Associated Press, 2007, para. 4). Goodell's severe punishment reflects his understanding of the potential of new technologies to ruin the game.

As society changes, we periodically need to assess whether our current practices are in keeping with the values that underlie a just society or fair sport. Moral and ethical principles evolve over time. To make moral decisions in the sport industry, managers must understand the responsibilities and duties of their jobs. As discussed, people never hold only one position in society and therefore cannot simply adopt one set of moral guidelines. Managers have to assess their responsibilities and choose virtues to help them complete their work fairly and morally.

Key Skills

Although sport organizations tend to operate as a whole, sport managers must remember that all sport organizations are made up of individuals who have certain duties to perform. Each person brings something unique to the workplace and each person's job requires certain moral behaviors. Each and every individual in a sport organization has the ability to make a difference within that sport organization. At the same time, the organization can shape the behavior of individuals. How, then, can sport managers attempt to establish a moral work climate?

Ensuring Morality in the Workplace

The complexity of competing interests in sport makes moral and ethical dilemmas especially difficult to resolve. Sometimes athletes are simple participants in an athletic competition, whereas at other times they are businesspeople who have to reconcile endorsements or salaries relative to the game and their willingness to play. Rules designed to protect the integrity of sport operate uncomfortably alongside the business structure underwriting it. Increasingly, managers, athletes, and coaches have to operate under commercial and noncommercial principles simultaneously, and it is easy for the distinction between the two to become blurred.

This complexity makes decision making more difficult—and more critical—for sport managers. There are ways, however, to simplify the decision-making process and ensure decisions are made as intelligently and conscientiously as possible. Organizations can help individuals make moral choices by promoting and supporting moral reasoning in four ways:

1. Establish clear standards of moral behavior (such as codes of conduct) and publicize them within the organization.

2. Encourage employees to periodically examine and review their individual moral judgments through self-examination.

3. Provide support structures through which employees can consult each other during and after the decision-making process.

4. Make clear that violations of codes of conduct will not be tolerated and publicize a process for enforcing codes within the organization.

Self-Examination

One way to promote moral reasoning is to ask employees to think about hypothetical ethical dilemmas. This strategy assumes most people want to make the correct and moral decision. More people will do the right thing if they think about ethical behavior prior to making important decisions or if they think people in their organization care about their behavior. Self-examination is an effective tool to remind people of ethical actions and express institutional concern for ethical issues.

A self-examination does not have to be reviewed by management to be effective, nor is it necessary to take severe punitive measures against those who do poorly. The NCAA, for example, requires all coaches involved in recruiting to take and pass a test of their knowledge of recruiting rules (NCAA, 2002). It is not a difficult test, and most coaches pass it with little trouble. Coaches who fail the test can retake it until they pass. The test is not designed to keep immoral coaches from recruiting, but rather to remind coaches of "right" actions. The simple act of reviewing the rules reminds coaches of them and reinforces the view that abiding by the rules matters. Despite this, both the number of major violations and the severity of those violations are continually increasing (Mahony, Fink, & Pastore, 1999). It appears that self-examination may not be enough to make college coaches do the right thing, as they are constantly pressured to engage in questionable recruiting practices to remain competitive.

Self-examinations can be performed on the organizational level as well. The NCAA instituted an accreditation process mandating that athletic departments review their organizational practices (NCAA, 2002). A committee made up of outside experts reviews the athletic department and makes recommendations about how the department might better fulfill the mission of the NCAA. The real benefit of the accreditation program is the process of preparing for the review. It forces department administrators to examine their day-to-day practices in light of institutional goals. Such reflection might not happen otherwise, given the demands placed on most sport management professionals working in athletic programs.

© Photodisc

Forum for Moral Discourse

Isolation contributes greatly to immoral behavior. Because morality is tied to social situations, communication is critical in deterring corruption and resolving ethical dilemmas. Employees should be encouraged to get together to discuss where and how they face specific problems. These discussions help employees understand they are not alone in making difficult choices and that their colleagues can provide significant insight, perspective, and help. The process takes the pressure off individuals and clarifies the issues at stake. It also brings employees together to resolve problems. Discussions of ethical or moral behavior can be incorporated into normal management systems, such as staff meetings or sales meetings. Decisions should not be reviewed only after they have been made. Employees should be encouraged to consult with one another and with their supervisors during the decision-making process. This helps them avoid making wrong choices, leaving out important parts of the decision, or becoming overwhelmed by the weight and complexity of issues.

Forums for discussion should not be confined to individual organizations. This is especially true for managers. Because management is often the smallest branch of an organization, there may not be an effective forum for the exchange of ideas. Annual conventions, executive education, or management training may be employed as forums for ethical discourse. Informal settings such as lunches among friends, confidential calls to colleagues with similar responsibilities, or casual conversations at a golf outing also contribute to keeping the discussions alive.

Consequences

Finally, employees need to know there are consequences for immoral behavior. Even in the best organizations, some people will be motivated solely by self-interest. However, if people understand that corruption comes with certain risks, they become less likely to engage in immoral acts. Simply making consequences clearly understood can eliminate much poor judgment. People need to understand they will lose their jobs, customers, or eligibility if caught violating rules. By making the consequences of immoral acts clear, organizations help promote ethical actions.

To be effective, discipline must meet two criteria: It must be meaningful and it must be enforceable. One complaint about rules that impose fines on professional athletes or professional team owners is that some of these individuals earn so much money that fines of even thousands of dollars are of little consequence to them. Furthermore, sometimes an athlete's team will pay a fine imposed on the athlete. Thus, fines have limited impact on behavior and are not meaningful in many cases. All the rules in the world will be ineffective if they are not enforceable, which is the second criterion

of discipline. For example, prior to the 1980s, schools and coaches had little fear they would be punished by the NCAA because the NCAA enforcement staff was woefully inadequate to investigate charges of corruption (Mitchell, Crosset, & Barr, 1999).

Summary

Sport managers need to be aware of the importance of morality and ethics in the sport workplace. The decisions sport managers make on a daily basis affect many people, ranging from athletes to team owners to fans. Therefore, sport managers need to understand the far reaching effects of their decisions and how management structures and personal values shape those decisions. Incorporating codes of ethics, self-examinations, forums for moral disclosure, and statements of consequences for ethical violations into organizational documents helps ensure that sport managers and employees make the "right" decisions.

Key Terms

absolutism, code of conduct, code of ethics, ethical decision making, ethical dilemma, ethical reasoning, ethics, morality, moral principles, morals, relativism

References

Adelson, B. (1999). *Brushing back Jim Crow: The integration of minor league baseball in the American South*. Charlottesville, VA: University of Virginia Press.

Associated Press. (2007). NFL fines Belicheck, strips Patriots of draft pick. Retrieved from http://www.nfl.com/news/story ?id=09000d5d80251b7e&template =with-video&confirm=true

Australia Sports Commission. (n.d.). Officials code of behavior. Retrieved from http://www.ausport.gov.au/participating /officials/tools/safety_and_ethics/ethics /officials_code_of_behaviour

BC Athletics. (n.d.). BC Athletics codes of conduct. Retrieved from http://www .bcathletics.org/main/codesofconduct.htm

Cooke, R. A. (1991). Danger signs of unethical behavior: How to determine if your firm is at ethical risk. *Journal of Business Ethics, 10*, 249–253.

DeSensi, J. T., & Rosenberg, D. (1996). *Ethics in sport management*. Morgantown, WV: Fitness Information Technology.

England Basketball. (2002). Codes of conduct. Retrieved from http://www.copleybasketball.co.uk/Conduct.pdf

Fraleigh, W. P. (1993). Codes of ethics: Functions, form and structures, problems and possibilities. *Quest, 45*, 13–21.

Geelong Cricket Association. (2013). Code of conduct. Retrieved from http://gca.vic.cricket.com.au/content.aspx?file=2105|24421j

Gough, R. (1994). NCAA policy's strangling effect on ethics. *For the Record, 5*(3), 3–5.

Hums, M. A., & MacLean, J. C. (2013). *Governance and policy in sport organizations*. (3rd ed.). Scottsdale, AZ: Holcomb-Hathaway Publishing.

International Health, Racquet and Sports Club Association. (2010). IHRSA associate member code of conduct. Retrieved from http://www.ihrsa.org/associate-code-of-conduct/

Jacobs, J. (1992). *Systems of survival: A dialogue on the moral foundations of commerce and politics*. New York, NY: Random House.

Jordan, J. S., Greenwell, T. C., Geist, A. L., Pastore, D., & Mahony, D. (2004). Coaches' perceptions of conference codes of ethics. *Physical Educator, 61*(3), 131–145.

Josephson Institute of Ethics. (2013). The six pillars of character. Retrieved from http://www.josephsoninstitute.org/MED/MED-2sixpillars.htm

Mahony, D., Fink, J., & Pastore, D. (1999). Ethics in intercollegiate athletics: An examination of NCAA violations and penalties, 1952–1997. *Professional Ethics, 7*(2), 53–74.

Mahony, D., Geist, A., Jordon, J., Greenwell, T. C., & Pastore, D. (1999). Codes of ethics used by sport governing bodies: Problems in intercollegiate athletics. *Proceedings of the Congress of the European Association for Sport Management, 7*, 206–208.

Mitchell, R., Crosset, T., & Barr, C. (1999). Encouraging compliance without real power: Sport associations regulating teams. *Journal of Sport Management, 13*, 216–236.

National Collegiate Athletic Association. (2002). *2002–2003 NCAA Division I manual*. Indianapolis, IN: Author.

Petry, E. (2001). EOA survey: Companies seeking to integrate ethics through the whole organization. *Ethikos, 15*(1), 1–3, 16.

Sims, R. R. (1992). The challenge of ethical behavior in organizations. *Journal of Business Ethics, 11*, 505–513.

Solomon, R. C. (1992). *Above the bottom line: An introduction to business ethics*. Fort Worth, TX: Harcourt, Brace.

Speed Skating Canada. (2007). *Speed Skating Canada officials manual level 1*. Ottawa, ON: Author.

Youth Sports Research Council. (2002). Code of conduct law, 74 New Jersey Stat. Ann. C.5: 17-1, et. seq.

Zinn, L. M. (1993). Do the right thing: Ethical decision making in professional and business practice. *Adult Learning, 5*, 7–8, 27.

Part II

Amateur Sport Industry

Chapter 7 High School and Youth Sport

Chapter 8 Collegiate Sport

Chapter 9 International Sport

Chapter 7

Dan Covell

High School and Youth Sport

Learning Objectives

Upon completion of this chapter, students should be able to:

1. Evaluate the importance of school and youth sports in contemporary American society.

2. Illustrate the need for well-trained professionals such as administrators, coaches, trainers, and officials in the school and youth sport segment.

3. Describe the historical development of school and youth programs in the United States from the mid-19th century to the present.

4. Assess the role of local, state, and national governing bodies in school and youth sports.

5. Identify the various career opportunities available in the school and youth sports industry.

6. Apply basic management principles such as programmatic goal setting, performance evaluation, budgeting, and marketing to school and youth sports.

7. Assess the importance of ethics in school and youth sports and how ethics apply to current issues such as coaches as predators, promoting gender equity, and providing participation opportunities for disabled athletes.

8. Examine the legal issues surrounding athlete eligibility in school and youth sports.

Introduction

Consider the following recent statistics:

- More than 650,000 boys and girls ages 7–18 participated on more than 50,000 teams sanctioned by the American Youth Soccer Organization (AYSO, 2011).
- Pop Warner Little Scholars, Inc., provides youth football and cheer and dance programs in 42 states and several countries around the world for approximately 425,000 youths ranging in age from 5 to 16 years (Pop Warner Little Scholars, Inc., 2012).
- Nearly 4.5 million young men and more than 3 million young women participated in high school athletics during the 2011–2012 school year (National Federation of State High School Associations, 2012a).
- More than 2 million coaches have been certified by the National Alliance for Youth Sports (NAYS), more than 65,000 families have gone through the alliance's parents' program, and more than 2,000 administrators have earned their certification credentials through the NAYS Academy for Youth Sports Administrators (NAYS, 2010).

Tables 7-1 and 7-2 show the most popular high school sports by participant, as compiled by the **National Federation of State High**

Table 7-2 Total Participants in High School Sports, 1971, 1986, 2002, and 2012

Year	Male	Female
1971	3,666,917	294,015
1986	3,344,275	1,807,121
2002	3,960,517	2,806,998
2012	4,485,167	3,207,533

Data from: National Federation of State High School Associations. (2012a). 2011–12 High School Athletics Participation Survey. Retrieved from http://www.nfhs.org/content.aspx?id=3282.

School Associations (NFHS) (see the "Governing Bodies" section of this chapter) in 2012, and participation totals over the previous three decades.

The benefits of participating in youth athletics are many. High school students who participate in athletics are found to possess, on average, better GPAs, have more self-confidence, and demonstrate leadership abilities. Students who spend no time in extracurricular activities are 49% more likely to use drugs and 37% more likely to become teen parents than those who spend 1 to 4 hours per week in extracurricular activities (U.S. Department of Education, 2002).

So what do all these facts and figures mean? The conclusion is that school and youth sports are arguably the most influential sport

Table 7-1 Top Five Boys' and Girls' High School Sports by Number of Participants, 2011–2012

Boys		Girls	
Sport	Number of Participants	Sport	Number of Participants
Football (11 man)	1,095,993	Track and field (outdoor)	468,747
Track and field (outdoor)	575,628	Basketball	435,885
Basketball	535,289	Volleyball	418,903
Baseball	474,219	Soccer	370,023
Soccer	411,757	Fast-pitch softball	367,023

Data from: National Federation of State High School Associations. (2012a). 2011–12 High School Athletics Participation Survey. Retrieved from http://www.nfhs.org/content.aspx?id=3282.

programs in the United States today and directly reflect the importance Americans place on involving youth in sport activities. Although professionals working in school and youth league sport do not garner the limelight and national prominence that sport management professionals do, working in this industry segment brings significant and important challenges and substantial personal rewards. A coach, official, or administrator at this level never lacks for responsibilities, and every day brings a fresh set of issues to tackle to ensure that the educational framework of youth athletics is maintained. To work in this segment is to make a difference in the lives of young people.

History

The recognition of the positive educational and developmental aspects of athletic participation is not a recent phenomenon. The history of youth athletic participation predates the signing of the Constitution and the formation of the United States. Native Americans played a game that French Jesuit priests called "lacrosse," because players used a stick that resembled a bishop's cross-shaped crosier. European settlers brought tennis, cricket, and several early versions of what would become baseball to America, and Africans brought to North America as slaves threw the javelin, boxed, and wrestled. Despite all this, formally organized athletic participation, particularly those programs run under the auspices of secondary educational institutions, did not emerge until the mid-nineteenth century (Swanson & Spears, 1995).

School Athletics in the Nineteenth Century

In 1838, educator Horace Mann noted that in an increasingly urbanized United States outdoor recreation space was becoming scarce and children were at risk of physical deterioration. Urban populations were doubling every decade due to steady country-to-city migration as well as immigration from Europe. In response to the common popular appeal of baseball in the nineteenth century, schools and other agencies began to promote the sport as a solution to broad social problems such as ill health and juvenile delinquency (Seymour, 1990).

Private schools in the United States were the first to provide athletic participation opportunities. At many schools, activities were informal and organized by students, with little oversight from faculty or administrators. The Round Hill School in Northampton, Massachusetts, was the first institution known to have promoted the physical well-being of its students as part of its formal mission and curriculum. The school's founders appointed a German, Charles Beck, as the instructor of gymnastics, making him the first known physical education instructor in the United States. Many other early U.S. private schools followed the model of elite English boarding schools such as Eton, Harrow, and Rugby, where athletic programs were more formalized (although still managed by students) with the intention of promoting the ideal of "muscular Christianity," creating gentlemen who were morally and physically able to go out and take on the challenges of modern life. Campus-based club teams focused on intramural-type play, which formed the early models of competition in the United States. In 1859, the Gunnery School in Washington, Connecticut, became the first school to feature games against outside competition in athletic programs actively encouraged and promoted by an administrator, school founder Frederick Gunn. Students who attended the school at the time noted that students were required to play baseball, and that Gunn "encouraged and almost compelled every kind of rational exercise as part of his scheme of character-building" (Bundgaard, 2005, p. 74). In 1878, St. Paul's School in Concord, New Hampshire, hired the

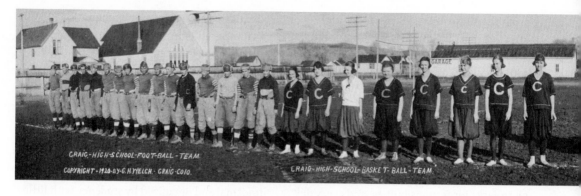

first full-time faculty member specifically to coach team sports, and in 1895, Phillips Exeter Academy, also in New Hampshire, appointed the first permanent faculty member as director of athletics (Bundgaard, 2005).

Educators at established **public schools** were much slower to embrace the value of exercise and play compared to their private school counterparts. As at the collegiate level, students organized the games. Interscholastic athletics, much as with the collegiate system after which they were patterned, were seen by students as not only an outlet for physical activity, but also as a vehicle for developing communal ties with classmates and alumni.

The acceptance of University of Chicago educator John Dewey's theories encouraging games helped to hasten the incorporation of athletics into school curricula. The State of New York required every public school to include an adjacent playground; citywide school baseball tournaments were held in the 1890s in Boston and in Cook County, Illinois; and students from several Boston area public and private schools formed the Interscholastic Football Association in 1888 (Hardy, 2003; Wilson, 1994). Concurrently, statewide high school athletic associations in Illinois and Wisconsin were formed to coordinate interscholastic competition.

School Athletics in the Twentieth Century

During the first two decades of the last century, youth athletics were popular vehicles through which newly formed secular government organizations sought to combat the proliferating ills of urban life. The social and political efforts of educators aligned with the **Progressive movement**, which touted athletics as a tool to prepare for the rigors of modern life and democracy and to assimilate immigrants into American culture. Progressives promoted child welfare by advocating for increased playground space, such as the development of year-round play spaces in Los Angeles in 1904 and in Chicago's congested South Side in 1905. Progressives also promoted formalized public school athletics as an antidote to regimented physical education curricula based on the German tradition of body-building through repetitious exercise (Dyreson, 1989).

Emerging city, state, and parochial school athletic associations coordinated competitions in baseball, track, and rifle shooting and emphasized sportsmanship and academic integrity. As a result of the movement promoting athletics as a critical part of the educational experience, government-funded educational institutions eventually assumed the

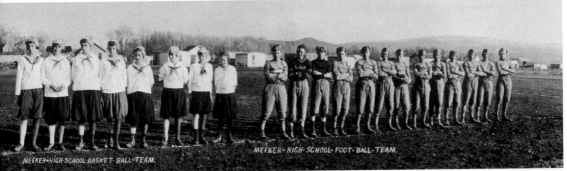

MEEKER-HIGH-SCHOOL-BASKET-BALL-TEAM.

MEEKER-HIGH-SCHOOL-FOOT-BALL-TEAM.

Courtesy of GH Welch, November 13, 1920, Library of Congress Prints and Photographs Division [LC-USZ62-127320]

administration and provision of the vast majority of athletic participation opportunities for youth in the United States (Vincent, 1994).

In the period during and immediately following World War I (1914–1918), school sports for males were promoted as a source of physical training for the armed forces without directly encouraging militarism. Sports were also seen as a means to develop social skills such as cooperation and discipline, which were valued by an increasingly ethnically diverse and industrial society. Sports also boosted student retention and graduation rates. This was important, because in 1918 only one-third of grade school students entered high school and only one in nine graduated (O'Hanlon, 1982).

During this period, athletics became entrenched in schools, and educators took control of athletics from students. However, educators had voiced concerns about their abilities to administer and teach athletics since the 1890s. Individuals such as Dudley Sargent, James Naismith, and Amos Alonzo Stagg made significant contributions toward meeting the burgeoning instructional and curricular development needs. Although students initially organized most teams, by 1924 state associations managed high school athletics in all but three states.

Nonschool Youth Sport Organizations

Athletics promoted by **nonschool agencies** emerged in various locations in the United States nearly simultaneously. The most prominent private agency to promote youth athletics was the Young Men's Christian Association (YMCA). Protestant clergyman George Williams founded the YMCA in England in 1844, and the organization established itself in the United States in 1851 to attract urban youth to Christianity through athletics. By 1900, the YMCA had grown to include 250,000 members (this number would double by 1915) at 1,400 branches, with a national athletic league under the direction of Dr. Luther H. Gulick (Putney, 1993). The Young Women's Christian Association (YWCA), established concurrently with the YMCA, began offering calisthenics in its Boston branch in 1877 and opened a new gym there in 1884. By 1916, 65,000 women nationwide attended gym classes and 32,000 attended swimming classes sponsored by the YWCA (Cahn, 1994).

From the 1930s through the 1950s, YMCA branches were opened in suburban areas that allowed female members to join, as determined by local policies. Family memberships were made available in an effort to retain and attract members. In the 1960s, the organization's leadership faced the issue of whether to reestablish its Christian evangelical elements and drift away from promoting its athletic programs, even as the exercise-seeking membership grew to over 5.5 million in 1969. The YMCA chose to emphasize individual values and growth, which dovetailed nicely with individual personal fitness goals (Putney, 1993).

The financial calamities of the Great Depression of the 1930s launched unprecedented government involvement in recreation. Private companies and businesses cut back on the athletic participation opportunities they had sponsored before the economic downturn, and government agencies were asked to fill the void. The Works Progress Administration (WPA) provided funds ($500 million by 1937) and labor for field and playground construction, and city recreation departments provided "schools" for athletic skill instruction and league coordination (Seymour, 1990).

Local government fostered participation as well. In 1931, 107 teams entered Cincinnati's boys' baseball tournament, and, in 1935, 75 teams of boys age 16 or younger played in a municipal baseball league in Oakland, California (Seymour, 1990). Many significant private and parochial youth sport organizations were also initiated during this period, including American Legion Junior Baseball in 1925, Pop Warner Football in 1929, the Catholic Youth Organization (basketball, boxing, and softball) in 1930, the Amateur Softball Association in 1933, and Little League Baseball in 1939.

Governance

The administration of school and youth sport is primarily a local affair, with most policy and procedural decisions made at the district, school, or youth-league level. However, the existence of local, state, and national **governing bodies** ensures the running of championships,

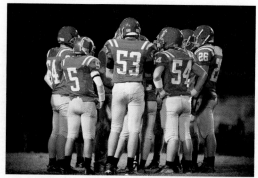
© Rena Schild/ShutterStock, Inc.

coordination of athlete eligibility, dissemination of instructional information, and implementation of certain coaching and administrative certification programs. Governing bodies also create and maintain stated rules and guidelines and apply them to all affiliated athletic programs equitably and consistently.

The National Federation of State High School Associations

The National Federation of State High School Associations (NFHS), a nonprofit organization headquartered in Indianapolis, Indiana, serves as the national coordinator for high school sports as well as activities such as music, debate, theater, and student council. NFHS encompasses all 50 individual state high school athletics and activity associations as well as the District of Columbia and a number of affiliate members. NFHS represents more than 11 million participants in more than 18,500 high schools, as well as coaches, officials, and judges through the individual state, provincial, and territorial organizations. In addition to compiling national records in sports and national sport participation rates, NFHS coordinates certification for officials; issues playing rules for 17 boys' and girls' sports; prints 8 million publications annually, including officials' manuals and case books, magazines, supplemental books, and teaching aids; holds national conferences and competitions; and acts as an advocate and lobbying agent for school-based youth sports. NFHS also maintains a high school Hall of Fame (NFHS, 2013).

Three facets comprise the organizational structure of the NFHS. The legislative body, the National Council, is made up of one representative from each member state, provincial, or territorial association. Each council member has one vote, and the council meets to conduct business twice each year. The administrative responsibilities are handled by the 12-member board of directors, elected by the National Council from professional staffs of member associations. Eight board members are elected to represent one of eight geographic regions, with the remaining four chosen on an at-large basis. The board of directors approves the annual budget, appoints an executive director, and establishes committees for conducting association business. NFHS has a paid administrative and professional staff, including the current executive director, Robert Gardner (NFHS, 2012b).

Other professional organizations and services offered by or affiliated with the NFHS include the following (NFHS, 2013):

- National Interscholastic Athletic Administrators Association (NIAAA)
- NFHS Coaches Association
- NFHS Officials Association
- NFHS Music Association
- NFHS Speech, Debate and Theatre Association

State Associations

The NFHS model is typically replicated at the state level by **state associations**. State associations, which are also nonprofit, have a direct role in organizing state championships and competitions in athletics and activities and are the final authority in determining athlete eligibility. The scope of activities, size of full-time administrative and support staff, and number of schools represented vary from state to state and are proportionally related to that state's population.

The legislative business of state associations is administered in much the same manner as the NFHS, with several general meetings each year attended by one voting representative from each member institution. Whereas championships and competitions are administered by the associations, committees consisting of coaches and administrators perform most of the actual duties associated with the events, including determining criteria for selection of event participants, event management, and the general rules pertaining to regular season competition.

National Youth League Organizations

National youth league organizations focus administrative efforts on promoting participation in a particular sport among children. The activities and duties of these organizations are illustrated by examining one such association, Little League Baseball, the best-known youth athletic organization in the United States. Factory worker Carl Stotz founded Little League Baseball in 1939 as a three-team league in Williamsport, Pennsylvania. The organization, initially for boys ages 9–12 (girls were admitted in 1974), grew to 867 teams in 12 states over the next decade. By 1963, Little League boasted 30,000 teams in 6,000 leagues on four continents. In 2012, there were 7,006 Little League programs in 79 countries (Little League, 2013).

The Little League governance structure is organized on four levels: local, district, region, and international. Each league program is organized within a community that establishes its own boundaries (with the total population not to exceed 20,000) from which it may register players. A board of directors guides each local league and is responsible for the league's day-to-day operations. Ten to 20 teams in a given area usually comprise a district. The district administrator organizes district tournaments. The district administrator reports to the regional director, of which there are five in the United States and four internationally. All Little League operations are led by the president and chief executive officer (CEO) who report to a board of directors comprising eight district administrators elected to rotating terms by their colleagues at the periodic International Congress. The current Little League CEO is Stephen Keener (Little League, 2013).

Career Opportunities

Courtesy of Mary Hufford, Archive of Folk Culture, Library of Congress [AFC 1999/008 CRF-MH-C101-13]

The employment opportunities in school and youth league sport are similar. What follows is a brief listing of the roles critical to the operation of school and youth league sport, including major job functions and responsibilities.

School Athletic Director/League Director

Supervising a school athletic program or youth league includes responsibilities such as hiring, supervising, and evaluating coaches; coordinating nearly all facets of contest management, including the hiring and paying of officials and event staff; setting departmental/league training and disciplinary policies; determining departmental/league budgets; overseeing all associated fund-raising; determining and verifying game scheduling and athlete eligibility; transmitting relevant publicity; and

handling public relations. In addition, most school athletic directors do not have the luxury of devoting their whole working day to this job. Most must also coach, teach, perform other administrative roles, or do some combination of all three.

Youth league directors must sometimes perform their duties on a completely voluntary basis, without compensation or work release time. Compared to coaches, **school athletic directors** have less direct involvement with athletes and perform their duties less publicly, but these administrators by no means have a less important role in successfully managing an athletic program. Some of their major responsibilities and concerns are risk management, insurance, employment issues, sexual harassment, gender equity, and fund-raising.

The job description for a school or youth league coach is indeed demanding. **Coaches** face complex human resource management issues, deal with constant and extreme pressure to perform successfully, and work long and irregular hours for low (or no) pay. Significant knowledge of injuries and physical training, equipment, and bus-driving skills are also highly recommended. High school coaches in most states are also required to pass certain certification requirements, many of which are delivered through the NFSH.

Because injuries inevitably occur in athletic activities, **trainers** and **physical therapists** are critical for school and youth sport operation. Most school districts and state associations require medical personnel and emergency medical transportation to be present at football games or other high-risk contact sports, although the dictates of youth leagues vary. Most schools and leagues do not have the personnel or financial resources to provide trainers or medical personnel (e.g., paramedics, certified athletic trainers, emergency medical technicians, physicians) for all contests, and such personnel are infrequently provided for practices.

Providing adequate medical treatment for injured athletes significantly reduces the risk of litigation against coaches, schools, and leagues and can reduce injury rates by 41%. However, because 62% of injuries occur during practices and training (PRWeb, 2010), some schools are looking to contract trainers or medical personnel to be present at all times and to set up year-round training and fitness programs.

Schools and leagues can contract trainers from a local hospital, physical therapy center, or fitness club. The position can also be linked to an internal job, such as a classroom or physical education teacher, a school doctor or nurse, or an athletic administrator. Such programs benefit the school athletic program and can provide a student-trainer with an educational opportunity. Salaries for this position vary widely, depending on the employment status (part time or full time) and the other job responsibilities linked to the post.

Officials and Judges

Officials and **judges** are vital to the proper administration of school and youth athletics, and they share much of the public scrutiny associated with coaches and administrators. Officials are employed by schools and leagues but are considered independent contractors because the school or league exhibits no supervisory capacity over officials. Depending on the locale, officials may require certification from national, state, and local sanctioning organizations to gain approval to work in interscholastic events. Most youth leagues rely on volunteers with such accreditation to officiate contests. Although this aids in the logistical operations, the use of such nonprofessionalized personnel can leave a league liable for litigation for the actions of these individuals. Officials possess a significant amount of control over game administration and supervision. In game situations, officials usually have the responsibility and authority to postpone and cancel games due to

inclement and dangerous weather situations, and they are responsible for controlling rough and violent play. At this level, officials work on a part-time basis, because compensation is not sufficient to cover full-time employment. Officials are also responsible for submitting documentation of their income to the IRS for tax purposes.

Application of Key Principles

Management

Programmatic Goals

Critics of highly organized youth athletics often cite that such activities create increased pressure to win and rob children of the opportunity to create and initiate their own play and competition. Professional physical educators and organizations such as the American Alliance for Health, Physical Education, Recreation and Dance (AAHPERD) decried the "win at all costs" approach as early as the 1930s (Berryman, 1978). Today, these concerns continue with many examples, some of which impact the health and safety of participants.

A recent issue that has garnered significant national attention is that of head injuries, not just in school and youth sport, but at all levels, especially in the sport of football. Concussions occur as a result of contact to the head, which leads to a series of changes in which the brain's nerve cells stop functioning as they should. Proper rest—meaning limited physical and mental activity—can lead to recovery in almost all circumstances. A recent study published in the *Journal of Sports Medicine* collected data from 100 high schools across the United States and found 544 concussions reported in the 2008–2009 academic year, 309 of which (56.8%) occurred in football and 65 (11.9%) in girls' soccer. It is estimated that 136,000 concussions occur in U.S. high school sports annually (Conaboy, 2011).

Concerns about the long-term effects of concussions and repeated head trauma have led to changes in practice and game operations. In Massachusetts in 2010, the state legislature passed a law requiring that all school-based team personnel—coaches, trainers, volunteers, players, and parents—be trained annually in concussion-recognition techniques. In addition, before every new season student-athletes must file a history of head injuries to be reviewed by school medical personnel, and participants who are diagnosed with a concussion must develop a plan with athletic and medical personnel for the resumption of athletic and academic activities. The new rules are "a great step in the right direction," according to Dr. William Meehan, director of the sports concussion clinic at Children's Hospital in Boston, but some school officials have criticized the rules, claiming that they create a whole new system of demands and requirements on programs already short on resources (Conaboy, 2011, p. G12). At other school districts, such as Fairfax County (Virginia), some athletic participants are required to submit to a baseline IMPACT (Immediate Post-concussion Assessment and Cognitive Testing) evaluation, similar to the one administered to NFL players. Fairfax County schools have administered 35,000 IMPACT evaluations in the last 4 years. The American Academy of Pediatrics recommends that all youth athletes participating in contact sports take the test (Brady, 2011).

Other sport managers are also seeking to decrease the number and severity of injuries, but think that reducing the equipment used is the correct approach. In the sport of women's lacrosse, helmets are banned (except for goalkeepers). Over 250,000 women are now playing the sport in the United States, and body checking at all levels of the sport is illegal. Mouth guards and eye guards are required. According to Dr. Margaret Putukian, chairwoman of U.S. Lacrosse's safety committee: "What we've seen is that behavior can change when athletes feel more protected, especially when it comes to the head and helmets . . . And they aren't as protected as they might think." Although the sport does have the third-highest rate of concussions (behind basketball and soccer) for girls' interscholastic sport, one player did admit, "I would be more likely to take risky checks . . . If (an opponent were) wearing a helmet, I don't have to worry about physically hurting her." U.S. Lacrosse president Steve Stenersen summarized the approach this way: "Everybody looks at equipment intervention as the end-all, be-all—but it's not, and the football discussion bears that out." He stated that the sport is better off emphasizing education and rules enforcement and to keep the game unchanged (Schwarz, 2011, p. B13).

Performance Evaluation and Supervision

Coaches are the principal supervisors of the athletic activities of their teams, and it is their responsibility to provide and ensure a reasonably safe environment for all participants. A coach can ensure a safe environment by issuing the proper equipment, maintaining issued equipment, ensuring that all participants have had physical examinations and been found fit to participate, and maintaining the various necessary forms of documentation (confirmation of physical status, confirmation of eligibility, proof of insurance, parent permission to participate). In terms of the actual play of participants, coaches are responsible for organizing drills, ensuring that physical mismatches are minimized, maintaining safe practice and playing grounds, suspending practice or play during dangerous weather conditions, and monitoring locker rooms during the time preceding and following activities. In play situations, coaches must monitor activities to be sure that student-athletes are not performing in an improper and dangerous manner that might harm themselves and/or other participants.

Financial Concerns

Although school and youth sport organizations are nonprofit enterprises, this does not mean that associated programs are not concerned with controlling costs and maintaining balanced budgets. This issue has been particularly problematic since 2008, as the global economic recession has meant that many school and youth programs across the United States have severely curtailed athletic offerings in light of reduced funding from local and state sources. At the youth sport level, parents are primarily responsible for footing the bill for the expenses related to participation, as organizations such as Little League are not generally publicly funded. Consider the sport of baseball and the cost for basic equipment items detailed in Table 7-3.

Mike May, spokesperson for the Sporting Goods Manufacturers Association, admits that the high prices can be a significant burden. "It's dizzying at times," he said of the associated cash outlay for purchases, adding that "the accessories make the experience more complete. Parents want their kids to look like Derek Jeter." Baseball and softball equipment purchases totaled just over $1 billion in 2010. One Cincinnati-area father of a baseball player reported that he spent a total of $11,704 for fees, travel, and equipment for his two children in 2011. "Looking back on it, you would not think we were sane people," the dad wrote, "but the circle we were in, we were normal." Travel costs for high-level leagues has been the fastest-growing slice of the participation expense pie, and the league seasons are growing longer and longer every year. As a result, these upward spiraling expenses can keep cash-strapped families from involving their kids in these types of sports (Tanier, 2012, p. B14).

But a few public school districts are bucking the austerity trend in light of substantial interest in programmatic success. Consider the case of Allen High School, the third-biggest high school in Texas (5,388 students in grades 9–12, with 1,200 football participants in grades 7–12), which in 2010 embarked upon construction of a $59.6 million football stadium. Town residents in the booming and affluent suburb (median household income is $100,843) north of Dallas approved a $119.4 million bond vote in 2009 to build a fine arts auditorium, a transportation service center for the district, and the 18,000-seat stadium, which is only the fifth largest in the state (there are 10 high school football stadiums in Texas with seating capacities over 16,000). The previous stadium seated a mere 14,000, with only 2,400 reserved seats, and had limited on-site parking, which meant that many fans had to take shuttle busses to the facility. The new venue—Eagle Stadium (no naming rights were sold, although there is scoreboard advertising, as at many high school facilities), is a sunken bowl with seating decks (bleachers, no individual seats or luxury boxes) on each side, a three-tiered press box with two hospitality rooms on the home side, and a giant video screen on an end-zone scoreboard. It also has an 84-yard-long weight room under the east stands (Bishop, 2011).

Even with the success of the program (the school won the 5-A state title in 2008, and 44 players from the 2010 team received college grant-in-aid offers) and popular support (families hold season tickets for decades, with a

Table 7-3 Cost of Basic Baseball Equipment

Item	Cost
Bat	$249.00
Helmet	$39.99
Batting glove	$19.99
Pants	$30.00
Socks	$9.99
Cleats	$51.99
Total	**$400.96**

Data from: M. Tanier. (2012, April 24). Young players, big costs. *New York Times*, pp. B11, B14.

cost of just $40 a season), some have criticized the project as fiscally irresponsible, especially as education budgets throughout the state and the country are being cut. "What do I say to that?" responds district athletic director Steve Williams. "I say we're in a community that overwhelmingly voted to build the stadium . . . Look, football has always been a big deal here. This is Texas . . . It's about tra-di-tion," added Williams, accentuating each syllable (Bishop, 2011, p. Y3).

Marketing

Corporations Profiting from School and Youth Sport Participation

Most of you are well aware of the impact of ESPN on the national and international sports landscapes and are probably also aware that ESPN's parent company is the Disney Corporation. Disney is also impacting the school and youth sport world through its Wide World of Sports Complex in Lake Buena Vista, Florida. In 1997, Disney Sports Enterprises created a $100 million sports facility to lure athletes and coaches and to steer more tourists to its Orlando-area theme parks. Today, the 255-acre complex encompassing a variety of indoor and outdoor venues hosts more than 350 amateur and professional events each year in 60 different sports (ESPN Wide World of Sports, 2013).

Expanding Participation Opportunities

More than 7 million students participate in athletic programs at NFSA-member schools, and there has been growing interest in developing participation opportunities for an even greater number of nontraditional youths, including home-schooled and special education students. Twenty-five states now allow the rising number of home-schooled students to play sports at public schools with varying restrictions, according to the Home School Legal Defense Association (HSLDA), a self-described "nonprofit advocacy organization established to

defend and advance the constitutional right of parents to direct the education of their children and to protect family freedoms" based in Virginia (HSLDA, 2011, p. 1).

In 2012, senators in the Virginia legislature opted to kill a proposed measure that had passed the state's Republican-controlled House of Delegates earlier that year. Patrick Foss, a top teenage soccer player from Virginia, wanted to try out as a kicker on the football team at Freedom High School in South Riding, his local public high school, but because he was home-schooled he was ineligible. "My parents pay the same exact taxes as my next-door neighbor who plays varsity sports," he said. "I just want to be part of the community. You shouldn't have to pick between athletics and academics" (Longman, 2012, p. 1). Virginia state officials say that nearly 32,000 children are home-schooled in the state, but the HLSDA claims there are twice that number (Kumar, 2012).

At Grandview High School, a public school of 2,700 students near Denver, Colorado, a collaboration with the Special Olympics has allowed nearly two dozen special education students to participate on "unified" basketball and cheerleading squads. More than 2,000 schools in 42 states have similar unified teams, which have been promoted with money from the U.S. Department of Education. With unified basketball, modified rules require at least three players with cognitive disabilities for each team be on the court. The remaining players can be partner athletes, who typically do not take over game plays. In Colorado, 20 high schools field unified programs, with 325 special education students participating (Frosch, 2012).

At Grandview, unified games are usually played between varsity and junior varsity contests. School principle Kurt Wollenweber stated that the teams have "transformed the culture of this school. It was almost as if these kids weren't noticed before we began doing this. I don't think anyone realized how power-ful (the teams) are." Assistant Principle Jon Hoerl helped start the program there when he was the athletic director. "The kids get to wear the same uniforms, the same warm-ups. We announce the lineups. The whole idea is to get them the mainstream experience of a high school athlete. They just want to be included," Hoerl said. Georgi McFail, who suffers from Apert Syndrome, a genetic disease character-ized by severe physical deformities, joined the unified spirit squad at the urging of her mother. "I get to go cheer for the games," she said, "and the varsity cheerleaders have become my good friends." The experience is also transformative for partner athletes. Payton Soicher, a senior at Grandview, also plays on the unified team. "These guys are not my teammates anymore; they are more my friends," he said. Grandview unified coach Cory Chandler, who also coaches baseball and football at the school, stated, "It's unlike any coaching experience I've ever had. I never got teary-eyed during basketball or foot-ball. With this, I fight back tears during every game" (Frosch, 2012, p. D7).

Ethics

Coaches as Predators

Many today are quite familiar with the sad and sickening case of decades of child sexual abuse perpetrated by Jerry Sandusky during and after his tenure as an assistant football coach at Penn State University. In 2012, a jury in a Pennsylvania state court found Sandusky guilty of repeatedly sexually assaulting 10 boys, all of them from disadvantaged homes and backgrounds. In addition, several members of the Penn State athletic and university adminis-tration, including university president Graham Spanier and longtime head football coach Joe Paterno, were fired for failing to report their knowledge of Sandusky's actions to law enforce-ment personnel (Drape, 2012).

Unfortunately, such incidents of sexual predation have not been restricted to the Penn State campus. Numerous examples exist where youth league coaches acted similarly with male and female children. Experts note that youth coaches have close relationships with their child participants, periods of unsupervised access, and hold a position of trust and authority that can often keep children from reporting inci-dents to parents or other authority figures. "It's not new," says Dr. Sandra Kirby, a researcher who has examined such incidents, "but in sports it seems we are doomed to be shocked and appalled all over again" (Zinser, 2011, p. Y1). To support Kirby's point, across Pennsyl-vania at about the time the Sandusky allega-tions broke, Francis Murphy, athletic director and baseball and football coach at Archbishop Carroll High School in Radnor Township, was arrested and charged with seeking sexual favors from a former male student at the school in exchange for sneakers and other athletic gear. Murphy was taken into custody outside a local ice cream store where he said he expected to meet the teen for sex. He later pleaded guilty to the charge, for which he faced up to 14 years in prison (Martin, 2011).

All sport organizations, especially those managing school and youth sport programs, have been impacted by the Sandusky and other similar cases. In light of these incidents, legislators in more than a dozen states, includ-ing California, Pennsylvania, West Virginia, and Washington, have introduced bills add-ing coaches and athletic directors to the list of "mandatory reporters" of suspected child abuse. Some bills would impose significant punishments, including fines, felony charges, and potential prison time (McKinley, 2012). Background checks of coaches are also on the rise. The National Council of Youth Sports (NCYS), an umbrella organization of 200 youth sport organizations, has recommended adding expanded and tightened criteria to such background checks (NCYS, 2012). Other national governing bodies have moved to set specific guidelines as well. In response to sexual molestation abuse allegations against former CEO and president Robert "Bobby" Dodd, the Amateur Athletic Union (AAU) also announced mandatory background checks for the 50,000-plus coaches and volunteers in their programs. The organization, which lacks the oversight and enforcement of many national governing bodies and has struggled in the past to curb recruiting and athlete exploitation in sports such as boys' basketball, did not explain how the background checks would be conducted ("AAU to Announce," 2012).

Beyond these legal and procedural dictates, reaction to these incidents has caused more subtle changes in how coaches interact with participants. "I have become even more careful about being the initiator of hugs," admitted Dug Barker, a coach of a variety of youth sports in Louisville, Kentucky. "And I am very careful with words and phrases that can have double meanings." Other coaches are equally wary, including Karen Ronney, a professional tennis instructor in San Diego, California. "One potentially negative situation can destroy a career or life. Possibly my own." Such concerns may cause many able adults to forgo involvement in school and youth sport, but some managers discount such misgivings. Sally S. Johnson, executive director of NCYS, stated flatly: "I'm sure there's other people out there who want to coach." That might be true, but any meaningful background check system, like tests for performance-enhancing drugs, must protect against falsely accusing innocent parties. In the town of Mill Hall, near the Penn State campus, Little League coach Bill Garbrick agreed. "How it affects coaching Little League? It's certainly going to make it a little more difficult" (McKinley, 2012, p. 18).

© bikeriderlondon/ShutterStock, Inc.

Gender Equity

Most sex discrimination challenges in high school athletics have been based on state or U.S. Constitution equal protection clauses, state equal rights amendments, Title IX of the Education Amendments of 1972, or a combination thereof. Gender equity is a flashpoint of controversy for schools, but less so for youth leagues, unless they depend on municipal funding or utilize public facilities. Administrators are responsible for ensuring that athletic programs treat boys and girls equally. The NFHS states as one of its legal foundations for the administration of high school athletics that interscholastic athletic programs must demonstrate equity or substantive and continuous progress toward equity in all facets of girls' and boys' athletics.

However, even though Title IX is the law of the land, certain factors influence how girls play. A recent study indicated that in suburban locations girls play sports at essentially the same rate as boys, but in urban areas only 36% of girls surveyed describe themselves as moderately involved athletes. Some of this difference can be attributed to money, as schools struggle with resources to sustain basic programs. Another factor is that many urban families, many of whom are recent immigrants and have low incomes, see the benefits of participation for their sons but not for their daughters, believing that girls have more responsibilities in the areas of family care, such as babysitting. The work schedules of players' parents also means that often no one gets to games to see their children play (Thomas, 2009).

All of these factors have come into play for the girls' basketball team at Middle School 61 (MS 61), a public school in the Crown Heights section of the New York City borough of Brooklyn. For one road game against Public School 161 in the Bronx, head coach Bryan Mariner had to borrow his nephew's car to drive his team through snarled city traffic to the game—with only five players—and paid the cousin of his best player $2 to cover her babysitting responsibilities for the afternoon. He also had to stop during the trip and convince the father of one player that it was safe to travel to the Bronx after the parent caught up to the car in traffic and wanted to pull his daughter off the trip. Once they made it to the school, they found out the game had to be cancelled because the other team didn't have enough players (Thomas, 2009).

There are also very real financial disparities between suburban and inner-city girls' programs. At MS 61, Mariner asks his players to contribute $80 for uniforms, transportation, and other expenses. Only half could pay in full, with most paying $1 or $2 at a time. Most nearby suburban middle schools on Long Island have a full complement of programs, and children can play at no cost. Participants are so plentiful that many schools field separate teams for seventh and eighth graders, with some schools playing extended games so that all participants can get into games. Coaches are paid as much as $5,000 a season. Mariner's salary was $2,500 (Thomas, 2009).

These differences mean that the level of play at MS 61 is somewhat ragged. Girls sometimes dribble the wrong way and often miss layups. Some are good enough to play in high school, such as Olivia Colbert, who competed in a citywide girls' tournament at Hunter College. When Olivia later gained acceptance to a local private parochial high school, there was concern over whether her mother, a single mother working as a school crossing guard, could afford the $5,600 tuition (Thomas, 2009).

Legal

Student-Athlete Eligibility

The pursuit of wins and championships are part of the goals and objectives for many school and youth sport organizations. Sometimes the desire to win is so overwhelming that participants and managers accidentally misinterpret or willfully ignore eligibility rules to create competitive advantages for their programs. Such was the case in 2010, when Cheverus High School, a private Catholic all-boys secondary day school in Portland, Maine, won the state's Class A basketball title. Before this, however, the Maine Principals' Association (MPA), the association that governs interscholastic sport in the state, had ruled that Cheverus's star player, Indiana Faithfull (his real name)—a transfer student from Australia whose father is American and claims his son is a U.S. citizen—had violated the MPA's "four seasons rule." The MPA ruled against Faithfull because he had participated in eight consecutive semesters, dating back from the beginning of his high

Case Study 7-1 Boarding Student-Athletes at Cardinal Ruhle Academy

Derron Damone is the athletic director at Cardinal Ruhle Academy (CRA), a private Catholic high school of 350 boys, located in Akropolis, a fading industrial city of 75,000 people in northwest Ohio. CRA has a strict jacket-and-tie dress code, a traditional curriculum focusing on math and science (along with religious education), a 90-year-old classroom building that has seen better days, and a mix of students, many of whom are first-generation immigrants from Central America, Russia, and Somalia, and some of whom travel more than 2 hours a day on the city's transportation system to attend. Sixty-five percent of the school's students are ethnic minorities.

When he took the job in 2007, Damone had been charged by CRA's head, Monsignor Gennaro (Johnny) DiNapoli, to improve the school's profile and enrollment (which had been falling due to concerns about the school's dangerous surroundings and fallout from the clergy sex-abuse scandals that had rocked the U.S. Catholic church) by expanding its athletic programs, specifically boys' basketball. At that point, he learned the school was about to undertake a significant fund-raising campaign (with a goal to raise $40 million) to refurbish its crumbling facilities. The creation of a nationally ranked boys' basketball team was going to be part of the public relations campaign to generate interest amongst alumni and prospective students. Initially the move to create a nationally prominent program had gone well. CRA had sent several players to top NCAA Division I men's basketball programs, and even had one player currently in the NBA, Jim Higgins, who played collegiate basketball for 1 year and then entered the NBA draft. Higgins, unfortunately, brought some unwanted attention as well. In the last few years, "high school" institutions have sprouted up across the United States: Lutheran Christian Academy and Rise Academy in Philadelphia; Boys to Men Academy in Chicago; God's Academy in Irving, Texas; One Christian Academy in Mendenhall, Mississippi; and Stoneridge Prep in Simi Valley, California, among others. Some of these alleged "schools," none of which have been accredited by the appropriate state education oversight organizations, have actual classes, although often for only 2 hours a day, and their students in most cases are African American male basketball players looking to become eligible to play in college.

Although CRA has never been one of these fly-by-night operations, whispers about its academics have gotten louder with each player who transfers to the school and then plays his way to a Division I grant-in-aid. Also, the hoped-for fund-raising boost that the ascendant program would bring has yet to materialize. The long-serving and much-beloved DiNapoli died in 2009, and his replacement, the much-younger and less-charismatic Walter McMullen, is well-meaning but has not been able to connect with the alumni and other potential donors to meet the lofty $40 million goal.

On a gray January morning in 2013, as he waited in the drive-through line for his morning coffee, Damone's phone buzzed. It was a text message from McMullen informing him that the school's trustees were about to approve a plan to gut an adjacent decrepit factory building and convert it into a 100-bed dormitory in an effort to coax boarding students to the school. "I believe this can be a boon to our athletic programs, especially basketball, the fortunes of which have faded since the departure of Mr. Higgins." Damone knew why McMullen and the school's trustees were considering the move. The $40 million fund-raising goal had yet to be realized, and the basketball program, while still a state power, has not won a title since Higgins had left. Would all this really help further the school's fund-raising initiatives, or was this just a short-term measure to keep the school afloat financially? "Seems pretty risky," Damone thought to himself. But he also knew the gamble could work. In his first job out of college, he had worked as a math teacher, coach, and dorm parent at Shattuck-St. Mary's School, a private, coeducational boarding and day preparatory school for grades 6–12 located in Faribault (pronounced "FAIR-eh-bow"), Minnesota. The school is affiliated with the Episcopal Dioceses of Minnesota, and currently enrolls about 450 students. Although Shattuck-St. Mary's (SSM) is a high school, its programmatic aspirations in hockey caused it to leave behind competition in the Minnesota State High School League for affiliation with USA Hockey, the national governing body for the sport sanctioned by the U.S. Olympic Committee. SSM squads are registered as a "noncommunity-based team" and can represent Minnesota in the USA Nationals playoffs every year. Today, the school fields seven teams—five for boys, two for girls. The 2011–2012 Prep team—the most advanced level—boasted a roster of players from 11 U.S. states, a Canadian province, and Latvia. On its website, the school describes the benefits of its program: A 7-month schedule, with 50 to 75 games a year and tournament play throughout the United States and Canada; player on-ice access 5 to 7 days a week, with 75 minute practices; and proficient instruction from former NHL and NCAA Division I coaches (Hunter, 2010; Shattuck-St. Mary's School, 2012).

Damone marveled at the SSM program today, based on what it was when he was there, when the hockey program was so weak that the school had been forced to enter a cooperative program with the local public high school and only five SSM players made the roster. Today it is undoubtedly a breeding ground for future college and NHL stars, including Sidney Crosby, Zach Parise, and Jonathan Toews. "But this is CRA," Damone wondered aloud. "Our facilities are crummy, and we're located in the toughest part of a very depressed city. What do we have to offer that some of these other more established programs and schools don't? There's a lot more competition for recruiting basketball talent than hockey talent, and most of the families of basketball prospects aren't exactly made of money. And who's going to live in the dorm with these kids?"

McMullen's text asked Damone to send back an initial response on how the move would impact their basketball fortunes. Damone put the phone down and drove ahead to pick up his large hazelnut coffee with cream and two sugars. He then pulled ahead to a parking spot, picked up his phone, and texted his response.

(continues)

Case Study 7-1 Boarding Student-Athletes at Cardinal Ruhle Academy (Continued)

Questions for Discussion

1. How does the issue of developing a boarding program reflect a change in CRA's program goals and focus?

2. Is the phenomenon of creating boarding programs consistent with marketing trends impacting school and youth sports?

3. With which governing bodies will Damone need to interact to determine how a boarding program might impact CRA's athletic programs?

4. With whom, if anyone, should Damone confer with to determine his action on this issue?

school career in Sydney, Australia. After using three semesters of eligibility, Faithfull transferred to Cheverus in the fall of 2007 to begin his sophomore year, and the MPA ruled he had used his final semester of eligibility in the fall of 2009. Faithfull missed the last five games of the regular season after the school reported the error (and did not contest the MPA's ruling), but he had been allowed to participate in the postseason because a state judge granted a temporary injunction restraining the MPA from barring Faithfull from playing after his parents had filed a lawsuit claiming their son had been discriminated against. Faithfull was reinstated only hours before the school's first round playoff game and went on to score 23 points in the state final as Cheverus edged Edward Little High School of Auburn, 55–50. Faithfull was later named the state's outstanding boys' basketball player for 2010 (Chard, 2011; Maxwell, 2010; Jordan, 2011; Soloway, 2010, 2012). Cheverus coach Bob Browne, who has held coaching clinics in Australia and whose son Brett was the head coach of the 2012 Australian Olympic men's basketball team, was unapologetic about the win, stating, "We went and played and the results are the results . . . We had a court order and our understanding is that you follow the court orders" (Chard, 2010, p. 2).

In May of 2011, after reviewing the case at the request of the trial judge, the Maine Human Rights Commission voted not to support Faithfull's claim that the MPA discriminated against him based on his country of origin or that the MPA's actions were retaliatory because Faithfull sued the organization, sending the case back to the trial court. In the spring of 2012, the state judge lifted the temporary restraining order, finding in favor of the MPA. Cheverus and MPA officials were scheduled to meet on August 20, 2012, to resolve the issue, but the meeting was cancelled. Early in the proceedings, MPA Executive Director Richard Durost stated that Cheverus would forfeit the state title if the MPA won its case (Jordan, 2011; "MPA Meeting," 2012).

Cheverus did indeed forfeit the title when the MPA's Interscholastic Management Committee voted 11–0 in October 2012 to strip the Stags of their 2009–2010 Class A boys' basketball title. Cheverus also was stripped of its 2009–2010 Western Maine regional title. Edward Little did not garner the title as Durost has promised, because championships were not awarded to the teams that Cheverus beat in the regional and state finals. "We certainly would have liked to have settled this long ago," said the MPA's Durost, "but the court system does not move quickly" (Jordan, 2012, p.1). Edward Little coach Mike Adams said the decision provides some closure for him and his players. "We've moved on. We've gotten past it," he said. "Nobody has called me up and offered me a Gold Ball [state championship trophy]." Adams said the majority of the players on that team do not want the title. If the offer ever came to him, he would decline it. "It still hurts to lose a game like that, and it still hurts and it will probably always hurt because we were so close," Adams added. "But for somebody to say, 'Here's a Gold Ball now,' I can't bring that moment back and bring the crowd back and say, 'Here's your crowd, here's your moment that you've worked so hard for so you can hold that ball over your head, hug your parents and jump around and have a good time'" (Whitehouse, 2012, p.1). After leaving Cheverus, Faithfull went on to play an additional season at a prep school in Connecticut, and then enrolled to play at Wofford College, an NCAA Division I member located in Spartanburg, South Carolina.

It is reasonable that the MPA, on behalf of its member schools, pursued this case, given the fact that an increasing number of international students are entering Maine schools, especially those schools that are a unique public–private hybrid, with privately chartered high schools serving a local population much in the manner of a public school. At one such school, Foxcroft Academy in Dover-Foxcroft, more than 100 students, many from China, are now enrolled, paying tuition and living in dorms built by the school. This issue is all the more problematic because the MPA permits public schools, private schools, and the public–private hybrids to join and compete in state championship competitions it administers. This mixed membership means that a school like Cheverus can, in effect, draw students from around the world to compete against public schools that draw students from a specifically circumscribed and limited geographic area, leading to potential friction in terms of determining fairness in eligibility rules and procedures.

Summary

School and youth sport has evolved from its modest beginning in New England private schools in the early 1800s to incorporate boys and girls of all ages in a multitude of sports and activities. These participation opportunities have expanded as administrators, coaches, and other associated personnel have developed the skills and expertise to deal with the challenges and issues that have accompanied this booming expansion. Although some contemporary issues complicate today's high school and youth sport landscape, the need and demand for well-run sport programs has never been greater. As long as there are boys and girls, the need for play and competition will exist, as will the need for well-trained professionals to ensure these needs will be met.

Resources

American Alliance for Health, Physical Education, Recreation and Dance (AAHPERD)
> 1900 Association Drive
> Reston, VA 20191-1598
> 800-213-7193
> http://www.aahperd.org

American Sport Education Program (ASEP)
> Box 5076
> Champaign, IL 61825-5076
> 800-747-5698; fax: 217-351-2674
> http://www.asep.com

American Youth Soccer Organization
(AYSO)

    12501 South Isis
    Hawthorne, CA 90205
    800-USA-AYSO
    http://www.soccer.org

Little League Baseball International

    P.O. Box 3485
    Williamsport, PA 17701
    570-326-1921; fax: 570-322-4526
    http://www.littleleague.org

National Federation of State High School
Associations (NFSA)

    P.O. Box 690
    Indianapolis, IN 46206

    317-972-6900; fax: 317-822-5700
    http://www.nhfs.org
    *Each state, Canadian province, and U.S.
    territory also has a high school athletic and
    activity association.*

Pop Warner Little Scholars, Inc.

    586 Middletown Blvd., Suite C-100
    Langhorne, PA 19047
    215-752-2691; fax: 215-752-2879
    http://www.popwarner.com

YMCA of the USA

    101 N. Wacker Drive
    Chicago, IL 60606
    312-977-0031
    http://www.ymca.net

Key Terms

coaches, governing bodies, judges, National Federation of State High School Associations
(NFHS), national youth league organizations, nonschool agencies, officials, physical therapists,
private schools, Progressive movement, public schools, school athletic directors, state associations, trainers, youth league directors

References

AAU to announce screening policy. (2012, June
    11). *USA Today*, p. 3C.
American Youth Soccer Organization. (2011).
    History of AYSO. Retrieved from http://ayso
    .org/AboutAYSO/history.aspx
Berryman, J. W. (1978). From the cradle to
    the playing field: America's emphasis on
    highly organized competitive sports for
    preadolescent boys. *Journal of Sports History*,
    5(1), 31–32.
Bishop. G. (2011, January 29). A $60 million
    palace. *New York Times*, pp. Y1, Y3.
Brady, E. (2011, May 26). Changing the game on
    youth concussions. *USA Today*, pp. 1C–2C.
Bundgaard, A. (2005). *Muscle and manliness: The
    rise of sport in American boarding schools*.
    Syracuse, NY: Syracuse University Press.

Cahn, S. K. (1994). *Coming on strong: Gender and
    sexuality in twentieth century women's sport.*
    New York: The Free Press.
Chard, T. (2010, March 4). Cheverus title forfeit
    is possible. *Portland (Maine) Press Herald*.
    Retrieved from http://www.pressherald.com
    /news/Cheverus-title-forfeit-is-possible
    -2010-03-04.html
Chard, T. (2011, January 28). Faithfull back in
    Maine for prep school tourney. *Portland
    (Maine) Press Herald*. Retrieved from http://
    www.pressherald.com/news/Indiana
    -Faithfull-case-still-in-limbo-2011-01-28.html
Conaboy, C. (2011, August 1). Heading off
    problems. *Boston Globe*, pp. G12–G13.
Drape, J. (2012, June 22). Sandusky found guilty
    of sexual abuse of 10 boys. *New York Times*.
    Retrieved from http://www.nytimes.com
    /2012/06/23/sports

Dyreson, M. (1989). The emergence of consumer culture and the transformation of physical culture: American sport in the 1920s. *Journal of Sport History, 16*(5), 3.

ESPN Wide World of Sports. (2013). ESPN Wide World of Sports Complex. Retrieved from http://espnwwos.disney.go.com/complex/venues/

Frosch, D. (2012, February 13). Unified teams take Special Olympics approach to school sports. *New York Times*, p. D7.

Hardy, S. (2003). *How Boston played: Sport, recreation, and community, 1865–1915.* Knoxville, TN: The University of Tennessee Press.

Home School Legal Defense Association. (2011). About HLSDA. Retrieved from http://www.hslda.org/about

Hunter, K. (2010, July 15). Shattuck-St. Mary's School—Center of hockey excellence. The Hockey Writers. Retrieved from www.thehockeywriters.com

Jordan, G. (2011, May 17). Indiana Faithfull case still in limbo. *Portland (Maine) Press Herald*. Retrieved from http://www.pressherald.com/news/Indiana-Faithfull-case-still-in-limbo-2011-05-17.html

Jordan, G. (2012, October 2). Cheverus stripped of 2010 basketball titles due to ineligible player. *Portland (Maine) Press Herald*. Retrieved from http://www.pressherald.com/news/MPA-vacates-Cheverus-basketball-titles-from-2009-10.html

Kumar, A. (2012, February 5). Bill aims to give home-schooled students access to public high school sports. *Washington Post*. Retrieved from http://www.washingtonpost.com/local/dc-politics/bill-aims-to-give-home-schooled-students-access-to-public-high-school-sports/2012/02/03/gIQAedHLsQ_story.html

Little League. (2013). Media guide. Retrieved from http://www.littleleague.org/Assets/forms_pubs/media/2013-LL-MediaGuide.pdf

Longman, J. (2012, February 9). Home schoolers are hoping to don varsity jackets in Virginia. *New York Times*, pp. A1, B12.

Martin, J. P. (2011, November 23). Former Archbishop Carroll athletic director pleads guilty to corrupting a minor. Philly.com. Retrieved from http://www.philly.com/2011-11-23/news

Maxwell, T. (2010, June 11). Faithfull lawyer whistles foul on MPA officials. *Portland (Maine) Press Herald*. Retrieved from http://www.pressherald.com/news/Faithfull-lawyer-whistles-foul-on-MPA-officials-2010-06-11.html

McKinley, J. (2012, April 15). After Penn State case, coaches face new scrutiny. *New York Times*, p. 18.

MPA meeting with Cheverus postponed. (2012, August 21). *Lewiston (Maine) Sun Journal*. Retrieved from http://www.sunjournal.com/news/local-sports/2012/08/21/mpa-meeting-cheverus-postponed/1239318

National Alliance for Youth Sports. (2010). Frequently asked questions. Retrieved from http://www.nays.org/Who_We_Are/frequently_asked_questions.cfm#1

National Council of Youth Sports. (2012). About NCYS. Retrieved from http://www.ncys.org/about/about.php

National Federation of State High School Associations. (2012a). 2011–12 high school athletics participation survey. Retrieved from http://www.nfhs.org/content.aspx?id=3282&linkidentifier=id&itemid=3282

National Federation of State High School Associations. (2012b). NFHS handbook 2012–13. pp. 5–9.

National Federation of State High School Associations. (2013). About us. Retrieved from http://www.nfhs.org/Activity3.aspx?id=3260

O'Hanlon, T. P. (1982). School sports as social training: The case of athletics and the crisis of World War I. *Journal of Sport History, 9*(1), 5.

Pop Warner Little Scholars, Inc. (2012). About Us. Retrieved from http://www.popwarner.com/About_Us.htm

PRWeb. (2010). Playing through the pain is not OK. Young athletes should play it safe to avoid injury. Retrieved from http://www.prweb.com/releases/2010/08/prweb4438484.htm

Putney, C. W. (1993). Going upscale: The YMCA and postwar America, 1950–1990. *Journal of Sport History, 20*(2), 151–166.

Schwarz, A. (2011, February 17). The best helmet may be no helmet. *New York Times,* pp. B13–B14.

Seymour, H. (1990). *Baseball: The people's game.* New York: Oxford University Press.

Shattuck-St. Mary's School. (2012). Shattuck-St. Mary's hockey. Retrieved from http://www.hockey.s-som.org

Soloway, S. (2010, February 27). Standing up when his son was told to sit. *Portland (Maine) Press Herald.* Retrieved from http://www.pressherald.com/news/standing-up-when-his-son-was told-to-sit-2010-02-27.html

Soloway, S. (2012, August 8). Discretion, for a Cheverus basketball title long past. *Portland (Maine) Press Herald.* Retrieved from http://www.pressherald.com/sports/discretion-for-a-title-long-past_2012-08-08.html

Swanson, R. A., & Spears, B. (1995). *Sport and physical education in the United States* (4th ed.). Dubuque, IA: Brown & Benchmark.

Tanier, M. (2012, April 24). Young players, big costs. *New York Times,* pp. B11, B14.

Thomas, K. (2009, June 14). A city team's struggle shows disparity in girls' sports. *New York Times,* pp. 1, 23.

United States Department of Education (2002). "No Child Left Behind: The facts about 21st century learning." Washington, D.C.

Vincent, T. (1994). *The rise of American sport: Mudville's revenge.* Lincoln, NE: University of Nebraska Press.

Whitehouse, R. (2012, October 1). MPA vacates Cheverus' 2010 Class A basketball title; EL still runner-up. *Lewiston (Maine) Sun Journal.* Retrieved from http://www.sunjournal.com/news/local-sports/2012/10/01/mpa-vacates-cheverus-2010-class-basketball-title-e/1258746

Wilson, J. (1994). *Playing by the rules: Sport, society, and the state.* Detroit, MI: Wayne State University Press.

Zinser, L. (2011, December 11). Opportunity and authority attract abusers to coaching. *New York Times,* pp. Y1, Y4.

Chapter 8

Carol A. Barr

Collegiate Sport

Learning Objectives

Upon completion of this chapter, students should be able to:

1. Assess the social and economic importance of modern intercollegiate athletics.

2. Describe the historical development of intercollegiate sport from 1852 to the present.

3. Evaluate the scope of the various governing bodies of intercollegiate athletics such as the NCAA, NAIA, and NJCAA.

4. Appraise the unique characteristics of NCAA Division I, II, and III athletic programs as well as the differences between FBS and FCS football within Division I.

5. Diagram the organizational structure of the NCAA and understand how that structure may influence the organization's decision making.

6. Identify the primary functions of the NCAA including the administration of championships, determining eligibility, promoting the welfare of student-athletes, and enforcement.

7. Analyze the importance of conference structure to intercollegiate athletics, with special emphasis on the implications of and the reasons for the recent flurry of conference realignments.

8. Recognize the various career opportunities available in intercollegiate athletics and the skills required to succeed in each of them.

9. Debate current issues of importance in intercollegiate sport such as conference realignment, the effect of Title IX, the concept of paying student athletes to participate, and hiring practices for minorities and women.

10. Assess the organizational, managerial, financial, and legal changes that are occurring in intercollegiate athletics.

Introduction

Intercollegiate athletics is a major segment of the sport industry. The number of student-athletes participating in intercollegiate athletics at all divisional levels surpassed 450,000 in 2011–2012 (Brown, 2012). Intercollegiate athletic contests are garnering increasingly more television air time as network and cable companies increase coverage of sporting events and athletic conferences create their own networks (e.g., Big Ten Network, Pac-12 Network). They are also attracting more attention from corporations seeking potential sponsorship opportunities. Television rights fees have increased dramatically. Sport sponsorship opportunities and coaches' compensation figures have escalated as well. The business aspect of collegiate athletics has grown immensely as administrators and coaches at all levels have become more involved in budgeting, finding revenue sources, controlling expense items, and participating in fund development activities. The administrative aspects of collegiate athletics have also changed. With more rules and regulations to be followed, there is more paperwork in such areas as recruiting and academics. These changes have led to an increase in the number of personnel and the specialization of positions in collegiate athletic departments. Although the number of athletic administrative jobs has increased across all divisions, jobs can still be hard to come by because the popularity of working in this segment of the sport industry continues to be high.

The international aspect of this sport industry segment has grown tremendously through the participation of student-athletes who are nonresident aliens (a term used by the NCAA for foreign student-athletes). Coaches are more aware of international talent when recruiting. Athletic teams are taking overseas trips for practice and competitions at increasing rates. College athletic games are being shown internationally, and licensed merchandise can be found around the world. It is not unusual to stroll down a street in Munich, Germany, or Montpellier, France, and see a Duke basketball jersey or a Notre Dame football jersey.

The evolution of collegiate athletics has also involved a proliferation of changes involving institutional membership in an athletic conference. These changes have significant financial implications, especially for the Bowl Championship Series (BCS) football conference affiliations, although this, too, will change with the College Football Playoff introduced in 2014–2015. But these changes have also led to historic team rivalries being dissolved. At least Ohio State and Michigan are still members of the Big Ten Conference (which currently has 12 members, not 10, and will be expanding to 14 members in 2014–2015), and Williams and Amherst are still members of the New England Small College Athletic Conference (NESCAC). These topics will be explored later in the chapter, but first let's take a look at where it all started.

History

Courtesy of George Grantham Bain Collection, 1915, Library of Congress [LC-USZ62-95947]

On August 3, 1852, on Lake Winnipesaukee in New Hampshire, a crew race between Harvard and Yale was the very first intercollegiate athletic event in the United States (Dealy, 1990).

What was unusual about this contest was that Harvard University is located in Cambridge, Massachusetts, and Yale University is located in New Haven, Connecticut, yet the crew race took place on a lake north of these two cities, in New Hampshire. Why? Because the first intercollegiate athletic contest was sponsored by the Boston, Concord & Montreal Railroad Company, which wanted to host the race in New Hampshire so that both teams, their fans, and other spectators would have to ride the railroad to get to the event (Dealy, 1990). Thus, the first intercollegiate athletic contest involved sponsorship by a company external to sports that used the competition to enhance the company's business.

The next sport to hold intercollegiate competitions was baseball. The first collegiate baseball contest was held in 1859 between Amherst and Williams (Davenport, 1985), two of today's more athletically successful Division III institutions. In this game, Amherst defeated Williams by the lopsided score of 73–32 (Rader, 1990). On November 6, 1869, the first intercollegiate football game was held between Rutgers and Princeton (Davenport, 1985). This "football" contest was far from the game of football known today. The competitors were allowed to kick and dribble the ball, similar to soccer, with Rutgers "outdribbling" its opponents and winning the game six goals to four (Rader, 1990).

The initial collegiate athletic contests taking place during the 1800s were student-run events. Students organized the practices and corresponded with their peers at other institutions to arrange competitions. There were no coaches or athletic administrators assisting them. The Ivy League schools became the "power" schools in athletic competition, and football became the premier sport. Fierce rivalries developed, attracting numerous spectators. Thus, collegiate athletics evolved from games being played for student enjoyment and participation to fierce competitions involving bragging rights for individual institutions.

Colleges and universities soon realized that these intercollegiate competitions had grown in popularity and prestige and thus could bring increased publicity, student applications, and alumni donations. As the pressure to win increased, the students began to realize they needed external help. Thus, the first "coach" was hired in 1864 by the Yale crew team to help it win, especially against its rival, Harvard University. This coach, William Wood, a physical therapist by trade, introduced a rigorous training program as well as a training table (Dealy, 1990). College and university administrators also began to take a closer look at intercollegiate athletics competitions. The predominant theme at the time was still nonacceptance of these competitive athletic activities within the educational sphere of the institution. With no governing organization and virtually nonexistent playing and eligibility rules, mayhem often resulted. Once again the students took charge, especially in football, forming the **Intercollegiate Football Association** in 1876. This association was made up of students from Harvard, Yale, Princeton, and Columbia who agreed on consistent playing and eligibility rules (Dealy, 1990).

The dangerous nature of football pushed faculty and administrators to get involved in governing intercollegiate athletics. In 1881, Princeton University became the first college to form a faculty athletics committee to review football (Dealy, 1990). The committee's choices were to either make football safer to play or to ban the sport all together. In 1887, Harvard's Board of Overseers instructed the Harvard Faculty Athletics Committee to ban football. However, aided by many influential alumni, the Faculty Athletics Committee chose to keep the game intact (Dealy, 1990). In 1895, the **Intercollegiate Conference of Faculty**

Representatives, better known as the **Big Ten Conference**, was formed to create student eligibility rules (Davenport, 1985). By the early 1900s, football on college campuses had become immensely popular, receiving a tremendous amount of attention from students, alumni, and collegiate administrators. Nevertheless, the number of injuries and deaths occurring in football continued to increase, and it was evident that more legislative action was needed.

In 1905 during a football game involving Union College and New York University, Harold Moore, a halfback for Union College, died of a cerebral hemorrhage after being crushed on a play. Moore was just one of 18 football players who died that year. An additional 149 serious injuries occurred (Yaeger, 1991). The chancellor of New York University, Henry Mitchell MacCracken, witnessed this incident and took it upon himself to do something about it. MacCracken sent a letter of invitation to presidents of other schools to join him for a meeting to discuss the reform or abolition of football. In December 1905, 13 presidents met and declared their intent to reform the game of football. When this group met 3 weeks later, 62 colleges and universities sent representatives. This group formed the **Intercollegiate Athletic Association of the United States (IAAUS)** to formulate rules that would make football safer and more exciting to play. Seven years later, in 1912, this group took the name **National Collegiate Athletic Association (NCAA)** (Yaeger, 1991).

In the 1920s, college and university administrators began recognizing intercollegiate athletics as a part of higher education and placed athletics under the purview of the physical education department (Davenport, 1985). Coaches were given academic appointments within the physical education department, and schools began to provide institutional funding for athletics.

The **Carnegie Reports of 1929**, produced from results obtained by the Carnegie Foundation after visiting 112 colleges and universities, painted a bleak picture of intercollegiate athletics, identifying many academic abuses, recruiting abuses, payments to student-athletes, and commercialization of athletics. One of the disturbing findings from this study was that although the NCAA "recommended against" both recruiting and subsidization of student-athletes, these practices were widespread among colleges and universities (Lawrence, 1987). The Carnegie Reports stated that the responsibility for control over collegiate athletics rested with the president of the college or university and with the faculty (Savage, 1929). The NCAA was pressured to change from an organization responsible for developing playing rules used in competitions to an organization that would oversee academic standards for student-athletes, monitor recruiting activities of coaches and administrators, and establish principles governing amateurism, thus alleviating the paying of student-athletes by alumni and booster groups (Lawrence, 1987).

Intercollegiate athletics experienced a number of peaks and valleys over the next 60 or so years as budgetary constraints during certain periods, such as the Great Depression and World War II, limited expenditures and growth among athletic departments and sport programs. In looking at the history of intercollegiate athletics, though, the major trends during these years were increased spectator appeal, commercialism, media coverage, alumni involvement, and funding. As these changes occurred, the majority of intercollegiate athletic departments moved from a unit within the physical education department to a recognized, funded department on campus.

Increased commercialism and the potential for monetary gain in collegiate athletics led to increased pressure on coaches to win. As a result, collegiate athletics experienced various problems with rule violations and academic abuses involving student-athletes. As these

© Aspen Photo/ShutterStock, Inc.

abuses increased, the public began to perceive that the integrity of higher education was being threatened. In 1989, pollster Louis Harris found that 78% of Americans thought collegiate athletics were out of hand. This same poll found that nearly two-thirds of Americans believed that state or federal legislation was needed to control college sports (Knight Foundation, 1993). In response, on October 19, 1989, the trustees of the Knight Foundation created the **Knight Commission**, directing it to propose a reform agenda for intercollegiate athletics (Knight Foundation, 1991). The Knight Commission was composed of university presidents, corporate executive officers and presidents, and a congressional representative. The reform agenda recommended by the Knight Commission played a major role in supporting legislation to alleviate improper activities and emphasized institutional control in an attempt to restore the integrity of collegiate sports. The

Knight Commission's work and recommendations prompted the NCAA membership to pass numerous rules and regulations regarding recruiting activities, academic standards, and financial practices.

Whether improvements have occurred within college athletics as a result of the Knight Commission reform movement and increased presidential involvement has been debated among various constituencies over the years. Proponents of the NCAA and college athletics cite the skill development, increased health benefits, and positive social elements that participation in college athletics brings. In addition, the entertainment value of games and the improved graduation rates of college athletes (although men's basketball and football rates are still a focus of concern) in comparison with the student body overall are referenced. Those critical of college athletics, though, cite the costs of fielding athletic teams (for the large majority of teams and schools), continual recruiting violations, academic abuses, and behavioral problems of athletes and coaches. These critics are concerned with the commercialization and exploitation of student-athletes as well. The "haves versus the have nots" debate in college athletics is not new. Many of the NCAA rules and regulations currently in place governing intercollegiate athletics were an attempt to level the playing field so that the richest athletic programs would not dominate.

Women in Intercollegiate Athletics

Initially, intercollegiate sport competitions were run by men for men. Sports were viewed as male-oriented activities, and women's sport participation was relegated to physical education classes. Prevailing social attitudes mandated that women should not perspire and should not be physically active so as not to injure themselves. Women also had dress codes that limited the type of activities in which they could physically participate. Senda Berenson of Smith College introduced basketball to collegiate women in 1892, but she first made sure that appropriate modifications were made to the game developed by James Naismith to make it more suitable for women (Paul, 1993). According to Berenson, "the selfish display of a star by dribbling and playing the entire court, and roughhousing by snatching the ball could not be tolerated" (Hult, 1994, p. 86). The first women's intercollegiate sport contest was a basketball game between the University of California–Berkeley and Stanford University in 1896 (Hult, 1994).

The predominant theme of women's involvement in athletics was participation. Women physical educators, who controlled women's athletics from the 1890s to the 1920s, believed that all girls and women, and not just a few outstanding athletes, should experience the joy of sport. Playdays, or sportsdays, were the norm from the 1920s until the 1960s (Hult, 1994). By 1960, more positive attitudes toward women's competition in sport were set in motion. No governance organization for women similar to the NCAA's all-encompassing control over the men existed until the creation of the **Commission on Intercollegiate Athletics for Women (CIAW)** in 1966, the forerunner of the **Association for Intercollegiate Athletics for Women (AIAW)**, which was established in 1971 (Acosta & Carpenter, 1985).

The AIAW endorsed an alternative athletic model for women, emphasizing the educational needs of students and rejecting the commercialized men's model (Hult, 1994). The AIAW and NCAA soon became engaged in a power struggle over the governance of women's collegiate athletics. In 1981, the NCAA membership voted to add championships for women in Division I. By passing this legislation, the NCAA took its first step toward controlling women's collegiate athletics. The NCAA convinced women's

athletic programs to vote to join the NCAA by offering to do the following (Hult, 1994):

- Subsidize team expenses for national championships
- Not charge additional membership dues for the women's program
- Allow women to use the same financial aid, eligibility, and recruitment rules as men
- Provide more television coverage of women's championships

Colleges and universities, provided with these incentives from the NCAA, began to switch from AIAW membership for their women's teams to full NCAA membership. The AIAW immediately experienced a 20% decrease in membership, a 32% drop in championship participation in all divisions, and a 48% drop in Division I championship participation.

In the fall of 1981, NBC notified the AIAW that it would not televise any AIAW championships and would not pay the monies due under its contract (a substantial percentage of the AIAW budget). Consequently, in 1982, the AIAW executive board voted to dissolve the association (Morrison, 1993). The AIAW filed a lawsuit against the NCAA (*Association for Intercollegiate Athletics for Women v. National Collegiate Athletic Association*, 1983), claiming that the NCAA had interfered with its commercial relationship with NBC and exhibited monopolistic practices in violation of antitrust laws. The court found that the AIAW could not support its monopoly claim, effectively ending the AIAW's existence.

Much has changed within women's college athletics since Title IX took effect in 1972. Since 1981, women's participation in collegiate athletics has increased from 74,239 to 198,103 student-athletes in 2011–2012 (NCAA, 2012a). The 2013 NCAA Division I Women's Final Four was watched by 2.3 million domestic viewers (and viewed internationally as well), with men being the majority of fans watching on TV

(Bowman, 2013). The popularity and importance of successful women's basketball programs is also reflected in the coaching salaries being provided, Geno Auriemma at the University of Connecticut receives around $2 million a year, although coaches of women's teams are paid much less than their counterparts on the men's side (Gentry & Alexander, 2012). The growth in women's sports provides evidence that college athletics today is both a men's and a women's game and has come far from its birth in 1852.

Organizational Structure and Governance

The NCAA

The primary rule-making body for college athletics in the United States is the NCAA. Other college athletic organizations include the **National Association of Intercollegiate Athletics (NAIA)**, founded in 1940 for small colleges and universities and having close to 300 member institutions (NAIA, 2013), and the **National Junior College Athletic Association (NJCAA)**, founded in 1937 to promote and supervise a national program of junior college sports and activities and currently having over 500 member institutions (NJCAA, 2013).

The NCAA is a voluntary association with 1,273 institutions, conferences, and related associations. NCAA **Division I** consists of 340 member institutions (120 in the Football Bowl Subdivision, 122 in the Football Championship Subdivision, and 98 in Division I sponsoring no football program), **Division II** comprises 290 member schools, and there are 436 active institutions within **Division III** (these NCAA division classifications are defined later in this chapter) (NCAA, 2013a). More than 430,000 student-athletes participate in NCAA sports involving 89 national championships in 23 sports (NCAA, 2013a). All collegiate athletics teams, conferences, coaches, administrators, and athletes

participating in NCAA-sponsored sports must abide by the association's rules.

The basic purpose of the NCAA as dictated in its constitution is to "maintain intercollegiate athletics as an integral part of the educational program and the athlete as an integral part of the student body and, by so doing, retain a clear line of demarcation between intercollegiate athletics and professional sports" (NCAA, 2013b, p. 1). Important to this basic purpose are the cornerstones of the NCAA's philosophy: namely, that college athletics are amateur competitions and that athletics are an important component of the institution's educational mission.

The NCAA has undergone organizational changes throughout its history in an attempt to improve the efficiency of its service to member institutions. In 1956, the NCAA split its membership into a University Division, for larger schools, and a College Division, for smaller schools, in an effort to address competitive inequities. In 1973, the current three-division system, made up of Division I, Division II, and Division III, was created to increase the flexibility of the NCAA in addressing the needs and interests of schools of varying size ("Study: Typical I-A Program," 1996). This NCAA organizational structure involved all member schools and conferences voting on legislation once every year at the NCAA annual convention. Every member school and conference had one vote, assigned to the institution's president or CEO, a structure called **one-school/one-vote**.

In 1995, the NCAA recognized that Divisions I, II, and III still faced "issues and needs unique to its member institutions," leading the NCAA to pass Proposal 7, "Restructuring," at the 1996 NCAA convention (Crowley, 1995). The restructuring plan, which took effect in August 1997, gave the NCAA divisions more responsibility for conduct within their division, gave more control to the presidents of member colleges and universities, and eliminated the one-school/one-vote structure. The NCAA annual convention of all member schools still takes place, but the divisions also hold division-specific miniconventions or meetings. In addition, each division has a governing body called either the Board of Directors (Division I) or Presidents Council (Division II and III), as well as Leadership and Legislative Councils (Division I) or a Management Council (Division II and III) made up of presidents, chancellors, and athletic administrators and faculty athletics representatives from member schools who meet and dictate policy and legislation within that division (**Figure 8-1**). The NCAA Executive Committee, consisting of representatives from each division as well as the NCAA president (nonvoting) and chairs of each divisional Leadership or Management Council (nonvoting), oversees the Presidential Boards and Leadership or Management Councils for each division.

Under the unique governance structure of the NCAA, the member schools oversee legislation regarding the conduct of intercollegiate athletics. Member institutions and conferences vote on proposed legislation, thus dictating the rules they need to follow. The **NCAA National Office**, located in Indianapolis, Indiana, enforces the rules the membership passes. The NCAA National Office has six primary units: administrative services, championships and

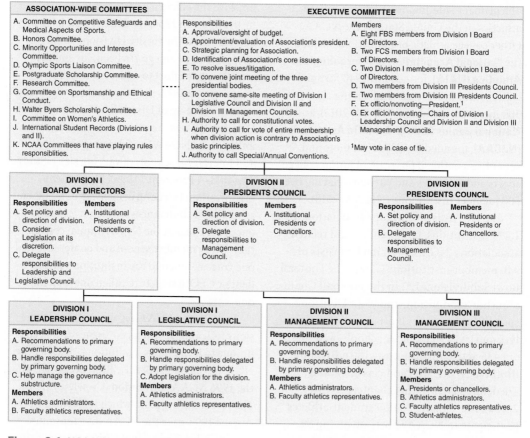

Figure 8-1 NCAA Governance Structure

alliances, communications, the NCAA Eligibility Center, enforcement, and membership and student-athlete affairs (NCAA, 2013c).

One of the more prominent areas within the NCAA administrative structure is the enforcement program. The **enforcement** area of the NCAA was created in 1952 when the membership decided that such a mechanism was needed to enforce the association's legislation. The process consists of allegations of rules violations being referred to the association's investigative staff. The NCAA enforcement staff determines if a potential violation has occurred and, if so, launches an investigation. If evidence of a major violation is discovered, the institution is notified of the allegations and the case moves to the Committee on Infractions (a committee of peers drawn from the NCAA membership and the public). The institution may also conduct its own investigation, reporting its findings to the Committee on Infractions. After hearing the case from both the enforcement staff and the institution, the Committee on Infractions releases its report and determination of penalties (if appropriate). The institution has an opportunity to appeal to the Infractions Appeals Committee (NCAA 2013d).

Up until August 1, 2013, the NCAA had a two-tiered approach to rule violations, secondary or minor violations and major violations. Following a call for reform in the enforcement model, a working group of Division I presidents, athletic directors, and commissioners developed a new Division I infractions process. This process includes a four-level violation structure, allowing for more flexibility in defining the severity and thus penalties associated with a case. In addition, accountability by the head coach has been enhanced such that potential consequences of rule violations can include suspensions that can range from 10% of the season's games to an entire season (Potter, 2013).

The NCAA also has in place committees at the various divisional levels to oversee sports rules and conduct championships. There are also association-wide groups, such as the Committee on Women's Athletics and the Committee on Competitive Safeguards and Medical Aspects of Sports, which examine issues specific to certain segments of the NCAA membership, as well as the Student-Athlete Advisory Committee, which provides student-athletes at each divisional level representation in the NCAA's governance structure.

Divisions I, II, and III

The NCAA is made up of three membership classifications designated as Divisions I, II, or III. Each division creates its own rules, with some of the more prominent differences occurring in the amount of athletic scholarships that are allowed, recruiting rules, and playing and practice seasons. The sport management student interested in pursuing a career in intercollegiate coaching or athletic administration should be knowledgeable about the differences in legislation and philosophies among the divisions so as to choose a career within the division most suited to his or her interests. Students should be aware that each institution has its own philosophy regarding the structure and governance of its athletic department. In addition, generalizations regarding divisions are not applicable to all institutions within that division. For example, some Division III institutions, although not offering any athletic scholarships, can be described as following a nationally competitive, revenue-producing philosophy that is more in line with a Division I philosophy. The student should thoroughly research an athletic department to determine the philosophy that the school and administration embraces.

Division I member institutions, in general, support the philosophy of competitiveness, generation of revenue through athletics, and national success. This philosophy is reflected in the following principles taken from the Division I Philosophy Statement (NCAA, 2013e):

- Strives in its athletics program for regional and national excellence and prominence
- Recognizes the dual objective in its athletics program of serving both the university or college community (participants, student body, faculty/staff, alumni) and the general public (community, area, state, nation)
- Sponsors at the highest feasible level of intercollegiate competition one or both of the traditional spectator-oriented, income-producing sports of football and basketball

Division I athletic departments are usually larger in terms of the number of sport programs sponsored, the number of coaches, and the number of administrators. Division I member institutions have to sponsor at least seven sports of all-male or mixed-gender teams and seven all-female teams, or six sports of all-male or mixed-gender teams and eight all-female teams (NCAA, 2013f). Division I athletic departments also have larger budgets due to the number of athletic scholarships allowed and larger operational budgets needed for the number of sport programs sponsored, recruiting budgets, and the salary costs associated with a higher number of coaches and administrators.

Division I schools that have football are further divided into two subdivisions: **Football Bowl Subdivision (FBS)** is the category for the somewhat larger football-playing schools in Division I and was formerly called Division I-A, and the **Football Championship Subdivision (FCS)** is the category for institutions playing football at the next level and was formerly called Division I-AA. FBS institutions must meet minimum attendance requirements for football (an average of at least 15,000 in actual or paid attendance for all home football games once every 2 years) as well as higher standards

for sports sponsorship (16 teams rather than the minimum of 14 teams required of Division I members), whereas FCS institutions are not held to any attendance requirements and follow the minimum sports sponsorship rule for Division I. Division I institutions that do not sponsor a football team do not have a FBS or FCS classification (NCAA 2013g).

Division II institutions usually attract student-athletes from the local or in-state area who may receive some athletic scholarship money but usually not a full ride. Division II athletics programs must offer at least 10 sports (at least 4 to 5 for men and 5 to 6 for women) and sponsor at least 2 team sports for each gender (NCAA, 2013h).

Division III institutions do not allow athletic scholarships and encourage participation by maximizing the number and variety of athletics opportunities available to students. Division III institutions must offer at least five sports for men and five for women (for institutions with enrollment of 1,000 students or fewer) or six sports for both men and women (for institutions with enrollment of more than 1,000 students) (NCAA, 2013i). Division III institutions emphasize the participant's experience, rather than the experience of the spectator, and place primary emphasis on regional in-season and conference competition (NCAA, 2013h).

Conferences

The organizational structure of intercollegiate athletics also involves **member conferences** of the NCAA. Division I multisport conferences must have a minimum of seven member institutions and the conference shall sponsor a minimum of 12 Division I sports, including both men's and women's basketball (NCAA, 2013j). Conferences provide many benefits and services to their member institutions. For example, conferences may have their own rules compliance director and run seminars regarding NCAA rules and regulations in an effort to better educate member schools' coaches and administrators. Conferences also have legislative power over their member institutions in the running of championship events and the formulation of conference rules and regulations. Conferences sponsor championships in sports sponsored by the member institutions within the conference. The conference member institutions vote on the conference guidelines to determine the organization of these conference championships. Conferences may also provide a revenue-sharing program to their member institutions in which revenue realized by the conference through NCAA distributions, TV contracts, or participation in football bowl games is shared among all member institutions. The increase in TV contracts with conferences over the years has contributed substantially to the revenue-sharing plans within conferences, but of even greater significance has been the emergence of conferences owning their own television networks. The Big Ten Conference is the most valuable college athletic conference, bringing in television revenue of $250 million, football bowl game revenue of $40 million, and NCAA tournament revenue (men's basketball predominantly) of $20 million (Smith, 2013). When shared with member schools through the conference revenue-sharing program, Big Ten institutions average between $20 and $25 million each per year.

Conferences have their own **conference rules**. Member institutions of a particular conference must adhere to conference rules in addition to NCAA rules. It is important to note, though, that although a conference rule can never be less restrictive than an NCAA rule, many conferences maintain additional rules that hold member institutions to stricter standards. For example, the Ivy League is a Division I NCAA member conference, but it prohibits its member institutions from providing athletic scholarships to student-athletes. Therefore, the Ivy League schools, although competing against other Division I schools that allow athletic scholarships, do not allow their athletic departments to award athletic scholarships.

Conference realignment is an issue that occurs periodically, affecting the landscape of college athletics. Some of the reasons for a school's wanting to join a conference or change conference affiliation are (1) exposure from television contracts with existing conferences, (2) potential for more revenue from television and corporate sponsorships through conference revenue sharing, (3) the difficulty independent schools experience in scheduling games and generating revenue, and (4) the ability of a conference to hold a championship game in football, which can generate millions of dollars in revenue for the conference schools. Conference realignment is discussed further in the "Current Issues" section of this chapter.

© Photodisc

Career Opportunities

For many decades, the traditional route followed for a career in collegiate athletics was to be an athlete, then a coach, and then an athletic administrator. It was a very closed system, with college athletic administrators selecting from among their own who would coach teams and then move into administrative positions. A 1992 study of Division I and Division III athletic directors found that 86% of the athletic directors in both divisions had been athletes at the collegiate level, while 78% in Division I and 90% in Division III had collegiate coaching experience (Barr, 1992). Yet, when asked whether more emphasis in the hiring process was placed on the athletic participation and coaching experience or the educational background of the applicant, the athletic directors in both Division I and Division III emphasized the importance of educational background over athletic participation and coaching experience (Barr, 1992). Much has changed since the original apprentice system used in college athletics, though, with athletic administrators being able to understand the financial and legal complexities that are a part of college athletics today.

Coaches and Athletic Directors

Differences exist among the divisions in terms of coaching and administrative duties and responsibilities. When moving from the smaller Division III institutions to the larger Division I institutions, the responsibilities and profiles of coaches within these athletic departments change. At the smaller Division III institutions, the coaches are usually part time or, if full time, they serve as coach to numerous sport programs. These coaches may also hold an academic appointment within a department, an administrative appointment, or teach activities classes. The Division III coach's budget on average is smaller than that of a Division I coach because most competition is regional and recruiting is not as extensive. Athletic scholarships are not allowed in Division III. Division III athletic directors may sometimes also coach or hold an academic appointment. Depending on the size of the athletic department, the Division III athletic director may wear many hats, acting as manager of the athletic department and coaches, business manager of the athletic department budget, media relations staff person, fund-raiser, and compliance officer. Some Division III athletic directors (ADs), due to the size of the athletic department, have a staff of assistant or associate athletic directors

providing administrative help in these various areas.

Athletic department budgets at the Division I, and especially FBS, level are in the tens of millions of dollars. It is common at this level to find coaches and assistant coaches employed full time coaching one sport program. Athletic scholarships are allowed, increasing the importance of recruiting, travel, and other activities geared toward signing blue-chip athletes. Individual sport program budgets are larger, providing more resources for recruiting and competitive travel opportunities. Division I athletic departments usually employ a large number of associate and assistant athletic directors with specialized responsibilities. The athletic director usually attends public relations and fund-raising events, participates in negotiating television contracts, and looks out for the interests of the athletic department in the development of institutional policies and financial affairs.

As college athletics has become more complex and businesslike, colleges and universities have looked to the corporate world for CEOs or administrators with business backgrounds to run their athletics department. University of Florida President Bernard Machen, in talking about Florida AD Jeremy Foley, states, "The athletic director is more like a CEO of a corporation than a guy who hires coaches. Jeremy oversees everything from the sale of bonds for capital construction to tickets and sponsorships, and he manages more than 500 employees" (Eichelberger, 2009). Similar to the stock options and performance-based bonuses used in the business world, college athletic directors also are negotiating bonus clauses in their contracts based on performance in areas such as wins and postseason appearances for high-profile teams, fiscal management within the athletic department, graduation rates of student-athletes, and lack of NCAA violations and probation of teams, to name a few (Bennett, 2003).

Assistant or Associate Athletic Director Areas of Responsibility

Reporting to the athletic director are assistant and associate athletic director positions functioning in specialized areas, such as business manager, media relations director, social media coordinator, ticket sales manager, fund development coordinator, director of marketing, sport programs administrator, facilities and events coordinator, academic affairs director, or compliance coordinator. Depending on the student's interest, various educational coursework will be helpful in preparing for a position in these areas. For example, business courses will prepare the student for positions working within the business aspect of an athletic department, communications courses will prepare the student for a position working with public relations and the media, educational counseling coursework is beneficial for positions within academic affairs, and a legal background will be helpful to administrators overseeing the compliance area.

Areas of growth where increased attention is being directed within collegiate athletic departments are **student-athlete services**, **fund development**, and **compliance**. Student-athlete services addresses the academic concerns and welfare of student-athletes, overseeing such areas as academic advising, tutoring, and counseling. Fund development has increased in importance as athletic departments seek new ways to increase revenues. Fund development coordinators oversee alumni donations to the athletic department and also oversee fundraising events. Compliance is the term used to describe adherence to NCAA and conference rules and regulations. The compliance coordinator works closely with the coaches to make sure they are knowledgeable about NCAA and

conference rules. The compliance coordinator also oversees the initial and continuing eligibility of the student-athletes as well as being directly involved in preventing or investigating any violations that take place within the athletic department.

Two other positions important to the collegiate athletic department are the **senior women's administrator (SWA)** and the **faculty athletics representative (FAR)**. The SWA is the highest-ranking female administrator involved with the conduct of an NCAA member institution's intercollegiate athletics program (NCAA, 2013k). The FAR is a member of an institution's faculty or administrative staff who is designated to represent the institution and its faculty in the institution's relationships with the NCAA and its conference (NCAA, 2013l).

Conference/NCAA or Other Association Opportunities

Opportunities for students interested in a career in college athletics exist within the NCAA member conferences as well as within the NCAA itself. With the specialization of positions and increased activities taking place within the athletic department, conference administration and management activities have followed a similar path. The size of athletic conference staffs has increased over the years, with conference administrators being hired to oversee growth areas such as conference championships, television negotiations, marketing activities, and compliance services offered to member schools.

The NCAA, as well as other college athletic associations such as the NJCAA and NAIA involved in the governance of college athletics, employs numerous staff members. Students may be interested in pursuing a career in college athletics at the NCAA, NJCAA, or NAIA national office level.

At whatever level or area in which the student is interested, one thing must be kept in mind: A job in college athletics is hard to come by because many people are trying to break into this segment of the sport industry. Therefore, students should set themselves apart from all the other applicants for the position to get noticed and hired. The way to do this is to prepare yourself academically by taking appropriate coursework and excelling in the classroom; to volunteer or help out in any way possible with the athletic department at your institution to gain valuable experience that you can include on your resume; to network and get to know people working in the industry, because it is an industry that relies on who you know and word-of-mouth during the hiring process; and to complete an internship. Even if unpaid, the internship gives you a valuable first step into the industry, where you then have the ability to prove yourself so that you can be hired into that first job.

Current Issues

Current issues affecting collegiate athletics abound and are constantly changing. Coaches and athletic administrators must be aware of the financial, legal, managerial, and ethical impacts of these issues.

Conference Realignment

Television contracts, football bowl payouts in the BCS games, and conference revenue sharing are the key reasons for much of the conference realignment that has been taking place within the NCAA over the past three decades. One of the first major conference realignments took place in 1994. This involved the movement of nine institutions and led to the demise of the 80-year-old Southwest Conference (Mott, 1994; "Western Athletic," 1994). In 2003–2004, 18 institutions changed conference affiliation involving the Big East, ACC, Conference USA, Atlantic 10, Mid-American, Western Athletic, and Sun Belt conferences (Lee, 2003; C-USA,

2010). In 2010, four large institutions changed conferences: Nebraska from the Big 12 to the Big Ten, Colorado from the Big 12 to the Pac-10, Utah from the Mountain West to the Pac-10, and Boise State departing the Western Athletic Conference (WAC) and joining the Mountain West Conference. With the loss of most of the conference's football-playing institutions to other conferences, the WAC discontinued football as a sponsored sport after the 2012–2013 season (Bullinger, 2012).

A similar result occurred with the Big East conference in 2011–2012 when Syracuse, Pitt, and Notre Dame (all sports but football) indicated their intent to leave the Big East Conference for the ACC, West Virginia decided to join the Big 12, Maryland and Rutgers accepted invitations to join the Big Ten, and Louisville accepted an invitation to join the ACC (Lessner, 2013). The remaining seven institutions (known as the "Catholic 7"—Marquette, Georgetown, Villanova, St. John's, Seton Hall, Providence, and DePaul) formed a new conference but retained the Big East name. This had the effect of dissolving the Big East football conference status. The new basketball-focused Big East Conference added Butler and Xavier from the Atlantic 10 and Creighton from the Missouri Valley and commenced operations on July 1, 2013 (Darcy, 2013). The remaining football-playing schools joined with several other schools to form a new conference called the American Athletic Conference (Gatto, 2013). Ironically the Big East Conference has come full circle, as it was originally formed in 1979 as a basketball-focused conference (O'Neil & Nevins, 2013). Since the spring of 2010, there have been 84 institutional moves affecting 28 Division I conferences (see **Figure 8-2**).

Coach Sandusky and Penn State

On November 5, 2011, former football assistant coach at Penn State Jerry Sandusky was

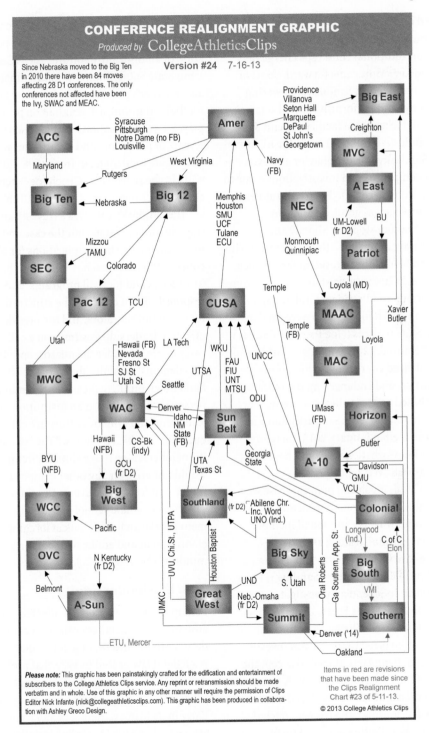

Figure 8-2 Conference Realignment

Reprinted with the permission of College Athletics Clips.

arraigned on 40 criminal counts involving sexual abuse of minors. A month later he was arrested on additional child rape charges as more alleged victims came forward. Some of the incidents involved Sandusky showering with the boys and performing sexual acts in the football locker room facility at Penn State ("Jerry Sandusky Trial," 2012). As the history of Jerry Sandusky's prior behavior and even previous complaints and investigations came to light, questions were raised as to who at Penn State knew what was going on and why Sandusky was not stopped. Shortly after Sandusky's arraignment, Athletic Director Tim Curley and Senior Vice President for Finance and Business Gary Schultz stepped down from their positions and President Graham Spanier and football coach Joe Paterno were fired by the Penn State trustees ("Joe Paterno, Graham Spanier Removed," 2011). Spanier, Curley, and Schultz all faced charges of perjury, obstruction of justice, and endangering the welfare of children based on their alleged awareness of incidents involving Jerry Sandusky and a minor. Joe Paterno died in January 2012; therefore, we do not know whether he would have been indicted as well (Wetzel, 2012).

The NCAA's involvement in this case was based on the NCAA Constitution and Bylaw principles and what is expected of member institutions, administrators, and coaches. While the case was being investigated for criminal prosecution of Jerry Sandusky, Penn State hired an independent investigator, former FBI Director Louis Freeh, to perform an investigation as well. The NCAA enforcement staff was not involved in the NCAA investigation. Instead, Penn State agreed to accept the findings of the Freeh report for NCAA violation determination and sanctions. Based on Freeh's report and its findings, the NCAA concluded that there was a significant lack of institutional control and a failure of institutional integrity that led to a culture in which the football program was held in such high esteem that there was an imbalance of power and perpetuation of an unhealthy culture. The NCAA fined Penn State $60 million (the approximate average of 1 year's gross revenue from the Penn State football program), a 4-year ban on postseason play, a 4-year reduction in athletic scholarships, 5 years of probation, and vacating all wins of the Penn State football team from 1998–2011, which will also be reflected in Coach Joe Paterno's career coaching record (NCAA, 2012b).

The Sandusky case was a travesty and a tragedy for Penn State, but the case and NCAA involvement also had implications for all of college athletics. Coaches' behavior, the culture of athletics and football programs, and the responsibility of coaches, the athletic director and administrators, and the president and others in leadership positions on a college campus are all under the microscope. This case also demonstrated the ability of the NCAA to hand down punitive measures for individual personal conduct when an institution's athletic leadership and athletic culture are called into question. The NCAA states, "The NCAA and its members hope that a similar circumstance would not arise on any other campus in the future—indeed, these events should serve as a call to every single school and athletics department to take an honest look at its campus environment and eradicate the 'sports are king' mindset" (NCAA, 2012c).

Title IX/Gender Equity

Perhaps no greater issue has affected collegiate athletic departments over the past couple of decades than **Title IX,** or gender equity. Title IX is a federal law passed in 1972 that prohibits sex discrimination in any educational activity or program receiving federal financial assistance. Early in its history, there was much confusion as to whether Title IX applied to college athletic departments. Title IX gained its enforcement power among college athletic departments with the passage of the 1988 Civil Rights Restoration Act. In 1991, the NCAA released the results of a gender-equity study that found that although the undergraduate enrollment on college campuses was roughly 50% male and 50% female, collegiate athletic departments on average were made up of 70% male and 30% female student-athletes. In addition, this NCAA study found that the male student-athletes were receiving 70% of the athletic scholarship money, 77% of the operational budget, and 83% of the recruiting dollars available (NCAA Gender Equity Task Force, 1991). In response to such statistics, an increase in the number of sex discrimination lawsuits took place, with the courts often ruling in favor of the female student-athletes.

© Adam Tinney/ShutterStock, Inc.

Collegiate athletic administrators started to realize that Title IX would be enforced by the Office for Civil Rights (OCR) and the courts, and as athletic administrators they would be required to provide equity within their athletic departments. The struggle athletic administrators are faced with is how to comply with Title IX given institutional financial limitations, knowing that lack of funding is not an excuse for not complying with Title IX. To bring male and female participation numbers closer to the percentage of undergraduate students by sex at the institution, numerous institutions are choosing to eliminate sport programs for men, thereby reducing the participation and funding on the men's side. Another method selected by some institutions is capping roster sizes for men's teams, known as **roster management**, thus keeping the men's numbers in check while trying to increase women's participation. A third, and most appropriate, option under Title IX is increasing participation and funding opportunities for female student-athletes. Of course, in selecting this option, the athletic administrator must be able to raise the funds necessary to add sport programs, hire new coaches, and provide uniforms for the new sport programs.

The most recent issue involving Title IX compliance involves the definition of what constitutes a qualified sport program for women. In July 2010, a federal judge ruled that Quinnipiac University was violating Title IX by failing to provide equal athletic opportunities to female students. In March 2009, Quinnipiac University in Hamden, Connecticut, announced that the school was cutting three sport teams: women's volleyball, men's golf, and men's outdoor track. The school also stated that it was establishing varsity cheerleading beginning in the 2009–2010 season. Five female student volleyball players and the coach of the volleyball team filed suit claiming that Quinnipiac was violating Title IX (Mahony, 2010). In his ruling, U.S. District Judge Stefan Underhill stated that the competitive cheerleading team does not qualify as a varsity sport for the purposes of Title IX and, therefore, its members may not be counted as athletic participants under the statute (*Biediger et al v. Quinnipiac University*, 2010). The U.S. Court of Appeals for the Second Circuit upheld this ruling, stating that cheerleading cannot be counted as a varsity sport under Title IX and that its athletes may not count toward gender-equity requirements (Grasgreen, 2012).

Hiring Practices for Minorities and Women

Minority hiring has long been an issue of concern and debate within collegiate athletics. In 1993–1994, the NCAA's Minority Opportunity and Interests Committee found that African Americans accounted for fewer than 10% of athletic directors and 8% of head coaches, and when predominantly African American institutions were eliminated from the study, the results dropped to 4% representation in both categories (Wieberg, 1994). The University of Central Florida Institute for Diversity and Ethics in Sport releases an annual Race and Gender Report Card that assesses the diversity and demographics of college athletics. In 2012, college sports earned a "B" for race and gender hiring. Results indicated that 12.5% of FBS head coaches and 18.6% of Division I men's basketball coaches were African American. The results for Division I men's basketball were the lowest percentage since 1995–1996. The results for women's basketball teams were not much better, with African Americans comprising only 14% of coaches. Women also represented only 8.2% of Division I athletic director positions, and 100% of FBS conference commissioners were white men (Uthman, 2013). This issue continues to demand—appropriately so—the attention of college athletic directors in the hiring of coaches and of institutional presidents in the hiring of athletic directors.

Pay-for-Play Debate

The debate about whether college athletes should be paid is not a new one. Ever since the escalation of television contract rights fees (both in football and basketball) and the ability of colleges to fill their football stadiums with up to 100,000 or more spectators, many have argued that the source of this revenue, the student-athletes themselves, should be compensated. Ed O'Bannon, a former basketball player at UCLA, filed suit in 2009 alleging that the NCAA, EA Sports, and the Collegiate Licensing Co. are in violation of antitrust laws. The lawsuit seeks compensation for the use of players' likenesses in EA Sports/NCAA-licensed video and was later amended to seek 50% of conferences' TV revenues as well (Hinnen, 2013). The five most valuable conferences (Big Ten, Pac-12, ACC, SEC, and Big 12) collect approximately $1.4 billion from bowls, tournaments, and television (Smith, 2013). Yet, only 23 out of 228 Division I athletic programs showed a surplus in 2012 (Berkowitz, Upton, & Brady, 2013). The NCAA has been considering a $2,000 stipend to college athletes, but support from NCAA member institutions seems to be lacking. If college athletes were allowed to be paid, a bidding war would certainly result, leading to a larger gap between the "haves" and the "have nots."

Many argue that an athletic scholarship covering tuition, room and board, books, and fees provides an opportunity for college athletes to receive a college education at little to no cost. The students' athletic talent is allowing them an opportunity to go to college for free. In addition, the top athletic programs provide additional support to these athletes, including academic and tutoring assistance, the latest in athletic training and nutrition guidance, and the necessary coaching that will enable them to excel and prepare for a professional (paying) career in their sport. This debate will surely continue as the NCAA, college athletic departments, college athletes, and the general public weigh in on whether college athletes should be paid.

Summary

Sport management students and future athletic department employees need to be aware that intercollegiate athletics, as a major segment of the sport industry, is experiencing numerous organizational, managerial, financial, and legal issues. The NCAA, first organized in 1905, has undergone organizational changes throughout its history to accommodate the needs of its member institutions. Knowing the NCAA organizational structure is important because it provides information about the power and communication structures within the organization. The NCAA has also undergone major reform over the years in its academic rules, legislative and enforcement division, and its membership structure. These will surely continue as the world of college athletics evolves.

It is also important for students to know the differences that exist among the various divisions within the NCAA membership structure. These differences involve the allowance of athletic scholarships, budget and funding opportunities, and competitive philosophies. Distinct differences exist among divisions, and even among schools within a particular division. Students, future collegiate athletic administrators, and coaches must become informed of these differences if they hope to select the career within a school or NCAA membership division that best fits their interests and philosophies.

In pursuing an administrative job within collegiate athletics, the sport management student should be aware of and work on developing skills that current athletic directors have identified as important. These skills include marketing expertise, strong public speaking and writing skills, creative and problem-solving abilities, the ability to manage complex financial issues, and the ability to manage and work

Case Study 8-1 The Role of an Athletic Director

Rebecca Jones has thoroughly enjoyed her job as athletic director at a Division I FCS institution. She has always enjoyed the day-to-day activities of managing a $25 million athletic budget, overseeing 25 sport programs (well beyond the minimum 14 needed for NCAA Division I membership), and interacting with the 15 assistant and associate athletic directors. But when she came into work one spring Monday morning she knew some very difficult days were ahead of her that would test her managerial, financial, and communication skills. At the lacrosse game on Saturday, the chancellor cornered Rebecca to let her know of an emergency meeting the state legislators had had the previous day. The governor was forwarding, with the legislators' endorsement, a budget that called for a 10% reduction to the university's budget starting July 1. The chancellor, in turn, told Rebecca that she would need to reduce the $25 million athletic budget by 10% (or $2.5 million). Word spread quickly of this impending budget cut, and there in her office early on this spring morning were three head coaches (men's soccer, men's swimming, and women's volleyball). Rebecca has always employed an open-door philosophy, encouraging any coach, student-athlete, student, or faculty member at the university to stop by and talk to her whenever he or she had a question or concern. Rebecca

(continues)

Case Study 8-1   The Role of an Athletic Director (Continued)

could tell by the faces of these three coaches that they were worried that their sport programs, and their jobs, would be eliminated as part of the budget reduction.

Rebecca invited the coaches into her office and began to listen to what they had to say. The men's soccer coach was concerned that his was a low-profile sport and therefore easily expendable. The men's swimming coach was concerned that even though he had been modestly successful over the years, the pool was in drastic need of repair—an expense the university could not afford—which he felt made the men's swimming program a target for elimination. The women's volleyball coach was concerned because of the high cost of volleyball (a fully funded sport at the university), with a huge potential savings possible by cutting just this one sport program. Also, volleyball was not a popular sport in the region and therefore was not drawing a lot of fan support.

As Rebecca was talking to the coaches, her administrative assistant interrupted to tell her that the local newspapers had been calling for a comment and that a local television station was camped outside the basketball arena interviewing coaches as they came to work. The administrative assistant overheard one of the questions being asked by the reporter: "Should the Division FCS football program, which has been running a deficit of between $1.3 million and $2.2 million per year over the past couple of years, be dropped completely or go nonscholarship?" Rebecca knew she had two initial concerns: one of an immediate nature, dealing with the media, and the second of a communication nature, regarding the coaches and administrators within the department. The chancellor asked her to submit a preliminary report in 2 weeks, so she had a little bit of time to address the bigger issue: What to do?

Questions for Discussion

1. Put yourself in Rebecca's position. What is the first thing that you should do with regard to the media? With the coaches and other athletic department administrators?

2. What types of information and data does Rebecca need to collect to make a decision on how to handle cutting $2.5 million from the athletic department's budget?

3. If you were Rebecca, would you involve anyone in the decision-making process or make the decision by yourself? If involving other people, who would they be, and why would they be an important part of the process?

4. What types of communication need to take place, and how would you go about communicating this information?

5. What are some potential solutions in terms of budget reduction? What are the possible ramifications surrounding these solutions?

6. If you choose to eliminate sport programs, what criteria would you use to determine which teams are eliminated?

with parents, students, faculty, alumni, booster groups, and sponsors. Appropriate course-work and preparation in these areas can better prepare the student interested in a career in collegiate athletic administration.

Probably the most important quality a coach or administrator needs to possess is being informed and knowledgeable about issues currently affecting this sport industry segment. Recently, these include coaches' behavior and the school's athletic culture (e.g., Sandusky and Penn State), conference realignment, the pay-for-play debate, Title IX compliance, and hiring practices for minorities and women. Staying on top of these and other issues affecting college athletics is important for all coaches, administrators, and people involved in the governance and operation of this sport industry segment.

Resources

National Association for Intercollegiate Athletics (NAIA)

> 1200 Grand Blvd.
> Kansas City, MO 64106
> 816-595-8000
> http://www.naia.org

National Association of Collegiate Directors of Athletics (NACDA)

> 24651 Detroit Road
> Westlake, OH 44145

> 440-892-4000
> http://www.nacda.com

National Association of Collegiate Women's Athletic Administrators (NACWAA)

> 2024 Main Street, #1W
> Kansas City, MO 64108
> 816-389-8200
> http://www.nacwaa.org

National Collegiate Athletic Association (NCAA)

> 700 W. Washington Street
> P.O. Box 6222
> Indianapolis, IN 46206-6222
> 317-917-6222
> http://www.ncaa.org

National Junior College Athletic Association (NJCAA)

> 1631 Mesa Ave. Suite B
> Colorado Springs, CO 80906
> 719-590-9788
> http://www.njcaa.org

Women's Sports Foundation

> Eisenhower Park
> 1899 Hempstead Turnpike, Suite 400
> East Meadow, NY 11554
> 516-542-4700
> http://www.womenssportsfoundation.org

Key Terms

Association for Intercollegiate Athletics for Women (AIAW), Big Ten Conference, Carnegie Reports of 1929, Commission on Intercollegiate Athletics for Women (CIAW), compliance, conference re-alignment, conference rules, Division I, Division II, Division III, enforcement, faculty athletics representative (FAR), Football Bowl Subdivision (FBS), Football Championship Subdivision (FCS), fund development, Intercollegiate Athletic Association of the United States (IAAUS), Intercollegiate Conference of Faculty Representatives, Intercollegiate Football Association, Knight Commission, member conferences, National Association of Intercollegiate Athletics (NAIA), National Collegiate Athletic Association (NCAA), National Junior College Athletic Association (NJCAA), NCAA National Office, one-school/one-vote, roster management, senior women's administrator (SWA), student-athlete services, Title IX.

References

Acosta, R. V., & Carpenter, L. J. (1985). Women in sport. In D. Chu, J. O. Segrave, & B. J. Becker (Eds.), *Sport and higher education* (pp. 313–325). Champaign, IL: Human Kinetics.

Association for Intercollegiate Athletics for Women v. National Collegiate Athletic Association. 558 F. Supp. 487 (D.D.C. 1983).

Barr, C. A. (1992). A comparative study of Division I and Division III athletic directors: Their profiles and the necessary qualifications they deem as essential in their positions. Unpublished master's thesis, University of Massachusetts, Amherst.

Bennett, B. (2003, July 13). Athletic directors: In the money; bonus clauses pay for wins, good grades, bottom line. *The Courier-Journal*, p. C11.

Berkowitz, S., Upton, J. & Brady, E. (2013, July 1). Most NCAA Division I athletic departments take subsidies. *USA Today.com*. Retrieved from http://www.usatoday.com/story/sports/college/2013/05/07/ncaa-finances-subsidies/2142443/

Biediger et al v. Quinnipiac University. Case No. 3:09cv621 (SRU), (U.S. Dist. Ct., 2010).

Bowman, J. (2013, June 17). The Ackerman white paper, part I: Concerns about college women's basketball. Retrieved from http://www.swishappeal.com/2013/6/17/4438912/the-ackerman-white-paper-part-i-concerns-about-college-womens

Brown, G. (2012, September 19). NCAA student-athlete participation hits 450,000. *NCAA.org*. Retrieved from http://www.ncaa.org.wps/wcm/connect/public/NCAA/Resources/Latest+News/2012/September/NCAA+student+athlete+participation+hits+450,000

Bullinger, J. (2012, August 21). How conference realignment wiped WAC football off the map. *SI.com*. Retrieved from http://sportsillustrated.cnn.com/2012/football/ncaa/08/21/was-football-demise/index.html

Crowley, J. N. (1995, December 18). History demonstrates that change is good. *The NCAA News*, p. 4.

C-USA. (2010). C-USA milestones. Retrieved from http://conferenceusa.cstv.com/ot/c-usa-milestones.html

Darcy, K. (2013, March 20). New Big East adds Butler, 2 others. *ESPNNewYork.com*. Retrieved from http://espn.go.com/mens-college-basketball/story/_/id/9074722/new=big-east-adds-butler-bulldogs-creighton-bluejays-xavier-muskateers

Davenport, J. (1985). From crew to commercialism—the paradox of sport in higher education. In D. Chu, J. O. Segrave, & B. J. Becker (Eds.), *Sport and higher education* (pp. 5–16). Champaign, IL: Human Kinetics.

Dealy, F. X. (1990). *Win at any cost*. New York: Carol Publishing Group.

Eichelberger, C. (2009, January 6). Florida enters BCS title game with top-paid athletic director. Retrieved from http://www.bloomberg.com/apps/news?pid=newsarchive&sid=aYYY_mDwYMkY

Gatto, T. (2013, April 3). Conference realignment: Big East becomes American Athletic Conference. *Sporting News*. Retrieved from http://www.sportingnews.com/ncaa-football/story/2013-04-03/conference-realignment-big-east-american-athletic-conference-catholic-7

Gentry, J. K., & Alexander, R. M. (2012, April 2). Pay for women's basketball coaches lags far behind that of men's coaches. *The New York Times*. Retrieved from http://www.nytimes.com/2012/04/03/sports/ncaabasketball/pay-for-women's-basketball-coaches-lags-far-behind-mens-coaches.html?pagewanted=all&_r=0

Grasgreen, A. (2012, August 8). Appeals court upholds ruling on cheerleading at Quinnipiac. *Inside Higher Ed*. Retrieved from http://www.insidehighered.com/quicktakes/2012/08/08/appeals-court-upholds-ruling-cheerleading-quinnipiac

Hinnen, J. (2013, April 1). USC AD Haden: Schools should 'prepare' for O'Bannon suit loss. *CBSSports.com*. Retrieved from http://www.cbssports.com/collegefootball

/eye-on-college-football-/21989037/usc-ad-haden-schools-should-prepare-for-obannon-suit-loss

Hult, J. S. (1994). The story of women's athletics: Manipulating a dream 1890–1985. In D. M. Costa & S. R. Guthrie (Eds.), *Women and sport: Interdisciplinary perspectives* (pp. 83–106). Champaign, IL: Human Kinetics.

Jerry Sandusky trial: All you need to know about allegations, how case unfolded. (2012, June 11). *CNN.com*. Retrieved from http://news.blogs.cnn.com.2012/06/11/jerry-sandusky-trial-all-you-need-to-know-about-allegations-how-case-unraveled/

Joe Paterno, Graham Spanier removed. (2011, November 10). *ESPN.com*. Retrieved from http://espn.go.com/college-football/story/_/id/7214380/jow-paterno-president-graham-spanier-penn-state

Knight Foundation Commission on Intercollegiate Athletics. (1991, March). *Keeping faith with the student-athlete*. Charlotte, NC: Knight Foundation.

Knight Foundation Commission on Intercollegiate Athletics. (1993, March). *A new beginning for a new century*. Charlotte, NC: Knight Foundation.

Lawrence, P. R. (1987). *Unsportsmanlike conduct*. New York: Praeger Publishers.

Lee, J. (2003, December 8–14). Who pays, who profits in realignment? *SportsBusiness Journal*, pp. 25–33.

Lessner, Z. (2013, January 31). College basketball: How conference realignment killed the Big East. *Bleacher Report*. Retrieved from http://bleacherreport.com/articles/1509548-college-basketball-conference-realignment-led-to-the-dissolving-of-the-big-east

Mahony, E.H. (2010, July 21). Judge says Quinnipiac discriminates against female student athletes. Retrieved from http://articles.courant.com/2010-07-21/sports/hc-quinnipiac-decision-0721-20100721_1_title-ix-athletic-participation-opportunities-female-student-athletes

Morrison, L. L. (1993). The AIAW: Governance by women for women. In G. L. Cohen (Ed.), *Women in sport: Issues and controversies* (pp. 59–66). Newbury Park, CA: Sage Publications.

Mott, R. D. (1994, March 2). Big Eight growth brings a new look to Division I-A. *The NCAA News*, p. 1.

National Association of Intercollegiate Athletics. (NAIA). (2013). About the NAIA. Retrieved from http://www.naia.org/ViewArticle.dbml?DB_OEM_ID=27900&ATCLID=205323019

National Collegiate Athletic Association. (2012a). *1981–82—2011–12 NCAA sports sponsorship and participation rates report*. Retrieved from http://www.ncaapublications.com/productdownloads/PR2013.pdf

National Collegiate Athletic Association. (2012b, July 23). Binding consent decree imposed by the National Collegiate Athletic Association and accepted by the Pennsylvania State University. Retrieved from http://s3.amazonaws.com/ncaa/files/20120723/21207236PDF.pdf

National Collegiate Athletic Association. (2012c, July). NCAA authority to act. Retrieved from http://www.ncaa.org/wps/wcm/connect/public/ncaa/resources/latest+news/2012/july/21207233

National Collegiate Athletic Association. (2013a). About the NCAA. Retrieved from http://www.ncaa.org/wps/wcm/connect/public/ncaa/about+the+ncaa/membership+new

National Collegiate Athletic Association. (2013b). Article 1.3.1: Basic purpose. In *2013–14 NCAA Division I manual*. Indianapolis, IN: Author.

National Collegiate Athletic Association. (2013c). National office. Retrieved from http://www.ncaa.org/wps/wcm/connect/public/ncaa/about+the+ncaa/national+office+new

National Collegiate Athletic Association. (2013d). Investigations. Retrieved from http://www.ncaa.org/wps/wcm/connect/public/ncaa/enforcement/process/investigations

National Collegiate Athletic Association. (2013e). Article 20.9.2: Division I philosophy statement. In *2013–14 NCAA Division I manual*. Indianapolis, IN: Author.

National Collegiate Athletic Association. (2013f). Article 20.9.6: Sports sponsorship. In *2013–14 NCAA Division I manual*. Indianapolis, IN: Author.

National Collegiate Athletic Association. (2013g). Article 20.9.9: Football bowl subdivision requirements. In *2013–14 NCAA Division I manual*. Indianapolis, IN: Author.

National Collegiate Athletic Association. (2013h). Differences among the three divisions. Retrieved from http://www.ncaa .org/wps/wcm/connect/public/NCAA /About+the+NCAA+OLD/Who+We+Are /Differences+Among+the+Divisions/

National Collegiate Athletic Association. (2013i). Article 20.11.3: Sports sponsorship. In *2013–14 NCAA Division III manual*. Indianapolis, IN: Author.

National Collegiate Athletic Association. (2013j). Article 20.02.5 Multisport conference. In *2013–14 NCAA Division I manual*. Indianapolis, IN: Author.

National Collegiate Athletic Association. (2013k). Article 4.02.4.1: Senior woman administrator. In *2013–14 NCAA Division I manual*. Indianapolis, IN: Author.

National Collegiate Athletic Association. (2013l). Article 4.02.2: Faculty athletics representative. In *2013–14 NCAA Division I manual*. Indianapolis, IN: Author.

National Junior College Athletic Association. (2013). *Colleges*. Retrieved from http://www .njcaa.org/colleges.cfm

NCAA Gender Equity Task Force. (1991). *NCAA gender equity report*. Overland Park, KS: National Collegiate Athletic Association.

O'Neil, D., & Nevins, C. (2013, March 12). Last call for a garden party. Retrieved from http:// espn.go.com/espn/story/_/id/9002900 /last-call-garden-party

Paul, J. (1993). Heroines: Paving the way. In G. L. Cohen (Ed.), *Women in sport: Issues and controversies* (pp. 27–37). Newbury Park, CA: Sage Publications.

Potter, E. (2013, August 1). New reform efforts take hold August 1. *NCAA.org*. Retrieved from http://www.ncaa.org/wps/wcm/connect /public/ncaa/resources/latest+news/2013 /august+1#

Rader, B. G. (1990). *American sports* (2nd ed.). Englewood Cliffs, NJ: Prentice Hall.

Savage, H. J. (1929). *American college athletics*. New York: The Carnegie Foundation.

Smith, C. (2013, January 16). The most valuable conferences in college sports. *Forbes*. Retrieved from http://www.forbes.com/sites /chrissmith/2013/01/16/the-most-valuable -conferences-in-college-sports/

Study: Typical I-A program is $1.2 million in the black. (1996, November 18). *The NCAA News*, p. 1.

Uthman, D. (2013, July 10). College sports earns 'B' for race and gender hiring. *USA Today*. Retrieved from http://www.usatoday.com /sotry/sports/college/2013/07/10/race-and -gender-hiring-practices-study/2504745/

Western Athletic Conference to become biggest in I-A. (1994, April 27). *The NCAA News*, p. 3.

Wetzel, D. (2012, November 1). Indictment of ex-Penn State president reveals disturbing details of how PSU dealt with Sandusky. *Yahoo Sports*. Retrieved from http://sports.yahoo.com/news /ncaaf--indictment-of-ex-penn-state -president-reveals-disturbing-details-of-how -officials-dealt-with-jerry-sandusky01191010 .html

Wieberg, S. (1994, August 18). Study faults colleges on minority hiring. *USA Today*, p. 1C.

Yaeger, D. (1991). *Undue process: The NCAA's injustice for all*. Champaign, IL: Sagamore Publishing.

Chapter 9

International Sport

Mary A. Hums, Per Svensson, Sheranne Fairley, and Mireia Lizandra

Learning Objectives

Upon completion of this chapter, students should be able to:

1. Distinguish between the terms *globalization*, *internationalization*, and *Americanization* of sport.

2. Differentiate between the school-based system of sport organization in the United States and the club-based system more commonly used in the rest of the world.

3. Illustrate the historical development of international sport.

4. Appraise the role of technology in enhancing the ability of sport organizations to introduce their products and services to foreign markets.

5. Distinguish between the different methods that leagues can use to become involved in international sport including broadcasting, licensing and merchandising, playing games overseas, marketing foreign athletes, and engaging in expansion.

6. Describe the objectives of the United Nations Sport for Development and Peace program.

7. Analyze the mission of the Olympic and Paralympic Movements.

8. Differentiate between the roles of the various Olympic governing bodies such as the IOC, NOCs, OGOCs, IFs, and NGBs.

9. Inventory the various career opportunities available in international sport management and understand the specific skills needed for a sport manager to succeed in the global marketplace.

10. Critically evaluate current issues of interest in international sport management such as cultural awareness and sensitivity, the increase in foreign student-athletes attending U.S. colleges and universities, the growth of global marketing and sponsorship opportunities, and doping.

Editor's Note: Most of the world refers to soccer as "football," so throughout this international chapter we will do the same. When referring to football played in the National Football League (NFL), Canadian Football League (CFL), and NFL Europe, we will use the phrase "American football."

Introduction

Although sport has been played on an international level as early as the ancient Olympic Games in 776 BC, sport continues to see an increasing degree of interaction and expansion across national borders. The increasing reach of broadcast media, improvements in communication, the growth of social media, relaxation of trade barriers, and increased ease of international travel have helped sport further diffuse through the boundaries of countries and continents. Many sport events or competitions are now broadcast live or live streamed online in multiple countries around the world, allowing fans to watch their favorite teams' performance as it happens. Live scores, sport events, and statistics are generally available globally on the Internet. As a result, people around the world can more easily access major sport leagues and events. It is now easier than ever to stay up-to-date with the latest sport, team, or player information, regardless of where you are in the world—provided that the necessary technology is available.

Oftentimes when talking about international sport, we view the internationalization and globalization of sport as the influence of contemporary superpowers on spectator sports, with special attention given to those sports that are widely disseminated in the popular media (Lai, 1999). This view has contributed to the use of the term *globalization* being treated synonymously with *Americanization*. In other words, the process of globalization is often thought of

in terms of how spectator sport in the United States is communicated to, received by, and adopted by other parts of the world. In truth, the scope of international sport is much wider. The internationalization of sport can be seen on many different levels, which include, but are not limited to:

- The continual introduction of sport into new countries where the sport has not traditionally been played
- Countries competing against one another in international competition
- The international broadcasting of sport competition and events in traditional and nontraditional media platforms
- International coverage of sport events and competition through various forms of news and print media
- Travel to sport events in different countries as a spectator, participant, official, or volunteer
- The use of social media by athletes and sport managers around the world
- The expansion of "national" leagues to include teams based in different countries
- Teams touring foreign countries to generate interest and awareness of their sport or league
- Individuals competing alongside players from different countries in organized leagues
- The availability of licensed merchandise outside of the country of the team or player
- Global companies sponsoring international sport events
- The use of sport as a social and political tool

As a result of the increasingly global nature of sport, abundant career opportunities exist for sport management students. Further, today's sport managers should have a general knowledge of the global platform in which sport is performed and consumed, as challenges for sport managers inevitably accompany the industry's continual expansion.

This chapter first examines the historical development of sport in the international marketplace. It then looks at the factors behind the global expansion of sport, addressing the growth of sport-related corporate activities, professional sport, sport tourism, grassroots sport, sport for development and peace, and the diffusion of sport into new cultural settings. The chapter next focuses on the growth of sport tourism. It then examines the Olympic Movement, including its organization and primary responsibilities. Finally, because the international emphasis on sport will continue to grow, resulting in an increased number of job opportunities in international sport, this chapter concludes by addressing the variety of potential employment opportunities in international sport. Although many of the examples in this chapter involve North American sports or leagues, this trend is not meant to suggest that international sport is in any way limited to the United States and Canada. The examples are included for illustrative purposes only.

Additionally, it is useful to know that the organization of sport in the United States is not typical of the organization of sport throughout the world. Unlike the school-based (high school or college) sport system in the United States, the club system form of sport organization is more common throughout the rest of the world. The club-based system is separate and distinct from the education system (i.e., one does not have to attend college to play at the elite level). The primary purpose of the club sport system is to fulfill social and fitness functions, rather than to promote superior athletes. The club system allows anyone to participate and take advantage of good facilities that are often maintained by

local or state government. Given the social and fitness benefits the club-based system provides, governments contribute substantially to the sport system. Thus, the funding structure for sport in many countries outside the United States entails much more government involvement, with some countries even having their own federal minister for sport (e.g., Canada and Australia).

Another difference between sport in the United States and other countries is the use of the promotion and relegation system in leagues. According to Li, MacIntosh, and Bravo (2012):

> Promotion and relegation works by having a multitiered system of connected sport leagues in which teams are exchanged from one league to the next based on performance. That is, teams finishing at the bottom of a higher league will be relegated to a league one tier down, and teams finishing at the top of a lower league will be promoted to the league in the next tier up. (para. 1)

Typically, this means the movement of the bottom three or four teams from one league down to the lower league, and the elevation of the top three or four teams in a lower league to the next league a level up. Here is an example from a hypothetical league setup. Let's say at the end of the 2013–2014 season, the final standings looked like this:

A League	B League
Anderlecht	Lierse
Cercle B	Lokeren
Charleroi	Mechelen
FC Brugge	Waregem
Genk	OH Leuven
Gent	Oostende
Kortrijk	S Liege

Using promotion and relegation, at the start of the 2014–2015 season, the league membership would look like this:

A League	B League
Anderlecht	Gent
Cercle B	Kortrjk
Charleroi	Mechelen
FC Brugge	Waregem
Genk	OH Leuven
Lierse	Oostende
Lokeren	S Liege

As you can see, the bottom teams from the A League were relegated to the B League, while the top teams in the B League were promoted to the A League. This system allows for leagues to have different member teams each season, and motivates teams at the bottom of the standings to keep playing hard in order to avoid relegation. This differs from U.S. leagues, where league membership rarely changes and teams at the bottom of the standings may see an advantage to finishing at the bottom because of the ability to have a high draft pick the following season.

To have a better understanding of the international sport scene, it helps to have at least a brief knowledge of sport across international borders. It is an interesting story to examine.

© JuliusKielaitis/ShutterStock, Inc.

History

Sport first spread across international borders through imperialistic efforts. As nations such as Great Britain colonized various areas throughout the world, sport was used to impose the conquerors' culture on the colonized land. For example, the British introduced cricket, rugby union, and rugby league to Australia when they colonized that continent. Today, cricket, rugby union, and rugby league are immensely popular in Australia, and an intense rivalry exists between Australia and Great Britain. Additionally, this colonization is reflected when you look at the sports and countries involved in today's Commonwealth Games. In this way, sport has fueled a feeling of pride in one's country, also known as **nationalism**. Nationalistic sentiments have also assisted in the growth of international sport to where it is today. In some instances, a win on an international level has led to increased interest and participation in a particular sport. The United States' victory over the Soviet Union's ice hockey team in the Olympic Games in 1980, for example, increased nationalistic pride as well as interest in hockey toward the end of the Cold War. Greece's victory in the Euro2004 football championship was a major factor in increasing national pride in the country right before the Athens Summer Olympic Games the same year.

Similarly, Australia's advancement to the 2006 Fédération Internationale de Football Association (FIFA) World Cup for the first time in 32 years produced an increased interest in football in that country. In other cases, lack of success at an international level has served as the catalyst for the further development of sport. For example, the Australian Institute of Sport (AIS), a center designed to train and develop elite athletes and teams, was established in 1981 as a result of Australia's disappointing performance at the 1976 Montreal Olympic Games. In Canada, disillusionment over low medal productivity prompted the formation of the Own The Podium (OTP) program, aimed at securing Canadian victories in the 2010 Olympic and Paralympic Games in Vancouver (Helliker, 2009).

Given the international exposure and media attention it attracts, sport is often used as a platform for political and social protests and boycotts. Various human rights groups have staged protests and disruptions of international sport events to bring international attention to their causes (Hums & Wolff, 2008). To protest against the practice of apartheid, the Stop the Seventy Tour Committee (STST) was established in 1970, staging mass demonstrations and disruptions when white South African cricket and rugby union teams toured the United Kingdom. The protest was not about sport, but rather used sport as a platform to promote human rights and showcase that apartheid was unacceptable.

Athletes have also used their positions to protest various issues. During the medal ceremony for the 200-meter track event at the 1968 Mexico Olympic Games, Tommie Smith and John Carlos staged a silent protest against racial discrimination of black people in the United States. During the victory ceremony, Smith and Carlos stood with their heads bowed, no shoes, black scarves around their necks, and black-gloved fists raised during the U.S. national anthem—an image that earned international recognition for the fight against racial discrimination.

© Photos.com

Concurrent with the growth of the Olympic Games, professional sport leagues and corporations have seized the opportunity to sell their products in international markets. Of the North American professional sport leagues, Major League Baseball (MLB) has the longest history of attempting to export its product. In 1888, driven by Albert Spalding's desire to sell more sporting goods, a group of professional baseball players traveled overseas to play exhibition games and introduce the sport of baseball through clinics in places such as Egypt, Scotland, Ireland, and England. Such practices continued following the turn of the century as Babe Ruth and other stars of the time regularly toured Canada, Latin America, and Japan (Field, 1997).

The major North American leagues now play actual league games overseas. In 1986, the NFL became the first North American professional sport league to export an exhibition between two teams. Exhibition games by North American league clubs now occur regularly overseas, primarily in Europe and Asia. In 2008, MLB played its first Opening Day series in Japan, and the 2014 season opened in Australia. In 2007, the NFL hosted a regular-season game in England, and the league's Jacksonville Jaguars are now committed to playing one home game per year for the next 4 years in London beginning in October 2013. Other leagues now have teams positioned in different countries and continents. For example, the Investec Bank Super 14s Rugby Union competition has teams placed in Australia, New Zealand, and South Africa.

Although each of the four major North American professional sport leagues aggressively attack the international marketplace, the world's most popular sport is still football (soccer). In fact, just as American football, basketball, baseball, and hockey leagues are attempting to spread the popularity of their sport overseas, so, too, is football attempting to spread its popularity. However, in the case of football, recent efforts have focused on increasing the interest and participation in the United States. Efforts have included the North American Soccer League (NASL), the 1994 World Cup, and Major League Soccer (MLS), the first Division I professional football league on U.S. soil in 12 years. Many large companies have signed on as MLS sponsors, including adidas, Pepsi, Visa, Bimbo, Gatorade, Volkswagen, and Anheuser-Busch. In an attempt to capitalize on its growing popularity, the league is now televised on NBC and has an ongoing relationship with ESPN (Vertelney, 2013).

The Globalization of Sport

To capitalize on the global marketplace, corporations have begun to adopt a **global strategy** for selling their products. The premise for a global strategy is basic: create products with the same appeal and that generate the same demand in all corners of the world. Early proponents of this strategy were Coca-Cola, Levi's, and Disney (with theme parks in Tokyo, Paris, Hong Kong, and one under construction in Shanghai). Cooper (2010) of *Marketing Week* suggests the following five strategies for a successful global brand:

1. Build a strong consistent brand culture.

2. Be borderless in your marketing.

3. Build yourself an internal hub.

4. Adopt a "glocal" structure.

5. Make customers your co-creators.

The ability to be both global and local is of the essence for international sport organizations. Hundreds of different languages and dialects are spoken throughout the world. For example, the term *footy*, a word commonly used in Australia to describe the sport of football (rugby league, rugby union, and Australian Rules Football), has little to no meaning in the North American sport context. In the United States, people often use baseball phrases such as "hit a home run" or American football terms such as asking someone to "quarterback a project." These terms would be meaningless in the international business setting.

To maximize profits, corporate leaders have realized they must look outside their boundaries to sell their products. Technological advances and increased access to technology worldwide drive the globalization of sport. The presence of satellite and digital technology as well as the popularity of the Internet and social media has made the transmission of visual images worldwide simple and virtually simultaneous. Globalization of sport is largely influenced by the contemporary superpowers that dominate these media. As a result, high-profile spectator sports in those countries with media dominance receive greater media exposure and, therefore, are the sports typically associated with globalization. Although spectator sports that attract greater media attention have an advantage in reaching global markets, globalization and diffusion are not dependent on media alone. This makes sense given the fact that only about 310 million of the world's 6.86 billion people live in the continental United States (U.S. Census Bureau, 2010). Clearly, to sell more products corporations must sell their products globally. This presents a challenge not just to mainstream businesses, but also to sport organizations.

Increasingly, sport organizations are eyeing a global strategy. Why does a Nike commercial for the Air Jordan running shoe have no spoken or printed words? Why does it include only visual images followed by Nike's trademark symbol, the Swoosh, at the end of the commercial? The answer to these questions is simple. These ads are created for a global audience. People in the United States will see the same ad as people in Japan. Further, the ad will have the same impact on American and Japanese consumers. Unfortunately, exporting the sport product is not always this easy. As with mainstream consumer products, adaptations based on cultural preferences often must be made. For example, the style of basketball played in the National Basketball Association (NBA) is not in adherence with Fédération Internationale de Basketball (FIBA) rules, and is not indicative of how the way the sport is played in the rest of the world and at international competitions. Efforts at globalizing the sport product can be seen on numerous fronts: corporations attempting to utilize the sport theme and sport products to enter the international marketplace; professional sport leagues attempting to spread the popularity of their leagues and associated products (e.g., televised games, licensed products) overseas; event and destination marketers leveraging events as sport tourism opportunities; and sport being used on a global scale as a medium that can aid in health and social issues.

Corporate Involvement with International Sport

People attend and watch sporting events expecting a good experience. With advances in technology, the Internet, and social media, audiences worldwide now have access to the top sporting events. Realizing that such access exists, corporations are increasingly using sport to sell their products to consumers on other continents. Generally, such activities can be grouped into two categories: (1) efforts by manufacturers of sport-related products, such as athletic shoes, athletic equipment, and sport drinks, and (2) efforts by non-sport–related companies that sponsor international sporting events, teams, and athletes to gain name recognition and thus sell their products in new global markets.

International Efforts of Sport Product Manufacturers

Similar to many corporations throughout the world, manufacturers of sporting goods and sport-related products are increasingly attempting to capitalize on potential international sales. The reason for such efforts is very simple: North American markets are becoming saturated. Today, many companies compete for the North American sporting enthusiasts' dollars because North Americans are sport oriented and have money to spend on sport products.

As a result, sport corporations are attempting to broaden their product distribution. For example, since 2000 Nike has sold more products overseas than in the United States. To do so, Nike not only focused on its most popular product lines, such as running and basketball shoes, but also looked to other products, such as golf shoes and apparel, hockey equipment, and football cleats and apparel. Because more people play and watch football than any other sport in the world, it was logical for Nike to expand its operations and focus on increasing its share of the football market. To meet this goal, Nike has signed with great teams like the Brazilian national football team, Manchester United, Manchester City, Juventus, Inter Milan, and F.C. Barcelona. It is also sponsoring the world's best football players, such as Ronaldo.

International Development via Sponsorship of Sporting Events

Non-sport–related corporations are also attempting to use sport to sell products internationally. Primarily, this is done through the sponsorship of international athletes and teams. Generally, such efforts are geared toward increasing awareness and sales overseas. By sponsoring prominent international sport efforts, corporations hope to benefit from the increased interest in sport. Coca-Cola is another large U.S. corporation that attempts to increase its popularity worldwide through international event sponsorship. Coca-Cola is a long-time International Olympic Committee (IOC) sponsor, and sponsors other sport organizations such as FIFA, Special Olympics, and the NBA.

Professional Sport Leagues' International Focus

Today, most professional sport leagues aggressively seek to increase the popularity and consumption of their respective products overseas. International travelers who see people in other countries wearing Miami Heat t-shirts or New York Yankees hats are witnessing the potential impact of new distribution channels for the major professional sport leagues.

Organizationally, each of the leagues has created an international division to guide such efforts. Within these divisions, each league maintains offices in cities throughout the world. For example, MLB International has offices in Australia, China, Japan, and London, in addition to the headquarters in New York City.

These divisions and international offices focus on increasing the popularity of North American professional sport by utilizing several common techniques and strategies: (1) broadcasting, (2) licensing and merchandising, (3) playing exhibition and regular season games, (4) cultivating participation in sport throughout each country (**grassroots efforts**), and (5) placing teams in international markets. In addition to increasing the popularity of the sport and the league on an international level, the leagues hope to increase participation in the sport. This increased participation should eventually increase the talent pool from which they can then recruit for the professional ranks.

Broadcasting

Many people around the world are introduced to sport from outside their home countries through television broadcasts of games and highlights. Visual images are easily exportable commodities. It is much easier for a professional sport league to reach international markets by first exporting its product through visual images. This strategy is aided by the fact that access to television sets and the Internet is increasing at a rapid pace.

Mergers in the mass media industry have also spurred growth. Major corporations now own major media outlets in numerous countries throughout the world. Perhaps the most notable conglomerate is the series of networks owned by Rupert Murdoch. Murdoch owns media outlets throughout Australia, Asia, Europe, and North America. In this case, MLB games televised by Murdoch's Fox Sports in the United States can also be packaged for overseas viewers on other Murdoch–owned stations such as BSkyB and Star-TV. Similarly, the English Premier League and Champions League are broadcast around the globe, primarily on networks owned and/or controlled by NewsCorp, as seen in the United States on Fox Soccer.

ESPN is also a heavy player in the international distribution of sport broadcasting. Its international division, ESPN International, has grown to include whole or partial ownership of 35 television networks outside of the United States. It also owns a variety of additional businesses that enable it to reach sport fans in more than 184 countries and territories around the world. ESPN International owns entities involved in all facets of sport entertainment. It has offices and production facilities around the world, including Bangalore, Buenos Aires, Hong Kong, London, Melbourne, Mexico City, Miami, Mumbai, New York City, Rio de Janeiro, São Paulo, Singapore, Sydney, and Toronto (ESPN, 2014).

Professional sport leagues have seized the opportunity to capitalize on such trends. Many professional sport leagues around the world are aggressively seeking to increase the popularity and consumption of their respective products overseas. The NFL's Super Bowl XLV in 2012 was televised in 180 countries and territories in 25 languages. The 2012–2013 NBA Finals were telecast in 215 countries around the world and translated into 47 languages.

Another tool for the NBA is NBA TV, a 24-hour television network that offers NBA news and information, live games, draft information, NBA Summer League, and behind-the-scenes specials that fans can access 365 days a year through their local cable company or satellite provider.

The Internet has also played a major role in spreading leagues' messages to new fans. All the major professional leagues have elaborate websites offering up-to-the-minute information on their respective leagues that are accessible to everyone with a computer. In addition to providing information, leagues also provide live coverage via various websites.

More leagues are also providing fans with access to games and information on their smartphones and mobile devices. The MLB At Bat app provides an MLB game of the day, live audio, exclusive in-game highlights, condensed games, and more. NFL Mobile includes live NFL games, the NFL Network, and the NFL Red Zone. The Barclay's Premier League offers an app, as does Bundesliga. FIFA provides a number of World Cup apps.

Licensing and Merchandising

Another tactic typically used to expand a sport to international markets is to sell **licensed merchandise**. Team-logoed merchandise provides people with a means to identify and associate with their favorite teams. However, sales of team-logoed items traditionally were isolated to the country in which the sport team competed. Increasingly, though, sport leagues are utilizing the sales of logoed merchandise as a means to increase league popularity internationally. The increase in popularity of online shopping has also increased the sales of team-related merchandise. Further, the sale of licensed merchandise serves as a promotional vehicle for teams or leagues. People purchasing and wearing Houston Rockets t-shirts and hats in Beijing serve to increase the awareness

of both the NBA and the Houston Rockets in China. When David Beckham chose to wear the number 23 on his shirt (the same number made famous by Michael Jordan), he had an eye on the U.S. market ("New Balance," 2003). Today, one can buy the jerseys of well-known football clubs as well as sport brands such as Ferrari in airports and malls around the world.

Exhibition and Regular-Season Games

The most obvious step a professional sport league can take in exporting its product is to actually hold matches or games on foreign soil. In this way, people in different countries have the opportunity to witness the sport in person. The NFL has played exhibition games outside the United States since 1986 and is now committed to playing at least one regular-season game on foreign soil each year. Other North American professional sport leagues have also undertaken significant efforts to export their product in game format.

MLB now features an Opening Day series in Japan, a practice that started in 2008, and, as mentioned earlier, the 2014 season opened in Australia. The NBA Global Games have now become an annual event. In the 2013–2014 season, the Minnesota Timberwolves took on the San Antonio Spurs in Mexico City and the Brooklyn Nets faced the Atlanta Hawks in London (NBA, 2013).

Marketing Foreign Athletes

As trade barriers between countries have diminished, so, too, have barriers preventing the top players in the world from playing in various professional sport leagues. The presence of foreign players has enabled these professional leagues to increase their popularity overseas. Specifically, by marketing these players in their homelands, professional leagues are able to increase the popularity of both the players and their respective sports overseas. The 2012–2013 NBA season set a record, with teams having a total of 84 international players from 37 countries and territories. Twenty-nine of the 30 NBA teams have at least one international player. In MLB, 28% of players on 2012 opening day rosters were born outside the United States, representing 15 different countries and territories. Further, 47.8% of minor league baseball players under contract in 2009 were born outside the United States.

The rise of satellite television, the Internet, mobile devices, and social media have aided this diversification. Improving technology allows worldwide audiences to see Emanuel (Manu) Ginóbili play for the San Antonio Spurs and Andrew Bogut play for the Golden State Warriors. The 2013 NBA Draft saw the Cleveland Cavaliers select Canadian Anthony Bennett as the first pick. These players increase the popularity of basketball throughout Argentina, Australia, and Canada, respectively. Increasingly, exhibition games featuring some of these foreign stars are being held in other countries.

Sport Tourism

An element of international sport involves travel to different countries to participate in, watch, or volunteer at various sport events or competitions or to view sport halls of fame, stadia, or museums. Participation in sport tourism is not a recent phenomenon, but the increased ease and convenience of international travel have made it more popular. Although the numbers vary on the financial impact of sport tourism, it was evident that visitors to the London 2012 Olympic and Paralympic Games spent more on average than the typical non-Games tourist (Telegraph Staff, 2012). As a result of media exposure from hosting the London 2012 Olympic and Paralympic Games, "the 2012–2017 legacy phase is expected to see an additional 1.1 million visitors worth £900m [$13,824,000]" (Wells, 2012, para. 6).

Three types of sport tourism are commonly identified: (1) travel to participate in a sport activity; (2) travel to view a sport activity; and

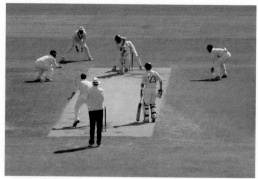

© Lance Bellers/ShutterStock, Inc.

(3) travel to visit a sport hall of fame, sport facility, or museum. Additionally, recent research has noted that individuals do, in fact, travel internationally to volunteer at sport events, including the Olympic and Paralympic Games. For example, the 2004 Athens Olympic and Paralympic Games received more than one-third of its applications of interest to volunteer at the Games from outside Greece, and 5% of the Vancouver Olympic Games volunteer workforce came from outside of Canada, indicating that many individuals were willing to travel internationally to volunteer for the event.

Sport for All

The Sport for All movement is an international movement that seeks to promote mass participation in sport without discrimination. The movement began in Europe in the 1960s and has since expanded globally. Unlike most forms of elite and professional sport, the purpose of Sport for All is not competition, but rather participation for participation's sake, as sport is viewed as both a human right and a key component of a healthy lifestyle. Specifically, the Sport for All movement seeks to involve all sectors of the population in physical activity regardless of age, gender, social or economic distinction, or physical or mental ability. The movement is, therefore, seen as a proponent of social integration. One of the goals of Sport for All is to make sport affordable and available to all communities, including underserved populations (e.g., children and youth, girls and women, the elderly, and people with disabilities). Many organizations working with these populations implement social marketing campaigns to increase levels of participation.

Regional, national, and international Sport for All organizations have been created to provide individuals with opportunities to participate in sport. The movement has been relatively successful in Europe, Australia, some parts of Latin America, and Africa, but has had limited impact in the United States.

The IOC Sport for All Commission was created in 1985 to integrate grassroots sport into the goals of the Olympic Movement and to globally disseminate sport as a basic human right. The Eleventh World Sport for All Congress was held in Havana, Cuba, in 2006; the theme of the conference was "Physical Activity: Benefits and Challenges." The conference was sponsored by the IOC and had the support of the World Health Organization (WHO) and the General Association of International Sport Federations (AGFIS). The 2010 Congress was held in Jyväskylä, Finland and featured the theme, "Promoting Sport for All as a Strategy for a Better 21st Century Society." In 2013, Lima, Peru, hosted the conference with three interwoven themes of social benefits, sport facilities and public spaces, and partnerships.

Sport for Development and Peace

The United Nations presents annual themes to bring attention to issues UN members believe the world should recognize. Thus, it designated the year 2005 as the International Year of Sport and Physical Education, with the goal of stimulating growth in organizations that use sport as a tool to promote positive social change (Beutler, 2006). This area of international sport is referred to as sport for development and peace (SDP).

Although the formal use of sport to promote social change has only emerged within the past 10 to 15 years, the use of sport to address social issues is not a new phenomenon (Kidd, 2008). For example, in 1922 the IOC and the UN International Labour Organization began a collaborative partnership (Beutler, 2006). One of the world's leading SDP programs, the Mathare Youth Sports Association (MYSA), has been using sport as tool to empower youth in the poor suburbs of Nairobi, Kenya, since 1987. MYSA uses football to educate youth about HIV/AIDS, provide leadership opportunities, and bring communities together to help others less fortunate.

Sport is at the core of what sport professionals do, but it can be hard to define. The UN Inter-Agency Task Force on Sport for Development and Peace suggests that *sport*, in the context of SDP, refers to "all forms of physical activity that contribute to physical fitness, mental well-being and social interaction. These include: play; recreation; organized, casual or competitive sport; and indigenous sports or games" (United Nations, 2003, p. 2). Although there are other definitions of sport, the one cited above highlights the broad scope of sport in the sense of SDP.

Development is also difficult to define, but important to address in order to gain a better understanding of SDP. In its Declaration of Right to Development, the United Nations (1986) defined *development* as a:

> comprehensive economic, social, cultural and political process, which aims at the constant improvement of the well-being of the entire population and of all individuals on the basis of their active, free and meaningful participation in development and the fair distribution of benefits there from.

Gilbert and Bennett (2013), in contrast, suggest that development in the context of SDP is primarily focused on human development.

Peace is another term with a broad range of definitions. The *Merriam-Webster Dictionary* has multiple definitions of *peace*, ranging from absence of war to "harmony in personal relations" (n.d.). Peace in the SDP context is primarily focused on conflict resolution and facilitating multicultural understanding. As highlighted in the challenges of defining these terms, SDP describes a broad range of programs and organizations that use sport as a tool to promote positive social change. SDP programs can be divided into several categories based on their primary purposes, including peace-building; post-disaster response; empowerment of girls and women; sport for persons with disabilities; health, education, and economic development; and career development. Questions arise as to whether these programs actually work and whether there is a template to follow for success.

Effective management of SDP organizations is imperative for their long-term sustainability. Many sport-based programs are operated in low- or middle-income countries but funded by organizations from high-income countries. Managers of both the grassroots organizations implementing the programs and funding partners (e.g., professional sport teams, corporate sport organizations, national sport federations, and governing bodies) need to critically reflect on their underlying reasons for engaging in these international development partnerships. Beacom (2007) suggests that greater transparency and open communication are crucial for mutually beneficial donor–recipient partnerships in SDP.

Managers of SDP organizations also must be aware of the need to support local capacity building and ownership in communities where sport-based programs are operated (Schulenkorf, 2012). Sport managers should develop strategic short- and long-term plans on how their organizations will empower local communities to develop the knowledge and skills needed to take control and manage grassroots SDP programs. Sport in and of itself is neither inherently good nor bad; how sport is used will determine whether outcomes are positive or negative (Coakley, 2011; Hums & Wolff, 2014; Schulenkorf, 2012). Therefore, Armour and Sandford (2012) suggest that sport should be considered a potential process for positive development rather than an inherently positive tool for solving social issues.

Sport can be viewed as a "hook" to appeal to the interest of youth, but the outcomes of these programs depend on the strength of their non-sport components (Hartmann, 2003; Hartmann & Kwauk, 2011). For example, A Ganar—meaning "to win" or "to earn" in Spanish—is an SDP program operated by the Partners of the Americas in 15 countries across Latin America. A Ganar is a sport-based employment-training program where sport is used as a tool in the initial program phase to teach employment skills. The latter stages, however, are focused on technical job training, gaining practical experiences, entrepreneurship, and mentoring by local business leaders to address the issue of youth (ages 16–24) unemployment. Thousands of youth have participated in the program, and more than 65% of program graduates secure a full-time job, return to school, or start their own business within 1 year. A Ganar is a good example of an organization focused on facilitating long-term change through self-help programs whereby participants are not simply provided with donated goods, but supported with opportunities to pursue careers in local business communities.

Sport 4 Socialisation International (S4S)—winner of the 2010 Beyond Sport Award for Best New Program—provides another valuable example of how an SDP program may be structured. S4S was founded by Isabel De Vugt in 2007 to promote social inclusion of children with disabilities and their families in Zimbabwe. Given that 80% of people with disabilities live in low- and middle-income countries and are often denied fundamental human rights and opportunities to education, health care, employment, and sport, S4S uses sport as a tool to empower youth with disabilities. The organization also operates support groups, awareness programs, and advocacy efforts targeting families of youth with disabilities and local communities to promote sustainable social change and social inclusion of people with disabilities.

Furthermore, the importance of SDP has been recognized by the United Nations. In 2014, April 6 was designated as the initial International Day of Sport for Development and Peace (IDSDP). The day was marked by celebrations of SDP around the world by large organizations such as the International Olympic Committee, the International Paralympic Committee, UNESCO, Magic Bus in India, The International Working Group on Women in Sport, Right to Play, and Sport Accord.

In summary, SDP is an emerging area of international sport whereby organizations and managers use sport as a tool to address social issues in communities worldwide. The number of SDP organizations has increased rapidly during the last decade with a broad range of programs. Sport managers need to be aware of the importance of their program structure, the promotion of local ownership, and the nature of funding partnerships for long-term sustainability of SDP organizations.

The Olympic Movement

The Olympic Games have played an important role in the development of international sport. Modern **Olympism** was conceived by Baron Pierre de Coubertin, on whose initiative the International Athletic Congress of Paris was held on June 23, 1894. There the **International Olympic Committee (IOC)** was constituted as the supreme authority of the Olympic Movement. Beginning with the inaugural modern Olympic Games in 1896 in Athens, Greece, the IOC has been entrusted with the control and development of the modern Olympic Games. In this capacity, the IOC has been quite successful. The Olympic Games are the largest multisport international sporting event today. Approximately 10,500 athletes from 204 National Olympic Committees competed in the 2012 Summer Olympic Games in London.

Although familiarity with the Olympic Games as a sport event is global, the key philosophy behind the Games, termed *Olympism*, is less well known. The Olympic Charter states that Olympism is:

> a philosophy of life, exalting and combining in a balanced whole the qualities of body, will, and mind. Blending sport with culture and education, Olympism seeks to create a way of life based on the joy found in effort, the educational value of good example and respect for universal fundamental ethical principles. (IOC, 2011, p. 10)

The Olympic Games extend well beyond the actual sport competition, corporate sponsorships, media broadcasts, and commercialism. The Olympic Games provide a space where countries from around the world can unite through a shared interest in festival and sport, a space where traditional status barriers are commonly transcended. Although the description of Olympism makes no mention as to whether the athletes competing should be amateurs or professionals, prior to the 1980s, a major mission of the Olympic Movement was to ensure that only amateurs competed. However, as the Games grew, the cost of financing the Games increased, and thus Games organizers were forced to rely more heavily on commercial enterprises.

The 1984 Summer Olympic Games in Los Angeles marked the turning point for commercial involvement with the Olympic Games, generating a profit of more than $200 million, largely due to corporate involvement (Graham, Goldblatt, & Delpy, 1995). Those Games marked the launch of **The Olympic Partner (TOP) Programme** sponsorship program. As corporations committed significant sums of money, they also saw the athletes and individual Olympic teams as opportunities through which to market their products. As such, it became very difficult to maintain amateurism as a standard for Olympic competition. All pretenses of amateurism were dropped in 1992, when professional basketball players from the NBA and other professional leagues around the world competed for their home nations on "Dream Teams" at the 1992 Summer Olympic Games in Barcelona.

For a better understanding of the Olympic structure, see **Figure 9-1**. At the top is the IOC, which is responsible for overseeing the Olympic Movement throughout the world. Beneath the IOC, the Olympic structure splits into two arms. On one side are the **National Olympic Committees (NOCs)**, the organizations responsible for the development and protection of the Olympic Movement in their respective countries. The NOCs promote the fundamental principles of Olympism at a national level within the framework of sports. On the other side of the

Olympic structure are the **international federations (IFs)**, the organizations responsible for the administration of individual sport competitions throughout the world. For example, the International Amateur Athletics Federation (IAAF) oversees the World Track and Field Championships, FIFA oversees football, and FIBA is the IF for basketball.

Related to both arms are the national federations (NFs)—also called **national governing bodies (NGBs)** or sometimes national sport organizations (NSOs)—and the **organizing committees for the Olympic Games (OCOGs)**. The NGBs operate within the guidelines set forth by their respective IFs to administer a specific sport in a given country. USA Track and Field is the NGB in the United States that selects athletes to compete in the World Track and Field Championships. The OCOGs are the organizations primarily responsible for the operational aspects of the Olympic Games. In essence, they are the event management arm for the Games. The OCOGs have to converse with the NOC of the country hosting the Games as well as with the IFs. Each of these organizational entities is explored in depth in the following discussion.

The International Olympic Committee

The defined role of the IOC is to promote Olympism in accordance with the Olympic Charter. The IOC is a nongovernmental, nonprofit organization based in Lausanne, Switzerland. The Olympic Charter is the codification of the fundamental principles, rules, and by-laws adopted by the IOC. The Olympic Charter governs the organization and operation of the Olympic Movement and stipulates the conditions for the celebration of the Olympic Games. As such, the IOC has a key role because it is the final authority on all questions concerning the Olympic Games and the Olympic Movement.

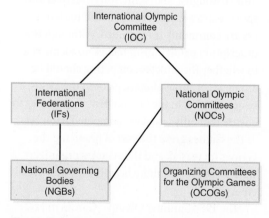

Figure 9-1 Organizational Structure of the Olympic Movement

Data from J.M. Gladden.

The IOC owns exclusive rights to the Olympic Games, the Olympic symbol (the five rings used alone, in one or in several colors), the Olympic flag (white background with the Olympic symbol in its five colors located in the center), the Olympic anthem, the Olympic motto ("Citius, Altius, Fortius," meaning "swifter, higher, stronger"), the Olympic flame, and the Olympic torch. Corporations wanting to use any of these marks must first pay the IOC a rights fee.

The IOC is governed by its members, who are self-selected (i.e., there is no outside vote on who is an IOC member). IOC members are its representatives in their respective countries and not delegates of their countries within the IOC. IOC members must speak at least one of the languages used at the IOC sessions (French, English, German, Arabic, Spanish, and Russian). There cannot be more than one member elected per country, except in the case of countries that have hosted an Olympic Games. In this case, countries are allowed two members. The IOC initially consisted of 14 members, with Demetrius Vikelas of Greece as its president. Today it has 104 members, 32 honorary members, and 1 honor member. The late Juan Antonio Samaranch was an Honorary President for Life.

The IOC is governed by three bodies: the Session, the Executive Board, and the president. The IOC Session, the general meeting of IOC members, is held at least once a year and is the supreme operating entity of the IOC. However, the president can call an extraordinary session if necessary. In these general sessions, the IOC members elect 1 president, 4 vice presidents, and 10 additional members to form the Executive Board. The main function of the Session is to adopt, modify, and interpret the Olympic Charter. Its decisions are final. Two other major responsibilities of the Session are to award the host cities for the Olympic Games and to determine which sports will be included on the official Programme for the Games. Both of these latter responsibilities have often sparked controversies and debates.

The Executive Board meets several times a year outside the Session to fulfill the duties assigned to it by the Olympic Charter. The Executive Board manages the affairs of the IOC, including approval of the IOC internal organization, management of the IOC's finances and preparation of the annual budget, presentation of a report to the Session on any proposed change of rules or by-laws, submission to the IOC Session of the names of persons it recommends for IOC membership, supervision of the procedure for acceptance and selection of candidatures for the organization of the Olympic Games, and performance of all other duties assigned to it by the Session.

The president heads the IOC and is elected by IOC members by secret ballot for an initial term of 8 years, renewable once for 4 additional years. The president presides over all activities of the IOC, acting as its permanent representative. In addition, the president can nominate special commissions to study certain specific subjects and submit recommendations to the Executive Board. Some of these special commissions are joint, comprising members of the IOC, representatives of the IFs and NOCs, technicians, consultants, and specialists. Examples of these commissions include the IOC Radio and Television Commission, Press Commission, Finance Commission, Medical Commission, and Athletes Commission.

© Photodisc

National Olympic Committees

The NOCs are responsible for developing and protecting the Olympic Movement in their respective countries, in accordance with the Olympic Charter. Specifically, NOCs are responsible for the following:

- Supporting the fundamental principles of Olympism in their countries
- Ensuring the observance of the Olympic Charter in their countries
- Encouraging the development of high-performance sport as well as sport for all within their respective countries
- Assisting in the training of both athletes and sport administrators
- Representing their respective countries at the Olympic Games and at regional, continental, and world multisport competitions patronized by the IOC

In addition, NOCs have the authority to designate cities that may bid to host Olympic Games in their respective countries. For example, the United States Olympic Committee (USOC) made the decision to put Chicago forward rather than Houston, Los Angeles, Philadelphia, or San Francisco as the bid city from the United States for the 2016 Summer Games. Those Games were ultimately awarded to Rio de Janeiro, Brazil.

The NOCs are organized regionally. The umbrella organization is the Association of National Olympic Committees (ANOC). Underneath ANOC, the NOCs are organized into five regional NOC organizations: the Association of National Olympic Committees of Africa (ANOCA), the Olympic Council of Asia (OCA), the Pan American Sports Organization (PASO), the European Olympic Committees (EOC), and the Oceania National Olympic Committees (ONOC). There are currently 204 NOCs spanning five continents. Before existing as an NOC, an organization must be recognized by the IOC. Recognition can be granted only to an NOC whose jurisdiction coincides with the limits of the country in which it is established and has its headquarters.

The United States Olympic Committee

The NOC for the United States is the United States Olympic Committee (USOC). The USOC is the organization mandated by Congress under the Amateur Sports Act of 1978 (as amended by the Stevens Amendment of 1998) to govern activities in the United States related to the Olympic Games, Paralympic Games, and Pan American Games. The USOC represents Olympic, Paralympic, and Pan American sport athletes, coaches, administrators, and the people of the United States who support the Olympic Movement. Most important, the USOC is responsible for sending the U.S. Olympic teams to the Olympic Games, Paralympic Games, and Pan American Games. USOC-affiliated organizations include four categories: Olympic and Paralympic Training Sites, Community Olympic Development Programs, community partners, and multisport organizations. According to the USOC (2013, para. 2), "The USOC has two primary responsibilities in its oversight of Olympic and Paralympic sport in the United States. The first is to generate resources in support of it mission, which is to help American athletes achieve sustained competitive excellence. The second is to ensure organizational resources are wisely and effectively used to that end."

The organizational structure of the USOC includes an executive committee and a board of directors. The executive committee meets as often as needed and is responsible for supervising the conduct of the business affairs of the USOC, according to the policy guidelines prescribed by the board of directors. The board of directors carries out the purposes and objectives of the USOC. It meets twice a year, unless otherwise decided by the constituency.

Organizing Committees for the Olympic Games

The honor of hosting the Olympic and Paralympic Games is entrusted by the IOC to the city designated as the host city of the Olympic and Paralympic Games. This honor is given to a city after it has gone through the bidding process. The bidding process has become increasingly complex due to the enhanced interest in hosting the Games.

The corruption crisis in 1998 in Salt Lake City brought many changes at the IOC. The crisis revealed that the IOC faced serious problems regarding its composition, organization, and role, as well as some of its procedures—in particular the selection of host cities for the Olympic and Paralympic Games. Criticism came when Salt Lake City admitted having influenced the votes of critical IOC members in its pursuit of hosting the Olympic and Paralympic Games.

The crisis brought a positive side because it allowed the formation of a commission that studied the crisis and brought solutions to the table (IOC, 2002). As a result of its work, a new procedure was adopted by the 110th IOC Session in December 1999 for the selection of the host city.

Once a city has been awarded the Games, it forms an organizing committee for the Olympic Games (OCOG). At this time, the IOC enters into a written agreement with the host city and the host country's NOC. From that moment, the OCOG is responsible for planning, implementing, and staging the Games. The responsibilities of the OCOG are enormous. The OCOG is ultimately responsible for the construction of all the venues, arrangement of accommodations for the athletes and coaches, accreditation, logistics, host broadcasting, security, medical services, technology, tickets, transportation, communications, finances, risk management, government relations, protocol, volunteer services, operations, and sports competition,

among other duties. It must also establish a marketing program and sign sponsorship agreements separate from those implemented by the IOC. The OCOG is also responsible for staging the Paralympic Games. As mentioned earlier, the OCOG is the event management arm for staging the Games. The OCOGs usually take on the name of the city. Recent examples include London Organizing Committee for the Olympic Games (LOCOG), the Sochi 2014 Organizing Committee, Rio2016, and the PyeongChang 2018 Organizing Committee (POCOG).

© Herbert Kratky/ShutterStock, Inc.

International Federations

International federations are the international governing bodies for one or several sports throughout the world. They are nongovernmental organizations recognized by the IOC to administer one or more sports at the world level and encompass organizations administering such sports at the national level. IFs must petition for formal recognition by the IOC. To be recognized, these organizations must incorporate the Olympic Movement Anti-Doping Code and conduct effective out-of-competition tests in accordance with the established rules. The IOC then grants 2 years (or any other period fixed by the Executive Board) of provisional recognition during which the IOC observes the federation to determine whether it deserves official recognition. At the end of such a period, the recognition automatically lapses in the absence of definitive confirmation given in writing by the IOC.

After each Olympic Games, the IOC reviews the Olympic Programme and determines whether new sports or new events should be added. At this time, IFs recognized by the IOC but not included on the Olympic Programme can petition to be included. For a sport to be included on the Summer Olympic Programme, it must be practiced by men in at least 75 countries on four continents and by women in at least 40 countries on three continents. To be included on the Winter Olympic Programme, a sport must be practiced in at least 25 countries on three continents.

The IFs can be classified under different categories:

- All the recognized IFs whose sports are not part of the Olympic Programme form the Association of IOC Recognized International Sports Federations (ARISF).
- All the recognized IFs whose sports appear on the Olympic Programme are known as International Olympic Federations. The ones whose sports appear on the Summer Olympic Programme are grouped under the Association of Summer Olympic International Federations (ASOIF). The ones whose sports appear on the Winter Olympic Programme are grouped under the Association of International Winter Sports Federations (AIWF). In addition, there is the Sport Accord, which also includes other sports federations.
- All the federations are grouped under the General Association of International Sports Federations (GAISF).

The IFs are run as international organizations, with their staffs determined by financial resources and objectives. **Table 9-1** presents a listing of the IFs. **Table 9-2** provides their website addresses. Sports such as basketball and football have large IFs, sometimes employing more than 25 people. In contrast, IFs for sports such as field hockey and team handball have very few employees.

In addition to actual Olympic competitions, each IF sanctions international competitions and establishes its own eligibility rules. An IF can have one set of eligibility rules for the Olympic Games, which must be approved by the IOC, and another set of rules for all other international competitions. For example, the International Ice Hockey Federation (IIHF) could decide to use different eligibility standards during the World Cup of Hockey than during the Olympic Games.

© Nicholas Rjabow/ShutterStock, Inc.

National Governing Bodies

National governing bodies (NGBs), national sports federations (NFs), or national sports organizations (NSOs) are the organizations governing a specific sport within each country. Each IF recognizes a single NGB in each country participating in the sport. For example, in the United States, USA Basketball is the NGB for basketball, and in Canada, Canada Basketball is the NSO for basketball, and both of these are recognized by Fédération Internationale de Basketball (FIBA), the international federation for basketball. An NGB's membership must be open to all national organizations concerned with promoting the sport.

Table 9-1 International Sport Federations (Recognized Olympic Sports)

Sport	International Federation	Abbreviation
Aquatics	Fédération Internationale de Natation	FINA
Archery	International Archery Federations	FITA
Athletics	International Association of Athletics Federation	IAAF
Badminton	Badminton World Federation	BWF
Baseball	International Baseball Federation	IBAF
Basketball	Fédération Internationale de Basketball	FIBA
Biathlon	International Biathlon Union	IBU
Bobsleigh	International Bobsleigh & Tobogganing Federation	FIBT
Boxing	International Boxing Association	AIBA
Canoe/kayak	International Canoe Federation	ICF
Curling	World Curling Federation	WCF
Cycling	Union Cycliste Internationale	UCI
Diving	Fédération Internationale de Natation	FINA
Equestrian	Fédération Équestre Internationale	FEI
Fencing	Fédération Internationale d'Escrime	FIE
Football	Fédération Internationale de Football Association	FIFA
Golf	International Golf Federation	IGF
Gymnastics	International Gymnastics Federation	FIG
Handball	International Handball Federation	IHF
Hockey	International Hockey Federation	FIH
Ice hockey	International Ice Hockey Federation	IIHF
Judo	International Judo Federation	IJF
Luge	International Luge Federation	FIL
Modern pentathlon	Union Internationale de Pentathlon Moderne	UIPM
Rowing	International Federation of Rowing Associations	FISA
Rugby	International Rugby Board	IRB
Sailing	International Sailing Federation	ISAF
Shooting	International Shooting Sport Federation	ISSF
Skating	International Skating Union	ISU
Skiing	International Ski Federation	FIS
Swimming	Fédération Internationale de Natation	FINA
Softball	International Softball Federation	ISF
Table tennis	International Table Tennis Federation	ITTF
Taekwondo	World Taekwondo Federation	WTF
Tennis	International Tennis Federation	ITF
Triathlon	International Triathlon Union	ITU
Volleyball	Fédération Internationale de Volleyball	FIVB
Weightlifting	International Weightlifting Federation	IWF
Wrestling	International Federation of Associated Wrestling Styles	FILA

Data from: http://www.olympic.org/uk/sports/index_uk.asp (2007), http://www
.internationalgolffederation.org (2010), and http://www.irb.com (2010).

Table 9-2 Web Addresses for International Federations of Olympic Sports

Federation	Sport	Web Address
Fédération Internationale de Natation (FINA)	Aquatics	http://www.fina.org
Fédération Internationale de Tir à l'Arc (FITA)	Archery	http://www.archery.org
Badminton World Federation (BWF)	Badminton	http://www.bwfbadminton.org
International Biathlon Union (IBU)	Biathlon	http://www.biathlonworld.com
Fédération Internationale de Bobsleigh et de Tobogganing (FIBT)	Bobsleigh and skeleton sports	http://www.fibt.com
Association Internationale de Boxe Amateur (AIBA)	Boxing	http://www.aiba.org
International Canoe Federation (ICF)	Canoe/kayak	http://www.canoeicf.com
World Curling Federation (WCF)	Curling	http://www.worldcurling.org
Fédération Equestre Internationale (FEI)	Equestrian	http://www.horsesport.org
Fédération Internationale d'Escrime (FIE)	Fencing	http://www.fie.ch
International Golf Federation	Golf	http://www.internationalgolffederation.org/
Fédération Internationale de Gymnastique (FIG)	Gymnastics	http://www.fig-gymnastics.com
International Handball Federation (IHF)	Handball	http://www.ihf.info
International Judo Federation (IJF)	Judo	http://www.ijf.org
Fédération Internationale de Luge de Course (FIL)	Luge	http://www.fil-luge.org
Fédération Internationale des Sociétés d'Aviron (FISA)	Rowing	http://www.worldrowing.com
International Rugby Board (IRB)	Rugby	http://www.irb.com
International Sailing Federation (ISAF)	Sailing	http://www.sailing.org
International Shooting Sport Federation (ISSF)	Shooting	http://www.issf-sports.org
International Table Tennis Federation (ITTF)	Table tennis	http://www.ittf.com
World Taekwondo Federation (WTF)	Taekwondo	http://www.wtf.org/wtf_eng/main/main_eng.html
International Weightlifting Federation (IWF)	Weight lifting	http://www.iwf.net
Fédération Internationale des Luttes Associées (FILA)	Wrestling	http://www.fila-wrestling.com

Data from: http://www.olympic.org/sports/index_uk.asp, 2007.

Each NGB is responsible for approving and sanctioning competitions open to all athletes in its country (USOC, 2010). For example, USA Track and Field is responsible for the coordination and administration of the USA Track and Field Championships. In addition, NGBs set national policies and eligibility standards for participation in their respective sports. Finally, NGBs are responsible for the training, development, and selection of the Olympic teams in their respective sports. USA Track and Field uses the USA Track and Field Trials to select the Olympic team for every Summer Olympic Games.

The Paralympic Games

The Paralympic Games, where the world's elite athletes with physical disabilities compete, represent one of the world's largest sporting extravaganzas. In 2004, 3,806 athletes from 136 countries competed at the Athens Paralympic Games (IOC, 2010). The Beijing Paralympic

Games hosted 3,951 athletes from 146 countries (International Paralympic Committee, 2010a). In 2012 in London, 4,237 athletes from 164 countries competed (IPC, 2013). A wide variety of athletes compete in the Paralympic Games, including amputees, athletes who use wheelchairs, the visually impaired, dwarfs, athletes with cerebral palsy, athletes with spinal cord injuries, and a limited number of athletes with intellectual disabilities. Introduced in Rome in 1960, the Summer Paralympic Games have been held every Olympic year since. The Winter Paralympic competition began in 1976 in Sweden (Hums & MacLean, 2013). The 2006 Torino Paralympic Games had 474 athletes from 39 nations (International Paralympic Committee, 2010b), the Vancouver Paralympic Games featured 502 athletes from 44 countries (International Paralympic Committee, 2010c), and the 2014 Winter Paralympic Games in Sochi included 547 athletes from 45 countries (BBC, 2014). Starting in 1988 in Seoul, South Korea, the Paralympic Games immediately followed the competition dates of the Olympic Games and shared common facilities.

Organizers of the Paralympic Games face the same major challenge as organizers of the Olympic Games: raising money to cover operating costs. With the Paralympic Games increasing in size and scope, the Games must generate revenues from corporate sponsorships, licensing agreements, and ticket sales. For example, in 2003 the International Paralympic Committee (IPC) signed an exclusive partnership agreement with VISA. VISA's agreement to become a Worldwide Partner is evidence that Paralympic sponsorship has grown. The IPC also added three other Worldwide Partners—Otto Bock, Samsung, and Atos. Other levels of sponsorship include International Partners (Allianz) and Government Partners (The Germany Ministry of the Interior, the Regional Government of North Rhine-Wesfalia, and the City of Bonn). The Paralympic Games are not governed by the IOC, and thus do not share in the millions generated by the Olympic Movement. Instead, the Paralympic Games are governed by the IPC, which is headquartered in Bonn, Germany.

The Paralympic Games have an organizational structure similar to that of the Olympic Games. The IPC oversees national Paralympic committees (NPCs). In May 2001, U.S. Paralympics became a division of the USOC. This structure is not the case in other countries, which usually have an independently operating NPC. Since the 2004 Athens Games, the management of the Olympic and Paralympic Games has been overseen by the site's OCOG. For example, in 2012 the London Organizing Committee for the Olympic Games (LOCOG) was responsible for staging both the Olympic and Paralympic Winter Games. As it stands now, the Paralympic Games are included as a required element of a candidate city's bid proposal to host the Olympic Games.

Career Opportunities

The sport management industry continues to evolve internationally, and potential job opportunities exist with a broad range of organizations in the private, public, and nonprofit sectors. International career opportunities in sport management may vary between regions and countries. The following discussion highlights some of these potential opportunities and provides examples of organizations and events from countries around the world.

Sport Agencies

The number of agencies or corporations specializing in sport continues to grow as the sport industry evolves. These specialized agencies provide services related to sport marketing, media, event operations, facility management, sales, licensing, athlete management, sponsorship activation, organizational management consulting, and more. Multidimensional agencies such as the World

Sport Group--employing more than 150 staff members in eight locations throughout Asia and the Pacific, including its headquarters in Singapore--provide customized solutions to clients by leveraging expertise in core sport management areas. The emerging role of technology in sport has also resulted in agencies such as Finnish-based Uplause and CrowdWave in Canada providing interactive crowd games for large sport teams and events worldwide to engage spectators through innovative technology. These types of agencies need passionate and knowledgeable managers to organize and lead partnerships with professional sport teams and major event organizers.

Professional Sport Leagues and Clubs

Professional sport leagues provide another avenue for potential career opportunities in international sport. These job positions require a detailed understanding of the sport, the organization, and the local culture and business environment. Many of the world's top sport leagues are in football (soccer) due to its global popularity. The top leagues include Bundesliga (Germany), Premier League (England), La Liga (Spain), Serie A (Italy), Ligue 1 (France), Serie A (Brazil), and Liga MX (Mexico). Opportunities in other sports include the Australian Football League (Australia), Nippon Professional Baseball (Japan), and Super Rugby (Australia, New Zealand, and South Africa). The largest professional sport clubs competing in these leagues also have front office staff members who specialize in marketing, communication, legal issues, accounting, finance, operations, facility management, licensing, and crowd management. Many of these opportunities require prospective employees to be fluent in the local language. Employers in many English-speaking countries are also increasingly looking for bilingual or multilingual skills due to the globalization of sport. For example, Manchester

United recently signed sponsorship agreements with two major Chinese companies and is strategically targeting new global markets to grow its brand.

Sport Mega-Events and International Sport Competitions

Large-scale sport events are organized by local organizing committees (LOCs). The Olympic and Paralympic Games are the most well recognized, but several other international sport events provide similar career opportunities. Sport managers are often hired years ahead of time due to the logistical demands of large-scale sport events. Therefore, it is important to stay updated on the bidding for sport-mega events in order to be familiar with future sites and potential job opportunities. Upcoming events include the 2015 Pan and Para-Pan American Games in Toronto, Canada; the 2018 Commonwealth Games in Gold Cost City, Australia; and the 2019 Asian Games in Hanoi, Vietnam. These events involve between 6,000 and 10,000 athletes. Those interested in pursuing a career with international sport competitions should also consider working with sport agencies specializing in event management, because services are often outsourced to these organizations.

International Sport Federations

International federations serve as the governing bodies for their respective sport. These organizations develop uniform rules, oversee and provide support to regional and national governing bodies, and promote their given sport. IFs also organize international competitions and world championship events for their discipline. International football (soccer) provides opportunities for those interested in sport event management with the upcoming FIFA World Cups in Russia (2018) and Qatar (2022). Other sport-specific events range from the FEI World Equestrian Games held every 4 years (2014 France; 2018 Canada) to biannual events such as the FINA World Championships (2015 Russia; 2017 Mexico). SportAccord––an umbrella organization for IFs––is a useful source for anyone interested in learning more about sport governing bodies.

National Sport Confederations

A national sport confederation is an umbrella organization for all national sport federations and is responsible for a nation's elite and amateur sports. This includes representing and advocating for its members in national and international matters. The broad range of responsibilities of these organizations requires staff members with expertise in many different areas. For example, the Swedish Sport Confederation has departments dedicated to communication, marketing, legal issues, political affairs, finance, sport development (elite, youth, and recreation), anti-doping, and education. Similar to professional sport leagues and clubs, working for national sport confederations often requires knowledge of the local language.

Sport for Development and Peace

The growth of organizations using sport to promote social change provides a broad range of potential job opportunities. These career opportunities are primarily with nonprofit organizations operating grassroots programs. Fundraising and monitoring and evaluation of programs are two of the biggest challenges facing SDP organizations. Strong analytical and critical-thinking skills are also important attributes as a greater emphasis is being put on the strategic management of SDP organizations. Other potential career opportunities exist with funding agencies such as the Nike Foundation or UK Sport––the national sport governing body of the United Kingdom––which has supported sport-for-development programs in almost 20 countries over the past two decades. Recently, UK Sport was responsible for implementing International Inspiration,

the international legacy program of the 2012 London Olympic and Paralympic Games aimed at reaching 12 million children with sport for development programs. Additional career opportunities exist with the UN Office on Sport for Development and UNICEF. The UN Office on Sport for Development website provides a list of international job and volunteer opportunities in sport for development.

Sporting Goods

Sporting goods companies such as Nike, adidas, and Puma provide career opportunities in many areas, including sales, marketing, and environmental sustainability. Li-Ning––one of the largest sporting goods companies in China––is expanding across international boundaries. In 2012, Li-Ning signed an endorsement contract with the NBA Miami Heat's Dwayne Wade. The World Federation of Sporting Goods Industry (WFSGI) is a valuable resource for those interested in learning more about potential international career opportunities in the sporting goods industry. The WFSGI website provides a comprehensive list of its members.

Corporate Sponsors

Prospective sport management professionals sometimes overlook career opportunities with corporate sponsors because these organizations do not operate sport events or services. Sport-specific positions, however, have emerged within many of these organizations as a result of the growth in sport sponsorships. Corporations such as Coca-Cola, Gillette, Barclays, and Nike employ full-time staff members with marketing and sales expertise to manage and activate their sport-related sponsorships.

Organizing Committees for the Olympic Games

Jobs become available with the organizing committees for the Olympic Games from the time the committee is formed (about 6 years prior to the Games). However, the 3 years before the Games are a crucial time for recruiting the right staff to work the Olympic and Paralympic Games. The available jobs can be related to any of the aspects needed to organize the Games, including administration, hospitality, international relations, logistics, protocol, technology, transportation, and ticketing. Usually jobs with OCOGs are temporary, lasting until the Games are over. However, some people work for one organizing committee after another because they have become experts in a specific area and enjoy living in a variety of different settings. The most appealing part of working for an organizing committee is receiving a unique experience. The drawback is that it is temporary and usually there is not much opportunity to grow inside the organization. Most of the time, an employee is hired to perform a specific task, and there is not much room for advancement.

National Olympic Committees

Different job opportunities exist within a National Olympic Committee. Depending on its size, an NOC can have anywhere from zero to 100 or more employees. In the United States, the USOC is a large organization, employing approximately 100 people. This number can increase with temporary jobs during Olympic/Paralympic years. In the case of the USOC, many employees are hired via internships. The USOC offers a formal internship program, soliciting applications and conducting interviews prior to hiring interns. Job opportunities at the USOC vary, but include positions in athlete development, broadcasting, coaching, corporate sponsorship, fund-raising, government relations, grants, human resources, international games preparation, international relations and protocol, legal aspects, licensing, management information systems, marketing, national events and conferences, public

information and media relations, sports medicine, sports science, sports for people with disabilities, and training centers. In addition, the NOC may be helpful in securing a position with one of the many NGBs within each country's sport movement. Again, the number of opportunities will vary greatly from country to country and from sport to sport.

International Paralympic Committee

The IPC is headquartered in Bonn, Germany. Similar to the IOC, the IPC offers employment opportunities for sport managers, including interns. Sport managers interested in working for the IPC should contact its office directly for additional information. Just as with the IOC, language fluency is necessary.

Current Issues

Cultural Awareness and Sensitivity

Individuals and organizations conducting business in different cultures need to appreciate differences and understand how the same sport can be interpreted differently from country to country, and from culture to culture. Therefore, when selling products overseas, some degree of adaptation to the local or regional culture is necessary.

In undertaking any international sport management effort, the sport manager must always be sensitive to **cultural differences**. Nike tailors the presentation of its product to the markets it serves. For example, Nike has always portrayed an antiestablishment image, allying with athletes who were prone to challenge conventional wisdom or accepted traditions. However, as Nike attempts to expand into the global marketplace, it has found that such a brash stance is frowned upon in many countries throughout the world (Thurow, 1997). Rather than attempting to buck established tradition, Nike must instead focus on respecting the cultures of other countries. Thus, in its initial efforts to sell more shoes in Europe, Nike featured a number of popular professional athletes in opera-themed ads. Incorporating one of Europe's most popular traditions, the opera, into its advertising enabled Nike to sell products to Europeans.

Foreign Student-Athletes in U.S. Colleges and Universities

In addition to the presence of international players in U.S. professional sport leagues, U.S. colleges and universities have seen an increase in the number of foreign student-athletes competing in intercollegiate athletics (Popp, Hums, & Greenwell, 2009). Foreign student-athletes have been participating in intercollegiate athletics since the early 1900s. In the late 1950s and early 1960s, college coaches began recruiting older foreign student-athletes who had several years of experience with international teams from their respective countries. Today, participation by foreign student-athletes is on the rise. Although some people argue there are too many foreign student-athletes, others suggest the presence of foreign student-athletes improves the caliber of play in U.S. college sport and provides universities with a more diverse student body.

Marketing the Olympic Games

Today, all levels of the Olympic Movement rely heavily on revenues from broadcasting and sponsorship agreements.

Broadcasting Rights

Broadcasting rights fees are significant for the IOC, accounting for 47% of all Olympic revenue (IOC, 2013). Broadcast revenues for the 2008 Beijing Summer Games were $1.739 billion and for the 2010 Vancouver Winter Games $1.279 billion (IOC, 2012). Broadcasting revenue has supported the Olympic Organizing Committees, NOCs, the World Anti-Doping Agency, the IPC, and international federations (IOC, 2013).

The IOC's long-term broadcasting strategy is to increase revenue and secure a consistent sum for the Olympic Movement and future host cities while avoiding market fluctuations. Establishing long-term rights fees contracts with profit-sharing arrangements and commitments to provide additional Olympic programs and guaranteed improved global coverage are related goals. Finally, a specific marketing strategy is to forge stronger links among sponsors, broadcasters, and the Olympic family to promote an agenda that goes beyond the Games to support the entire Olympic Movement.

Recently, there have been discussions between the IOC and USOC with regard to appropriate allocation of broadcast revenues. Based on an open-ended contract dating to 1996, the USOC receives 20% of global sponsorship revenue and 12.75% of revenue from U.S. broadcast rights deals. However, the IOC believed that this amount was excessive and sought to reduce the share received by the USOC. Based on negotiations between the IOC and USOC, the current U.S. share will remain the same until new contract terms come into effect in 2020. The new terms state that the USOC will receive a smaller share of the revenue once certain minimum amounts have been met. Talks on the issue had been on-going for 2 years, and there was talk the United States was not putting any host city candidates up for consideration until the dispute was settled (Associated Press, 2012). In 2014 NBC Universal agreed to pay $7.75 billion for the exclusive broadcast rights to the six Olympic Games from 2022 to 2032, the most significant broadcast deal in Olympic history (Sandomir, 2014).

Sponsorship Sales

All levels of the Olympic Movement (IOC, NOCs, OCOGs, IFs, and NGBs) rely on sponsorship sales to finance their operations. Following the IOC principles established in the Olympic Charter, there are three levels of sponsorship for the Olympic Games: The Olympic Partner Programme, NOC sponsorship programs, and OCOG sponsorship programs.

The Olympic Partner Programme

As touched on previously, the Olympic sponsorships sold by the IOC and its selected agencies are referred to as The Olympic Partner (TOP) Programme. Based on the success of the 1984 Los Angeles Olympic Games, in 1985 the IOC established TOP, under which corporations pay millions of dollars for status as an official Olympic sponsor for a 4-year period (quadrennium). Some current TOP members include McDonald's, Coca-Cola, Samsung, and VISA, among others. Recent costs to be a TOP sponsor were estimated at $100 million for the London 2012 Summer Games ("London 2012 Olympic Sponsors," 2012). This does not include the cost of supplies, materials, or personnel, but rather the cost of the fee to be a "member" of this exclusive club. TOP sponsors are the official worldwide partners of the IOC.

NOC Sponsorship Programs

NOCs have their own sponsorship programs as well. The NOCs usually use these programs to target domestic companies in an effort to generate funds for the development and travel of their Olympic teams. The TOP sponsors are encouraged to sign agreements with each of the NOCs. A preference in each category will be given to the TOP sponsor before the NOC signs with another company to protect its rights.

OCOG Sponsorship Programs

An OCOG also identifies and targets its own sponsors. However, it needs approval from both the IOC and the host-country NOC. BMW, BP, and British Airways were sponsors of LOCOG, the London Games Organizing Committee. For this right, they paid $63 million (Associated Press, 2012).

Doping

Doping allegations have dominated the media coverage of several international sports, including Olympic events, the Tour de France, World Cups, and many others. The Lance Armstrong story provided fodder for the media for years. Doping is "the deliberate or inadvertent (accidental) use by athletes of banned substances or methods that may enhance performance" (Sports Medicine Australia, 2006, p. 44). Many athletes in competitive sports have turned to doping as a means of gaining an advantage. Famous cases, such as the East German swim team of the 1970s, the cycling bust on the eve of the 2006 Tour de France, and the Lance Armstrong saga, may lead some to believe that doping is problematic only in certain sports and in certain countries, but this is not the case. In recent years, cases of doping have arisen across a variety of sports and in numerous countries.

After a drug scandal in cycling in 1998, the IOC recognized the severity of the doping issue, and in 1999, the World Anti-Doping Agency (WADA) was established with the goal of coordinating and promoting the fight against doping on an international scale. WADA was set up as an independent international agency funded by the world's governments and sport programs and remains universally accepted as the authority in anti-doping efforts. Guidelines and principles developed by WADA (known as the Code) have been adopted by the IOC, the IPC, all Olympic and Paralympic sports, national Olympic and Paralympic committees, athletes, national anti-doping organizations, and international agencies (WADA, n.d.).

WADA works with both athletes and organizations to protect athletes from the potentially harmful effects of performance-enhancing drugs and strives to create an equal playing field for athletic competition. In addition, WADA coordinates anti-doping programs at the international and national levels (WADA, 2003).

One of WADA's most visible functions is as a testing agency. It conducts "out-of-competition," or "year-round," testing for athletes. It also provides independent observers to monitor procedures at events such as the Olympic Games, Paralympic Games, FIBA World Championships (basketball), and Commonwealth Games. In addition to testing, the agency provides education, funds research, and conducts athlete outreach to connect one on one with athletes worldwide.

The IOC has stated that the fight against doping is its top priority. As a consequence, the IOC is adopting a zero-tolerance policy at Olympic events. Through a concerted effort among governments, WADA, and the world of sport, the IOC strives to educate athletes about the detrimental effects doping can have on health, the credibility of sport, and the athlete's career.

Summary

Today, more than ever, corporations, sport leagues, and sport governing bodies are attempting to increase their popularity and revenues in international markets. Technology, particularly with respect to the transmission of visual images and use of social media, greatly enhances the ease with which sport managers can introduce their products to foreign markets. In effect, the world is becoming smaller. Corporations are attempting to capitalize on this trend by sponsoring international sporting events in an effort to increase the distribution channels for their products. Major professional sports worldwide are attempting to utilize the shrinking marketplace to increase exposure for their respective leagues and sports in an effort to expand their revenue bases. This is true for both the popular North American professional sports as well as for the world's most popular sport, football. Ultimately, both corporations and professional sport leagues are attempting to improve the global appeal of their products, and to do so they must hire people with experience in international sport management.

The Olympic Movement also offers career opportunities for sport managers. Whether at the top with the IOC, or with an NOC, NGB, or OCOG, opportunities within the Olympic Movement continue to grow.

Such growth creates an increased need for revenues. Financing, most often in the form of sponsorships, is heavily reliant on the corporate sector. Thus, sport managers are needed to sell sponsorships and assist the corporations in implementing their sponsorship programs.

There is clearly a diversity of opportunities for the sport manager interested in international sport. Further, because technology will continue to improve and trade barriers between countries will continue to diminish, the volume of opportunities in international sport will increase. However, to capitalize on these opportunities, the sport management student must become knowledgeable about and sensitive to the cultures of other countries. The prospective international sport manager should also be prepared to learn new languages, because multilingual capabilities are necessary at the highest levels of international sport.

Case Study 9-1 Growing Australian Rules Football in the United States

© max blain/ShutterStock, Inc.

Australian Rules Football (Aussie Rules) is the number one spectator sport in Australia, but only recently has it been seen on an international scale. In 1997, the United States Australian Football League (USAFL) was founded with the mission of growing Aussie Rules in the United States. In particular, the USAFL's stated mission is to develop Australian Rules Football through "promoting awareness and knowledge of the Australian culture, by promoting a sense of community among USAFL clubs and club members, and by fostering women's and junior programs across the United States" (USAFL, 2010).

In April 2007, when the USAFL Board met in Louisville, Kentucky, it was noted that in 10 years the league had expanded to the point where it had more than 35 teams, located in nearly every major market in the United States, with over 2,000 players. At the meeting, the board discussed the league's goals for the next 10 years. It agreed on three primary goals for the next decade: (1) to grow the league to more than 10,000 participants, (2) to have 1% of the U.S. population become aware of and interested in Aussie Rules, and (3) to secure four new league sponsors.

A. J. Hudson, director of development, was put in charge of devising a plan to create and foster awareness and increase participation in Australian Rules Football. Hudson walked away from the meeting and started asking himself, "How will I generate interest in a game that only a limited number of people have heard of? How will I convince Americans to participate in a sport that is relatively new to the country? How will I position Aussie Rules to compete against baseball, American football, basketball, and hockey? Which community stakeholders could I get involved to help me with this project?"

Hudson knew that his budget was limited, because the USAFL is a nonprofit organization. He had to find a way to spread the word about the USAFL with a very limited budget.

Questions for Discussion

1. How could Hudson create awareness and interest in Aussie Rules?

2. What could Hudson do to inform the public of the league?

3. How should Hudson position Aussie Rules so that it is seen as an attractive alternative to American football, baseball, basketball, and hockey?

4. Which community groups could Hudson target to become involved with Aussie Rules?

5. Toward which target markets should Hudson focus his marketing campaign?

6. Which stakeholders (or sponsors) could Hudson approach to help to reach the USAFL's goals?

Resources

IMG International Headquarters
McCormack House
Hogarth Business Park
Burlington Lane
Chiswick London W4 2TH
(44) 208-233-5300; fax: (44) 208-233-5301

International Olympic Committee (IOC)
Chateau de Vidy
Lausanne CH 1009
Switzerland
(41) 21-612-6111
http://www.olympic.org

International Paralympic Committee (IPC)
Adenauerallee 212-214, 53113
Bonn, Germany
(49) 228-2097-200
http://www.paralympic.org

Major League Baseball International Partners
245 Park Avenue
New York, NY 10167
212-350-8304
http://mlb.mlb.com/mlb/international/

Major League Soccer/Soccer United Marketing
110 E. 42nd Street, Suite 1000
New York, NY 10017
212-687-1400
http://www.mls.com
http://www.sumworld.com

National Basketball Association International
Olympic Tower
645 Fifth Avenue
New York, NY 10022
212-407-8000; fax: 212-832-3861
http://www.nba.com

Octagon
1 Dag Hammarskjold Plaza 7th Floor
New York, NY 10017
212-597-8170
http://www.octagon.com

PyeongChang Organizing Committee for the 2018 Winter Olympic and Paralympic Games
325 Solbong-ro, Daegwanryeong-myeon,
Pyeongchang-gun, Gangwon-do 232-951
South Korea
(82) 33-350-3803
http://www.pyeongchang2018.org

Rio 2016 Organising Committee for the Olympic Games

Avenida das Américas 899
Barra da Tijuca
Rio de Janeiro, Brazil
22631-000
(55) 21-3433-5777
http://www.rio2016.com

United States Olympic Committee (USOC)

27 South Tejon
Colorado Springs, CO 80903

719-578-4654
http://www.olympic-usa.org

World Anti-Doping Agency (WADA)

Stock Exchange Tower
800 Place Victoria, Suite 1700
P.O. Box 120
Montreal, Quebec H4Z 1B7
Canada
514-904-9232; fax: 514-904-8650
http://www.wada-ama.org

Key Terms

cultural differences, global strategy, grassroots efforts, international federations (IFs), International Olympic Committee (IOC), licensed merchandise, national governing bodies (NGBs), nationalism, National Olympic Committees (NOCs), Olympism, organizing committees for the Olympic Games (OCOGs), The Olympic Partner (TOP) Programme

References

Armour, K., & Sandford, R. (2012). Positive youth development through an outdoor physical activity programme: Evidence from a four-year evaluation. *Educational Review, 65*(1), 1–24.

Associated Press. (2012, May 24). IOC, USOC resolve differences over revenues. Retrieved from http://espn.go.com/olympics/story/_/id/7967000/ioc-usoc-resolve-differences-revenues

BBC. (2014, March 7). Sochi Paralympics: Russia ready for biggest ever Winter Games. Retrieved from http://www.bbc.com/sport/0/disability-sport/26447291

Beacom, A. (2007). A question of motives: Reciprocity, sport and development assistance. *European Sport Management Quarterly, 7*(1), 81–107.

Beutler, I. (2006). *Sport for a better world: Report on the international year of sport and physical education.* New York: United Nations.

Coakley, J. (2011). Youth sports: What counts as "positive development?" *Journal of Sport & Social Issues, 35*(3), 306–324.

Cooper, L. (2010). Five strategies for a successful global brand. *Marketing Week.* Retrieved from http://www.marketingweek.co.uk/five-strategies-for-a-successful-global-brand/3015220.article

ESPN. (2014). Worldwide locations. Retrieved from http://espncareers.com/about-us/location.aspx

Field, R. (1997). Play ball: Just whose pastime is it anyway? *Play Ball*, 109–117.

Gilbert, K., & Bennett, W. (2013). *Sport, peace, and development.* Champaign, IL: Common Ground Publishing.

Graham, S., Goldblatt, J. J., & Delpy, L. (1995). *The ultimate guide to sport event management and marketing.* Chicago: Irwin Publishing.

Hartmann, D. (2003). Theorizing sport as social intervention: A view from the grassroots. *Quest, 55*(2), 118–140.

Hartmann, D., & Kwauk, C. (2011). Sport and development: An overview, critique, and reconstruction. *Journal of Sport and Social Issues, 35*(3), 284–305.

Helliker, K. (2009, Dec. 1). Canada flexes its Olympic muscles in Vancouver. *Wall Street Journal*. Retrieved from http://online.wsj .com/article/SB1000142405274870393940457 4566164171812676.html

Hums, M. A., & MacLean, J. C. (2013). *Governance and policy development in sport organizations* (3rd ed.). Scottsdale, AZ: Holcomb Hathaway Publishers.

Hums, M.A., & Wolff, E.A. (2014, April 3). Power of sport to inform, empower, and transform. *Huffington Post*. Retrieved from http://www .huffingtonpost.com/dr-mary-hums /power-of-sport-to-inform-_b_5075282 .html?utm_hp_ref=sports&ir=Sports

Hums, M. A., & Wolff, E. A. (2008). Sport and human rights. In J. Borms (Ed.), *Directory of sport science* (5th ed.), pp. 467–487. Berlin, Germany: International Council on Sport Science and Physical Education.

International Olympic Committee. (2002). *Report by the IOC 2000 Commission to the 110th IOC session*. Lausanne, Switzerland: Author.

International Olympic Committee. (2010). Official site of the Olympic Movement. Retrieved from http://www.olympic.org

International Olympic Committee. (2011). *Olympic charter: Fundamental principles of Olympism*. Lausanne, Switzerland: Author.

International Olympic Committee. (2012). *Olympic marketing fact file—2012 edition*. Lausanne, Switzerland: Author.

International Olympic Committee. (2013). Revenue sources and distribution. Retrieved from http://www.olympic.org/ioc-financing -revenue-sources-distribution?tab=sources

International Paralympic Committee. (2010a). Beijing 2008. Retrieved from http://www .paralympic.org/Paralympic_Games/Past _Games/Beijing_2008/index.html

International Paralympic Committee. (2010b). Paralympic Games, Torino 2006. Retrieved from http://www.paralympic.org /Paralympic_Games/Past_Games /Torino_2006/index.html

International Paralympic Committee. (2010c). Paralympic Games Vancouver 2010. Retrieved from http://www.paralympic.org /Paralympic_Games/Past_Games /Vancouver_2010/index.html

International Paralympic Committee. (2013). Great Britain. Retrieved from http://www .paralympic.org/paralympic-games /london-2012

Kidd, B. (2008). A new social movement: Sport for development and peace. *Sport in Society, 11*(4), 370–380.

Lai, F. Y. (1999). Floorball's penetration of Australia: Rethinking the nexus of globalisation and marketing. *Sport Management Review, 2*, 133–149.

Li, M., MacIntosh, E., & Bravo, G. (2012). Organization of European sport leagues. Excerpt from *International sport management*. Retrieved from http://www .humankinetics.com/excerpts/excerpts /european-model-causes-unique-on-field -and-financial-outcomes-for-sport-leagues.

London 2012 Olympic sponsors list: Who are they and what have they paid? (2012). *The Guardian*. Retrieved from http://www. guardian.co.uk/sport/datablog/2012/jul/19 /london-2012-olympic-sponsors-list

Merriam-Webster's online dictionary. (n.d.). Peace. Retrieved from http://www.merriam-webster .com/dictionary/peace

National Basketball Association. (2013). NBA Global Games expands with regular season games in London and Mexico City for 2013– 14 season. Retrieved from http://www.nba .com/global/nba_global_regular_season _games_london_mexico_city_2013_06_24 .html

New Balance liking strategy more and more. (2003). *SportsBusinessDaily*. Retrieved from http://www.sportsbusinessdaily.com /article/77620

Popp, N., Hums, M. A., & Greenwell, T. C. (2009). Do international student-athletes view the purpose of sport differently than United States student-athletes at NCAA Division I universities? *Journal of Issues in Intercollegiate Athletics, 2*, 93–110.

Sandomir, R. (2014, May 7). NBC extends Olympic deal into the unknown. *The New York Times.* Retrieved from http://www.nytimes.com /2014/05/08/sports/olympics/nbc-extends -olympic-tv-deal-through-2032.html?_r=0

Schulenkorf, N. (2012). Sustainable community development through sport and events: A conceptual framework for Sport-for-Development projects. *Sport Management Review, 15*(1), 1–12.

Sports Medicine Australia. (2006). *Sport medicine for sport trainers.* Australia: Author.

Telegraph Staff. (2012, October 11). Tourist spending spree at London Olympics boosts UK economy. *Telegraph.* Retrieved from http://www.telegraph.co.uk/finance /economics/9601918/Tourist-spending -spree-at-London-2012-Olympics-boosts -UK-economy.html

Thurow, R. (1997, May 5). In global drive, Nike finds its brash ways don't always pay off. *The Wall Street Journal,* pp. A1, A10.

United Nations. (1986). Resolution 41/128: Declaration on the Right to Development. Adopted at the 97th Plenary Meeting of the General Assembly. Retrieved from http://www .un.org/documents/ga/res/41/a41r128.htm

United Nations. (2005). *Sport as a tool for development and peace. Towards achieving the United Nations Millennium Development Goals.* Retrieved from http://www.un.org /sport2005/resources/task_force.pdf

United Nations. (2007). Sport for development and peace. Our mandate: What does sport have to do with the UN? Retrieved from http://www .un.org/themes/sport/intro.htm

United States Australian Football League (USAFL). (2010). About the USAFL. Retrieved from http://www.usafl.com

United States Olympic Committee. (2010). The United States Olympic Committee history. Retrieved from http://www.teamusa.org /about-usoc/usoc-general-information /history

United States Olympic Committee. (2013). Inside the USOC. Retrieved from http:// www.teamusa.org/About-the-USOC /Inside-the-USOC

U.S. Census Bureau. (2010). Home page. Retrieved from http://www.census.gov/

Vertelney, S. (2013). Will Major League Soccer ever have major league television ratings? Retrieved from http://www.goal.com/en-us /news/1110/major-league-soccer/2013/01/21 /3688186/seth-vertelney-will-major-league -soccer-ever-have-major

Wells, M. A. (2012, November 15). London 2012 Olympics: What is London's tourist legacy? *Telegraph.* Retrieved from http://www .telegraph.co.uk/travel/ultratravel/9680322 /London-2012-Olympics-what-is-Londons -tourism-legacy.html

World Anti-Doping Agency. (n.d.). *Play true.* Montreal: Author.

World Anti-Doping Agency. (2003). *World anti-doping code.* Montreal: Author.

Part III

Professional Sport Industry

Chapter 10 Professional Sport

Chapter 11 Sports Agency

Chapter 10

Lisa P. Masteralexis

Professional Sport

Learning Objectives

Upon completion of this chapter, students should be able to:

1. Compare and contrast the league structure and philosophy of the five major North American professional team sport leagues (NFL, MLB, NBA, NHL, and MLS).

2. Identify the primary sources of revenue of professional sport organizations: gate receipts, media rights fees, licensed product sales, and stadium revenues.

3. Illustrate the history of professional sport leagues in the United States and how the leagues organized themselves using a system of self-governance rather than a corporate governance model.

4. Appraise the ownership rules of each league, and understand basic concepts such as franchise rights, territorial rights, and revenue sharing.

5. Analyze the role of the league commissioner in team sport and individual sport.

6. Distinguish the operational and philosophical differences between individual professional sport and team sport.

7. Examine the role that labor relations have played in the development and relative welfare of owners and players in North American professional sport leagues.

8. Understand that legal issues are an important part of the professional sport industry, particularly contract, antitrust, labor, and intellectual property law.

9. Recognize the various career opportunities available in professional sport and the key managerial skills needed for success.

10. Debate current issues in professional sport such as salary caps; racial diversity among players, coaches, and administrators; globalization; concussion litigation; drug testing; and analytics.

Introduction

The professional sport industry creates events and exhibitions in which athletes compete individually or on teams and are paid for their performance. The events and exhibitions are live, include a paying audience, and are sponsored by a professional league or professional tour. The professional sport industry is a major international business, grossing billions of dollars each year. Although leagues and events derive revenue from **gate receipts** (ticket sales) and **premium seating** (personal seat licenses, luxury suites, club seating) sales, the bulk of their revenue comes from the sale of media rights. Professional sport has moved into new markets with the Internet and increased demand for television sports programming. Through the drafting of more international players by North American sport leagues and increased social media opportunities, professional sport has sought new international markets. The international sale of professional

sport teams' licensed products (e.g., apparel, videos, books, memorabilia) and the worldwide availability of online services add to the industry's international growth.

North America is home to five preeminent professional leagues: Major League Baseball (MLB), the National Basketball Association (NBA), the National Football League (NFL), the National Hockey League (NHL), and Major League Soccer (MLS). As of 2013, those five leagues included 141 franchises. Each year new leagues, such as the Arena Football League (AFL), Major League Lacrosse (MLL), the National Lacrosse League (NLL), the Women's NBA (WNBA), and the National Women's Soccer League (NWSL), emerge—some survive, and others do not. The minor leagues in baseball, basketball, soccer, and hockey are far too numerous to list here. Table 10-1 gives a breakdown of the number of major and minor league professional sport franchises operating in North America as of 2013.

Table 10-1 Numbers of Professional Sport Teams in North America, 2013

Sport	League	Number of Teams
Baseball	Major league (MLB)	30
	Minor league affiliates	189
	Minor league independents	55 (includes Mexican League)
Men's basketball	Major league (NBA)	30
	Minor leagues	16
Women's basketball	Major league (WNBA)	12
Men's football	Major league (NFL)	32
Men's ice hockey	Major league (NHL)	30
	Minor leagues	84
Men's soccer	Major league outdoor (MLS)	19 (2 to 3 expansion teams planned)
	Minor leagues (NASL, USL Pro)	24
Women's soccer	Major league outdoor (NWSL)	9
Men's lacrosse	Outdoor	8 (MLL)
	Indoor	11 (NLL and PLL)
Tennis	World Team Tennis	8
NASCAR	Sprint Cup	20 full time; 11 part time
	Nationwide Cup	21 full time; 11 part time
	Camp World Trucks Cup	18 full time; 10 part time

Numerous professional leagues also operate throughout South America, Europe, the Middle East, Asia, Australia, and Africa in the sports of rugby and rugby union, cricket, baseball, basketball, Australian Rules and American football, soccer, hockey, and volleyball. Professional athletes in leagues are salaried employees whose bargaining power and ability to negotiate salaries vary. In some cases, athletes are unionized, enabling them to negotiate collectively for better wages, benefits, and conditions of employment. In other cases, professional players may have little bargaining power. For instance, in the (MLB-affiliated) minor leagues, unless the player has prior major league experience, the player has little leverage to negotiate. Minor league baseball salaries are relatively uniform across the league, and for many players wages fall below what would be considered a living wage. For example, a typical Single A-level player's salary starts at $1,100 per month during the season plus a small amount of per diem money for meals incurred when on the road ($25 per day). Assuming that in an average week half of the team's games are home and half away, a player works (travel, practice, games, and community/fan relations) approximately 60 hours. Players generally have 1 to 2 days off per month. At the lower levels of baseball, this is hardly a living wage. Players with some level of major league experience earn higher monthly wages ($10,000 to $15,000 per month in season and nothing out of season). A good comparison is to look to minor league hockey players in the American Hockey League (AHL) and the ECHL (formerly the East Coast Hockey League), where conditions are far more favorable because the league is subject to antitrust laws and the players are unionized. Through their collective bargaining agreements, the minimum salary in the AHL for 2013–2014 is $41,500 (but $32,500 for players on loan to the AHL from lesser leagues) with $67 day per diem (PHPA, 2010).

The ECHL has a minimum weekly salary due to its frequent player movement. The 2013–2014 weekly minimum falls between $400 and $450 (depending on player's experience level), and the daily per diem is $42 per day (PHPA, 2013). However, teams are also held to a weekly salary floor of $8,900. If a team does not spend a minimum of $8,900 weekly on player salaries, the difference is paid by the club in equal allotments to all players on its roster. In sum, the AHL and ECHL through unionization have achieved very different working conditions for hockey's minor leaguers than that available for baseball's minor leaguers.

Countless professional sports events are also staged around the world in individual sports, including action sports, boxing, fencing, figure skating, golf, tennis, racquetball, running, and track and field. Individual sports are generally organized around a tour, such as the NASCAR (National Association of Sports Car Auto Racing Sprint Cup Series), the PGA (Professional Golfers Association) Tour, or the LPGA (Ladies Professional Golf Association) Tour. An athlete on a professional tour earns prize money, and a top (seeded) player considered a "draw" might earn an appearance fee. Athletes on some tours are also required to play in pro-ams the day before the tournament. For some tours, like the LPGA, the pro-ams are the lifeblood of the sport, because they are a place where players cater to their sponsors, and players are disqualified for failing to participate or for showing up late (Crouse, 2010). Sponsorship provides income and the products necessary for individual athletes to compete (e.g., golf clubs, tennis racquets, and shoes). The value of sponsorship to athletes is easily apparent with just a quick look at a NASCAR vehicle or the apparel worn by a tennis player such as Serena Williams. A tour stops at various sites for events and exhibitions that are usually sponsored by one named corporation (the title sponsor) and a number of other sponsors. Some tours also have television, cable, and/or radio contracts.

Tours or exhibitions have also been created for athletes by sport agencies in sports such as tennis, golf, and figure skating. These events serve many purposes, such as generating revenue for the athletes and their agencies as well as satisfying fan interest. For instance, the 2014 "Smucker's Stars on Ice" annual tour began shortly after the Sochi Olympic Games and featured many medalists and competitors hoping to capitalize on their Olympic achievements and name recognition. Sochi Olympic ice dancing gold medalists Meryl Davis and Charlie White competed on "Dancing with the Stars." Television and cable networks have also created exhibitions for programming purposes in action sports (ESPN's X-Games and NBC's Alli Dew Tour), golf (ABC's Skins Game), and other sports (ESPN's Outdoor Games). These tours and exhibitions generate income for athletes, sport management firms, and the broadcasting industry primarily from sponsorship, media, and ticket sales. Occasionally, some of the income generated from these events is donated to charity.

History

Professional Sport Leagues

In 1869 the first professional team, the Cincinnati Red Stockings, paid players to barnstorm the United States. The 10-player team's payroll totaled $9,300. At the time, the average annual salary in the United States was $170, so the average player's salary of $930 shows that as early as 1869 a professional athlete's income exceeded an average worker's wages (Jennings, 1989).

In 1876 North America's first professional sport league, the National League, was organized (Jennings, 1989). Among the principles from the National League's Constitution and By-Laws that continue as models for professional sports today are limits on franchise movement, club territorial rights, and a mechanism for expulsion of a club. Interestingly, these rules also allowed a player to contract with a club for his future services (Berry, Gould, & Staudohar, 1986). It did not take long—just 3 years—for owners to change that rule.

Following the National League's lead, other professional leagues have organized themselves into a system of **self-governance**, as opposed to a **corporate governance model** (Lentze, 1995). Under a corporate governance model, owners act as the board of directors, and the commissioner acts as the chief executive officer (CEO). Although it may appear that leagues have adopted a corporate governance model, Lentze (1995) argues that the commissioner's power over the owners does not place the commissioner under the direct supervision and control of the owners in the same manner that a CEO is under the direct supervision and control of a corporate board. This distinction is made because the commissioner in professional sport possesses decision-making power, disciplinary power, and dispute resolution authority (Lentze, 1995). The commissioner's role is discussed in greater detail later in this chapter.

Learning from the fiscal challenges facing a new sport league, MLS was structured as a limited liability company with owners initially investing $50 million in the league as a single entity to avoid financial and antitrust liability (Garber, 2004). Other leagues, namely the WNBA, AFL, MLL, and NLL, to name a few, have followed this trend to establish themselves as single entities to avoid antitrust liability and to create centralized fiscal control. The legal definition of a single entity is governed by substance, not form. In other words, to determine if a league operates as a single entity, and thus not subject to Section 1 Sherman Antitrust Act liability, one must evaluate whether the league joins together separate economic factors that would be actual or potential competitors (*American Needle v. NFL*, 2010).

Soon after the MLS was established, the **single-entity structure** was scrutinized in a lawsuit. The structure withstood an antitrust challenge from MLS players who argued that it was a sham created for the purpose of restraining competition and depressing player salaries (*Fraser v. MLS*, 2002). Although the First Circuit Court of Appeals disagreed with the players' allegations, it did not conclusively find that the MLS was a single entity, instead construing it as a hybrid that settled somewhere between a traditional sports league and a single company (*Fraser v. MLS*, 2002). As a strategy, the MLS players chose not to unionize because doing so and negotiating a collective bargaining agreement would allow the league access to the labor exemption defense in an antitrust suit. After losing the lawsuit, the players established the Major League Soccer Players Union (MLSPU). Interestingly, while the WNBA maintained a similar structure, its players chose to unionize rather than pursue an antitrust challenge. Shortly after the union negotiated its second collective bargaining agreement with the league, the WNBA abandoned the single-entity league structure in favor of a traditional team ownership model. In 2010, the U.S. Supreme Court ruled that traditionally structured leagues with separate owners having individual control of their teams are not single entities for antitrust purposes (*American Needle v. NFL*, 2010).

Franchise Ownership

Historically, sport team ownership was a hobby for the wealthy, with many teams being family owned "Mom and Pop" businesses. While no longer operated as "Mom and Pop" businesses, family ownership continues. The owners of NFL clubs are listed in **Table 10-2**. For these owners, the investment is not simply a hobby, but a profitable business venture and status symbol. In the NFL, family or individual ownership is still the norm, but the focus of these owners is

on running the team like a business rather than a hobby.

Family or individual ownership is successful in the NFL because it engages in far more revenue sharing than do the other professional leagues. Teams in other leagues with less revenue sharing are more dependent on groups of potential owners coming together to fund the purchase and operations of a team. That system of "haves" and "have nots," however, has been under fire as more of the newer owners who have paid hundreds of millions of dollars for their teams are seeking to maximize their local revenue to make a return on their investments (Foldesy, 2004). Jerry Jones, who paid $140 million for the Dallas Cowboys, began the challenge to this system by entering into marketing deals through his stadium, some of which ambushed the league's exclusive deals and led to a legal battle with the NFL (*National Football League Properties, Inc. v. Dallas Cowboys Football Club, Ltd.*, 1996). The chasm lies in the fact that some owners have paid as much as $600 million (Steve Bisciotti, Baltimore Ravens), $700 million (Bob McNair, Houston Texans), and $800 million (Daniel Snyder, Washington Redskins), whereas others have inherited their franchises and have no acquisition costs to recover (Brown family, Cincinnati Bengals; Halas-McCaskey family, Chicago Bears; Mara family, New York Giants; Rooney family, Pittsburgh Steelers). Although a vote in 2004 extended for 15 years the NFL's Trust, which owns all team logos and trademarks, oversees and administers the league properties rights, and distributes revenue for those rights to each club, there is a growing number of owners clamoring for more local control over the potential marketing revenues from using team logos, trademarks, and sponsorships. Although not the sole factor in determining that the NFL was not a single entity for purposes of licensing, the battle for local control of licensing revenues undermined the NFL's argument that it was a single entity

Table 10-2 NFL Ownership

NFL Team	Ownership	Year Ownership Began
Arizona Cardinals	Bidwell Family	1972
Atlanta Falcons	Arthur Blank	2004
Baltimore Ravens	Steven Bisciotti, Jr.	2004
Buffalo Bills	Ralph Wilson	1959
Carolina Panthers	Jerry Richardson*	1993
Chicago Bears	McCaskey (Halas) Family*	1983
Cincinnati Bengals	Mike Brown*	1991
Cleveland Browns	Jimmy Haslam	2012
Dallas Cowboys	Jerry Jones	1989
Denver Broncos	Pat Bowlen	1984
Detroit Lions	William Clay Ford	1964
Green Bay Packers	Publicly owned	1923
Houston Texans	Bob McNair*	1999
Indianapolis Colts	James Irsay	1997
Jacksonville Jaguars	Shahid Kahn	2012
Kansas City Chiefs	Hunt Family	1960*
Miami Dolphins	Steven M. Ross	2008
Minnesota Vikings	Zygi Wilf/Wilf Family	2005
New England Patriots	Bob Kraft/Kraft Family	1994
New Orleans Saints	Tom Benson	1985
New York Giants	Mara* Family & Tisch Family	1925, 1991
New York Jets	Robert Wood "Woody" Johnson	2000
Oakland Raiders	Carol & Mark Davis	2011
Philadelphia Eagles	Jeffrey Lurie	1994
Pittsburgh Steelers	Rooney Family*	1933
San Diego Chargers	Spanos Family	1984
San Francisco 49ers	DeBartolo/York Family	1977
Seattle Seahawks	Paul Allen	1997
St. Louis Rams	Stan Kroenke	2010
Tampa Bay Buccaneers	Glazer Family	1995
Tennessee Titans	Estate of Bud Adams	2013
Washington Redskins	Daniel Snyder	1999

*Denotes original owner or descendant of original owner.

Data compiled from http://www.nfl.com and team websites.

with licensed properties controlled at the league level in *American Needle v. NFL* (2010). There was evidence that the Dallas Cowboys, Miami Dolphins, and Oakland Raiders had different arrangements for their licensed properties than the other teams in the NFL, undermining their argument of a single entity.

Ownership Rules

Not just anyone can become a sports franchise owner. It takes a great deal of capital, but even having the financial capacity and the desire to purchase a team does not guarantee eventual ownership of a team. Permission to own a sports franchise must be granted by a league's ownership committee. Each league imposes restrictions on ownership, including a limit on the number of **franchise rights** granted and restrictions on franchise location. Franchise rights, the privileges afforded to owners, are granted with ownership. These include such rights as **territorial rights**, which limit a competitor franchise from moving into another team's territory without league permission and providing compensation to the rightsholder; and **revenue sharing**, which gives a team a portion of various league-wide revenues (e.g., expansion fees, national television revenue, gate receipts, and licensing revenues). Owners also receive the right to serve on ownership committees. Ownership committees exist for such areas as rules (competition/rules of play), franchise ownership, finance, labor relations/negotiations, television, and expansion. Ownership committees make decisions and set policies for implementation by the commissioner's office.

Leagues may also impose eligibility criteria for franchise ownership. For instance, MLB has no formal ownership criteria, but it does have key characteristics it looks for when granting ownership rights (Friedman & Much, 1997). Key considerations include substantial financial resources, a commitment to the local area where the franchise is located, a commitment to baseball, local government support, and an ownership structure that does not conflict with MLB's interests (Friedman & Much, 1997).

The NFL has the strictest ownership rules. It is the only league to prohibit **corporate ownership** of its franchises, which it has done since 1970. The NFL has made one exception to its rule for the San Francisco 49ers. In 1986, then-owner Eddie DeBartolo, Jr., transferred ownership of the team to the Edward J. DeBartolo Co., a shopping mall development corporation. Although the NFL fined DeBartolo $500,000 in 1990, it let the corporate ownership remain (Friedman & Much, 1997). The team is currently operated by DeBartolo's nephew, Jed

York. The NFL also bans **public ownership** with one exception—the Green Bay Packers, which were publicly owned prior to the creation of the 1970 rule and thus were exempted from it.

Until March 1997, the NFL strictly banned **cross-ownership**; that is, ownership of more than one sport franchise (Friedman & Much, 1997). The NFL softened, but reaffirmed, its rule on cross-ownership to allow Wayne Huizenga, then-majority owner of MLB's Florida Marlins and the NHL's Florida Panthers, to purchase the Miami Dolphins, and Paul Allen, majority owner of the NBA's Portland Trailblazers, to purchase the Seattle Seahawks. The new rule allows an NFL owner to own other sports franchises in the same market or own an NFL franchise in one market and another franchise in another market, provided that market has no NFL team (Friedman & Much, 1997). This change also paved the way for NFL owners to become investors in multiple MLS teams. The Kansas City Chief's Lamar Hunt became an investor-operator of the Kansas City Wizards, Dallas Burn, and Columbus Crew. The New England Patriots' Bob Kraft became investor-operator of the New England Revolution and the now defunct San Jose Earthquakes. Paul Allen became the investor-operator of the Seattle Sounders. Although the clubs are in NFL markets, soccer club ownership does not violate the rule because investors in MLS invest in the league as a single entity, not in individual teams. The investors then operate the club locally and retain a percentage of local revenue.

The Commissioner

The role of the **commissioner** in professional sport leagues has evolved over time. Until 1921 a three-member board, the National Commission, governed baseball. In September 1920, an indictment was issued charging eight Chicago White Sox players with attempting to fix World Series games, an incident commonly known as the Black Sox scandal (*Finley* *v. Kuhn*, 1978). To squelch public discontent, baseball owners appointed Judge Kennesaw Mountain Landis the first professional sport league commissioner in November 1920. Landis was signed to a 7-year contract and received an annual salary of $50,000 (Graffis, 1975). Landis agreed to take the position on the condition that he was granted exclusive authority to act in the best interests of baseball; then, in his first act, he issued lifetime bans to the eight "Black Sox" players for their involvement in the scandal. In his first decade in office, he banned 11 additional players, suspended Babe Ruth, and said no to any attempts to change the game by introducing marketing strategies or opening baseball to black players (Helyar, 1994).

In North American professional sport leagues, the league's constitution and by-laws set forth commissioner powers. Players associations have used collective bargaining to limit the commissioner's powers by negotiating for grievance arbitration provisions that invoke a neutral arbitrator and for procedures to govern disputes between the league or club and a player. Players view the commissioner as an employee of the owners and believe that he or she will usually rule in the owners' favor for fear of damaging his or her standing with them. For example, many people cite former MLB Commissioner Fay Vincent's intervention in the lockout of 1990—which he did because of his belief that it was in the best interest of baseball and the best interest of the fans—as the beginning of the end of his term as commissioner.

Team owners have tried court challenges to limit the power of the commissioner. Three cases have upheld the baseball commissioner's right to act within the best interests of the game, provided that the commissioner follows league rules and policies when levying sanctions. In *Milwaukee American Association v. Landis* (1931), Commissioner Landis' disapproval of an assignment of a player contract from the major league St. Louis Browns to a minor league Milwaukee team was upheld. In *Atlanta National League Baseball Club, Inc. v. Kuhn* (1977), the court upheld Commissioner Kuhn's suspension of owner Ted Turner for tampering with player contracts, but found that the commissioner's removal of the Braves' first-round draft choice exceeded his authority because the MLB rules did not allow for such a penalty. In *Finley v. Kuhn* (1978), the court upheld Commissioner Kuhn's disapproval of the Oakland A's sale of Vida Blue to the New York Yankees and of Rollie Fingers and Joe Rudi to the Boston Red Sox for $1.5 and $2 million, respectively, as being against the best interests of baseball. *Finley v. Kuhn* (1978) is particularly interesting when viewed against some recent moves made by team management to liquidate talent that have gone unchecked by the current commissioner. Following Fay Vincent's departure, MLB operated without a permanent commissioner. Its current commissioner, Bud Selig, has been accused of operating with a conflict of interest due to his former ownership of the Milwaukee Brewers.

To this day commissioners maintain some of the original authority granted by baseball, particularly the authority to investigate and impose penalties when individuals involved with the sport are suspected of acting against the best interests of the game. The commissioner generally relies on this clause to penalize players or owners who gamble, use drugs, or engage in behavior that might tarnish the league's image. The commissioner no longer has the power to hear disputes regarding player compensation, except in the MLS, where compensation is determined at the league level by the commissioner's staff. Because the MLS is a single entity, compensation and personnel decisions are made centrally. Commissioners continue to possess discretionary powers in the following areas:

- Approval of player contracts
- Resolution of disputes between players and clubs

- Resolution of disputes between clubs
- Resolution of disputes between player or club and the league
- Disciplinary matters involving owners, clubs, players, and other personnel
- Rule-making authority (Yasser et al., 2003, p. 381)

Commissioners in other professional sports were modeled after baseball's commissioner; however, not all embraced the role of disciplinarian as did Landis. Modern sport commissioners are as concerned with marketing as they are with discipline. For example, in the 1960s Pete Rozelle took the NFL to new levels of stability with his revenue-sharing plans. Rozelle introduced NFL Properties, an NFL division that markets property rights for the entire NFL instead of allowing each team to market its own property rights. This idea was consistent with the **"league think"** philosophy he introduced to the NFL. With league think, Rozelle preached that owners needed to think about what was best for the NFL as a whole, as opposed to what was best for their individual franchises (Helyar, 1994).

Labor Relations

John Montgomery Ward, a Hall of Fame infielder/pitcher and lawyer, established the Brotherhood of Professional Base Ball Players as the first players association in 1885 (Staudohar, 1996). Although the Brotherhood had chapters on all teams (Staudohar, 1996), it became the first of four failed labor-organizing attempts. Ward fought the reserve system, salary caps of between $1,500 and $2,500 per team (depending on the team's classification), and the practice of selling players without the players' receiving a share of the profits (Jennings, 1989). Under the reserve system, players were bound perpetually to their teams, so owners could retain player rights and depress players' salaries.

When owners ignored Ward's attempts to negotiate, 200 players organized a revolt, which led to the organization of the Players League, a rival league that attracted investors and was run like a corporation, with players sharing in the profits. The Players League attracted players by offering 3-year contracts under which the salary could be increased but not decreased. The Players League folded after its first year, but only after the National League spent nearly $4 million to bankrupt it and after the media turned on the Brotherhood. Most players returned to their National League teams, and collective player actions were nonexistent for about 10 years (Jennings, 1989).

In the six decades following the Players League, three organizing attempts were unsuccessful largely due to the owners' ability to defeat the labor movement or the players' own sense that they did not belong to a union. Players were somewhat naive in their thinking, and they viewed their associations more as fraternal organizations than trade unions (Cruise & Griffiths, 1991). Cruise and Griffiths noted that NHL players started the organizations to acquire information and improve some working conditions, but feared that if they positioned themselves as a trade union their relationship with the owners would be so adversarial that it would damage their sport.

Formed in 1952, the Major League Baseball Players Association (MLBPA) was initially dominated by management, and its negotiations were limited to pensions and insurance (Staudohar, 1996). However, in 1966, things changed when Marvin Miller, an executive director with a trade union background, took over. Miller's great success is attributed to, among other things, organizing players by convincing all players that each of them (regardless of star status) was essential to game revenues and by bargaining for provisions that affected most players (minimum salary, per diem, pensions, insurance, salary and grievance arbitration, etc.) (Miller, 1991).

Miller also convinced the players to develop a group promotional campaign in order to raise funds for the players association. Players authorized the association to enter into a group licensing program with Coca-Cola in 1966, which provided $60,000 in licensing fees. Miller also encouraged the players to hold out with Topps Trading Card Company. By holding out, the players association doubled the fees for trading cards from $125 to $250 per player and contributed a percentage of royalties to the union (8% on sales up to $4 million and 10% thereafter). Twenty-five years later, the players association brought in approximately $57 million in licensing fees and $50 million in trading card royalties from five card companies (Miller, 1991).

The National Basketball Players Association (NBPA) was established in 1954, but it took 10 years for the NBA to recognize it as the players' exclusive labor union. In 1964, the average annual salary was $8,000, and there was no minimum salary. Players did not receive pensions, per diems, or healthcare benefits. The 1964 All-Star team, led by union leaders and future hall of famers Bob Cousy, Tommy Heinsohn, and Oscar Robertson, threatened not to play in the NBA's first televised all-star game, resulting in a players association victory (NBPA, 2010).

NHL players attempted to unionize in 1957 when Ted Lindsay, Doug Harvey, Bill Gadsby, Fernie Flaman, Gus Mortson, and Jimmy Thomson sought to protect the average hockey player and establish a strong pension plan. They received authorization from every NHL player but one. After the owners publicly humiliated players, fed false salary information to the press, and traded or demoted players (including Lindsay) in retaliation for their involvement with the union, the NHL finally broke the players association. Many average players feared for what would happen to them, because the NHL

owners seemed to have no problem humiliating, threatening, trading, and/or releasing superstars such as Lindsay for their involvement in the players association (Cruise & Griffiths, 1991).

The Professional Hockey Players Association (PHPA), established in 1967, is the oldest union for minor league players. It has represented minor league hockey players in the AHL and ECHL. More recently, newer leagues' unions were created as divisions of more established unions. For example, the Women's National Basketball Players Association (WNBPA) became part of the NBPA in 1998, and the Arena Football League Players Association (AFLPA) became part of the National Football League Players Association (NFLPA) in 2001.

In sum, labor relations did not play a major role in professional sports until the late 1960s but has become a more dominant force in recent times. By the early 1970s, the professional sport industry had begun its transformation to a more traditional business model. Growing fan interest and increased revenues from television and sponsorship transformed leagues into lucrative business enterprises that lured additional wealthy business owners looking for tax shelters and ego boosters. New leagues and expansion provided more playing opportunities and thus more bargaining power to the players. The increased bargaining power and financial rewards led players to turn increasingly to agents and players associations (Staudohar, 1996). Players associations, once "weak or nonexistent, became a countervailing power to the owners' exclusive interests" (Staudohar, 1996, p. 4).

Under labor law, once players have unionized, professional sport league management cannot make unilateral changes to hours, wages, or terms and conditions of employment. These items are mandatory subjects for bargaining and must be negotiated between the league and the players association. The contract that results from these negotiations is called a **collective bargaining agreement (CBA)**. Collective bargaining in professional sports is far messier than in other industries. Players are impatient in negotiating provisions in the CBA. They have short careers and need to earn as much as possible in a short period of time, thus shifting their priorities to the wage provisions; therefore, more is financially at stake for both sides. The owners seek cost containment through restrictions on free agency, salary caps, and other wage restrictions, whereas players seek payment and player movement through a free market.

Strikes and lockouts are also far more disruptive in professional sport than in other industries, because players possess unique talents and cannot be replaced. Thus, a strike or lockout effectively shuts the business down. A good example of the difference can be seen in the nationwide United Parcel Service (UPS) strike of 1997. Although the strike severely disrupted UPS's service, it did not completely shut down business because managers could deliver packages and hire replacement workers. In contrast, it would be very difficult to find a replacement for a Derek Jeter, Kobe Bryant, Peyton Manning, or Sidney Crosby. Fans will not pay to see unknown players on the field, and television networks and sponsors would pull their financial support from the league. In the 1995 MLB strike, the owners' attempt to use replacement players failed. The one time that replacement players did make an impact was during the NFL strike of 1987 shortly after the United States Football League (USFL) disbanded. The owners were able to break the strike by using replacement players from the available labor pool of marquee, unemployed, talented USFL players.

When the collective bargaining process reaches an **impasse** (a breakdown in negotiations), the players can opt to strike or the owners can opt to "lock out" the players in order to spur the process along. Over the three-decade history of labor relations in professional sports, there have been numerous strikes (involving the MLB, NFL, and NHL) and lockouts (involving the MLB, NBA, NFL, and NHL). It is unique to sport that often prior to negotiating to impasse, owners will announce an inevitable lockout or players will announce a strike. In other industries, the lockout or strike is an economic weapon of last resort after bargaining to impasse. Another aspect unique to professional sport is the leagues' interest in players unionizing. Universally, in other industries, management prefers their workplaces to be free from unions. However, in professional sport, with a union in place, the league can negotiate with the players associations for acceptance of restrictive practices through the collective bargaining process. Under antitrust law, any restrictive practices that primarily injure union members and that are negotiated in a collective bargaining agreement are exempt from antitrust laws. All of the restrictive practices in professional sport included in the collective bargaining agreement—the draft, salary cap, restrictions on free agency, and the like—are thereby immune from antitrust lawsuits, saving the owners millions of dollars in potential antitrust damages.

Individual Professional Sports

Individual professional sports generally exist around a tour of events, meets, or matches. This chapter discusses the history of just one professional tour, the PGA Tour, as a case study of the different structures that are possible and the challenges facing individual sport governance and tours.

The first U.S. Open was held in 1895, but the PGA was not born until January 1916, when a New York department store magnate called together golf professionals and amateur golfers to create a national organization to promote the game and to improve the golf professional's vocation ("History of the PGA Tour," 1997). Its constitution, by-laws, and rules were modeled after those of the British PGA and were completed in April 1916 (Graffis, 1975). The PGA's objectives were as follows:

- To promote interest in the game of golf
- To elevate the standards of the golf professional's vocation
- To protect the mutual interest of PGA members
- To hold meetings and tournaments for the benefit of members
- To establish a Benevolent Relief Fund for PGA members
- To accomplish any other objective determined by the PGA ("History of the American PGA," 1997)

During the PGA's formative years (1916–1930), much of its energy was focused on developing rules of play, establishing policies, cleaning up jurisdictional problems with manufacturers and the U.S. Golf Association, standardizing golf equipment, and learning its own administrative needs. In 1921, the PGA hired an administrative assistant and began a search for a commissioner. Unlike MLB, the PGA was not looking for a disciplinarian, but rather for an individual with strong administrative capabilities to conduct its daily operations. Nine years later, the PGA hired Chicago lawyer and four-time president of the Western Golf Association Albert R. Gates as commissioner for a salary of $20,000. Gates' guiding principle in making decisions was to ask the question, "What good will it do golf?" (Graffis, 1975).

The practice of charging spectators began at fund-raisers by top male and female golfers to benefit the Red Cross during World War I. The PGA later adopted the practice for its tournaments to raise money for the PGA's Benevolent Fund. Soon golfer Walter Hagen began to charge for his performances (Graffis, 1975). Today, each PGA Tour event is linked to a charity. Some, like the Deutsche Bank Classic (DBC) are run by the charity. In the case of the DBC, it is the Tiger Woods Foundation (Antolini, 2104). In other cases, the tournament may be run by an agency, such as IMG. In either case, the proceeds of the Tour event go to charity. To date, the PGA Tour has contributed over $2 billion to charity (PGA Tour Charities, 2014).

© Duard van der Westhuizen/ShutterStock, Inc.

When the PGA was founded there was no distinction between club and touring professionals. Tournaments were small and manageable until television began paying for golf programming. The influence of television made golf more of a business than a game. In the early to mid-1960s, a number of factors created a growing tension between the PGA tournament professionals and country club professionals, because the two groups' interests clashed. Questions were raised concerning the mission of the

PGA. Was it to operate PGA Business Schools for local club professionals, primarily given the task of promoting interest in golf and golf-related products locally? Or was it to work with professionals coming through the Qualifying School (Q-School) for the PGA Tour circuit?

At annual meetings held from 1961 to 1966, the PGA became a house divided over control and power. Tour professionals claimed they had the support of a majority of golf's sponsors and threatened to leave the PGA to form a new association and tour. At the 1966 meeting, the PGA identified two different constituencies in professional golf: first, the club professionals who served the amateur players, and, second, the showcase professionals who provided the entertainment for golf's spectators (Graffis, 1975). Two years later, the PGA tournament players broke away to form a Tournament Players Division, which in 1975 was renamed the PGA TOUR ("History of the American PGA," 1997). The PGA TOUR, headquartered in Ponte Vedra, Florida, operates five tours: the PGA Tour, the Champions (Senior) Tour, PGA Tour Canada, NEC Series Latinoamérica, and the Web.com Tour (PGA TOUR, 2014a). Television revenues and corporate sponsorship have increased the purses for players on the PGA Tour ("History of the PGA Tour," 1997). The PGA Tour now schedules events year round, and tournament purses have grown. Purses for PGA Tour events range from $1.35 to $9 million per tournament (PGA TOUR, 2014). The purses for the other tournaments are as follows: Championship Tour events range from $1.6 to $2.5 million (PGA TOUR, 2014), Web.com tour purses are $550,000 to $1 million (PGA TOUR, 2014), tour purses for the PGA Tour Canada are all CAN$150,000 (PGA TOUR Canada, 2014), and tour purses for NEC Series Latinoamérica are all $150,000 (PGA Tour Latinoámerica, 2014). Purses (or winnings) are paid for by the title sponsor and the PGA Tour. The PGA Tour makes the majority of its revenue from television contracts (Antolini, 2014).

For six decades, players had to qualify annually for the PGA Tour through a grueling qualifying tournament known as Q-School, unless they earned an exemption by winning a tournament or one of the four majors. After the 2012 Q-School, the top 25 finishers no longer move to the PGA Tour, but instead go to the developmental Web.com Tour (Ferguson, n.d.). Players now qualify based on their prior year's performance on the PGA Tour or by moving up through the ranks on the Web.com Tour. The change was made as a result of the PGA Tour studying data on the comparative performance of players coming off the developmental tour versus the Q-School from 1990–2012. The data showed that the developmental tour better prepared players for the competitive challenges in playing on the PGA Tour, including the toll that travel takes on players. By making the developmental tour the primary path to the PGA Tour, the plan is also to create better branding between the two tours, as well as create more excitement for the Web.com Tour (Ferguson, n.d.).

Tours in the various individual sports have their own rules and regulations. In tennis, the 50 top-ranked players are required to submit their tournament schedules for the following year to their respective governing bodies by the conclusion of the U.S. Open "so decisions can be made on designations and fields can be balanced to meet the commitments the WTA and ATP have made to their tournaments" (Feinstein, 1992, p. 392). Throughout Wimbledon and the U.S. Open, players' agents and tournament directors negotiate appearance fees and set schedules for the top-ranked players' upcoming seasons, while the other players are left to make decisions about whether to return to the tour the following year.

Key Concepts

League Revenues

Leagues derive revenue from national television and radio contracts, league-wide licensing, and league-wide sponsorship programs. Leagues do not derive revenue from local broadcasting, gate receipts, preferred seating sales, or any of the stadium revenues. All those forms of revenue go to the teams, and disparities in local markets have caused competitive balance problems among teams. These problems are most pronounced in MLB, which has the least amount of national revenue sharing and no salary caps.

Franchise Values and Revenue Generation

In all leagues but the NFL, today's franchise costs make family or single ownership a challenge. Most franchise owners need to diversify investments to protect against the financial risk of franchise ownership. Many owners purchase teams as a primary business investment, whereas others purchase them as an ancillary business to their primary business. Still others are fulfilling a dream with a number of co-owners. Due to rising franchise fees, expansion fees, player salaries, and the leveling off of or decrease in television revenues, there is too much at risk for one owner if that person does not have diverse pools of money to cover a team's operating costs. For instance, when the Boston Red Sox and New England Sports Network (NESN) were sold for $660 million, more than 20 individuals made up the ownership group led by John Henry (Bodley, 2002).

Currently, franchise values for major league clubs are in the hundreds of millions of dollars. Much and Gotto (1997) note that the two most important factors in determining a franchise's value are the degree of revenue sharing and the stability of the league's labor situation. Revenue sharing is a factor in creating competitive balance among the teams in the

league. The NFL shares virtually all national revenues, but does not share stadium revenue. In an effort to generate greater revenues, teams have used their leverage to negotiate favorable lease agreements that provide the teams with revenue from luxury boxes, personal seat licenses, club seating, and other revenues generated by the facility, including facility sponsorship (signage and naming rights), concessions, and parking. As a result of the race for these revenues, a strategy called **franchise free agency** emerged in the 1990s. Under this strategy, team owners threaten to move their teams if their demands for new stadiums, renovations to existing stadiums, or better lease agreements are not met. In other sports, such as hockey and basketball, teams have moved with the lure of better facilities and local deals. As a result, in the NHL there is a very strict franchise relocation policy with numerous factors that must be satisfied before a team can move, including evidence of a lack of fan support over three seasons prior to the request to move. Baseball has less relocation due to its exemption from antitrust, enabling it to restrict relocation. Without antitrust liability, owners interested in moving do not have the leverage to threaten a treble-damage antitrust suit in response to a no vote on a relocation request. At the same time, this exemption from antitrust has allowed MLB teams leverage over their home cities to demand stadium renovations at their current sites (knowing the cities cannot sue on antitrust grounds either).

Like never before, sport managers are at work to maximize revenue streams. A case study lies in the strategy of the Boston Red Sox to maximize the revenue potential in every inch of Fenway Park while adding to the fans' Fenway experience. Since taking over the Red Sox in 2002, the management team has turned Yawkey Way into a fan-friendly concourse to market the club and sell more concessions and licensed products. Because demand exceeds supply for tickets, the club has built additional seating in box seats near the dugout, on top of the Green Monster section of the park, and on the rooftop and in front of the grandstand. After adding the seats, the Red Sox discovered "dead space" used for media parking and laundry. They then moved those uses off-site to create more concourse space for revenue-generating opportunities, plus an improved fan experience, because there is less congestion around the concourse and restrooms (Migala Report, 2004).

Outside of Fenway Park, the Red Sox have created other innovations intended to maximize revenues. One marketing innovation was to show games live at stadium-style movie theaters in select locations throughout New England. The movie theater experience came complete with vendors. The team has worked to stretch its market by hosting "state" days at Fenway Park and taking the Sox players and World Series Trophies on tour throughout New England. The team has spent the past few years pitching itself as New England's team and has spent the past decade battling the New York Yankees for territory in the state of Connecticut.

Another marketing innovation involves the Fenway Sports Group (FSG) that works from the built-in Red Sox Nation fan base. FSG is a venture of New England Sports Ventures (NESV), the holding company that also owns and operates the Red Sox, Fenway Park, and NESN (Fenway Sports Group, 2010a). FSG is a sports agency created with the goals to diversify interests of the parent company and to drive more revenue into the venture. Its pioneers were Red Sox staff moonlighting at FSG (Donnelly & Leccese, 2007). In addition to working with the Red Sox, FSG represents sports properties such as Boston College, MLB Advanced Media, Fulham Football Club, and Athletes Performance. Additionally, it engages in corporate consulting and event business for clients such as Stop and Shop, Dunkin Donuts, Cumberland Farms, and Gulf Oil (Fenway Sports Group, 2010b). It also is entrepreneurial, operating FSG sports-related properties such as the Salem (VA) Red Sox (minor league baseball team), Fanfoto (a fan-centric sports photography business), Red Sox Destinations (travel agency), and Roush Fenway Racing (NASCAR) (Fenway Sports Group, 2010c). In maximizing revenue, FSG has a goal

© Beelde Photography/ShutterStock, Inc.

of leveraging the audience of 12 million Red Sox fans for crossover marketing, while reaching beyond that with new properties, new ventures, and ultimately new revenue streams.

A second issue affecting franchise values is particular to MLB: the large-market to small-market dichotomy created by the disparity in local broadcast revenues. MLB does not share local broadcast revenues. This means that a team in a large media market, such as the New York Yankees, derives far more broadcast revenues than does a small-market team, such as the Kansas City Royals. This disparity results in an unfair advantage for a large-market team in terms of operating revenue and franchise valuation. Due to this disparity, small-market teams, such as the Pittsburgh Pirates, are constantly building from their farm systems and often losing franchise players to the free market because they lack sufficient revenue to meet players' salary demands.

To meet the challenge of competitively operating a small-market club, teams like the Oakland A's, under the leadership of General Manager Billy Beane, are focusing on efficiency and a new value system now termed *moneyball* after the book by that name. In a nutshell, the concept is to win games with a small budget. Put simply, it is a system that involves focusing on less commonly used statistics, drafting wisely, and drafting players who are "signable" in an effort to take away some of the uncertainty of drafting and developing players. According to Lewis (2003), Beane did not create the theories but effectively used the ideas of the baseball statistical wizard Bill James and those of some of today's best baseball writers and websites and put them all together. Despite much vocal opposition from the establishment in the baseball fraternity (long-time general managers, scouts, and baseball writers), a significant number of general managers have adopted many of these theories in building their teams. In fact, James is a consultant to the Boston Red Sox and has

led the team to the use of more quantitative analysis of player performance and evaluation alongside its traditional qualitative observations of players (Neyer, 2002). Only time will tell if these theories to create greater certainty in cost containment and player development will pan out. However, the book has inspired employees and fans alike in other professional sports to try to rely on new statistical theories. In this way, it has brought more innovative management to all professional sport organizations and in the process created a few new jobs for individuals focused on using statistics to bolster decisions on player development, investment, and acquisition.

The other piece of the franchise value equation is labor stability. A long-term CBA creates cost stability for teams. The combination of strong leadership from commissioners, shared revenue, and cost stability has enabled a league like the NFL to market what is arguably the strongest brand in North American professional sports. A quality product and the knowledge of long-term labor peace (and thus a lack of interruption in games) translate into media revenues in the billions.

Legal Issues

Almost all areas of law are relevant to the professional sport industry, but those most prevalent are contracts, antitrust, labor, and intellectual property (trademark and licensing). Historically, many high-profile cases have developed either when players and owners (current and prospective) have challenged league rules or when rival leagues have tried to compete against the dominant established league that possesses market power.

Over time many contract issues have been resolved, and all team-sport athletes now sign a standard player contract particular to each league. This does not mean that contract disputes are eliminated. Occasionally there will be cases if the commissioner refuses to approve a player's contract if it violates a league rule or policy. For instance, sometimes player contracts contain provisions that the commissioner finds will circumvent the salary cap. The team and player may either renegotiate the contract or challenge the commissioner's finding. A good example is the rejection of the New Jersey Devils' 17-year contract with star left winger Ilya Kovalchuk. The NHL rejected the 17-year, $102 million deal, which would have been the longest contract in its history. The NHL's rejection of the contract was upheld by an arbitrator who found many problems with the contract, particularly the significant frontloading of salary and the length, which would have had Kovalchuk playing until he was 44. Only 1 player has played past age 43, and only 6 of 3,400 players in the past 20 years have played at age 42, making it unrealistic that Kovalchuk would still be an active contributing player on the roster at 44 (*National Hockey League and National Hockey League Players Association*, 2010). The Devils and Kovalchuk did submit a new 15-year, $100 million contract that the NHL did approve. However, the NHL allegedly in the process issued the NHLPA an ultimatum on long-term deals, conditioning them on changing the salary cap hit for contracts that end with the player over 40 years of age and a new formula that counts the five highest years of salary in long-term (over 5-year) deals carrying additional weight in the cap calculation (Brooks, 2010). Such a change in the salary cap during the term of the CBA is unusual and shows the depth of the commitment by the NHL to the cap and actions they perceive will harm competitive balance.

In a global market, contract disputes also arise over which team retains the rights to a particular player who is attempting to move from one league to another. Such disputes may lead to legal battles between teams and players of different countries. To avoid these types of disputes, North American leagues and those abroad are continually evaluating their player transfer agreements.

Antitrust law is a second area where disputes arise. Antitrust laws regulate anticompetitive business practices. MLB is exempt from antitrust laws. All professional sport leagues adopt restrictive practices to provide financial stability and competitive balance between their teams. The game would not be appealing to fans if the same teams dominated the league year after year because they had the money to consistently purchase the best players. Similarly, fans and front office staff would not like to see their teams change player personnel year after year. It is the nature of sport that teams must be built and that players and coaches must develop strong working relationships. However, restrictive practices such as drafts, reserve systems, salary caps, free agent restrictions, and free agent compensation developed for competitive balance may have another effect, such as depressing salaries or keeping competitor leagues from signing marquee players. Therefore, players and rival leagues have used antitrust laws to challenge such practices as anticompetitive, arguing that they restrain trade or monopolize the market for professional team sports. Additionally, in the past decade, owners have sued their own leagues on antitrust grounds to challenge restrictive practices. Antitrust laws carry with them a treble damage provision, so if a league loses an antitrust case and the court triples the amount of damages, the league could effectively pay millions or billions in damages.

Race and Gender in the Professional Sport Industry

In his book *In Black and White: Race and Sport in America*, Shropshire (1996) stresses pointedly that integration of more diverse employees into management positions will not happen without a concerted effort by owners, commissioners, and those in positions of power. He suggests that to combat racism in professional sport there must be recognition of what "both America and sport in reality look and act like" as well as what both "should look and act like in that ideal moment in the future [when racism is eliminated]" (Shropshire, 1996, p. 144). Between these two phases is an intermediate period of transition. During that transition the black community's youth must alter its focus away from athletic success as being a substitute for other forms of success. Second, athletes must take a stronger united stand against racism. Third, league-wide action evidencing a commitment to address diversity is needed. An example of this is the **Rooney Rule** in the NFL. Named for Steelers owner Dan Rooney, the rule requires NFL teams with coaching openings to interview minority coaches as part of the search process. As Table 10-3 shows, the NFL now has 19% minority coaches. The final step is a combination of continued civil rights political action coupled with legal action to combat racism through lawsuits and government intervention by such organizations as the Department of Justice and the Equal Employment Opportunity Commission.

Critics have argued that because there is great racial diversity among athletes on the field, more people of color should be represented in management positions. By the year 2004, the four major leagues had marked their fiftieth anniversaries of integration. In 2003, the NBA and MLB achieved major milestones by welcoming minority owners African American Bob Johnson and Mexican American Arte Moreno to the Charlotte Bobcats and Los Angeles Angels, respectively. Lapchick and colleagues in 2009 reported that for the first time in the 20-year history of publishing his Racial and Gender Report Card, each of the five major leagues received a grade of "A" for hiring people of color (Lapchick, et. al, 2009). All leagues showed increases for women in management positions, so it appears some positive movement forward is occurring. For current data on racial and gender representation by league, see Tables 10-3 and 10-4.

Table 10-3 Racial Diversity in Professional Sports (Percentage)

Segment	NBA	NFL	MLB	MLS	WNBA
Player	82	72	39	51	86
League office	34	30	31	46	29
Head coach	53	19	13	11	33
Assistant coach	44	33	39	19	40
CEO	13	0	0	10	0
Principal	26	19	10	11	42
Vice president	12	9	14	15	12
Senior administrator	22	15	20	19	21
Professional administrator	25	12	22	24	27

Data from: Lapchick, R., Bernstine, C., Nunes, G., Okolo, N., Snively, D., and Walker, C. (2013, May 21). The 2013 Racial and Gender Report Card: Major League Baseball. Retrieved from http://www.bus.ucf.edu /sportbusiness/?page=1445; Lapchick, R., Milkovich, M., & O'Keefe, S. (2012, September 5). The 2012 Women's National Basketball Association Racial and Gender Report Card. Retrieved from http://www.bus.ucf.edu /sportbusiness/?page=1445; Lapchick, R., Lecky, A., & Trigg, A. (2012, June 26). The 2012 Racial and Gender Report Card: National Basketball Association. Retrieved from http://www.bus.ucf.edu/sportbusiness/?page=1445; Lapchick, R., Costa, P. Sherrod, T., & Anjorin, R. (2012, September 13). The 2012 Racial and Gender Report Card: National Football League. Retrieved from http://www.bus.ucf.edu/sportbusiness/?page=1445; Lapchick, R., Gunn, O., & Trigg, A. (2012, November 8). The 2012 Racial and Gender Report Card: Major League Soccer. Retrieved from http://www.bus.ucf.edu/sportbusiness/?page=1445.

Table 10-4 Gender Diversity in Professional Sports (Percentage)

Segment	NBA	NFL	MLB	MLS	WNBA
Player	0	0	0	0	100
League office	42	40	36	51	71
Head coach	0	0	0	0	42
Assistant coach	0	0	0.4	0	64
CEO	4	3	0	0	13
Principal	0	0	0	0	33
Vice president	18	15	18	13	25
Senior administrator	25	20	27	21	52
Professional administrator	39	30	26	31	44

Data from: Lapchick, R., Bernstine, C., Nunes, G., Okolo, N., Snively, D., & Walker, C. (2013, May 21). The 2013 Racial and Gender Report Card: Major League Baseball. Retrieved from http://www.bus.ucf.edu/sportbusiness/?page=1445; Lapchick, R., Milkovich, M., & O'Keefe, S. (2012, September 5). The 2012 Women's National Basketball Association Racial and Gender Report Card. Retrieved from http://www.bus.ucf.edu/sportbusiness/?page=1445; Lapchick, R., Lecky, A., & Trigg, A. (2012, June 26). The 2012 Racial and Gender Report Card: National Basketball Association. Retrieved from http://www.bus.ucf.edu/sportbusiness/?page=1445; Lapchick, R., Costa, P. Sherrod, T., & Anjorin, R. (2012, September 13). The 2012 Racial and Gender Report Card: National Football League. Retrieved from http://www.bus.ucf.edu/sportbusiness/?page=1445; Lapchick, R., Gunn, O., & Trigg, A. (2012, November 8). The 2012 Racial and Gender Report Card: Major League Soccer. Retrieved from http://www.bus.ucf.edu/sportbusiness/?page=1445.

Career Opportunities

Commissioner

The role and responsibilities of a league commissioner were detailed earlier in this chapter. A wide variety of skills are required to be an effective commissioner. They include an understanding of the sport and the various league documents (league constitution, by-laws, rules and regulations, standard player contract, and CBA); negotiating skills; diplomacy; the ability to work well with a variety of people; an ability to delegate; a good public image; an ability to handle pressure, crises, and the media; an ability to make sound decisions; and, in general, a vision for the league. These are not skills that are easily taught. For the most part, they evolve over time through a combination of education and life experience.

Other League Office Personnel

Each league has an office staff working in a wide variety of positions. Although the number of positions in league offices varies, most leagues have literally hundreds of employees in a range of areas, from the commissioner's staff to the legal department to properties and marketing divisions to entertainment to communications to research and development. For instance, departments in the NBA's Commissioner's Office include administration, broadcasting, corporate affairs, editorial, finance, legal, operations, player programs, public relations, security, and special events (**Figure 10-1**). Departments in the NBA Properties Division include business development, finance, international offices, legal, licensing, marketing, media and sponsor programs, and team services. Departments in NBA Entertainment include administration, accounting, legal, licensing, operations, photography, production, and programming. Thus, a wide variety of opportunities in league offices are available for individuals with degrees in sport management and business and for those who couple their initial degrees with a graduate degree in a field

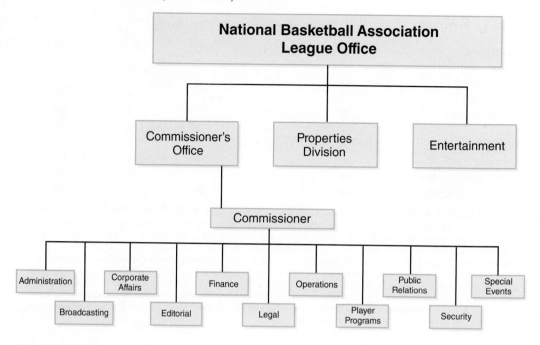

Figure 10-1 NBA League Office/Team Front Office Flowcharts

such as law, sport management, or business administration. Skills necessary for working in a league office vary with the position, yet a few universal skills include having a working knowledge of the sport, the teams in the league, and the professional sport industry in general; good customer relations skills; and a willingness to work long hours (especially during the season and postseason).

Team General Manager

A team general manager is in charge of all player personnel decisions, including overseeing the scouting and drafting of players, signing free agents, trading players, and negotiating contracts with players and their agents. The general manager must understand the sport and be able to assess talent. He or she must also possess a working knowledge of all league documents (constitution, by-laws, rules and regulations, CBA, standard player contract). A career path for a general manager has traditionally been

to move into the position from the playing or coaching ranks. As the position has become more complex, individuals with graduate degrees in sport management, business administration, law, or a combination of these have become desirable employees. Some teams will have a general manager who has risen from the playing or coaching ranks, and then hire one or more assistant general managers to deal with complex contract negotiations and to decipher league rules and policies, such as salary caps, as well as to interpret and develop statistical models that have become commonplace in the moneyball era.

Other Team Front Office Personnel

Like league office staffs, team front offices offer a wide variety of positions. In the past decade, the number of positions and specialization of jobs has increased greatly. When the first edition of this text was published, the Miami Heat front office staff provided a glimpse of the variety of positions available. At that time the team possessed 40 full-time employees, 4 partners, and 4 limited partners (Miami Heat, 1993–1994). Compare that to a current Miami Heat directory (**Figure 10-2**) and the Philadelphia 76ers, whose website listed 100 front office employees in 2010. The employees included the following positions: a chairman (owner); a president/chief operating officer; 2 executive vice presidents; 3 senior vice presidents; 2 vice presidents; a director of player personnel; a sales staff of 17 (including director and managers); a customer service staff of 6 (including directors and managers); a marketing and promotions staff of 3; a game operations staff of 6; a communications staff of 6 (includes community relations and public relations); and numerous other employees, such as coaches, scouts, broadcasters, accountants, and administrative assistants throughout the basketball and business operations (NBA, 2010a). It is noteworthy that the basketball operations staff is considerably smaller than the business operations side. The business side drives the revenue into the operation and, therefore, there tend to be more opportunities for employment on that side of the "house."

Front office entry level positions tend to be in the sales, marketing, community relations, and media/public relations departments. Salaries tend to be low, because many people would love to work for a professional team; therefore, supply always exceeds demand. Salaries are often higher in the sales department because

Executive Office

Managing General Partner President of Basketball Operations General Manager President of Business Operations

Executive Vice Presidents: Chief Marketing Officer, HEAT Group Enterprises, Sales, General Manager, Chief Financial Officer, General Council

Vice Presidents

Senior VP of Basketball Operation Senior VP/Chief Information Officer

Vice Presidents: Sports Media Relations, Arena Bookings and Marketing, Marketing Division, Operations, Assistant General Manager, Finance, Corporate Partnerships, Ticket Operations and Services, Human Resources, Player Personnel

Basketball Operations

Senior Director of Team Security

Directors: Sports Media Relations, College/International Scouting, Team Services, Team Security, Pro/Minor League Scouting

Other: NBA Scout, Scout, Assistant Director of Sport Media Relations, Sport Media Relations Assistant, Business Media Relations Assistant, Scouting and Information Coordinator

Figure 10-2 Miami Heat Front Office Directory Chart

Data from: http://www.nba.com/heat/contact/directory_list.html (December, 2006).

employees earn a base salary plus commissions for ticket, corporate, or group sales productivity. As with league office positions, skills necessary for working in a front office are knowledge of the sport and the professional sport industry, good customer relations abilities, and a willingness to work long hours (particularly during the season and postseason). As for educational requirements, a sport management degree and, depending on the position, possibly an advanced degree, such as a JD or an MBA, are appropriate for someone looking to break into a front-office position.

Tour Personnel

Tours such as the PGA Tour and the Association of Tennis Professionals (ATP) Tour employ many sport managers. The Dew Tour, which debuted in June 2005, consists of five major multisport events with a cumulative points system, a $2.5 million competitive purse (the largest in action sports), and an additional $1 million bonus pool based on participants'

year-end standings. As with league sports, the positions vary from commissioner to marketer to special events coordinator.

For example, in 2009 the ATP Tour held 65 tournaments in 32 countries and was organized into three main offices: Player Council, Board of Directors, and Tournament Council. Each office is led by an executive and has a number of staff positions available. The ATP has offices located in several countries, including Monaco, Australia, the United Kingdom (London), and the United States (Florida). An executive organizational chart is shown in **Figure 10-3**.

As with league sports, the positions vary from commissioner to marketer to special events coordinator. Much of the event management work for the actual site operations for the tour is, however, often left to an outside sports agency. Tours and sites contract with event marketing and management agencies to take care of all of the details of putting on the event at a particular country club or other event location.

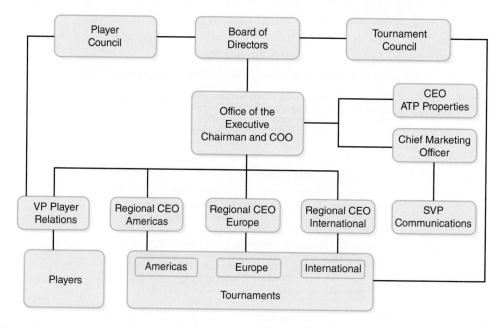

Figure 10-3 Executive Organizational Chart

Agents

Almost all team and individual athletes in the professional sport industry have sports agents representing them and coordinating their business and financial affairs. In addition, a growing number of professional coaches rely on sports agents.

Current Issues

Salary Caps

In an effort to contain player personnel costs, salary caps continue to be the rage in professional sport. They are used in the AFL, NBA, NFL, NHL, MLS, WNBA, ECHL, and NLL. Salary caps are intended to create parity among teams by capping how much a team can spend on its players' salaries. Salary caps are adjusted annually for changes in revenue.

To impose a salary cap in a league in which a union exists, owners must negotiate with the players (because the cap impacts wages). In the negotiation process, the union will inevitably negotiate for some exceptions to the salary cap. These exceptions have in reality created loopholes for creative general managers and agents representing players. For instance, in the NFL, signing bonuses are applied to the cap by prorating them across the life of the contract. Another problem with the caps is that they routinely force teams to cut established players or renegotiate their contracts to make room under the cap to sign another player. A third problem is that the caps provide a team with spending minimums, so low-revenue teams are prevented from cutting their payrolls to stay competitive (Fatsis, 1997). In the WNBA, the combination of a tight salary cap and a minimum salary scale negatively impacts veterans, whose minimum salaries are higher based upon years of service. Thus, in the case of a talented veteran competing for a spot against an equally talented rookie, the club may choose the rookie

because the athlete takes up less room under the cap (Bergen, 2004).

Globalization

All major leagues are drafting and signing players from other nations and moving into those countries with marketing efforts. MLB has an office in Tokyo to oversee its efforts in Japan, Taiwan, and China, plus the league has been playing one game to open the season in Japan for the past few years. The NFL no longer operates NFL Europe, but has begun playing a marquee regular season game in Europe, and the NBA has expanded throughout the globe with probably the most international movement of all the North American leagues. Currently the NBA hosts 14 international NBA websites in addition to its main North American site (NBA, 2010b). Following the NFL and MLB, the NBA has also moved away from an exhibition game in Europe, scheduling a regular season game there for the 2010–2011 season (NBA, 2010c).

An interesting case study exists in examining NBA China and NBA India. NBA International is following its game plan in China to move into the Indian market. For China, the NBA spent two decades building courts, teaching youth the game, and hosting promotions. Now over 300 million people in China play basketball. The league notes that 89% of Chinese aged 15 to 54 are aware of the NBA brand and NBA.com/China averages 2 million unique users a month. Games are shown in China on 51 outlets, drawing 1.6 billion viewers in 2008–2009 (34% more than in 2006–2007). China is now the NBA's biggest foreign market for its branded merchandise. Outside investors—including Disney/ESPN, Bank of China Group, Legend Holdings, China Merchant Group, and the Li Ka-shing Foundation—bought 11% of NBA China in January 2008 for $2.3 billion with a goal of launching a professional league (Van Riper & Karmali, 2009). However, NBA

China had a setback when AEG Facilities pulled out of its plan to build and/or operate NBA arenas in Beijing, Shanghai, and Guangzhou.

NBA International began bringing NBA stars to India in 2006. Since November 2008, the NBA has been staging youth tournaments in Mumbai, New Delhi, and Bangalore. NBA games on ESPN in India reach 120 million homes, nearly a third of the country. That said, becoming the second most popular sport in India (behind cricket) will be a challenging goal, because India has not fielded an Olympic basketball team since 1980 (Van Riper & Karmali, 2009).

Journalists credit the global interest in the NBA to the 1992 Dream Team (Crowe, 2004), but it must also be a product of the NBA's strategy of integrating international stars into its teams. To continue its global expansion, many NBA teams have drafted and signed players from other nations. NBA official rosters in the 2009–2010 season included 83 players from 36 different countries or U.S. territories, such as Puerto Rico and the Virgin Islands. Fans of these players open new revenue sources for the NBA. Foreign markets generate as much as 20% of the $900 million the NBA earns in television revenue, and they provide about 20% of merchandise sales (Crowe, 2004). In 2010, the NBA Finals were broadcast in 215 countries and in 41 languages (NBA, 2010b).

The interest may also be stemming from overtures made by former Commissioner David Stern indicating that the NBA is looking to move into Europe. These overtures have encouraged AEG Facilities to build NBA-style arenas in London and Berlin (McCosky, 2002). Stern noted the opening up the arenas in London and Berlin allowed the NBA to consider many options, ranging from exhibitions to games to permanent homes for franchises (McCosky, 2002). As mentioned earlier in this section, the NBA held its first regular season game in Europe during 2010–2011 season (NBA, 2010c).

Concussion Litigation

Among the most hotly debated current issues in professional sport is how professional leagues have managed concussions and how they will address player safety in the future. Retired NFL and the NHL players have filed suit against the leagues. The retired players and their families allege that they have developed chronic traumatic encephalopathy (CTE) and other brain diseases, such as Alzheimer's and dementia, due to head trauma they received while playing professional football and ice hockey. The NFL has proposed a settlement with the 4,500 plaintiffs in the amount of $765 million, but the judge has denied the initial proposal. The judge's reason for rejecting the settlement is that she fears that it is not enough money to cover the future costs the plaintiffs may face and that the court needs more time to assess the fairness and adequacy of the settlement amount (Brinson, 2014). NHL players also are suing their league over concussions. The lawsuit involves 75 plaintiffs and has the complicating matter of the role of fighting in causing the head trauma. Tied to the issue of whether head trauma that occurs to players while playing the sport of hockey is the question of whether fighting causes more head trauma, and thus more brain damage, *and* whether by having fighting as part of the professional game the NHL is condoning these injuries.

Drug Testing and Human Growth Hormone

Another current issue that will need to be addressed is human growth hormone (HGH) testing in professional sport. The four major leagues have adopted drug testing policies and have adopted the penalties noted in **Table 10-5**. The question will be how the leagues manage HGH, which has still to be addressed.

Table 10-5 Disciplinary Penalties for Performance Enhancing Drug Use in the MLB, NBA, NFL, and NHL

	MLB	NBA	NFL	NHL
1st Offense	50-game suspension	5-game suspension and mandatory attendance in NBA anti-doping program	4-game suspension	20-game suspension without pay
2nd Offense	100-game suspension	10-game suspension plus counseling	8-game suspension without pay	60-game suspension without pay
3rd Offense	Lifetime ban	25-game suspension plus counseling	1-year suspension without pay	Lifetime ban
4th Offense		Minimum 2-year suspension		

In MLB, the issue of the commissioner's power to suspend a player based on evidence gathered by means other than a drug or HGH test was at issue in the Alex Rodriguez arbitration case. MLB obtained documents from an anti-aging clinic then used information from those documents to suspend Rodriguez for 211 games under a provision in the CBA. The arbitrator reduced the Commissioner's penalty to 160 games.

Analytics

Professional sport is becoming more and more dependent on analytics. The moneyball era ushered in the use of analytics such as **sabermetrics** in player development. Sabermetrics is the empirical study of baseball. Analytics have moved from baseball into other sports, namely basketball, where it is used to analyze all play on the court (Goldsberry, 2014), to football, and hockey. Beyond the use of analytics in player evaluation, player development, and team operations, teams have started to use analytics on the business side, using it in marketing, market research, customer relationship management, and other aspects of decision making. Leagues such as the NBA and MLS have league-level analytics departments that analyze data on the teams. The league departments then send their staff out to work with clubs as "consultants" to improve and assist the team to do better.

Summary

The professional sport industry involves the sale of the entertainment value of sport events and exhibitions. Revenue is generated primarily through media rights fees, licensed product sales, gate receipts, and stadium revenues. The leagues and tours face a number of challenges, including keeping fans satisfied in light of their perceptions regarding the "highly paid athlete." Directly related to this is finding a means for achieving labor stability in the leagues while developing methods of keeping a fan base that is representative of society as ticket prices continue to skyrocket. The dominant major professional leagues (MLB, MLS, NBA, NFL, and NHL) also face a challenge in market share from the new upstart leagues (e.g., arena football), women's sports, expansion in the minor leagues, and the growing professionalization and commercialization of collegiate sport.

The professional sport industry is entering an exciting period. Innovations in technology are making professional sport more global, particularly as leagues look for unsaturated markets and new revenue streams. This exciting environment, coupled with the perception of

Case Study 10-1   Is the NFL Conduct Policy Working?

In response to the murder charges levied against Baltimore Ravens linebacker Ray Lewis, the NFL owners established a personal conduct policy in 2000. Former Commissioner Paul Tagliabue used it to issue short suspensions. In 2007, the NFL invoked the integrity of the game powers to lengthen the suspensions a commissioner could levy and even allowed for indefinite ones if the player's actions involved violent or criminal behavior that undermines the NFL's integrity, erodes public confidence, or results in tragic consequences to perpetrator and/or victim (Maravent, 2010).

From January 2006 through April 2007, more than 50 players were arrested (Bell, 2007a). Two—Tennessee Titans cornerback Adam "Pacman" Jones and Cincinnati Bengals wide receiver Chris Henry—were among the worst offenders. Jones had been arrested five times and questioned an additional five times since he had been drafted in 2005. Jones' arrests involved felony and misdemeanor charges involving fights and other incidents, including one in which a security guard was left paralyzed after being shot by someone in Jones' party. Over a 14-month period, Henry had been arrested four times in three different states for charges involving firearms use and concealment, as well as driving recklessly, DUI, and providing alcohol to minors. After 7 months on the job, NFL Commissioner Roger Goodell held hearings with Jones and Henry to determine their fate (Bell, 2007a). Following the hearings, Goodell announced a 1-year suspension of Jones and an 8-game ban on Henry as well as a strengthened NFL conduct policy. Goodell stated: "We hold ourselves to higher standards of responsible conduct because of what it means to be part of the National Football League" (Associated Press, 2007, par. 4). The Commissioner also mentioned that the NFL has always had a commitment to ensuring that players live up to these standards and that the new policy would continue to support this goal (Associated Press, 2007).

The updated policy resulted from NFL officials' frustration with the players' behavior. As owner, Bob McNair of the Houston Texans remarked, "[f]ines are such a small part of a player's total compensation. They don't pay attention to it . . . A $50,000 fine, [it's like], 'I spent that last night when I got arrested. That's what I gave *one* girl'" (Bell, 2007b). Many NFL players were equally frustrated, according to Gene Upshaw, then-Director of the NFLPA, who supported Goodell's approach. "The conduct of some players is what got us to this point," Upshaw said. "But I think the insistence of a lot of players also drives the need for a stronger policy. This is a grass-roots movement" (Bell, 2007b). "The NFL Players Association and the Player Advisory Council have been discussing this issue for several months," Upshaw said. "We believe that these are steps that the commissioner needs to take and we support the policy. It is important that players in violation of the policy will have the opportunity and the support to change their conduct and earn their way back" (Associated Press, 2007). Goodell called former players for input and put together a six-player advisory panel on conduct issues (Bell, 2007b).

The conduct policy Goodell introduced applies to all NFL employees. The definition of NFL employees is broad, including players under contract plus those drafted and undrafted players about to commence negotiations with teams. It also includes coaches, officials, owners, front office, and league personnel (NFLPA, 2008).

In 2010, 3 years into the policy, the NFL continued to battle its image problem. In response to sexual assault allegations being raised against Pittsburgh Steelers quarterback Ben Roethlisberger in March 2010, Commissioner Goodell reconfirmed how seriously he takes the conduct policy. He sent a memo to all NFL teams to clarify that the new policy was not just a warning against criminal behavior, but a requirement, and that all representatives of the NFL brand must behave responsibly. Goodell stressed that any hint of improper or unlawful behavior would risk the loss of the respect of the fans and business from the partners. Thus, even if the bad behavior does not occur with one's own team, if bad behavior occurs with any team, it impacts all teams and the league as a whole (La Canfora, 2010, par 5).

Questions for Discussion

1. Once a players association (union) is in existence, any changes in the workplace that involve mandatory subjects for bargaining may not be unilaterally implemented by the league (management) but must be negotiated with the players. Mandatory subjects for bargaining are hours, wages, and terms and conditions of employment. Should this new conduct policy have been negotiated with the NFLPA through collective bargaining?

2. Commissioners have long held power to make decisions to maintain the integrity of the game. Historically, the integrity of the game decisions have involved gambling, drug use, on-field bad behavior, and bad behavior toward fans. Does this conduct policy fit within the integrity of the game provision? Does regulating off-field behavior go too far? Because the commissioner can act simply when someone in the organization is arrested, how do we reconcile it with the concept of innocent until proven guilty?

3. What will be some of the challenges in enforcing the policy? How will the league impose fairness?

4. As a manager, what strategies would you adopt to keep from having this policy invoked against members of your team (players and staff)?

5. What suggestions do you have for Commissioner Goodell and the NFLPA about player conduct and discipline issues when they sit down to negotiate their next CBA?

6. Using Google, examine the news over a 2- to 3-year period to determine if the NFL policy is working. Does it apply to team and league management and coaches as well as players? What is your assessment as a fan? Does the behavior of players on and off the field influence your decision to follow the NFL? Do you think it would affect the decisions of sponsors to be associated with the NFL? Individual teams? Individual players?

the glamour of working for a team or league, attracts many job seekers to professional sports. Therefore, landing an entry-level position is competitive, and salaries tend to be lower than in other segments of the industry. Those who are persistent, are willing to intern in the industry, and are committed to keeping abreast of this fast-paced industry will be rewarded. Professional sports are constantly changing and are often addressing challenges. The sport manager who can adapt to change and resolve problems and who possesses a vision for the professional sport industry in the twenty-first century will find success in this field.

Resources

Professional Sport Leagues

American Hockey League (AHL)
One Monarch Place
Springfield, MA 01069
413-781-2030
http://www.theahl.com

ECHL
116 Village Boulevard, Suite 304
Princeton, NJ 08540
609-452-0770
http://www.echl.com

Major League Baseball (MLB)
350 Park Avenue
New York, NY 10022
212-339-7800
http://www.mlb.com

Major League Soccer (MLS)
110 East 42nd Street
New York, NY 10017
212-450-1200
http://www.mlsnet.com

Minor League Baseball (MLB)
201 Bayshore Drive, S.E.
St. Petersburg, FL 33701
727-822-6937
http://www.milb.com

National Basketball Association (NBA)
645 Fifth Avenue
New York, NY 10022
212-407-8000
http://www.nba.com

National Football League (NFL)
410 Park Avenue, 6th Floor
New York, NY 10022
212-758-1500
http://www.nfl.com

National Hockey League (NHL)
1251 Avenue of the Americas
New York, NY 10020-1198
212-789-2000
http://www.nhl.com

National Professional Fastpitch (NPF)
4610 S. Ulster Drive, Suite 150
Denver, CO 80237
303-290-7494
http://profastpitch.com

National Women's Soccer League (NWSL)
1801 S. Prairie Ave.
Chicago, IL 60616
312-808-1300
http://nwslsoccer.com

Women's National Basketball Association (WNBA)
645 Fifth Avenue
New York, NY 10022
212-688-9622
http://www.wnba.com

Professional Sport Tours

Association of Tennis Professionals (ATP) Tour
200 ATP Boulevard
Ponte Vedra Beach, FL 32082
904-285-8000
http://www.atptennis.com

Dew Tour

Alli (Alliance of Action Sports)
150 Harvester Dr., Suite 140
Burr Ridge, IL 60527
630-908-6300
http://www.allisports.com

Indy Racing League (IRL)
4565 W. 16th Street
Indianapolis, IN 46222
317-492-6526
http://www.indycar.com

Ladies Professional Golf Association
(LPGA)
100 International Golf Drive
Daytona Beach, FL 32124
386-274-6200
http://www.lpga.com

National Association for Stock Car Auto
Racing Inc. (NASCAR)
1801 W. International Speedway Boulevard
Daytona Beach, FL 32114
386-253-0611
http://www.nascar.com

Professional Golfers' Association
(PGA) Tour

Champions Tour

NEC PGA Tour Latinoamérica

PGA Tour Canada

Web.com Tour
112 PGA Tour Boulevard
Ponte Vedra, FL 32082
904-285-3700
http://www.pgatour.com

Women's Tennis Association (WTA) Tour
One Progress Plaza, Suite 1500
St. Petersburg, FL 33701
727-895-5000
http://www.sonyericssonwtatour.com

XGames/ESPN
ESPN Events
ESPN Plaza
Bristol, CT 06010
http://www.sports.espn.go.com

Players Associations

Canadian Football League Players'
Association (CFLPA)
603 Argus Road
Oakville, Ontario, Canada L6J G60
306-525-2158
http://www.cflpa.com

Major League Baseball Players
Association (MLBPA)
12 E. 49th Street, 24th Floor
New York, NY 10017
212-826-0808
http://www.mlbplayers.mlb.com

National Basketball Players Association
(NBPA)
1775 Broadway, Suite 2401
New York, NY
212-463-7510
http://www.nbpa.com

National Football League Players
Association (NFLPA)/Arena Football
League Players Association (AFLPA)
2021 L Street, N.W.
Washington, DC 20036
202-436-2200
http://www.nflpa.org
http://www.aflplayers.org

National Hockey League Players
Association (NHLPA)
20 Bay Street, Suite 1700
Toronto, Ontario, Canada M5J 2N8
416-408-4040
http://www.nhlpa.com

Professional Hockey Players' Association (PHPA)

One St. Paul Street, Suite 701
St. Catherines, Ontario, Canada L2R 7L2
905-682-4800
http://www.phpa.com

Women's National Basketball Players Association (WNBPA)

2 Penn Plaza, Suite 2430
New York, NY 10121
(212) 655-0880
http://www.wnbpa.org

Key Terms

collective bargaining agreement, commissioner, corporate governance model, corporate ownership, cross-ownership, franchise free agency, franchise rights, gate receipts, impasse, "league think," premium seating, public ownership, revenue sharing, Rooney Rule, sabermetrics, self-governance, single-entity structure, territorial rights

References

American Needle v. NFL, 130 S.Ct. 2201 (2010).

Antolini, M. (2014, February 11). Presentation on the golf industry. Mark H. McCormack Department of Sport Management, Isenberg School of Management, University of Massachusetts–Amherst.

Associated Press. (2007, April 10). Goodell unveils new conduct policy. *ESPN*.com. Retrieved from http://sports.espn.go.com/nfl/news /story?id=2832098

Atlanta National League Baseball Club, Inc. v. Kuhn, 432 F. Supp. 1213 (N.D. Ga. 1977).

Bell, J. (2007a, April 11). Conduct unbecoming: NFL sets new standards with suspensions. *USA Today*. Retrieved from http://www .usatoday.com/sports/football/nfl/2007-04 -10-pacman-henry-suspensions_N.htm

Bell, J. (2007b, April 10). NFL will confront discipline issue, unveil new policy within days. *USA Today*. Retrieved from http://www .usatoday.com/sports/football/nfl/2007-04 -09-conduct-policy_N.htm

Bergen, M. (2004, May 7). Salary issues scuttle WNBA veterans' chances. *Seattle Post-Intelligencer*. Retrieved from http://www .seattlepi.com/wnba/172352_storm07.html

Berry, R. C., Gould, W. B., & Staudohar, P. D. (1986). *Labor relations in professional sports.* Dover, MA: Auburn House Publishing.

Bodley, H. (2002, January 16). Baseball owners approve sale of Red Sox to Henry. *USA Today*. Retrieved from http://www.usatoday.com /sports/baseball/redsox/2002-01-16-sale-ag .htm

Brinson, W. (2014, January 14). Judge rejects initial $765 million concussion settlement. *CBS Sports*. Retrieved from http://www.cbssports .com/nfl/eye-on-football/24409040/judge -rejects-initial-765m-nfl-concussion-lawsuit -settlement

Brooks, L. (2010, Sept. 2). NHL gives union ultimatum on Kovalchuk, Luongo, Hossa. *New York Post*. Retrieved from http://www.nypost.com/p/sports/devils /nhl_gives_players_assn_ultimatum _UEbYgwfB6I4E4y7xGbE1OP

Crouse, K. (2010, April 1). Absences worsen LPGA's headache. *New York Times*. Retrieved from http:// www.nytimes.com/2010/04/02 /sports/golf/02wgolf.html

Crowe, J. (2004, June 15). Outside influence. *Los Angeles Times*. Retrieved from http://articles .latimes.com/2004/jun/15/sports/sp-nba15

Cruise, D., & Griffiths, A. (1991). *Net worth.* Toronto: Viking Penguin Group.

Donnelly, G., & Leccese, M. (2007, April 23). Q&A: Dee leads Red Sox parent's drive to diversify. Retrieved from http://boston.bizjournals .com/boston/stories/2007/04/23/story9.html

Fatsis, S. (1997, June 25). Is battle looming over salary caps? *The Wall Street Journal*, p. B9.

Feinstein, J. (1992). *Hard courts.* New York: Villard Books.

Fenway Sports Group. (2010a). About us: Who we are. Retrieved from http://www .fenwaysportsgroup.com

Fenway Sports Group. (2010b). Clients. Retrieved from http://www.fenwaysportsgroup.com

Fenway Sports Group. (2010c) Ventures. Retrieved from http://www.fenwaysportsgroup.com

Ferguson, D. (n.d.). PGA Tour makes sweeping changes to Q-School, season schedule, and more. Retrieved from http://www.pga.com /news/pga-tour/pga-tour-makes-sweeping -changes-q-school-season-schedule-and-more

Finley v. Kuhn, 569 F.2d 527 (7th Cir. 1978).

Foldesy, J. (2004, June 17). NFL owners fear death of golden goose. *Washington Times*. Retrieved from http://www.washingtontimes.com /sports/20040617-120824-5896r.htm

Fraser v. Major League Soccer, 284 F.3d 47 (1st Cir. 2002).

Friedman, A., & Much, P. J. (1997). *1997 Inside the ownership of professional sports teams.* Chicago: Team Marketing Report.

Garber, D. (2004). Major League Soccer: Establishing the world's sport in a new America. In *Inside the minds: The business of sports* (pp. 109–129). Boston, MA: Aspatore Books.

Goldsberry, K. (2014, February 6). Databall. *Grantland*. Retrieved from http:// grantland.com/features/expected-value -possession-nba-analytics/

Graffis, H. B. (1975). *The PGA: The official history of the Professional Golfers' Association of America.* New York: Crowell.

Helyar, J. (1994). *Lords of the realm.* New York: Villard Books.

History of the American PGA. (1997). *WorldGolf. com.* Retrieved from http://worldgolf.com /wglibrary/history/ampgahis.html

History of the PGA Tour. (1997). *WorldGolf.com.* Retrieved from http://www.worldgolf.com /wglibrary/history/tourhist.html

Jennings, K. (1989). *Balls and strikes: The money game in professional baseball.* Greenwich, CT: Praeger Publishing.

La Canfora, J. (2010, April 15). Goodell issues memo highlighting NFL's personal conduct policy. Retrieved from http://www.nfl.com /news/story/09000d5d8178bb24/article /goodell-issues-memo-highlighting-nfls- personalconduct-policy

Lapchick, R., Bartter, J., Diaz-Calderon, A., et al. (2009). *2009 Racial and gender report card.* Retrieved from http://web.bus.ucf.edu /documents/sport/2009_RGRC.pdf

Lapchick, R., Bernstine, C. Nunes, G. Okolo, N. Snively, D., and Walker, C. (2013, May 21). The 2013 Racial and Gender Report Card: Major League Baseball. Retrieved from http:// www.bus.ucf.edu/sportbusiness/?page=1445

Lapchick, R., Milkovich, M., & O'Keefe, S. (2012, September 5). The 2012 Women's National Basketball Association Racial and Gender Report Card. Retrieved from http://www.bus. ucf.edu/sportbusiness/?page=1445

Lapchick, R., Lecky, A., & Trigg, A. (2012, June 26). The 2012 Racial and Gender Report Card: National Basketball Association. Retrieved from http://www.bus.ucf.edu /sportbusiness/?page=1445

Lapchick, R., Costa, P. Sherrod, T., & Anjorin, R. (2012, September 13). The 2012 Racial and Gender Report Card: National Football League. Retrieved from http://www.bus.ucf .edu/sportbusiness/?page=1445

Lapchick, R., Gunn, O., & Trigg, A. (2012, November 8). The 2012 Racial and Gender Report Card: Major League Soccer.

Retrieved from http://www.bus.ucf.edu/sportbusiness/?page=1445

Lentze, G. (1995). The legal concept of professional sports leagues: The commissioner and an alternative approach from a corporate perspective. *Marquette Sports Law Journal, 6,* 65–94.

Lewis, M. (2003). *Moneyball: The art of winning an unfair game.* New York: W.W. Norton.

Maravent, B. (2010, July 27). Big Ben and the conduct policy. *The Biz of football.* Retrieved from http://bizoffootball.com/index.php?option=com_content&view=article&id=474:big-ben-and-the-nfl-conduct-policy&catid=44:articles-and-opinion&Itemid=61

McCosky, C. (2002). Overseas markets interested in NBA. *Detroit News Online.* Retrieved from http://www.detnews.com/2002/pistons/0206/10/f06-511202.htm

Miami Heat. (1993–1994). *Miami Heat media guide.* Miami, FL: Author.

Migala Report. (2004, May). Trading spaces: How to examine new revenue opportunities that exist within your facility. Retrieved from http://www.migalareport.com/may04_story2.cfm

Miller, M. (1991). *A whole different ballgame.* New York: Birch Lane Publishing.

Milwaukee American Association v. Landis, 49 F.2d 298 (D.C. Ill. 1931).

Much, P. J., & Gotto, R. M. (1997). Franchise valuation overview. In A. Friedman & P. J. Much (Eds.), *1997 Inside the ownership of professional sports teams* (pp. 6–7). Chicago: Team Marketing Report.

National Basketball Association. (2010a). Philadelphia 76ers. Front office directory. (n.d.). *NBA.com.* Retrieved from http://www.nba.com/sixers/front_office/index.html

National Basketball Association. (2010b). Global sites. *NBA.com.* Retrieved from http://www.nba.com/global/

National Basketball Association. (2010c). NBA to stage first-ever regular season games in Europe. *NBA.com.* Retrieved from http://www.nba.com/global/europe_games_100809.html

National Basketball Players Association. (2010). About the NBPA. Retrieved from http://www.nbpa.org/about-us

National Football League Players Association. (2008). NFLPA 2008 player conduct policy. Retrieved from http://images.nflplayers.com/mediaResources/images/oldImages/fck/NFL%20Personal%20Conduct%20Policy%202008.pdf

National Football League Properties, Inc. v. Dallas Cowboys Football Club, Ltd., 922 F. Supp. 849 (S.D.N.Y. 1996).

National Hockey League and National Hockey League Players Association. (2010). The full document: Richard Bloch's ruling in the Ilya Kovalchuk arbitration case. Retrieved from http://www.sbnation.com/2010/8/10/1614815/arbitration-ruling-ilya-kovalchuk-full-document

Neyer, R. (2002, November 5). Red Sox hire James in advisory capacity. ESPN.com. Retrieved from http://espn.go.com/mlb/s/2002/1105/1456563.html

PGA Tour Canada. (2014). Tournament schedules. Retrieved from http://www.pgatourcanada.com/leagues/cantour_events.cfm?clientid=3776&leagueid=0

PGA Tour Charities. (2014, January 22). PGA Tour reaches $2 billion in charitable giving. Retrieved from http://together.pgatour.com/stories/2014/january/pga-tour-announces-2-billion.html

PGA TOUR, Inc. (2014). Tournament schedules. Retrieved from http://www.pgatour.com/tournaments

PGA Tour Latinoámerica (2014). NEC Series Latinoámerica tournament schedules. Retrieved from http://www.pgatourla.com/tournaments/2014/

Professional Hockey Players' Association. (2010). AHL-PHPA collective bargaining agreement.

Professional Hockey Players' Association. (2013). ECHL-PHPA collective bargaining agreement.

Shropshire, K. (1996). *In black and white: Race and sports in America*. New York: New York University Press.

Staudohar, P. M. (1996). *Playing for dollars: Labor relations and the sports business*. Ithaca, NY: ILR Press.

Van Riper, T., & Karmali, N. (2009, June 22). The NBA's next frontier. Retrieved from http://www.forbes.com/global/2009/0622/china-india-adidas-nba-next-frontier.html

Yasser, R., McCurdy, J., Goplerud, P., & Weston, M. A. (2003). *Sports law: Cases and materials* (5th ed.). Cincinnati, OH: Anderson Publishing.

Chapter 11

Lisa P. Masteralexis

Sports Agency

Learning Objectives

Upon completion of this chapter, students should be able to:

1. Describe the reasons why the sports agency industry has grown so rapidly over the past several decades.

2. Discuss the history of the sports agency industry and identify some of the key personalities who defined the industry, such as C. C. Pyle and Mark McCormack.

3. Compare and contrast the differences involved in representing team sport athletes, individual sport athletes, coaches, and management professionals.

4. Illustrate differences that exist when representing athletes in different sports.

5. Distinguish between the various types of sports agency organizations, such as freestanding sport management firms, law practice only firms, sport management firms affiliated with a law firm, and superagencies.

6. Illustrate the various fee structures that sports agencies may utilize.

7. Appraise the career opportunities available in the sports agency industry and be aware of the skills and education needed to qualify and succeed in each of them.

8. Analyze the various roles of a sports agent including negotiating playing or coaching contracts, marketing, negotiating marketing and endorsement contracts, financial planning, career and post-career planning, dispute resolution, legal counseling, and personal care.

9. Discuss some of the unethical behavior that may occur in the sports agency industry including income mismanagement, incompetence, conflicts of interest, charging of excessive fees, and overly aggressive client recruitment.

10. Describe some of the methods that governing bodies, players associations, leagues, and government have utilized to regulate the activities of sports agents.

Introduction

This chapter focuses on the field of sports agency, examining how athlete management and marketing firms operate. Many sports agency firms started by representing athletes, evolved to also include sports marketing and event management segments, and continue today to evolve as the sports agency business responds to competition.

A quick examination of IMG (International Management Group), one of the very first sports agencies, shows this evolution. IMG began in 1960 when its founder and sports agency industry innovator **Mark H. McCormack** began representing iconic golfer Arnold Palmer; he soon added Gary Player and Jack Nicklaus to his list of clients before moving into tennis with Rod Laver in 1968 (IMG, 2004a). In more than 40 years of leading IMG, McCormack transformed the company into the leader in managing golfers as well as "running tournaments all over the world in both golf and tennis, even controlling the computer that assigns worldwide rankings to golfers" (Feinstein, 1992, p. 131). "The business of representing people—whether models, opera singers or rugby players—is the essence of IMG's business" (Christy, 2002). Beyond representing talent, IMG owns and runs events for its talent, and then produces, distributes, and markets television programming of those events, as well as others. Shortly after McCormack's passing in 2003, IMG's web site had a letter posted from its new co-CEOs describing the company as "[t]he world's largest athlete representation firm [that], through its broadcast division, TWI, is both the world's largest independent producer of televised sports programming and distributor of sports television rights." (Johnston & Kain, 2004). The letter also noted the diversity of IMG's areas of business, listed below, which Johnston and Kain (2004) attempted to pull together with the term "multi-faceted sports and lifestyle businesses":

- An event management division for sports, classical music, and other unique events, such as the Nobel Prize celebrations;
- A consulting division that served major corporations, major products, and sports properties
- A division that developed golf courses and resort properties
- A sports training academy
- A sports media division specializing in digital and interactive media
- A top modeling agency
- A top literary agency
- A top licensing agency
- A classical music agency

Excluding TWI, prior to its $750 million sale to Ted Forstmann in 2004, IMG listed 26 areas of business on its website (IMG, 2004b). Forstmann reinvigorated IMG by streamlining the organization and its cost structure by eliminating that which was not vertically integrated throughout the company, such as its representation of team-sport athletes, artists, and celebrities. In doing so, IMG allowed agents of team sport athletes to move on to competitors while investing in new areas of business, such as IMG College and creating joint ventures in the emerging markets in India, Brazil, China, and Turkey (IMG, 2014). Also, as you'll learn later in the chapter, team-sport athlete representation has more costs for fewer financial rewards. Forstmann expanded IMG's focus to a more global one, acquiring only new companies that complement IMG's strengths. These moves again position IMG as the innovator in the field. IMG currently has a staff of 3,500 employees in 30 countries (IMG, 2014). After Forstmann's passing and at the time of IMG's sale to WME (William Morris Endeavor), IMG had 12 identified areas of expertise, plus 4 joint ventures in emerging markets for a total of 16 divisions (down from 26 a decade earlier) (IMG, 2014):

- IMG Academy
- IMG Art+Commerce
- IMG Clients
- IMG College
- IMG Consulting
- IMG Events and Federations
- IMG Fashion
- IMG Golf
- IMG Licensing
- IMG Media
- IMG Performance
- IMG Tennis
- IMG joint ventures: IMG Reliance (India); IMX (Brazil); IMGCCTV (China), IMG Dogus (Turkey)

How does a smaller agency compete with such a behemoth? It is a logical question to ask at a time when many agency firms are operating in an environment of mergers and acquisitions. In the past decade and a half, the sports agency business has seen SFX Sports come and go; built through the acquisition of more than 20 different sports and entertainment firms, it was later sold to Clear Channel and spun off with Live Nation. Many of the original agents whose firms were bought by SFX (such as Arn Tellem, the Hendricks brothers, and David Falk) bought back their firms to make a fresh start as SFX Sports became lost within the entertainment giant Live Nation. Others that sought vertical integration in the sports and entertainment media and marketing businesses, such as Octagon, have outlasted SFX. Octagon is the sports arm of Interpublic Group, a large advertising and marketing communications agency developed through similar acquisitions of established sports agencies. Octagon boasts over 800 employees in 68 offices across 22 countries on 6 continents (Octagon, 2014b). Octagon manages 13,480 events annually, up from 3,200

events in 2007 (Octagon, 2014). It also represents more than 900 professional athletes and celebrities in music and entertainment in its personalities division (Octagon, 2007a). In its marketing research side, it maintains a database of fans that it calls "Passion Drivers" and claims to have managed or influenced $300 billion in sponsorship investments (Octagon, 2014a). Still others—namely, Creative Artists Agency (CAA Sports) and Wasserman Media Group (WMG)—are trying to dominate and shape the industry segment created by IMG. The concept of developing a sports agency business through such acquisitions will be discussed in greater detail later in this chapter. This chapter primarily focuses on representatives of athletes and coaches.

A **sports agent** is difficult to define. As Ruxin (2004) points out, the term *sports agent* covers a broad range of relationships with an athlete, including friend, lawyer, teacher, or coach. In some aspects, a sports agent is similar to a talent agent in the entertainment industry in that both serve as personal managers who find the best outlet for the client's talent (Ruxin, 2004). When an agent acts as a representative of an athlete or coach, the law of agency imposes certain fiduciary duties on the agent.

Many people hold themselves out as sports agents. The exact number of sports agents out there is hard to pinpoint, but one thing is certain: because the client pool is limited there are far more people claiming to be agents than there are potential clients. The four major leagues have more than 4,300 professional athletes. There are between 1,600 and 1,800 agents registered or certified with the respective players associations. Currently, over 300 agents are certified by the Major League Baseball Players Association (MLBPA) to represent the 1,200 players on a 40-man roster in Major League Baseball (MLB) (MLBPA, 2014), 174 agents in the National Hockey League (NHL) (NHLPA,

2014), 350 agents in the National Basketball Association (NBA), and 800 to 1,000 agents in the National Football League (NFL) (Martino, 2009). Shropshire and Davis (2003) estimate that fewer than 100 NBA agents have clients, and only 50% of agents represent a client in the NFL (Levin, 2007). Many agents either have no clients or are doing agency work part time while supplementing their incomes through other professions, such as law, marketing, accounting, or financial planning. The fact that some athletes have more than one person representing their interests may contribute slightly to the high number of agents. For instance, one agent may be retained for contract negotiations; another employed for marketing, public relations, and media work; and yet another for financial advising. In any case, the number of sports agents clearly exceeds the number of potential clients, creating an environment ripe for unscrupulous conduct by sports agents. Ironically, often those who resort to unethical conduct during the recruiting process do not end up with the clients they were pursuing. This chapter discusses in detail the field's challenges to entry and clarifies the role of the sports agent and agency firms in the sport industry and in the lives of the athletes they represent.

Due to the competition in the industry, potential agents look for other areas in which to do business. The representation of coaches and management personnel in professional sports and big-time Division I college programs is one such emerging area. The reasons for this growth will be explored in greater detail later in the chapter. Another area for growth of representation in the United States is in soccer due to the growth in its popularity and Major League Soccer (MLS). The MLS relies on Fédération Internationale de Football Association (FIFA)

regulations. FIFA has not certified agents since 2001. Instead, member associations do, by relying on FIFA regulations. Currently, 6,861 soccer agents are registered worldwide, including 160 in the United States, 13 in Mexico, and 44 in Canada (FIFA, 2014). In South America, Brazil (245) and Argentina (219) are way ahead of the other countries in number of agents registered. Europe has the most agents per continent with England (451), France (226), and Germany (470) standing out, but Italy holding not only the largest number of any country in Europe, but in the world with 1,060 (FIFA, 2014). The Canadian Football League (CFL) is yet another market explored by agents and their players. For this reason, the CFL Players Association (CFLPA) currently lists 159 registered agents on its site, many of whom also are registered with the National Football League Players Association (NFLPA) (CFLPA, 2014).

History

Theater promoter C. C. "Cash and Carry" Pyle is often called the first sports agent. In 1925, Pyle negotiated a deal with George Halas' Chicago Bears for Red Grange to earn $3,000 per game and an additional $300,000 in endorsement and movie rights (Berry, Gould, & Staudohar, 1986). A few years later, New York Yankee George Herman "Babe" Ruth allegedly consulted sports cartoonist Christy Walsh to serve as his financial advisor through the Great Depression (Neff, 1987). Until the 1970s, it was extremely rare for a player to have a sports agent because teams generally refused to deal with agents. Some players even found that having an agent turned out to be a detriment to their contract negotiations. One often-told story involves a Green Bay Packers player, Jim Ringo, who, in 1964, brought his financial advisor to help him negotiate his contract with legendary coach and general manager Vince Lombardi. Lombardi immediately excused himself for a minute. When Lombardi returned he told the

agent he was negotiating with the wrong team, for he had just traded Ringo to Philadelphia (Hofmann & Greenberg, 1989). Interestingly, although the story is *not* true, Vince Lombardi publicly encouraged the story to go on in the hopes that it would dissuade players from hiring agents or becoming difficult in contract negotiations. But privately, about the story Lombardi stated, "Hell, no, the trade didn't take place in 5 minutes. That's no way to general-manage a football team" ("Sports Legend Revealed," 2011).

This type of treatment and the inability to negotiate on what the players believed was a level playing field led the Dodgers' star pitchers Sandy Koufax and Don Drysdale to hire Hollywood agent Bill Hayes to represent them in 1965. Hayes orchestrated Koufax and Drysdale's joint holdout in which they each demanded a 3-year, $1 million contract, up from the $85,000 and $80,000 the Dodgers had paid them the season before (Helyar, 1994). The idea of a joint holdout, the amount of money the two demanded, and the prospect of other players trying the tactic outraged the Dodgers, and Hayes lined up an exhibition tour for Koufax and Drysdale in Japan and threatened to get Drysdale a movie contract. Although the two had immense talent, they had little bargaining power because the rules in MLB did not allow them to negotiate with other major league teams. As a result, Koufax and Drysdale ended up settling for $125,000 and $115,000, respectively (Helyar, 1994). It was a great deal less than they sought, but more than they would have received had they bargained individually and without an agent.

Few players in team sports had agents until the late 1960s. In that era, even those who had agents used them more as advisors than as agents. In 1967 Bob Woolf counseled Detroit Tigers pitcher Earl Wilson. Wilson went to the front office of the Tigers alone while Woolf stayed in Wilson's apartment; whenever Wilson had a question he excused himself from the room and called Woolf for more advice (Woolf, 1976). Despite the fact that the door to representation in team sports began to open in 1970 when the MLBPA negotiated for a player's right to be represented by an agent, it did not fully open until free agency was won in 1976 through the Messersmith-McNally arbitration decision.

Players in individual sports such as golf and tennis have relied on agents for a longer time. C. C. Pyle also made his mark in professional tennis when, in 1926, he guaranteed French tennis star Suzanne Lenglen $50,000 to tour the United States (Berry et al., 1986). At the time people were startled by the sum, but by the end of the tour Pyle had helped popularize professional tennis, and all involved earned a handsome share of the revenue it generated (Berry et al., 1986). Mark H. McCormack, founder of IMG and one of the first agents to represent individual athletes, was known as the pioneer of the sports marketing industry. He revolutionized the sport industry by "establishing athlete representation as a distinct business discipline" (IMG, 2003). A college golfer at William & Mary, McCormack became "famous for launching the modern sports-marketing business when he packaged and marketed Arnold Palmer, endorsement king of the pre-Michael Jordan era" (Katz, 1994, p. 231). Although golfers such as Bobby Jones and Walter Hagen pitched products such as cigarettes and liquor long before Palmer came along, McCormack and Palmer took a different approach to sport marketing, because Palmer told McCormack he would not endorse a product he didn't like or use. In a brilliant move, McCormack did not tie Palmer's endorsements to his success on the golf course, but rather to his traits, such as character, endurance, reliability, and integrity (Palmer, 2014).

This formula has worked well; in 2012 Arnold Palmer was ranked the third most successful golfer on the annual income ranking of golfers, despite the fact that he stopped golfing in 2006 and has not won a tournament in more than 25 years (Warner, 2013). Palmer is most successful with garnering endorsements and licensing, two areas where he generates all of his income. Palmer also possesses the third largest net worth of anyone involved in sports behind Vince McMahon, a professional wrestling promoter, and Formula One racer Michael Schumacher (Celebrity Net Worth, 2014). He is also currently ranked third in annual income amongst golfers, behind Tiger Woods (#1) and Phil Mickelson (#2) (Warner, 2013).

The reason Palmer continues to earn so much annually is due to his long-standing popularity and the resulting licensing fees, endorsement deals, and incredible thirst from customers for the Arizona Ice Tea drink that bears his name (Palmer, 2014; Rovell, 2013). Palmer's success over 60 years stands as a testament to Palmer's traits, business sense, and the work done by his agency, IMG, to turn him into a corporate enterprise. Palmer truly was the first athlete to become a brand, through his Arnold Palmer Enterprises. The partnership of Palmer and McCormack created a model followed by other top athletes, such as Maria Sharapova, Gary Player, Jack Nicklaus, and Michael Jordan.

Beyond his work with Palmer, McCormack developed new opportunities for revenue streams for individual athletes by branching into the marketing of events in which they could participate. From there he developed TWI, a broadcast division that is currently the largest independent producer of televised sports programming and distributor of sports television rights (IMG, 2003). McCormack's innovations created the model of today's multiservice sports agency, a business model that is engaged in many facets of the sport industry, from representation to events to media development and corporate consulting, licensing, and other ventures.

Growth of the Sports Agency Business

By the late 1970s, most segments of the sport industry had acknowledged the role that agents had come to play in professional sports. According to Sobel (1990), five factors accounted for the growth of the sports agency business: the evolution of players associations, the reserve system, players' need for financial advice, the development of competing leagues, and an increase in the number of available product endorsement opportunities.

Evolution of Players Associations

Expounding on Sobel's factors, we first examine the evolution of the players associations in the late 1960s and early 1970s that opened the doors of the team front offices to sports agents. In negotiations of their second collective bargaining agreement, the MLBPA received a written guarantee for the players to have a right to use an agent in contract negotiations with management (Lowenfish, 1991). In its negotiations with MLB's Management Council, the MLBPA also achieved the right to labor grievance arbitration. Labor grievance arbitration is a system that allows both players and management to settle work-related conflicts in a hearing before a neutral arbitrator. Players achieved free agency through such an arbitration award in 1975.

Achieving free agency enabled sports agents to negotiate better contracts for players. Players associations opened the door for the agents to have more power, and they often monitor and work with agents through negotiations and arbitrations because both represent the players' interests. The difference between the two is that the union represents the collective interests of all players, whereas an agent represents the individual interests of a particular player. As such, the union negotiates a collective bargaining agreement for all players in the league and the agent negotiates a contract for the player he or she represents, called the **standard or uniform player contract**. Through collective bargaining, players associations establish salary and benefit minimums, and agents try to negotiate salaries and benefits above and beyond those minimums for the athletes they represent. This is unique to sport and entertainment, because in most labor relationships the union represents all employees. Players associations support agents by sharing a great deal of salary and contract data and information to support contract negotiations and by providing invaluable guidance in salary and labor arbitrations.

The Reserve System

Until the mid-1970s, players in MLB were bound perpetually to their teams by the **reserve system**. Each league used a restrictive system to limit a free and open market so that the owners could retain the rights to players and depress salaries. Baseball's reserve system was the first and serves as a great example. The system consisted of the reserve clause and the reserve list. The **reserve clause** in the players' standard contracts gave teams the option to renew players for the following season. Each contract contained a reserve clause, and thus a player could be renewed season after season at the team's option. The **reserve list** was a list sent to each team in the league. League rules entitled each team to place its reserved players on a list, and the teams had a "gentlemen's agreement" not to offer contracts to any other teams' players reserved on the list. This two-part system kept players bound to their teams, depressing their salaries and bargaining leverage. Once the 1976 Messersmith-McNally arbitration toppled the reserve system, free agency descended on baseball, and agents such as Jerry Kapstein (who represented 60 baseball players) elevated salaries by holding auctions for talented ones (Helyar, 1994). Kapstein played to the owners' lust for talent by driving them into bidding wars for his free agents (Schwarz, 1996). As salaries increased, so, too, did the players' demand for agents.

Athletes' Need for Financial Planning

As athletes' salaries increased, tax planning (Sobel, 1990), financial planning (Grossman, 2002), and other forms of business advice became vital to a player's financial success. Agents help athletes negotiate more favorable contract clauses for increased income, tax breaks, and postcareer income. According to Shropshire (1990), an agent also provides a level of parity in negotiations with the athlete and the team, event, or sponsor. Sports team or event management people have a great deal of experience, negotiating many contracts each year, whereas an athlete may have just one opportunity to negotiate, and thus should hire an agent with comparable negotiating experience to level the playing field (Shropshire, 1990). This is particularly important when complex systems such as salary caps are involved. It is highly likely that most athletes have not seen a player's contract before, let alone a collective bargaining agreement. Without an agent's help, an athlete might be at a severe disadvantage.

Agents allow athletes to focus their attention on performing in their sport while the agent acts as a shield to outside distractions. The shield is the transparent bubble that agents build around their clients to protect them from such distractions as tax and insurance forms, payment of bills, travel arrangements, the media, and the emotional challenges of being a professional athlete (Schwarz, 1996). Further, according to Grossman (2002), an athlete's long-term financial success requires the conversion of current income into longer-term financial resources. The dynamics are such that an athlete's career earnings debut at a rate far exceeding those of his or her peers in other industries. Often an athlete may be transformed from relative poverty to wealth almost overnight but may lack the wisdom and maturity to control spending and save for the future. Grossman (2002) suggests that an athlete's financial team should consist of an accountant or tax advisor,

business attorney, banker, investment advisor, insurance professional, and estate attorney. These individuals are separate from the agent representing the athlete's interest in contract negotiations or marketing.

Development of Competing Leagues

The development of competing leagues from the 1960s through the 1980s furthered the growth of the sports agency business (Sobel, 1990). Competing leagues such as the American Football League (AFL, 1960–1966), the American Basketball Association (ABA, 1967–1976), the World Hockey Association (WHA, 1972–1978), and the United States Football League (USFL, 1982–1986) offered higher salaries to induce marquee players to join the leagues, and these offers provided leverage during contract negotiations. As players jumped to competing leagues their salaries increased, and correspondingly the salaries of players that owners were trying to keep in the dominant leagues increased. Agents often played a crucial role in locating interested teams in the new leagues, sifting through players' offers, and negotiating contracts. This concept can be taken one step further, as sport has become more of a global phenomenon over the past two decades. With more athletes moving into a worldwide market for team sport, agents with an understanding of leagues and teams on a global scale and with international contacts are critical to athletes moving into playing opportunities in other countries.

Growth of Product Endorsement Opportunities

As professional sport grew into a nationally televised business and its entertainment value increased, so, too, did opportunities for athletes to increase their income through product endorsements (Sobel, 1990). Martin Blackman pioneered the negotiation of endorsement contracts for athletes with his deals for retired athletes to star in Miller Lite's television commercial series (Shropshire, 1990). Today, many athletes hire sports marketing experts to help them create images, market their images and services, and negotiate endorsement deals.

Beyond product endorsement, agents for athletes are involved in parlaying their images into entertainment and celebrity. Some athletes, such as Mike Tyson, Dwayne Johnson ("The Rock"), Reggie Jackson, Michael Jordan, and Shaquille O'Neal, have starred in movies, whereas others, including Michael Strahan, Tiki Barber, Rocco Mediate, Peyton Manning, Derek Jeter, and Serena Williams, have appeared on television shows. Bernie Williams, Shaquille O'Neal, and Tony Parker recorded music professionally. Professional athletes have also moved into the popular reality television genre. Former NFL stars Emmitt Smith and Jerry Rice, former NBA star Clyde Drexler, boxers Laila Ali and Evander Holyfield, auto racer Helio Castroneves, and Olympians Apolo Anton Ohno, Kristi Yamaguchi, Meryl Davis, and Charlie White have appeared on *Dancing With the Stars*. NFL stars Chad Ochocinco and Terrell Owens had TV shows, *Ochocinco: The Ultimate Catch* and *The T.O. Show*, respectively. A number of former sports stars have appeared on *Celebrity Apprentice* (e.g., Scott Hamilton, Jenny Finch, Dennis Rodman, etc.), putting them back into the spotlight and playing to their competitive fire. Shaquille O'Neal hosts his own show called, *ShaQ Vs.* in which he challenges other star athletes and entertainers to competitions in their expertise, harkening back to popular shows from the late 1970s, such as ABC's *Wide World of Sports Superstars* and *Battle of the Network Stars*, that featured athletes and entertainers competing. The latter two were joint productions between IMG's television production arm and ABC Sports, once again demonstrating IMG's branding of the athlete as celebrity and the integration of sports and entertainment. The sports agent often obtains opportunities for their clients to be involved in entertainment and then navigates the public relations needs for their celebrity status.

Still other athletes get into entrepreneurial ventures such as golf course design, product development, theme restaurants, sports bars, and music clubs. The sports agent often performs a crucial role carrying out business transactions to establish these ventures.

Evolution of Sports Agencies

The name of the game in the sports agency world in the late 1990s was to create "uberagencies." This trend was spawned by SFX founder Robert F.X. Sillerman's attempted corporate acquisition revolution in 1998. At the time, Sillerman's two companies, the Marquee Group and SFX Entertainment, were international leaders in marketing, concert promotion, and live entertainment production. He moved into the sporting world by buying up sports agencies, spending $150 million in just 18 months. As the line between sports and entertainment blurred, Sillerman believed SFX Sports Group could provide athletes with one-stop shopping for marketing and negotiation. SFX Sports could use its resources to achieve vertical integration (Wertheim, 2001). Octagon jumped into the fray, pursuing multiple acquisitions of smaller agencies to keep up with SFX Group and IMG, already the model of vertical integration that Sillerman sought to achieve.

SFX was brought down by internal strife. What Sillerman did not effectively plan for is the idea that these agencies that were fiercely competitive would now have to work together in a cooperative manner. What ensued were numerous power struggles and a sale of SFX in August 2000 to Clear Channel that made Sillerman $4.4 billion. However, the move weakened SFX, because sports accounted for less than 10% of SFX's business, and SFX was less than 10% of Clear Channel's core business (Wertheim, 2001). As SFX Sports disintegrated and many began to think that the era of agency mergers and acquisitions was over, along came Wasserman Media Group (WMG) and CAA Sports.

WMG grabbed Arn Tellem's agency, which he had recently bought back from SFX (WMG, 2006a); Touring Pro, an events firm (WMG, 2006b); soccer representation firm SportsNet, SFX's European soccer division (WMG, 2006c, 2006d); Reich and Katz's baseball agency (Mullen, 2007b); sport and entertainment marketing agency OnSport (WMG, 2007); and two agents from Octagon and one agent from IMG who represent athletes in the areas of women's sports, action sports, and golf (Mullen, 2007b). Meanwhile, CAA Sports acquired IMG's baseball, football, and hockey divisions, along with SFX's football division, and Leon Rose's basketball division, which represents LeBron James (Mullen, 2006, 2007a). More recently, CAA has picked off some of IMG's executives, and their clients have followed (Futterman, 2010a; Mullen, 2010a, 2010b). IMG settled its lawsuit against former coaches' agent Matthew Baldwin over his defection to CAA Sports and an alleged attempt to steal its coaching representation business (Futterman, 2010a; Mullen, 2010c). Incidentally, CAA dismissed Baldwin prior to his settlement with IMG (Futterman, 2010b).

These aggressive moves to merge and acquire agencies caught many observers by surprise, because this approach seemed to fail in the SFX experiment. However, according to Randy Vataha, president of Boston-based Game Plan, "If it was a complete failure the first time, it wouldn't be happening now . . . The agent world is extremely entrepreneurial" (Mullen, 2006). Companies such as the old SFX Entertainment and the former Assante Corporation, which also bought a number of top sports agencies about a decade ago only to dissolve the business a few years later, saw a big opportunity initially. "But once the dust cleared, they had to manage all these mavericks," Vataha said. "I think the people doing this now think they

have learned from the mistakes of the earlier deals" (Mullen, 2006). Some industry experts, including agents and others who have talked to CAA President Richard Lovett, who is leading the sports agency acquisition charge, note that that company may be able to avoid some of the pitfalls of the past because, after all, talent representation is CAA's core business (CAA represents such entertainment stars as Tom Cruise, George Clooney, and Steven Spielberg).

Tellem, who was one of the agents acquired by the old SFX Entertainment and is now the head of athlete management for WMG, knows about the mistakes of the past firsthand. "Our plan is not to do a roll-up of sports agencies. I have been there and that is a recipe for disaster," said Tellem. SFX's aggregation of sports agencies "was done as a way of building up a company of critical mass and then selling it," Tellem said (Mullen & Broughton, 2008). Tellem added that he decided to join WMG because the company's owner, Casey Wasserman, is committed to building something that lasts and because the company's core business is sports. CAA Sports and WMG were the top two sports agencies in brokering player salaries in the four major team sports according to a list published in the summer of 2008 by *SportsBusiness Journal* (Mullen & Broughton, 2008). Only time will tell if WMG and CAA Sports are leading the next wave of firms to have the lasting impact of an IMG, but it appears they are not going the way of SFX.

In December 2013, the sports agency world had yet another acquisition. Entertainment talent agency William Morris Endeavor (WME) and Silver Lake Partners purchased IMG for $2.3 billion. The combination of WME and IMG will make it a challenge to compete with when it comes to talent recruitment and acquisition. This acquisition by WME will bring together the sports and entertainment worlds, strikingly similar at least on paper to CAA Sports and Roc Nation, Jay-Z's new sports representation venture (Ozanian, 2013).

A further challenge that SFX faced was an issue noted by Donald Dell, sports agency pioneer and founder of ProServ, "[w]e had 15 companies bought in 2-1/2 years, … [so, w]e had 15 egomaniacs, all strutting around telling everyone what to do, and nothing happened" (Mullen & Broughton, 2008). Finally, as noted by AEG president and CEO Tim Leiweke, another difference between the SFX example and CAA Sports is that CAA Sports has aligned with a sports medicine and performance institute to help athletes get drafted to a higher position or signed onto a team (Mullen & Broughton, 2008). Some sport agencies may be working more on talent development in order to compete with large competitors such as IMG, which owns a multisport training academy in Florida. As the agency business has evolved, many athletes have begun to expect that agents will pick up much of the cost of training for them. For instance, one football agent suggested that the NFL Combine preparation runs at least $1,000 per week for training, plus an athlete will need housing, a stipend, a car, and food; thus, an agent may invest close to $20,000 on preparing one player for the Combine (Kuliga, 2007). Creating alliances or partnerships with training facilities and car dealerships is one method of limiting the costs or even deriving some revenues from the relationships for sports agencies.

A key difference between firms that represent individual athletes and those that primarily represent team-sport athletes is that the firms doing individual representation are intimately involved in all aspects of the sport, from running the sports' tournaments to televising them. Such involvement can create a conflict of interest. As Brennan (1996) points out, athletes often decide that the conflict created when their agent becomes their employer is not as trying as the conflict created when their training and traveling bills come due and they have generated no income from their sport.

As the Olympic Movement has moved away from its rigid rules on amateurism, top-level Olympic athletes have increasingly found that they, too, have a greater need for sports agents. In figure skating, for example, new revenues from television rights increased the athletes' earning opportunities. Senior manager/agent Michael Rosenburg, two-time Olympic medalist and ice skating commentator Dick Button, and the management firm IMG had worked to develop professional skating careers for athletes such as Dorothy Hamill, Janet Lynn, and doubles partners Tai Babilonia and Randy Gardner. WMG, in particular, is focused on this business (Mullen & Broughton, 2008). Octagon's Peter Carlisle created a niche in representation of Olympians, starting with Winter Olympic snowboarders and skiers and then moving into the Summer Games with swimmer Michael Phelps. Carlisle's work with Phelps resembles the partnership of McCormack and Palmer. Like Palmer, Phelps was clear in what his marketing goal was. Phelps wanted to bring swimming into the mainstream, for instance, to get it on ESPN's *Sports Center*. Carlisle worked to create marketing opportunities that would bring Phelps and his sport into the mainstream. Phelps, our most decorated Olympian, continues to keep the sport and himself on that global stage through such activities as his VISA sponsorship relationship and his development of the Michael Phelps Swim School, both of which emphasize his community work in swimming (Carlisle, 2012).

Representing Individual Athletes

Representing the individual athlete differs significantly from representing the team-sport athlete. Much of what the individual athlete earns is dependent on consistent performance in events, appearance fees from events, and the ability to promote and market his or her image. Therefore, an agent representing an individual athlete often travels with the athlete, tending to daily distractions so the athlete can stay focused on winning. For instance, as Ivan Lendl's agent for 7 years, Jerry Solomon of ProServ spent nearly 24 hours a day, 7 days a week traveling and representing Lendl. This takes a toll on one's social and personal life, but often is necessary to retain a client. When Solomon eventually pulled away from this relationship with Lendl, Lendl resented it and moved from ProServ to IMG (Feinstein, 1992). An agent of an individual-sport athlete is often more involved in managing the individual player's career, much like business managers hired by entertainers.

Management tasks include booking exhibitions and special competitions to supplement the athlete's winnings from regular tour or circuit events as well as managing training, travel, lodging, and the athlete's personal life. For the team-sport athlete, the professional team takes care of many of these details. However, this may be changing a bit, because competition in acquiring and retaining clients is causing agents to offer more services. Some agents are taking a more active role in their athletes' training regimens by providing access to trainers and coaches (Helyar, 1997), or even signing an alliance with their Olympic appearances (Brennan, 1996). As figure skating's popularity has increased, so has the amount of money flowing into the sport, legitimately creating an increased need for agents. Like other national governing bodies, the U.S. Figure Skating Association expects stars to be out participating in promotions, interviews, tours, and various competitions, and as a result these young athletes are now hiring agents to promote them and to protect them from the "blastfurnace media" (Brennan, 1996, p. 126). In previous years a family struggled financially to enable a daughter or son to pursue the Olympic dream, but now, with the help of an agent, an Olympic athlete may earn money to help pay some of his or her training and traveling expenses (Brennan, 1996).

Marketing is similar for agents of individual- and team-sport athletes. Marketing is critical for individual-sport athletes who are dependent on sponsorship contracts to provide product and earn income for travel and training costs. Although not a recent development, today there is greater emphasis on branding all athletes. Although branding is not exclusive to individual athletes, the opportunities for branding are greater due to the individual nature of their performances. Although branding is the current buzzword, innovative sport marketing agencies such as IMG have been doing it for years. For instance, in a 2004 interview with BusinessWeek, Arnold Palmer demonstrated that even in the 1960s, IMG was thinking about the development of the Arnold Palmer brand. Palmer explained that he posed a question to his IMG agent about how a very intense commercial shoot could be replicated when he was old, and the agent responded, "[w]e will have established you as a business, and you personally will not be so important" (Brady, 2004). This answer was given long before "branding" was a focus in the marketing world. Judging by Palmer's success, Mark McCormack's identification of Palmer's marketing appeal and his ability to manage Palmer's off course ventures lead to Palmer's success (Hack, 2008). Despite not having a major tour victory since 1973, Palmer is the second highest paid retired athlete, earning $40 million in 2013 (Badenhausen, 2014). The Arnold Palmer name has been licensed in a way that continues to reap benefits for him. For instance, the Arizona Ice Tea drinks that bear his name bring in 25% of the company's $200 million in revenues; in Asia 400 stores bear his name; and IMG continues to manage 50 Palmer licensees in Asia. (Badenhausen, 2014).

Building a brand out of an athlete does not work for every athlete. The athlete must be good enough at the sport to command interest. Mark McCormack would create brands for those clients that had talent, but also a marketing ability away from the field, court, or ice (Hack, 2008). In addition, the client must have what Brian Dubin, head of WMA's East Coast commercial division and brand expert for skateboarder Tony Hawk, calls "intangible assets: a name, a reputation, a credibility, and an image." Dubin suggests those intangible assets, marketed properly can be turned into a product or service, making them a tangible brand. (Towle, 2003).

However, there are challenges in athlete branding. For instance, if the advertisements and products are not a fit with the athlete's personality or do not work to raise an athlete's image, it can work against the athlete. A good example of this dilemma was former 7-foot, 6-inch Chinese Houston Rocket star Yao Ming, who was criticized for not maintaining better control of his image outside of China. Ming did advertisements that furthered cultural stereotypes (VISA check cards) and positioned him as freakishly tall (Apple Computer), rather than as a premier athlete. By doing advertisements that pandered to his height or foreignness, he moved away from his image in China—that of a premier basketball superstar—an image that should have been the linchpin of his branding in the United States and beyond (Sauer, 2003). To change this perception, some marketers, such as branding expert Wendy Newman, advocate an approach called *person-centered branding*, in which an authentic brand is created based on who the person is, focusing on the person's identity to establish an enduring brand as opposed to capitalizing for the short term on an athlete's game or performance and contriving an image to fit a product or brand. The first strategy promises to last a lifetime, whereas the second will likely fade away with the end of the athlete's playing career (Newman, 2007).

Another challenge that arises from athlete branding "is that, while it trades on the allure of a personality, it is vulnerable to the public's acceptance of that personality" (Towle, 2003). Some observers argue that, in sports, where celebrity branding originated, a backlash already has occurred. Jim Andrews, Editorial Director at IEG Sponsorship Report, suggests that corporations are moving away from exlusively tying all their marketing to one athlete for fear of the damage to the company's reputation that might occur when the athlete's performance dwindles or does something illegal or unethical. (Towle, 2003).

Representing Coaches and Management Professionals

A handful of sports agents represent professional and collegiate coaches. Not all coaches have sports agents, but the number who have representation is growing. The growing income of coaches is one reason. The top 10 NCAA men's college basketball coaches contracts fall in the range of $2 to $7 million, with Mike Krzyzewski of Duke leading the group with a 2013 salary of $7,233,976, up $2,534,406 from 2012 (Berkowitz, Upton, Dougherty, & Durkin, 2013a). Compensation for NCAA college football coaches has increased substantially, with the top 10 2013 salaries ranging from $3.7 to $5.5 million (Berkowitz et al., 2013a). The agent for Alabama football coach Nick Saban renegotiated his contract in December 2013, and his new deal will pay $7 million, an increase of $1.5 million (Vint, 2013). To compare how these salaries stack up with the professional coaching ranks, in 2013 the NFL's Sean Payton of the New Orleans Saints leads the group with an annual salary of $8 million, the NBA's Doc Rivers of the Clippers earns $7 million, MLB's Mike Scioscia of the Los Angeles Angels earns $5.5 million, and the NHL's Alain Vigneault and Joel Quenneville of the New York Rangers and Chicago Blackhawks, respectively, earn $2 million (Vint, 2013). Agents can earn a respectable commission off of those salaries, and these clients often come with fewer problems and headaches due to their age and life experience.

A second reason for the increased use of agents by coaches may be the increased job movement and added pressures on coaches to succeed (Greenberg, 1993). The increased complexities of the position of head or top assistant coach may make having an agent to rely on for advice and counsel almost a necessity. One agent credited with growing the salaries of NFL coaches, Bob LaMonte, views the modern-day coach as a CEO; he therefore prepares the coach to be a CEO while at the same time negotiating CEO-like pay from club owners (Wertheim, 2004). For these same reasons, management professionals, such as general managers in professional sports, are also turning to sports agents and attorneys to assist in their contract negotiations with clubs. The "Career Opportunities" section later in this chapter discusses specific details regarding coaching contract negotiations.

Sports Agency Firms

There is no blueprint for how a sports agency firm should be structured. In small firms, an agent works alone or with a small group of employees, and work may be outsourced to other professionals. In larger firms, the agent may be part of an international conglomerate representing many athletes in a broad range of sports and working on many aspects of an athlete's career. Often these divisions will have a big-name agent as the head of the division, with a number of subordinate agents working to make the operation run smoothly.

In a presentation before the American Bar Association's Forum Committee on the Entertainment and Sports Industries, law professor Robert A. Berry stated that there are three models for the sports agency business (Berry, 1990). The first and most popular model is the **freestanding sport management firm**. It is established as a full-service firm providing a wide range of services to the athlete. Although each sport management firm may not perform all the services discussed in the "Career Opportunities" section, it is likely that a firm performs several, including contract negotiations, marketing, and some financial planning. These freestanding sport management firms may be further divided into two categories: (1) those that represent athletes only, such as the Scott Boras Corporation (baseball) and Newport Sports Management (hockey), and (2) those that combine athlete representation, event management, and industry consulting, such as IMG, Octagon, CAA Sports, and WMG, all of which have many divisions across many sports and events (Berry, 1990).

According to Shropshire (1990), a freestanding sport management firm's benefits are as follows: (1) the athlete is presumably able to receive the best service without having to shop around for many experts and (2) the agent retains all aspects of the athlete's business. The firm benefits because the athlete usually pays fees for any services provided beyond the contract negotiation. Fees will be discussed in greater detail later in this chapter.

Berry (1990) identifies a second type of firm as a **law practice only**. In this type of firm, "lawyer sports representatives often participate as principals in a sports management firm, but opt to include this as just one aspect of their law practice" (Berry, 1990, p. 4). In this practice, the lawyer performs many legal tasks for the athlete, such as contract negotiation, legal representation in arbitration or other proceedings, legal counseling, dispute resolution, and the preparation of tax forms. Often the lawyers do not undertake financial management, marketing, or investing of the athlete's money; the sports lawyer may, however, oversee the retention of other needed professionals to advise the athlete and protect him or her from incompetent service (Berry, 1990). Lon Babby, formerly a partner at the Washington, D.C., law firm of Williams & Connolly, was known for charging clients an hourly rate and represented such basketball players as NBA stars Grant Hill and Tim Duncan as well as WNBA stars Alana Beard and Tamika Catchings. This practice was first popularized by Babby before he became the president of Basketball Operations for the Phoenix Suns. Babby also introduced the hourly rate to baseball representation. Williams & Connolly continue the practice of hourly representation on behalf of the firm.

The third type of firm identified by Berry (1990) is the **sport management firm affiliated with a law firm**. Many sports lawyers who represent athletes originally developed a law practice, and as their businesses grew they recognized the advantages of expanding the services they offered the athlete beyond legal services. Some have abolished their law practices in favor of a freestanding sport management firm, but others have retained a law practice and created a sport management subsidiary within the practice to provide those services not traditionally offered by lawyers. A trend in the past 20 years has been for law firms to create an affiliate relationship whereby the law firm remains its own entity but creates a working relationship with a freestanding sport management firm, each filling the void by providing the services the other does not offer (Berry, 1990).

Small firms find greater success representing athletes in one sport and focusing on one or two services for the athletes or coaches. The work outsourced to other professionals by smaller firms is generally tax planning and preparation, financial investing, public relations, and, more recently, physical and psychological career preparation. Large firms employ professionals from many disciplines to provide services ranging from negotiating contracts to marketing the athlete's image to financial planning and developing outside business interests (Ruxin, 2004). Most agents fall somewhere in between, although the large multifaceted firm with offices worldwide is becoming an increasingly dominant force in the athlete representation market (Ruxin, 2004).

The different types of firms are market driven. Some athletes prefer association with a large firm, whereas others prefer the individual attention of a small firm. Those who choose the large firms often do so for the following reasons: (1) a large firm provides one-stop shopping by employing many skilled professionals to take care of all services; (2) a large firm may have a more established history, reputation, and industry contacts; (3) many athletes prefer representation by firms representing other star players (it's similar to being on the same team); and (4) some athletes believe that being with an agent who represents many players helps their own bargaining position. For instance, some athletes choose an agency such as Octagon on the assumption that the sheer number of athletes it represents (over 900) must translate into contacts with a large number of general managers or events and a larger number of marketing opportunities. Still others may choose to go with an agent due to the perceived or real influence that person has on the industry. For example, over the past 25 to 30 years **Scott Boras** has built an agency in baseball that some have argued influences the entire baseball industry. He has revolutionized the approach to player–team negotiations by relying on a deep understanding of the game and the business of baseball that enables him to wield baseball statistics, tough negotiating tactics, knowledge of the rules, and a free-market philosophy to change the market for players (Anderson, 2007; Pierce, 2007). In fact, it has been argued that Boras' player signings and deals with the owner of the team (to the chagrin of the club's general manager) influenced the ability of the Detroit Tigers to make it into the 2006 World Series (Kepner, 2006). Athletes have been known to choose Boras on the basis of this reputation (Pierce, 2007), as they are very aware that they have limited opportunities to get their value in the market. Other athletes might prefer to be one of the few individuals represented by a person with whom they build a bond or whom they trust rather than becoming one of a number of clients at a large firm (Steadman, 2004).

Athletes who choose small firms often do so because of the attention they receive from such a firm. At large firms, the attention of the more established agents will often go to their superstar clients. Those professional athletes on the bottom of the priority list may be assigned an assistant to deal with or may have trouble getting telephone calls returned. Even established athletes may have difficulty with the large firms. For example, golfers Greg Norman and Nick Price moved away from the large IMG and formed their own management companies to focus solely on their own needs because they found that calls to IMG often took a couple of days to be answered—not because IMG was irresponsible, but because it had so many clients to service. Both golfers also thought it more cost-effective to hire their own staff than to pay IMG's 20% to 25% commissions on business deals (Feinstein, 1995). Interestingly, Greg Norman returned to IMG as a client and has since switched to CAA Sports.

Fees Charged by Sports Agents

Fees charged by agents vary because fees are market driven and depend on whether the players association limits the fees. Fees are usually based on one of four methods: the flat fee, the percentage of compensation, an hourly rate, or a combination of an hourly rate with a percentage of compensation cap (McAleenan, 2002). The first method, the flat fee arrangement, requires an athlete to pay the agent an agreed upon

amount of money before the agent acts for the athlete (McAleenan, 2002).

The second method, the percentage of compensation, is by far the most popular arrangement. Although it is criticized as being inflated, agent Leigh Steinberg defends it. Steinberg "dismisses those who bill by the hour as 'egg-timer agents' and argues that such a fee structure militates against an important aspect of the agenting: developing a personal relationship with clients" (Neff, 1987, p. 83). The fee often covers not just the negotiation, but all of the work related to the provisions of the contract over its term.

There is a drawback to the percentage formula, though. There may be no guarantee that the agent receives his or her expected percentage, in that the agent is paid as the athlete earns the money. For instance, the NFLPA limits the agent's fee to 3% of the contract, and in the NFL there is no such thing as a guaranteed contract. An agent may negotiate a contract and then the athlete may be cut during training camp, with the team owing nothing more than a signing or reporting bonus (if that was in the contract). Thus, despite the time invested, the agent may never see the full 3% of the contract he or she negotiated. Another example is in baseball, where the agent regulations limit an agent from earning any income from an athlete in the minor leagues. An agent may charge a fee for negotiating a signing bonus when a player is drafted, but the regulations prohibit an agent from receiving a percentage fee until the athlete has exceeded the league minimum salary (usually in the player's second season in the majors). While representing players in the minor leagues, an agent incurs a number of expenses, among them equipment, travel, and telephone expenses, and costs associated with negotiating trading card and in-kind product deals. In fact, because of the way the sporting goods industry has evolved, the agent actually supplies the products (e.g., gloves, cleats, bats, and apparel) a minor leaguer needs to succeed out of his or her own budget. Thus, until an agent makes it by landing a top-round client, the agent is often left paying dues and investing a great deal of time, energy, and money into clients who may not provide a financial return. To make matters worse, some established agents make it their practice to market themselves to players only once those players are legitimate prospects or once the players are called up to the major leagues. As a result, players may leave their agent from the minors for a more established one once they reach the majors, never having paid a cent to the agent who invested in him in the minors. There are also numerous examples of agents in the NFL losing clients between the time of the draft and the actual signing of the contract. The recruiting by competitors does not stop simply because someone is drafted. In such a case, though, if there was a signed representation contract, the agent has the ability to pursue an arbitration case against the athlete for services rendered and perhaps a lawsuit against the other agent for tortious interference with a contractual or advantageous business relationship.

The third method, the hourly rate, is often not used for the reasons stated previously by Leigh Steinberg. For a high-round draft pick or a superstar free agent, however, McAleenan (2002) suggests that an hourly rate will provide the lowest fee. For example, assume the agent charges $450 per hour and works 40 hours negotiating a 3-year $1 million compensation package. Working on a 4% fee structure, the agent would receive $40,000, but working the hourly rate the agent would receive only $18,000 (McAleenan, 2002). What this example fails to recognize, though, are the numerous hours spent on the telephone with the athlete in career counseling or working out details of the contract with the team or athlete, which does not usually occur with, for example, a corporate client. The relationship between athlete and agent is such that for most athletes it would probably sour the relationship to turn on the clock every time an athlete called to ask his or her agent a question or tell the agent about the previous night's game. The relationship between the athlete and agent is as much a personal one as a business one.

The fourth method, the hourly rate with a compensation cap, addresses the athlete's concern that the agent may pad the billable hours and inflate the fee. This option provides an hourly rate, the total of which will not exceed a certain percentage of the athlete's compensation, called the percentage cap (McAleenan, 2002).

A key component of the MLBPA, the NFLPA, the National Hockey League Players Association (NHLPA), and the National Basketball Players Association (NBPA) regulations governing agents is the limitation on agent fees. Players associations have set ceilings for agents' fees at between 3% and 6%. The fierce competition for clients has driven the average fees down closer to 2% to 3%, although well-established agents still charge the maximum percentages (Burwell, 1996). The NFLPA and NBPA have set maximum fees. The NBPA's regulation sets the maximum fee an agent can charge for negotiating a minimum salary at $2,000, or 4% for those contracts above the minimum. The NFLPA has a similar measure that limits an agent's fee to between 1% and 3% of the player's compensation based on the player's contract and status/designation (i.e., free agent, franchise, transition player). The MLBPA and NHLPA do not limit the fee charged by an agent. However, the MLBPA does not allow an agent to charge a fee unless the agent negotiates a contract above the minimum salary, which was $500,000 in 2014. Then, the MLBPA prefers that an agent only charge a fee from the amount that exceeds the minimum. This would mean that if a baseball player's salary was $550,000 in 2014, the union would prefer the agent charge his or her percent on $50,000 (the amount of value that the agent actually added to the minimum contract). Therefore, if the agent's fee was 5%, it would mean the agent would earn $2,500. Because that amount is so low, agents tend to favor taking 5% of the total contract. Another stipulation is that the agent's fee cannot bring the athlete's compensation below the minimum. Also, an agent can only be paid as the athlete is paid, and can only be paid off the bonus if the athlete actually earns the bonus. Other aspects of player association regulations are discussed later in the chapter.

The fee limitations, though, exist only for the fees the agents can charge for negotiating the athlete's contract. In an attempt to undercut competition, occasionally some agents will charge the same fee percentage for negotiating the athlete's marketing deals as for negotiating the player's contract. That is definitely not the norm, as marketing fees charged by agents generally range between 15% and 33%. Although this is much higher than the team contract negotiation compensation, a great deal of work goes into creating an image for an athlete in the media and then selling that image to marketers at companies to create a positive fit for the athlete and the product. Imagine being the agent responsible for marketing athletes in the midst of scandals, such as Tiger Woods, Lance Armstrong, or Alex Rodriguez. These high-profile scandals force agents to put a great deal of time and energy into crisis management at the time of the incident and then into resurrecting images and convincing corporations to invest in endorsement opportunities with athletes whose images come with some baggage. Beyond the marketing fees, agents may also charge for other services rendered, such as tax planning, financial planning, and investment advising.

For athletes in other sports and for coaches, there are no regulations regarding fees, so the fees tend to be higher. The athlete or coach and the agent negotiate these fees individually, so the fee will depend on market factors and bargaining power. In tennis, for example, the standard fee players pay agents when they first become professionals is 10% of their prize money and 20% to 25% of all other revenue, whereas superstars usually will have their prize money fee waived and off-court fees cut to 10% or less (Feinstein, 1992). For example, when Ivan Lendl was a ProServ client, his contract provided for a flat fee of $25,000 and 7.5% of all earnings (Greenberg, 1993).

Career Opportunities

A sports agency is a business and, as with any other business, there are a range of opportunities available to potential employees. As many sports agencies have evolved, they have hired employees similar to those in mainstream consulting businesses. These employees include individuals with expertise in marketing, management, finance, accounting, operations, and the like. They may be working to keep the agency business afloat or they may be working as consultants to the agency's clients. A quick look at job listings for one of the larger agencies on its website includes openings for accountants, a finance executive, account executives (sales/marketing), production assistants (broadcasting), communications specialists, event specialists, and more.

Sports Event Manager

Some sport management firms also control the rights to sporting events and hire **sports event managers** to run these events. Event managers generally have no involvement with the representation of professional athletes. Event managers must be very detail oriented, organized, and able to work in an environment that can be stressful at times.

Sports Marketing Representative

The **sports marketing representative** coordinates all of the marketing and sponsorship activities for sport properties. Sport properties include sporting events run by the agency firm and the athletes the agency represents. A sports marketing representative's responsibilities may include conducting market research, selling sponsorships for an event, promoting an event and the athletes participating in it, or making calls to find endorsement opportunities for athletes who are clients of the firm. As sports agencies face greater competition in the market, more firms are focusing their energies on marketing activities and even consulting in marketing because marketing activities generate significant new revenue streams and there are no restrictions on fees charged for them.

Sports Account Executive

An account executive for a sports agency will be involved with the agency's corporate clients servicing their needs and leading sales and marketing efforts. The position may involve revenue generation, consulting activities, and customer management.

Sports Agent

Sports agents often refer to themselves as athlete representatives or sports lawyers. To some, the term *sports agent* has a negative connotation. Not all sports agents are lawyers. While they need not be lawyers, most are required by the players associations to hold a bachelor's degree.

The functions of sports agents vary more widely than do the types of firms. Keep in mind that some agents perform just one function and others may have a number of employees performing these functions for clients. The ability to offer a broad range of services depends on an agent's education, skills, and training, and the amount of time he or she can devote to these tasks. The amount of time spent per athlete is also dependent on the number of athletes the agent represents and their needs at the time. The number of agents or employees in the firm and

the variety of skills each has to offer will influence the ability to offer many services. The eight essential functions performed by sports agents are as follows:

- Negotiating and administering the athlete's or coach's contract
- Marketing
- Negotiating the athlete's or coach's marketing and endorsement contracts
- Financial planning
- Career and postcareer planning
- Dispute resolution
- Legal counseling
- Personal care

These eight functions are discussed individually in the following sections.

Negotiating and Administering the Contract

The Athlete's Contract

Contract negotiation varies depending on whether the agent is negotiating a contract for an individual athlete to participate in an exhibition or event or negotiating a team-sport contract. When negotiating a contract for an individual athlete, the agent must be familiar with the sport and the rules, regulations, and common practices of its governing body. When negotiating a contract for a team-sport athlete, the agent must understand the value of the player's service, be knowledgeable about the sport, and know the collective bargaining agreement, the standard or uniform player contract, and other league documents.

Some examples of negotiable terms for team-sport athletes include the following:

- Bonuses (signing, reporting to training camp, attendance, incentives)
- Deferred income (income paid after the player has retired from the sport)
- Guaranteed income (income guaranteed to be paid to the player even if he or she has retired)

- A college scholarship plan (available for MLB players leaving college early)
- Roster spots (generally not available, but positions on the 40-man roster in baseball are negotiable)

Although it appears that with standard player contracts and many contractual limitations, such as restrictions on rookie contracts, anyone could negotiate an athlete's contract, such a thought loses sight of all that is involved in contract negotiations. For instance, a player's value should drive the negotiating process, and a great deal of preparation goes into knowing and maximizing the player's value. Understanding how that value and the team's needs create leverage on one side or another is also a key to preparation. It will be important to assess the role that salary caps will play in the contract negotiation. Negotiations differ based on where an athlete falls in the span of his or her career, because there are differences in rookie versus veteran contract negotiations. Such a discussion exceeds the scope of this chapter, but please do give the differences in the types and context of negotiations some thought.

After negotiating the contract, the agent's work continues. Agents must administer the contract. This involves ensuring that the parties comply with their contract promises. If promises are not kept, the agent may become involved in conversations, negotiations, and ultimately dispute resolution between the player and the club. The agent may have to resolve unanticipated situations through informal channels, such as partial or full contract renegotiation, or through formal ones, such as alternative dispute resolution systems or the courts. As the representative of the player and the negotiator of the contract, when problems arise, it is the agent's responsibility to represent the athlete's interests.

The Coach's Contract

Due to the lack of job security for coaches in the Division I college and professional ranks, it has become increasingly important for coaches to have well-drafted contracts and a representative available to administer the deal (Greenberg, 1993). When negotiating a contract for a college coach, an agent must be familiar with the sport, the NCAA and conference rules, any applicable state open records laws, and common concerns of collegiate athletic directors and university presidents (Greenberg, 1993). It has also become standard that coaches' contracts contain a clause restricting coaches from seeking endorsements outside of university apparel contracts without consent from the university.

When negotiating a contract for a professional coach, an agent must understand the league's constitution and by-laws, as well as the coaching and management environment of a particular team or league. There is no uniform coaching contract, so there may be more flexibility in negotiable terms.

Examples of negotiable terms in coaches' contracts include the following (Greenberg, 1993):

- Duties and responsibilities
- Term of employment and tenure
- Compensation clauses (guaranteed, outside/supplemental, endorsement, and deferred income; bonuses; moving expenses; retirement; and fringe benefits)
- Termination clause
- Buyout/release of contractual obligations by either side
- Support of the team by athletic program or ownership
- Support staff (assistant coaches, other personnel)
- Confidentiality (to the extent allowable under law, the promise to keep terms confidential)
- Arbitration of disputes

In the past decade, representing coaches has become far more lucrative for agents, particularly for those representing Division I college football and basketball coaches and NBA coaches. In the NBA coaches' salaries and terms to be higher and longer than those of the athletes on their teams (Boeck, 1997). Agents have also played an important role in negotiating for coaches to serve in dual roles as general managers or team presidents. Such clauses give the coach more power in player personnel decisions and presumably more control over the athletes and the direction in which the team is headed in achieving its goals. This trend is a direct reaction to athletes' apparent loss of respect for their coaches and the athletes' temptation to remove the coach due to athletes' leverage and financial clout with the team (Boeck, 1997). It is also a reaction to the coaches having to take the brunt of the blame for a losing season. The long-term multimillion-dollar deals for coaches may well change the dynamics in the locker rooms and on the basketball courts (Boeck, 1997).

Coaches' agents, such as Lonnie Cooper, president and CEO of Career Sports and Entertainment, who represents eight head NBA coaches, numerous assistant NBA coaches, and 14 Division I college coaches, also are the beneficiaries of these deals. Another example is Bob LaMonte, who operates the boutique firm Professional Sports Representation, Inc. (PSR) with his wife and has cornered the market on head football coaches, including among his clients Mike Holmgren, Brad Childress, John Fox, Mike Nolan, Charlie Weiss, and Andy Reid's numerous NFL assistant coaches, coordinators, and front office staff. During his career, he has negotiated well over $250 million in coaching contracts (Farmer, 1999). LaMonte notes that in the mid-1980s salaries for NFL head coaches ranged from $100,000 to $150,000 (CBS News,

2004), whereas by the end of 2009 the average salary was $3,226,565 (Top NFL News, 2010). The higher salaries reflect the greater importance placed on the role of head coach as leader. The game is far more complicated and strategic than in years past owing to the greater reliance on statistics, video, scouting, and the like (CBS News, 2004). Further, the head coach must manage a fluid team whose roster changes frequently due to salary caps, free agency, and the occasional disciplinary problem.

Marketing the Athlete

The sports agent should develop a plan in which each endorsement creates an image consistent with the athlete or coach's ambitions and long-range goals (Lester, 2002). At the same time, the agent must keep in mind that the client's career and public persona may be short-lived, and thus "every opportunity should be assessed according to its potential to maximize the [client's] earnings and exposure during and after his or her active playing [or coaching] career" (Lester, 2002, p. 27-2). The sports agent must also be familiar with restrictions that may limit an athlete or coach's marketing opportunities. Restrictions include limitations on compensation set by the NCAA, national governing bodies, professional sports regulations, group licensing programs, and rules prohibiting the endorsement of alcohol or tobacco products (Lester, 2002).

Group licensing programs are very popular among professional sports unions, where often a major share of the players association's funding comes from trading card deals or marketing arms, such as the NFLPA's Player's, Inc. Under these group licensing programs, the players pool their bargaining power and licensing resources in exchange for a prorated (proportionate) share of any surplus income. It allows licensees one-stop shopping for multiplayer promotions. The definition of a group varies by league.[1] Most athletes agree to participate in these programs, the recent exceptions being Michael Jordan (NBA), Barry Bonds and Alex Rodriguez (MLB), and LaVar Arrington (NFL). Keeping in mind that agents do not receive compensation from group licensing programs, the movement away from group licensing by superstars may provide additional revenues for agents. It is also likely to damage the unions' revenue generation.

Agents usually seek product endorsements (goods necessary for the athlete to play the sport) before nonproduct endorsements because they are easier to obtain (Lester, 2002). Before targeting potential endorsements, the agent should assess the athlete's marketability. The assessment should include the athlete's desire for endorsements, willingness to make appearances, likes/dislikes of products, and his/her strengths and weaknesses (Lester, 2002). In addition, an agent must analyze his or her client. To determine an athlete's marketability, an agent must be sure that the athlete has a positive image and a clean reputation and on and off the field achievements (Lester, 2002). An agent must also consider the level of appeal of the athlete—will they be successful in a local, regional, national, or international level and with a brand that has the same level of reach (Lester, 2002).

The agent should also conduct a market assessment. Some agents have well-developed networks of contacts with sports product and non-product endorsement companies. For those who do not, the agent should choose a product the athlete would align well with, and determine that product's manufacturers and whether or not they invest in athlete endorsements. (Lester, 2002). To determine the products an athlete

will align with, the agent should consider the athlete's reputation, personality, and image and make a match with a product line that fits with the athlete's characteristics.

Marketing an athlete or coach may include creating or polishing a public image for that person. To assist with image building, some agents are beginning to hire "sports-media coaches" to train athletes or coaches for meeting the press and public. Sports-media coaches offer training sessions that mix lectures, mock interviews, question-and-answer sessions, and videotapes of other athletes or coaches to critique (Dunkel, 1997). For instance, Jerry Stackhouse's media coach, Andrea Kirby, began his session with an exercise in which he wrote down a list of his personal positive qualities (Thurow, 1996). Stackhouse's list included "friendly, caring, talkative, athletic, well-dressed . . . good son, good family person, a leader, warm, respectful, generous" (Thurow, 1996, p. A4). Kirby copied the list and told Stackhouse to carry it with him and review it every time he faced fans, the media, or commercial cameras so that he would consistently portray the image he had of himself. Beyond the media coaching, Stackhouse's training also included taking a couple of college drama courses, practicing speaking with a smoother cadence, and shaving his mustache (Thurow, 1996). This image building supports the standard sport marketing practice for athletes, brand building. As branding for athletes becomes more sophisticated, sport marketers are taking new approaches to it. For instance, Wendy Newman is a personal branding coach and has created Person-Centered Branding, which she claims endures because it is not contrived or based on temporary factors, but rather authenticates who the athlete is as a person. Newman's system has been embraced by the LPGA, who hired her to work with elite golfers to develop personal narratives and individual brands (Dell, 2007). **Table 11-1** sets forth the differences in her system versus traditional branding.

---

[1] The numbers of players necessary in group licensing programs are as follows: at least 6 for the NFLPA, at least 3 for MLBPA, at least 6 for NBPA, and 5 to 10 for the NHLPA (Lester, 2002).

Table 11-1 Traditional Versus Person-Centered Branding

Traditional Branding	Person-Centered Branding
Outside-in	Inside-out
Brand with shelf life; burns out	Brand built for endurance
Strategy dictates image	Identity dictates strategy
Short-term revenues; fad	Long-term revenues; consumer/brand loyalty
Starts with athlete's performance	Starts with athlete's life
Only as good as the last win	Sustains image regardless of performance
Starts with desired image of who/what athlete is being told to be	Starts with the identity of who athlete is
Revenues first; then happiness and fulfillment	Happiness and fulfillment first; then revenues
Brands athlete	Brands person
Athlete trying to be something	Being who athlete is
Contrived	Authentic
Endurance = sport, tenure, performance	Endurance = sustainable brand personality
Temporary	Permanent

Courtesy of Wendy Newman, MA, Founder Developer, Person-Centered Branding®

© Yuri Arcurs/ShutterStock, Inc.

Another solution to the challenge is being championed by the firm Sports Identity and is called BrandMatch. The goal with BrandMatch is to create a profile of the athlete to find out who he or she is, then to use that unique image to strategically market the athlete based on where he or she is professionally and personally. Once that task is accomplished, the sports marketers at Sports Identity match the athlete with brands that will create opportunities and experiences for both the athlete and the company that are meaningful promotional experiences. This practice differs from that of some sport marketers who will just "dial for dollars," calling any and every company just to deliver an endorsement

opportunity for the athlete, with no thought being paid to the long-term value or relationship between the athlete and the company. Sports Identity has also created a BrandMatch process for businesses, but that goes beyond the scope of this chapter (Sports Identity, 2007).

Finally, the agent should determine the athlete's market value. Many factors influence an athlete's market value, including the athlete's skill/success in sport, individual characteristics (image, charisma, physical appearance, and personality), how badly the organization wants the athlete, and any negative factors (crimes, drug use, public scandal) (Lester, 2002).

Negotiating the Athlete's or Coach's Marketing and Endorsement Contracts

Due to salary caps and rookie wage scales, an agent's ability to supplement a team salary with lucrative endorsement contracts has gained greater importance in athlete representation (Thurow, 1996). Economically, agents fare far better in the amounts of compensation they can command from marketing work. As far as the specifics of marketing deals go, the agent must first know any limitations the sport places on an athlete's ability to endorse products. For instance, all major professional sport leagues prohibit the use of team names and logos in endorsements, and most professional sport leagues ban the endorsement of alcoholic beverages and tobacco products (Lester, 2002). Agents representing athletes in individual sports, such as golf, tennis, racquetball, figure skating, and auto racing, should examine the rules and regulations of the sport. Restrictions vary from the simple requirement of the PGA Tour that endorsements be "in good taste" to the specific limitations in tennis and racquetball that limit the number and size of patches displayed on players' clothing and equipment bags (Lester, 2002).

Negotiation of endorsement deals has been a lucrative supplement to Division I coaches' income. University athletic departments, however, have begun to examine the coaches' outside endorsement deals and to negotiate contracts with athletic shoe, apparel, and equipment companies that benefit the entire athletic department. NCAA rules also require that the university's chancellor or president approve coaches' endorsement deals. To get a sense of how much money is at issue, the top 10 Division I NCAA football coach's outside pay falls in the range of $31,000 to $300,000 (Berkowitz et al., 2013b). For the top 10 men's Division I NCAA basketball coaches, the range for outside pay is $38,000 to $895,000 (Berkowitz et al., 2013a). Outside pay is defined as self-reported athletics-related income outside of what the institution pays the coach (Berkowitz et al., 2013b).

When negotiating an endorsement contract, an agent should be certain to maintain the client's exclusive rights and control over his or her image and other endorsements. The agent must also be familiar with the terms typically negotiable in athlete endorsement contracts. After reviewing numerous endorsement contracts, the following list emerges:

- Grant of rights regarding the distribution, marketing, advertising, promotion and sale of products.

- Grant of rights regarding the design, development, creation, manufacture, production, distribution, marketing, advertising, promotion, and sale of licensed products in all channels of trade.
- Exclusivity.
- Compensation, including bonuses for sales or bonuses for awards achieved in sport. May also include compensation for:
  - Appearances.
  - Commercials (print, television, other media).
- In-Kind products. May include in-kind products for family. May include clause barring sale, loan, or trade of in-kind products.
- Athlete's agreement to maintain the value of the endorsement. This clause may include:
  - The need for the athlete's visible use and endorsement of the product(s) in the contract.
  - A morals clause where the athlete acknowledges the role that his/her actions or behavior play in the value of the relationship.
  - The athlete's agreement to stay in good physical condition.
  - The athlete's agreement not to break rules or regulations of the sport.
  - The athlete's agreement not to promote alcohol or tobacco.
- Terminations, including reasons for termination such as not complying with exclusivity, no longer being an athlete of a certain status (i.e., major leaguer vs. minor leaguer), morals clause violation, or damaging statements against the product. The termination clause may also include the terms of termination.
- Liquidated damages.
- Rights of first refusal and renegotiation terms.
- Confidentiality.
- Indemnities.
- Governing laws.
- Dispute resolution. This is often an agreement to pursue mediation and arbitration, as opposed to a court of law.

Financial Planning

Financial planning covers a wide range of activities, such as banking and cash flow management, tax planning, investment advising, estate planning, and risk management (Grossman, 2002). Many lawsuits concerning sports agents' incompetence, fraud, and breaches of fiduciary duties involve financial planning and investing. These cases have exclusively involved athletes, so financial planning for athletes will be the focus in this section. Many sports agents have made mistakes because of the complex nature of the financial affairs of athletes. Sports agents often attempt to take on this function without proper skills and training; this can lead to allegations of incompetence and negligence. Also enticing to a less scrupulous agent is access to the athlete's money. There are many allegations of agents "double dipping" into athletes' funds, investing money into businesses from which the agent derives benefit, and outright embezzlement of an athlete's money. This behavior is discussed in greater detail later in the chapter.

An athlete earning a multimillion-dollar salary should adopt a budget (Willette & Waggoner, 1996). Without a budget, athletes who earn sudden wealth face risks (Waggoner, 1996), one of which is rushing into an investment. Athletes often receive many unsolicited prospectuses and requests for investments, and many have lost money in failed business ventures. Thus, planners often advise athletes to see a written business plan and have the plan analyzed by a professional before investing—and even if an investment seems to be worthy, planners advise an athlete to commit no more than 5% to 20% of the his or her portfolio to it (Willette & Waggoner, 1996). The second risk is making a radical lifestyle change. NBA agent Curtis Polk shares this example: For a client earning $10 million per year, he gives the athlete a budget of $1 million per year and invests $4 million, leaving the remaining $5 million for local, state, and federal taxes (Willette & Waggoner, 1996). The third risk is guilt, which often leads athletes to make bad loans to family and friends or to hire them as an entourage; to overcome guilt, advisors suggest that athletes raise money for charities (Waggoner, 1996).

Athletes should be aware of the recent surge of companies reaching out to athletes with predraft lines of credit. One such company, Datatex Sports Management, a division of Huntleigh Securities in St. Louis, uses its own in-house football analysts to calculate predraft lines of credit for potential draft picks. Those projected to go in the first round qualify for $100,000, and those in the seventh qualify for $1,500. Obviously, problems arise for athletes who do not end up drafted. Southern Mississippi offensive lineman Torrin Tucker and New York City high school guard Lenny Cooke were given predraft lines of credit and neither was drafted. For Cooke, taking the line of credit also eliminated his ability to play for the University of Louisville because it violated NCAA rules for two reasons: He arranged it through a sports agency firm, Immortal Sports, and the line of credit through CSI Capital Management was based on Cooke's future earnings potential. Some, such as Louisville's head basketball coach Rick Pitino, fault the agents and banks for acting irresponsibly, but others, such as CSI Capital Management's Chairman Leland Faust and a runner for agents, Ernest Downing, Jr., argue that lines of credit are now so common that athletes request them before hiring the agent (Farry, 2003).

Finally, insurance plays a key role in an athlete's financial planning. Star athletes in the major professional team sports usually invest in disability insurance plans to protect themselves during and after their playing career. In contract negotiations with a professional team, the agent may negotiate for the team to cover the cost of this policy. Athletes in individual sports also insure against these types of injuries. Many insurance companies, though, will only insure an athlete after that athlete is likely to achieve a certain level of income.

© LiquidLibrary

Career and Postcareer Planning

An agent must help an athlete with the transition to a professional career and again with the transition into retirement from the sport. The average career length varies by sport, but generally it is under 5 years. Thus, the agent must maximize the athlete's earning potential during and after his or her playing career. An agent must also "insure" the athlete's future earnings by building and protecting the athlete's image against damage, such as overexposure. An agent must balance the need to capitalize on opportunities while doing what is best personally and professionally for the athlete. The handling of 1994 Olympic Silver medalist Nancy Kerrigan provides an example of these dangers. Nancy Kerrigan had a reputation for being nervous and painfully inarticulate (Longman, 1994). On January 6, 1994 she was attacked and clubbed on the knee by a competitor's bodyguard in a conspiracy. When attacked, her screams were characterized as whiney. She was criticized, even though she was the victim. In the next seven weeks, Kerrigan was named to the U.S. national team; she recovered, and won an Olympic silver medal and was overheard criticizing the gold medalist. Already an athlete with an inaccurate media portrayal as an ice princess, her comments exposed her flaws. Kerrigan should

have been given a rest. Instead, her agent swept her away from the Olympic Games prior to the closing ceremonies to participate in a parade at Disney World for her $2 million sponsor. During the parade, Kerrigan complained that it was dumb and corny and that she didn't want to be there (Lowitt, 1999). She moved on to hosting Saturday Night Live and more. Saying yes to every opportunity, especially those not suited to her personality, created pressure for Kerrigan and subjected her to criticism for verbal missteps made while exhausted and under stress. According to Hersch, Kerrigan was unprepared and uncomfortable with celebrity, but did nothing to respond to her missteps, which led to an image meltdown (1994). Hersh noted, ". . .her agent and companion Jerry Solomon. . . . made her fabulously wealthy, but at what cost?" (1994). Although it is important to capitalize on opportunities in the short window post-Olympics, an agent must balance the athlete's long term interests against the prospect of short term earnings.

Career planning may also involve the agent investing time, energy, and money into a player's career while the player is training in the minor leagues or training toward events, exhibitions, or the Olympics. While in the minor leagues or while trying to make it into the professional ranks, more and more athletes have come to expect that agents will cover costs of products, some training and coaching costs, and even travel. This has evolved due to a number of factors, among them athletes who have come to expect a certain level of treatment and a competitive industry in which those trying to recruit clients will throw many inducements their way. Further, the product companies have taken note of this, and until a player makes it into the major leagues, in lieu of giving products in-kind, the manufacturers and suppliers have created agent accounts to purchase products for athletes. Often this investment is required when the agent is also trying to break into the business, and it creates a financial barrier to entry. The agent may reap little financial benefit from this invest-ment if the athlete does not make it or if he or she is wooed away by a bigger-name agent who has made no investment in the athlete's career.

Another aspect of career planning the agent may take on is the establishment of sports camps or charitable organizations under the athlete's name. Running sports camps and charitable organizations does many positive things for the athlete. Camps provide additional income, but beyond that camps and chari-ties create goodwill for the athlete's name and image; give the athlete contact with his or her community; give something back to children, communities, or a worthy cause; provide a use-ful outlet for the athlete's energy and time in the off-season; and may provide a hefty tax break. The camps and charitable organizations are also activities the athlete can stay involved with after his or her playing career is finished.

During the career transition out of sport, the agent must address the potential for a financial crisis (Grossman, 2002). Proper financial plan-ning that includes income investment, insurance coverage, and contracting for deferred income can avert a disaster. Beyond the financial aspect, the athlete needs a sense of purpose. Participa-tion in sport has defined many athletes' lives and self-images, and agents can be helpful in prepar-ing athletes for the psychological difficulties that may accompany retirement. By exploring career and business opportunities for the athlete inside and outside the sport industry, such as in broad-casting, the agent can help the athlete make a more successful transition.

Dispute Resolution

It is the sports agent's responsibility to resolve disputes the athlete or coach may have with his or her league, team, teammates, fans, referees or umpires, press, endorsement companies, and the like. Baseball agent Dennis Gilbert likens the role of the agent to a "shield," stating that it is the agent's task to protect the athlete from the headaches that go along with resolving disputes

(Schwarz, 1996). The shield allows the athlete to focus solely on playing or coaching to the best of his or her ability without distractions. To resolve disputes, the sports agent may find himself or herself in a labor or commercial arbitration forum, or occasionally in court.

Legal Counseling

If the sports agent is a lawyer, the agent may provide legal counseling. Legal counseling may include contract negotiation, legal representation in court, arbitration or sport-related administrative proceedings, estate planning, and the prepara-tion of tax and insurance forms. However, the nature of the legal work may dictate that a lawyer specializing in a particular area is better suited for providing the actual legal services. For instance, a given sports agent may be very confident in provid-ing negotiation and contract advice on any matter in his or her client's life, yet that same agent will not likely be the best lawyer to handle the client's divorce proceedings. For such a dispute, the best advice an agent can give is to encourage the client to find an attorney experienced in high-profile, high-income divorce proceedings.

Personal Care

The tasks required under this function are personal in nature. They include such respon-sibilities as assisting when an athlete is traded, arranging transportation, finding and furnish-ing a house or apartment for the season or training camps, purchasing cars, and helping the athlete's family and friends.

Key Skills Required of Sports Agents

Although there are no established educational standards to becoming an agent, some unions are now requiring a bachelor's degree. Some are lawyers, some are certified public accountants, and others are investment advisors or financial planners. With the various services demanded of agents by athletes and in light of competition in the field, a professional degree is practically a necessity.

Primarily, the sports agent must have a good working knowledge of the sport industry, particularly the specific sport in which he or she practices. This knowledge should include an understanding of the economic picture of the sport industry, insight into the inner workings of the industry, the sport the athlete plays, the documents used in the industry (e.g., contracts, policies, rules and regulations, constitutions and by-laws, and collective bargaining agreements), and a great network of contacts in the industry. Although the skills needed by sports agents vary depending on the services provided, all agents must possess good listening and counseling skills. The agent works for the athlete and must invest time in getting to know the athlete on a personal level. This builds trust and a stronger relationship between the two. Agents must make decisions according to the athlete's desires and goals. The agent should act only after consulting the athlete and must always act in the athlete's best interest.

Excellent oral and written communication skills are also essential, because the agent represents the athlete in many forums. Many of the agent's functions require polished negotiation skills. An agent must also be loyal to the athlete and be strong enough to shield the athlete from the media and even from his or her own front office staff. Professional athletes, like entertainers, find their lives scrutinized by the press, and the agent must help the athlete adjust to the pressure that accompanies fame and counsel the athlete to properly deal with the media. When the athlete has to negotiate a contract or go into arbitration against his or her team, the relationship is adversarial. This is not always the best situation for professional athletes, for whom psychology plays a key role in their on-field success. The agent must shelter the athlete from the derogatory statements made about him or her in those forums, because often those statements can damage the athlete's confidence.

Current Issues

Unethical Behavior

In the five decades that the sports agency field has been active, there has been a great deal of criticism and a public perception that the behavior of those in the profession is excessively unethical. There are, in fact, many ethical agents who run their businesses professionally; however, there have been many high-profile cases of unethical and illegal behavior reported, tainting the image of the profession. In addition, sports agency is a field in which outsiders perceive there is quick, easy money to be made and a field in which clients are scarce. These two factors combine to bring an element of corruption to the profession. According to Sobel (1990), there are five key problems in the profession: (1) income mismanagement, (2) incompetence, (3) conflicts of interest, (4) charging of excessive fees, and (5) overly aggressive client recruitment. Of the five, **income mismanagement** is probably the most devastating to the athlete. Because the agent is often dealing with the income of a multimillion-dollar athlete, the losses can be great, and it is unlikely the athlete will be able to reclaim the money from the agent or earn back the amount lost. Although many reported cases stem from incompetence, others begin with incompetence and further deteriorate to fraud or embezzlement (Sobel, 1990). A good example is the case of agent Tank Black, who was sentenced to 5 years in prison for swindling millions of dollars out of the NFL players he represented and also sentenced to more than 6 years in jail for laundering $1.1 million for a drug ring in Detroit. In abusing his clients' trust, Black stole in excess of $12 million from them by encouraging them to invest in bogus investments and pyramid schemes (Fish, 2002a). The Tank Black saga has made the NFLPA more vigilant in its efforts to regulate agents. As a result, in 2003 the NFLPA created the first registration system for financial advisors who work with NFL players.

Agents have also been accused of performing their responsibilities negligently because of sheer incompetence. As the industry has become more complex, some agents have run into problems because they are incapable of figuring out their clients' worth, working with the complex documents necessary to effectively negotiate, or carrying out the tasks they promise athletes they will do. It is likely this problem has been compounded by the competition in the industry. Agents may make promises they cannot keep for fear of losing a client or may exaggerate when trying to land a client. If they are not, for example, trained as lawyers or do not have experience in arbitration, they may be more likely to settle a case to avoid having to proceed to the actual arbitration. Due to fear of losing a client to a competitor, many are afraid to outsource a labor or salary arbitration case.

Conflicts of interest raise serious questions about the fiduciary duty of loyalty required of all agents under agency law. A conflict of interest occurs if there is a situation in which the agent's own interest may be furthered over that of the athlete's (principal's) interest. Keep in mind that an agent works for an athlete and possesses a fiduciary duty to put the athlete's interest first. It is clear, though, that in business settings there are bound to be conflicts of interest. If the agent fully discloses the conflict and allows the athlete to direct the agent, or in some cases suggests that the athlete hire a neutral party to see the athlete through the conflict, the agent will not have breached his or her fiduciary duties.

There are many examples of conflicts of interest in the sports agency business. Conflicts may arise for agency firms that also run events. Those firms have a fiduciary duty to fully reveal the extent of the conflict of interest and to allow the athlete to bring in a neutral negotiator to negotiate with that particular event. Some, such as Jerry Solomon, however, argue that these companies operate as diverse entities (athlete representation versus event management) and

that as a result the two groups have built invisible walls between them that prevent such a conflict from arising (Feinstein, 1992; Solomon, 1995). Another conflict may arise when an agent is representing two players on the same team or two players who may be vying for the same position on a team. Clearly, in these situations there may be a tendency for the agent to give greater attention to the athlete who will better serve the agent's own interest. Another example is dual representation. It occurs when an agent represents both a coach and a player or represents a player and is also the head of the union. The NBPA and NHLPA prohibit representation of both a coach and player, but it is allowed in the NFL and MLB. The days of representation by an agent who also leads the union in the major leagues are past, but the potential for it to exist again in the future with emerging sports is real.

The complaint of charging excessive fees occurs when agents charge fees that do not fairly represent their time, effort, and skills. To an extent, this complaint has been addressed by players association regulations mentioned earlier and also by competition in the market. Competition for clients has forced some agents in the market to reduce their fees to entice clients. However, although the fees have dropped for the negotiation of team-sport contracts, many agents continue to charge what may be considered excessive fees in the marketing area. Another complaint is charging the athlete for every service the agent performs, when the athlete may believe that all services are provided in the fee charged for the contract negotiation. Such confusion may arise because some agents do not use written representation agreements. This problem is also being overcome as the players associations are insisting that players use standard-form representation agreements that clearly establish fees and contractual promises; however, in individual sports or emerging leagues there are no such requirements.

Overly aggressive client recruitment is a problem that has plagued the amateurism requirement of collegiate athletics. First, it can wreak havoc with NCAA rules because an athlete loses his or her eligibility if he or she signs with a sports agent or accepts anything of value from a sports agent. In fact, in 2008, collegiate pitcher Andy Oliver was ruled ineligible for simply engaging advisors who contacted a MLB team on his behalf after being drafted in 2006. In the competition for clients, many agents have resorted to underhanded tactics such as paying athletes to encourage them to sign with agents early. The difficulty in becoming an agent or obtaining clients has led some to offer inducements. For example, World Sports Entertainment (WSE), an athlete representation firm operated by entertainment agent Norby Walters and partner Lloyd Bloom, spent approximately $800,000 to induce athletes to sign representation agreements with them before their NCAA eligibility expired. Walters argued that what he did broke no laws (just NCAA rules) and was a common practice in the music industry, where entertainers often received financial advances from their agents (Mortensen, 1991). The athletes, too, are to blame, because some encourage this type of activity from the agent, believing that their skills and talent should enable them to make this money for signing. For instance, when football player Ron Harmon signed with WSE as a junior at the University of Iowa, the FBI investigation discovered he ran up expenses of over $54,000 in cash, plane, concert tickets, and other entertainment. Clearly, Harmon was taking advantage of the situation for his own entertainment and was not using the money, as other athletes did, for bills and family expenses (Mortensen, 1991). Notorious agent Tank Black was accused of paying athletes up to $15,000 while in college to sign with him when they became professionals (Fish, 2002b).

Second, it has created a very ugly side to the sports agency industry. Most agents can tell stories about the dirty recruiting that goes on in the industry as competitors vie for clients. The behavior mirrors the recruiting scandals prevalent in big-time college athletics. Many veteran agents claim the unethical recruiting has reached epidemic proportions that will have a lasting negative effect on the industry (Mullen, 2004). In addition to the promises of prohibited inducement, among the noted lasting negative impacts from unethical recruiting are the following: (1) representatives are spending more time on retaining clients, so it cuts back on their time to develop new business opportunities for current clients; (2) recruiters are targeting teenagers in the sports of basketball, baseball, and hockey, making promises that may not come to fruition; and (3) in an effort to compete with the large conglomerates, smaller agencies are promising late-round picks marketing guarantees in the six-figure range that will be difficult to achieve (Mullen, 2004).

It became so intense that the MLBPA and its Executive Board (made up of active players) examined how to curb the behavior. As a result, the MLBPA put new agent regulations into effect on October 1, 2010. The 48 pages of regulations are so sweeping in their changes that all certified agents had to reapply for certification and those who are operating as recruiters or handlers for the players must also apply for certification. That requirement signals that the union is going to more seriously monitor contact between players and competitor agents. In addition, agents must inform the MLBPA if they speak to a player they do not represent, or intend to do so, or travel to meet a player they do not represent (MLBPA, §5(A)(11), 2010). Often, agents attempt to recruit players away from their current agent as they are eligible for free agency or salary arbitration because that is when a player will receive a significant increase in compensation and, thus, the agent will receive a fee increase. The new regulations prevent a player in this stage in his career from changing agents "unless they first consult with the MLBPA." (MLBPA, §6(L), 2010) This consultation requirement is an attempt by the MLBPA to monitor the recruitment of their members and an attempt to limit overly aggressive recruitment by agents seeking clients.

The regulations also limit the players' freedom to switch agents at whim because any player facing salary arbitration or free agency must consult with the union before switching agents during those critical periods of the player's career (Clifton & Toppel, 2010). The final two areas of significant change in the regulations involve the areas of restrictive covenants and the use of arbitration to settle disputes among the MLBPA's player-agent group. Historically, the union's position has been focused on the player's choice of agent being a priority over supporting an agency's restrictive covenant against an agent who has left the firm and taken the player. These new regulations permit employers to utilize "reasonable" restrictive covenants in agent employment agreements. The determination of the reasonableness of each covenant will be made on a case-by-case analysis. Lastly, the union is requiring all disputes involving agents to be resolved in arbitration rather than litigation (Clifton & Toppel, 2010).

The NFLPA has been the most active in disciplining agents and through its Committee on Agent Regulations and Discipline has imposed discipline on 130 agents between 1993 and 2008 (Golka, 2008). One of the challenges faced by the players associations in going after agents is that it is difficult to find proof unless athletes are willing to testify against agents. In addition, pursuing these cases takes a great deal of energy and personnel away from the main mission of the union. Still, the NFLPA is continuing to take the lead in this area, as in 2004 it announced that all registered agents must also list their runners with the NFLPA so it may keep better tabs on the individuals who recruit clients for agents. This step is another first in the regulation of the agency industry, and it will be interesting to see if the other unions follow the NFLPA's lead.

Another step some regulatory groups are taking is the requirement of professional liability insurance, which is now required by the NFLPA and FIFA and is under consideration by CFLPA.

Regulation of Sports Agents

In the words of Lionel Sobel (2002), "sports agents today must maneuver through a maze of conduct governing regulations" set forth by college governing bodies and university athletic departments, players associations, state ethics boards, state legislatures, and the federal government.

Of these forms of regulation, the NCAA or other college and university regulations carry the least weight with agents. Because agents are not NCAA members, the NCAA cannot enforce its rules against them. Instead, NCAA agent regulations are intended for the athletes and member institutions to stop athletes from having contact with agents.

NCAA by-laws permit student athletes to retain the service of an attorney or an outside consultant provided that this personal representative does not consult with professional teams. In *Oliver v. NCAA* (2009), pitcher Andy Oliver was ruled ineligible by the NCAA for a violation of this by-law. The Ohio state district court upheld Oliver's argument that the NCAA's ruling was against public policy and affected an attorney–client relationship, with the court adding that the by-law was "capricious . . . [and] . . . arbitrary." Oliver settled with the NCAA prior to appeal, thus limiting the precedential value of this case. In a similar case that followed the Oliver decision, a baseball player from University of Kentucky was deemed ineligible after he had relied on an agent to unsuccessfully sign him to a contract with the Toronto Blue Jays.

Agents representing athletes in MLB, the NFL, the NBA, the NHL, and the CFL are regulated by players associations. The MLS has adopted the FIFA agent regulations, but neither MLS nor MLSPA regulate agents. Instead MLS and MLSPA defer to FIFA's certification program.

Application fees to become registered or certified by the players associations are as follows:

MLBPA $500 application fee
NBPA $1,500 annually, plus $100 application fee
NFLPA $1,200 annually if representing less than players; $1,700 for more than 10 players
NHLPA $1,500 annually

Agents must annually submit to the union uniform athlete–agent representation agreements that set forth the terms of the relationship and contain clauses mandating the arbitration of disputes between players and their agents. The uniform agreement is renewable annually by the player, but the player is free to abolish it at any time to go to another agent. This puts the players associations on notice about who is representing the athlete and also allows the agent access to union assistance with salary information, dispute resolution, and the like.

Currently, 43 states have some form of athlete–agent regulation. The National Conference of Commissioners, with prodding and backing from the NCAA and the Sports Lawyers Association, created a uniform agent registration law, called the Uniform Athlete Agent Act (UAAA), that can be adopted by all states. Forty states, plus the District of Columbia and the Virgin Islands, have adopted this legislation. In addition, three states have their own statutes on athlete–agent relationships that predate the UAAA.

After many attempts at federal legislation, the Sports Agent Responsibility and Trust Act (SPARTA) was enacted in 2004. The act seeks to "designate certain conduct by sports agents relating to the signing of contracts with student athletes as unfair and deceptive acts or practices to be regulated by the Federal Trade Commission (FTC)" (SPARTA, 2004). SPARTA prohibits agents from directly or indirectly recruiting or soliciting a student to enter into an agency contract by providing false or misleading information, making false promises, or providing anything of value to amateur athletes or their families. It also prohibits agents from entering into an oral or written agency contract with a student without providing a required disclosure document both to the student-athlete and to the athlete's academic institution. Finally, SPARTA prohibits the act of predating or postdating an agency contract (SPARTA, Sec. 3, 2004). Each violation of SPARTA is deemed an unfair or deceptive act or practice under the Federal Trade Commission Act, or the FTCA (SPARTA, Sec. 4, 2004). Further, SPARTA authorizes civil actions by the FTC, state attorneys general, and educational institutions against violators. It supplements, but does not preclude, other actions against agents taken under other federal or state laws (SPARTA, Sec. 5, 2004).

With the enactment of this law, the maze of legislation regulating sports agents grows deeper. The goal of the law is to protect student-athletes from deceptive practices and keep the athletes eligible to play NCAA sports. Senator John McCain noted that SPARTA serves as federal backstop for the ongoing effort by the NCAA, college coaches, university presidents, and athletic directors to support state level legislation (Associated Press, 2004). The UAAA legislation requires that sports agents be registered with the states in which they operate and provide uniform state laws addressing their conduct and practices.

One challenge for agents is that the law is one-sided; only the agents are regulated, and the athletes are perceived as playing no role in the practice of inducements being given to athletes to sign with agents. In fact, stories abound of athletes and families of athletes literally "selling" their services to the highest bidder among the myriad of agents competing to sign a high-round pick to an agency agreement. If little or no penalty is assessed against the athlete, it will be interesting to see if the federal law actually addresses the unethical recruitment of athletes. To date, legal action under UAAA and SPARTA has been scarce.

Finally, athletes and others abused by agents can seek recourse under tort, criminal, agency, and consumer protection laws. More agents are resorting to the courts, filing 12 lawsuits for unfair competition, tortious interference with contract, libel, and slander in the past couple of years (Mullen, 2004). The willingness to resort to the courts may be a result of the large amount of money involved and the fact that in a legal proceeding witnesses can be subpoenaed, and thus witness testimony may be more easily obtainable than in a complaint filed with a players association.

Case Study 11-1   King Sport Management

King Sport Management (KSM) is a sports agency firm based in Chicago that has been in business for 5 years. KSM is owned and operated by law school graduate Jake King. KSM has suddenly arrived on the sports business radar screen as the company having one of the largest stables of clients in baseball behind the Scott Boras Corporation, WMG, and ACES, which have been in business for many more years. As the owner of Baseball Talent, Inc., an agency in business for just over a decade, Nate Baxter was bewildered about how an agency with so little experience in the industry grew so quickly. Soon that would change. Nate's Baseball Talent represented 30 players, 25 of whom were in the minors and 5 who were on major league rosters. Two of the players on the 40-man roster were still in the minor leagues at the AAA level.

One day Nate received a call from Mark Hartman, one of his top prospects in AA, telling him that he had just met with an agent from KSM. The agent told Hartman that he could get him a Topps trading card deal worth $10,000 and that if his current agent couldn't deliver that kind of money, then he must not know what he was doing in the trading card business. Nate knows that Topps is the exclusive baseball card licensee of Minor League baseball ("MiLB") and that the MiLB license provides Topps the right to include every player who is playing in the minors. Minor league players are not compensated for inclusion in these products, so Nate told Mark that he doubted KSM could arrange such a deal. Nate told the client to ask KSM to show him a trading card contract with those figures on it. The client said, "I really don't care where the money comes from because at this point I could really use the $10,000. If you can't find a similar deal, I may have to leave. Besides, KSM has been to visit my dad, and the KSM representative and my dad wait for me after every game with a KSM contract to sign. I think they have given my father some money to cover some of his bills and I can't let my own father down." Two weeks later, Nate received a standard form letter terminating their business relationship postmarked from Chicago, even though the prospect was playing for a team on the West Coast.

The next day Nate called one of his clients, Terrence Sharpe, to talk about the client's outing the day before. Sharpe was an all-star high school athlete in Florida and a top pitching prospect for the Tampa Bay Devil Rays. Sharpe struggled the first few years in baseball, but had suddenly begun winning and had just been moved from A-ball to AA. When Nate

(continues)

Case Study 11-1 King Sport Management (Continued)

reached Sharpe, he was on the golf course with his roommate Mike Hanson and some agents. Sharpe told Nate about the brand-new golf clubs he had just purchased at the club's pro shop. Sharpe told Nate that he really didn't feel like talking about yesterday's outing and, because he had just purchased a laptop computer, Nate should e-mail him at IMSharpe@gmail.com so he could get back to his golf game. Nate hung up the phone and thought, "Where would Terrence get the money for golf clubs and a laptop?" Nate knew that Terrence barely had enough money to get by because he came from a poor background and had given his signing bonus to his grandmother, who had raised him. Nate had a terrible feeling that he was going to lose Terrence to KSM. Nate sent a few e-mails to Terrence, but received no response. A week later, Nate received the same form letter in the mail from Terrence that he had received from Mark. It, too, was postmarked from Chicago.

Two months later Nate was visiting Josh Bartley, a catcher and a 40-man roster player for the Atlanta Braves. Josh told Nate that he knew he was great defensively and if he could just hit more homeruns he was told he'd make the major league roster the next year. Josh felt that if he could use steroids and bulk up then he'd make that goal. Josh asked Nate to help him get steroids. Nate told Josh that there were many reasons he should not use steroids, top among them being his own health and the violation of baseball's rules. Nate assured Josh that the best way to better his hitting ability was to work with a hitting coach. Nate suggested that Josh work more closely with his club's hitting coach, and Nate told Josh that he'd happily invest in a hitting coach and nutritionist for Josh to work with in the off-season. Nate also suggested some books for Josh to read on hitting. Josh said that he was convinced steroids were the answer to his hitting problems. Nate ended the evening worried about Josh. Three days later Nate received a call from Josh's dad that began, "So I understand you won't help my son bulk up . . ."

Shocked, Nate took a moment to respond. "Excuse me, is this Ken Bartley, Josh's dad?"

"Yes, Nate, you know it's me. I thought you were on our side. Here to help Josh make it to the 'bigs,' and now you won't get him steroids or HGH (human growth hormone)."

Nate said, "Ken, you are aware of the health risks to your son and the fact that baseball conducts tests for steroid and HGH use . . ."

Ken said, "Sure, I know, I know. But Josh just needs it to get to the majors, then he'll stop. Short-term use should not be that big a deal. I don't understand your reasoning. I thought you were here to help us. Isn't that what you said when you recruited Josh as a client?"

Nate said, "I did say that. Yet, none of us know the real risks of steroid or HGH use. Besides, using steroids and HGH violates the rules of baseball. And steroids are illegal substances. As a lawyer, I'm not going to lose my license trying to acquire steroids for your son—end of story! I told Josh I'd happily invest in a hitting coach for him in the off-season. In my professional judgment, that is his best way to the majors. Besides, haven't you been following the recent suspension of Alex Rodriguez for HGH use? MLB is getting serious about cheating."

At that point, Ken ended the conversation by saying, "Nate, we like your service, but you're making a big mistake. If you want to compete with the big dogs, sometimes you have to bend the rules. A-Rod may be out a year, but think of all the money he's made in the process. Money for himself and his agent. Out of all those players who have been suspended, most have earned more money than they'd have made without using these substances. And besides, no penalties have come to their agents. So, I'd suggest you find an anti-aging clinic to help you get what these guys need to make it. You'll make more money and these guys will live their dreams."

Nate immediately called Josh. Josh told him that if Nate wouldn't find him performance enhancers, he'd find an agent who would. A month later, Nate received a letter from Josh postmarked from Chicago terminating their contractual relationship.

As the baseball season was nearing an end, Nate couldn't help but worry about his business. He had lost three of his top prospects to KSM, and two of his better clients were off to the Arizona Fall League, long known as a place where clients are ripe for the picking by unscrupulous agents. One of his clients, Chad Kramer, was like a son to Nate, and Nate had a heart-to-heart with him before he left about the types of inducements Chad should expect to receive while in Arizona. Chad left by saying, "Nate, you should know by now, you have nothing to worry about."

A few weeks later Nate flew to Arizona to see Chad. With a smile on his face, Chad said, "Have I got a story for you!" Chad went on to explain that he had relented about going to dinner with a KSM runner only after the runner had asked him to dinner numerous times. Chad figured that after that much badgering he deserved a free steak! At dinner the runner offered him money to leave Nate for KSM. Chad said, "I have all the money I need." Then the runner offered a car. Chad said, "I have a nice car and don't need another." Then the runner coyly offered a prostitute. Chad said, "I'm engaged and am not interested." The runner said, "Then why are we having dinner?" Chad said, "You tell me—you're the one who made the invitation." So the runner went on to tell Chad that at the beginning of the year KSM hired 10 runners under a 1-year contract and gave them a list of prospects to recruit. The two runners who recruited the most clients from that prospect list would then be hired into full-time positions. Nate thought he had heard it all.

As he arrived home from the trip, he opened up his *SportsBusiness Journal* to see a special edition on sports agents. There staring up at him was a picture of Jake King with the headline, "KSM Principal Lobbies for New Ethical Standards to Govern Agents." Nate angrily thought, "Sure, now that he's broken the rules and built his business by stealing our clients, he wants to clean up the industry."

Questions for Discussion

1. Should Nate contact the MLBPA to pursue a claim against KSM? What about the state of Illinois (which has an agent regulation statute)? What about the Illinois bar association?

2. Should Nate engage in legal action against KSM for unfair competition or tortious interference with contractual or advantageous business relations? Should Nate consider legal action against the players who have left him for KSM?

(continues)

Case Study 11-1   King Sport Management (Continued)

3. Should Nate contact the police, the Chicago U.S. attorney's office, or the state or federal legislators about the steroid allegation against KSM?

4. Do you think the actions taken by Jake King to build KSM are the norm in the industry? What would be your response if Jake King were to tell you that to compete in this industry you must give the athletes what they want or someone else will?

5. What do you think about the athletes and their decisions? What is their role and responsibility in the sports agency business?

6. If you were a partner to Nate, what would be your strategy going forward to retain current clients and to recruit new ones?

Summary

The field of sports agency can be exciting. Landing a first-round draft pick and negotiating a playing contract or creating an image and negotiating major marketing deals for a Wimbledon champion can bring an incredible thrill for an agent. Servicing clients' needs exposes agents to the world of these elite athletes; as a result, it is a highly competitive business. Those seeking an entry-level position face an uphill battle, because there are tremendous barriers to entry, among which is fierce competition for a scarce number of potential clients. Recruiting a client is just part of the struggle, because keeping the client in this competitive market is an equally competitive battle. Furthermore, it is estimated that more than 80% of athletes are represented by approximately 20% of agents. Many agents work part-time supplementing their income through other professions, such as law, marketing, or financial planning. Nevertheless, there are a handful of large, dominant multiservice firms engaged in athlete representation and

event management that may provide a good launching point to break into the field. On the representation side, few entry-level positions at these firms are in client recruitment. In reality, employment exists if the entry-level agent can deliver a client. With the trend toward mergers and acquisitions, many entry-level positions seem to be limited to those who have a few clients already in hand. This competitive environment may lead new agents to act in an overly aggressive manner while recruiting clients.

Resources

Professional Associations

American Bar Association Forum Committee on the Entertainment & Sport Industries

    321 N. Clark Street
    Chicago, IL 60654
    312-988-5000
    http://www.abanet.org/forums/entsports
    /home.html

Sports Lawyers Association

12100 Sunset Hills Road, Suite 130
Reston, VA 20190
703-437-4377
http://www.sportslaw.org

Agency Firms

BDA Sports

700 Ygnacio Valley Road, Suite 330
Walnut Creek, CA 94596
925-279-1040
http://www.bdasports.com

Beverly Hills Sports Council

131 S. Rodeo Drive, Suite 100
Beverly Hills, CA 90212
310-858-1872
http://bhscouncil.com

CAA Sports

2000 Avenue of the Stars
Los Angeles, CA 90067
424-288-2000
http://www.sports.caa.com

Career Sports and Entertainment

150 Interstate North Parkway, SE
Atlanta, GA 30339
770-955-1300
http://www.groupcse.com

Gaylord Sports Management

13845 N. Northsight Boulevard,
Suite 200
Scottsdale, AZ 85260
480-483-9500
http://www.gaylordsports.com

IMG

U.S. Headquarters
200 5th Avenue, 7th Floor
New York, NY 10010
212-489-8300; fax: 646-558-8399
International Headquarters
McCormack House
Hogarth Business Park

Burlington Lane
Chiswick London W4 2TH
(44) 208-233-5300
http://img.com/home.aspx

Newport Sports Management, Inc.

201 City Centre Drive, Suite 400
Mississauga, ON L5B 2T4, Canada
905-275-2800
http://www.thehockeyagency.com

Octagon Worldwide

7950 Jones Branch Drive, Suite 700N
McLean, VA 22107
703-905-3300
http://www.octagon.com

Priority Sports and Entertainment

325 N. LaSalle, Suite 650
Chicago, IL 60654
312-664-7700
http://www.prioritysports.biz

PSR, Inc.

1220 Plumas Street
Reno, NV 89509
775-828-1864
http://www.psr-inc.net

Roc Nation

1411 Broadway, 38th floor
New York, NY 10018
212-292-8500
http://rocnation.com/sports/

The Scott Boras Corporation

18 Corporate Plaza Dr.
Newport Beach, CA 92660
949-833-1818
http://www.borascorp.com

Wasserman Media Group (WMG)

10960 Wilshire Boulevard, Suite 2200
Los Angeles, CA 90024
310-407-0200
http://www.wmgllc.com

For a more definitive list of sports agencies, go to: http://www.sportsagentblog.com/agencies
/agencies-by-alphabetical-order/

Key Terms

Scott Boras, conflicts of interest, freestanding sport management firm, income mismanagement, law practice only, Mark H. McCormack, overly aggressive client recruitment, reserve clause, reserve list, reserve system, sports agent, sports event managers, sport management firm affiliated with a law firm, sports marketing representative, standard or uniform player contract

---

References

Anderson, J. (2007, May 22). The Boras factor. *LA Weekly*. Retrieved from http://www.laweekly.com/2007-05-24/news/the-boras-factor/

Associated Press. (2004, September 10). Legislation aims to protect student athletes. Retrieved from http://sports.espn.go.com/espn/news/story?id=1878699

Badenhausen, K. (2014, Feb. 27). The highest paid retired athletes. Retrieved from http://www.forbes.com/sites/kurtbadenhausen/2014/02/27/the-highest-paid-retired-athletes/

Berkowitz, S., Upton, J., Dougherty, S., & Durkin, E. (2013a). NCAAB College coach salaries. *USA Today*. Retrieved from http://www.usatoday.com/sports/college/salaries/ncaab/coach/

Berkowitz, S., Upton, J., Dougherty, S., & Durkin, E. (2013b). NCAAF College coach salaries. *USA Today*. Retrieved from http://www.usatoday.com/sports/college/salaries/

Berry, R. C. (1990). Representation of the professional athlete. In American Bar Association Forum on the Entertainment and Sports Industries (Ed.), *The law of sports: Doing business in the sports industries* (pp. 1–6). Chicago: ABA Publishing.

Berry, R. C., Gould, W. B., & Staudohar, P. D. (1986). *Labor relations in professional sports.* Dover, MA: Auburn House Publishing.

Boeck, G. (1997, September 25). Cooper cashes in for NBA coaches: Agent snags rewarding deals. *USA Today*, pp. C1–C2.

Brady, D. (2004, July 12). Arnold Palmer: With IMG from the start. *BusinessWeek Online*. Retrieved from http://www.businessweek.com/magazine/content/04_28/b3891131.htm

Brennan, C. (1996). *Inside edge: A revealing journey into the secret world of figure skating.* New York: Doubleday.

Burwell, B. (1996, June 28). David Falk: The most powerful man in the NBA? *USA Today*, pp. C1–C2.

Canadian Football League Players Association (CFLPA)(2014). Players agents. Retrieved from http://www.cflpa.com/players-agents.html

Carlisle, P. (2012, November 27). "Marketing an Olympic icon: Behind the business of a global sports superstar," Lecture at University of Massachusetts, Amherst.

CBS News. (2004, December 26). The secret of their NFL success. Retrieved from http://www.cbsnews.com/stories/2004/09/16/60minutes/main643894.shtml

Celebrity Net Worth (2014). Top 50 richest athletes list. Retrieved from http://www.celebritynetworth.com/list/top-50-richest-athletes/

Christy, J. H. (2002, July 8). The alchemy of relationships. *Forbes*. Retrieved from http://www.forbes.com/global/2002/0708/026_print.html

Clifton, G., & Toppel, J. (2010, September 24). MLBPA issues new sweeping regulations governing agents. Retrieved from http://www.hackneypublications.com/sla/archive/001133.php

Dell, K. (2007, Apr. 26). New driver at the LPGA. *Time*. Retrieved from http://www.time.com/time/magazine/article/0,9171,1615197-1,00.html

Dunkel, T. (1997, March). Out of the mouths of jocks. *Sky*, 97–103.

Farmer, S. (1999, September 29). Teacher has history of being good sports agent. *The Holland Sentinel*. Retrieved from http://www.thehollandsentinel.net/stories/092999/spo_teacher.html

Farry, T. (2003, August 28). Bank(rupting) on the future. *ESPN.com*. Retrieved from http://sports.espn.go.com/espn/print?id=1605207&type=story

Federation International de Football Association (FIFA). (2014). About FIFA: Player agents list. Retrieved from http://www.fifa.com/aboutfifa/organisation/footballgovernance/playeragents/list.html

Feinstein, J. (1992). *Hard courts*. New York: Villard Books.

Feinstein, J. (1995). *A good walk spoiled: Days and nights on the PGA tour*. Boston: Little, Brown and Co.

Fish, M. (2002a, May 7). A black eye: Headed to prison, Black should be a lesson to agents. Retrieved from http://sportsillustrated.cnn.com/inside_game/mike_fish/news/2002/05/07/tank_black/

Fish, M. (2002b, May 7). Q&A with Tank Black. Retrieved from http://sportsillustrated.cnn.com/football/college/news/2002/05/07/black_qa/

Futterman, M. (2010a, May 7). Talent agencies cry foul, lawsuits fly. *Wall Street Journal*. Retrieved from http://online.wsj.com/article/NA_WSJ_PUB:SB10001424052748703686304575228314238507620.html#articleTabs%3Darticle

Futterman, M. (2010b, May 28). CAA dismisses talent agent hired from rival firm. *Wall Street Journal*. Retrieved from http://online.wsj.com/article/SB10001424052748703630300575270912343901640.html

Golka, J. (2008). Golka's athlete regulation blog. NFLPA—Basics of agent certification. Retrieved from http://www.gaarb.com/2008/06/nflpa-basics-of-agent-certification.html

Greenberg, M. J. (1993). *Sports law practice*. Charlottesville, VA: The Michie Co.

Grossman, J. W. (2002). Financial planning for the professional athlete. In G. A. Uberstine (Ed.), *Law of professional and amateur sports* (pp. 3-4–3-11). St. Paul, MN: West Group.

Hack, D. (2008, Dec. 15). McCormack and Palmer changed world of sports and business forever. *Golf.com*. Retrieved from http://www.golf.com/tour-and-news/mccormack-and-palmer-changed-world-sports-and-business-forever#ixzz37AUp0uI3

Helyar, J. (1994). *Lords of the realm*. New York: Villard Books.

Helyar, J. (1997, June 25). Net gains? A Providence guard leaves college early, hoping for NBA gold. *Wall Street Journal*, pp. A1, A8.

Hersch, P. (1994, December 11). Commentary: Kerrigan's off-ice spins create "image meltdown." *The Seattle Times*. Retrieved from http://community.seattletimes.nwsource.com/archive/?date=19941211&slug=1946743

Hofmann, D., & Greenberg, M. J. (1989). *Sport$ biz*. Champaign, IL: Leisure Press.

IMG. (2003). IMG chairman's letter. Retrieved from http://www.imgworld.com/chairmansletter/default.htm

IMG. (2004a). IMG history. Retrieved from http://www.imgworld.com/history/

IMG. (2004b). IMG home. Retrieved from http://www.imgworld.com/

IMG. (2014). About us. Retrieved from http://img.com/about-us.aspx

Johnston, A. J., & Kain, R. D. (2004). CEO message. Retrieved from http://www.imgworld.com/message/

Katz, D. (1994). *Just do it: The Nike spirit in the corporate world*. New York: Random House.

Kepner, T. (2006, October 21). Baseball; The Boras bunch. *New York Times*. Retrieved from http://select.nytimes.com/search/restricted

/article?res=F20815F93D5B0C728EDDA909
94DE404482

Kuliga, K. (2007, April 4). Interview as part of the "Someone to be Proud of Series." University of Massachusetts Club, Boston, MA.

Lester, P. (2002). Marketing the athlete; endorsement contracts. In G. A. Uberstine (Ed.), *Law of professional and amateur sports* (pp. 27-2–27-39). St. Paul, MN: West Group.

Levin, M. (2007, February 12). Telephone conversation with Director of Salary Cap and Agent Administration of NFLPA.

Longman, J. (1994, February 6). Focus on sports: The whole world is watching. *New York Times*. Retrieved from http://www .nytimes.com/1994/02/06/sports/focus -on-sports-the-whole-world-is-watching .html?pagewanted=print&src=pm

Lowenfish, L. (1991). *The imperfect diamond* (rev. ed.). New York: Da Capo Press.

Lowitt, B. (1999, November 29). Harding, Kerrigan are linked forever by skating incident. *The St. Petersburg Times*. Retrieved from http://www .sptimes.com/News/112999/Sports/Harding __Kerrigan_are.shtml

Major League Baseball Players Association (MLBPA). (2014). Frequently asked questions. Retrieved from http://mlb.mlb.com/pa/info /faq.jsp#certified

Martino, R.J. (2009, November 22). Sports agents: Changing the compensation method. Retrieved from http://www.scribd.com /doc/22951011/Sports-Agents-Changing-the -Compensation-Method

McAleenan, G. (2002). Agent-player representation agreements. In G. A. Uberstine (Ed.), *Law of professional and amateur sports* (pp. 2-10-2-12). St. Paul, MN: West Group.

MLBPA (2010). Regulations governing player agents. Retrieved from http://reg.mlbpaagent.org

Mortensen, C. (1991). *Playing for keeps: How one man kept the mob from sinking its hooks into pro football*. New York: Simon & Schuster.

Mullen, L. (2004, April 19–25). Dirty dealings spark debate. *Street & Smith's SportsBusiness Journal*, 23–27.

Mullen, L. (2006, October 16–22). New players emerge in athlete rep business: Ranking the agencies. *Street & Smith's SportsBusiness Journal*, p. 26.

Mullen, L. (2007a, January 15). LeBron's agent close to CAA deal. *Street & Smith's SportsBusiness Journal*, p. 1.

Mullen, L. (2007b, January 8). Two agents exit Octagon for WMG. *Street & Smith's SportsBusiness Journal*, p. 5.

Mullen, L. (2010a, May 17). Lawsuits may affect big-name sports agencies. *Street & Smith's SportsBusiness Journal*, p. 1.

Mullen, L. (2010b, May 17). Bear with them: CAA Sports signs to represent Jack Nicklaus. *Street & Smith's SportsBusiness Journal*, p. 14.

Mullen, L. (2010c, September 16). IMG, Matthew Baldwin both claim victory in lawsuit settlement. Retrieved from http://www .sportsbusinessdaily.com/Daily/Issues /2010/09/Issue-4/Sports-Industrialists /IMG-Matthew-Baldwin-Both-Claim -Victory-In-Lawsuit-Settlement.aspx

Mullen, L. and Broughton, D. (2008, August 25). Survey puts CAA tops in player salaries. *Street & Smith's SportsBusiness Journal*, p. 1.

National Hockey League Players Association (NHLPA). (2014). Certified agents. Retrieved from http://www.nhlpa.com/inside-nhlpa /certified-player-agents/find-an-agent?ln=Z

Neff, C. (1987, October 19). Den of vipers. *Sports Illustrated*, 74–104.

Newman, W. (2007). Person-centered branding: Coaching to create an authentic brand. Retrieved from http://www .personcenteredbranding.com

Octagon. (2007). About us. Retrieved from http:// www.octagon.com/AboutUs/42

Octagon. (2014a). Who we are: By the numbers. Retrieved from http://www.octagon.com /who_we_are/by_the_numbers/

Octagon. (2014b). Who we are: Offices. Retrieved from http://www.octagon.com/who_we_are/offices/

Oliver v. NCAA, 2009 Ohio 6587 (2009).

Ozanian, M. (2013, December 18). IMG sold for $2.3 billion to William Morris Endeavor and Silver Lake Partners. Retrieved from http://www.forbes.com/sites/mikeozanian/2013/12/18/img-sold-for-2-3-billion-to-william-morris-endeavor-and-silver-lake-partners/

Palmer, A. (2014). Arnold Palmer Enterprises. Retrieved from http://www.arnoldpalmer.com/BUSINESS/ap_enterprises.aspx

Pierce, C. (2007, April 1). Why Scott Boras is the best (and worst) thing to happen to baseball. Retrieved from http://www.boston.com/news/globe/magazine/articles/2007/04/01/why_scott_boras_is_the_best_and_worst_thing_to_happen_to_baseball/

Rovell, D. (2013, March 21). How golfer Arnold Palmer became a drink to an entire generation. ABC News. Retrieved from http://abcnews.go.com/blogs/business/2013/03/how-golfer-arnold-palmer-became-a-drink-to-an-entire-generation/

Ruxin, R. (2004). An athlete's guide to agents (4th ed.). Sudbury, MA: Jones & Bartlett Publishers.

Sauer, A. D. (2003, March 17). Yao Ming falls short. brandchannel.com. Retrieved from http://www.brandchannel.com/features_profile.asp?pr_id=116

Schwarz, A. (1996, March 4–17). Agents: What's the deal? Baseball America, 14–19.

Shropshire, K. (1990). Agents of opportunity. Philadelphia: University of Pennsylvania Press.

Shropshire, K. L., & Davis, T. (2003). The business of sports agents. Philadelphia: University of Pennsylvania Press.

Sobel, L. (1990). The regulation of player agents and lawyers. In G. A. Uberstine (Ed.), Law of professional and amateur sports (pp. 1-1–1-107). Deerfield, IL: Clark, Boardman, and Callaghan.

Sobel, L. (2002). The regulation of player agents and lawyers. In G. A. Uberstine (Ed.), The law of professional and amateur sports (pp. 1-1–1-6). St. Paul, MN: West Group.

Solomon, J. (1995, April 26). Guest lecture: Professional sports and the law class. University of Massachusetts, Amherst.

Sports Agent Responsibility and Trust Act, Pub. L. No. 108-304. (2004) (enacted).

Sports Identity. (2007). BrandMatch® for athletes. Retrieved from http://sportsidentity.com/bm_athletes.php

Sports legend revealed: Did Vince Lombardi trade a player five minutes after learning the player hired an agent? (2011, February 8). L.A. Times. Retrieved from http://latimesblogs.latimes.com/sports_blog/2011/02/sports-legend-revealed-did-vince-lombardi-trade-a-player-five-minutes-after-learning-the-player-hire.html

Steadman, T. (2004). Owens faithful to his agent in Triad. News and Record. Retrieved from http://www.news,record.com/cgi,bin/print_it.pl

Thurow, R. (1996, February 9). The 76ers are lowly, but Jerry Stackhouse scores big in marketing. Wall Street Journal, pp. A1, A4.

Top NFL News (2010). 2009 NFL salaries of coaches. Retrieved from http://www.topnflnews.com/2009-nfl-salaries-of-coaches/01/2010/

Towle, A. P. (2003, November 18). Celebrity branding: Making the brand. Hollywood Reporter. Retrieved from http://www.hollywoodreporter.com/hr/search/article_display.jsp?vnu_content_id=2030984

Vint, P. (2013, December 14). Twelve ways of understanding Nick Saban's new $7 million salary. Retrieved from http://www.sbnation.com/college-football/2013/12/14/5209876/nick-saban-alabama-contract-salary

Waggoner, J. (1996, July 12). Walk, don't run, after a windfall. USA Today, p. 5B.

Warner, B. (2013, January 22). The 20 highest paid golfers of 2012. CelebrityNetWorth.com. Retrieved from http://www.celebritynetworth

.com/articles/entertainment-articles/10
-highest-earning-golfers-2012/

Wertheim, L.J. (2001, November 5). SFX needs an Rx. *Sports Illustrated*. Retrieved from http://sportsillustrated.cnn.com/vault/article/magazine/MAG1024185/index.htm

Wertheim, L.J. (2004, May 3). The matchmaker: Agent Bob LaMonte represents NFL coaches on the rise. Retrieved from http://sportsillustrated.cnn.com/vault/article/magazine/MAG1031945/index.htm

Willette, A., & Waggoner, J. (1996, July 12). Rich can't afford to dismiss budget: Even superstars need financial coaching. *USA Today*, p. 5B.

WMG. (2006a, January 27). Wasserman Media Group acquires Arn Tellem's prominent baseball and basketball athlete representation business. Retrieved from http://www.thefreelibrary.com/Wasserman+Media+Group+Acquires+Arn+Tellem's+Prominent+Baseball+and...-a0141346234

WMG. (2006b, May 11). Wasserman Media Group forms WMG Events via acquisition of Touring Pro. Retrieved from http://wmgllc.com/news/wmgevents.html

WMG. (2006c, June 5). Wasserman Media Group acquires SportsNet, the nation's premier soccer management business. Retrieved from http://wmgllc.com/news/sportsnet.html

WMG. (2006d, November 9). Wasserman Media Group becomes market leader in soccer—acquires SFX Sports Group European soccer practices. Retrieved from http://wmgllc.com/news/soccerleader-11_09_06.html

WMG. (2007, June 25). Wasserman Media Group acquires sport and entertainment marketing leader, OnSport. Retrieved from http://wmgllc.com/news/onsport.html

Woolf, B. (1976). *Behind closed doors*. New York: New American Library.

Part IV

Sport Industry Support Segments

Chapter 12 Facility Management

Chapter 13 Event Management

Chapter 14 Sport Sales

Chapter 15 Sport Sponsorship

Chapter 16 Sport Communications

Chapter 17 Sport Broadcasting

Chapter 18 The Sporting Goods and Licensed Products Industries

Chapter 12

Facility Management

Mary A. Hums and Lisa P. Masteralexis

Bananaur/Thinkstock

Learning Objectives

Upon completion of this chapter, students should be able to:

1. Describe the history of sport facilities with an emphasis on the recent trend toward more single-purpose stadiums and arenas.

2. Categorize the various types of public assembly facilities such as arenas, stadiums, convention centers, university venues, metropolitan facilities, or local/civic venues.

3. Identify some of the different types of events that may be held at public assembly facilities.

4. Distinguish between public and private financing of sport facilities and discuss the advantages and disadvantages of each.

5. Analyze the arguments for and against government subsidization of public assembly facilities.

6. Understand the importance of the relationship between facility ownership and management staff.

7. Describe the basics of marketing and promoting events.

8. Identify the sources of revenues and expenses of sport facilities.

9. Appraise the career opportunities available in the sport facility management segment and be aware of the skills needed to succeed in each.

10. Analyze some of the current issues in the public assembly facility industry, including enhanced security, sustainability, access for persons with disabilities, and universal design.

Introduction

People congregate in large groups for a number of reasons. Public assembly facilities must be big enough to accommodate the large numbers of people who want to be entertained at a sport or entertainment event or who meet together for social or business purposes. The facilities designed and built to accommodate these large groups of people include arenas, stadiums, convention centers, theaters, performing arts facilities, racetracks, and amphitheaters. Arenas and stadiums are the primary venues for professional and amateur **sports events**. Although convention centers and theaters are not designed primarily to host sports events, they are utilized and marketed for this function. The growth in popularity of sports such as volleyball and mixed martial arts (MMA) has created a new market for these venues because they offer the large, unobstructed space that is vital for successful functions. Additionally, convention centers host sport-related conventions, such as sporting goods expositions, recreation and boat shows, and league meetings. Management principles are similar for all types of these facilities, and their managers are eligible for membership in the **International Association of Venue Managers (IAVM)**, the professional trade association for this field. In this chapter, the discussion of public assembly facilities considers arenas, stadiums, convention centers, and theaters. Facility managers provide the public with a safe, enjoyable experience while providing a cost-effective and efficient means for the venue owner. This chapter focuses on significant areas in facility management to identify the structure and reasons why facilities are managed in certain ways.

History

Public assembly facilities have existed since ancient times. In fact, the word **stadium** is derived from the ancient Greek *stade*, a site for early Olympic-style athletic competition, such as the early Olympic Games first held in Olympia, Greece. Many of today's famous facilities bear the names of ancient and medieval facilities (e.g., Forum, Coliseum, Globe Theater). Throughout recorded history, people have gathered to witness sporting competitions and live theater at their era's version of public assembly facilities. From a sport management perspective, today's version of public assembly facilities evolved during the late nineteenth and early twentieth centuries in the United States, coinciding with the development of professional and intercollegiate athletics.

Early stadiums saw professional baseball and football teams sharing the same facilities. There was once a time when both the Chicago Cubs and Chicago Bears called Wrigley Field their home! Professional hockey moved to arenas first, followed by basketball, which hockey owners used to fill dark days when the hockey teams did not play.

The Modern Era of Stadium and Arena Construction

Basketball and hockey, as tenants of one arena, are much more compatible in terms of building design and sightlines than are baseball and football. Stadium quirks and fan annoyance factors were never as critical in developing arenas capable of hosting both indoor sports as they were in stadiums attempting to host both outdoor sports. Still, it is clearly advantageous for sports facility owners (whether indoor or outdoor) to have two prime sport tenants. Baseball-only stadiums that had served their owners and fans for more than 40 years became obsolete during the 1960s. Some were too small, and most lacked modern amenities such as wide seats, leg room, easy access to concession stands, and artificial turf. Several new stadiums were built during the 1960s and 1970s, but not by the team owners.

Team owners at that time were beginning to learn a lesson they would use to their advantage in the future: they could save a great deal of money by having their host city build their stadium rather than building it themselves. Cities, driven by the civic pride that "big league" status endows, built shiny new facilities to keep their teams as enthusiastic about their hometowns as were the civic leaders. It made sense for the cities to build facilities with both their football and baseball tenants in mind because more activity justified the public investment. The result was the so-called "cookie-cutter stadiums," such as Veterans Stadium in Philadelphia, Three Rivers Stadium in Pittsburgh, and Riverfront Stadium in Cincinnati. They were new, they were modern, they had artificial turf (so field maintenance was easy), and they all looked alike. Arena construction boomed during this era, too. Civic centers and civic arenas sprang up in a number of major and secondary markets as cities competed for major and minor league sport teams by building suitable facilities. This period also marked the dawn of the touring concert industry, and concerts became an extremely lucrative addition to a facility's schedule. City leaders generally believed that a publicly built stadium with both baseball and football tenants or a publicly built arena with both basketball and hockey tenants, along with the concert and family show tours, was a good investment. Such facilities contributed to the city's quality of life by providing sports and entertainment for the citizens and spin-off benefits for the local economy.

Eventually, team owners, and many of their fans, decided that multipurpose facilities were not quite good enough. Stadiums designed to be acceptable for both baseball and football ended up being desirable for neither. The trend over the past two decades has been single-purpose stadiums. This specialization has extended to facilities built solely for soccer teams, called **soccer-specific stadiums (SSS)**. SSS have become the legacy of soccer investor, Lamar Hunt, late owner of the Columbus Crew, whose SSS in Columbus, Ohio, was the first venue of its size to be built in the United States and has fueled SSS growth. The Crew Stadium opened in 1999 and has become a model for all Major League Soccer (MLS) franchises. Now, SSS in MLS are the norm.

Financing these facilities has become an interesting dilemma, particularly given team owners' desire to use facility revenues to compete for free-agent players and boost their own profits. Some cities have constructed (or have promised to construct) facilities that will provide team owners the design and revenue streams they need to be successful. Team owners have traditionally sought lucrative stadium leases that provide revenue from four sources: preferred seating (i.e., luxury suites, club seating, and personal seat licenses), parking, concessions, and stadium sponsorship (i.e., signage and naming rights) (Greenberg & Gray, 1993). New technology has created additional revenue streams. For example, in the Dallas Cowboys' AT&T Stadium, there is now emphasis on second-screen viewing. According to Stephen Jones, son of the Cowboys owner Jerry Jones, "This is about smartphones, pads, computers and technology . . . we have targeted them from the get-go. This was not just about settling for a naming rights deal. . . . This is a bigger deal" (Jacobson, Robinson-Jacobs, & Moore, 2013). As a result, franchise free agency has developed. Team owners flee their traditional locations for greener pastures not because of market size and growth, but because of more profitable facility deals. In fact, the facility in which a professional sport team plays has the most significant impact on its profitability and is often the primary consideration in choosing to remain or move to a new location.

Types of Public Assembly Facilities

Arenas

Arenas are indoor facilities that host sporting and entertainment events. They are usually built to accommodate one (or more) prime sports tenant(s) or to lure a prime tenant to the facility. Colleges and universities typically build an arena for their basketball teams and occasionally their hockey teams, as at the University of Notre Dame's Compton Family Ice Arena. These arenas may also be used for volleyball, such as the Bob Devaney Center at the University of Nebraska, and gymnastics as well as concerts and other touring shows. Intercollegiate facilities are financed by private donations, endowments, student fees, fund-raising campaigns, and, in the case of public institutions, public grants or capital bonds.

Some NBA and NHL teams have built their own arenas. In other cases, municipalities, state governments, or public authorities have built them. Sometimes the public owner manages its facility, and sometimes it contracts out for private management. The public or private manager then negotiates a lease with the prime sports tenant. If the arena is privately built, commercial lenders issue loans to the team, which pledges facility revenue streams as collateral. Public financing typically involves issuing bonds that can be tied to direct or indirect facility revenue, but more often are a general obligation of the governmental entity.

Basketball and hockey teams can generally peacefully coexist in the same arena without either being forced into unacceptable compromises. Arenas also host indoor soccer leagues, arena football, concerts, ice shows, family shows, graduations, other civic events, and some types of conventions. Recent trends in

facility construction include adjacent practice facilities for the primary tenants. The NHL's Columbus Blue Jackets and New Jersey Devils both have this arrangement. The Minnesota Timberwolves and WNBA Minnesota Lynx have their practice facility across the street from their home arena, and Mayo Clinic will open a sports medicine clinic on the site as well (NBA Media Ventures, 2014).

Stadiums

The ownership, financing, and management issues discussed in the arena section also apply to stadiums. Like their arena counterparts, stadium managers try to maximize bookings, but it is more difficult. First, far fewer nonsport events can play in stadiums, primarily because stadiums are significantly larger than other venues and most other events cannot attract stadium-sized crowds. The main nonsport events for stadiums are outdoor concerts given by performers who have the drawing power to fill a stadium. The large parking facilities that are adjacent to most stadiums have long been utilized for pregame tailgating. However, now on nongame days they are being utilized and marketed to fairs, festivals, circuses, carnivals, outdoor marketplaces, and drive-and-buy car shows. They are also sometimes rented out for staging areas for new cars in transit to dealers or for parking for nearby events such as state fairs or major civic events such as the Kentucky Derby.

Convention Centers

Convention centers are almost always built and owned by a public entity. Convention centers are built to lure conventions and business meetings to a particular municipality. They are publicly financed because the rents and fees they charge do not always cover their costs. However, the municipality they serve benefits in other ways, namely through the economic impact the conventions or business meetings

have on the municipality. Organizations such as the International Association of Convention and Visitors Bureaus evaluate the economic impact of various events, considering spending that includes hotel, meal, entertainment, and related expenditures.

Convention centers are typically located near the downtown districts of large cities. The convention business is extremely competitive, and municipalities (and states) offer significant financial inducements to convention and meeting planners for the opportunity to host visitors. The conventioneers and meeting attendees stay in local hotels, eat in local restaurants, shop in local stores, and patronize local tourist attractions, all of which support business and employment in the region. Conventioneers also are typically taxed, so the state and municipality receive indirect revenue from the events. The increased business, employment opportunities, and fiscal revenue justify the public entity's construction and continued subsidy of convention centers.

In addition to the nontraditional sporting events previously discussed, convention centers host a wide variety of events, such as volleyball and basketball tournaments; trade shows, such as car, boat, and home shows; corporate meetings; banquets; and similar functions.

University Venues

University venues consist of stadiums and arenas that operate under different economic factors. The market for university and college venues is generally dictated by the student population. Universities and colleges have different geographic locations, but the general intent when selling tickets is to market to the student population and, therefore, certain types of events will play better than others. Universities tend to provide the venue with tenant teams as well as a certain amount of content through the university. Providing the university with the content that may be routing through the area can sometimes prove to be difficult based on the occupied dates scheduled for university programs.

Metropolitan Facilities

Metropolitan facilities are venues located in large cities such as Madison Square Garden in New York, the Wells Fargo complex in Philadelphia, and the Staples Center in Los Angeles. Venues like these are generally referred to as a *must play* based on the size of the potential audience. The three venues just listed can present as many as 400 events a year if the scheduling allows for it. They often have multiple tenants, including NHL, NBA, WNBA, NBA Development League (NBA D-League), and arena football leagues. Typically the staffs operating these venues are larger based on the event load, whereas a smaller venue will generally run a more streamlined staff.

A must-play venue is popular with promoters for several reasons. Promoters with established routing have a variety of local staff, making tour travel less expensive and more efficient. Metropolitan venues often have larger capacities, allowing for greater ticket sales. Skilled labor in metropolitan venues is almost always unionized. In smaller venues, specific labor may be mandated to be contracted to the unions, but there is often a component that can be nonunion. The venues located within city limits utilize skilled labor from the union, but their expertise often costs more than hiring a private contractor. Venue managers often are required to use union labor because of contracts negotiated before the venue opened that were based on funding and economic impact studies.

Local/Civic Venues

Local/civic venues may have a smaller capacity and are located in towns or small cities. The Sun National Bank Center in Trenton, New Jersey, and the Santander Arena in Reading, Pennsylvania, are examples of local or civic

venues. They have a smaller surrounding population and seating capacity. The venues themselves are able to host large-scale events and concerts but tend to host smaller-capacity events due to artist costs. The venue manager needs to identify what works for venues in the 5,000 to 10,000 seat range. Although the venue may have an NBA or NHL minor league affiliate (such as the Reading Royals in Reading) as a tenant, it is essential to have the additional events to fill the calendar. Facility-operating teams have been successfully hosting events that play to local groups, such as cheerleading competitions, political conventions, and church conferences. The civic venue has a niche that is based in the surrounding community, and the support the venue receives is critical to its success.

Types of Events

Many different types of events are possible. Some are mainstream, such as Disney On Ice, whereas others may be somewhat nontraditional, such as the X Games or Dew Tour. Venue managers should know a wide variety of genres and be able to quickly access the type of event that would have the biggest impact on the community and the venue. When looking at event types, the promoter and facility director must consider the market in order to ensure the success of an event. Family events, such as the Harlem Globetrotters, are always popular. The well-known Harlem Globetrotters act encompasses comedy, athleticism, and pop culture. The Globetrotters travel throughout the world and are well received in every venue they play. Family events such as traveling circuses may not do as well, because some activist groups believe that the animals involved in such programs are being treated unethically. Venue managers and promoters need to take market concerns such as this into consideration prior to booking a routing event. The facility manager also has to be aware of the specifics of his or her market in order to provide the public with the desired event at the best time of the year to avoid undue competition with other events that may be occurring simultaneously. The following are some event genres and how they operate.

Sport Events

Sports have seasons that allow events to be scheduled approximately 8 months out. Several venues will have primary tenant teams that play a home schedule and require certain dates contractually. For example, the primary tenants in Chicago's United Center are the NBA Bulls and NHL Blackhawks. Facility managers walk a fine line when budgeting shows around team games because of playoffs. Should the tenant team make the playoffs, it will require that home days be available. A close eye needs to be kept on the booking calendar to make sure conflicts or double bookings do not occur. Nontenant events must be booked around the primary tenants. Examples of these types of sport events may include AAU basketball tournaments or high school all-star games.

Family Events

Family events are products geared toward the toddler through the "tween" markets. Often these are acts produced from television or movie programs that are run on mainstream television or in movie theaters. Sesame Street, Nickelodeon, and Disney are among the top names in the family genre. They produce the artists that children identify with. When playing a venue, the show normally has a multiple-day run and generates large demands for food and beverages as well as merchandise sales. Booking can be challenging based on the amount of preparation the venue will need and how long of a run the show will have. Ice programs will need ice specifically tailored to the artists and the performance. Preparation for changes to an ice sheet from hockey usage to ice show usage can take time and commitment

from the operations team. Should the schedule be tight and a quick turnaround necessary, the venue manager may need to look at the event and try to find alternate dates that work.

Concerts

Concerts are booked on average 6 months before the performance date. Tours and routings are established, and the dates are promoted after an agreement is reached. When booking concerts it is important to look at the potential ticket sales and the intended market. Size, age of the arena, and the building's technology capacity can dictate the types of performers who will appear. Booking Lady Gaga, Eminem, or Bruno Mars would only be possible in the most state-of-the-art facility.

Timing also is critical when scheduling a concert. Consider university students, for example. Students have breaks throughout the year that generally include a fall, winter, and spring break. It would not make sense to schedule a big name performer when the students are on winter break. In addition, some schools are more of a commuter type and do not have a central location where students are housed in large numbers. These are all critical factors when looking at booking a venue with a show geared toward a student body.

Some cities have amphitheaters that host outdoor music events. These are particularly popular in the summer season when the evenings are warm and comfortable.

Trade Shows

Trade shows are mostly multiple-day events held annually in the same location. Trade shows work best in convention centers because hotel and exhibition space are specifically intended for that usage, but they can also play in stadiums and arenas that can be converted to accommodate the event. An example is the Phoenix Convention Center in Arizona that hosts an annual expo for outdoor enthusiasts and fans of recreational vehicles. This venue utilizes its retractable roof and stadium field in order to fill dates, which gives the promoter the ability to expand the show into a larger, more unique space.

Religious Events

Religious events encompass mass worship. These events are generally booked as a rental with expenses guaranteed. The rental structure is preferred because religious organizations generally do not charge for tickets. Some groups, such as the Jehovah's Witnesses, can provide a good opportunity to utilize a venue when bookings for the facility are slow. Arenas have been able to schedule religious events in the summer to fill dates that would otherwise go vacant. Concerts and tours tend to play outdoor facilities in the summer, so religious events present a nice opportunity to make a small profit on days that would otherwise not be utilized.

Convocations

Convocations, graduations, and speaking engagements are great ways to get community involvement and interaction with the venue. Venue managers generally approach these types of events with the understanding that graduations happen in the spring and weather conditions may present certain challenges to hosting them outside. Another plus is the capacity of the venue and the graduates' ability to have additional tickets for friends and family. Graduations can be a busy time of year depending on the number of local schools hosting at the facility and the size of the class.

Seasonal Events

Seasonal events are defined as events that take place during a specific time frame. Summer tours are a perfect example of a seasonal event. In the past, large summer music tours were held mostly at outdoor theaters, but more recently stadiums are hosting large country music

festivals and touring programs. One event that seems to mark the beginning of the summer for many concert goers is Jimmy Buffet. Jimmy Buffet and his Margaritaville tour is one of the most heavily attended summer touring events. The shows are generally held at outdoor facilities so the fans can experience the music in an outdoor and relaxed fashion. Other types of seasonal programming that the facility manager may consider are seasonal programs directed at holidays, such as the Radio City Music Hall Rockettes touring holiday program or the Tran-Siberian Orchestra. Both programs tour around the November–December holiday season and attract good attendance from families looking to get into the holiday spirit.

Facility Financing

Facility financing starts with the federal government, which allows state and local governments to issue tax-exempt **bonds** to help finance sports facilities. Tax exemption lowers interest on debt, thereby reducing the amount that cities and teams must pay for a stadium. Public assembly facilities can be financed in a variety of ways, but the specific financing decision is always preceded by a single fundamental question: Will the facility be financed publicly or privately? The answer depends on a number of factors, including the type of facility being constructed. Convention centers are almost always financed publicly because they are not intended to make money. Convention centers do not book events to make a profit for themselves; rather, they book events that maximize the impact on the local economy, particularly the hospitality industry. Because of their "public" focus, the public sector pays for them, often by initiating or raising taxes on the state or local hospitality industry (e.g., hotel room taxes, restaurant meal taxes, and rental car fees).

Arena and stadium financing is not as clear-cut, particularly when a major league professional sport team is a prime tenant. Professional sport teams are in business to make money—sometimes enormous amounts of money. Some argue that any for-profit enterprise should build its own facility where it conducts its business. At the same time, a number of studies have shown that sports facilities provide significant economic benefits to their host communities, and teams are undeniable sources of civic pride and community spirit. Attracting a sport team can provide a public relations boost to a city, too, particularly one attempting to prove it is "major league."

Controlling stadium revenue streams such as concessions, advertising, sponsorship, premium seating and suites, and seat licenses has become the primary means to the owners' ends. Single-purpose facilities designed to the specifications of a particular sport with one team as primary tenant are desirable to team owners because revenue streams do not have to be shared.

For the cities, states, stadium authorities, and other representatives of the public sector, these issues have become increasingly problematic. The public benefits justifying stadium construction remain, but costs continue to rise, particularly if two teams are each looking for its own stadium or arena. Cities, in particular, face hard choices, because most have stable or declining tax revenues and increasing municipal government costs. Building public assembly facilities means that other services have to be neglected. In many locations, the question of publicly financing a stadium has been put to a vote.

Facility Financing Mechanisms

The facility arms race for college and professional sports continues to push forward with new arenas and stadiums across the country. The question arises of how these facilities are being funded and for how much. From the 1960s through the early 2000s, professional

sport venues of the Big Four (MLB, NHL, NBA, and NFL) have cost approximately $24 billion, with 64% of this being funded through tax dollars (Crompton, 2004; Crompton, Howard, & Var, 2003). This trend has continued, with the industry seeing the first $1 billion dollar stadiums, including MetLife Stadium, Yankee Stadium, AT&T Stadium, and Wembley Stadium.

A team or city has a variety of options in funding a new facility or financing a renovation. As previously stated, public financing has accounted for 64% of costs for professional facilities. This is available through bonds, hard taxes, or soft taxes.

A bond is defined as "an interest-bearing certificate issued by the government or corporation, promising to pay interest and to repay a sum of money" (Samuelson & Nordhaus, 1985, p. 828). A variety of bonds are available for facility financing. Tax-exempt bonds used by government entities are available in two types: general obligation and nonguaranteed. General obligation bonds are bonds that are repaid with a portion of the general property taxes and requires voter approval (Sawyer, 2006). Stadiums funded by these bonds include AT&T Stadium in Dallas, Texas; Time Warner Cable Arena in Charlotte, North Carolina; and the Tampa Bay Times Forum in Tampa, Florida (Kuriloff & Preston, 2012). Another example of a tax-exempt bond in use is in Cleveland. Jacobs Field (MLB Indians) and Gund Arena (NBA Cavaliers) both opened in 1994 and saw great early success after opening. The new venues were also credited with sparking the revitalization of downtown Cleveland. Gateway Development Corporation (GDC), which owns both venues, was not collecting enough money from the leases to pay on the debt service on the $120 million in bonds that helped finance the project (Burke, 1997). In turn, Cuyahoga County, the guarantor of the debt, was forced to cover the costs through its taxpayers (Burke, 1997). Nonguaranteed bonds are sold on the basis of repayment from designated revenue sources (i.e., concessions, naming rights, parking revenue, etc.) (Sawyer, 2006). Although nonguaranteed bonds do not generally require voter approval, the interest rate is higher compared to general obligation bonds (Sawyer, 2006).

Another form of bond is a taxable bond issued by private entities. There are two forms of this type of bond: private-placement bonds and asset-backed bonds. Both types of bonds are sold by the team, but private-placement bonds provide a lien on all future revenues generated by the team, whereas asset-backed bonds are secured through specific assets (Sawyer, 2006). Pepsi Center, home of the Denver Nuggets, Colorado Mammoth, and Colorado Avalanche, was financed through asset-backed bonds in the 1990s (Kaplan, 1999).

Another bond option that has become popular is tax-increment financing, or TIF. TIF is available in a specific square mileage of land around the facility (usually an urban area that has been identified for renewal or redevelopment) where the tax base is frozen and any additional taxes added are used to repay the TIF bonds (Sawyer, 2006). For example, the KFC Yum! Center is owned by the Louisville Arena Authority, Inc. and is home of the University of Louisville men's and women's basketball teams and women's volleyball team, and is surrounded by a TIF district with a 6-square-mile radius.

The public can also help finance a new venue through additional taxes. Hard taxes include taxes on local income, real estate, personal property, and general sales and often require voter approval because the burden of payment becomes that of the public (Sawyer, 2006). Soft taxes include added taxes to car rentals, taxis, hotels/motels, restaurants, "sin" (alcohol, tobacco, gambling, etc.), and players (additional tax imposed on visiting professional athletes)

and affect a much smaller portion of taxpayers, making it easier to levy (Sawyer, 2006). The Minnesota Vikings helped fund its new stadium by imposing an additional tax on tobacco products (Bradley, 2013).

Another option for financing a new facility is private funding. Many universities across the country go this route through their athletic development and fund-raising departments. Ways to gain private funding for a facility project include naming rights, food and beverage rights, luxury suites and premium seating, advertising rights, and so on. The University of Maryland was able to pen a 25-year agreement with Comcast Cable for the naming rights of its basketball arena (Howard & Crompton, 2004). Private donors to university athletic departments also will provide funding and have their names placed on the new facilities. Recent examples include the University of Louisville's $18.5 million Dr. Mark and Cindy Lynn Stadium (soccer), slated to open in 2015; Oklahoma State's Boone Pickens Stadium (football), which opened in 2009; and the University of Notre Dame's Compton Family Ice Arena, which began operations in 2011.

Many municipalities will not support additional taxes for stadium projects, so team owners have to seek private funding. A prime example of a team that successfully built an arena with limited tax support was the Utah Jazz. Team owner Larry H. Miller received minimal public financing support for the team's new home, and he ended up supporting the project with his own money (Jensen, 2000). As a result, he built a cost-efficient arena on land given to him by the state of Utah while taxpayers saw no new direct tax increases from this project (Jensen, 2000). The Palace at Auburn Hills, home of the Detroit Pistons, opened in 1988 as one of the first single-purpose venues, was funded wholly through private sources (Crompton et al., 2003).

Oftentimes, opportunities are available to combine private and public funding in order to build a new facility. For example, Denver voters approved to subsidize $300 million for the construction of a new football stadium for the Broncos while the ownership was required to provide $100 million of their own funds and cover the cost of any overruns (Crompton et al., 2003).

The desire for new facilities continues as teams, universities, and cities try and upgrade their status. Whether used as a recruiting tool for college athletes, a state-of-the-art destination for pro sport fans, or a visible sign of civic pride, sport managers will need to work creatively to find the best sources of revenue to meet this ongoing demand.

Why Cities Subsidize Sports Facilities

The economic rationale for cities' willingness to subsidize sports facilities comes from the thought that sports facilities will improve the local economy in four ways. First, building a facility creates construction jobs. Second, people who attend games or work for the team generate new spending in the community, expanding local employment. Third, a team attracts tourists and companies to the host city, further increasing local spending and jobs. Finally, all this new spending has a "multiplier effect" as increased local income causes still more new spending and job creation (Noll & Zimbalist, 1997). Advocates argue that new stadiums spur so much economic growth that they are self-financing in that subsidies are offset by revenues from ticket taxes, sales taxes on concessions and other spending outside the stadium, and property tax increases arising from the stadium's economic impact.

Unfortunately, these arguments contain bad economic reasoning that leads to overstatement of the benefits of stadiums. Economic growth takes place when a community's resources—people, capital investments, and natural resources such as land—become more productive. Building a stadium is good for the local economy only if a stadium is the most productive way to make capital investments and use an area's workers (Noll & Zimbalist, 1997). According to Reed (2014):

> Urban populations need to get past that "civic pride" foolishness and put their governments "in check." League-wide, 70% of the capital cost of NFL stadiums is being provided by taxpayers. Many governments also pay stadiums' ongoing costs, by providing power, sewer services, and other infrastructure improvements.

No recent facility appears to have earned anything approaching a reasonable return on investment. In addition, no recent facility has been self-financing in terms of its impact on net tax revenues (Noll & Zimbalist, 1997). According to Demause (2011), "Owners of teams in the 'big four' sports leagues . . . have reaped nearly $20 billion in taxpayer subsidies for new homes since 1990. And for just as long, fans, urban planners and economists have argued that building facilities for private sports teams is a massive waste of public money."

Prospects for cutting sports subsidies are not good. Although citizen opposition has had some success, without more effective intercity organizing or more active federal antitrust policy, cities will continue to compete against each other to attract or keep artificially scarce sports franchises. Given the profound penetration and popularity of sports in U.S. culture, it is hard to see an end to rising public subsidies of sports facilities. A great example of this is the relationship of the city of New York to its professional sports teams. Despite the current economic challenges, the city helped to subsidize the building of new stadiums for the Yankees and the Mets. Mayor Michael Bloomberg nixed the plan of his predecessor Rudy Giuliani to spend $800 million in city funds due to the recession. However, 3 years later, Bloomberg's own plan, while calling on the two teams to pay for the construction of their stadiums, provided for the city to build parks, parking garages, and transit stations near the stadiums at a cost of $485 million to the city and another $201 million to the state. These totals do not also include an estimated $480 million in tax breaks to the teams; while the teams are also receiving use of city-owned land tax free (Bagli, 2008).

Facility Ownership and Management Staff

The relationship between the owner of a facility and management is critical, with efficiency and profitability determined by the purpose of the building (Farmer, Mulrooney, & Ammon, 1996). Facility ownership generally falls into three categories: community or state, which may have a "plethora of regulations and procedures in place"; colleges, where "funding is based on continued student growth, gifts, and institutional subsidies"; and private facilities, whose motive is solely for profit (Farmer et al., 1996).

Responsibilities of the management staff include serving tenants' needs and providing a clean, safe, and comfortable environment for patrons. Various functions performed by the management team include security, cleanup, marketing and sales, scheduling and booking, operations, event promotions, and finance and box office operations.

Private Management Options

The growth of private management in the operation of public assembly facilities in the past decade is indicative of the pressure to achieve maximum operating results by municipal and private ownership entities. Private management offers expertise and resources not usually available to individual venue managers. Most private management companies have a network of facilities that create leverage in cultivating key event relationships and, in turn, event bookings. Additionally, these companies have dedicated corporate personnel who are available to provide oversight and assistance that otherwise would most likely have to come from other municipal departments. Other examples of the benefits of private management include increased operating efficiencies, purchasing leverage for supplies and maintenance items, and labor negotiation resources. Some of the larger private facility management companies include Global Spectrum, which manages facilities ranging from Philadelphia's Wells Fargo Center to the United Arab Emirates Zayad Sport City in Abu Dhabi, and AEG, which manages a wide array of facilities, ranging from the Barclay's Center in Brooklyn, New York, to the O2 Centers in London and Berlin, to the Brussels National Arena in Belgium.

Private management companies have also added many career options for individuals entering the venue management field. With a network of facilities, these companies may offer growth and advancement opportunities to their employees across a wide geographic area. Companies such as Global Spectrum have also widened their reach by acquiring PACIOLAN ticketing systems and Ovations Food Systems.

Facility Marketing

Marketing

Identifying the market and the specifics of the venue are critical to successfully marketing the facility and its events. Facility managers need to focus on several aspects of marketing, including marketing new facilities, securing anchor tenants, attracting events, and developing relationships (Fried, 2010). The facility manager needs to account for the location of the venue, the types of events that best fit the community and culture of the facility, and how those events will be produced. Routing shows and artists are key elements to making a new or existing venue a sustainable option for the community and the facility's owners. Concerts generally confirm dates several months out, whereas family programs such as Disney On Ice, Sesame Street, Ringling Brothers and Barnum and Bailey's Circus book annual dates. These two types of events book in the manner that they do for several reasons. Annual events generally have a several-day run and provide groups such as schools, churches, Boy and Girl Scouts, and other clubs the ability to budget for the program. Concerts oftentimes rotate off the release of an album or an event that sparks public interest.

The information culture that has developed as a result of the Internet and social media outlets gives the facility manager the ability to access information much more quickly than in the past. These critical advances in technology also increase the demand for the manager to utilize his or her facility's calendar and team in the most efficient and effective manner. By using online tools, the manager can quickly react to inquiries for available dates and can establish a routing for a program or show.

The geographic location of a facility is a critical factor in the routing of artists and acts. *Saturated markets* are markets with several venues in a close proximity to one another. When booking programs, some acts may have radius clauses prohibiting the same act from playing another venue within 50 miles. These types of clauses are very difficult when defining a geographic market, because state lines often are crossed and in certain circumstances communities will not travel across state lines to see a program. Markets tend to define themselves, but the venues can define the market and how and what types of programs to host.

Finally, the local economy will be the driving force behind ticket sales and ticket price points. Promoters need to earn a base amount to cover the artist guarantees and venue expenses depending on the way the deal is negotiated.

Promoting

Shows and events can be promoted in several different ways. The facility manager may have a series of rules or guidelines to use when negotiating a contract for an event or program for the facility. His or her task is to keep financial risks low and profit margins high. Deal structures can be negotiated between promoters and venue managers to share revenue streams and risk certain profits such as rent, facility fee, or parking. A deal structure where risk and revenue are shared is generally defined as a *co-promotional model*. Should the venue manager be prohibited from taking risk in holding events, most likely he or she will operate under a rental agreement guaranteeing a specified rental amount with the external costs being covered by the promoter. Co-promotional agreements can provide a greater profit, but they also carry the risk of loss should ticket sales not be favorable. The rental is a fixed cost for the venue but it relies on ancillary revenue to help increase the profit margin.

Generally, the majority of shows are brought to venues by professional promoters. Live Nation, AEG Live, and Feld Entertainment are three of the largest promoters in the world. Live Nation works with talent such as Bruno Mars, Jay Z, Katy Perry, and the Dave Matthews Band. Large promoters such as Feld own their products and tour them internationally or regionally. Feld's most recognizable program is Disney On Ice.

Venues often rely on the local center for visitors bureau (CVB) to help push certain types of events. The CVB has better synergies with convention centers, but is able to work with most public facilities in order to promote a city and help to create commerce.

Facility Revenues and Expenses

The majority of facilities generate revenues from tickets, luxury suites and club seating, concessions, parking, sponsorships, and facility rentals. The primary expenses are mortgage and rent, maintenance and repairs, utilities, taxes, marketing and sales, personnel, and insurance (Ammon, Southall, & Nagel, 2010). This section highlights some of these areas.

Ticket sales generate the majority of revenues when promoting events. Venues can have ticket deals with ticketing agents, and artists and promoters can have deals that can be tied into the facility's contract with those artists and promoters.

Strategies to provide ticketing are developing quickly, and new profit centers are being realized daily. The most common ticketing profit center is the **ticket rebate**. The rebate is part of the surcharge that consumers must pay when they purchase a ticket to an event. This is an additional fee that is structured based on the ticket price, and it is returned to the facility or venue as a result of the sale. Most ticketing contracts are awarded based on the size of the rebate and the number of points of sale available to the consumer. Ticketing to the public is more convenient now than it has ever been. Internet tickets or print-at-home tickets are frequently used, comprising the majority of purchases.

Ticketing and event promotion can make or break a program. The promoter and the venue manager need to work together to ensure that tickets are priced reasonably. If the artist has packages for fan clubs or the venue holds a number of tickets for sponsors, these need to be accounted for prior to any tickets going on sale to the public. Certain groups mandate that fan club members get the first opportunity to buy tickets to the program. These groups are contacted by band representatives and are given codes to access a *presale* prior to the ticket sale to the general public. The code grants the buyer access to better seats in the facility and lower price points for the tickets. When the tickets go on sale to the general public, it is possible that the capacity of the program is less than initially estimated based on the size of the fan group in that area.

When promoters are establishing ticket prices, they look at the guarantee from the artist, the venue expenses, and the capacity of the venue to find a price point for the program. Should one of these numbers be too little or too great, the promoter will need to decide how or if it makes sense to host a particular show or artist at a venue. This type of market knowledge makes the difference between venues that host successful programs and those that do not. An additional factor is the demographic that the show is playing to. As previously discussed, the audience for a family program is not necessarily same as the audience for a rock show. Ticket prices for the rock concert can be higher and the audience will have different event behavior that would affect how a facility would prepare for the show. Family events geared towards children will have lower ticket prices and security costs because of the nature of the events and the event culture.

Ancillary revenue occurs from the sale of concessions, parking charges, ticket fees, and sponsorships. These fees are useful to the venues not only for their obvious income, but their profit margins allow venue managers to get creative with promoters when developing their deal structures.

Markets are becoming more and more saturated with venues hosting large-scale events. Facility managers are forced to constantly reevaluate the model they are using to fill the venue. One plan of action is to allow the promoters to share in profits from the ancillary revenues. Depending on the deal structure, all or only certain revenues can be included in the mix. Promoters are incentivized to bring larger acts to an area based on the potential revenue they will earn. Ticket sales are the first attempt at making a show profitable, but promoters have realized that opportunities exist beyond the standard ticket price. The bond fee or facility fee can be increased and rebated back to the promoter, or there can be a ticket rebate to the promoter based on the venue contract deal. Companies such as Ticketmaster, New Era, Eventim, and Ticket Pro all return a percentage based on the ticket price back to the facility as part of the program. Venues are incentivized to sell tickets because of the added fees that will return to the bottom line.

In the case of in-house promotion, some of the catering companies have joined forces with the venues to set aside a marketing fund. This **marketing fund** is a pool of money that is set aside from the profits of other shows. The concessionaire and the venue director each agree to a certain share of the percentage of sold goods, and they use the pool to help invest in future programs. The investment by both parties allows each to earn more money in the future.

One of the largest revenue drivers in venues today is the sale of alcohol. Alcohol sales are effective drivers of sponsorship dollars as well as being very popular at sporting and entertainment events. Alcohol sales have brought about changes in the venue's structure, which include sponsored areas, such as suites, as well as renovations for sports-themed bars and pubs. Alcohol and the culture that goes with selling it do open more liability to the concessionaire, but experienced and trained venue operators should be well aware of the dangers that present themselves as well as prepare for the artists and acts that may be a higher risk. Alcohol sales may be prohibited for intercollegiate athletic events such as basketball or football games depending on conference rules. The Southeastern Conference (SEC), for example, bans alcohol sales at events.

Sponsorship is also an important part of the equation. Naming rights are a particularly robust manner for driving revenues, typically generating millions of dollars per year for a facility. For example, the average annual value of Citi Group's sponsorship of Citi Field, home of the New York Mets, is approximately $400 million over 20 years. A 25-year deal at MetLife Stadium in New Jersey produces approximately $17 to $20 million annually, with an overall value estimated up to $625 million ("Top 10 Stadium," 2014).

In terms of expenses, a facility usually carries with it an obligation to pay a mortgage, just like one would have to do on a home—a monthly fee. Facility managers have to make sure these fees are managed appropriately, because revenues may ebb and flow during the year. These expenses are quite predictable, as are annual taxes and insurance; however, other expenses may not always be. Maintenance and repairs may take place on a regular schedule, but some items may not be predictable. For example, flooding from extreme snowmelt or natural disasters such as a tornado may result in higher than anticipated costs. Utilities also are somewhat predictable, but climate change and extreme weather conditions may affect the monthly bill as well. Personnel expenses can add up with the number and size of events. In order to put on one NFL home football game, a facility may require up to 1,000 workers, most of whom are part-time employees. Finally, facility managers need to spend money in order to make money; hence, the application of trade for services is always a bonus, but cash is always the preferred medium. Sponsorship needs to be approved by the promoter and act prior to its sale, but is a sure-fire means of event revenue generation. When applied correctly, the revenue can be the deciding factor between a break even and a loss.

When looking at a calendar, a facility manager should always be trying to fill nonevent days with some type of function. Events that break even are still good events to hold.

Career Opportunities

College graduates seeking career opportunities in the facility management industry will be pleasantly surprised at the wide variety of options available in arenas, convention centers, stadiums, and performing arts centers. No matter what their job title, facility managers need to master a set of managerial skills that the IAVM refers to as core competences (Russo, Esckilsen, & Stewart, 2009):

1. Administration (people and organization)

2. Sales and marketing (selling time and space and event activity)

3. Fiscal management (financial performance)

4. Facility services and operations (physical plant and event management)

5. Leadership and management

The career opportunity areas in facility management are shown in Table 12-1 and discussed in the sections that follow.

Marketing Director

Being the **marketing director** for an arena, performing arts center, or other venue is one of the more exciting careers in facility management. It is a fast-paced, highly stressful, enormously challenging career track that can

Table 12-1 Career Opportunity Areas in Facility Management

Marketing
Public relations/communications
Event management
Booking
Operations
Advertising, signage, and sponsorship sales
Group ticket sales
Box office

lead a successful individual all the way to the executive suite.

Facility marketing directors act primarily as in-house advertising agents for the various events booked into facilities. Buying media (e.g., TV, radio, print, billboards, Internet), coordinating promotions, working with social media, and designing marketing materials (e.g., TV commercials, brochures, flyers, newspaper advertisements, websites) are some of a marketing director's primary responsibilities. A typical day in the life of a facility marketing director may include creating a marketing plan and ad budget for Sesame Street Live, meeting with radio and TV sales staff to discuss cross promotions with McDonald's for the Harlem Globetrotters, and designing a print ad for Sunday's newspaper.

The more successful marketing directors are multiskilled performers who possess excellent people skills, sales ability, and written and oral communication skills. Most important, a successful marketing director possesses an almost uncanny ability to consistently earn profits for facilities or promoters. The quickest way to become a facility general manager or executive director is to showcase the talents and skills it takes to improve the bottom line. Moneymakers are few and far between, so proven producers will get noticed—and promoted.

Public Relations/Communications Director

A good **public relations (PR) or communications director** is essential for facilities as they deal with the media on a wide variety of issues. A talented PR or communications director can "spin" the news, good or bad, and position a facility in the best possible light. This is a very important skill to have when the media are banging on the door wanting to know why the arena's $2 million scoreboard just came crashing down on the ice, why attendance is down 20%, or why the box office is missing

$25,000 and the director has just left for a long trip out of the country. One of the primary goals for a facility's PR department is to forge solid working relationships with TV and radio news directors, newspaper editors, and reporters so that when bad news hits, the media report a balanced story. Good rapport with local media helps a great deal when seeking publicity for positive stories, and at times it can mean the difference between receiving front-page coverage or being buried next to the obituaries.

A typical day in the life of a facility PR director may include coordinating a live TV broadcast from the arena with the local sports anchor to publicize that evening's basketball game, writing a press release announcing that tickets are going on sale that weekend for a Katy Perry concert, discussing an upcoming Twitter campaign to promote an event, and arranging a publicity stunt for Bert and Ernie to visit the local children's hospital while they are in town for an upcoming Sesame Street Live tour. The most important attributes of a good PR director are a strong writing ability, a creative mind, and an ability to respond rationally while under pressure. Excellent training grounds for facility PR people are college and daily newspapers, TV stations, and internships in corporate PR departments.

Event Director

Events are the lifeblood for all types of facilities. Hundreds of events may be booked at a facility in the course of a year. With thousands of people in the venue at any given time, it is imperative that there be excellent crowd control and exceptional customer service at all times. The **event director** acts as the point person for

© Ken Inness/ShutterStock, Inc.

the facility during each show. Supervising a full staff of ushers, police officers, firefighters, emergency medical technicians, and private concert security staff, the event director manages the show from start to finish.

The event director must be able to think and react quickly to any problems arising during the event and must be able to deal with show promoters, angry customers, lost children, intoxicated patrons, and other situations calmly but forcefully. He or she must handle all this pressure while thousands of guests are in their seats enjoying the show. Being in charge of the safety and satisfaction of so many people is an immense responsibility, and for this reason the event director's position is not for everyone.

A typical day in the life of an event director might begin as early as 8:00 a.m. with six tractor-trailer trucks pulling up to the facility to begin the load-in for a major concert. The event director supervises and schedules traffic, parking, and security personnel to help ensure that the concert load-in runs as smoothly as possible. Later that day, he or she meets with the band road manager and reviews all security requirements for that evening's show. As the concert time draws near, the event director will meet with all ushers, police, and private security staff, giving instructions on how to handle that evening's event. During the concert, he or she will likely deal with customers, emergency situations, intoxicated patrons, and perhaps an altercation or two. By the end of the night, he or she will have been at the facility for 18 long hours.

Booking Director

Events in smaller facilities are booked by the general manager or executive director. In larger venues, however, there is usually a separate position devoted to booking events. This person works in tandem with the general manager or executive director to land as many events as

possible. This is an exciting career path involving much time spent talking on the telephone to agents and promoters and attending conventions to solicit events.

A facility **booking director** can land events in several different ways. Most concerts and Broadway shows are booked by dealing directly with agents who represent the acts or by negotiating with promoters who rent the facility and deal directly with agents on their own. The booking director may choose to rent the facility to a promoter, to co-promote an event, or to purchase the show directly from an agent. There are advantages and disadvantages associated with all three methods. Renting the facility to a promoter is a risk-free way to increase the number of events; however, it limits the amount of income a building may receive from an event. For some events with limited income potential or risky track records (e.g., conventions, trade shows), this method is the smartest way to do business. For potentially highly lucrative events (e.g., concerts, family shows, Broadway shows), partnering with a promoter in a share of the profits or purchasing the event directly from an agent may be the more profitable strategy—albeit also the one with the greatest risk to lose money if the show is not successful.

A typical day in the life of a booking director might begin at 8:00 a.m. with telephone calls to local radio program directors gauging the current popularity of a specific concert act. At 10:00 a.m. the constant phone calls back and forth with Broadway agents in New York begin as the booking director tries to fill up next year's Broadway lineup for the performing arts center. Lunch with a local concert promoter cutting a rental deal for an upcoming show will be followed by telephone tag the rest of the day with other agents and promoters. Negotiating contracts and getting them out in the mail completes a typical facility booking director's day.

Operations Director

Facility operations departments are the heart and soul of this industry. The **operations director** supervises facility preparation for all types of events. He or she typically spends the lion's share of a facility's annual expense budget on labor, maintaining and repairing all equipment and purchasing all the necessary supplies (e.g., toilet paper, cleaning materials) events require on a weekly basis.

Perhaps the most important part of an operations director's job is coordinating, scheduling, and supervising the numerous changeovers that constantly take place as one show moves in and another moves out. An operations director faces logistical problems daily because the facility may change over from hockey to basketball, then to a concert, and then to a Broadway show, all in one week. The job requires a mechanical knowledge of a facility's inner workings. A good operations director must be an expert on heating, ventilation, and air conditioning equipment, ice making, and structural issues, such as how many pounds of pressure can be rigged to the roof without it collapsing. An operations director must also possess superior people skills, because he or she is directly in charge of the majority of the facility's staff, including foremen, mechanics, laborers, stagehands, and the 50 to 500 part-time workers required to set up events and clean up after them.

A typical day in the life of an operations director likely begins early in the morning with a check of the previous night's changeover from basketball to hockey. Inspecting the overnight cleanup and the temperature and condition of the ice surface and discussing any problems with assistants will keep the operations director busy most of the morning. Then it will be time to plan ahead for next week when the circus rolls into town with 30 elephants, 14 tigers, and other assorted animals and equipment. The circus will take over the entire facility and two square blocks in the downtown business district for 6 days. Meetings with circus managers and city officials to plan for the event, as well as scheduling, will complete the day for the person with his or her hand constantly on the pulse of the facility operation.

Advertising, Sponsorship, and Signage Salesperson

Advertising and sponsorship revenue represent a significant total of a facility's annual revenue. Most facilities, depending on size, designate a staff person or an entire department to sell signage and event sponsorships to corporations. College graduates who perform well in high-pressure sales environments can make a substantial amount of money selling signage and sponsorships. This area offers good entry-level positions. Most facilities hire sales staff on a commission-only basis. Commissions can range from 5% to 20% depending on the size of the deal.

Salespeople must possess excellent interpersonal and presentation skills. They also must be able to handle plenty of rejection on a daily basis. For every 100 telephone calls a salesperson makes to corporations, an average of only 5 or 10 will result in actual business. Sales is a numbers game, and only strong, thick-skinned personalities are successful in such an environment. Successful salespeople generate money for themselves and the facility—and that will be noticed at the executive level. It is common for good salespeople to ultimately end up in the general manager's or executive director's chair.

A typical day in the life of an aggressive signage and sponsorship salesperson will include at least 25 cold calls to corporate decision-makers, two to four face-to-face sales presentations, and plenty of writing. A good salesperson must have strong writing skills because he or she must create outstanding sales proposals, follow up meetings with thank-you letters and to-do lists, and draft contracts once deals have been finalized.

Group Ticket Salesperson

Many college graduates begin their facility management careers in the group sales department. Entry-level opportunities are numerous because there is fairly high turnover. Group salespeople are primarily responsible for selling large blocks of tickets for various events to corporations, charity organizations, schools, Boy Scout and Girl Scout troops, and other parties. Group sales for certain types of shows (e.g., Sesame Street Live, Disney On Ice, the Ringling Brothers and Barnum & Bailey Circus, the Harlem Globetrotters, professional sport teams) contribute significantly to an event's success. Similar to the successful signage and sponsorship staff person, a good group salesperson is tenacious and excels on the telephone and in face-to-face presentations. Usually paid on a commission basis (typically 10% to 15%), group sales is also a numbers game. However, renewal business is usually strong, and solid personal relationships with key decision makers at area corporations, agencies, and other organizations can result in excellent sales year after year. A good group salesperson is an important asset to a facility.

Box Office Director

This facility position is responsible for the sale of all tickets to events as well as the collection of all ticket revenue. The facility box office is typically the first impression patrons have of the venue, making good customer service critical. The **box office director** must be a patient, understanding individual with a great mind for numbers. He or she must also have good supervisory skills. Within most venues, the box office is usually the second largest department, after operations. Made up of a combination of full- and part-time help, the box office personnel must be completely trustworthy, because millions of dollars

and thousands of credit card numbers flow through the department each year.

A typical day for a box office director begins at 9:00 a.m. On any given day, event tickets may be going on sale, and the telephones and lobby windows are generally extremely busy. Meetings with promoters to set up scaling of shows and filling ticket orders for advertisers and very important persons (VIPs) takes up a good portion of the day. Scheduling staff for all of the shows and daytime hours is also a time-consuming job. The box office director will be in his or her office for most of the day, but the real work begins when the event starts.

Dealing with customers who have lost their tickets, are unhappy with their seats, or have other concerns will occupy the box office director's time during the event. The box office will usually close halfway through the event so the staff can begin their paperwork. Counting all the money, preparing settlement documents for the promoter's review, and completing other tasks take up the rest of the evening. By the time all is said and done, the box office director will have worked 12 to 18 hours.

Current Issues

Security

The area of security was propelled to the highest level of importance for facility management after the terrorist attacks of September 11, 2001. Bag checks, pat downs, and metal detectors are now normal, regular functions in day-to-day operations. Large arenas and stadiums have placed barricades, posts, and fencing around the perimeters of facilities to create a "moat" effect to keep potential threats and terrorist activities away from crowds and buildings. Special attention is being given to the U.S. Homeland Security system of rating possible threats and to facility managers implementing procedures to safeguard patrons during events as well as the facility itself. Facility managers must evaluate every event for its security risk, taking into account the performer and crowd attendance profiles as well as the anticipated media coverage.

The National Center for Spectator Sports Safety and Security has put forth a tripartite approach to stadium and arena security. The formula involves video security surveillance combined with personnel training and implementing processes that balance safety with creating a positive experience for fans. This strategic stadium security plan protects stadiums and arenas from attack while providing a fan-friendly experience (Titch, 2010).

Large international events such as the Olympic Games have garnered worldwide attention because of security issues. Security costs for the Sydney Summer Games in 2000 were estimated at $176.9 million. These costs skyrocketed at the first–September 11 Summer Games, held in Athens, Greece in 2004, with organizers paying out approximately $1.5 billion for security (Epstein, 2012). Cost estimates for securing the Sochi Winter Games were $900 million and the London 2012 Summer Games ran to just over $1 billion (Lundy, 2014).

The best management tool for crowd management is a **crowd management plan**. This plan encompasses categorizing the type of event; knowing the surrounding facilities and environment, team or school rivalries, threats of violence, and the crowd size and seating configuration; using security personnel and ushers; and having an emergency plan.

In November 2004, an on-court fight during a Detroit Pistons–Indianapolis Pacers NBA game ended up spilling into the stands, involving members of the attending crowd as well. In response, then NBA Commissioner David Stern stated that the NBA would set new security guidelines for its arenas, an area previously left to individual teams to control ("League to Set," 2004). Shortly thereafter, the NBA issued arena guidelines that included policies dealing with

the deployment of security personnel, alcohol sales, and a new Fan Code of Conduct (NBA, 2005). The NCAA has also gotten involved with this issue by publishing a Crowd Control Global Check List/Tool Kit that institutions can use when they plan for and put in place crowd control policies (NCAA, 2006). Despite the NCAA's tool kit, worries abound as to whether colleges and universities are prepared in the event of an attack at one of its facilities. Because more than 48 million spectators attend NCAA football games in a given season, the issue is one that needs to be addressed to create risk management plans, training, and emergency services (Associated Press, 2007). Rules are also in place to deter fans from rushing the court after a big win. The SEC rule against court storming reads, "For the safety of participants and spectators alike, at no time before, during or after a contest shall spectators be permitted to enter the competition area." A $5,000 fine can be assessed to a school on a first offense; additional offenses can bring fines of up to $50,000 (Auerbach, 2013).

Sustainability

Public facilities, such as convention centers, stadiums, and arenas, consume more energy per square foot than any other retail industry (Jackson, 2008). As a result, the facility management industry is working to build green buildings, create "green management teams," reduce waste, cut energy usage and pollution, and implement recycling programs (Jenkins, 2007; Jackson, 2008). For facilities, it not only makes good environmental sense, it also makes good business sense. In the words of Scott Jenkins, vice president of Ballpark Operations at SAFECO Field, the Seattle Mariners stadium, "[g]oing green makes good financial sense in that it reduces operating expenses and builds a socially responsible brand. Besides, consumers and government are starting to demand that we operate in environmentally responsible ways" (Jenkins, 2007). Further, Jenkins shared that the team was able to save $250,000 by reducing the stadium's natural gas bill by 36% and electric bill by 18%, simply by paying attention to how the ballpark was operated and by investing in water controls, a $6,200 cost (Jenkins, 2007).

The Olympic and Paralympic Games require extensive facility construction and can also have an environmental impact. The London 2012 Olympic Stadium set new standards for sustainability. The stadium used recycled materials, including an unused gas pipe from a North Sea oil project. Approximately 40% of the concrete used was made of recycled aggregate. The London organizers (LOCOG) also saved energy by transporting materials to the site by boat or train. LOCOG analyzed the carbon footprint of the stadium and concluded that it had the lowest carbon footprint of any stadium ever built (IOC, 2013). The London Games were billed as the greenest Games on record (Singh, 2012). However, the same cannot be said for the 2014 Winter Olympic and Paralympic Games in Sochi, Russia, which were surrounded by reports of 1,500 unsanctioned waste dumps and encroachment into protected wildlife areas for construction of venues and transport (Luhn, 2014).

A gold standard today for facilities is **LEED certification**. LEED, which stands for Leadership in Energy and Environmental Design, helps facility operators identify green building design, construction, operation, and maintenance. LEED certification includes an examination of the following elements: sustainable site development, water savings, materials and atmosphere, energy efficiency, and indoor environmental quality (U.S. Green Building Council, 2014). Based on a point system, four levels of LEED certification are possible: platinum, gold, silver, and certified. MLB's Washington Nationals' Park was the first major sport stadium to be silver certified. The San Francisco 49ers new Levi's stadium became the first NFL certified

stadium when it opened in 2014. As of 2013, 25 North American professional sport facilities were LEED certified, including the American Airlines Arena and Soldier Field, in addition to Nationals' Park (Environmental Leader, 2013). Colleges and universities are slowly following suit, with the University of North Texas opening the first major college football stadium that is LEED certified.

Access for Persons with Disabilities

On July 26, 1990, President George H. W. Bush signed into law the **Americans with Disabilities Act (ADA)**. The intent of the ADA is to prevent discrimination against qualified people with disabilities in employment, public services, transportation, public accommodations, and telecommunications services According to Pate and Waller (2012):

> the ADA was adopted to prevent discrimination against persons with physical disabilities. Accessibility problems continue to exist despite ADA regulations, and they may be brought to light at athletic events when individuals with physical disabilities experience accessibility problems. Therefore, it is essential that athletic facility managers be knowledgeable of the ADA regulations and accessibility to address the needs of individuals with physical disabilities who attending sporting events. (p. 4)

The ADA defines an "individual with a disability" as a "person who has a physical or mental impairment that substantially limits one or more major life activities, who has a record of such an impairment, or who is regarded as having such an impairment" (Connecticut Department of Social Services, 2014). In 2011, the ADA was updated with a number of changes directly applicable to stadiums and arenas.

For example, ADA guidelines about tickets and seating include the following (Clifton & Lynett, 2014):

Accessible Seating

Covered entities must comply with the following requirements:

- 500 to 5,000 seats: Six wheelchair spaces and companion seats plus one additional wheelchair space for each additional 150 seats (or fraction thereof) between 501 through 5,000.
- More than 5,000 seats: At least 36 wheelchair spaces and companion seats plus one additional wheelchair space for each 200 seats (or fraction thereof) over 5,000.
- Premium seating standards: Each luxury box, club box and suite in an arena, stadium or grandstand is required to be wheelchair accessible and to contain wheelchair and companion seating.
- Sightlines: Significant new technical requirements for providing lines of sight over seated and standing spectators.

Ticket Sales

Tickets for disabled seating must be available for purchase during the same hours, stages, through the same methods of distribution, in the same types and numbers of ticketing sales outlets, and under the same terms and conditions as other tickets sold for the same event or series of events.

Other accessible features include concession areas, public telephones, restrooms, parking areas, drop-off and pick-up areas, entrances and exits, water coolers, visual alarms, and signs. Assisted-listening systems must also be provided when audible communications are integral to the use of the facility. The law requires that a facility adapt, but only to the extent that the reasonable accommodation does not cause an undue burden on the facility.

Universal Design

A new concept that extends the ADA and makes facilities more accessible for all people is **universal design**. A new arrival on the sport facility scene, the concept of universal design is best seen in places such as art galleries, museums, and airports. Facility design is essential for accessibility for all regardless of factors such as disability, age, or language spoken. The Institute for Human Centered Design (2014) in Boston suggests the following principles for universal design:

- *Equitable use:* The design does not disadvantage or stigmatize any group of users.
- *Flexibility in use:* The design accommodates a wide range of individual preferences and abilities.
- *Simple, intuitive use:* Use of the design is easy to understand, regardless of the user's experience, knowledge, language skills, or current concentration level.
- *Perceptible information:* The design communicates necessary information effectively to the user, regardless of ambient conditions or the user's sensory abilities.
- *Tolerance for error:* The design minimizes hazards and the adverse consequences of accidental or unintended actions.
- *Low physical effort:* The design can be used efficiently and comfortably, and with a minimum of fatigue.
- *Size and space for approach and use:* Appropriate size and space is provided for approach, reach, manipulation, and use, regardless of the user's body size, posture, or mobility.

When placed in the context of access to stadiums or arenas, these principles provide guidance for facility managers who wish to enhance the in-house experience for all customers. Universal design takes the ADA one step further and looks to enhance the total customer experience at a sport facility. Sport managers who incorporate universal design into their stadiums and arenas will be ahead of the curve in terms of the customer service experience they provide.

Case Study 12-1   The Booking Process in a University Venue

The Mullins Center is a 10,000-seat multipurpose facility with an attached ice rink located on the campus of the University of Massachusetts in Amherst, Massachusetts. The Mullins Center is managed for the University of Massachusetts by Global Spectrum. As part of the management contract, the general manager for the Mullins Center is responsible for the booking of the main facility and the attached practice rink. The Mullins Center has three tenant teams: the university's men's hockey, women's basketball, and men's basketball teams.

The campus and surrounding five-college area have up to 30,000 students from September to May. During that time frame, the Mullins Center is busy hosting athletic events and entertainment programs. In order to be successful, the general manager utilizes several different setups and capacities in order to provide the university and the community with entertaining programs. Concert seating capacities are set at a 7,200, 8,500, or 9,000 seats. Comedy or theater programs are set at 1,700 to 3,500 seats. Basketball events are set at 9,400 seats. Hockey or ice show events have 8,400 seats. Using this information and the topics discussed in the chapter, please answer the following questions.

Questions for Discussion

1. As the general manager of the Mullins Center, what specific genre of entertainment do you think would do well in this venue, taking into account the demographics, available time frames, and seating capacities?

2. Identify a group, act, team, or entertainer that will be touring with available dates to play the Mullins Center and specify who will be acting as the promoter for the event.

3. Assume that the act will cost $75,000 and the venue will be rented for an all-inclusive package of $35,000. Provide ticket prices that will appeal to the target demographic market in a spreadsheet that reflects the total costs and the balance according to estimated ticket sales.

4. Explain the impact of ancillary revenue on the event, including the potential role food and beverage, ticket fees, and parking play when negotiating a deal with a promoter.

5. Provide an event recap and explain why you did or did not book this event at the Mullins Center, noting why it would have been successful or unsuccessful.

Summary

Public assembly facilities provide a site for people to congregate for entertainment, social, and business purposes. The many types of facilities range from stadiums and arenas to convention centers and theaters. The key challenges facing facilities are financing new facilities or renovations, retaining the revenue generated by the facility, preparing fully integrated security programs, retaining tenants, and addressing the ADA. Facility management provides a career field that is fast-paced and exciting, though filled with long hours and, at times, pressure and stress.

Resources

AEG Corporate Headquarters
800 West Olympic Blvd., Suite 305
Los Angeles, CA 90015
213-763-7700
http://www.aegworldwide.com

ARAMARK Corporation
1101 Market Street
Philadelphia, PA 19107
215-238-3000
http://www.aramark.com

European Association of Event Centers (EVVC)
Eschersheimer Landstraße 23
D-60322 Frankfurt am Main
Germany
49 (0) 69/915-096-98-0
http://www.evvc.org

Global Spectrum
3601 South Broad Street
Philadelphia, PA 19148
215-389-9587
http://www.global-spectrum.com

International Association of Venue Managers (IAVM)
635 Fritz Drive, Suite 100
Coppell, Texas 75019
972-906-7441
http://www.iavm.org

International Association of Convention Centres (AIPC)
Marianne de Raay 1060
Brussels, Belgium
[32](496) 235327
http://www.aipc.org

SMG
300 Conshohocken State Road, Suite 450
West Conshohocken, PA 19428
(610) 729-7900
http://www.smgworld.com

Stadium Managers Association
525 SW 5th Street, Suite A
Des Moines, IA 50309
515-282-8192
http://www.stadiummanagers.org

Venue Management Association Limited
30-34 Gladstone Road, Suite 1
Highgate Hill
QLD 4101 Australia
61-0-7-3870-4777
http://www.vma.org.au

Key Terms

Americans with Disabilities Act (ADA), ancillary revenue, arenas, bonds, booking director, box office director, concerts, convention centers, convocations, crowd management plan, event director, family events, International Association of Venue Managers (IAVM), LEED certification, local/civic venues, marketing director, marketing fund, metropolitan facilities, operations director, public relations (PR) or communications director, religious events, seasonal events, soccer-specific stadium (SSS), sports events, stadium, theaters, ticket rebate, trade shows, universal design, university venues

References

Ammon, R.A., Southall, R.M., & Nagel, M.S. (2010). *Sport facility management* (2nd ed.). Morgantown, WV: Fitness Information Technology.

Associated Press. (2007, December 26). Stadium security a concern at colleges. *New York Times*. Retrieved from http://www.nytimes.com/2007/12/26/sports/ncaafootball/26stadiums.html

Auerbach, N. (2013, February 7). The forecast for college basketball: Storming the court. *USA Today*. Retrieved from http://www.usatoday.com/story/sports/ncaab/2013/02/05/storming-rushing-the-court-college-basketball/1890851/

Bagli, C. (2008, November 4). As stadiums rise, so do costs to taxpayers. *New York Times*. Retrieved from http://www.nytimes.com/2008/11/05/nyregion/05stadiums.html?_r=1

Bradley, B. (2013, August 21). Minnesota using tobacco tax to pay off debt on new Vikings stadium. Retrieved from http://nextcity.org/equityfactor/entry/minnesota-using-tobacco-tax-to-pay-off-debt-on-vikings-new-stadium

Burke, D. (1997). The stop tax-exempt arena debt issuance act. *Journal of Legislation, 23*(1), 149–157.

Clifton, G. E., & Lynett, J. J. (2014). Top ten ADA regulatory changes. Retrieved from https://www.acc.com/legalresources/publications/topten/ADA-Title-III-Changes.cfm

Connecticut Department of Social Services. (2014). DSS: ADA—Americans with Disabilities Act. Retrieved from http://www.ct.gov/dss/cwp/view.asp?a=2349&q=304658

Crompton, J. L. (2004). Beyond economic impact: An alternative rationale for the public subsidy of major league sports facilities. *Journal of Sport Management, 18*(1), 41.

Crompton, J. L., Howard, D. R., & Var, T. (2003). Financing major league facilities: Status, evolution, and conflicting forces. *Journal of Sport Management, 17*(2), 156–184.

Demause, N. (2011, Aug. 5). The nation: Stop the subsidy-sucking sound. *NPR*. Retrieved from http://www.npr.org/2011/08/05/139018592/the-nation-stop-the-subsidy-sucking-sports-stadiums

Environmental Leader. (2013). USBGC, Green Sports Alliance, team up for LEED certified stadiums. Retrieved from http://www.environmentalleader.com/2013/08/22/usgbc-green-sports-alliance-team-up-for-leed-certified-stadiums/

Epstein, D. (2011, September 9). Olympic Games after 11 September: More expensive, less patriotic. *Sports Illustrated*. Retrieved from http://sportsillustrated.cnn.com/2011/writers/david_epstein/09/08/olympics.after.september.11/

Farmer, P., Mulrooney, A., & Ammon, R. Jr. (1996). *Sport facility planning and management*. Morgantown, WV: Fitness Information Technology.

Fried, G. (2010). *Managing sport facilities*. Champaign, IL: Human Kinetics.

Greenberg, M. J., & Gray, J. T. (1993, April/May). The stadium game. *For the Record*, 2–3.

Howard, D. R., & Crompton, J. L. (1995). *Financing sport*. Morgantown, WV: Fitness Information Technology.

Institute for Human Centered Design. (2014). Principles of universal design. Retrieved from http://www.adaptenv.org/universal-design/principles-universal-design

International Olympic Committee (IOC). (2013). Flexible and sustainable London's Olympic Stadium sets new standards. Retrieved from http://www.olympic.org/news/flexible-and-sustainable-london-s-olympic-stadium-sets-new-standards/170181

Jackson, A. (2008). Sustainability baby steps. *Facility manager*. Retrieved from https://www.iaam.org/Facility_manager/Pages/2008_Feb_Mar/BusinessFinance.htm

Jacobson, G., Robinson-Jacobs, K., & Moore, D. (2013). Cowboys-AT&T Stadium deal pioneers new revenue source for big-time sports. *Dallas Morning News*. Retrieved from http://www.dallasnews.com/business/headlines/20130725-cowboys-att-stadium-deal-pioneers-a-new-source-of-revenue-for-big-time-sports.ece

Jenkins, S. (2007). Going green makes good business. *Facility manager*. Retrieved from https://www.iaam.org/Facility_manager/Pages/2007_Dec_Jan/Stadiums.HTM

Jensen, S. A. (2000). Financing professional sports facilities with federal tax subsidies: Is it sound tax policy? *Marquette Sports Law Review, 10*(2), 425–460.

Kaplan, D. (1999, February 22). Rating agency backs private arena bonds. *Sports Business Journal*. Retrieved from http://m.sportsbusinessdaily.com/Journal/Issues/1999/02/19990222/No-Topic-Name/Rating-Agency-Backs-Private-Arena-Bonds.aspx

Kuriloff, A., & Preston, D. (2012, September 5). In stadium building spree, U.S. taxpayers lose $4 Billion. *Bloomberg News*. Retrieved from http://www.bloomberg.com/news/2012-09-05/in-stadium-building-spree-u-s-taxpayers-lose-4-billion.html

League to set new security guidelines. (2004, December 1). *Indianapolis Star*. Retrieved from http://www2.indystar.com/articles/3/198833-9753-245.html

Luhn, A. (2014, January 22). The hidden environmental and human costs of the Sochi Olympics. *The Nation*. Retrieved from http://www.thenation.com/article/178051/hidden-environmental-and-human-costs-sochi-olympics#

Lundy, M. (2014, February 7). Why the Sochi Olympics are the most expensive games ever.

Yahoo Sports. Retrieved from ca.sports.yahoo.com/blogs.en-game/why-Sochi-hosting-most-expensive-loympics-ever-133051945.html

National Basketball Association (NBA). (2005, February 17). NBA establishes revised arena guidelines for all NBA arenas. Retrieved from http://www.nba.com/news/arena_guidelines_050217.html

National Collegiate Athletic Association (NCAA). (2006, June 8). Crowd control global check list/tool kit. Retrieved from http://www.ncaa.org/sportsmanship/crowd_control_checklist.pdf

NBA Media Ventures. (2014). Timberwolves, Lynx to open new practice facility. Retrieved from http://www.nba.com/2014/news/02/04/timberwolves-practice-facility.ap/

Noll, R. G., & Zimbalist, A. (1997). "Build the stadium—Create the jobs!" In R. G. Noll and A. Zimbalist (Eds.), *Sports, jobs, and taxes: The economic impact of sports teams and stadiums* (pp. 1–54). Washington, DC: Brookings Institution Press.

Pate, J. R, & Waller, S. N. (2012). Measuring athletic facility managers' knowledge of access and the Americans with Disabilities Act: A pilot study. *International Journal of Sport Management, Recreation, and Tourism. 9*, 1–22.

Reed, W. (2014). Cities pressured to subsidize sports stadiums. Retrieved from http://atlantadailyworld.com/2014/01/01/cities-pressured-to-subsidize-sports-stadiums/

Russo, F. E., Esckilsen, L. A., & Stewart, R. J. (2009). *Public assembly facility management: Principles and practices* (2nd ed.). Coppell, TX: International Association of Assembly Managers.

Samuelson, P. A., & Nordhaus, W. D. (1985). *Economics*. New York: McGraw-Hill.

Sawyer, T. (2006). Financing facilities 101. *Journal of Physical Education, Recreation & Dance, 77*(4), 23–28.

Singh, T. (2012, August 14). The London 2012 Summer Games were the greenest Olympics ever. Inhabitat. Retrieved from http://inhabitat.com/the-london-2012-summer-games-were-the-greenest-olympics-ever/

Titch, S. (2010, October 8). Convergence adds new dimension to stadium security. *Security squared*. Retrieved from http://www.experteditorial.net/securitysquared/2010/10/convergence-adds-new-dimension-to-stadium-security.html

Top 10 stadium, arena naming rights deals. (2014). *San Francisco Business Times*. Retrieved from http://www.bizjournals.com/sanfrancisco/blog/2013/05/stadium-naming-rights-deals-49ers-levis.html?s=image_gallery

U.S. Green Building Council. (2014). About LEED. Retrieved from http://www.usgbc.org/articles/about-leed

Chapter

13

Carol A. Barr

Event Management

Learning Objectives

Upon completion of this chapter, students should be able to:

1. Describe the emergence and history of the sport event management industry.

2. Identify the various roles of sport management/marketing agencies such as client representation and marketing, event development, event management, television production, sponsorship solicitation, hospitality services, grassroots programming, market research, and financial planning.

3. Differentiate between full-service, specialized, and in-house sport management/marketing agencies.

4. Analyze critical event management functions including budgeting, risk management, operations, registration, volunteer management, and event marketing.

5. Recognize that when multiple agencies work together to produce a sporting event, coordination and cooperation between agencies is critical to the event's success.

6. Appraise the career opportunities available in the event management industry and understand the skills necessary to succeed in each of them.

7. Critically evaluate current issues of interest in the field of event management such as the heightened awareness of event security and the growth of niche sports.

Introduction

A local Young Men's Christian Association (YMCA) basketball game, the State Junior Golf Championship, and the Super Bowl are all examples of events that are managed. They all also share one common element: the need for educated and trained managers and marketers to ensure success. Further, the critical event management functions are quite similar, although different in scope, whether the event is small (e.g., a local 5K road race) or large (e.g., Major League Baseball's All-Star Game). For the purposes of this chapter, we define sport event management as all functions related to the planning, implementation, and evaluation of a sport event.

This chapter presents an overview of the event management segment of the sport industry. First, the historical evolution of event management is discussed. Then, because many large and small events are managed and marketed by sport management/marketing agencies, the types and roles played by these unique sport organizations are explored. Successful event management requires the appropriate application of all the management functions, thus this chapter reviews finance/budgeting, risk management, tournament operations, registration, volunteer management, and event marketing within the context of event management. The next-to-last section explores career opportunities in event management, including information on educational backgrounds appropriate for those in sport event management. Finally, current issues surrounding the management of events are discussed.

History

Although even the earliest documented sport event probably required management, it was not until the late 1800s that the focus turned to the professional aspects of managing sport events. A desire to increase profits was the catalyst for such an emphasis. Following his retirement as a professional baseball player in the 1870s, Albert Spalding organized tours throughout North America to promote baseball to create a larger market for his products. Spalding's tours were an early example of what were called **barnstorming tours**. The touring of star athletes and teams to promote the popularity of a particular sport soon became exercises in event management. George Halas, longtime owner of the Chicago Bears, used his star player, Red Grange, to increase the popularity of professional football in the early 1900s (Schaaf, 1995). Professional boxing also provided a platform for professional event management. With the stakes of boxing events reaching more than $1 million by the turn of the twentieth century, boxing event promoters were forced to attend to the business aspects of managing such events.

Just as the need for a business focus prompted the creation of the sport management discipline, so, too, profit motives spurred the creation of professional event managers in the 1960s and 1970s. The growth of sport event management led to the emergence of multifaceted companies called **sport management/marketing agencies**. A **sport management/marketing agency** is defined as a business that acts on behalf of a sport property. A **sport property** can be a person, company, event, team, or place. Sport management/marketing agencies were initially established to represent the legal and marketing interests of athletes. International Management Group (now known as IMG), for example, was founded in 1960 by Mark McCormack to locate endorsement opportunities for professional golfer Arnold Palmer. As the sport industry evolved, agencies expanded to incorporate a myriad of functions beyond representing athletes. For example, as IMG signed more athletes as clients, its business soon expanded to include managing and promoting events in which its athletes competed. Agencies capitalized on the concurrent growth of and public's interest in televised sporting events to rapidly increase the revenues generated through events of all sizes. Agencies also started to create their own made-for-TV events (content creation) that they both owned and managed. Today, hundreds of sport management/marketing agencies are intricately involved with the creation and promotion of most events. A number of these agencies have also expanded beyond sporting events to other entertainment or charitable types of events, such as IMG has done with its entertainment division. The sport event management industry has also evolved with its very own industry conference. The Eighth International Sports Event Management Conference took place in London, bringing together sport industry professionals, international and national federations, and representatives of local and national governments who are involved in the planning and delivery of sports events (Eighth International Sports Event Management Conference, 2013).

Sport Management/ Marketing Agency Functions

Table 13-1 provides a list of the various roles sport management/marketing agencies play. It should be noted that although some agencies

Table 13-1 Sport Management/ Marketing Agencies' Roles

Client representation
Client marketing
Event development
Event management
Television production
Sponsorship solicitation
Hospitality services
Grassroots programs
Market research
Financial planning

perform all of the functions on this list, many of these sport agencies may specialize in only one or a few of these functions. The first function listed in Table 13-1, client representation, refers to acting on behalf of a client in contract negotiations. Contract negotiations can take place with any type of sport property, such as a franchise, an event, the media, or a licensee. The function of client marketing is closely related to client representation. Marketing includes locating appropriate endorsement opportunities, booking personal appearances, and developing entertainment extensions. For example, golfer Tiger Woods' career earnings since turning pro in 1996 are just over $100 million, whereas his total career income, including endorsement and licensing deals is more than $1 billion (Kelley, 2012).

In addition to representing the interests of individuals, agencies are involved in event development and management. Given the increased number of outlets for events, such as satellite and digital television and the Internet, a variety of events have been created to provide programming. The X Games (summer and winter), for example, are a direct result of the growth in sports television. ESPN created the X Games to provide programming and elects to manage the six X Games in-house. (The term *in-house* refers to producing a product or service within the organization.) Alliance of Action Sports (Alli) is an organization that "brings together the best sports properties, athletes, and brands globally for the fans of action sports" and is involved in properties such as the Dew Tour, the Lucas Oil Pro Motocross, the Octane Academy, the Red Bull Signature Series, and the World of Adventure Sports (Alli Sports, 2013).

A majority of sport agencies play a role in soliciting corporate sponsorships. With 2012 corporate sponsorship spending at $18.91 billion in North America and $51.1 billion worldwide (IEG, 2013), a viable market has been created for organizations skilled in identifying and acquiring sponsors. Likewise, corporations often hire sport management/marketing agencies to locate and negotiate sponsorship agreements with teams and events whose fans match their target markets. In each of these cases, the sport agency is paid a set percentage of the sponsorship fee. It should be noted, though, that the economic recession caused the dollar amount being spent on sponsorship to decrease in 2009 for the first time, although the market has subsequently rebounded. To facilitate matching corporations with sport properties, Team Marketing Report publishes the annual *Sports Sponsor FactBook*. This publication lists and provides detailed information on the activities of sport sponsors, advertisers, facility naming rights, and promotional sponsors (Team Marketing Report, 2010).

© Eric Limon/ShutterStock, Inc.

Another function of sport management/marketing agencies is to develop and market **grassroots programs**. These programs are created by organizations attempting to target individuals at the most basic level of involvement, sport participation. A number of professional sport leagues are involved in grassroots programming, including the National Football League (NFL) Punt, Pass, & Kick national skills competition; the NFL Flag Football league (NFL, 2013); and the Urban Youth Academy program of Major League Baseball (MLB) (MLB, 2013). In addition, the National Hockey League (NHL) has joined in a partnership with the North American Roller Hockey Championships (NARCh) (NHL, 2013a), and the National Basketball Association sponsors the NBA FIT program (NBA, 2013).

Although one result of the growth in televised sports has been the creation of new events, another impact has been increasing demand for television production and development work. Potential revenue streams from television have led to the creation of television production divisions within some of the larger agencies. For example, IMG Media is the world's largest independent producer and distributor of sports programming (IMG, 2013). IMG distributes more than 300 events and thousands of hours of live and finished programming each year.

Sport organizations require market research to evaluate the success of events and initiatives. By implementing mail surveys, focus groups, on-site surveys, and sponsorship/economic impact surveys, sport management/marketing agencies assist sport properties in documenting the relative success or failure of programs and pinpointing areas that need improvement. Market research is particularly crucial for corporations wanting to know the impact of their sponsorship activities. This function is usually handled by sport marketing agencies that specialize in market research. For example, IFM Sports Marketing Surveys provides sport market research to clients, including sponsorship evaluations, economic impact studies, return on investment modeling, retail and consumer behavior, and attitude surveys, among others (Sports Marketing Surveys, 2010).

Types of Sport Management/ Marketing Agencies

Sport management/marketing agencies vary widely in terms of numbers of employees, revenue generation, scope of services provided, and types of target clients. Sport agencies can be categorized as full-service agencies, specialized agencies, or in-house agencies. These types of agencies are briefly described in this section.

© Ryan McVay/Photodisc/Thinkstock

Full-Service Agencies

Full-service agencies perform the complete set of agency functions discussed in the previous section. Although a number of firms fall into this category, the largest are IMG and Octagon. IMG, for example, has

3,500 employees in 30 countries throughout the world (IMG, 2013). With operating divisions for athlete management services, event management services, licensing, broadcasting (both production and negotiation), Internet consulting, and marketing and consulting services, this firm covers the entire gamut of sport event and athlete functions. IMG's clients include athletes such as Peyton Manning (football), Venus Williams (tennis), and Luke Donald (golf). Octagon, by contrast, has more than 800 employees globally in 68 offices across 22 countries (Octagon, 2013).

Specialized Agencies

Specialized agencies limit either the scope of services performed or the type of clients serviced. For example, Redmandarin is a London-based sport marketing agency that focuses on advising corporations on how to maximize their involvement with sponsorship opportunities. Redmandarin takes pride in the fact that it helps provide support at all stages of the sponsorship life cycle, from strategy development through campaign planning and execution (Redmandarin, 2013).

In-House Agencies

A trend to be discussed later is the formation within major corporations of separate departments or divisions dealing with event management, typically called **in-house agencies**. For example, MasterCard Worldwide has a department solely dedicated to identifying sponsorship opportunities, creating activation programs, and overseeing the implementation of the sponsorship. These in-house agencies exist to coordinate the sponsorship function across the various divisions of the company.

Critical Event Management Functions

Regardless of the size of the event or the responsible agency, nearly all events must attend to a variety of critical functions. These functions include the following:

- Finance/budgeting
- Risk management
- Tournament operations
- Registration
- Volunteer management
- Event marketing

The remainder of this section examines these six functions in depth.

Finance/Budgeting

The complexity of managing events, coupled with the need to constantly monitor financial conditions, places the functions of budgeting and finance at the forefront of successful sport event management. **Budgeting** is the process of developing a written plan of revenues and expenses for a particular accounting cycle. For events, an *accounting cycle* is usually the time period necessary to plan, organize, and operate the upcoming event. This cycle can be as short as a month or, in the case of an organization such as the United States Olympic Committee (USOC), budgeting can attempt to predict revenues and expenses for the following 4 years of activity.

Although there are a number of different types of budgets and budgeting processes, two that are particularly important for events are zero-base budgeting and cash-flow budgeting. **Zero-base budgeting** requires a review of all activities and related costs of an event as if it were taking place for the first time. Previous budgets and actual revenues and expenses are ignored. All projected revenues and expenses have to be justified prior to becoming part of the overall budget. This type of budget process forces managers to view their event from a fresh perspective, never taking elements for granted and always searching for ways to become more efficient and effective. **Cash-flow budgeting** refers to accounting for the receipt and timing

of all sources and expenditures of cash. Cash-flow budgeting informs the manager of the cash amount needed to pay expenses at predetermined times throughout the accounting cycle. Events often expend sizable amounts of cash during the planning and organizing phases, while only receiving cash just prior to the actual execution of the event; therefore, planning carefully to avoid cash shortfalls is critical.

Risk Management

According to Prairie and Garfield (2004), **risk management** is defined as "the function or process by which [an organization] identifies and manages the risks of liability that rise from its activities" (p. 13). Usually this refers to personal injury risk management, although the sport event manager should broaden this definition to also include financial loss, equipment or property damage, loss of goodwill (customers becoming unhappy based on their experience), and loss of market share, to name a few.

Thus, risk management is broader than just protecting one's organization from a lawsuit. It essentially encompasses protecting the organization from anything that could possibly go wrong and lead to a loss of revenue or customers.

A common tool used by events to reduce the potential for a lawsuit from a participant or volunteer is the *waiver and release of liability*. This is a form signed by participants and volunteers that releases the venue and event organizers from a negligence action in case of accident or injury. If the participant is a minor, the signature of a parent is suggested. The validity of a waiver is determined by the law in each state; therefore, the best practice for event organizers to follow is to consult with an attorney to determine whether waivers are recognized in a particular state and, if so, what important phrases and description of activities need to be included within the waiver. Event organizers must remember that a waiver or release of liability does not exonerate them from all responsibility and liability regarding the event.

Waivers and releases of liability can only be used to waive or release a defendant from negligence claims. Event organizers are still responsible for running an event in a responsible, safe manner or they may be found liable for any injuries or problems that may occur.

Another approach necessary when handling risk factors associated with an event is to purchase insurance. Insurance can be purchased not only to cover safety concerns, but also to provide security to an event regarding potential financial losses as well as to cover buildings or other structures/contents involved in the event. For example, an outdoor event that collects sponsorship dollars and registration fees from participants in advance may need to refund a portion, if not all, of this revenue if the event is cancelled due to inclement weather. The event organizers, though, still incurred expenses in getting ready to host the event. Purchasing cancellation insurance can help to offset some of these expenses. Most venues require that the promoter, sponsor, or organizer of the event maintain a minimum level of insurance. The premiums for these types of insurance are based on the level of risk.

Risk management and insurance are of primary importance to event organizers and should never be overlooked when running an event. Appropriate advance planning in these areas can help alleviate problems when the event actually takes place. In addition, event organizers should realize the importance of addressing risk management and insurance concerns surrounding an event to limit the legal liability of the event.

Tournament Operations

Tournament operations can be described as the nuts and bolts of an event. The tournament operations staff stage the event, meet facility and equipment needs, and provide any operational items for the event. Tournament operations can be divided into pre-event, actual event, and postevent activities.

Pre-event tournament operations require appropriate planning and information collection to ensure that all aspects and details surrounding the actual event are identified. Depending on the size and scope of the event, pre-event tournament operations planning may start 4 months prior to an event, as is common for local events such as bike races or basketball tournaments, or 8 to 10 years prior to an event, as is common with large events such as the Olympic Games. During the pre-event planning stages, it is important for the tournament operations staff to be clear as to the type of event being planned and the event's goals. This information is critical in determining how the tournament will be organized and run—components central to the responsibilities and concerns of the tournament operations staff.

Items that should be addressed in the pre-event planning stages include the following:

- Venue plan and layout
- Equipment and facility needs
- Schedule of activities
- Sponsorship needs
- Signage commitments and locations
- Food and beverages
- Merchandise sales
- Media concerns

© Lowe R. Llaguno/ShutterStock, Inc.

- Promotional activities and needs
- Transportation concerns
- Housing of athletes
- Staff communication
- Personnel responsibilities
- Lines of authority
- Security issues
- Americans with Disabilities Act requirements
- Policies to address other legal concerns such as alcohol use
- Crowd control

This list is not all-inclusive, because the items handled by the tournament operations staff will vary depending on the type, goals, size, and scope of the event.

During the actual event, the tournament operations staff are responsible for ensuring that the event takes place as planned. This includes attending to the activities and needs relating to participants, sponsors, and spectators. To help in this area, many events utilize a script of activities. The **script** is a specific, detailed, minute-by-minute (or even second-by-second) schedule of activities throughout the day, including information on the tournament operations responsibilities for each activity. This script provides information relative to (1) the time of day and what is taking place, (2) the operational needs (equipment and setup) surrounding each activity, and (3) the event person(s) in charge of the various activities. During the actual event, the tournament operations staff implement the tournament script while also troubleshooting as needed. Advance preparation and planning can certainly assist in running an event, but the tournament operations staff must also be prepared to troubleshoot and to be flexible and adaptable to change when an unforeseen problem arises.

The post-event stage consists of the activities surrounding the completion of an event. Areas covered during the post-event stage include the following:

- Tear-down of the venue
- Storage of equipment and supplies
- Trash pickup and disposal
- Return of borrowed equipment, sponsorship signage, and other items
- Final financial accounting regarding expenses relative to the operations portion of the event
- Thank-you notes sent to appropriate constituencies who assisted in the tournament operations area

It is important for the tournament operations staff to realize that the completion of the actual event does not signal the end of their responsibilities. Numerous items such as those just listed still need to be addressed before the event is wrapped up.

Registration

Registering participants for an event is of the utmost importance because this is the first time event staff members come into contact with participants. An efficient **registration system** is crucial for making a good first impression on the event's clientele. Appropriate advance planning and attention to information needed from participants guide the development of a registration system that is appropriate for the event and convenient for participants.

In developing a registration system, event managers must consider the following:

- Number of participants who will be registering
- Information that needs to be collected from or disseminated to the participants (e.g., waiver forms, codes for sportsmanship conduct, inclement weather policy, event schedule)
- Registration fees that must be collected
- Whether identification is needed (e.g., regarding age limitations)

- Whether information will be collected manually or via a computer system
- Whether the event involves minors, who require the signature of a parent or guardian on a waiver form

This list is not all-inclusive, because the event will dictate the items that need to be covered during the registration process.

Different systems can be used to accommodate the participants and alleviate congestion during the registration process while still collecting or disseminating appropriate information. Examples of such registration systems include using a staggered schedule that provides times when certain divisions of participants for an event should register or using different registration sites for different categories of participation. Note that it is important to create or establish security measures if registration fees are being collected.

The registration process for numerous sporting events has evolved to incorporate online registration processes. Also, an increasing number of sport events are choosing to outsource their registration process instead of developing and servicing an online platform themselves. One of the more successful online registration and database management companies is Active Network, which hosts Active.com, an online event search and registration website. Active Network works with over 55,000 organizations worldwide (Active Network, 2013).

Volunteer Management

The importance of volunteers to an event cannot be emphasized enough. Most events cannot be successfully executed without volunteers. This is a good opportunity for sport management students looking to gain experience. You should always be able to find an event in your area that is in need of a volunteer. Events from the smallest local bike race to those as large and complex as the Olympic Games rely on volunteer help.

Volunteer management staff supervise the volunteers involved with an event. **Volunteer management** can be divided into two areas: (1) working with event organizers and staff to determine the areas in which volunteers are needed and the quantity needed and (2) soliciting, training, and managing the volunteers. Once again, advance planning and preparation are critical in determining how many volunteers are needed and in what capacities they will serve. The volunteer management staff must communicate with every division or area within an event to determine its volunteer needs. Information must include the number of volunteers a particular area may need, qualifications of volunteers, and the type of work to be performed. This information is important when scheduling volunteers because the volunteer management staff would not want to assign a volunteer to work moving heavy equipment, for example, if the volunteer were not physically capable.

Once the volunteer management staff have calculated or estimated the number of and areas of work where volunteers are needed, the staff can make sure that recruitment efforts are appropriate to solicit that number of volunteers. Volunteer recruitment should begin well in advance of the event to ensure that the appropriate number of volunteers are recruited. In addition, the volunteer management staff should be aware of the method in which volunteers are being recruited. (For example, if adult volunteers are needed, the recruitment efforts obviously should not be aimed at area middle schools.)

After the recruitment of volunteers takes place, appropriate training sessions must be held. Training sessions typically include several components, starting with a general information session and progressing to more specialized direction on how to manage the specific responsibilities in each of the individual event departments. Items covered in the basic educational component training session may include how the volunteers should dress or obtain their volunteer uniforms, how they can obtain food and beverages during the event, and how the communication system will be used so they know whom to contact in case of a problem; in addition, all volunteers should be trained concerning risk management and the procedures they should follow in case of an injury or accident. Specific department training may include a description of volunteer duties, how to carry out these duties, when and where volunteers should check in, the name of their direct supervisor, and any other information specific to the volunteer work they will be performing. For example, for a professional golf tournament, people working in the box office would be trained in the printing of passes and the handling of money, whereas people working at each of the holes would be trained on how to create space for the golfers and how to quiet the crowds when the golfers are ready to take their shots.

Event organizers must also understand the importance of volunteers to the continual operation and success of an event. It is important for the volunteer management staff and event organizers to make sure certain things are done to keep the volunteers happy so they will keep coming back year after year. First, volunteers should not be scheduled into too many time slots so they do not become tired. The schedule should also include appropriate food and bathroom breaks. Second, volunteers need to be recognizable to participants and spectators. Uniforms can help the volunteers be more recognizable while increasing the professional perception of the event. Additionally, uniforms help build goodwill with volunteers in that they are the only ones able to wear the special volunteer uniform. Finally, volunteers need to be recognized for their assistance and contribution to the event. This can be done in a number of different ways, including constant recognition during the event, holding a volunteer party

after the event is over, and running volunteer raffles in which the volunteers have a chance to win prizes or receive some benefits in exchange for volunteering.

Event Marketing

Sport and special events cannot be successful without carefully planned **event marketing** programs. There are nine areas on which event marketers must focus:

- Sales of corporate sponsorship
- Advertising efforts
- Public relations activities
- Hospitality
- Ticket sales
- Broadcasting
- Website development and management
- Licensing/merchandising
- Fundraising

These nine areas are intricately linked. Efforts toward soliciting corporate sponsors will affect advertising strategies, and broadcasting agreements will influence ticket sales. Because these areas are so interrelated, the event marketer must employ an integrated marketing approach. **Integrated marketing** entails long-term strategic planning to manage functions in a consistent manner. For example, ticket sales strategies should be formulated considering the potential sales promotion efforts of sponsors. Similarly, tickets and/or registration should be possible on the website. With this in mind, each of the nine event marketing areas will now be explored.

Corporate Sponsorship

As already discussed in this chapter, the number of events has grown significantly in recent years. With this growth, the competition for sponsors (and other marketing revenues such as ticket sales) has increased. At the same time, events have become increasingly reliant on sponsorship. This is true of small events as well as large events. The 10 biggest sponsors of events and sports in the world are presented in Table 13-2.

Typically, corporate sponsorships are either sold by the event (in-house) or by an outside sport marketing agency. Sport marketing agencies are hired by a sport property because the property does not have sufficient personnel or expertise in selling sponsorships. In the early 1980s, the International Olympic Committee (IOC) decided the Games were becoming too reliant on broadcasting fees for funding. In response, it decided to sell worldwide sponsorships for the Olympic Games. However, it did not have the expertise or personnel to approach global companies asking for multimillion-dollar sponsorship commitments. Therefore, in 1983 the IOC turned to ISL Marketing, which raised $100 million for the 1988 Olympic Games (Simson & Jennings, 1992). In an effort to generate more revenue and garner more control over sponsorship sales, the IOC partnered with Chris Welton and Laurent Scharapan to form the sport marketing agency Meridian in 1997 (Woodward, 2003). Meridian was responsible for finding and servicing IOC sponsors. In 2003, the IOC brought its sponsorship effort completely in-house when it purchased the Meridian Agency. This move allows the IOC to earn more money from its sponsorship sales because it no longer has to pay fees to an outside agency (Woodward, 2003).

Advertising

Many events operate on very tight budgets. As a result, such events are not able to allocate significant expenditures for advertising through the traditional forms of media. Most often advertising expenditures are a very minor portion of an event's expenses. However, this does not mean that events do not expend energy devising alternative means for mass media advertising. Events typically seek advertising

Table 13-2 Top 10 Biggest Sponsors of Events and Sports

Company	2013 Spending	Sponsorships (sample)
Barclay's	$525.5 million	English Premier League, NBA Brooklyn Nets arena
Adidas	$498 million	2012 Summer Olympics, German national football team, several athlete endorsers
General Motors	$388.4 million	MLB, NFL, NBA, NHL, MLS, WNBA, CFL teams; PGA golf tournament; NASCAR
Anheuser Busch InBev	$309.2 million	MLB, NBA, NFL, NHL teams; World Cup; PGA; LPGA; Major League Lacrosse
MillerCoors	$272 million	MLB, NBA, NFL, NHL teams; Hockey Canada; Milwaukee stadium
Toyota	$245.5 million	Arenas in Houston, Chicago, Los Angeles, etc.; NASCAR and Indycar series, professional and college sport teams
Verizon	$228.2 million	Stadium in New Hampshire, Washington DC, etc.; professional sport teams; partner of U.S.A. Luge
AT&T	$226.7 million	Arenas and stadiums, Cotton Bowl, golf tournaments, professional and college sport teams
Yum!	$210 million	Kentucky Derby, sport teams, U.S. Amateur Softball Association, AVP Pro Beach Volleyball Tour
Sprint	$205 million	NASCAR's premier series (Sprint Cup series), U.S. Ski and Snowboard Association, U.S. Tennis Association, professional and college sport teams

Reproduced from Said, S. (2013, August 6). The 10 biggest event and sport sponsorships. Valnet Inc.

through one of two means: (1) media sponsors or (2) attachment to corporate sponsor advertisements.

In addition to selling corporate sponsorships, nearly all successful events sell sponsorships to media outlets. Such sponsorships are often referred to as in-kind sponsorships. **In-kind sponsorships** rarely involve a cash exchange. Instead, an event provides the typical sponsorship benefits to a newspaper, magazine, radio station, or television station in exchange for a specified number of free advertising spots or space. Event promoters will also work with sponsors to promote their events through traditional forms of mass media. Most often, such advertising is geared toward promotions. For example, a shoe company might purchase a newspaper ad to inform potential customers that it will be selling shoes at an upcoming 3-on-3 basketball tournament. In this case, the advertising would serve to promote the basketball tournament as well.

Public Relations

Because events are so constrained in their advertising efforts, generating free publicity is extremely important. Most important to attaining publicity is developing a good working relationship with the members of the media. Hospitality efforts can greatly assist in this endeavor and will be discussed later in this section. In addition, regular communication with media outlets helps enhance the publicity an event receives. However, because members of the media seek stories of interest to the masses, the event must be creative.

Hospitality

Hospitality refers to providing a satisfying experience for all stakeholders of the event. This includes participants, spectators, media, and sponsors. Most events occur on a regular basis, and providing good hospitality is one way of improving event loyalty. The sport manager should take strides to ensure that prominent

event participants receive private housing, meals, changing areas, and warm-up space. If the participants are also celebrities, the sport manager must ensure that extra security is available to shield them from the public. If hospitality is not successfully implemented, the participants are less likely to return to the event. With respect to spectators, hospitality entails attempting to ensure that people attending the event have an enjoyable time. This includes clear signage directing participants to their seats, to restrooms, and to concession stands. In addition, training all support staff personnel is imperative so that interpersonal interactions with event staff are always positive.

The event manager will often expend the most energy providing hospitality to members of the media, to corporate sponsors, and to other VIPs. Because the event manager is seeking positive publicity from the media, there should always be a separate, prime seating location for the media. In addition, members of the media are accustomed to having private meals and accessibility to a private room where they can complete their work. Increased spending on corporate sponsorships has led to growing awareness and interest in hospitality services. Sport sponsors utilize hospitality for a variety of reasons, including the following:

- To reward and build relationships with current customers
- To generate business from new customers
- To reward employees for good performance
- To reward suppliers for excellent sales

For these reasons, hospitality has become one of the 10 most common functions of a sport management/marketing agency (as presented in Table 13-1).

Ticket Sales

Sporting events rely on ticket sales to varying degrees. For larger events, such as college football games, ticket sales are a very important revenue stream. For example, the football stadium at the University of Michigan has a seating capacity of over 109,000, generating a large amount of ticket revenue. However, for medium-sized and smaller events, ticket sales are a less effective way to generate revenues. Much of the ability to charge admission for these events is dependent on where the event occurs and how easily the event manager can control entry to the event. For example, many professional golf tournaments experience difficulty generating revenues through ticket sales because it is hard to control entry to the course and because so many tickets are given away to corporate sponsors. In these cases, the event is more reliant on sponsorship or broadcasting revenues. However, event managers have discovered creative ways to increase revenues tied to ticket sales. In exchange for a higher monetary outlay, golf tournaments have begun offering preferred viewing lanes whereby spectators receive premium seating in front of the typical gallery areas.

Advancements in technology also have had an impact in the ticket sales area. A number of professional sport franchises have recently adopted usage of Flash Seats, a paperless ticketing system in which spectators gain entrance to a sporting event via an encrypted code that can be placed on a driver's license, credit card, or other form of identification. This technology has aided in eliminating fraud and duplicate tickets and has decreased spectator no-show rates (Sutton, 2010).

Broadcasting

Radio and television broadcasts of an event add credibility to the event and provide increased exposure benefits to sponsors. A wide variety of broadcast outlets are available for sporting events:

- National television networks (e.g., ABC, NBC, CBS, Fox)
- National sports networks (e.g., ESPN, ESPN2, Fox Sports Net)
- National cable outlets (e.g., TNT, TBS, TNN, The Golf Channel)
- Local television stations
- Regional sports networks (e.g., Big Ten Network, New England Sports Network)
- National radio (e.g., CBS, ESPN, XM/Sirius)
- Local radio stations
- Websites (e.g., mlb.com coverage of base-ball games)

Although the increased number of sport outlets has accelerated the demand for sport event programming, a sport property must still meet certain criteria to interest a radio or television broadcast outlet. In fact, only the most valuable sport properties, such as the Super Bowl, the Olympic Games, Wimbledon, the Masters, professional sports, and Division I college athletics, are able to secure direct rights fee payments from broadcasting affiliates. It is important to remember that television and radio stations are funded by advertising sales. Advertisers purchase advertising time during programs that will attract large viewing or listening audiences. Therefore, if a broadcast outlet does not believe an event will be attractive to a large audience, which limits the ability to sell advertising time, then the outlet will not be willing to pay a rights fee to televise or broadcast an event.

Sport organizations and governing bodies have also pursued access to consumers through broadcasting of games and highlights via popular video-sharing sites such as YouTube and social-networking sites such as Facebook, MySpace, and Second Life. The NBA Channel, which shows game and user-generated highlights, debuted on YouTube in February 2007. In 2012, the NBA Development League (NBA D-League) struck a deal with Google to broadcast over 350 live games on YouTube ("NBA and YouTube to Partner," 2012). The National Hockey League (NHL) struck a similar deal with YouTube in November 2006 (Lombardo, 2007).

Website Development and Management

Because access to the Internet is now widespread and the connection speeds associated with such access are no longer an issue, people are becoming more reliant on websites for information. For this reason, it is imperative that every event, no matter the size, has an online presence to promote important information about the event. Ideally, the website's uniform resource locator (URL) will be the name of the event or something very similar. In terms of content, the website can include a wide variety of information. At the very least, it should include the basic details of when and where the event is occurring and how tickets can be purchased. If the event charges admission, it is sometimes easier for customers to purchase tickets through a website than by phone or at the event. The website can also be a source for the most up-to-date information about the event. For example, it can include news releases about the event, or it can provide real-time updates of event results. In the event of inclement weather during an outdoor event, the website can serve to inform participants and spectators about whether the event is actually occurring.

Licensing/Merchandising

The sale of **licensed merchandise**—that is, items that display an event's name or logo—is beneficial in a number of ways, including advertising and brand recognition of the event as well as a potential revenue source through sales generated. For popular events such as the Olympic Games and the Super Bowl, there will be significant demand for licensed merchandise. However, for smaller, less recognizable events, such as a high school football game or a 10K road race, the effort and expense needed to sell merchandise may be higher than the revenue generated from such sales. To cover the costs of inventory, staffing, and space allocation, significant sales must be achieved for the event to make a profit. Typically, selling tens or even hundreds of pieces of merchandise will not allow the event promoter to record a profit from merchandise sales.

Fundraising

When an event is classified as **not-for-profit**, another marketing tool is fundraising. Fundraising differs from sponsorship in that it does not offer advertising benefits associated with a donation. Most often, not-for-profit events center around raising money for some charitable enterprise, such as the Susan G. Komen Race for the Cure, which generates money for breast cancer research. The Komen Race for the Cure is the largest series of 5K runs/fitness walks in the world, with more than 1.6 million participants in more than 140 races across four continents (Susan G. Komen for the Cure, 2013a). Another successful event is the Tough Mudder. Created in 2010 by former members of the British Special Forces, the 10- to 12-mile events have grown exponentially, with over 460,000 participants in 2012 and more than $6 million raised for The Wounded Warrior Project (Tough Mudder, 2013).

Cause-related marketing efforts by corporations are another instance in which fundraising may be appropriate. For example, the CVS Caremark Charity Classic is a men's professional golf tournament sponsored by CVS, a drugstore chain, for the purpose of generating money for charity. Since its inaugural event in 1999, the CVS Caremark Charity Classic has raised more than $16 million for charities throughout Rhode Island and Southeastern New England (CVS Caremark Charity Classic, 2013). Similarly, since 1993, the V Foundation has awarded more than $100 million to more than 100 facilities nationwide for cancer research with events such as the Jimmy

V Basketball Classic and the ESPY Awards (The V Foundation, 2013). Sport teams and leagues are engaged in their own charitable type of activities. The NHL currently endorses the Ace Bailey Children's Foundation Got Skills Challenge for pee wee–aged youth hockey players (ages 11–12). Skills tournaments take place in local rinks across the United States (NHL, 2013b).

Career Opportunities

Event management offers a diverse array of career possibilities. Any event, from the local 3-on-3 basketball tournament to the Olympic Games, requires event management expertise. As a result, the event management field offers one of the most fertile areas for career opportunities. However, to successfully run a sporting event, the event manager's day often begins before dawn and concludes late at night. In addition, because events are usually held on weekends, employment in event management often requires extensive travel and work over weekends. Thus, to be successful in event management, one must be prepared to work long and typically inconvenient hours. Career opportunities in event management center on working with one of three types of organizations: sport management/marketing agencies, events, and charities.

Sport Management/Marketing Agencies

Because of the wide range of tasks carried out by these agencies, job responsibilities within such agencies vary. Typically, an entry-level position with a sport marketing agency will require a person to implement programs on behalf of corporate clients. These programs can include any combination of the key event management functions already discussed. Although an entry-level person is usually not responsible for recruiting corporate clients, he or she is required to successfully manage events

and programs created for specific sponsors. For example, an account manager might be responsible for supervising hospitality at an event or for ensuring that a corporation's signs are properly placed throughout an event site. To move beyond an entry-level position within an agency, a person is usually required to accept more business development responsibilities. For example, most vice presidents of sport management/marketing agencies are responsible for attracting new clients for the agency. This function is typically called **business development**.

Events

Although sport management/marketing agencies are typically involved with any sport event, many events have their own offices of full-time employees. This is most often true for events to which a corporation or sport management/marketing agency does not own the rights. Instead, the rights to the event may be owned locally. In this case, the management team for the event would not be from an agency or corporation. However, because most events are seasonal in nature, the full-time year-round staffs for such events are not very large; in other cases, the full-time staff for an event may be only one person.

Charities

Many charities view events as a way to increase revenues. To raise money and manage the events, staff is needed. For example, the Komen Foundation is led by more than 100,000 survivors and activists in nearly 200 countries (Susan G. Komen for the Cure, 2013b). The Tiger Woods Foundation lists over 50 staff members on its website who are dedicated to running the various events and programs of the Foundation (Tiger Woods Foundation, 2013).

Key Skills

As this chapter illustrates, an event manager assumes a variety of responsibilities. To successfully execute these responsibilities, the sport manager must have the necessary skills and experience. First, the sport manager must possess the proper educational background. Therefore, students interested in event management should seek a sport management program or business school that will provide them with coursework in areas such as sport marketing, event management, sport management, business, and finance. Many events are created by one person and begin as a small business, so classes in entrepreneurship and accounting are also appropriate for the prospective event manager.

In terms of experience, an internship is almost always required prior to being hired for an entry-level position in event management. In many cases, sport management/marketing agencies will turn to their most effective interns when seeking to fill full-time entry-level positions. Because agencies are charged with supporting corporate clients, new accounts often mean that agencies will need to hire additional personnel. Therefore, students must put themselves in a position to be hired when new accounts are acquired. In addition, it is never too early to begin working for events. A number of volunteer and paid opportunities exist in any university community: the athletic department, intramural department, community recreation programs, charity events, and so on. Nearly all of these activities can help improve a student's background in event management, making him or her more knowledgeable and marketable.

Current Issues

Event Security/Boston Marathon

After the terrorist attacks of September 11, 2001, there was a heightened security presence at sporting events and facilities, including metal detectors that spectators needed to pass through, searches of purses for suspicious objects, and even a ban placed on backpacks

and larger bags being brought into certain facilities. Event security has escalated to an even higher level of importance and scrutiny after the bombing during the 2013 Boston Marathon, which claimed three lives and injured hundreds more, predominantly spectators attending the event.

Providing appropriate security to outdoor events is very difficult, especially for events such as marathons that involve a large area. But even events held within stadiums have felt increased scrutiny regarding the security being provided. Oftentimes event management companies or facility operators will hire a private security firm to provide security guards for the event/facility. However, these security guards are often low-paid, part-time employees with little to no training in security techniques. As of 2013, 7 states do not require security guards to be licensed, and 23 states do not require security guard applicants to complete any training (Schrotenboer, 2013). The U.S. Department of Homeland Security has been advising stadium officials for years and has conducted assessments to detect vulnerabilities in the security being provided. However, professional and major sport teams and facility operators often hire private security firms for games and may select them based on cost or through a low-bid process (Schrotenboer, 2013). This is an area that will continue to receive increased attention from national, state, and local governments as additional training and licensing gaps are addressed and minimal expectations for security of events are put in place.

Olympic Games in Russia

Russia had not hosted an Olympic Games since 1980, when Moscow hosted the 1980 Summer Olympic Games. At that time, the United States, along with a select group of other countries, including Japan, West Germany, and China, boycotted the Olympic Games due to the 1979

Soviet invasion of Afghanistan. When Russia hosted the 2014 Winter Games in Sochi, the debate was whether countries with human rights issues should host the Olympic Games. On the eve of the 2014 Games, President Vladimir Putin signed a law prohibiting the promotion of nontraditional sexual relationships to minors, interpreted by many as banning gay pride parades and preventing any discussion of homosexuality (Lally, 2013). The law was questioned by many as discriminatory, with some calling for athletes to boycott the Sochi Olympic Games. Others claimed that the Russian law was in violation of the Olympic charter. The IOC determined that the Russian law banning "gay propaganda" did not violate its charter. Although President Obama condemned the Russian law, he did not support an Olympic boycott (Lally, 2013).

Another group brought into this debate was the Olympic sponsors themselves. Civil rights groups and advocates applied pressure to Coca-Cola, McDonald's, General Electric, and other corporate sponsors to make a statement and perhaps even pull their sponsorships. It will be interesting to see the impact of the intersection between human rights issues and sporting events, including corporate sponsorship involvement, in the years to come.

Niche Sports

Horse jumping, sailing, Le Mans road racing, and action sports, such as skateboarding and snowboarding, are considered by many to be niche sports. The most popular niche sport today seems to be UFC MMA, or Ultimate Fighting Championship Mixed Martial Arts. **Niche sports** are unique and appeal to a distinct segment of the market, whether defined by age, such as the Millennial Generation or Generation Y (the teenagers and 20-somethings of today), or socioeconomic class, as is seen with the appeal of sailing and polo to those

with higher incomes. Niche sports can be very valuable to an organization from a sponsorship perspective. Alltech, a worldwide leader in animal nutrition, health, and performance, paid $10 million to be a title sponsor for the 2010 World Equestrian Games in Kentucky and $14 million to be a title sponsor of the 2014 World Equestrian Games in Normandy, France (Jaffer, 2011). And even sports too small for cable can find a strong viewership through online broadcasting or video.

New events have spawned from the appealing nature of these sports to their respective demographic groups. The Dew Tour was established in 2005 and has three events scheduled around a beach–city–mountain (Winter Tour) format with TV coverage on NBC, NBC Sports Network, and Dew Tour Live on DewTour.com (Dew Tour, 2013). In 2013, the Dew Tour's biggest competitor, the X Games, expanded to six international events throughout the year. Embracing the international participants and audiences, ESPN expanded from the original two events held in Los Angeles, California, and Aspen, Colorado, to add events in Munich, Germany; Barcelona, Spain; Fox de Iguaçu, Brazil; and Tignes, France (O'Neil, 2012).

With the exception of the action sports, many of these niche sports suffer from a lack of exposure and corporate support beyond their small demographic cohort. For example, in 2009 the World Croquet Championship was held in the United States for the first time, but organizers did not spend much time worrying about crowd control because they were fearful that attendance would be quite small even with offering free admission (Show, 2009). The growth and popularity of niche sporting events targeting specific demographic cohorts will continue. What will be interesting to follow, though, is which sports are able to secure the needed sponsorship, spectator interest, and network coverage in order to make it.

Case Study 13-1   Planning for a New Event

David Tompkins sat in his third-floor office contemplating the new challenge dropped in his lap by his employer, Excellent Events, Inc. David has been working for Excellent Events as Northeast Regional Director of 3-on-3 Basketball Operations for the past 4 years. David's job responsibilities involve overseeing all operational details and sponsorship properties of the 3-on-3 basketball tournaments run by Excellent Events. This morning at a meeting with the company's CEO, David had been presented with a new challenge. Excellent Events wants to expand into the soccer market, hosting soccer tournaments throughout the Northeast region. Excellent Events has been in the 3-on-3 basketball tournament business for over 10 years. The company has seen participation in these tournaments start to fall in recent years, so it is looking to introduce a new sporting event. After researching various potential events, such as beach volleyball and lacrosse, the company decided to go with soccer. It was up to David Tompkins to organize and run these soccer tournaments in his territory.

Raised in Minnesota, David had never played organized soccer while growing up. But while working in the Northeast over the past 4 years, he had realized that soccer was a popular sport in the area. Just how popular, though, he wasn't sure, and he made a note on the notepad in front of him to find out. David also wasn't familiar with the rules of soccer, the equipment that would be needed, the different formats used for soccer tournaments, the age classifications used for playing divisions, risk management or liability concerns surrounding the sport of soccer, or even the types of youth soccer leagues and organizations that might already exist in the area. Again, the pen was busy scratching down ideas and thoughts on the pad of paper in front of him.

David was also well aware of the financial goals of Excellent Events. He realized that the financial success of the soccer events was contingent on a combination of team registration fees and corporate sponsorships. But he also knew that the demographics for soccer participants might differ from what he knew regarding participants and spectators for the 3-on-3 basketball tournaments. David also wanted to explore the possibility of the event giving back to the community, perhaps through a connection with a local charitable organization. Once again David made note of these thoughts.

David had never felt so challenged in his life. Although he considered himself a great event manager, he was not sure how much of his success at running 3-on-3 basketball tournaments would transfer to this new venture. However, one thing he had learned in his 4 years as an event manager was that attention to details sprinkled with creativity could carry an event manager far.

Questions for Discussion

1. David decided the first thing he needed to do was to research the sport of soccer in his area. What types of information would you suggest that David research and collect?

2. Although David is well aware of the equipment and supplies necessary to run a 3-on-3 basketball tournament, he lacks familiarity with the sport of soccer. Depending on the age divisions of the participants, the equipment might vary (e.g., a smaller soccer ball and goal size might be used for younger age divisions that play on a smaller field). Provide a comprehensive list of all equipment required to successfully operate a soccer event.

3. Given the demographics and psychographics of soccer participants and spectators, what types of corporations should David target for sponsorship solicitation?

4. What suggestions would you have for David in terms of a marketing strategy? How should David market these new tournaments?

Summary

By virtue of the continued increase in sporting events, sport event management offers a wide variety of career opportunities for young sport managers. Most of these opportunities exist within sport management/marketing agencies, the entities that most often organize, manage, and market sport events. Due to the variety of event management functions, it is possible for multiple agencies to work together on a sporting event. For example, a professional golf tournament may have one sport agency responsible for the operational aspects of the event and another agency responsible for the sponsorship sales, public relations, and hospitality of sponsors and VIPs. Yet another agency could be financially and legally responsible for the event and thus be in charge of implementing budgeting and risk management practices. In some cases, one large agency will handle all of these aspects and perhaps even produce a television broadcast of the event. Regardless of how these functions are delegated, each is crucial to the sporting event's success. With the proliferation of made-for-TV events, opportunities for sport managers in event management will continue to grow. To enter the event management field, however, a student must have a strong background in sport management, marketing, entrepreneurship, finance, and accounting. The good news is that the student can begin immediately by seeking both volunteer and paid opportunities with sporting events on campus and in the local community.

Resources

16W Marketing, LLC
   75 Union Avenue, 2nd Floor
   Rutherford, NJ 07070
   201-635-8000
   http://www.16wmktg.com

Alli (Alliance of Action Sports)
   http://www.allisports.com

Bronskill & Co.
   55 Fieldway Road
   Toronto, Ontario M8Z 3L4
   Canada
   416-703-8689
   http://www.bronskill.com

Fuse Integrated Marketing, Inc.
P.O. Box 4509
Burlington, VT 05406
802-864-7123
http://www.fusemarketing.com

Genesco Sports Enterprises
1845 Woodall Rodgers Freeway, Suite 1250
Dallas, TX 75201
214-303-1728
http://www.genescosports.com

GMR Marketing
5000 South Towne Drive
New Berlin, WI 53151
262-786-5600
http://www.gmrmarketing.com

IEG, Inc.
350 North Orleans Street, Suite 1200
Chicago, IL 60654
312-944-1727
http://www.sponsorship.com

IMG
U.S. Headquarters
200 5th Avenue, 7th floor
New York, NY 10010
212-489-8300
http://www.imgworld.com

Octagon Marketing
800 Connecticut Avenue, 2nd floor
Norwalk, CT 06854
203-354-7400
http://www.octagon.com

Redmandarin
Somerset House, West Wing
Strand
London, England
WC2R 1LA
+44 (0) 207 566 9410
http://www.Redmandarin.com

Team Championships International
10497 Centennial Road
Littleton, CO 80127
303-948-7108

Velocity Sports and Entertainment
230 East Avenue
Norwalk, CT 06855
203-831-2000
http://www.teamvelocity.com

Key Terms

barnstorming tours, budgeting, business development, cash-flow budgeting, cause-related marketing efforts, event marketing, full-service agencies, grassroots programs, hospitality, in-house agencies, in-kind sponsorships, integrated marketing, licensed merchandise, niche sports, not-for-profit, registration system, risk management, script, specialized agencies, sport management/marketing agencies, sport property, tournament operations, volunteer management, zero-base budgeting

References

Active Network. (2013). Our story. Retrieved from http://www.activenetwork.com/about-us/our-story

Alli Sports. (2013). allisports.com. Retrieved from http://www.allisports.com

CVS Caremark Charity Classic. (2013). Charity. Retrieved from http://www.cvscharityclassic.com/content/charity

Dew Tour. (2013). Dew Tour announces 2013 dates and locations. Retrieved from http://www.allisports.com/dew-tour/event/ocean-city-beach-championship-2013/news/dew-tour-announces-2013-dates-and-locations

Eighth International Sports Event Management Conference. (2013). Retrieved from http://www.iirme.com/isem/home

IEG. (2013, January 7). 2013 sponsorship outlook: Spending increase is double-edged sword. *IEG Sponsorship Report*. Retrieved from http://www.sponsorship.com/IEGSR/2013/01/07/2013-Sponsorship-Outlook-Spending-Increase-Is-Dou.aspx

IMG. (2013). About us. Retrieved from http://img.com/about-us-aspx

Jaffer, N. (2011, July 8). Alltech to sponsor 2014 world equestrian games in Normandy, France. Equisearch.com. Retrieved from http://www.equisearch.com/news/alltech-and-normandy-join-forces-alltech-to-sponsor-2014-weg/

Kelley, B. (2012). What are Tiger Woods' career earnings? About.com Guide. Retrieved from http://golf.about.com/od/tigerwoods/f/tiger-woods-career-earnings.htm

Lally, K. (2013, September 29). Russia anti-gay law casts a shadow over Sochi's 2014 Olympics. *Washington Post*. Retrieved from http://articles.washingtonpost.com/2013-09-29/world/42510859_1_sochi-russia-anti-gay-law-olympic-boycott

Lombardo, J. (2007, February 27). NBA giving YouTube a tryout. *Street & Smith's SportsBusiness Journal*, p. 36.

Major League Baseball. (2013). Urban youth academy. Retrieved from http://mlb.mlb.com/community/uya.jsp

National Basketball Association. (2013). NBA FIT. Retrieved from http://www.nba.com/nbafit/kids/home.html

National Football League. (2013). NFL flag football. Retrieved from http://www.nflrush.com/play/nflflag

National Hockey League. (2013a). NHL tourneys. Retrieved from http://www.nhl.com/tourneys/

National Hockey League. (2013b). Kids special programs. Retrieved from http://www.nhl.com/kids/subpage/sp_skills.html

"NBA and YouTube to partner to present NBA D-League games live on YouTube." (2012, November 20). NBA D-League news. Retrieved from http://www.nba.com/dleague/news/nba_youtube_partner_to_present_nbadleague_games_youtube_2012_11_20.html

Octagon. (2013). Who we are. Retrieved from http://www.octagon.com/who_we_are/offices

O'Neil, D. (2012, December 10). X Games expands globally. ESPN.com. Retrieved from http://xgames.espn.go.com/cities/article/7862758/x-games-grow-three-six-events-2013

Prairie, M., & Garfield, T. (2004). *Preventive law for schools and colleges*. San Diego, CA: School & College Law Press.

Redmandarin. (2013). Approach. Retrieved from http://www.redmandarin.com/redmandarin/approach

Said, S. (2013, August 6). The 10 biggest event and sport sponsorships. The Richest. Retrieved from http://www.therichest.com/sports/the-10-biggest-event-and-sport-sponsorships/

Schaaf, P. (1995). *Sports marketing: It's not just a game anymore*. New York: Prometheus Books.

Schrotenboer, B. (2013, May 2). *USA Today* sports investigation: Holes in stadium security. *USA Today Sports*. Retrieved from http://www.usatoday.com/story/sports/2013/05/02/stadium-security-boston-marathon-kentucky-derby/2130875/

Show, J. (2009, April 13). Top-shelf sports. *Street & Smith's SportsBusiness Journal*, p. 15.

Simson, V., & Jennings, A. (1992). *Dishonored games: Corruption, money and greed at the Olympics*. New York: S.P.I. Books.

Sports Marketing Surveys. (2010). About us. Retrieved from http://www .sportsmarketingsurveys.com/about-us

Susan G. Komen for the Cure. (2013a). About the race. Retrieved from http://apps.komen.org /raceforthecure/

Susan G. Komen for the Cure. (2013b). Our people. Retrieved from http://ww5.komen.org /AboutUs/OurPeople.html

Sutton, B. (2010, May 10–16). Using technology to build ticket database can boost bottom line. *Street & Smith's SportsBusiness Journal*, p. 11.

Team Marketing Report (TMR). (2010). *Sports Sponsor FactBook*. Retrieved from http:// www.teammarketing.com/fact/

The V Foundation. (2013). Our story. Retrieved from http://www.jimmyv.org/about-us /our-story/

Tiger Woods Foundation. (2013). About the foundation. Retrieved from http://web .tigerwoodsfoundation.org/aboutTWF/staff

Tough Mudder. (2013). Tough Mudder facts and figures. Retrieved from http://toughmudder .com/press-room/tough-mudder-facts -and-figures

Woodward, S. (2003, May 26). IOC does a 180, buys Meridian agency in move to take marketing in-house. *Street & Smith's SportsBusiness Journal*, p. 5.

Chapter 14

Stephen McKelvey

Sport Sales

Learning Objectives

Upon completion of this chapter, students should be able to:

1. Recognize that there are more entry-level job opportunities in sales than any other segment of the sport industry.

2. Evaluate the relative importance of the factors that influence the sport consumer's purchase decision: quality, quantity, time, and cost.

3. Apply the concept of customer relationship management to the sales process.

4. Identify traditional sales methods such as direct mail, telemarketing, and personal selling and know the advantages and disadvantages of each.

5. Apply the techniques of benefit selling, up-selling, eduselling, and aftermarketing to the personal selling process.

6. Analyze the effect of technology and social media on the sales process.

7. Evaluate the key skills that make a good salesperson.

8. Distinguish between the various items in a typical sport organization's sales inventory, including tickets, hospitality, advertising, signage, naming rights, promotions, community programs, and sponsorships.

9. Recognize that regardless of your occupation, you will always be selling yourself and your ideas, so selling is an integral part of your career growth and success within the sport industry.

Introduction

Few, if any, avenues within the sport industry hold more job opportunities, particularly at the entry level, than sales. Chances are, many of you reading this now are already sufficiently discouraged: Sales?! However, as you read on within this chapter, you will begin to realize three important things about sales. First, sales is the lifeblood of any sport organization. Whether it is season tickets, outfield signage, advertising spots on the team's local radio station, print advertisements in the game-day magazine, online advertising, or multiyear sponsorship deals, the sales function accounts for the vast majority of revenues for any sport organization. Those who can learn to master the art of selling become invaluable, and often irreplaceable, assets to their organizations.

Second, sales can be fun! Contrary to popular notions, successful salespeople are not born; they are developed through training, experience, and enthusiasm. Sales involves interacting and communicating with other people—typically people who are predisposed to like and even admire your product or service. The successful salesperson wakes up each morning not bemoaning sales as a drudgery, but enthusiastic about the opportunity to help meet the wants and needs of his or her potential customers!

Third, regardless of your job in the industry, it will entail some element of sales. Baseball executive Mike Veeck, the son of the legendary founder of sport promotion, Bill Veeck, provides a quote that he attributes to "17,325 failed potential major-minor league executives": "Oh, I love marketing. But you won't catch me selling. It's just not something I do" (Irwin, Sutton, & McCarthy, 2002, p. ix). The point of Veeck's quote is that whether you are employed in the marketing department, the public relations department, or the operations department, you will always be selling: selling yourself and selling your ideas!

Regardless of the sport, organizations—from the major professional leagues and colleges/universities to sports broadcasting companies and teams at the lowest rungs of the minors—are being challenged daily to better utilize traditional sales methodologies, employ innovative sales tactics, create new inventory, and discover new ways of packaging their sales inventory to provide not only new revenues to the organization, but also longer-term value to their customers.

In today's world, consumers have more and more options for spending their discretionary entertainment dollars, and companies have more and more options for investing their advertising and sponsorship dollars. In this competitive environment, how then do sport organizations use the sales process to attract and retain consumers? What do sport organizations have to sell? Which methodologies do they use to sell it? What does it take to be a successful salesperson in sport? In exploring the evolving world of sport sales, this chapter provides an introduction to the range of sales approaches and methodologies that sport organizations are embracing in the increasingly competitive sport marketplace. Among them is a shift in emphasis from product-oriented to consumer-oriented sales and recognition of the importance of building long-term relationships with customers. But first, it is important to understand how we arrived at this point.

History

As sport management as a discipline has become more sophisticated, so, too, has the sales process within sport. What was once viewed as a form of "hucksterism"—one-size-fits-all ticket packages and short-term gimmicks to "put fannies in seats"—has evolved into a dynamic discipline. Historically, sport sales consisted of simple tactics such as handing out season ticket brochures or mailing out simple two-page proposals listing a range of advertising and sponsorship options that could be purchased by companies. As noted by Mullin, Hardy, and Sutton (2007), sport marketing, including the sales function, has historically fallen victim to an array of "marketing myopias," defined as "a lack of foresight in marketing ventures" (p. 12). However, today's leading-edge sales departments have adopted the following "truisms" with regard to the sales function:

- A winning team can certainly be a selling advantage; however, a sales staff needs to be trained and prepared to sell either a winning *or* a losing team.
- The major emphasis should be on identifying and satisfying consumers' wants and needs instead of focusing simply on selling the sport organization's goods and services.
- A priority needs to be placed on the collection and effective use of customer data. This includes initiatives to seek to identify each and every consumer who attends the sport organization's events, an initiative made easier by the advent of digital (or paperless) ticketing. Digital ticketing serves several valuable functions for the sport organization, including helping to eliminate waste and fraud, as well as streamlining fan entry into stadiums. However, perhaps most important for the sales force, digital ticketing not only helps to identify each and every fan who attends the event, but also can create a wealth of data on consumer behavior and preferences (Fisher, 2012).
- Simply handing out free tickets to a sporting event sends a distinct message to fans about the perceived quality of the product: *If it's free, it can't be worth all that much.* Although distributing blocks of "complimentary" tickets to charity groups is one exception to this caveat, the most effective

means of doing this is to secure a local business to underwrite the cost of these tickets and distribute them as part of a community goodwill initiative.

- Success begins with an organizational commitment to the ongoing training, motivating, and evaluating of each and every salesperson, premised on an understanding that the first line of interaction and communication between the sport organization and its potential customers is typically the entry-level salesperson making the initial phone calls and selling tickets at the ticket window. One example of this is Major League Soccer (MLS), which in 2010 launched the first-ever league-wide ticket sales training center in Minnesota (Mickle, 2010). The MLS National Sales Center provides a 45-day curriculum designed to train beginners in ticket sales in preparation for them to then join an MLS team and is a model that other sport leagues should consider implementing. Since its inception, the training center has placed 85 graduates with 16 different MLS teams (MLS National Sales Center, 2013).

The ever-increasing competition for consumers' discretionary dollars, the influx of professionally trained sport marketers, and the continued evolution of sport management and marketing as a scientific discipline have gradually eradicated these myopias. This has resulted in a much higher level of sophistication and understanding of the sales process and its importance to the overall success of any sport organization. As you read on, you will hear more about how sport organizations are changing their attitudes toward sales as well as enhancing their ability to succeed in selling in an increasingly competitive environment through the use of new technologies and creative innovation.

Sales in the Sport Setting

Sales is the revenue-producing arm of a sport organization. It has been defined as "the process of moving goods and services from the hands of those who produce them into the hands of those who will benefit most from their use" (Mullin et al., 2007, p. 280). Any discussion of sport sales might best begin with Mark McCormack, the industry-proclaimed "founder of sport marketing" who built IMG (formerly International Management Group) into one of the world's premier sport management conglomerates. McCormack (1996) explained that selling consists of four ingredients: (1) the process of identifying customers, (2) getting through to them, (3) increasing their awareness and interest in your product or service, and (4) persuading them to act on that interest.

As suggested by Honebein (1997), sales can also be viewed as "customer performance: When a customer purchases your product, he or she performs the act of buying" (p. 25). As Mullin, Hardy, and Sutton (2007) further elaborate, there are four main factors that cause sport consumers to purchase (or not purchase) a sport organization's product or service:

1. *Quality:* Teams' win–loss records are one obvious example of identifying the quality of the product or service and influencing consumers' purchase-behavior decisions.

2. *Quantity:* An individual might wish only to purchase an eight-game ticket plan from an NBA team rather than a full-season ticket package, so the numbers (the units) in which the product is sold can become an influencing factor.

3. *Time:* Family obligations, work schedules, and everyday life can dictate whether the consumer has the time to consume the product. For instance, to make a season ticket purchase worthwhile, the individual must have the time available to attend the majority, if not all, of the team's home games.

4. *Cost:* Each year, *Team Marketing Report* (*TMR*), one of the leading industry trade publications, publishes a Fan Cost Index (FCI). The FCI measures the cost of taking a family of four to a game for each of the major professional sport leagues and includes not only the cost of tickets but also the other costs that consumers likely incur, including the purchase of parking, concessions, and souvenirs. Although the average cost of tickets for a family of four to attend a Major League Baseball (MLB) game in 2011 was $107 (by far the lowest of the three major professional sport leagues), the overall cost of attending the game, factoring in the other elements including parking and concessions, was $197 for the 2011 season (*Team Marketing Report*, 2011). Thus, the price of game tickets is just part of the equation that influences consumers' purchase decisions. In addition to direct out-of-pocket expenses, the concept of cost also relates to such aspects as payment options, value received for the purchase price, and the investment of time required to attend the event.

One element that distinguishes sport sales from the selling of other traditional consumer products or services such as cereal or mobile phone services is the presence of emotion (Mullin et al., 2007). The emotion inherent in sport adds a special excitement to the sales process. Think about it: Would you rather work the phones calling Boston residents to sell them a new credit card or to sell them Red Sox tickets?

Sales Strategies and Methods

Innovation in the sales process and methodologies within the sport industry have often lagged behind those in other service industries,

due in part to the myopias described earlier in this chapter. However, in recent years, certain innovative sales methodologies have begun to be more widely utilized throughout the sport industry. Historically, sport organizations communicated with customers once it was time to "renew the order." With the increased competition for the loyalties of the sport consumer, organizations have recognized the need to expand and enrich their relationships with current and potential customers. This section provides an overview of the methodologies and terminology that have become the linchpins of the sales process in the sport industry today.

Two of the most critical determinants of success of a sales department are (1) the ability to accurately identify and understand the needs of potential and current customers and (2) the ability to maximize the generation of sales leads. One key to achieving these objectives is through the maintenance of a **customer relationship management (CRM)** system that enables sport organizations to build and utilize a database of demographic (e.g., age, gender, education level, occupation, and ethnicity) and psychographic (e.g., motivations, interests, and opinions) information, as well as past purchase behaviors, for existing and potential customers. CRM systems enable sales departments to more effectively and efficiently segment their various target markets.

The evolution of sales analytics, readily retrievable through CRM systems and software, has dramatically changed the landscape of sport sales over the past decade. One of the first CRM products designed for sports sales departments was Archtix, a Ticketmaster product enabling teams to consolidate their sales and marketing operations into a single operating suite. More recently, Veritix introduced a paperless ticketing product called Flash Seats that enables customers to enter the stadium or arena via an encrypted code that can be placed on a driver's license, credit card, or other form of identification. "What I have loved about this product . . . is the data-capture ability that enables the venue or the team to know the identity of every person in the building on any given night," said Bill Sutton, a leading sport industry sales expert. "The value of the data for future marketing and sales efforts along with cross-promotional opportunities is a significant revenue opportunity" (Sutton, 2010, p. 11).

A second new technology is a product called Prospector, developed and owned by Turnkey Sports & Entertainment (Sutton, 2010). Prospector is a program that analyzes and "scores" sales leads, thus increasing the efficiencies of selling tickets in a variety of ways. For instance, the program can prioritize leads based upon customer segments and also allows the sales manager to better understand who is best at selling different types of inventory (i.e., season tickets, partial plans, premium seating) by measuring the revenue generated in direct correlation to the leads the salesperson is assigned. The Prospector program also increases accountability in terms of assigned leads and the revenue produced by those leads, and it allows the sales manager to rotate assigned leads equally or to create a system whereby the best leads (those with five stars) can be assigned to those salespeople who meet their sales goals the previous week (Sutton, 2010). "[Prospector] is all about improving the efficiency of the sales staff and trying to move from a 1 percent success rate of outbound calling to a rate of 3 or 4 percent or perhaps higher," said Turnkey Sports & Entertainment executive Haynes Hendrickson (Sutton, 2010, p. 11).

Sport organizations utilize their CRM systems to generate sales through three primary methods: direct mail, telemarketing, and personal sales. **Direct mail** solicitations are widely used in the sport industry. As suggested by Mullin, Hardy, and Sutton (2007), the major advantage of using direct mail campaigns is that they reach only those people the organization wants to reach, thus minimizing the expense of circulating a sales offer to individuals who would have little interest in the offer. Organizations often promote season tickets, partial season ticket plans, and single-game tickets through direct mail campaigns. Through the wonders of computers, the information stored in the database can be merged to create letters that are personalized for each individual. Furthermore, because you can easily measure the effectiveness of direct mail, organizations can devise accurate head-to-head tests, formats, pieces, terms, or so forth, to better ensure the success of future direct mail initiatives. Of course, one potential drawback of the direct mail approach is that, unlike the telemarketing and personal selling methodologies discussed next, direct mail solicitations do not provide an opportunity to verbally explain the sales offer, counteract objections, or answer questions. Thus, the organization must clearly communicate the sales offer so that it is easily understood by the recipient.

Telemarketing is also widely used within the sport industry. Whereas in the past, sport organizations literally handed their sales interns a phone book ("dialing for dollars," as it was often called), the advent of CRM systems has brought a greater degree of sophistication and training to the sales process. Telemarketing utilizes telecommunications technology as a part of a well-planned, organized, and managed sales effort that features the use of non-face-to-face contact (Mullin et al., 2007). Telemarketing can be one-dimensional, such as the software that enables sport organizations to handle literally tens of thousands of inbound calls from consumers in response to a promotional offer through the use of a toll-free number. The other approach is two-dimensional, whereby salespeople use the phone to prospect for customers, follow up leads, or solicit existing customers for repeat or expanded business. Telemarketing involves training the sales personnel to "follow a script,"

become effective listeners, and complete the sales process by countering any objections and best meeting the specific needs of the customer. More and more teams, however, are realizing that telemarketing is just the start of the sales process. For instance, the Arizona Diamondbacks are training their sales representatives to use the phone only as a starting point to gather information about a prospect. To close the sale, they are meeting in person with the prospect or, better yet, inviting the prospect for a tour of the stadium (King, 2010a). "People aren't going to make purchases over the phone anymore," predicts Diamondbacks CEO Derrick Hall. "They're not going to commit. We've got to get them here [to the stadium for a tour] and then we have success" (King, 2010a, p. 1).

© Monkey Business Images/ShutterStock, Inc.

Personal selling describes face-to-face, in-person selling and again usually incorporates the use of the sport organization's CRM system. Although personal selling is often more costly than direct mail or telemarketing, personal selling can be more precise by enabling sales executives to more closely target the most promising prospects. Personal selling is often necessary, and more effective, for successfully selling higher-priced inventory such as luxury suites and sponsorship packages because these items involve a greater financial investment by the prospective customer. It is rare indeed that a company would ever purchase a team sponsorship package over the phone!

As the race to obtain—and retain—the business and the loyalties of both consumers and corporations has intensified over the past decade, successful sport organizations have also adopted proactive sales approaches, or philosophies, that are premised on the concept of relationship marketing. These include benefit selling, up-selling, eduselling, and aftermarketing. Each of these concepts is introduced in the following section.

Benefit Selling

What should a sport organization do when the product or service package it is selling doesn't meet the specific wants or needs of a consumer? One approach, called **benefit selling**, "involves the promotion and creation of new benefits or the promotion and enhancement of existing benefits to offset existing perceptions or assumed negatives related to the sport product or service" (Irwin, Sutton, & McCarthy, 2008, p. 107). The first step in benefit selling is to understand what objections customers have to your product or service, and why. This can be achieved through customer surveys and focus groups. Once benefits have been identified, they must be publicized and must be judged by the consumer to have worth or value.

The concept of the *flex book* is one example of benefit selling in action (Irwin et al., 2008). This concept arose in response to the frequent objection by potential customers, when being pitched partial season ticket plans, that they were not able to commit to a certain number of games on specific dates well in advance of the season. Flex books (sometimes also called *fan flex plans*) contain undated coupons for a specified number of games that can be redeemed for any games of the customers' choosing (subject to seating availability). It is an example of creating a new benefit to offset existing perceptions or assumed negatives related to the sport product or service. Another increasingly popular example is *open houses*, in which teams allow potential consumers into their venues to get a feel for the "experience" and the benefits associated with it.

Up-Selling

Successful sport organizations are never satisfied with simply renewing a customer at his or her current level of involvement. By effectively managing and maintaining their CRM system and by embracing the sales philosophies of relationship selling and aftermarketing, sales personnel should be well positioned to **up-sell** current customers. When it comes to tickets, the idea of **up-selling** corresponds to the "escalator concept," whereby sport organizations are continually striving to move customers up the escalator from purchasing single-game tickets to purchasing mini-ticket plans, and then to full-season ticket packages (Mullin et al., 2007). For those involved in sponsorship sales, the goal should always be to increase, over time, the company's involvement with the sport organization. Relationship selling and aftermarketing put the salesperson in an advantageous position when it comes time to renew and up-sell a client.

Eduselling

At this point, one thing should be clear to you, the reader and future sales executive: *The customer rules!* Product- or service-focused sales activities that emphasize the product (its benefits, quality, features, and reputation) or the sport organization itself have been replaced by the mantra of customer-focused selling that stresses the needs and requirements of the customer (Irwin et al., 2008). A salesperson engaged in customer-focused selling views himself or herself as a consultant to the prospective customers, helping to provide them with a *solution*, rather than simply trying to convince them to purchase a product or service they may not want or need. Irwin and colleagues (2008) specifically describe the importance of **eduselling** in the context of selling corporate sponsorships; they define *eduselling* as "an instructive process that continually and systematically supplies information and assistance to the prospective sponsorship decision maker in order to enhance product knowledge, facilitate understanding of product benefits, and establish a sense of partnership between rights holder and buyer" (p. 175). Eduselling is more than just educating a customer before the sale, or providing short-term service after the sale. Eduselling is a continual process that involves the sales staff monitoring consumer utilization and satisfaction through regular communication. Through this monitoring process the sport organization is able to ensure that the product or service is being utilized properly. By ensuring the product is being utilized properly and to its fullest extent, the sales staff is able to maximize customer satisfaction and ultimately the lifetime value of the client.

One way a salesperson engages in eduselling is by proactively assisting customers in developing ways to better utilize and leverage their investment with the organization. For instance, more and more teams are providing corporate season ticket holders with something as simple as a chart that allows the company to more easily keep track of who has use of which tickets for which games. Other teams are providing a means for season ticket holders to forward unused tickets to worthy local charities, through which the company can derive

some goodwill. Tactics such as these are aimed at helping to make sure that the season tickets don't end up buried in a desk drawer, unused—a scenario that would make the season ticket renewal process quite difficult. Furthermore, sport organizations committed to eduselling will themselves develop promotional ideas showing how their sponsors can utilize the team's game tickets and other merchandise to help generate new business opportunities and sales. Remaining in constant communication with customers, and displaying a vested interest in achieving customers' business goals, helps ensure that both parties, if they live up to their commitments, will benefit from the relationship in both the short and the long term.

Aftermarketing

Direct selling, telemarketing, and personal selling are the most widely used methodologies for prospecting and achieving initial sales. As competition for customers intensifies and the emphasis shifts from acquiring customers to retaining customers, the ability to provide consistent high-quality service is a source of competitive advantage for sport organizations (McDonald, 1996). **Aftermarketing**, defined by Vavra (1992) as "the process of providing continued satisfaction and reinforcement to individuals or organizations who are past or current customers" (p. 22), is a critical consideration because of the significant competition for the sport consumer's entertainment dollars. It has become critical for sport organizations to have an aggressive plan for retaining their market share of fans. From a practical business standpoint, aftermarketing serves to encourage an organization to view a season ticket holder not as a one-time $3,000 customer, but, based on a potential span of 10 years, as a $30,000 client. Mullin and colleague (2007) have referred to the concept of viewing customers as an organizational asset as "lifetime value" (LTV) (p. 309). Through this lens, every single season ticket holder becomes much more worthy of cherishing! "It's all about relationships," said Mullin. "If you didn't build the relationship with a sponsor or season-ticket holder or fan back when things were good, it's very hard to all of a sudden do it now" (King, 2010a, p. 1).

Given the fact that it takes exponentially more money and manpower to get *new* customers onto the frequency escalator than it takes to retain current customers, successful sport sales organizations have also embraced the importance of customer service as a critical component of the sales process. A goal of exceedingly superior customer service should permeate the sales culture of a sport organization. A successful customer service program, adapted from one professional team sport organization, includes the following elements:

- Personal calls by sales account reps to 50 season ticket holders per week
- E-mails to 50 season ticket holders per week
- Personal notes to 25 season ticket holders per week
- Direct-dial phone numbers and e-mail addresses given to each season ticket holder for contacting his or her personal service representative
- In-seat visits by sales account reps during home games
- Maintenance of a customer sales and service booth in the arena that is staffed by sales and service team members
- Invitations to attend "Fan Forums" with the team's general manager and team president
- A handbook or manual sent to season ticket holders describing the goals and values of the team's on-ice product
- A complimentary team magazine sent to season ticket holders and fans on the season ticket holder waiting list

- Advance sale opportunities for season ticket holders for other nonsporting events held at the team's facility (e.g., concerts)
- Special events for season ticket holders (e.g., an opportunity for them to visit the team locker rooms or practice on the team's court and field)
- Automated phone calls from players and team front office personnel to season ticket holders identified in the team's database
- A holiday card from the team with a redemption coupon for a gift, such as a team cap

Finally, teams should continually seek to encourage feedback on customer satisfaction through regular customer surveys, online polls, monitoring of chat rooms, and focus groups. All comments and feedback should be logged on individual accounts in the CRM system to enable the sales staff to track patterns and uncover opportunities to improve service.

Ticket Sales and Social Media

Social media has become an increasingly effective tool for sport organizations to enhance their ticket sales revenues. Today, sport organizations are routinely using social media not only to connect and engage with fans by sharing news, posting videos, and hosting contests, but they also are using social media platforms such as Facebook, Twitter, YouTube, and Pinterest to drive ticket sales. For instance, every year the University of Michigan athletic department conducts a social media–only ticket presale campaign for its football program during a 2-week period in July; the campaign generated a reported $75,000 in ticket sales in 2011 (Maddox, 2013). As another example, in 2010, the NBA Golden State Warriors conducted a "Warriors Draft Challenge" contest on Facebook, Twitter, and YouTube that resulted in a reported $440,000 in ticket sales generated from contest registrants (Cohen, 2010). The benefit of such social media–driven campaigns is that they enable sport organizations to keep their products readily accessible on a computer, smartphone, or iPad. The increasing reliance on social media in the sales process has also created many new entry-level sales positions for those who are particularly savvy in the use of social media.

Key Skills: What Makes a Good Salesperson?

It is the rare breed of person who is "born to sell." It takes a certain degree of confidence to pick up the phone and cold call strangers to interest them in purchasing season tickets or an Internet advertising package. If you are engaged in personal selling, it takes a certain degree of courage to knock on a company door, ask yourself in, and pitch a group sales or sponsorship package. More often than not, successful salespeople develop their skills through training, trial and error, and experience.

Mark McCormack (1984), a salesman who mastered his craft by selling clients such as Arnold Palmer, Jack Nicklaus, and Tiger Woods to corporate America, has stated:

> Effective selling is directly tied to timing, patience, and persistence—and to sensitivity to the situation and the person with whom you are dealing. An awareness of when you are imposing can be the most important asset a salesman can have. It also helps to believe in your product. When I feel that what I am selling is really right for someone, that it simply makes sense for this particular customer, I never feel I am imposing. I think that I am doing him a favor. (p. 92)

The following is a "Top 10 Rules for Successful Selling" list that incorporates McCormack's sage advice (McCormack, 1996) in addition to experience gleaned by this author during 15 years in the sport sales business:

1. *Laugh.* It never hurts to have a sense of humor. Remember, sports is entertainment!

2. *Use a commonsense fit.* Make sure that what you are selling makes sense for your prospective customer. Never try to shoehorn inventory down a prospect's throat.

3. *Wear Teflon.* The most successful salespeople believe that being told "no" is the *start* of the sales process; they don't take rejection personally, and they accept it as a challenge. (Beware, however, of rule 2!)

4. *Know the prospect.* There's an old adage: Knowledge is power. Undertake to know as much as you can about the sales prospect *before* making the initial sales call. If you're calling on an individual, does your CRM system show that he or she has attended games in the past? If you're pitching a local company for sponsorship, do you know if that company is currently sponsoring other sports properties? Is the person you're going to meet with a sports fan? Find out in advance (ask his or her assistant!). Knowing that, alone, can make the sales process easier.

5. *Pump up the volume.* Sales is a numbers business. As a rule of thumb, 10 phone calls to solicit a meeting may result in 1 actual sales call. For every 10 meetings, you might get 1 sales nibble. Sales is about volume—making a lot of calls and seeing a lot of people (see rule 3).

6. *Knock on old doors.* Don't abandon potential customers just because they turned you down the first time. Individual consumers' interests and financial circumstances change, as do companies' business strategies and personnel, and when they do you

don't want to be a stranger. Be polite, but persistent.

7. *Consult, don't sell.* Successful salespeople seek to learn potential customers' wants and needs, and then work with them to find solutions that are mutually beneficial. They let the sale come to them.

8. *Listen!* Perhaps the best skill a salesperson can develop is the art of listening. If you ask, prospective customers will always provide clues that open avenues toward an agreement, if not today, then somewhere down the road (see rule 6). Good listeners pick up on these clues.

9. *Have two kinds of belief.* Successful salespeople have an unwavering belief in what they are selling and in themselves.

10. *Ask for the order.* This sounds self-explanatory, but closing the sale is one of the toughest steps to successful selling. You will never know if a potential customer wants to buy your product until you ask!

Chad Estis cut his teeth in an entry level sales position with the then down-trodden Cleveland Cavaliers and eventually worked his way up through a series of sport sales positions to become the vice president of sales and marketing for the Dallas Cowboys. He describes ticket sales as a grind-it-out business, and to be successful those in the business must have a focused, dedicated, skilled, well-trained, and highly professional sales team approaching the market in a strategic way (King, 2010a).

Sales Inventory

Because sales is the lifeblood of a sport organization, for many a position in sales is often the first step into the industry. **Sales inventory** is "the products available to the sales staff to market, promote and sell through sales methodologies" discussed earlier (Mullin et al.,

2007, p. 286). Sport organizations have a broad range of sales inventories, each of which entails different sales methodologies as well as levels of sales experience. The typical front office of a team sport organization includes the following staff positions reporting to the vice president of sales and marketing: manager (or director) of season ticket sales, manager of group sales, manager of advertising sales (print, broadcast, and Internet), manager of sponsorship sales, and manager of luxury suite/premium seating sales. It is important to note, as we review the sales inventory of a typical sport organization in this section, that many of the inventory items discussed are often packaged together when being presented to a company (Mullin et al., 2007).

Tickets and Hospitality Inventory

People traditionally get their start in the industry in the ticket sales department, first staffing the ticket booth and then advancing up the sales ladder to group sales and partial- or full-season ticket plans. Mullin and colleagues (2007) describe the game ticket inventory as a "club sandwich" (p. 305) consisting, from the bottom up, of community promotional tickets, tickets bought through day-of-game "walk-up" sales, advance sales, group tickets, and partial plans, topped off by full-season tickets. The authors suggest the following "recipe" for a good-tasting and profitable "club sandwich" through which to maximize ticket sales revenue (Mullin et al., 2007, p. 305):

Ingredient	Percentage of Customers
Season ticket equivalencies (full and partial plans)	50
Advance ticket sales	25
Group sales	20
Day-of-game/walk-up sales	5

Although historically the "sizzle" in sport sales was in selling sponsorships and advertising, sport organizations have come to realize that the "steak" is in ticket sales. As the lifeblood of most franchises, sales from tickets and club seats make up more than half of a typical franchise's local revenue in all of the four major sport leagues, ranging as high as 80% for some teams (King, 2010a). Bernie Mullin, former CEO of the NBA Atlanta Hawks and NHL Thrashers and senior vice president of team marketing for the NBA, described how resources from teams were traditionally pumped into sponsorship sales and services, and yet most teams' locally generated revenue was coming from tickets sales. This has since changed as teams have realized the economic realities of tickets sales. Ticket sales have become a more sophisticated endeavor and teams, utilizing technology and other ticket sales strategies, are doing a much better job in the ticket sales arena (King, 2010b).

Sport organizations' continued emphasis on customer accommodation and hospitality has expanded the sales inventory over the past decade to include club seats (with personal waiter service), luxury suites complete with catered food service, private seat licenses (PSLs), and VIP parking, among other perks.

Advertising Inventory

Advertising inventory includes both electronic and print inventory. Electronic advertising inventory includes television, radio, and team websites. Although most sport organizations still sell their local broadcast rights to media outlets (called *rightsholders*) in exchange for an annual rights fee, some teams have brought their television or radio rights or both in-house. Although in this latter situation the team bears the production costs of its broadcasts, it also has the opportunity to retain all of the advertising sales revenues. The New York Yankees provides an example of a team willing to bear this risk, having taken control of its television broadcasts through the creation of the YES Network and the hiring of its own in-house sales staff to sell the advertising inventory. Print inventory includes advertising in game programs, media guides, and newsletters as well as on ticket backs, ticket envelopes, scorecards/roster sheets, and team faxes, and other items.

Signage Inventory

Signage inventory has traditionally been limited to dasherboards, scoreboards, outfield signs, and concourses. However, the quest for new revenue streams has expanded the signage sales opportunities to include the playing surface itself, the turnstiles, and the marquees outside the venue, among other locations.

Naming Rights

Naming rights provide a sport organization the opportunity to sell the title of its arena or stadium, practice facility, or the team itself. The corporate naming of stadiums and arenas has resulted in a significant new revenue stream for sport organizations. In some instances, naming rights agreements have also caused issues for the sport organizations that sold the rights and/or the companies that have purchased the rights. Consider the embarrassment and financial hardship sport organizations endured during the 1990s as a result of entering into naming rights deals with companies such as Enron, PSINet, TWA, and Pro Player that eventually went bankrupt. On the heels of this string of bankruptcy filings, one industry expert commented: "When the naming rights craze started . . . there was such excitement that a lot of discipline hadn't been put into the deals. In hindsight, there probably wasn't as much due diligence" (Radcliffe, 2002, p. 26). Today, facility naming rights deals often include clauses designed to ensure that sport organizations get back, for free, their ability to sell their facility's name if the signing company becomes insolvent. On the other side of the arrangement, some companies that have bought naming rights from sport organizations have also experienced major issues. Soon after the financial meltdown in late 2008 (and subsequent government bank bailout), many members of Congress criticized Citibank's naming of Citi Field in New York City. Congress questioned how Citibank could afford a $20 million annual naming rights agreement with the Mets yet require a government bailout to continue day-to-day operations. These are just a few of the issues that must be considered when selling naming rights. The top 10 most valuable U.S.–based sport facility naming rights deals, as of spring 2013, can be found in Table 14-1.

Online Inventory

Websites hosted by sport organizations represent attractive platforms for companies to advertise the products and/or services they sell. Banner ads, blogs, instant messaging applications, and pop-up ads are all common online inventory sport organizations can sell. The high traffic that many sport websites attract makes this online inventory both valuable and important for a sport organization's bottom line. Often online inventory (e.g., banner ads, company links) is included as an important value add in a larger sponsorship deal.

Promotions Inventory

Promotions inventory ranges from premium giveaway items and on-floor/on-field promotions to DiamondVision scoreboard promotions and pre- or postgame entertainment. Popular examples include sponsored "T-shirts blasts," in which team-logoed T-shirts are shot up into the stands by a specially designed, handheld cannon, and the fan-favorite sponsored "Dot Races" that appear between innings on the DiamondVision scoreboard. Many sport organizations also sell the rights to local companies to "present" postgame entertainment, such as the ever-popular fireworks displays.

Community Programs

Community programs offer a wealth of inventory for sport organizations to sell to local organizations, including, but not limited to,

Table 14-1 Top 10 Most Valuable Sport Facility Naming Rights Agreements

Venue	Location	Years	Annual Value (Millions)	Total Value (Millions)
Citi Field	Flushing, NY	20	$20.0	$400
Farmers Field	Los Angeles, CA	30	$20.0	$600
MetLife Stadium	East Rutherford, NJ	25	$17.0 to $20.0	$425 to $625
Levi's Stadium	Santa Clara, CA	20	$11.0	$220
Barclay's Center	Brooklyn, NY	20	$10.0	$200
Reliant Stadium & Arena	Houston, TX	31	$10.0	$310
Philips Arena	Atlanta, GA	20	$9.25	$185
Gillette Stadium	Foxboro, MA	15	$8.0	$240
University of Phoenix Stadium	Glendale, AZ	20	$7.72	$154.5
FedEx Field	Landover, MD	27	$7.59	$205

Data from: Leuty, R. (2013, May 8). Top 10 stadium, arena naming rights deals. *San Francisco Business Times*. Retrieved from http://www.bizjournals.com/sanfrancisco/blog/2013/05/stadium-naming-rights-deals -49ers-levis.html.

school assemblies, camps and clinics, awards and banquets, kick-off luncheons, and golf tournaments.

Miscellaneous Inventory

Miscellaneous inventory is often up to the ingenuity and resourcefulness of the sport organization. Miscellaneous inventory can include fantasy camps, off-season cruises with players, locker room tours, and road trips. Sport organizations have gotten increasingly creative in developing new inventory and thus generating new revenue streams by selling companies the opportunity to associate with their sanctioned events. For instance, many teams now conduct off-season "fanfests" involving interactive games and exhibits, which provide an entirely new source of sponsorship and advertising inventory.

Several professional sport teams have been successful in selling companies the entitlement to their individual playoff games. For example, Cub Cadet, a manufacturer of lawn mowers, served as the presenting sponsor of the Cleveland Cavaliers' 2010 playoff run. As a result of the sponsorship, Cub Cadet received a number of banner ads on the Cavaliers' website, and the designation "Cleveland Cavaliers Playoffs Presented by Cub Cadet" was used on all local radio broadcasts. The New Jersey Nets broke new ground in this regard following the 2009–2010 season, selling a local auto insurance company the presenting sponsorship of the team's *off-season*! The sponsorship included brand exposure in all Nets' off-season communications, including press releases, e-mail campaigns, advertising on the team's website, and sponsorship of a sweepstakes tied to the NBA draft (Brennan, 2010).

Sponsorships

Of all the inventory that a sport organization has available to sell, sponsorships often are the most involved and time consuming. Before even presenting a sponsorship proposal, the property must do extensive homework on the targeted company. Who is the decision maker? Who are its competitors? What have the company and its competitors done in the past in the area of sport sponsorship? Based on your research, who are the company's primary customers and how does your property or event deliver this audience? Is the company on solid financial ground? (After all, you don't want to sign a sponsor that either can't afford to properly leverage its sponsorship or that may be out of business in a year!) What are some top-line promotional ideas that you might suggest that can reinforce the company's marketing objectives or its company slogan? Why do you believe the targeted company would be a good fit for your organization, and why would the company believe this?

Sponsorship packages typically incorporate some, if not all, of the various inventory described previously. The sponsorship sales process requires a great deal of up-front research, creativity, sales acumen, and patience. First, sponsorship packages often entail a much larger emotional and financial commitment on the part of the potential customer. Second, because of the many inventory elements typically included in sponsorship packages, they often require input, review, and sign-off by a number of departments within the company, including advertising, sales, promotions, and public relations. Third, because the company will want to fully utilize and effectively leverage its sponsorship, the process of selling sponsorship packages must allow the company sufficient lead time, particularly if the company needs to plan retail promotions.

For instance, if a company were interested in sponsoring its local NFL team, which begins play in September, the deal would ideally have to be completed by the prior April (at the latest!) to allow the company sufficient lead time to develop and begin to implement its sales promotion and advertising campaign by the start of the season. In short, it is much easier for an individual to decide to purchase a ticket package than for a corporation to decide to invest in a sponsorship package.

In selling sponsorship packages, Mullin and colleagues (2007) have suggested the following sales process:

1. Schedule a meeting with the sponsorship decision-maker. Remember, don't accept a "no" from someone who is not empowered to say "yes."

2. At the first meeting, listen 80% of the time and sell only when you have to. You are there to observe and learn. Where does the potential sponsor spend its marketing dollars right now? What is working? What isn't working? What other sport organizations or events does the company sponsor or support? What does the company like or dislike about these relationships?

3. Arrange a follow-up meeting for the presentation of your proposal before leaving this initial meeting (ideally, within 1 week).

4. Create a marketing partnership proposal. Give the potential sponsor a promotional program that can be proprietary to that company. Act more like a marketing partner than a salesperson.

5. Present the proposal as a "draft" that you will gladly modify to meet the company's needs. Custom-tailored proposals are much more likely to succeed than generic proposals.

6. Negotiate the final deal and get a signed agreement. Close the deal when you have the opportunity—ask for the order! Be sure that the final signed deal has agreed-upon deliverables, payment terms, and mutually agreed-upon timetables.

Case Study 14-1   The Outsourcing of College Ticket Sales Operations

For decades, colleges and universities have relied upon the expertise of consulting companies to handle the development and management of their various marketing assets. For instance, industry-leading firms such as Collegiate Licensing Corporation (now a division within IMG College) and Licensing Resource Group have been representing the licensing interests of colleges and universities since the 1970s. The former Host Communications (also now a division of IMG College) was on the forefront of representing colleges and universities for their broadcasting rights. These and other industry players, including Learfield, CBS College Sports, ISP (now absorbed into IMG College), and Nelligan Sports Marketing, have also been retained by collegiate institutions to develop, manage, and sell their sponsorship programs, because so many of these partnerships are driven in large part by media/advertising sales. In most cases, one outside firm may handle all three areas of assets for the college or university.

These consulting arrangements typically provide the collegiate institution with a guaranteed annual cash rights fee payment (and in some cases a percentage of revenues above a certain monetary threshold) in exchange for allowing the outside company with the rights to reap the potential monetary benefits from the sales of the collegiate institution's broadcast advertising, sponsorship packages, and licensed products. It has historically been viewed as a win–win relationship for both parties. The focus of colleges and universities is typically on the educational mission; hence, many athletic departments lack the sales personnel and resources that one would typically find within a professional sport organization.

In the spring of 2009, Georgia Tech announced the hiring of The Aspire Group to handle ticket marketing and sales for football and men's basketball (Lombardo & Smith, 2009). It was the first such arrangement in college sports involving the outsourcing of ticket sales, and the publicity attendant to the announcement suggested the ushering in of a new trend in the collegiate marketplace. The same factors that drove collegiate merchandising/licensing, and then later broadcast media and sponsorship rights, to outsourcing have also driven the outsourcing of ticket marketing and sales—lack of expertise within the athletic department staff. However, in the case of outsourced ticket marketing, sales, and service, a few additional factors appear to be driving this growth. Many universities during the recent economic downturn have not been able to fund the significant number of new full-time positions that labor-intensive proactive outbound phone sales demands. Further, the payment of commissions to sales staff and bonuses to managers is frequently prohibited by state law. Finally, existing athletic administrative staff invariably have their time spread so thinly across multiple ticketed sports that they cannot allocate the time necessary to recruit, train, develop, and closely manage the ticket sales staff.

The arrangement called for The Aspire Group to handle full- and partial-season ticket sales and group ticket sales in exchange for expense reimbursement plus a percentage of any increase in ticket sales. Georgia Tech's athletic department maintains control of ticket prices and season ticket plans as well as ticket sales of premium seating and suites. After signing the agreement with Georgia Tech, The Aspire Group set up a full-time sales staff of around 15 people who work on Georgia Tech's Atlanta campus, which has subsequently grown to over 20 sales consultants, a director, and two managers.

"It boils down to cost containment and efficiency," said Mullin. "Traditionally, schools have a smaller number of year-round sales staff, but we can put more staff and resources behind the sales efforts. The school is providing the infrastructure and we are providing the management, systems, and procedures" (Lombardo and Smith, 2009, p. 1). Added Georgia Tech's Athletic Director Dan Radakovich, "We look at this as the next frontier for what we need to do to sell tickets" (Lombardo and Smith, 2009, p. 1).

Although the outsourcing of college ticket sales is a relatively new concept, in just 4 years since Aspire started the trend there are now over 80 NCAA Division I programs that have outsourced and an additional 30 NCAA Division I Athletic programs that have developed their own outbound ticket sales capabilities in-house. Additionally, several schools have outsourced their ticket marketing functions, responsibility for season ticket renewals, plus athletic donation renewals, and new sales. At Rutgers, University of California-Riverside, and University of Louisiana-Monroe, they have even outsourced ticket office/box office management and all day-of-game gate sales responsibilities to The Aspire Group.

To Outsource or Not to Outsource? That Is the Question

From the 2005 to 2008 Georgia Tech football seasons, attendance at the 55,000-seat Bobby Dodd stadium declined from an average of 51,607 per game to an average of 47,489 (a nearly 8% decline in attendance). In the season in which Georgia Tech outsourced its ticket sales to The Aspire Group, attendance increased by over 12% to a per game average of 51,584 (Table 14-2). Additionally, during the first 4 months of 2010, The Aspire Group had sold more than 770 new season-ticket packages, representing over $240,000 in additional revenue (Roberson, 2010). In each year that the Aspire Group has been selling Georgia Tech's tickets, the amount of new and incremental ticket revenues has grown each year, including a total of

Table 14-2 Georgia Tech Football

Year	Average Attendance	Percent of Capacity	Change from Previous Season
2012	43,955	79.9%	−8.8%
2011	48,232	87.7%	+3.8%
2010	46,449	84.45%	−9.9%
2009	51,584	93.78%	+12.43%
2008	47,489	86.34%	−5.55%
2007	50,280	91.42%	−0.67%
2006	50,617	92.03%	−1.92%
2005	51,607	93.83%	+10.23%

Data from: National Collegiate Athletic Association. (n.d.). Retrieved from http://www.ncaa.org.

(continues)

Case Study 14-1   The Outsourcing of College Ticket Sales Operations (continued)

$2 million in the 2012–2013 season. But perhaps more important, when the "annuity value" or "lifetime asset value" (LAV) is factored in, the residual revenue streams to Georgia Tech of these new ticket purchasers repeating their purchases in future years is extremely large. Georgia Tech has identified that approximately 67% of these new buyers renew each year, and therefore the LAV is 300% of each year's new ticket revenues, which over the 4-year period of outsourcing to The Aspire Group is estimated to be $15.3 million.

Revenue generated from football and men's basketball ticket sales is the lifeblood of collegiate athletic departments. Consider that during the 2006 fiscal year, ticket sales accounted for nearly 30% of the revenue generated by members of the NCAA's Football Bowl Subdivision, the single largest source of revenue (Fulks, 2008). Research has indicated that a number of factors influence consumer demand for collegiate sport (Groza, 2010). Although a number of these factors are outside of the control of the sales department, the ticket sales department must nonetheless strive to promote and ultimately sell tickets by highlighting the value to the customer. For high-demand games (e.g., the home team is having a successful season and/or is playing a quality opponent), creating a value proposition for the customer is not difficult. However, selling tickets to low-demand games (e.g., the home team is having an unsuccessful season and/or is playing an undesirable opponent) represents a much more challenging task for the ticket sales department.

© Photos.com

The art of selling is becoming increasingly scientific and technology driven. Today, advanced analytics such as consumer demand modeling and CRM systems allow sales managers to intelligently predict demand and sales personnel to better understand the individual customer.

Although The Aspire Group originally hired and managed 15 salespeople who were physically located within the Georgia Tech athletic facility, an increasingly prevalent mode, especially with smaller and emerging athletic programs, is for outside firms to handle all ticket sales from their corporate headquarters. For instance, The Aspire Group has up to 22 salespeople working out of its National Sales Center in Atlanta, where, for example, it sells over $1 million in ticket inventory for the NCAA and six of its National Championships, including men's and women's basketball; women's softball; women's volleyball; FCS football; and men's lacrosse.

Questions for Discussion

1. The outsourcing of licensing, media, and sponsorship rights is a business-to-business (so-called B2B) operation. Outside firms such as IMG College, Learfield, CBS, and Nelligan endeavor to find local, regional, and national businesses to buy advertising and sponsorships. Selling tickets is, in contrast, primarily a business-to-consumer (so-called B2C) endeavor. Assume you are the athletic director for a midsized Division I university. What would you see as some fundamental differences in and challenges to these two sales approaches?

2. Assuming the same situation, what concerns might you have about an outside firm selling tickets for your university from a sales call center in another location, perhaps even another state?

3. Assume you are the athletic director for a major Division I football powerhouse. Would you recommend that your athletic department outsource its ticket operations? Why or why not? What factors would influence your decision?

Summary

The steadily increasing competition for customers—both individuals and corporate—has sparked an evolution in sales methodologies within the sport industry. Today, smart sport organizations build and manage well-trained sales staffs that are committed to the philosophy of customer-focused relationship building. If you choose to begin your sport management career with a team sport organization, as so many do, chances are you will find yourself situated somewhere within the organization's sales department. In addition to positions in actual sales, more and more sport organizations are also looking for students with the strong analytical skills needed to manage and mine the organization's customer relationship management system. Additionally, as sport organizations further split their sales function from their customer retention function, opportunities exist for students to begin their careers within customer retention departments.

Regardless of your specific role within the sales department, there is arguably no better place to begin! Sales are the lifeblood of any sport organization, and regardless of your career path—from ticket sales to suite sales to sponsorship sales and perhaps into other disciplines within a sport organization—you will always be selling. The tools and experience garnered from responsibilities as unromantic as telemarketing—a sport industry form of "paying one's dues"—will pay big dividends as you move up in your career. The past few years have seen the emergence of so-called "sports sales combines," multiday seminars in which the organizers bring in sales executives from professional teams to coach and evaluate the attendees, while looking to also identify new young sales talent (King, 2010b). Students who attend these "combines" are essentially auditioning for entry-level sales positions.

A recent article entitled "The Changing Environment of Selling and Sales Management," although not specific to the sport industry, illuminates many of the challenges salespeople face today (Jones, Brown, Zoltners, & Weitz, 2005). For instance, potential and current customers today have higher expectations of salespeople; among other things, they expect salespeople will have a better understanding of and concern for their needs, be it soliciting a small business for a season-ticket package or attempting to sell a major corporation a multiyear sponsorship package. As such, sport organizations and their sales staffs need to become increasingly adept at customer-focused selling. Additionally, sales managers and salespeople are required to have much higher levels of technological aptitude, including, but not limited to, the willingness to adapt to technological advances and the ability to utilize selling tools ranging from CRM software to social media.

When asked to comment on the concerns and trends within the sport sales industry, a panel of sport industry executives expressed the difficulty they experienced in determining pricing of their product because the sport industry still revolves around fans' emotional responses, including popularity of the team, players, and owners. Social media and the understanding of its importance to fans is another trend impacting sport organizations (Industry Insider: Sales Panel, 2011). In addition, the consumption of the sport product has rapidly evolved to include digital ticketing and various other ways to purchase a ticket. Brent Stehlik, Executive Vice President and Chief Revenue Office for the Cleveland Browns, observed:

> Tickets have become a commodity like wheat or copper; think about the secondary ticketing market and how many outlets there are to purchase a ticket to the same event. It's changed dramatically in the last 3, 5, and 10 years, as there are dozens of places you can go to purchase a ticket. How we can keep the lifeblood of our business (ticket sales) strong in the future is of the utmost importance.

Sport organizations need to constantly be aware of these changes, and respond accordingly so as to stay current with how their sport product is consumed.

As discussed throughout this chapter, many factors are fueling new levels of complexity and sophistication within the realm of sport sales. The constantly changing competitive environment for sport sales of everything from online advertising to season tickets to sponsorship provides many skills-enhancing challenges for those who decide to begin their career in sport sales.

Resources

Major League Soccer National Sales Center
http://www.mlsnationalsalescenter.com

Ticketmaster
http://www.ticketmaster.com

Turnkey Sports & Entertainment
9 Tanner Street
Haddonfield, NJ 08033
856-685-1450
http://www.turnkeyse.com

Key Terms

aftermarketing, benefit selling, customer relationship management (CRM), direct mail, eduselling, personal selling, sales inventory, telemarketing, up-selling

References

Brennan, J. (2010, June 9). Insurer the "cure" for Nets' sponsorship needs in off-season. *Bergen (NJ) Record*. Retrieved from http://www.northjersey.com/news/nets-a-good-investment-cure-says-1.190315

Cohen, M. G. (2011). Golden State Warriors—Using social media to drive ticket sales. Retrieved from http://www.michaelgcohen.com/2012/04/golden-state-warriors-using-social-media-to-drive-ticket-sales/

Fisher, E. (2012, March 19). MLB FanPass to make paperless ticketing push. *Street & Smith's SportsBusiness Journal*, p. 1.

Fulks D. L. (2008). *2004–06 NCAA revenue and expenses of Division I Intercollegiate Athletics Programs Report*. Indianapolis, IN: National Collegiate Athletic Association.

Groza, M. D. (2010). NCAA conference realignment and football game day attendance. *Managerial and Decision Economics, 31*(8), 517–529.

Honebein, P. (1997). *Strategies for effective customer education*. Lincolnwood, IL: NTC Business Books.

Industry Insider: Sales Panel. (2011). *Sport Marketing Quarterly, 20*(2), 69–74.

Irwin, R., Sutton, W. A., & McCarthy, L. (2002). *Sport promotion and sales management*. Champaign, IL: Human Kinetics.

Irwin, R., Sutton, W. A., & McCarthy, L. (2008). *Sport promotion and sales management* (2nd ed.). Champaign, IL: Human Kinetics.

Jones, E., Brown, S., Zoltners, A., & Weitz, B. (2005). The changing environment of selling and sales management. *Journal of Personal Selling & Sales Management, 25*(2), 105–111.

King, B. (2010a, March 15). Always be closing. *Street & Smith's SportsBusiness Journal*, p. 1.

King, B. (2010b, March 15). Combine puts sales skills to true test. *Street & Smith's SportsBusiness Journal*, p. 13.

Leuty, R. (2013, May 8). Top 10 stadium, arena naming rights deals. *San Francisco Business Times*. Retrieved from http://www.bizjournals.com/sanfrancisco/blog/2013/05/stadium-naming-rights-deals-49ers-levis.html

Lombardo J., & Smith M. (2009, May 25). Ga. Tech hands ticket sales to Aspire Group. *Street & Smith's SportsBusiness Journal*, p. 1.

Maddox, J. (2013, January 3). Impact of social media on ticket sales. Retrieved from http://businessofcollegesports.com/2013/01/03/impact-of-social-media-on-ticket-sales/

McCormack, M. (1984). *What they don't teach you at Harvard Business School*. New York: Bantam.

McCormack, M. (1996). *On selling*. West Hollywood, CA: Dove Books.

McDonald, M.A. (1996). Service quality and customer lifetime value in professional sport franchises. Unpublished doctoral dissertation, University of Massachusetts, Amherst.

Mickle, T. (2010, May 24). MLS will be first league to run extensive ticket sales training. *Street & Smith's SportsBusiness Journal*, p. 5.

MLS National Sales Center. (n.d.). Retrieved from http://www.mlsnationalsalescenter.com/

Mullin, B., Hardy, S., & Sutton, W.A. (2007). *Sport marketing* (3rd ed.). Champaign, IL: Human Kinetics.

National Collegiate Athletic Association. (n.d.). Retrieved from http://www.ncaa.org/Docs/stats/football_record/Attendance

Radcliffe, J. (2002, April 29–May 5). Name game gets more complicated for teams. *Street & Smith's SportsBusiness Journal*, p. 26.

Roberson, D. (2010, April 28). Tech season-ticket sales improving. *Atlanta Journal Constitution*. Retrieved from http://blogs.ajc.com/georgia-tech-sports/2010/04/28/tech-season-ticket-sales-improving

Sutton, B. (2010, May 10). Using technology to build ticket database can boost bottom line. *Street & Smith's SportsBusiness Journal*, p. 11.

Team Marketing Report. (2011). *Fan cost index*. Retrieved from https://www.teammarketing.com/public/files/2011_mlb_fci.pdf

Vavra, T. G. (1992). *Aftermarketing: How to keep customers for life through relationship marketing*. New York: Irwin.

Chapter 15

Stephen McKelvey

Sport Sponsorship

Helmut/Thinkstock

Learning Objectives

Upon completion of this chapter, students should be able to:

1. Recognize the reasons for the rapid growth of the sport sponsorship segment over the past three decades.

2. Assess why companies are eager to engage in sport sponsorship and the benefits that can accrue to sponsors.

3. Appraise the effect that the commercial success of the 1984 Los Angeles Olympics had on the sport sponsorship industry.

4. Evaluate the role of sales promotion in sponsorship programs with particular emphasis on the increasing use of cross-promotion.

5. Identify the broad range of sponsorship platforms that are available, including governing body, team, athlete, media, facility, and event sponsorships.

6. Examine the challenges that are faced when measuring the return on investment from sport sponsorships.

7. Debate current issues in the sport sponsorship industry, such as ethnic marketing through sport sponsorship, the overcommercialization of sport, and the marriage of vice and sport.

8. Recognize that within the spectrum of sales jobs, selling sponsorships is regarded as the most glamorous of sales positions, and these positions are usually reached after gaining experience selling other types of sales inventory.

Introduction

When the Dayton Dragons of minor league baseball's Class A Midwest League first opened the gates of the newly minted Fifth Third Field in April 2000, a standing-room-only crowd was greeted by what the team dubbed the "world's largest outdoor billboard." Instead of continuing the age-old minor league baseball tradition of plastering the outfield walls with upwards of 50 hand-painted sponsor signs—the epitome, some might argue, of advertising "clutter"—the Dragons had constructed one outfield sign (240 feet long by 6 feet high) to cover the entire outfield wall. The sign is backlit and rotates every half-inning with a wall-to-wall advertisement from one of the team's major sponsors. Thus, at any time during the game only one company is promoted to the entire crowd.

This innovative strategy for selling the team's outfield wall signage was meant to create and deliver, as the Dragons call it, a "dominant identity" for its sponsors. The Dragons carried the concept of "dominant identity" even further by limiting the total number of team sponsors to just 30. This approach to sponsorship represents a dramatic shift in strategy from the traditional minor league team that boasts anywhere from 75 to 300 sponsors. The Dragons' approach to sponsorship—sell fewer sponsorships and give those sponsors incrementally more benefits, exposure, and "identity" to consumers—illustrates just one type of approach, or philosophy, that sport organizations can take with respect to corporate sponsorship. This chapter provides an introduction to sponsorship within the sport industry. What is sport sponsorship all about? What benefits can sport organizations provide to sponsors? What are the key elements of a sponsorship package?

As you proceed, one common theme will emerge throughout this chapter. The Dayton Dragons' example illustrates the growing challenge for sport organizations to think outside the box in terms of attracting corporate sponsors in an increasingly competitive sport marketplace. The continuing influx of new sport leagues, teams, and events has created more and more options for companies large and small to engage in sport sponsorship. Ultimately, sport organizations that can best meet the needs and objectives of companies, and deliver on their promises, will be the ones that are most successful in attracting and retaining sponsorship partners.

Sponsorship is one of the most prolific forms of sport marketing. It has been defined as "a cash and/or in-kind fee paid to a property . . . in return for access to the exploitable commercial potential associated with that property" (Ukman, 1995, p. 1). For the major professional sport leagues and associations, sponsorship fees can often exceed $5 million per year per sponsor and are often structured as multiyear deals. Sponsorship provides a company with the right to associate with a sport property. A sponsorship agreement also gives the company the opportunity to leverage its affiliation with the sport property to achieve marketing objectives that range from generating incremental sales to entertaining key customers to generating positive awareness for the company and its products or services. Sponsorship is more integrated than other promotion activities and contains a variety of marketing-mix elements designed to send messages to a targeted audience, including, but not limited to, advertising, sales promotion, grassroots event programs, public relations and publicity, cause marketing, and hospitality.

A Brief History of Sport Sponsorship

Although we can trace some semblance of sport sponsorship back to the ancient Greek Olympics—local businesses paid charioteers to wear their colors—the increasing commercialization of sport has led to a tremendous growth in the area of sport sponsorship. Whereas $300 million was spent on sport sponsorship in 1980 (Mullin, Hardy, & Sutton, 2007), that number had grown to $11.28 billion by 2009 (IEG, 2010). The number of U.S. companies spending $15 million or more on sport sponsorship grew from 77 in 2010 to 86 in 2011 (IEG, 2012). Table 15-1 lists the top 15 sport sponsors in 2011.

Industry pundits have identified the 1984 Los Angeles Olympic Games as a watershed event in the evolution of sport sponsorship. The Los Angeles Olympic Organizing Committee, under the direction of its president, Peter Ueberroth, brought a new commercial mind-set to the L.A. Games in its effort to make its Games the first Olympic Games to ever turn a profit for the host city. Employing a "less is more" sales strategy, Ueberroth and

his marketing team signed a limited number of companies to exclusive official sponsorship contracts, with fees ranging from $4 million to $15 million per company. AT&T alone paid $5 million to sponsor the first-ever cross-country Olympic torch relay. Fuji Photo Film USA paid $9 million to outbid goliath Kodak for the official sponsorship rights in the film and camera category in an effort to firmly entrench itself in America as a major player (Dentzer, 1984). The publicity surrounding this highly successful commercial venture not only resulted in Ueberroth being named *Time* magazine's "Man of the Year," but also ushered in a new era of sport sponsorship by demonstrating that companies could gain tremendous benefits from sponsorships.

Although the commercial success of the 1984 Los Angeles Olympics put a new spotlight on sport sponsorship, several other factors have contributed to the tremendous growth in sport sponsorship over the past three decades. One influence is the increased media interest in sport, both traditional and online, which has provided companies with a highly visible mechanism for promoting their sponsorship involvements. This has assured sponsors that there is a better chance that their sponsorship will be publicized. Sponsorship is also being viewed as a way for companies to break through the clutter of traditional advertising. Through sponsorship, companies are able to derive numerous in-venue, in-broadcast, retail, and online promotion and publicity benefits that go far beyond the impact of a 30-second commercial spot in connecting with and influencing consumers.

Further, companies have begun to realize the impact that sponsorship could have in reaching their target consumers through their lifestyles (Mullin et al., 2007). Corporate marketing executives have found that linking their messages to leisure pursuits conveys their

Table 15-1 Top 15 U.S. Sport Sponsors, 2011

Amount	Company
$340 to $345 million	PepsiCo, Inc.
$265 to $270 million	The Coca-Cola Co.
$255 to $260 million	Anheuser-Busch InBev
$215 to $220 million	Nike, Inc.
$175 to $180 million	AT&T, Inc.
$170 to $175 million	General Motors Co.
$150 to $155 million	Toyota Motor Sales U.S.A., Inc.
$135 to $140 million	MillerCoors LLC
$135 to $140 million	Ford Motor Co.
$105 to $110 million	Verizon Communications, Inc.
$80 to $85 million	Sprint Nextel Corp.
$80 to $85 million	The Proctor & Gamble Co.
$70 to $75 million	Bank of America Corp.
$65 to $70 million	FedEx Corp.
$60 to $65 million	UPS

Reproduced from: IEG, Inc. (2012, May 29). Following the money: Sponsorship's top spenders of 2011. Courtesy of *IEG Sponsorship Report*.

messages immediately, credibly, and to a captive audience. Targeted sponsorships also enable corporate marketers to reach specific segments, such as heavy users, shareholders, and investors, or specific groups that have similar demographics or psychographics or geographic commonalities. For instance, the director of marketing for Golden Flake Snack Foods, a regional snack food company, remarked in discussing his company's long-running sponsorship of Southeastern Conference (SEC) football: "College football is a religion in the Southeast. Sponsorship lets us tap into the emotions people have for these events and be part of something they value. Because we try to maintain long-term relationships, people recognize and appreciate that we're not a fly-by-night sponsor, but have a commitment to [the SEC]" (IEG, 2003a, p. 6). Another example of using sport sponsorship to target a specific geographic market is Glidden's sponsorship of the Big South Athletic Conference (Smith, 2010). Glidden, an Ohio-based paint company, sought to enhance awareness of its brand in the South by sponsoring a sport property based in that region. Through its agreement with the Big South Conference, Glidden is designated the conference's "official paint supplier" and will have access to all 10 of the league's schools throughout South Carolina, North Carolina, and Virginia (Smith, 2010). PepsiCo has long used sponsorship to reach specific target markets. Take for example, PepsiCo's title sponsorship of NBC's action sports series The Dew Tour. Through this sponsorship PepsiCo is able to reach a demographic that it has assessed as the typical Mountain Dew consumer: young, active, and daring (Mickle, 2010).

Last, but not least, the discipline of sport sponsorship has emerged as the decision-making process has been gradually transferred from the company's CEO to the company's team of marketing professionals. Historically, companies delved into a sponsorship program because the CEO wanted to; the CEO liked to golf, so he made sure his company became a sponsor of a PGA or LPGA tournament. Today, however, sport sponsorship involves in-depth consumer research, significant financial investment, and strategic planning. Buying decisions have become much more sophisticated, requiring sellers to provide compelling business reasons to the prospective sponsor (e.g., demographic information demonstrating that the property will deliver the right target audience for the company) and requiring potential buyers to demonstrate to their CEO that a sponsorship program will meet the company's specific marketing and sales objectives in some measurable way. This is commonly referred to as **return on investment (ROI)**, a topic that will be more fully discussed in the section entitled "Evaluating Sport Sponsorships."

The increased competition for the loyalties of sport consumers has also changed the priorities of sport properties in terms of the companies with which they choose to partner. Today, sport properties prefer not to partner with companies that simply purchase the sponsorship rights (thereby blocking out their category from their competitors) and then do little or nothing to utilize, or leverage, their sponsorship to the benefit of both the sponsor and the sport property itself. Thus, more and more sponsorship contracts now require that the sponsor commit financial resources in support of its sponsorship through promotion and advertising that thematically includes the sport property's imagery. This is a concept known as sponsorship **activation**. The oft-cited rule of thumb for activating a sponsorship is 3 to 1; that is, $3 in advertising/promotion support for every $1 spent in rights fees.

Concurrently, given the increased competition for corporate sponsorship dollars, prospective sponsors have gained leverage in negotiations. It's the age-old question: Who needs whom more? Thus, companies have become more demanding of sport properties in terms of the marketing rights and benefits they are provided. "Sponsors are pushing harder," noted the vice president of PepsiCo's Sports Marketing Division, "and leagues are working harder to add value and measurable results" (Solomon, 2002, p. 1). The National Hockey League (NHL), for example, allowed Pepsi to conduct a promotion in which the grand prize winner would have the Stanley Cup delivered to his or her house by Mark Messier, the NHL's second-leading all-time scorer. It is now commonplace for leagues and teams to allow their official sponsors to conduct sweepstakes that reward winners with aspirational opportunities, such as the chance to throw out first pitches at the World Series, drop the ceremonial puck at Stanley Cup Games, or participate in the ceremonial coin toss at a National Football League (NFL) game.

New themes and initiatives have also started to emerge in the sport sponsorship space over the past few years. One example has been the development and activation of sponsorships that support sustainability, or so-called "green" initiatives. The National Association for Stock Car Auto Racing (NASCAR), for instance, has built a Green Partners program that today numbers over 20 companies ranging from Eaton Electrical (which supplies electric vehicle–charging stations) to MillerCoors (Mickle, 2013). One of the fastest growing sources of sponsorship revenue is in the social media space. Among the most active sponsors is the location-based social networking site Foursquare, which over the past several years has inked sponsorship arrangements with sport properties ranging from the U.S. Open Tennis Championships to the NFL, NHL, and Major League Soccer (MLS) (Botta, 2013). In addition to its ability to generate millions of impressions for the sport organization, Foursquare also

provides the leagues and teams with a platform to offer discounts to fans. For example, during the opening weeks of the 2013 MLS season, fans who connected to Foursquare on their mobile devices received an offer for $10 off the $59.99 subscription price for MLS Live (the league's video-streaming service) (Botta, 2013). The National Basketball Association (NBA) has embraced social media–oriented sponsorships, which include B&H Photo's sponsorship of the Brooklyn Nets' Instagram destination; Esurance's sponsorship of the Golden State Warriors' "Social Media Night"; and Chevrolet's sponsorship of the Los Angeles Galaxy's social media hub, which aggregates the team's stats, highlights, Twitter-based voting, Instagram galleries, and other content (Fisher, 2013).

From electric vehicle–charging companies and fruit growers' associations to casinos and social media platforms, the range of commercial entities seeking to engage in sport sponsorship continues to expand. If your sport organization or property can deliver the audience that these and other companies are seeking to target, there is a sponsorship possibility for those with creative minds and strong sales skills.

Sales Promotion in Sport Sponsorship

Sponsorship programs are often built upon some type of promotional activity, generally referred to as sales promotion. **Sales promotion** is defined as "a variety of short-term, promotional activities that are designed to stimulate immediate product demand" (Shank, 2009, p. 312). Although aimed primarily at driving sales in the short term, typically over the course of a month or two, sponsors' sales promotion efforts may also be aimed at increasing brand awareness, broadening the sales distribution channels for their product or service, and getting new consumers to sample their product or service. A typical example of a sport-themed sales promotion is when a sponsoring company provides all fans with a free item featuring the company's logo (also known as a *premium item*) as they enter the arena. In addition to such in-venue activities, sales promotions are often implemented at the retail level (known as *in-store promotions*), such as an offer of a free game ticket when fans redeem a soft drink can at the box office. This section first discusses the implementation and benefits of in-venue promotions, and then describes in-store promotion tactics.

In-Venue Promotions

No other sport has utilized in-stadium promotion as widely as baseball. One major reason for this is that "putting fannies in seats" has traditionally been more of a priority in baseball than in the other major sports: Major League Baseball (MLB) teams have 81 home dates with thousands of seats to fill each game. At the opposite extreme, NFL teams have historically had little need to attract additional fans with "freebies" and giveaways because the majority of NFL teams sell out their stadiums for all home games. The trend across all sports, however, has been to increase the amount of "value-added" benefits that teams provide their paying customers, which has resulted in a growth in in-stadium promotions across the sport industry. In-stadium promotions run the gamut from traditional giveaway days, in which the sponsor underwrites the cost of a premium item in exchange for its logo on the item and advertising support that promotes the event, to themed-event days, such as nostalgia-driven "Turn Back the Clock Days," which are popular in MLB. Many teams have also created what are known as *continuity promotions,* which require fans to attend multiple games to obtain, for instance, each player card in a limited-edition trading card set, thus building attendance frequency.

Sport organizations are constantly on the prowl for the hottest fad in giveaway items. For instance, back in the late 1980s and early 1990s, baseball teams gorged on the collectible trading card craze. Fans would line up hours before games to ensure that they received the hottest new trading card–themed giveaway item, ranging from the Surf detergent–sponsored Topps Baseball Card books to the Smokey the Bear–themed collectors sets and the Upper Deck Heroes of Baseball card sheets. Beanie Babies emerged as the hot items in the late 1990s, and the bobblehead doll craze followed shortly thereafter. Table 15-2 lists MLB's most successful promotional giveaway items during the 2012 season.

The success of an in-venue promotion varies widely based on a number of factors, including time of season (and teams' current win–loss records), the day of promotion (weeknight versus weekend), opponent, and perceived quality of the giveaway item or themed promotion event day. Contrary to what one might expect, teams generally build their promotional calendars to feature their most attractive giveaways or events on their more attractive dates (in

Table 15-2 2012 MLB In-Stadium Giveaways

Rank	Category (number of teams)	Number of Dates
1	Bobbleheads (26)	94
2	T-shirt (24)	79
3	Headwear (28)	69
4	Backpack/bag (26)	50
5	Magnet schedule (29)	46
6	Photo (12)	43
7	Toy (22)	37
8	Poster (15)	33
9 (tie)	Jersey (17)	31
9 (tie)	Retail coupon (7)	31

Reproduced from: Broughton, D. (2012, November 12). Everybody loves bobbleheads: Popular giveaway climbs past T-shirts, headwear to top spot on promotions list. *SportsBusiness Journal*, p. 9. Courtesy of *SportsBusiness Journal*.

Table 15-3 Top MLB In-Game Promotions/Events for 2012

Rank	Category (number of teams)	Number of Dates
1	Fireworks (22)	186
2	Festival (16)	168
3	Ticket discount (9)	164
4	Concessions discount (13)	127
5	Autographs (6)	125
6	Family day (10)	103
7	Run the bases (16)	100
8	College night (10)	76
9	Team history tribute (21)	73
10	Kids day (16)	67

Reproduced from: Broughton, D. (2012, November 12). Everybody loves bobbleheads: Popular giveaway climbs past T-shirts, headwear to top spot on promotions list. *SportsBusiness Journal*, p. 9. Courtesy of *SportsBusiness Journal*.

terms of opponents and game times) because of the popular notion that a strong promotional giveaway or event typically attracts a larger *incremental* audience. For example, the Chicago White Sox staging a fan appreciation day against an unattractive opponent on a midweek night might attract an incremental 1,000 fans. That same promotion versus the Yankees on a Saturday afternoon might draw an incremental 10,000 fans. Table 15-3 shows a ranking of the most popular in-stadium promotions for MLB teams during the 2012 season.

In-Store Promotions

One of the primary reasons that companies secure sponsorships is to drive sales of their product or service. Hence, not surprisingly, companies often leverage their sponsorships at the retail level: in stores where their product is sold or within their own retail stores. In-store promotion encompasses a wide variety of tactics to incentivize consumers and to communicate offers, including premiums, contests and sweepstakes, sampling, point-of-sale or point-of-purchase marketing, and coupons.

Premiums

Premiums can be described as "merchandise offered free or at a reduced price as an inducement to buy a different item or items" (Block & Robinson, 1994, p. 876). One of the most popular tactics is offering premiums to consumers who redeem a certain number of proof-of-purchase seals (also known as UPCs) that are printed on the product itself. Premiums can also be delivered to consumers in-pack or on-pack. For example, a cereal company can activate its NASCAR sponsorship by offering consumers a free mini-race car inside specially marked boxes.

Contests and Sweepstakes

Contests and **sweepstakes** are other popular sales tools used in sales promotion. Contests are competitions that award prizes based on contestants' skills and ability, whereas sweepstakes are games of chance or luck. A sport team or company may require a purchase as a condition of consumers being entered into the contest (e.g., requiring contestants in a football accuracy throwing contest to enter by submitting proofs-of-purchase); however, contests typically appeal to a much smaller universe of potential customers than sweepstakes (where everyone has a *chance* to win). Companies and sport teams conducting sweepstakes may not require the purchase of a product or service for consumers to become eligible to win prizes (thus, the "No Purchase Necessary" notice that precedes all sweepstakes rules).

Sweepstakes typically offer trips to special sporting events, the opportunity for the winner to meet a celebrity athlete, or some other "aspirational" prize that would be difficult (if not impossible) for the winner to otherwise obtain. For example, Pepperidge Farms Goldfish Baked Crackers signed NBA star Dwayne Wade for a sweepstakes in which customers could sign up online to win prizes, including an all-expenses paid trip for four to the NBA

All-Star Game. Staples has leveraged its role as the NFL's "official office supply retailer" with a sweepstakes called the "Staples Score NFL Season Tickets Sweepstakes," offering one of 32 lucky winners season tickets to the team of his or her choice. Consumers entered by filling out a sweepstakes entry form at their local Staples store that also requested valuable demographic and purchase-decision information that surely went into Staples' customer database for use in future direct mail campaigns. Sport teams and companies have also increasingly turned to an online sweepstakes entry process as a means of driving traffic to their websites. After all, it is easier to post a sweepstakes entry form on one's own website than to hope that the sweepstakes entry forms get appropriately displayed in retail stores.

Sampling

Sampling is one of the most effective sales promotion tools to induce consumers to try a product; it is most often used in the introduction of a new product. Companies typically use sampling to leverage their sport sponsorship by gaining access to a major sporting event, such as the MLB All-Star FanFest or a college bowl game, at which they can hand out product samples to the captive and targeted audience that attends such events. Sampling is not without its hard costs. Although the product samples may be free to consumers, bear in mind when planning a sampling campaign that it still costs money for the company to produce the samples and hire individuals (usually a professional sampling firm) to distribute them to the 70,000 consumers attending, for instance, MLB's All-Star FanFest.

Point-of-Sale or Point-of-Purchase Marketing

Point-of-sale or **point-of-purchase marketing**, interchangeably referred to in industry lingo as POS or POP, is used by marketers to attract consumers' attention to their product or service and their promotional campaign at the retail level. POS display materials can include end-aisle units (large cardboard displays that sit on the floor and are featured at the end of retail store aisles), "shelf-talkers" (cardboard displays that hang on aisle shelves), and banners that are designed to attract potential customers. The life-sized cardboard cutouts of star athletes that you see in grocery and footwear stores are examples of POS materials. Typically these display pieces hold brochures, coupons, or sweepstakes entry forms.

Coupons

Coupons, certificates that generally offer reductions in price for a product or service, are another popular sales promotion tool. They most often appear in print advertisements such as **freestanding inserts (FSIs)**, which are the coupon sections that appear each week in Sunday newspapers. Coupons may also be delivered to consumers on the product package itself, inserted into the product itself, or mailed to consumers. In-store promotions are also typically supported by coupons that appear in the participating retailers' circular (the coupon magazines available in-store). Although coupons have been found to induce short-term sales, one disadvantage is that the continual use of coupons can detract from the product's image in the mind of consumers. In addition, studies have shown that most coupon redemption is done by consumers who already use the product, thereby limiting the effectiveness of coupons to attract new customers (Shank, 2009).

Putting It All Together: Kraft's "Taste of Victory" Promotion

Kraft Foods is one of the world's largest sport sponsorship spenders. Kraft's "Taste of Victory" promotion, a multifaceted corporate-wide engagement, perfectly illustrates the implementation of the various sales promotion tactics discussed previously. The promotion, thematically tied to Kraft's celebration of its 100 years in business, leveraged the company's sponsorship of Dale Earnhardt's NASCAR race team and was supported by a multitude of Kraft brands, including Country Time Lemonade, Miracle Whip, A1 Steak Sauce, and Grey Poupon mustard. Titled "Get a Taste of Victory," the promotion was communicated via in-store POS end-aisle displays, advertisements and coupons in retailers' circulars, and a full-page FSI in the nation's Sunday newspapers. The FSI included a mail-in form enticing consumers to mail in two proofs-of-purchase from any featured Kraft products (plus $4.00 shipping and handling) to receive a "free" premium: a Kraft 100th anniversary die-cast race car (miniature die-cast cars being one of the hottest collectibles in the auto-racing industry). The FSI also encouraged consumers to visit Kraftfoods.com to enter a sweepstakes to win the grand prize: a "street-legal" version of Kraft's 100th anniversary race car valued at $31,000. The POS displays served as a means to attract consumers to Kraft products in-store, the premium offer of the die-cast racing car served as a means of driving incremental sales (particularly among the extremely loyal race car fans), and the online sweepstakes served as a vehicle for collecting the names and addresses of Kraft customers (for future direct mailings). Finally, Kraft's purchase of advertisements and coupons in retailers' circular magazines served to ensure the retailers' in-store support of the promotion, in the form of providing Kraft with the most valuable "real estate" in any store: the end of aisles, where the bulk of impulse purchases take place. If this sounds like a creative form of blackmail, well, it is! It is how the game is played at the retail level.

The Emergence of Cross-Promotion

As companies tackle the need to break through the clutter, drive sales, and better leverage their sport sponsorship investments, they have sought to expand the scope of their sponsorships through **cross-promotion** with other companies or with other business units within the same company. This joining together of two or more companies to capitalize on a sponsorship is becoming increasingly popular and effective. Cross-promotion is viable in today's marketplace for a number of reasons, as suggested by Irwin, Sutton, and McCarthy (2008). Cross-promotions:

- Allow companies to share the total cost of the sponsorship and/or the promotional execution.
- Allow promotion of several product lines within the same company, often drawing from separate budgets, as illustrated in Kraft's "Taste of Victory" promotion.
- Enable companies to utilize existing business relationships.
- Enable a weaker company to "piggyback" on the strength and position of a bigger company to gain an advantage over its competitors.
- Allow testing of a relationship when future opportunities are under consideration.
- Create a pass-through opportunity, typically involving grocery chains that agree to a sponsorship and pass some or all of the costs (and benefits) to product vendors in their stores. For example, Kroger sponsors a NASCAR team but then passes most of the sponsorship rights fees on to vendors such as Pepsi and Nabisco. In exchange, Kroger then agrees to feature Pepsi and Nabisco products in-store.

© Beelde Photography/ShutterStock, Inc.

Sponsors team with other sponsors to create more bang for their buck under the premise that two sponsors working together can generate more interest and awareness among the targeted sport consumers. "Got Milk's" leveraging of its NASCAR sponsorship through a cross-promotion with Kellogg's illustrates the growing amount of sponsorship activation involving what has been dubbed "peanut butter and jelly" (PB&J) partners (IEG, 2003c). These PB&J partners illustrate cross-promotions by discrete brands that go together but can also stand alone.

Another increasingly popular cross-promotion tactic involves *codependent partners*, companies whose products or services are integral to each other, such as computer software and hardware manufacturers, teaming up to leverage a sport sponsorship (IEG, 2003a). For example, IBM, as a sponsor of the NBA, might offer a free NBA video game with the purchase of a new laptop. Finally, cross-promotions can be staged between *customer-partners*, two discrete brands that stand alone but do so much business with each other that they are almost siblings (IEG, 2003c). For example, to better leverage its sponsorship of MLB, Pepsi incorporated one of its biggest national customers, Subway restaurants, as a partner in an official All-Star Game balloting promotion. Such involvement between customer-partners not only greatly broadened the impact and awareness of MLB's All-Star balloting program nationwide but also enabled Pepsi to pass through an invaluable marketing asset to one of its largest national customers, thereby strengthening its business relationship with Subway.

As a sport marketer, whether on the property side or the corporate side, it has become increasingly important to think outside the box as to how sponsors can be joined together to increase the overall effectiveness of their sponsorship investments. Many of the official

sponsors of the major professional sport leagues are hard at work looking for creative ways to cross-promote their companies. **Tables 15-4** through **15-7** list some of the official sponsors for several of the major North American professional sport leagues; **Table 15-8** provides a list of the Worldwide IOC Olympic Partner Sponsors (TOP). Here's a challenge: See if you can develop a few effective cross-promotion opportunities for them! Would you classify them as PB&J promotions, codependent partner promotions, or customer-partner promotions?

Sponsorship Packages

In 2010 Bridgestone Tire signed a 5-year sponsorship deal with the NHL. Bridgestone's sponsorship of the NHL provides a good illustration of the benefits typically included in a league or team sponsorship package as well as the types of commitments the sponsoring company makes to the sport organization. Benefits typically include the following:

- *Exclusivity* in one's product or service category. For example, Bridgestone became the only company the NHL could sign as a national sponsor in the tire category.
- *"Official" designations* tie the sport to the sponsor's product or service category. For instance, Bridgestone became the "official tire of the NHL," the "official tire of the NHLPA," and the "official tire of the Hockey Hall of Fame." (Many sport organizations, embracing a relationship marketing mentality, today prefer the use of "official partner" designations.)
- *Rights* to utilize the sport organization's intellectual property in advertising and promotion campaigns. For Bridgestone this includes the rights to use the NHL logo in promotional activities. (Typically, the major professional sport league sponsorship departments do not have the authority, via their agreement with their member

Table 15-4 NHL Corporate Marketing Partners for the 2012–2013 Season

Sponsor	Category	Sponsor Since
North America		
Reebok	Outfitter	2003
PepsiCo (Pepsi, Gatorade, Aquafina, Frito-Lay)*	Soft drink, energy drink, water, snack	2006
Bridgestone*	Tire, Winter Classic naming rights	2007
SiriusXM	Satellite radio	2007
Ticketmaster	Secondary ticket provider	2007
Cisco	Technology/network solutions	2008
Compuware*	Global applications, Premiere Series naming rights	2009
Las Vegas Convention & Visitors Authority	Home of NHL Awards	2009
Starwood Hotels	Hotel	2009
Enterprise	Rental cars	2010
MillerCoors/MolsonCoors	Beer	2011
U.S. Only		
Verizon*	Wireless service provider	2006
McDonald's	Quick-service restaurant	2007
Honda	Automaker	2008
Discover	Credit/debit/affinity card	2010
Geico	Automotive insurance	2010
Canada Only		
Kraft (Nabisco)*	Cracker/cookie/snack mix	1999
Scotiabank*	Bank/financial services provider/affinity card	2007
Tim Horton's	Coffee/breakfast/donut	2008
Visa*	Credit/debit card	2008
Bell	Wireless service provider	2009
Hershey's	Confections	2009
Canadian Tire	Home improvement retailer	2010

* = Deal also extends to NHLPA.

Reproduced from: Spons-o-Meter: NHL boasts 23 official corporate sponsors this season. (2012, April 11). Retrieved from http://www.sportsbusinessdaily.com/Daily/Issues/2012/04/11/Marketing-and-Sponsorship/NHL -sponsometer.aspx. Courtesy of *SportsBusiness Journal*.

teams, to grant national sponsors the right to utilize team logos on an individual team basis; such rights must be obtained directly from the desired team or teams.)

- *Title naming rights* for the "Bridgestone NHL Winter Classic," an annual regular season outdoor hockey game typically played on or near New Year's Day.

- *In-stadium signage and promotional announcements* during NHL-controlled events such as the All-Star Game and the Stanley Cup Playoffs, often in the form of 30-second commercials and sponsor "thank you" messages via scoreboards, matrix boards, and public address (PA) announcements.

Table 15-5 NBA Corporate Marketing Partners

Sponsor	Category	Sponsor Since
Gatorade	Sports and energy drinks	1984
Coca-Cola	Soft drinks, juice and flavored drinks	1986
Nike	Footwear	1992
Anheuser-Busch	Beer (alcoholic and nonalcoholic malt beverages)	1998
Adidas	Apparel/footwear	2002
Southwest Airlines	Airline	2003
FedEx	Overnight delivery services	2004
Electronic Arts	Video game software	2005
Sirius/XM Radio	Satellite radio	2005
Spalding	Basketballs	2005
T-Mobile	Wireless service provider and handsets	2005
AutoTrader.com	Online auto retailer	2006
Haier America	High-definition TVs and consumer appliances	2006
Cisco	Information technology and networking solutions	2007
HP	Personal computers, printers, and IT services	2008
Kia Motors	Automotive	2008
Right Guard	Antiperspirant, deodorant, and body wash	2008
Taco Bell	Quick-service restaurant	2009
Bacardi	Rum	2010
State Farm	Insurance (all kinds)	2010

Reproduced from: Spons-o-Meter: NBA Boasts List of 20 Marketing Partners. Retrieved from http://www
.sportsbusinessdaily.com/Daily/Issues/2010/04/Issue-152/Sponsorships-Advertising-Marketing/Spons-O-Meter
-NBA-Boasts-List-Of-20-Marketing-Partners.aspx. Courtesy of *SportsBusiness Journal*.

- *Access to tickets* for NHL-controlled events, including the All-Star Game, and the Stanley Cup Playoffs.
- *Access to the use of* NHL player rights and images.

In exchange for these benefits, Bridgestone, again illustrative of most sport sponsorship contracts, made the following contractual commitments to the NHL:

- *A rights fee* in the form of a cash payment (typically spread out in periodic payments throughout the season).
- *A multiyear commitment* (most established sport properties insist on multiyear sponsorship deals to ensure stability for the league and a longer-term commitment by the sponsor; Bridgestone entered into a 5-year agreement with the NHL).

- *Advertising commitment* to spend a predetermined dollar amount on NHL-controlled media and/or with NHL's broadcast partners (i.e., NBC, CBC, and RDS).

Companies engaged in sport sponsorship use a wide variety of marketing elements, often collectively, to achieve their marketing objectives. The next section considers some possible sport sponsorship platforms.

Sport Sponsorship Platforms

A broad range of platforms are available upon which a company can become involved in sport sponsorship. As suggested by Irwin and colleagues (2008), these platforms are often integrated to expand the depth and breadth of the sponsorship.

Table 15-6 NFL Corporate Marketing Partners, 2012 Season

Sponsor	Category	Sponsor Since
Gatorade	Isotonic beverage	1983
Visa USA	Payment systems services	1995
Campbell's Soup	Soup	1998
FedEx	Worldwide package delivery service	2000
Frito-Lay	Salted snack/popcorn/peanuts/dips	2000
General Motors	Car and passenger truck	2001
Mars Snackfood	Confectioner	2002
Pepsi	Soft drink	2002
Dairy Management Inc.	Dairy, milk, yogurt, cheese	2003
Bridgestone	Tire sponsor	2007
National Guard	HSPD/7on7 (not a promotional sponsor)	2009
Procter & Gamble (Gillette, Head & Shoulders, Vicks, Old Spice)	Grooming products, fabric care/hair care, household needs	2009
Verizon	Wireless telecommunication service	2010
Barclay's	Official affinity card/rewards program (NFL extra points)	2010
Papa John's	Official pizza	2010
Castrol	Official motor oil	2010
Anheuser-Busch	Official beer	2011
USAA	Insurance/military appreciation	2011
Bose	Official home theater system	2011
Marriot	Official hotel	2011
Xbox	Video game console	2011
Quaker	Hot cereal	2012
Procter & Gamble (Tide, Duracell)	Household cleaning, battery power	2012
Lenovo	Computers (desktop, laptop, computer workstations)	2012

Reproduced from: Spons-o-Meter: NFL lines up 24 partners to start '12 season. (2012, September 7). Retrieved from http://m.sportsbusinessdaily.com/Daily/Issues/2012/09/07/NFL-Season-Preview/Sponsometer.aspx. Courtesy of *SportsBusiness Journal*.

Governing Body Sponsorship

A governing body sponsorship entails securing the "official sponsor" status with a national or international sport league or governing association. Companies that play upon this platform tend to be larger, international companies due to the size of the financial investment required. Governing bodies range from the IOC, which grants companies the right to be an "official worldwide partner" of the Olympic Games, to the major professional sport leagues (e.g., MLB, NFL), to organizations such as the National Collegiate Athletic Association (NCAA) and Little League Baseball. Most of these sponsorships, while providing "official sponsor" status across the entire organization, do not necessarily grant "official sponsor" status to the individual teams within the organization. These rights must be secured separately from the individual teams.

Team Sponsorship

Team sponsorship is often a more appropriate platform for local or regional companies or

Table 15-7 MLB Corporate Marketing Partners, 2012 Season

Sponsor	Category	Sponsor Since
Procter & Gamble (Gillette, Head & Shoulders)	Gillette (men's and women's razors/blades, pre/postshaving); Head & Shoulders (shampoo/conditioner)	1939
Anheuser-Busch (AL/NL Player of the Month Awards)	Alcoholic and nonalcoholic malt beverages	1980
Gatorade	Isotonic beverage	1990
MasterCard	Credit card/payment system	1997
Pepsi-Cola (Aquafina Pitch Hit & Run, "This Week in Baseball")	Beverage (nonalcoholic, nonisotonic)	1997
Nike	Athletic footwear and athletic eyewear	1998
Bank of America	Banking services/affinity card	2004 (1997 for MBNA affinity card)
SiriusXM (All-Star Futures Game)	Satellite radio network	2004
Taco Bell (All-Star Legends & Celebrity Softball Game)	Quick-service restaurant	2004
GM/Chevrolet (All-Star & World Series MVP Awards, Roberto Clemente Award, All-Star Red Carpet Parade)	Foreign and domestic vehicle	2005
Frito-Lay	Salty snack	2006
InterContinental Hotels Group/Holiday Inn	Hotel and resort	2006
State Farm (Home Run Derby)	Insurance	2007
Firestone (In-stadium All-Star balloting)	Tire	2010
Scotts (Retail All-Star balloting)	Lawn care, grass seed	2010
Bayer Healthcare/One-A-Day	Pain relief/multivitamin	2011

Reproduced from: Spons-o-Meter: MLB boasts 16 official corporate sponsors this season. (2012, April 4). Retrieved from http://www.sportsbusinessdaily.com/Daily/Issues/2012/04/04/MLB-Season-Preview/2012 -Sponsors.aspx. Courtesy of *SportsBusiness Journal*.

Table 15-8 The Worldwide IOC Olympic Partner Sponsors (TOP)

Company	Category
Atos	Information technology
Coca-Cola	Nonalcoholic beverages
DOW	Official chemistry company
General Electric	Energy generation systems; energy distribution systems; healthcare: diagnostic imaging, monitoring, and electronic medical records; technology; lighting fixtures and systems; aircraft engines; rail transportation; water treatment facilities and services; equipment and transportation management
McDonald's	Retail food services
Omega	Time pieces (watches, clocks, and official countdown clocks); timing systems/services; electronic timing, scoring, and scoreboards systems and services
Panasonic	Audio/TV/video equipment
Procter & Gamble	Personal care and household products
Samsung	Wireless communications equipment
VISA	Consumer payment systems (credit cards, etc.)

Reproduced from: The Olympic Partner (TOP) Program (2014). International Olympic Committee. Retrieved April 7, 2014 from http://www.olympic.org/sponsors

companies with smaller marketing budgets. Such sponsorships typically include the right to be the "official sponsor" of the team, the opportunity to conduct in-venue promotions, and access to team tickets and hospitality. Most governing bodies allow for competitors of their sponsorship partners to sign sponsorship deals with the local teams. For instance, although Bank of America is the "Official Bank of the NFL," many NFL teams have sponsorship deals with local banks.

This loophole has served as an avenue for ambush marketing for some companies. Take for example the 2010 Fédération Internationale de Football Association (FIFA) World Cup: Although Adidas was the "Official Licensee and Supplier of the FIFA World Cup," Nike was a sponsor (and jersey provider) of many national teams, including the United States, Brazil, and The Netherlands.

Athlete Sponsorship

Athlete sponsorship serves as a platform for companies to develop a sponsorship based on support of individual athletes (versus a team or a league). Such arrangements typically involve some type of endorsement of the sponsor's product or service. Athletes in individual sports, such as tennis and golf, tend to attract more sponsor interest because they are able to generate a greater number of visible, well-focused sponsor impressions on television. Perhaps the most prolific example of athlete sponsorship is Michael Jordan, who in his prime earned over $50 million annually through deals with Nike, Rayovac, and Ballpark Franks, among others.

One of the services that companies use to help determine which athletes to sponsor is the QScore, compiled by New York City–based Marketing Evaluations/TvQ, a research firm that has been measuring the notoriety of athletes, actors, and entertainers for over 40 years. The QScore uses a scale to measure celebrities'

familiarity and appeal among the general public. Based on 2010 QScore rankings, the five highest ranked athletes were Michael Jordan, Apolo Anton Ohno, Peyton Manning, Steve Nash, and Joe Montana (Pulver, 2010).

However, sponsoring an individual athlete can be riskier than sponsoring a league or team. Sport celebrities garner a great deal of attention and interest from the public, and thus the media is quick to report on any news involving the athlete. Unfortunately for sponsors, this news typically involves the sport celebrity getting into some sort of trouble. Take, for example, the personal issues golf great Tiger Woods experienced in late 2009. Although Woods was ranked as having the second highest QScore among sport celebrities in 2009, that ranking had dropped to 25 just 12 months later due to his highly publicized off-the-course infidelities (Lefton, 2010). Companies must carefully evaluate the risk associated with sponsoring an individual athlete prior to entering into any agreement. The problem is that the true risk is difficult (if not impossible) to calculate with any accuracy.

Media Sponsorship

Media sponsorship occurs most often in the form of broadcast sponsors; that is, companies that purchase advertising or programming during sport-related broadcasts. For several years, Home Depot has been the presenting sponsor of ESPN's *College GameDay* show, positioned as "College GameDay Built by the Home Depot" (a clever way to further entrench Home Depot's brand message in the minds of consumers). This media sponsorship includes commercial spots, on-site signage, and game tickets for hospitality and entertainment purposes. The sponsorship "helps Home Depot fortify its base of active, male, do-it-yourself customers," said a Home Depot marketing executive. "College football and home improvement projects are two things that people associate with the weekend, particularly Saturdays. This sponsorship allows Home Depot to strengthen that connection with our consumers" (Wilbert, 2003, p. 1D).

Often broadcast sponsors have no affiliation with the team or league being broadcast, a situation that can result in ambush marketing whereby the broadcast sponsor seeks to convey to consumers some "official" relationship that does not in fact exist. Although not illegal, one classic example was Wendy's advertising as an "official broadcast sponsor" of the Olympics, although McDonald's was the official sponsor of the Olympics in the fast-food category. Many sport organizations now either require their official sponsors to purchase advertising within their event broadcasts or, alternatively, provide them a "right of first refusal" to purchase broadcast advertising time, with the intent of eliminating or curtailing such ambush marketing activity.

Facility Sponsorship

Facility sponsorship is one of the fastest-growing sponsorship platforms, most notably in the form of naming rights agreements. Over the past 10 years, almost every professional sport facility (and many collegiate athletic stadiums and arenas) has sold naming rights to companies. For example, Citizens Bank signed a 25-year, $95 million naming rights deal that put its name on the Philadelphia Phillies' ballpark. As an example of platform integration, Citizens Bank was already an official sponsor of the team, and its naming rights deal also included a commitment to media sponsorship (i.e., advertising within Phillies television and radio broadcasts). Another example of platform integration is Red Bull's sponsorship of both the New York Red Bulls (an MLS team) and Red Bull Arena (the facility where the team plays). Essentially, facility sponsors typically sponsor the sport properties that play in the facility in some other capacity. Many sport

organizations are further slicing and dicing areas within the facility to attract incremental sponsorship revenue beyond the naming rights deal. For instance, most stadiums now sell corporate sponsorship to specific entryways, concourse areas, luxury box levels, and even practice facilities! For instance, prior to the 2013 football season, the NFL's New York Giants signed Quest Diagnostics as its training facility sponsor, replacing a 4-year deal with Timex valued at over $2 million per year (Vacchiano, 2013).

Event Sponsorship

Event sponsorship enables companies to tie directly into the event atmosphere over a relatively short time period, typically a few days or a weekend. Examples include sponsorship of triathlons and marathons, college football bowl games, extreme sports events such as the X Games, and professional golf tournaments, typically events that are locally based and annual.

Sport-Specific Sponsorship

Sport-specific sponsorship enables a company to direct its sponsorship efforts to a specific sport that best appeals to the company and its targeted consumers and provides a strong fit for generating brand identity. For instance, ING Group, a Dutch financial services company, identified sponsorship of marathons as a perfect platform to launch "Globe Runner," one of ING's worldwide financial services products. As part of this sponsorship strategy, ING Group purchased the first-ever title sponsorship of the New York City Marathon (a 3-year, $5 million deal), in addition to entitlement of other high-profile marathons in Brussels, Amsterdam, Taipei, and Ottawa. Such sport-specific sponsorships are often most effectively leveraged and enhanced through the additional use of governing body, athlete, and/or media channel sponsorships.

Evaluating Sport Sponsorships

There is a saying: "It you can't measure it, you can't manage it." Companies that fail to set clear and measureable objectives before entering into a sport sponsorship program are more likely to meet with failure. With the growing financial commitments necessary to sponsor and effectively activate sport sponsorship programs, the evaluation of sponsorships has become a necessary component of the sport sponsorship process. It is critical that sponsoring companies develop metrics to answer questions such as the following: Do consumers understand the sponsorship? Can consumers identify your sponsorship after being exposed to it? Has the sponsorship led to a meaningful connection with your target audience? How many media impressions has the sponsorship generated? And, last but certainly not least, has the sponsorship led to quantifiable new business opportunities?

Measuring ROI from sport sponsorships poses several challenges for sponsors. First, there is no one exact formula for measuring ROI, thus leaving companies to establish their own internal criteria. Companies use a wide range of criteria to help determine whether their sport sponsorship is a valuable asset in achieving their marketing objectives. These include internal feedback for sales departments, sales promotion bounceback measures, print media exposure, television media exposure, primary consumer research, dealer/trade response, and syndicated consumer research. Second, it is difficult to precisely determine how much incremental sales are directly attributable to a specific sponsorship program or how a sponsorship has directly affected consumers' awareness of the sponsoring company or brand.

Consumer surveys are often deployed as a first step in measuring sponsorship ROI. For example, a survey administered following the 2010 Winter Olympics found that over 45% of respondents identified Visa, a long-time Olympic sponsor, as an official partner of Team USA (Broughton, 2010). The same survey showed that only about 4% of surveyed consumers identified Hilton Hotels as an official partner of Team USA. Surveys such as the one just described provide sponsors a general understanding of the level of awareness consumers have of the sponsorship alliance. It is difficult, however, to use this type of survey research to conclude Visa's sponsorship of Team USA is 10 times more valuable than Hilton's sponsorship of Team USA. Thus, a more scientific approach to sponsorship evaluation is necessary to more accurately measure ROI.

Sponsorship evaluation has become a burgeoning business, and today many companies specialize in measuring sponsorship ROI. Research companies such as Performance Research, Nielsen Sports Marketing Service, Repucom, and Sponsorship Research International (SRi) have emerged to provide professional services for evaluating, through quantitative and qualitative research instruments, various aspects of a sponsor's involvement with a sport property. Some key questions in evaluating sponsorships include the following: Do consumers understand your sponsorship? Has the sponsorship made a connection with your target audience? How many media impressions has your sponsorship generated? Has your sponsorship resulted in new business opportunities?

Sport properties often hire professional research firms to perform evaluation research that examines the value the property provides to their sponsors. This is done to increase sponsor satisfaction and maximize potential sponsorship revenues. The NBA, for example, has worked with SRi to measure the effectiveness of basketball-themed promotions of commercials versus ones that are not themed around the sport (Show, 2009). The study indicated that the NBA does in fact provide a significant lift in promotions. The PGA Tour has also worked with research companies to show the value the Tour can provide sponsors. The PGA Tour worked with Repucom to evaluate the value in terms of international television exposure a title sponsor receives (Show, 2009). Repucom estimated the television exposure of a title sponsor of one PGA Tour event at over $20 million.

Students with an aptitude for and interest in the research process may find career opportunities with market research companies that specialize in sport marketing and sponsorship, such as those listed in the "Resources" section at the end of this chapter.

Sponsorship Agencies

As you are probably well aware, there is much that makes the sport product, sport consumers, and thus sport marketing unique. Hence, many companies engaged in sport sponsorship outsource the negotiation and/or implementation of their sponsorship programs and leave the nuances of sport marketing to the experts. You would not believe the number of corporate marketers, experts in marketing their own products and services, who don't know that the World Series is not played in the same location every year, or that you cannot just stick the Super Bowl logo in your advertisements without first obtaining the NFL's approval, or that using Babe Ruth in a commercial shoot may not be possible ("Uh, Babe Ruth is no longer with us"). These are all true tales from the front lines of sport sponsorship agency work that serve to reinforce the fact that sport marketing is a different animal and is sometimes better left to the experts! Many companies rely on agencies because they do not possess the expertise, the experience, or the resources to negotiate and implement sponsorship programs on their own. Thus, those charged with selling sport property sponsorships often will deal directly with sport

marketing and promotion agencies in pitching their sponsorship opportunities. Therefore, career opportunities exist for trained sport marketers to apply their skills on the agency side. A list of the major sport marketing and promotion agencies that specialize in the negotiation and implementation of sport sponsorships on behalf of their clients (the sponsoring companies) is provided in the "Resources" section of this chapter.

Issues in Sport Sponsorship

Ethnic Marketing Through Sport Sponsorship

The expanding market of ethnic consumers, coupled with the increasing globalization of sport, is compelling more and more corporations to direct a portion of their sport sponsorship spending to **ethnic marketing**. Likewise, sport organizations have begun to adopt strategies to more effectively target ethnic groups, particularly Hispanics and African Americans, who historically have represented only a small percentage of the sport spectator base in the United States. The Hispanic market, in particular, is the fastest-growing ethnic population in the United States. In some baseball markets, such as Anaheim, California, Hispanics account for 30% of ticket buyers (King, 2013). Additionally, an ESPN Sports Poll found that Hispanics living in English-dominant households are far more likely than the general U.S. population to be a fan of MLB, the NBA, the NFL, and action sports ("Demographics," 2007). Many of the companies that sponsor MLS, such as Sierra Mist, Kraft, and Budweiser, have identified an interest in reaching the largely Hispanic audience that attends these games.

The influx of Asian athletes into major U.S. professional sport leagues (particularly soccer, basketball, and baseball) has also fueled the interest of companies in using sport sponsorship to target Asian communities. The arrival of Yao Ming to the NBA in 2002 has become a classic example of the impact that athletes and their fans can have on local corporations' ethnic marketing initiatives. Shortly after Ming signed with the Houston Rockets, Harbrew Imports of New York, marketers of Yanjing Beer, signed a multiyear sponsorship deal with Ming's team (shortly thereafter the company also signed a sponsorship deal with the Los Angeles Clippers after that team signed Chinese player Wang Zhizhi). Ming's ability to resonate with Chinese consumers both in the United States and China quickly resulted in athlete sponsorship deals between Ming and companies that included Pepsi, Gatorade, Apple, and Visa. More recently, after Taiwanese American Jeremy Lin signed with the Houston Rockets, the team quickly signed five sponsorship deals with companies doing business in China (Gregory, 2012).

Companies have also recognized the ability of sport sponsorship to reach the African American market. Nike, for example, has through its sponsorship of high-profile African American athletes "demonstrated an understanding of how to effectively employ a culturally based approach to communicating with black consumers. Its promotional messages contain content that is tasteful and culturally appropriate for black consumers, yet also appealing to the mainstream market" (Armstrong, 1998). Russell Athletic (through its association with the Black Coaches and Administrators Association) and footwear marketer Converse (through its grassroots inner-city basketball tours "Converse Open Gym") are other examples of companies effectively utilizing sport sponsorship platforms to target the African American market.

Sport marketers, however, must be cognizant of key cultural differences among and between ethnic groups in terms of how sponsorship and its various tactics are communicated to and perceived by targeted ethnic groups (Cordova, 2009). For example, ethnic marketing cannot be, or be perceived as, a token effort by the company to reach out to a particular ethnic market. Sport marketers must also understand the difference between marketing to first-generation immigrants and those who, although identified as part of an ethnic group, are in fact well indoctrinated into American culture. Armstrong (1998) has identified a number of strategies that sport organizations and corporations should employ when marketing to black consumers, including involving the black media, demonstrating concern and respect for the black community and causes salient to it through socially responsible cause-related marketing, and patronizing black vendors. There remains, however, much research and work to be done in effectively reaching ethnic markets through sport sponsorship.

When Is Enough . . . ENOUGH?

There is, arguably, very little remaining space or inventory that cannot be sponsored somehow, somewhere, by some company. The increasing proliferation of advertising and sponsorship raises a critical question for sport marketers: When is enough . . . enough? Sport marketers have built a world in which their fans visit a stadium called Comerica Park and pass through a turnstile featuring Chevrolet ads to watch a team sponsored by Bank One in a game sponsored by Sprint. The fans then pass a luxury suite section sponsored by Papa John's Pizza, to witness a first pitch sponsored by ReMax, followed by an inning sponsored by Joe's Trucking. Add to this a plethora of sponsored scoreboard messages and between-innings promotions, and one begins to see the potential magnitude of the issue.

Even the most sacred of venues have not escaped sport marketers' quest for new revenue streams. For instance, beginning in 2002 corporate advertisements were placed on Fenway Park's famed outfield wall, the Green Monster.

A similar signage issue arose at a 2003 Chicago Cubs game in ivy-covered Wrigley Field when television rightsholders Fox and ESPN successfully lobbied MLB to place an electronic message-board on the brick wall behind home plate that for the first time exposed Cubs fans and viewers at home to ads from Budweiser, Subway, and a number of other sponsors during a *Saturday Game of the Week* telecast (Fisher, 2010). In June 2013, the NBA approved teams selling on-court advertising for high-profile space in front of team benches as well as the camera-visible areas on top of backboards (Lombardi, 2013a).

The potential overcommercialization of sporting events raises interesting questions as to whether sport consumers may have an emotional threshold or tolerance level for accepting a constant bombardment of corporate names, logos, and messages. Is there, as well, a point at which companies' sponsorship investments become so mired in clutter that they lose all effectiveness? As sport marketers continue to push the envelope in search of new revenue streams, one is left to wonder if, and when, sport sponsorship may reach a law of diminishing returns. Thus, sport marketers must always be careful and cognizant of how innovative sponsorship deals will be perceived by consumers and the media and, at the very least, take steps to proactively position such groundbreaking sponsorships in as positive a light as possible.

The Marriage of "Vice" and Sport

Sport organizations historically shunned affiliations with legalized gambling establishments (LGEs), fearing negative public perceptions and threats to the on-field integrity of the games. Gambling has, however, taken a strong hold in the United States over the past decade, as the number of LGEs (e.g., tribal casinos, state lotteries, riverboat casinos) has grown exponentially. One industry trade publication estimates that the number of casinos in the

United States increased 25% in 4 years, from 405 in 1999 to 508 in 2003, spanning 27 states (IEG, 2003b). In Massachusetts alone, there are no less than 35 different scratch-and-win lottery games operating at any one time. With increased government endorsement and public acceptance of gambling, sport organizations have embraced LGEs as a growing source of sponsorship revenue. For example, over the past several years, the relationship between LGEs and sport organizations has grown to include the following:

- The NBA, NHL, and MLB have all licensed their team logos to state lotteries for use in scratch-and-win games whose prizes include cash, trips to their championship games, and league-licensed merchandise. These leagues also allow their teams to sell or distribute lottery cards as in-arena premiums.
- In 2012, the NFL became the last of the four major U.S. sport leagues to allow in-stadium casino advertising (Kaplan, 2012).
- For the 2013 season, the Women's National Basketball Association (WNBA) Tulsa Shock signed a deal for the Osage Casino to be the marquee sponsor on the team's game jerseys (Lombardo, 2013b).
- The Sycuan Indian tribe, which operates one of the largest casinos in California, bought sponsorship of the San Diego Padres season that included in-stadium PA announcements and broadcast announcements referring to the "2003 Padres season, presented by Sycuan." Even the Padres' telephone welcome greeting invited consumers to purchase tickets to the "2003 Padres season, presented by Sycuan."

LGEs began aggressively engaging in sport sponsorship for much the same reasons as other traditional sport sponsors. One primary objective is to drive traffic to casinos. For example, Mohegan Sun activated a sponsorship of the

Boston Red Sox by sending "brand ambassadors" throughout the city with a book in which fans could write good luck messages to the team. Each person penning a note received a scratch-and-win game piece that could be brought to the casino for the chance to win $1 million as well as various Red Sox–related prizes (IEG, 2003b). Another objective is the desire of gaming establishments to retain and reward their premium players (the high rollers). Based on one study that showed that 5% of customers account for 40% of the casinos' gross gaming win, gaming establishments have turned to sports to provide an attractive lure. For instance, the best customers of Foxwoods Resort Casino in Connecticut are invited to private dinners with Boston Celtics stars (IEG, 2003b). Casinos are also turning to sport sponsorship as a means of fighting negative perceptions of gambling and to position themselves as concerned corporate citizens through community relations tie-ins. "When we put up a sign at Fenway Park, we are trying to tell people we're part of the crowd," said Mitchell Etess, executive vice president of marketing for Mohegan Sun (IEG, 2003b, p. 8).

Case Study 15-1 Introducing . . . The FedEx, I Mean, the Discover Orange Bowl!

For more than two decades, FedEx was the title sponsor of the Orange Bowl, one of college football's most prestigious holiday season bowl games and one of the four bowl games included in the Bowl Championship Series (BCS). Through this sponsorship, the FedEx name became synonymous with the Orange Bowl, and the game became FedEx's biggest hospitality platform. Each year, the company hosted hundreds of key customers and rewarded top employees with a 4-day party built around the Orange Bowl game in Miami.

However, in May 2010, after a 21-year run, FedEx publicly announced its decision to not renew its title sponsorship of the Orange Bowl, the longest-running title sponsorship of any of the BCS games, which include the Tostitos Fiesta Bowl, the Allstate Sugar Bowl, and the Rose Bowl presented by Citi (the bank). Why would FedEx, after two decades of building tremendous sponsorship equity in the FedEx Orange Bowl, suddenly decide to drop its sponsorship?

For one thing, the dynamics of the Orange Bowl deal had changed. After years of being televised by FOX and ABC, ESPN had recently acquired the rights to air all of the BCS games beginning with the 2010 season. In addition to the broadcast rights, however, ESPN had also secured the rights to sell all sponsorship and advertising inventory. Upon securing the rights to the BCS games, ESPN significantly increased the entitlement sponsor price tag over what BCS title sponsors had previously been paying FOX (ESPN was reportedly seeking $20 million annually over 4 years for any new BCS game entitlement deal). Furthermore, ESPN was requiring that the entitlement sponsor purchase a lengthy and more expensive college football advertising package that would start in September and would run throughout the entire college football season. Although the Orange Bowl game itself was important to FedEx, the company decided that it was not interested in committing to a larger college football platform.

(continues)

Case Study 15-1   Introducing . . . The FedEx, I Mean, the Discover Orange Bowl! (Continued)

The Orange Bowl had also lost some of its prestige in recent years because of lackluster matchups that had led to a steady decline in television ratings (Table 15-9). For instance, the 2009 game between Virginia Tech and Cincinnati drew a 5.4 rating and 9.3 million viewers, the lowest numbers ever for a BCS game. Although the FedEx Orange Bowl match-up between Iowa and Georgia Tech on January 5, 2010, generated a 6.8 rating and 10.9 million viewers, it still ranked as the smallest audience of the four BCS games in 2010.

Declining television ratings, coupled with a higher financial commitment as required by ESPN, were important factors in FedEx's decision to relinquish its title sponsorship of the Orange Bowl after 21 years. Furthermore, as a shipping company, FedEx had been especially hit hard by the recession and had to make tough decisions to cut back on sports marketing expenditures that were once routine, including its television advertisement that had appeared in 12 straight Super Bowls until 2009. It had also become increasingly expensive to host elaborate parties for hundreds of customers and employees at the Orange Bowl.

Despite having relinquished its Orange Bowl entitlement deal, FedEx still holds league deals with the NFL and NBA and has several other sponsorships, including naming rights for FedEx Field in suburban Washington, D.C., and FedEx Forum in Memphis. It also has several sponsorship positions with NFL, MLB, and NBA teams, as well as sponsorship on the No. 11 NASCAR Sprint Cup Series car at Joe Gibbs Racing.

Table 15-9 Orange Bowl Ratings in the Bowl Championship Series Era

Year	Network	Matchup	Rating	Viewers (millions)
2010	Fox	Iowa vs. Georgia Tech	6.8	10,879
2009	Fox	Virginia Tech vs. Cincinnati	5.4	9,319
2008	Fox	Kansas vs. Virginia Tech	7.4	11,958
2007	Fox	Louisville vs. Wake Forest	7.0	10,655
2006	ABC	Penn State vs. Florida State	12.3	18,557
2005*	ABC	USC vs. Oklahoma	13.7	NA
2004	ABC	Miami vs. Florida State	9.1	NA
2003	ABC	USC vs. Iowa	9.7	NA
2002	ABC	Florida vs. Maryland	9.5	NA
2001*	ABC	Oklahoma vs. Florida State	17.8	NA
2000	ABC	Michigan vs. Alabama	11.4	NA
1999	ABC	Florida vs. Syracuse	8.4	NA

NA: not available.

* BCS National Championship Game

Reproduced from: Durand, J., Smith, M., & Lefton, T. (2010, May 3). FedEx name will come off Orange Bowl. *Street & Smith's SportsBusiness Journal*, p. 1. Courtesy of *Sports Business Journal*.

The Orange Bowl 'Discovers' a New Title Sponsor

The Orange Bowl was not without an entitlement sponsor for very long. On the heels of FedEx's decision to end its long-running association with the game, ESPN announced the Orange Bowl's new entitlement sponsor: Discover Card, the credit card and financial services company.

The entitlement sponsorship of the Orange Bowl was viewed by Discover Financial Services, issuer of the Discover Card, as a way to enter the sport sponsorship landscape in a major way. The new entitlement deal was reported to be a 4-year contract worth just under $20 million a year. In addition to entitlement of the Orange Bowl ("The Discover Orange Bowl"), other marketing benefits include commercials within ESPN's Saturday afternoon college football telecasts, sponsorship of the "Discover Play of the Day" feature every Saturday afternoon of the college football season, over 100 on-air announcements promoting the "Discover Orange Bowl" leading up to the game, rights to use ESPN college football analyst Lee Corso in POS promotional materials, and 500 tickets to the Orange Bowl.

A marketing platform that stretches from the start of college football season in late August through the BCS games after New Year's Day provides Discover with a 4-month-plus platform, in addition to the game's entitlement rights. With the entitlement sponsorship package, Discover will put its brand on the rotating national championship game at least once during the 4-year deal (the Orange Bowl hosted the national championship in 2013).

Entitlement sponsorship of the Orange Bowl was deemed by Discover's marketing team as a way to significantly expand Discover's position in the sport sponsorship landscape. In the extremely competitive market of credit card services, competitors such as market leaders Visa and Master Card have long established portfolios of sport sponsorships. Visa, for example, sponsors the NFL, the Olympic Games, the FIFA World Cup, NASCAR, and the Kentucky Derby. MasterCard has been a long-time sponsor of MLB and is an active sponsor on the PGA Tour. These companies have been able to successfully leverage their sport sponsorships by issuing affinity cards (credit cards that allow customers to earn points that can be used to purchase tickets and officially licensed merchandise) and offering give-a-ways in which credit card users are entered into a drawing to win tickets to various sporting events. Discover hopes to capitalize on its new sponsorship by leveraging its association with the Orange Bowl as effectively as possible.

Questions for Discussion

1. Assume that you are the Director of Sport Sponsorship for FedEx. What other factors, beyond those stated in the case, would help inform your decision to continue with or relinquish your 21-year entitlement of the Orange Bowl? Would you also decide to relinquish it? Why or why not?

2. Now assume you are the Director of Sport Sponsorship for Discover and have been presented with this new entitlement sponsorship opportunity. Would you recommend Discover invest in entitlement sponsorship of the Orange Bowl? Why or why not?

(continues)

Case Study 15-1   Introducing . . . The FedEx, I Mean, the Discover Orange Bowl! (Continued)

3. The association of Discover's orange logo (the O in Discover is always presented as an orange figure) with the Orange Bowl is a very obvious and logical fit. However, other than this fit, what are some of the challenges you, as the Director of Sport Sponsorship for Discover, can expect to face in trying to leverage your new sponsorship?

4. FedEx leveraged its Orange Bowl sponsorship primarily as a B2B opportunity by using the event as a platform to entertain key corporate customers. As the Director of Sport Sponsorship for Discover, what are some of the promotional tactics you would recommend to leverage your entitlement of the Discover Orange Bowl to build your business?

The sponsorship of sport properties by hard liquor companies has also gained popularity in the last few years. In 2005, both NASCAR and the PGA Tour began permitting events and teams (or players) to sign sponsorship deals with hard spirit alcoholic beverage brands. By 2010, Diageo's Ketel One vodka was the PGA Tour's official distilled spirit and Crown Royal was the primary sponsor of the popular NASCAR driver Matt Kenseth's race car. In 2009, the NBA followed the trend when the league loosened its alcohol marketing regulations. Soon after, the league signed a sponsorship deal with Bacardi Gold rum in 2010 (Lefton & Lombardo, 2010). Just as gambling sponsorships gained acceptance in the late 1990s and early 2000, hard liquor sponsorships are now becoming more acceptable amongst sport marketers.

One of the key concerns for sport organizations entering sponsorship agreements with gaming establishments and hard liquor manufacturers is the possible negative perceptions fans may have toward these sport organizations. Another is the possible longer-term effects that such associations may have on impressionable youngsters through the tacit condoning or encouragement of gambling and drinking. One commentator has noted that the marriage of sport organizations and vices such as gambling "is the beginning of a slippery slope. As the search for revenues in sports becomes more acute, the intellectual distinction between negatives of gambling and the purism of sports becomes blurry, if not obliterated" (Heistand, 2003, p. C1). Only time will tell.

Summary

Over the past two decades, sport sponsorship has evolved into a billion-dollar industry that has grown increasingly competitive. The increase in the sheer number of sport organizations pursuing corporations' sponsorship dollars and the never-ending expansion of inventory—including everything from venue naming rights to turnstile signage to championship parades to social media sites—has sparked a heightened degree of sophistication in the sales, implementation, and servicing of sport sponsorships. At the same time, there has been a tremendous increase in the market of companies and industry trade associations eager to engage in sport sponsorship. These companies, although today much more attuned to the benefits of sport sponsorship, continue to put increasing emphasis on the evaluation and measurement of their sport sponsorship involvements to ensure a return on their investment. Thus, there is a broad range of opportunities for individuals seeking careers in the area of sport sponsorship, including the sport organization side, the corporate side, the sport marketing consulting agency side, and the sponsorship evaluation side.

Resources

Sport Research Firms

Performance Research
25 Mill Street
Queen Anne Square
Newport, RI 02840
401-848-0111
http://www.performanceresearch.com

Sponsorship Research International (SRi)
230 East Avenue
Norwalk, CT 06855
203-831-2060
http://www.teamsri.com

Turnkey Sports & Entertainment
9 Tanner Street, Suite 8
Haddonfield, NJ 08033
856-685-1450
http://www.turnkeyse.com

Sports Marketing and Promotion Agencies

ARC Worldwide
35 W. Wacker Drive, 15th Floor
Chicago, IL 60601
312-220-5959
http://www.arcww.com/

Championship Group, Inc.
1954 Airport Road, Suite 200
Atlanta, GA 30341
770-457-5777
http://www.championshipgroup.com

Edelman Worldwide Event and Sponsorship Marketing
250 Hudson Street, 16th Floor
New York, NY 10013
212-768-0550
http://www.edelman.com

Fuse Integrated Sports Marketing
P.O. Box 4509
Burlington, VT 05406
802-864-7123
http://www.fusemarketing.com

Genseco Sports Enterprises
1845 Woodall Rogers Freeway
Dallas, TX 75201
214-826-6565

GMR Marketing
5000 S. Towne Drive
New Berlin, WI 53151
262-786-5600
http://gmrmarketing.com

IEG, LLC
350 N. Orleans Street, Suite 1200
Chicago, IL 60654
312-944-1727
http://www.sponsorship.com

IMG
IMG Center
1360 E. Ninth Street, Suite 100
Cleveland, OH 44114
216-522-1200
http://www.imgworld.com

Ion Marketing
10 E. 38th Street, 11th Floor
New York, NY 10016
646-827-3300
http://www.ionmktg.com

Momentum, Inc.
250 Hudson Street, 2nd Floor
New York, NY 10013
646-638-5400
http://www.momentumww.com

Octagon

  800 Connecticut Avenue, 2nd Floor
  Norwalk, CT 06854
  203-354-7400
  http://www.octagon.com

The Strategic Agency

  70 W. 36th Street, 10th Floor
  New York, NY 10018

212-869-3003
http://www.thestrategicagency.com

Velocity Sports & Entertainment

  230 East Avenue
  Norwalk, CT 06855
  203-831-2000
  http://www.teamvelocity.com

Key Terms

activation, contests, coupons, cross-promotion, ethnic marketing, freestanding inserts (FSIs), point-of-sale/point-of-purchase marketing, premiums, return on investment (ROI), sales promotion, sampling, sweepstakes

References

Armstrong, K. (1998). Ten strategies to employ when marketing sport to black consumers. *Sport Marketing Quarterly, 7*(3), 11–18.

Block, T., & Robinson, W. (Eds.). (1994). *Dartnell sales promotion handbook*. Chicago, IL: Author.

Botta, C. (2013, March 18). MLS checks in with Foursquare, extends partnership with site. *Street & Smith's SportsBusiness Journal*, p. 6.

Broughton, D. (2010, March 15). Visa's visibility recognized by Olympics fans. *Street & Smith's SportsBusiness Journal*, p. 12.

Broughton, D. (2012, November 12). Everybody loves bobbleheads: Popular giveaway climbs past T-shirts, headwear to top spot on promotions list. *Street & Smith's SportsBusiness Journal*, p. 9.

Cordova, T. (2009, April 27). Success begins with understanding the demo. *Street & Smith's SportsBusiness Journal*, p. 17.

Demographics: Hispanics. (2007, January 22). *Street & Street's SportsBusiness Journal*, p. 18.

Dentzer, S. (1984, August 20). What price prestige. *Newsweek*, p. 28.

Durand, J., Smith, M., & Lefton, T. (2010, May 3). FedEx name will come off Orange Bowl. *Street & Smith's SportsBusiness Journal*, p. 1.

Fisher, E. (2010, March 29). Sponsorship growth a slippery slope at historic ballpark. *Street & Smith's SportsBusiness Journal*, p. 15.

Fisher, E. (2013, June 3). Social media sponsorship deals. *Street & Smith's SportsBusiness Journal*, p. 18.

Gregory, S. (2012, July 19). Can Jeremy Lin's appeal in China really help Houston's bottom line? Keeping Score blog. Retrieved from http://keepingscore.blogs.time.com/2012/07/19/can-jeremy-lins-appeal-in-china-really-help-houstons-bottom-line/

Heistand, M. (2003, June 19). As casino lures customers with NBA team, alliance creates concern about purity of sports. *USA Today*, p. C1.

IEG, Inc. (2003a, February 10). Sponsorship is key ingredient for venerable Southern snack brand. *IEG Sponsorship Report*.

IEG, Inc. (2003b, May 26). Casinos place their bets on sponsorship. *IEG Sponsorship Report*.

IEG, Inc. (2003c, February 10). Assertions. *IEG Sponsorship Report*.

IEG, Inc. (2010, January 26). Sponsorship spending receded for the first time in 2009. *IEG Sponsorship Report.*

IEG, Inc. (2012, May 29). Following the money: Sponsorship's top spenders of 2011. *IEG Sponsorship Report.*

Irwin, R., Sutton, W. A., & McCarthy, L. (2008). *Sport promotion and sales management* (2nd ed.). Champaign, IL: Human Kinetics.

Kaplan, D. (2012, April 16). NFL gives OK for teams to accept casino advertising. *Street & Smith's SportsBusiness Journal.* Retrieved from http://www.sportsbusinessdaily.com/Journal/Issues/2012/04/16/Leagues-and-Governing-Bodies/NFL-casinos.aspx?hl=casinos&sc=0

King, B. (2013, June 24). Angels seek messaging that will play across both the Hispanic and general markets. *Street & Smith's SportsBusiness Journal.* Retrieved from http://www.sportsbusinessdaily.com/Journal/Issues/2013/06/24/In-Depth/Los-Angeles-Angels.aspx

Lefton, T. (2010, June 7). Penalty drop: Tiger Woods plummets on Sports Q Scores list. *Street & Smith's SportsBusiness Journal,* p. 10.

Lefton, T., & Lombardo, J. (2010, April 5). NBA strikes sponsor gold with Bacardi. *Street & Smith's SportsBusiness Journal,* p. 1.

Lombardi, J. (2013a, June 10). NBA clubs to sell ads high, low. *Street & Smith's SportsBusiness Journal.* Retrieved from http://www.sportsbusinessdaily.com/Journal/Issues/2013/06/10/Leagues-and-Governing-Bodies/NBA-floor.aspx

Lombardi, J. (2013b, February 4). Shock signs casino as jersey sponsor, with assist from Richie. *Street & Smith's SportsBusiness Journal.* Retrieved from http//www.sportsbusinessdaily.com/Journal/Issues/2013/02.04/Franchises/Shock.aspx?hl=casino s&sc=0

Mickle, T. (2010, January 25). Dew keeps tour name through '11. *Street & Smith's SportsBusiness Journal.* Retrieved from http://www.sportsbusinessjournal.com/article/64648

Mickle, T. (2013, July 1). NASCAR charged up about latest addition to green partner list. *Street & Smith's SportsBusiness Journal,* p. 32.

Mullin, B., Hardy, S., & Sutton, W. A. (2007). *Sport marketing* (3rd ed.). Champaign, IL: Human Kinetics.

Pulver, T. (2010, September 29). The five most liked and five least liked athletes [according to Q Score], Retrieved from http://coed.com/2010/09/29/the-five-most-liked-and-disliked-athletes-according-to-q-score/

Shank, M. (2009). *Sports marketing* (4th ed.). Upper Saddle River, NJ: Prentice Hall.

Show, J. (2009, February 23). Properties try to show dollars well spent. *Street & Smith's SportsBusiness Journal,* p. 21.

Smith, M. (2010, May 24). Glidden hopes to make inroads in southern markets with Big South paint sponsorship. *Street & Smith's SportsBusiness Journal,* p. 8.

Solomon, J. (2002, April 21). The sports market is looking soggy. *New York Times,* p. 1.

Spons-o-Meter: MLB boasts 16 official corporate sponsors this season. (2012, April 4). Retrieved from http://www.sportsbusinessdaily.com/Daily/Issues/2012/04/04/MLB-Season-Preview/2012-Sponsors.aspx

Spons-o-Meter: NFL lines up 24 partners to start '12 season (2012, September 7). Retrieved from http://m.sportsbusinessdaily.com/Daily/Issues/2012/09/07/NFL-Season-Preview/Sponsometer.aspx

Spons-o-Meter: NHL boasts 23 official corporate sponsors this season. (2012, April 11). Retrieved from http://www.sportsbusinessdaily.com/Daily/Issues/2012/04/11/Marketing-and-Sponsorship/NHL-sponsometer.aspx

Spons-o-Meter: NBA boasts list of 20 marketing partners. (2010). Retrieved from http://www.sportsbusinessdaily.com/article/138724

The Olympic Partner (TOP) Program (2014). International Olympic Committee (2014, April 7). Retrieved from http://www.olympic.org/sponsors

Ukman, L. (1995). *The IEG's complete guide to sponsorship: Everything you need to know about sports, arts, events, entertainment and cause marketing.* Chicago, IL: International Events Group, Inc.

Vacchiano, R. (2013, July 30). The "Quest" begins at the Meadowlands. *New York Daily News.* Retrieved from http://www.nydailynews.com/blogs/giants/2013/07/the-quest-begins-at-the-meadowlands-0

Wilbert, T. (2003, June 24). Home Depot to sponsor ESPN college pregame show. *Atlanta Constitution*, p. 1D.

Chapter 16

Gregory Bouris

Sport Communications

© Hemera/Thinkstock

Learning Objectives

Upon completion of this chapter, students should be able to:

1. Recognize the vital role that communication plays in the success of a sport organization.

2. Appraise the historical development of sport communication and understand how technology has changed the methods used to communicate.

3. Compare and contrast the various methods that sport organizations use to disseminate information, such as press releases, press conferences, media guides, photography, videography, and conference calls.

4. Identify the basic legal issues pertinent to a sport communication professional, such as defamation and privacy laws.

5. Analyze the role of the new media industry in sport communication and understand that it is far more than just websites and email; it includes blogs, apps, podcasts, and social media.

6. Develop a crisis plan for a sport organization and understand the basic principles for communicating during a crisis.

7. Illustrate how the concept of integrated marking communications has brought together advertising, marketing, and public relations professionals to promote sport organization.

8. Appraise the career opportunities available in the sport communication industry and identify the skills necessary to succeed in each of them.

9. Recognize that beyond the traditional communications that occur between sport organizations and the media, it is important for a sport communication professional to understand the basics of community relations, internal communications, and government relations.

Introduction

According to Don Middleberg (2001), author of *Winning PR in the Wired World*, "public relations isn't just about 'ink' anymore. It's about a brilliant idea, creatively communicated by traditional and new media, in new ways" (p. xi). Like public relations, sport public relations has come a long way. With the ever-increasing growth of sport as big business, coupled with the Internet and other emerging technologies, the sport industry's need for highly skilled communications professionals has never been greater.

Because advances in technology have made the world much smaller as sport has moved onto the global stage, the sport industry has seen a dramatic shift in its communications needs and demands. The business has evolved from implementing passive methods of communicating with its fans, such as advertising a sport event, to more aggressive and proactive forms of communication that strive to build strong relationships through one-to-one communications—and today, in some cases, in real time. Sport organizations have found that more aggressive and strategic communication plans are vital to their overall success. This change in philosophy has resulted in positive media impressions, stronger relationships with core stakeholders—the fans, sponsors, media rightsholders, and alumni—and, in the case of professional team sports, stronger franchise valuations.

Today, the financial success of the sport organization and the media are inextricably linked. According to Nichols, Moynahan, Hall, and Taylor (2002), media sources "provide sport organizations with substantial revenue, as well as opportunities for increased public exposure" (p. 4). In fact, sport teams have attracted attention and investment from several media conglomerates, such as Cablevision, owner of the New York Rangers, Knicks, and Liberty, as well as Madison Square Garden and the Hartford Wolfpack; Time Warner, former owner of the Atlanta Braves and *Sports Illustrated*; and the Walt Disney Corporation, owner of ESPN and the former owner of the Mighty Ducks and Anaheim Angels. In a related twist to this phenomenon, in 2013 the owner of the Boston Red Sox, John Henry, purchased *The Boston Globe*, one of the country's oldest and most esteemed daily newspapers, for $70 million from The Times Co., owner of *The New York Times*. The Times Co. had bought the *Globe* for $1.1 billion 20 years earlier (Healy, 2013).

Sports and media have become so intertwined that leagues, professional teams, and college conferences have launched cable networks of their own, such as the National Football League (NFL) Network and the Big Ten Network. Despite steep costs involved in launching a cable network, these entities are leveraging their popularity and access to programming to tap into the local, regional, and national subscriber fees available to successful cable networks.

Advances in technology have resulted in fragmented viewing habits, as consumers now have the luxury of watching their favorite programs "on demand" with the option to skip the commercials. This has led advertisers to spend more of their media budgets on live sports programming. In turn, the value of sport broadcasting rights has increased once again. By way of example, in 2012 Major League Baseball's Los Angeles Dodgers sold for an unheard of $2 billion. The price tag was a reflection of the value the team's local cable TV rights would be worth on the open market—either through the creation of its own network or through the sale of its broadcast rights to a regional sports network. In addition to revenue generation through game broadcasts, these networks serve as lucrative branding and messaging vehicles to their legions of hard-core supporters. MLB launched its MLB Network to the largest audience in cable TV history when it debuted in January 2009. The National Hockey League (NHL), the New York Yankees, the New York Mets, and the Southeastern Conference (SEC) are examples of others that have entered the media side of the sport industry within the last decade.

Despite all the evolutionary changes the sport industry has experienced, one area that has remained part of the professional and amateur sport organizational chart since the beginning is public relations or, in today's sports vernacular, communications. For the purposes of this chapter, **communications** will be defined as all methods used by a sport organization to proactively deliver its key messages to a diverse universe of constituencies. In the past, communications was limited to contact with a select number of mostly print media representatives. However, today's sport organizations employ communications professionals to help deliver key messages to a greater number of stakeholders. **Stakeholders** are groups and individuals that have a direct or indirect interest in an organization. Newsom, Turk, and Kruckeberg (2004) state that stakeholders have "evolved to encompass employees, customers, government and investors" (p. 89). In sports, additional stakeholders include season ticket holders, sponsors, licensees, alumni, peer organizations (e.g., league offices), and the general public.

As in the past, the media continue to play an important role in how sport organizations deliver their messages. However, sport organizations have learned that in the changing media world it is better to communicate directly with a desired target than to rely upon the media to deliver (and run the risk of inaccurately retelling) their key messages. Additionally, economic pressures and generational changes in how people consume their news have impacted the newspaper industry. As they attempt to reinvent themselves and change their business model to adapt to an ever-changing marketplace in the Internet age, newspapers have cut back on their budgets and, as a result, their coverage. This is reflected in the example provided earlier involving *The Boston Globe* recently being purchased by John Henry for nearly 50% less than what it was purchased for 20 years ago, despite the fact that today more people read the print and online versions than at any other time in the newspaper's history.

Over the past decade, the sports departments of newspapers in major cities have been hit particularly hard. In certain cases, newspapers only assign writers to cover home games and opt for wire service coverage for away games. This trend should be watched closely by today's sport communications professional. Because of this, sport organizations now use an integrated marketing communications approach that includes advertising, direct marketing, and public relations to deliver messages directly to their stakeholders. Some organizations, such as the NHL's Los Angeles Kings, have taken this a step further by hiring writers away from their local newspapers to provide in-depth and constant coverage on team websites.

Not all communications activities are proactive. Gone are the days of once-daily news reports. The Internet has brought with it the 24/7 news cycle and a constant thirst by Web-based media outlets to constantly post "breaking" news reports. The lines are beginning to blur between hard news and information posted on **blogs**, which are diary-type entries (coined from the term "Web logs") that are regularly posted on the Internet. This adds further to the demands on sport communications professionals. They must stay up-to-date on emerging Internet-based news outlets while also assigning someone to monitor known sites from time to time to ensure their accuracy and to control their organization's branding efforts. The demand of the public, and subsequently the media, to know everything possible about a sport organization helps feed this 24/7 news engine, placing enormous pressure on an organization to protect its image. Therefore, today's sport communications professional needs to have a well-rounded understanding of the role communications plays in the successful operation of the twenty-first century sport organization, as well as a complete understanding of the role the Internet plays in the information and news cycles.

History of Sport Communication

Sport coverage in the United States dates back to 1773. The first outlet to cover a sporting event was the *Boston Gazette*, when it sent a reporter to London to cover a boxing match. Joseph Pulitzer was credited with introducing the first sports section in *The New York Herald* in 1896 (Nichols et al., 2002).

As a result of the continued growth in the sport industry, the variety of business activities practiced by professional and amateur sport organizations began to grow dramatically in the 1980s. This growth was brought on by the expansion of cable television and its need to use sports programming to lure subscribers, which substantially increased the rights fees organizations received for their game broadcasts. Prior to the 1980s, a professional sport team's organizational chart consisted of an owner, president, general manager, coaches, public relations director, ticket manager, and accounting staff. Noticeably absent, compared with modern-day organizations, were disciplines such as marketing, game operations, sponsorships and group sales staff, customer services, website staff, community relations, and, more recently, social media coordinator. Of these areas or disciplines, public relations has played, and continues to play, a major role in the structure and operation of every amateur and professional sport organization.

How the Media and Communications Have Changed

Sport communications has seen dramatic changes in terms of the number of stakeholders as well as the methods used to communicate. Times have changed. The media have changed. News coverage and the news cycles have changed, and the corporate world has taken notice of sports. Franchises are no longer run as secondary businesses, managed neatly on a game-to-game basis. Cable television introduced the concept of 24-hour news and later 24-hour sports programming and news. Sports radio has become one of the most profitable formats on the radio dial. Teams are now cashing in on their strong local brand awareness, and leagues are also cashing in on the national as well as international popularity of their sport. In the past, team public relations staffs worked almost exclusively on a seasonal basis with the newspaper reporters assigned to cover their respective teams. Today, sport communications professionals work with, and communicate to, a larger audience 12 months a year.

On the college level, the sport communications area has evolved from a one-person staff position known as a **sports information director (SID)** to a full media relations staff. Larger Division I athletic departments may have a media relations department with anywhere from 5 to 10 full-time staff members. Smaller athletic departments may have an assistant athletic director for media relations or even a coach with a dual appointment who also oversees media relations for the entire athletic department. A college athletics media relations department oversees game-day operations, including running the press box at football games or overseeing press row at basketball games. Other duties may include fielding calls from the media, coordinating press conferences, working with the athletic director on press releases about athletic department

announcements, designing and writing media guides for sport teams, developing and writing athletic department publications for print or the Internet, and maintaining social media accounts (e.g., Twitter, Facebook). A community relations staff position usually does not exist in the collegiate athletic department, although the athletic department does community relations projects. In a large Division I program, these community service–based activities may be carried out by coordination of the coaching staff, marketing, student-athlete services, and media relations departments.

Today's sport communications professional should possess a well-rounded knowledge of communications, including media relations, public relations, government relations, internal communications, advertising, and direct marketing. In addition, today's public relations professionals must keep abreast of all the communications opportunities available to them through emerging technologies. Related coursework includes journalism, public relations, public speaking, Web design, and audio/video production classes.

Current and future generations of professionals are entering the workforce with hands-on experience in social media and the ability to upload and download media to the Internet. These skills are useful when advising and assisting, for lack of better terms, the aging workforce.

Key Topics

Media Relations

Most sport organizations are blessed with so much mass appeal that media organizations are compelled to cover these entities on a regular basis. This popularity creates a "pull" from the media, whereas most other industries have to "push" their information to the media and hope to receive publicity for their efforts. In other words, it is highly unlikely that the local company has someone from the local newspaper showing up every day needing to fill a number of column inches in the paper. Most media outlets, especially newspapers, turn the public's insatiable desire to know all they can about their favorite team and players into revenue dollars by selling more papers and advertising to increase their own profits.

The media can be broken into categories, such as print, television, radio, and the Internet. Table 16-1 contains a working media list. Given the free publicity received, most sport organizations have developed strong working relationships with the media. It is a priority to determine the key media members (or reporters) as well as their individual needs. They are not all the same.

Print editions of daily newspapers have deadlines in the evening that must be met to guarantee coverage in the following day's paper. A writer working on a story with an approaching deadline must be given priority over a writer working for a weekly or longer-lead publication, such as *ESPN the Magazine* or *Sports Illustrated*. Most, if not all, sportswriters of major daily newspapers also have blogs on their paper's website that are maintained and updated throughout the day. Today, most, if not all, beat writers also maintain Twitter accounts that they use to weigh in on topics of interest and to share links to their online articles and articles of their coworkers.

Wire service reporters may not be very well known by name, but their stories have the potential to reach a large audience through a distribution network consisting of hundreds of newspaper, radio, television, and Internet outlets. Wire services should be given priority treatment because they have the potential to reach the widest audience. The main wire service is the Associated Press. Other wire services include Reuters, Bloomberg News, and the sport-specific wire service The Sports Network.

Table 16-1 Working Media List

Print Media

Local daily newspapers

Wire services (e.g., Associated Press, Reuters, Scripps Howard)

National daily newspapers (e.g., *USA Today, Wall Street Journal*)

Weekly newspapers (business journals, local town weeklies)

National sport magazines (e.g., *Sports Illustrated, ESPN the Magazine, Sporting News*)

Local magazines (city magazines, such as the *Washingtonian, Bostonian*)

Specialty pulp papers (e.g., *USA Today Sports Weekly, The Hockey News*)

Trade publications (e.g., *SportsBusiness Journal, Team Marketing Report*)

Television Media

Local over-the-air network affiliates (ABC, CBS, Fox, NBC)

National over-the-air networks

Regional sports networks (e.g., Madison Square Garden Network)

National cable sports networks (e.g., ESPN)

Local cable programs

National cable programs (e.g., Nickelodeon's G.A.S.)

National cable networks (e.g., CNN, MSNBC, CNBC)

On-demand programming

Radio Media

Local all-sports stations

Local nonsports radio

National sports radio networks (e.g., ESPN Radio, Fox Sports Radio, Sporting News Radio Network)

Nationally syndicated sports programs (e.g., Westwood One, Premier Radio Network, Jim Rome Show)

Satellite radio (e.g., XM and Sirius)

Internet Media

ESPN.com

SI.com

Yahoo! (yahoo.com)

CBS SportsLine (cbssportsline.com)

League sites (e.g., nfl.com, mlb.com, nba.com)

Team sites (e.g., atlanta.braves.mlb.com, newyorkjets.com)

Blogs (e.g., fanblogs.com, yankeefan.blogspot.com)

Communicating directly with the news media occurs in many ways. For example, the most common way for professional and major college sport teams to communicate is daily contact with the **beat reporter** assigned by the local media outlet to cover an organization, its games, and its practices. In most cases, this person is from the local newspaper and is known as the **beat writer**. According to Nichols and colleagues (2002), in the 1920s and 1930s newspapers assigned beat writers to baseball and these beat writers "traveled with their respective Major League Baseball team to cover them" (p. 5). In the eyes of the team owners, the coverage provided by their local newspapers was the lifeblood of the franchise. In those days, it was not uncommon for MLB club owners to cover the travel costs for their beat writers. At that time the newspaper was the only way most fans could follow their team, because radio and TV were in their infancy or not yet invented. Bear in mind that also back then there were no stadium lights, and therefore no night games, meaning most games were played on weekday afternoons while most people were working. Today, it is common for five or more beat reporters to be assigned to a particular professional or major collegiate sport team by the numerous local media outlets. This makes for a very competitive group all aiming to get a unique angle and story.

Press Releases

The main way a sport organization gets its news out is with a **press release** (also called a news release). Seitel (2001) states that press releases serve as "the basic interpretive mechanism to let people know what an organization is doing and are sent out to editors and reporters in hopes of stimulating favorable stories about their organizations" (p. 328).

News releases are written in the standard **inverted pyramid** style of writing. The inverted pyramid style presents the most important facts in the lead paragraph. The remaining paragraphs are arranged in descending order of importance. News releases should be written in a matter-of-fact fashion.

Press Conferences

For more important announcements, a press release may not be sufficient to get your message out. In that case the **press conference**, where the media are invited to a specific location, would be the chosen method of communicating. Seitel (2001, p. 345) suggests the following guidelines in preparation of a press conference:

1. Notify the media well in advance.

2. Don't play favorites.

3. Hold a news conference in an appropriate location.

4. Follow up early and often.

5. Keep the speaker(s) away from the media before the conference.

6. Remember TV.

In the ever-changing world of sports, advance notice might be as little as 2 hours. This usually is the case when a coach is fired or a major trade occurs. It may also be the case when something negative happens and you must act quickly to get your message out.

Regardless of where a press conference is held, accommodating the needs of the attending media is a top priority. There must be proper lighting, sound, enough electrical outlets, a backdrop with a logo, a raised platform in front of the room with a podium, a raised platform in the rear of the room for TV cameras, and a **multibox** device to allow multiple camera operators and radio reporters to plug into the audio feed without having to place an unwieldy number of microphones on the podium. A number of questions need to be answered just in planning the news conference, before the real questions are even asked. A brief outline of a press conference can be found in **Figure 16-1**.

© afaizal/ShutterStock, Inc.

Media Guides

It is routine to distribute packages of notes and other related pieces of information to the media. **Media notes** packages contain all the statistical information and biographical information about the two teams competing in a game, from

The following is a brief outline for a press conference to announce the hiring of a new coach:

1. PR (or media relations [MR]) director welcomes media and announces any ground rules to be followed.

2. PR or MR director introduces general manager (GM) or athletic director (AD).

3. GM or AD announces and introduces new coach.

4. Coach greets media, makes comments.

5. PR or MR director conducts questions and answers (Q&A) between GM or AD, coach, and media.

6. PR or MR director thanks media for attending and announces procedure for one-on-one or small group interviews with coach and/or GM or AD.

Figure 16-1 Press Conference Outline

individual athletes to coaches, as well as the team perspective.

Annual team **media guide** publications must be created and distributed to the media before the season begins. The media guide serves an invaluable role for all of a team's beat reporters and television and radio announcers, as well as for media members who are not as familiar with an organization. This publication contains all the information a reporter will need to know about the organization, including staff directories; biographies of all coaches, players, owners, and front-office staff; and team and individual records. When a fan listening at home hears a sportscaster recite some interesting facts or figures, it is a safe bet that the information was pulled together from the media guide or media notes package provided by the home team's media relations department.

Another example of how technology has influenced the area of sport communications is the migration from print publications (i.e., media guides) to electronic, or digital, editions. For example, for the 2010 MLB season, the league's communications department distributed its array of annual publications, such as the media information directory and the Red and Green Books, on flash drives. The popular Red and Green Books (in-depth guides to the American and National Leagues, respectively), published annually for decades, are no longer produced in print form. They are distributed exclusively in a digital format. Additionally, the National Basketball Association (NBA) has granted its teams permission to distribute their media guides exclusively in a digital format.

Photography

Photography is another key area for a sport communications professional. It is imperative to hire a capable photographer, preferably one who can attend press conferences, games, selected practices, community relations events, and other team functions requiring some level of photo capturing. Today, a team photographer must have the capability to shoot digitally. Digital images afford communications professionals an easier way to file, retrieve, and distribute photos than prints, slides, and negatives. Today, digital images can be taken, edited, and uploaded to websites, newspapers, and magazines for almost instantaneous usage.

Videography

Other forms of communicating with the media include the use of video. In the digital age, video has quickly become the public's chosen media.

© Hemera Technologies/AbleStock.com/Thinkstock

With the potential to reach millions of fans and potential fans through websites such as YouTube and Vimeo, not to mention an organization's own website, access to a professional videographer and/or video production house has become paramount. A written press release is most beneficial to the print and radio media. However, the Internet and television media live in a world of moving images and sound. It is becoming more common to see organizations offering their own video of special events and activities to the news media via Internet downloading. This helps get their message out while also easing the burden placed on the staff and financial resources of news organizations. That is why a **video news release (VNR)** is sometimes worth the price of production and distribution. A VNR is not produced for every announcement. However, a VNR with strong imagery will help your message get picked up by television outlets. A VNR is a preproduced piece that includes a written story summary or press release that is edited for broadcast, making it more attractive and time saving for a TV producer to air.

A cousin of the VNR is **b-roll**, a tape of raw footage, not a finished segment, that accompanies a written news release. The footage, which the organization selects, arms a news producer with proper video to support a written announcement. Keep in mind that anytime the use of video and video distribution is considered there are costs involved that may serve as a deterrent. In addition to the costs of hiring a video crew to shoot the material, which will run about $1,500 for a full-day shoot, the editing costs could run as high as $250 per hour, and the copying/tape-dubbing costs could be as high as $50 per Beta format tape (the preferred format of producers). There are additional charges to digitize the footage for uploading and downloading purposes. It is imperative that all video material be digitized for wider distribution and more efficient in-house archiving. With this in mind, one can expect more sport organizations to purchase the necessary equipment (digital camera with HD video capability, lighting, microphone, etc.) and employ public relations personnel with the skills to manage video needs in-house.

Conference Calls

In this day and age of high-tech gadgetry, one of the most successful ways of communicating with the media is to use the telephone. Now that virtually everyone has 24/7 access to a phone, telephone **conference calls** have become a very common and extremely convenient method of communication. A conference call can be organized by one of a number of service providers (e.g., AT&T, Sprint, or MCI) in a matter of minutes and scheduled for as early as 30 minutes after setting it up. Some organizations go so far as to have their own dedicated teleconference phone number. This allows the media relations department to organize a call in the time it takes to get the word out to the media. The media then dials in and participates in the call, and the organization is billed for the service just as it would be for any other phone usage. Many teams use this method when they have traded players late in the day or are on the road.

Some features to consider when setting up a conference call include having an operator record a list of call participants with their affiliations, having the callers in a listen-only mode (this reduces background noise and cell phone static), and using a question and answer (Q&A) moderator who introduces the media member before he or she asks a question. Conference calls can also be recorded and played back on a toll-free number for a predetermined amount of time following the call. This allows media unable to participate in the call a chance to hear the call in its entirety. Recordings from the calls are also available in electronic or digital formats, which allow for easy e-mail distribution, uploading to websites, and archiving. Full typed transcripts of the calls can be provided for accurate record keeping, archival purposes, and posting a print version on a team's website.

In the near future, one can imagine a day when the Web conference replaces the conference call. The Internet has the ability to provide the same audio quality capability as the telephone but provides all parties involved with the ability to enhance their communications with shared access to important documents and video. Many companies (e.g., WebEx, Skype, GoToMeeting.com) are gaining market share and penetration in this area.

Legal Issues

Sport communications professionals must be conscious of the laws affecting their work. For instance, defamation (libel and slander) may come into play if the sport communication professional provides information to the media that may not be accurate. Professionals working with intercollegiate athletics need to be aware of the Family Educational Rights and Privacy Act (FERPA), also known as the Buckley Amendment. FERPA sets the parameters for providing personal academic and medical information to the media. For years FERPA has required that student-athletes at universities receiving federal funding consent to release academic and medical information to

nonuniversity personnel, such as college conferences and the media. The Health Insurance Portability and Accountability Act (HIPAA) sets limits on providing medical information to others and has caused some confusion in college athletic departments about what sort of medical information can be released to the press. However, HIPAA addresses this point by excluding from the definition of "protected health information" a student's college or university education records. Thus, those records continue to be subject to FERPA (NCAA, 2003).

Public and Community Relations

There was a time in sports when public relations covered media relations, **community relations**, and public relations. Today, the role of the sport communications professional has become more specific and defined. For the purposes of this section, *public relations* is defined as all non-media-related communications efforts aimed at delivering a direct message to the fans.

Many public relations activities generate some media exposure and, it is hoped, portray an organization in a positive manner. However, most public relations activities are undertaken to have a positive impact on the community. They are not undertaken for the sole purpose of gaining publicity. Conventional wisdom dictates that if the public relations efforts are meaningful and sincere, then along the way positive media relations' benefits will result.

One of the most visible and common public relations practices is community relations. Community relations activities and departments are extensions of an organization's public relations department and, prior to the mid to late 1980s, were generally handled by the public relations department. In the era of specialization in the front offices of sport organizations, more emphasis was given to the effort of improving an organization's image through community involvement, such that it required the efforts of a full-time staff member(s).

Community relations objectives include developing substantive programs to benefit charitable causes as well as educational and outreach programs in an organization's local business area. These programs can include creating a 501(c)(3) nonprofit foundation to raise funds and distribute financial contributions to worthy causes or to serve as a link to a community's charitable organizations.

Community relations programs allow organizations and their athletes a chance to give back to the communities in which they live and work. These programs can also result in positive public relations and media coverage for both the players involved and their team.

Community relations departments also make in-kind contributions of licensed merchandise, game tickets, and autographed memorabilia to help a cause raise funds through auctions, special events, and raffles. Given the demands on the time of today's professional and amateur athletes, in-kind contributions tend to be the most popular method of supporting local charities. Charities auction or raffle these items to help raise funds.

In most cases, this type of support is not intended to generate any substantial publicity but rather to create a benevolent reputation for the organization in the eyes of its fans and community leaders. These relationships also offer organizations a chance to reach out to the general public and try to increase their recognition among people who may not be avid or even casual sports fans. Bear in mind that if a strong community relations program is allowed to mature, over time the program will likely generate media exposure to further enhance an organization's image within its community.

New Media and the Internet

The **new media industry** "combines elements of computing, technology, telecommunications, and content to create products and services which can be used by consumers and business users" (Thornton, 1999, Biomedical section). Most people think of new media as a **website** and the use of e-mail, but it is much more than that.

In terms of communications, websites are one of an organization's most valued public relations outlets. The time it has taken the Internet to grow from a fad to a mainstream media outlet has been astounding. Recent numbers put the wired world in North America at over 273 million home users, or 79% of the population. This is 11.4% of the 2.4 billion worldwide users (Internet World Stats, 2012). In terms of sports, Nielsen reported that sports websites attracted more than 87 million Americans and 36 million smartphone owners using a sports app during the month of September 2013 alone. This was primarily due to the start of the professional football season and the MLB playoffs taking place during this month ("Fantasy Big Leagues," 2013).

With those facts in mind, websites are clearly key tools for sport communications professionals to get their messages out and to interact one-to-one with stakeholders. Also, an organization's website allows a sport organization's message to be published in the way the organization wants it to be presented and not filtered by the media. To that end, it has become common for teams to make important announcements on their own sites before or at the same time as the information is distributed to the media.

The sport communications professional should do all he or she can to develop a trusted and resourceful website. Stakeholders should be able to go to an organization's website for all the latest information, including updated scores, ticket information, feature stories, photographs, audio and video clips, and merchandise. Today's sports websites "more than any other medium [have] the ability to feed the insatiable appetite of sports fans" (McGowan, 2001, p. 33). By building a trusted site, an organization reduces its need to rely upon the outside media to deliver its messages to its most valued customers.

Websites also provide organizations with the ability to distribute their message and product to a worldwide audience. Given the nearly boundless nature of the Internet, organizations can develop one-to-one relationships with fans from every corner of the globe. With only 11.4% of the Internet users residing in North America, there are plenty of opportunities for sport organizations to reach audiences in other parts of the world, including Asia (44.8% of Internet users), Europe (21.5%), and Africa (7.0%) (Internet World Stats, 2012). Many of these relationships may bring incremental revenue through the sale of licensed products such as hats, t-shirts, pennants, and posters. Additionally, a website has the ability to increase brand awareness as well as provide unique insights into the organization to the website user. This should explain why a number of North American sport leagues are eager to take their games abroad. In addition to serving as a repository of "all things" related to an organization, an organization's website should be viewed as the hub of all Internet-related activities, including social media sites such as YouTube, Twitter, and Instagram.

The Internet has also changed how sport communications professionals prepare and utilize publications, including newsletters, media guides, and annual yearbooks. The printed newsletter is rapidly becoming an endangered species as organizations move to utilize e-mail as a more personal and effective way to communicate with their publics. **Electronic newsletters** sent via e-mail are generally less costly, easier to produce, and more timely than printed newsletters and can include additional links to other Web-based information and various multimedia features, such as audio and video.

The delivery of these publications has changed as well. Printing and mailing costs have almost been eliminated with the creation of the electronic newsletter. Many organizations have produced media guides and yearbooks on CD-ROMs or in electronic PDF files delivered on flash drives, thereby decreasing the number of copies printed.

E-mail also has changed how sport organizations communicate with their numerous stakeholders, such as the media. News releases, previously mailed and faxed, can now be distributed almost instantly. Further, media members can be targeted by creating specific **media lists**, such as beat writers, editors, columnists, and news directors. E-mail has also enabled the sport organization to communicate directly with its key stakeholder—the fan—on a one-to-one basis.

© Vereshchagin Dmitry/ShutterStock, Inc.

New media can be defined as the emergence of digital, computerized, or networked information and communication technologies in the later part of the twentieth century. Examples of these technologies include websites and social media, blogs, podcasts, online video streaming, and mobile technology (Flew, 2008). Social media outlets such as Facebook, Twitter, and Instagram offer sport organizations the opportunity to communicate with their fans—or in the new media vernacular, their followers—in real time. These most often brief (in Twitter's case, 140 characters or fewer) interactions allow for a free-flowing exchange of commentary, ideas, and opinions, all of which help strengthen the bond between an organization and its followers. Specifically, Twitter has been embraced by all professional sport teams, leagues, colleges, and conferences, as well as most athletes, as a powerful communications vehicle, despite its character limitations. Twitter has allowed athletes to speak directly to their most passionate fans, and in doing so build stronger connections with their fan base, enhance their own images, and improve their marketability. Teams and leagues encourage their players to pursue social media interactions, because this form of new media has proven to be one of the most effective ways to heighten interest in and awareness of various aspects of the industry, from games and promotions to telecasts. For example, during MLB's 2013 All-Star Game players departing the game were ushered into social media stations where they could post to their Twitter and/or Facebook accounts. This effort helped the All-Star Game telecast generate 851,192 total social media comments among 477,795 unique users. At one point in the telecast, social media commentary peaked at 14,000 tweets a minute when Mariano Rivera entered the game in his last All-Star appearance ("MLB All-Star Game Wins," 2013). Media relations personnel may be tasked, as part of their job responsibilities, with following social media sites, including their team's coaches Facebook and Twitter accounts, and providing comments or "posts."

New media technology has also led to the development and launch of sports-specific software applications, or **apps**, for mobile devices, such as smartphones and tablets. These apps can be either league and/or team specific, and are generally available free of charge. Apps offer sport organizations an opportunity to migrate much of their website content, literally, into the palms of the hands of their fans through smartphones. This further enhances the communications benefits and opportunities to connect with a fan base in real time. Apps also can become an incremental profit center; if they are not free, they are usually priced at a modest 99 cents, and the low cost can result in mass consumption by those fans with an insatiable desire to know all there is to know about their favorite team.

Podcasts are another communications outlet available through new media. Generally speaking, **podcasts** are, in most cases, long-form audio broadcasts created by their producers to offer information that is not generally available through conventional media. However, many conventional media outlets also produce podcasts to further extend their reach and content distribution. For the sport communications professional, podcasts are a relatively inexpensive way to produce and broadcast in-house video feature-length programs without the need for a cable TV or over-the-air television broadcast partner.

Blogs have presented a relative challenge to the sport communications professional, as *bloggers*, as writers of blogs are known, have built up large followers and legions of loyal readers. Originally viewed with disdain by many sport communications professionals and most mainstream media members, bloggers have emerged as legitimate members of the new media brigade. For example, popular website, app, and blog publisher outlet Bleacher Report was started in 2007 by four sports fans and was picked by *Adweek* readers as 2011's "Best Sports Media Brand" (Beltrone, 2012). Bleacher Report is now a part of the Turner Sports and Entertainment Network, having been acquired in 2012. Today's sport communications professionals must judge bloggers based on their own merits, but as Bleacher Report shows, ignoring bloggers may not be a prudent communications strategy. Although anyone with a computer and an Internet connection can start a blog, some teams have attempted to embrace bloggers, going so far as to offer credentials to some. Most bloggers are diehard fans of a team, and most position the teams in a positive light, and therefore should not be overlooked by sport organizations when disseminating information to the media. The combined audience of a team's legion of bloggers may add up to an impressive number of the team's most ardent supporters.

New media also offers sport communications professionals with free and easy-to-use opportunities to distribute video content to their core communications targets via websites such as YouTube, Vimeo, and Daily Motion, to name a few of the most popular sites. These outlets provide sport communications professionals with the ability to engage targeted audiences through video, which remains one of the strongest and most effective forms of communications. For example, an organization can create its own channel on YouTube and post video highlights, promotional pieces, staged and humorous video content, and so forth. In some cases, videos have gone "viral," becoming very popular through the process of Internet sharing, social media, and e-mail. A viral video can attract a million or more viewers, which is an impressive number, regardless of the medium.

Although new media presents tremendous communications opportunities, it also brings with it challenges. Not all websites, bloggers, and social media outlets seek to promote or present teams, leagues, and athletes in a positive light. Some, such as Deadspin.com, have attracted millions of visitors and followers with their exposure of controversial issues involving teams and leagues and the "off the field" activities of athletes. Although new media continues to take the sport industry to unimaginable heights of exposure, in real or near real time, everyone involved in the industry has to be mindful of their actions nearly every waking moment. As long as a mobile device is nearby, what happens next can become a global Internet sensation—for good or bad—for eternity in a matter of seconds.

Preparing for the Interview

Sport communications professionals spend a great amount of time trying to generate publicity for their respective organizations. This is accomplished through interviews between the media and members of the organization, such as the president, general manager, athletic director, coaches, or athletes. An interview is a question-and-answer session employed by the media to gather information and present it to an audience. The interview provides insights into a sporting contest, event, or other announcement. The media members are looking to gain answers to the basic news questions of who, what, where, when, why, and how.

Nichols and colleagues (2002, p. 122) offer several common characteristics of an interview:

- An interview is an interchange of information between two or more parties. In the sport setting, it may involve an interaction between two parties, such as a one-on-one interview.
- An interview has a specific purpose or goal. The primary purpose of a newspaper story, radio interview, or television interview is to inform and/or entertain.
- Both parties in an interview exchange information by asking and answering questions.

To prepare the interviewee, the first item is for the sport communications professional to prepare **key messages** the organization wants to convey to the media during the interview. It is most effective to have two or three key messages. These messages are what should be included in responses to the questions the media ask during the interview.

In addition to the key messages, the sport communications professional should create a list of potential questions, including suggested responses. The sport communications professional needs to think like the media and anticipate what questions the media are likely to ask. What follow-up questions will flow from likely answers? How should answers be crafted to reinforce the key messages? In addition, the interviewee could be asked questions unrelated to the interview. These questions could refer to current events or events that happened in other places. The interviewee should be prepared for these types of questions as well. Lastly, the sport communications professional should meet in advance with the interviewee to review the probable questions and answers.

It is easy to take this aspect of the communications process for granted. Most senior-level front office people generally deal with the media on a regular basis and may feel they can handle themselves without help. However, even the most media-savvy individuals will do these preparatory exercises in their heads, if not by jotting down some thoughts on a piece of scrap paper or a napkin.

Crisis Management

For the most part, the day-to-day contact between the sport communications professional and the media focuses on the game, rivalries, the players' performances, player transactions, and the business of sport. However, crises in sport have become almost regular occurrences. Just follow the newspapers, radio, or television and it won't take long to find one. Some examples include Tiger Woods' extramarital affairs, the NFL's concussion issue and the safety/health of players, the BALCO drug inquiry leading to allegations of steroid use by professional and Olympic athletes, Michael Vick's involvement with a dog-fighting ring, the hazing and bullying charges levied against Miami Dolphins guard Richie Incognito by his teammate Jonathan Martin, and the child sex abuse scandal at Penn State University involving assistant football coach Jerry Sandusky.

A crisis is any nonroutine event that could be disruptive to the sport organization. It can also be an unusual short-term incident that has a real or perceived negative impact on the general welfare of the organization or its stakeholders. A crisis situation for a sport organization, individual athlete, or coach can create a very stressful time. It can also cause irreparable damage to an individual involved, a team, or a college athletic department. The damage can include damage to one's reputation and brand equity, which could erode endorsement and marketing opportunities and ticket and sponsorship sales. To combat these serious incidents, sport organizations should create a **crisis plan** in advance. The amount of reaction time saved when time is at a premium will pay off in the long run when a crisis occurs. Barton (2001) states that "because so many incidents have become mismanaged, new demands have emerged for corporations . . . to have a crisis plan in place" (p. 62).

In preparing for a potential crisis, identifying crises that may affect the organization, estimating the probability of their occurrence in advance, and creating a plan of action are the starting points to better management. A list of potential sport crisis areas appears in **Table 16-2**.

The most common mistake made during a crisis is overreaction. When a crisis occurs, it is important to not panic by simply reacting to the situation. Take a step back and gather as many of the facts as quickly as possible. Once the facts have been gathered, prepare a plan of action, not one of reaction. It should be done swiftly, but not before as much information as possible has been gathered. When preparing an action plan, be sure to deal with the issue head-on, promptly, and with honesty. Then, use the heightened level of media attention to get the message out.

Table 16-2 Potential Crises in Sports

Accident (crash of plane, train, bus, car)
Arena disaster (building collapse, object falls, power outage)
Criminal activity (DUI, drugs, domestic violence, gambling, weapons)
Customer relations (problems with ticket service)
Death of executive, coach, player
Employee/management misconduct (sexual harassment, sexual misconduct, sexual abuse, bribery, kickbacks, discrimination)
Employee problem (inappropriate comments or behavior by ownership, department staff, coaches, athletes)
Gambling
Hiring/firing
Investor relations (going public, IPO, merger, acquisition)
Labor relations (strike, lockout, contract negotiations, holdouts)
Lawsuits (ticket holders)
Natural disaster (earthquake, fire, tornado)
Product liability (jersey, hat)
Protestors at site of arena, stadium, team or athletic department offices
Rule violations
Social controversies/issues (hazing, drugs, alcohol, AIDS, diversity, domestic violence)
Terrorism
Ticket price increase

This list is meant as a starting point in assessing potential crises and crisis planning. Abbreviations: DUI = driving under the influence; IPO = initial public offering; AIDS = acquired immunodeficiency syndrome.

Seitel (2001, p. 214) offers 10 general principles for communicating in a crisis:

1. Speak early and often.

2. Don't speculate.

3. Go off the record at your own peril.

4. Stay with the facts.

5. Be open and concerned, not defensive.

6. Make your own point and repeat it.

7. Don't war with the media.

8. Establish yourself as the most authoritative source.

9. Stay calm, and be truthful and cooperative.

10. Never lie.

In addition to identifying potential crises and creating a crisis plan, a prepared sport organization should create a **crisis team**. The crisis plan should identify roles and responsibilities for members of the organization. Additionally, it should include a system to notify key members of the organization as soon as possible should a crisis arise. A crisis team is a group of key organizational individuals who will be responsible for managing the crisis effectively. A crisis team should include some of the following executives: president, general manager/athletic director, director of communications, director of marketing, director of finance, facilities manager, legal counsel, and other key technical experts of the organization.

Early on in a crisis, it is important for the organization to speak with one voice. That one voice should be communicated by the organization's spokesperson. The spokesperson should be a senior management person and be the only person to speak publicly on the crisis issue.

In a crisis situation, there are always at least two sides to a story. At times, the media look to create an environment that pits the sides against each other—tune into any cable news network and you will see ongoing examples. With that said, sometimes the best way to deal with a crisis is to tell your side of the story up front, ensure that it is easily understood, and refuse to take the bait to extend the story. Crises breed controversy and, in turn, sell newspapers, drive radio listenership, and increase television viewership. Contributing or responding to every claim made by the other side merely prolongs the coverage of the issue, which may not be in the organization's best interest. As long as the story has been told accurately, no one owes it to the media to sustain the story.

When dealing directly with the media, it is always helpful to keep in mind that the media are always looking for a "crisis" or hot-button issue to cover. Therefore, it is imperative to learn how to avoid falling into some traps regularly practiced by members of the media such as **speculation** and asking for off-the-record comments.

Speculation

The media will often ask questions that include the words "what if" or "suppose." These questions are highly speculative in nature, and it is seldom in anyone's best interest to speculate or offer a guess to a question. Politely respond by stating that you prefer not to answer a speculative or hypothetical question.

Off-the-Record Comments

Going **off the record** with the media is a very dangerous practice. If the information is very compelling or newsworthy, a reporter may use the information regardless of an off-the-record agreement. The level of trust with a media member has to be very high for a sport communications professional to engage in this practice.

Awareness

Whenever the media are around, a sport communications professional should be mindful of what is said and done. Words can be picked up by a turned-on tape recorder, a nearby television camera can record sound and actions, and so, too, can most smartphones and other handheld devices. It is the media's responsibility to report a story, and in many major markets members of the media, especially print journalists, are under extreme pressure to break exclusive stories. The more time that is dedicated to learning the needs and wants of the media covering an organization, including individual reporting styles, the easier it will be to do the job effectively.

Media Training

Several companies offer **media training** tips for communications professionals and for anyone likely to be dealing with the media. Several sport organizations have used these companies to provide players, coaches, athletic directors, and senior executives with tips on proper interviewing techniques, handling hostile interviewers, and shaping messages into sound bites. Many of these companies provide video analysis to compare the before and after performances. An experienced sport communications professional should be able to provide similar services or support to his or her organization's key personnel or should locate a company that can provide this service to the organization.

Internal Communications

One of the most overlooked forms of communications is **internal communications**. Organizations are often so involved with generating positive news, posting information on their websites, creating printed publications, and so on that communicating to the organization's staff is overlooked. This seemingly small issue can become a major problem for an organization, resulting in poor morale and decreased productivity. According to Barton (2001), employees are key stakeholders who can be especially valuable to the organization in a time of crisis.

The solution to this potential problem is rather simple and can be achieved in a number of ways. The president or general manager can distribute a daily or weekly e-mail that includes a status report on any existing projects, new hiring, new partnership agreements, ticket sales updates, employee of the month award, and anything else that engages the employees. Another common practice is a weekly or monthly breakfast where the staff can gather in an informal environment with senior staff and discuss organizational happenings. Always keep in mind the old adage that says your most important customers are your employees. If the employees don't feel strongly about the organization, how can they be expected to positively represent the organization in their day-to-day business relationships?

Integrated Marketing Communications

Demands placed on the sport communications professional continue to change. The new buzzword is **integrated marketing communications (IMC)**, which, according to Seitel (2001), is the symbiosis of advertising, marketing, and public relations. Today's sport communications professionals need to be knowledgeable in these areas because they will be called upon to participate in campaigns utilizing these areas to promote their organizations.

Advertising

Advertising often does not fall under the job responsibilities of the sport communications specialist, but it is an area of communications that must be fully understood. Cutlip, Center, and Broom (2000) define *advertising* as "information placed in the media by an identified sponsor that pays for the time or space. It is a controlled method of placing messages in the media" (p. 11). Public relations relies upon news outlets to convey its message. Although less expensive than advertising, public relations efforts are subject to whatever editing the media decides upon. There is no guarantee a press release will generate any publicity at all. In contrast, advertising guarantees the message will gain the space and coverage purchased. Although advertising promises to get the message out there, it does not ensure that message will be trusted or believed.

Perhaps the most significant difference between the two is that advertising is more costly to produce and place than media relations activities. For example, a successfully

placed news item published by *Sports Illustrated* will get the item in front of more than 3 million avid sports fans at virtually no cost other than staff time. To place a full-page ad in *Sports Illustrated* to reach the magazine's subscriber base would cost more than $238,000 (color) and $166,500 (black and white), not including the costs involved in creating the ad (*Sports Illustrated*, 2014).

There are, generally speaking, two types of ads: **image ads** and **call-to-action ads**. Image ads are created to reinforce an organization's brand imagery in the minds of consumers. These ads tend to highlight the quality of a service. Call-to-action ads aim to encourage consumers to do something, such as buy tickets.

Media Planning

Choosing the correct medium in which to place advertising requires a thorough examination of each potential outlet's ability to reach the most people fitting a target audience's demographic profile. This is known as **media planning**. Because advertising can be costly, it is imperative to make the effort to ensure that the advertising will be successful. Once the total advertising budget has been decided, it must be determined how the ad dollars will be effectively spent in the media of TV, radio, print (newspapers and magazines), and the Internet. A trained **media buyer**, who purchases advertising for clients, can provide the information required to make the right decision for each particular circumstance. Always keep in mind that the goal is to reach the greatest possible number of people who fit the targeted customer profile, not just the greatest number of people. A benefit to advertising on the Internet is the medium's ability to allow for cost-effective and near instantaneous monitoring of an ad's success. Checking a Web ad's click-through rate allows a marketer to alter the ad to generate an increase in clicks. Text copy, background colors, and everything in between can be tweaked and measured for success. When the winning formula is found, the ad, in theory, should wind up being more successful. Try doing that with traditional mediums of print, radio, and TV! It's too costly and time consuming to even try.

Direct Marketing

As previously discussed, reaching a targeted audience through advertising is not an easy process. With this in mind, another form of communications is **direct marketing**. As consumers, we have come to refer to this widely used practice as junk mail. However, thousands of very successful companies use this method of communication exclusively to sell their products or services, and the sport industry is just beginning to fully understand the powers of successful direct marketing campaigns, especially direct e-mail marketing campaigns.

Before beginning a direct marketing campaign, it is important to fully understand your key customers by creating a customer profile. Once the customer profile is developed, the proper message and the creative look or design that are likely to appeal to the audience for your direct marketing piece must also be developed. After the creative material has been carefully crafted so that it is visually appealing to the target audience, the next step is to acquire an appropriate mailing list of the people fitting the customer profile. In most cases, the names and addresses of people living within certain ZIP codes can be purchased from a list provider. In turn, the direct marketing material will be sent to these people and, if done properly, will capture their interest. The success rates of a direct marketing campaign vary widely, but successful campaigns return a positive response from approximately 2% of individuals targeted.

Direct marketing is now being utilized via the Internet. Similar to obtaining a mailing list, electronic mailing lists of qualified e-mail addresses can be purchased or created internally and utilized to send targeted messages and/or offerings. E-mail is a much more cost-effective method, can be sent instantaneously, and generates a faster and higher response rate. With that in mind, it is imperative for an organization's website to build a component to capture the e-mail addresses of its visitors.

Career Opportunities

Over the past 25 years, sport organizations have enjoyed tremendous growth in popularity thanks to expanded media coverage (cable television, magazines, 24-hour sports radio, and the Internet) as well as corporate support. This popularity has resulted in an explosion of sorts in the number of sport-related organizations, including professional sport leagues and teams, sport marketing and public relations firms, and the number of corporations employing sport-specific personnel.

This growth has been a boon to the area of sport communications. On the professional sport side, 25 years ago there were far fewer teams with fewer communications professionals. As this text went to print, there were 141 teams at the North American major league level (MLB, NBA, NFL, NHL, and Major League Soccer [MLS]) with hundreds of communications-related positions (media relations, public relations, community relations, and publications in print and online). This expansion on the professional level has also changed the structure of the department responsible for communications. Twenty-five years ago, a one- or two-person public relations staff handled a team, but today staffs consist of 6 to 10 individuals with titles ranging from the vice president level to directors, assistant directors, and other support staff, including more specialized positions such as assistant director of social media.

Additionally, auto racing (e.g., National Association of Stock Car Auto Racing

[NASCAR], Indy Racing League [IRL]) and minor league sports (e.g., Minor League Baseball, NBA Development League [NBDL], National Association of Professional Baseball Leagues [NAPBL], American Hockey League [AHL], East Coast Hockey League [ECHL]) have enjoyed tremendous growth over the same period of time. New professional sport leagues (e.g., Arena Football, Major League Lacrosse), women's leagues (e.g., Women's National Basketball Association [WNBA]), and nontraditional sports (i.e., X Games) have burst onto the scene in recent years, resulting in an increase in opportunities available to those interested in pursuing a career in sport communications. On the amateur level, sport communications professionals work in college athletic departments, college athletic conferences, Olympic committees, and other governing bodies. Finally, many sport facilities also have a communications professional working for the venue.

Even though opportunities in the area of sport communications have experienced tremendous growth over the past 30 years, obtaining one of these coveted positions is as difficult as ever. Because these jobs do not generally get listed in the local Help Wanted section of the newspaper, coursework and related work experience are required to obtain an internship, let alone a full-time position.

© SiuWing/ShutterStock, Inc.

Not all job candidates possess sport management degrees. As a matter of fact, many sport communications professionals possess degrees in communications, public relations, or journalism. It is important to accumulate coursework or volunteer or paid work experience to help you understand the fundamentals of public relations, communications, marketing, advertising, and journalism. Public speaking skills, writing skills, and knowledge of TV/video production and computer technology (Internet uploading, downloading, text posting, social media, etc.) are a must for all future sport communications professionals. Therefore, coursework rich in these areas will help prepare students for their internships.

There used to be a time when an internship offered students a chance to learn on the job. However, the competition for the most coveted internships is so intense that when an internship is available several applicants will have already amassed relative experience. Some will have written for their school or local newspaper. Some will have created their own websites and blogs. Many will have volunteered in their school's sports information department or served as public relations staffers for nonprofit organizations. It is no longer acceptable to enter the sport communications field, even as an intern, without some practical, firsthand experience.

The internship remains invaluable to starting a career in sport communications. It is important to choose an internship offering real opportunities to contribute to the communications activities of an organization. This does not mean that interns should be expected to make day-to-day strategic decisions. What this does mean is that internships should offer candidates a chance to get firsthand experience through actual tactical responsibilities. Interns should look for opportunities that promise more than "gofer" responsibilities. Interns should look for opportunities offering hands-on experience, but they should also choose an environment offering a complete learning experience, including a chance to work closely with proven professionals. Because most internships do not lead to full-time job offers, the internship will serve as the launching pad for your career. However, landing that desired entry-level position is a very difficult process. It will be a matter of timing, experience, and, to a large extent, who you know, and who knows you.

Make no mistake, the relationships and networks built during an internship will prove instrumental in gaining that first real job.

Despite the fact that men seem to dominate most sport organizations, women have an equal opportunity to gain internships and full-time opportunities in the area of sport communications. In fact, in 2013 women held no fewer than 45 positions in the public/media relations departments of the 30 MLB teams. This number does not even count the areas of sales, marketing, and community relations, which offer additional opportunities for women. Of all areas of the front office, public relations, media relations, and community relations are perhaps the most diverse.

Sport communications staffers at the professional and collegiate team levels get as close to the field of play as anyone outside of players and coaches. This makes for an exciting professional career full of memorable moments. If one wants to advance within the ranks of the organization's hierarchy, the ability to quickly establish oneself as a trustworthy employee who understands that what is heard and seen can often never be repeated is a necessity. Breaching this implied level of trust and confidentiality is sure to tarnish a reputation and result in a short-lived professional career.

Those fortunate enough to earn one of these coveted positions will soon learn that long hours, low starting pay, and slow-moving advancement come with this unique territory.

Most senior sport communications professionals, such as professional team public relations (PR) directors, have to attend every home game; most, if not all, road games; and most of the team's practices. This means that time for family and friends is extremely limited during the season, which can put a strain on most personal relationships.

Perhaps because most sport communications professionals share a lot in common, they are a close-knit group and communicate regularly with one another, formally, informally, intersport, and intrasport. It is common for a PR director from a team in one league to contact a peer in another league to ask for a favor or get an opinion on a writer, among other things. Although there are no real peer associations to speak of in professional sports, college sports offers its communications professionals a great opportunity for peer interaction through a professional association known as the College Sports Information Directors of America (CoSIDA). CoSIDA was founded in 1957 and has more than 3,000 members. The group holds an annual meeting with workshops. It also publishes monthly digests, and newsletters; offers an e-directory; sponsors scholarships; and boasts a well-developed website with useful professional information and a career center (CoSIDA, 2014). Other organizations can serve as resources as well as networking opportunities, such as the Public Relations Society of America (PRSA) and the International Association of Business Communicators (IABC). The PRSA has a Public Relations Student Society of America (PRSSA) to help students explore the field and enter the profession. In its 40th year, PRSSA has more than 11,000 college student members and more than 21,000 public relations and communications professionals worldwide. Its website boasts useful career information plus scholarship listings. The group also hosts an annual conference (PRSSA, 2014). In addition, the Association of Women in Sports Media

(AWSM) serves as "a support network and advocacy group for women who work in sports writing, editing, broadcast and production, and public and media relations" (AWSM, 2014).

Current Issues

Technology

As technology continues to have a great impact on the way we communicate with one another, expect Internet-based communications efforts to only increase. For example, social media websites such as Facebook, Instagram, Twitter, and YouTube offer organizations additional means to communicate directly with their current and future core fans almost anywhere in real or near-real time. However, social media sites also pose challenges, requiring constant monitoring and updating. In 2010, one MLB club hired a senior director of social media, and many more continue to add social media staff.

"Push" technologies, such as Twitter, allow individuals and organizations to communicate with their loyal or interested followers in real time. In some respects, today's technology has rendered a sport's organization's dependency on the media to get its message out obsolete. However, traditional mediums still reach more of the masses and provide organizations with an implicit third-party endorsement that organizations willing to bypass traditional media relations do at their own peril.

Web conferencing, as mentioned earlier, should become increasingly popular in the world of sport communications. Already popular with public companies and their investor relations activities with stock analysts, shareholders, and other important constituencies who may be dispersed throughout the world, Web conferencing allows for real-time exchange of audio, video, and text-based messaging. Additionally, Wi-Fi, a wireless Internet connection protocol, is also gaining in popularity and becoming a constant presence in and outside the sports world. Virtually all major sports league press boxes and press areas have Wi-Fi access, as do most stadiums. As Wi-Fi improves in strength and expands its reach in large public venues, it is easy to imagine real-time communications between teams and their fans from the moment they enter the stadium to the moment they leave, not to mention communications between fans and their social media "followers." With third-party service providers such as Skype, video Web conferencing is likely to enjoy continued growth in popularity and use.

Outside Agencies

A growing trend, especially at the league and association level, is hiring an outside public relations firm to help develop and administer public relations programs or special events. These agencies allow the staffs of the leagues and associations to concentrate on their day-to-day responsibilities, most of which are reactive in nature, and shift the implementation of these proactive public relations programs to someone else. These agencies, in essence, act as extensions of the hiring organization, allowing the organization to have greater impact in the area of public relations without being limited by its staff resources. These agencies can range from moderate or large companies with offices around the world to smaller agencies run by just an individual or two. The agencies can be hired on a **retainer** basis, whereby they are paid monthly to be of service to the organization, or they can be hired on a project-by-project basis.

Government Relations

One of the most recent trends in public relations activities focuses on government relations. **Government relations**, or lobbying, is used by all major sports leagues and players' unions, the NCAA, and in some cases by individual teams. Most organizations hire outside firms with legislative and other government contacts as well as more experience in this delicate area to represent their interests. Leagues, unions, and the NCAA have had lobbyists at the federal level for years. On the state level, the increased need to improve government relations has been influenced by the increase in new stadium and arena construction.

Needing to finance such costly projects, sport organizations have turned to their local legislators to help them gain access to federal, state, and local funds, as well as contributions from existing or specially created tax funds.

Case Study 16-1 Communications Strategies for the Cricket League

Congratulations! You have just graduated with a degree in sport management and have landed a job in professional sports. An overseas professional cricket league has hired you as its director of international communications. The premise behind your hire is that the United States is populated with numerous expatriates from several cricket-playing countries, and this cricket league wants to tap into that market. League officials want to host matches on U.S. soil and use the Internet to engage current cricket fans in their league and nurture new fans.

The cricket league is relying on you to help it choose the three markets in the United States that should host matches, and it wants you to generate local publicity to help sell tickets to these events. The league is also counting on you to generate national buzz in the United States for the purpose of increasing exposure for the remainder of the cricket season.

You must now develop and implement several strategies and tactics that incorporate traditional media and the Internet, including social media sites, to generate publicity for the league.

Questions for Discussion

1. Determine the three cities in the United States to host the matches during the cricket tour. What can be done in each market to engage local sports fans? How would you locate and communicate with fans from cricket-playing countries living in these markets? Would there be a benefit to engaging in a community-minded project while in each market? If so, what types of projects would you pursue and why? How would you go about gathering information from cricket fans in each local market for future communications purposes?

2. In order to make a national "splash," your bosses want you to plan a press conference in New York City upon the cricket team's arrival. Where would you host the press conference? League officials and the players are unfamiliar with the U.S. sports press. Prepare a background sheet with brief information on some national outlets likely to attend the press conference. What key messages will you craft and share with league officials and players? What kinds of questions will the media likely ask the officials and players? What other national media opportunities might you pursue while the teams are in New York?

3. Upon the conclusion of the series, you must sustain your superb efforts by creating and implementing an ongoing communications program during the cricket season. Relying heavily on the Internet as the main medium of communication, what types of communication elements will your plan include? Your main goals are to promote merchandise sales; to keep fans up-to-date on scores; and to provide player features, standings information, and live and on-demand Web viewing of matches and highlights.

Summary

As indicated by the breadth of information covered in this chapter, today's sport communications professional serves one of the organization's most vital roles. The sport communications professional has direct contact with local, national, and international media, the general public, the coaching staff, management staff, and the players, so it is imperative that this staff member know virtually all there is to know about an organization. Sport communications professionals must know all about an organization's ticket packages, sponsorship rates, history, rules of the game, community activities, players' interests and backgrounds, and on and on.

Sport communications professionals serve in the most vibrant area of the organization. In many cases, they travel to away games, may sit in on trade discussion meetings, and often offer input into how the team or athletic department will be marketed and promoted. In addition, they are the first to respond in a time of crisis. They will be quoted in the newspaper and will conduct television and radio interviews. They are the first people to whom others in the organization turn for information of all sorts. This is what makes sport communications an extremely challenging and exciting career choice. To be successful, sport communications professionals must remain cool, calm, and collected at all times. They need to be trustworthy, resourceful, and display common sense. If they do not know the answer to a question or a request, they need to know where to find it (and quickly). They must be good listeners, friendly, and approachable. Professional opportunities are numerous and growing, and an exciting future awaits those who choose this as a career path.

Lastly, today's sport communications professional must be technologically savvy. Rapidly advancing communications technologies provide the sport communications professional with ample opportunities to take matters into his or her own hands when developing and implementing organizational communications strategies and tactics.

Resources

Association for Women in Sports Media (AWSM)
7742 Spalding Drive, Suite 377
Norcross, GA 30092
http://awsmonline.org

College Sports Information Directors of America (CoSIDA)
P.O. Box 78718
Greenwood, IN 46142
http://www.cosida.com

International Association of Business Communicators (IABC)
601 Montgomery Street, Suite 1900
San Francisco, CA 94111
415-544-4700
http://www.iabc.com

Public Relations Society of America (PRSA)
33 Maiden Lane, 11th Floor
New York, NY 10038
212-460-1400
http://www.prsa.org

Public Relations Student Society of America (PRSSA)
33 Maiden Lane, 11th Floor
New York, NY 10038
212-460-1474
http://www.prssa.org

Key Terms

apps, beat reporter, beat writer, blog, b-roll, call-to-action ad, communications, community relations, conference call, crisis plan, crisis team, direct marketing, electronic newsletter, government relations, image ad, integrated marketing communications (IMC), internal communications, inverted pyramid, key messages, media buyer, media guide, media list, media notes, media planning, media training, multibox, new media, new media industry, news release, off the record, podcast, press conference, press release, retainer, speculation, sports information director (SID), stakeholder, video news release (VNR), Web conferencing, website

References

Association of Women in Sports Media. (2014). About. Retrieved from http://awsmonline.org/about/

Barton, L. (2001). *Crisis organizations II.* Cincinnati, OH: South Western College Publishing.

Beltrone, G. (2012, February 20). *Adweek* readers select the industry's star players. *Adweek.* Retrieved from http://www.adweek.com/news/advertising-branding/sports-media-and-marketing-mvps-138411

College Sports Information Directors of America. (2014). Our organization: What is CoSIDA? Retrieved from http://cosidacon.sidearmsports.com/sports/2013/7/25/general.aspx

Cutlip, S. M., Center, A. H., & Broom, G. M. (2000). *Effective public relations* (8th ed.). Upper Saddle River, NJ: Prentice Hall.

Fantasy Big Leagues: How fantasy sports are scoring with users. (November 26, 2013). *Nielsen.* Retrieved from http://www.nielsen.com/us/en/newswire/2013/fantasy-big-leagues-how-fantasy-sports-are-scoring-with-users.html

Flew, T. (2008). *New media: An introduction.* Melbourne, Australia: Oxford University Press.

Healy, B. (2013, August 4). John Henry adding Globe to his Boston constellation. *The Boston globe.* Retrieved from http://www.bostonglobe.com/business/2013/08/03/john-henry-bid-helped-local-profile-cash-offer/3SabclHyGeMKY7qoOaQqiN/story.html

Internet World Stats. (2012). Internet world statistics. Retrieved from http://www.internetworldstats.com/stats.htm

McGowan, A. (2001). Don't wait for a crisis to write a crisis plan. *Street & Smith's SportsBusiness Journal, 4*(23), p. 33.

Middleburg, D. (2001). *Winning PR in the wired world.* New York: McGraw-Hill.

MLB All-Star game wins the night on television and Twitter. (July 17, 2013). MLB.com. Retrieved from mlb.mlb.com/news/article.jsp?ymd=20130717&content_id=53967460&vkey=pr_mlb&c_id=mlb

NCAA. (2003, March 3). Privacy rules affect exchange of student-athlete medical records. *NCAA News.* Retrieved from http://fs.ncaa.org/Docs/NCAANewsArchive/2003/Association-wide/privacy+rules+affect+exchange+of+student-athlete+medical+records+-+3-3-03.html

Newsom, D., Turk, J., & Kruckeberg, D. (2004). *This is PR: The realities of public relations* (8th ed.). Belmont, CA: Wadsworth/Thompson Learning.

Nichols, W., Moynahan, P., Hall, A., & Taylor, J. (2002). *Media relations in sport*. Morgantown, WV: Fitness Information Technology.

Public Relations Student Society of America. (2014). About PRSSA? Retrieved from http://www.prssa.org/about/PRSA/

Seitel, F. (2001). *The practice of public relations* (8th ed.). Upper Saddle River, NJ: Prentice Hall.

Sports Illustrated. (2014). *Sports Illustrated* rate card #62. Retrieved from http://sportsillustrated.cnn.com/adinfo/si/ratecardframe.html

Thornton, T. V. (1999). Illinois has developed into the world's high tech hub. *Illinois Labor Market Review*. Retrieved from http://lmi.ides.state.il.us/lmr/hightech.htm

Chapter 17

Sport Broadcasting

Jim Noel

Learning Objectives

Upon completion of this chapter, students should be able to:

1. Recognize that broadcasting is an advertising medium and the very existence of that medium depends on the ability of the provider to produce advertising fees in excess of the fees that are paid to the rightsholders.

2. Trace the history of sport broadcasting from telegraph to radio, television, and cable television, through Internet streaming and understand how the industry has been shaped by technological change.

3. Identify the key personalities, programming, and organizations that have influenced the sport broadcast industry such as Roone Arledge, Pete Rozelle, *ABC's Wide World of Sports*, *Monday Night Football*, and ESPN.

4. Explain how rights fees for sporting events are valued and how those rights fees are distributed by the rightsholder.

5. Assess the way in which the broadcast of sporting events are produced

6. Illustrate how ratings are determined and how they affect the value of advertising time during a specific sporting event.

7. Differentiate between the various methods of sport broadcast distribution such as broadcast networks, syndication, cable networks, digital networks, and pay-per-view.

8. Recognize that American sport organizations are expanding their broadcast presence in foreign markets while their international counterparts are doing the same in the United States.

9. Debate some of the current issues of interest in the sport broadcast industry such as the potential market bubble for rights fees, the bundling of cable channels, the emergence of "cord-cutters," the widespread use of mobile devices, and the trend of audience fragmentation.

10. Identify the career opportunities available in the sport broadcast industry and recognize the skills needed to succeed in each of them.

Introduction

The coverage of sport by electronic media—television, radio, and digital technology—has grown into one of the biggest and most powerful forces in the business of sport. Today, fans can watch events unfold around the world as they happen, no matter where or when. The images and sounds of every major event—and many not-so-major ones—flash into our homes instantaneously, and we have come to expect the instant replays, dazzling computerized graphics, and expert commentary that accompany the events. When Usain Bolt won the Olympic 100-meter dash at the 2012 London Olympics, his performance was witnessed not only by 80,000 fans in Olympic Stadium, but by a global television audience of an estimated 2 billion people. Thanks to advanced technology, fans not only saw the race and Bolt's triumphant victory lap in high-definition video, they also saw multiple replays using slow motion, multiple camera angles, and extreme close-up images. Even the fans who witnessed the race in person were treated to replays on the large video boards in the stadium.

Not only has the electronic media impacted the way fans follow sport, they profoundly impact the economics of the sport industry. Television and related media pay billions of dollars for the rights to transmit coverage of various events to their audiences. **Rights fees** are a major source of revenue for sport leagues and organizations, and the volume of this revenue has exploded in recent years. Sport **rightsholders** rely on the rights fees they receive from broadcasters. In turn, sport programming makes money for broadcasters from the advertising contained in the programs and the distribution fees received from cable and direct-broadcast satellite companies.

In these ways, the sport industry and the broadcast media business are allied in a **symbiotic relationship**. It is a relationship that produces valuable, compelling programming content that has become an essential element of the worldwide sport industry.

History of Sport Broadcasting

The telegraph was the first electronic communications medium used for transmission of information about sport events. Samuel F. B. Morse created the first commercial telegraph service in 1844, a 40-mile circuit between Washington, D.C. and Baltimore. It sent messages along a wire by opening and closing an electrical circuit in a series of dots and dashes representing letters and numbers, which then were transcribed into text and hand delivered to recipients (Head, Sterling, & Schofield, 1994). The service quickly grew into the nation's first transcontinental electronic communications system.

By the early twentieth century, many newspapers had their own telegraph machines, which allowed them to provide play-by-play reports of important sport events as they happened. Public interest in the 1915 World Series between the Boston Red Sox and Philadelphia Phillies was so great that 10,000 people gathered in Times Square in New York City to watch a 50-foot-high mechanical scoreboard and baseball diamond depicting every play of the game, based on telegraph reports received in the *Times* newsroom (Fullerton, 1915).

The telephone was first demonstrated to the public in 1876 by Alexander Graham Bell, who used a microphone to transmit sound along wires (Head et al., 1994). Long-distance telephone service was relatively expensive for several decades thereafter, however, so the telephone was not a commercially viable means of transmitting game reports directly to consumers. Telephone lines later became an important means of connecting radio and television stations, enabling nationwide networks.

In the late nineteenth century, experimentation with the transmission of wireless sound waves led to the development of radio. By the time of the outbreak of World War I in 1914, the wireless (radio) was a standard method of communication for business, government, and the military. Ironically, one feature of radio was initially regarded as a drawback to commercial applications of the technology: Once a message was transmitted, anyone within range who had a receiver tuned to the proper frequency could hear it. Why would anyone want to send a message through the air that thousands, perhaps millions, of people could listen to? The answer came from a Westinghouse Electric Company executive named Harry Davis, whose company had a warehouse full of World War I surplus radio receivers. Perhaps, he reasoned, if a wireless station broadly transmitted entertainment and news programs every day on a fixed radio frequency—hence the term **broadcasting**—people would buy his receivers, tune into the specific frequency, and listen.

The first commercial radio broadcast occurred on November 2, 1920, when a radio station set up in a Westinghouse plant in Pittsburgh, Pennsylvania, with the "call letters" KDKA broadcast the returns of the 1920 U.S. presidential election. After the election of Warren G. Harding was duly reported, KDKA began broadcasting entertainment and news programming. Less than 6 months later, on April 11, 1921, KDKA broadcast the first live sport program, a boxing match between Johnny Dugan and Johnny Ray, and the first play-by-play coverage of a Major League Baseball (MLB) game (the Pittsburgh Pirates vs. the Philadelphia Phillies) on August 5, 1921 (KDKA, 2010). The radio boom of the 1920s began, and it took the United States (and the world) by storm (Barnouw, 1966–1970).

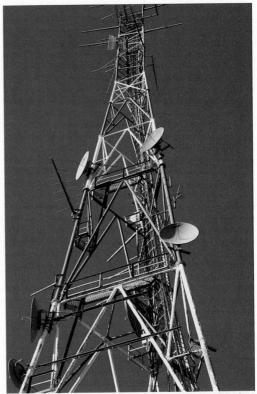
© AbleStock

The early radio industry was based on a business model that still underpins over-the-air electronic media—stations produce programs and transmit them on specific channels of the electromagnetic spectrum (because the airwaves are public property, the spectrum is regulated by the federal government), funded by advertisements sold by the stations and interspersed in the programs, and received by people having devices capable of converting the electronic signal into usable form.

The radio business grew dramatically during the 1920s. National broadcasts became feasible by linking individual stations via telephone wires to create **networks** that allowed multiple stations to broadcast the same program. This enabled the first nationwide sport broadcast in 1926, a heavyweight championship boxing match between Jack Dempsey and Gene Tunney. Within 2 years, Dempsey's promoter,

Tex Rickard, began demanding rights fees from broadcasters for the privilege of covering Dempsey's bouts (Dunning, 1998). The first national radio broadcast of a college football game, by the then-fledgling NBC network, was the Rose Bowl on New Year's Day, 1927, between Alabama and Stanford (which also demonstrated the early power of national media coverage as a recruiting tool—a young Arkansas farm boy named Paul Bryant, who had not yet earned his nickname "Bear," said that listening to that game was how he first learned of the University of Alabama, where he eventually went to play football and then meet his destiny as an iconic coach) (Schexnayder, 2009).

Radio's ability to reach a national audience also created national advertising opportunities. In 1926, the Royal Typewriter Company became the first national sport-related programming **sponsor,** by paying the now charmingly modest sum of $35,000 for exclusive sponsorship rights to the Dempsey–Tunney fight broadcast (Evensen, 1996).

Although the World Series was broadcast as early as 1923, MLB, the self-proclaimed "National Pastime," did not immediately embrace the new technology. Owners initially were concerned that free game broadcasts would make fans less likely to buy tickets to games. Throughout the 1930s, the three powerful New York teams—the Yankees, Giants, and Dodgers—banned all broadcasters (from the away teams as well as home teams) from their ballparks (Smith, 1995).

Nevertheless, the trend of more extensive coverage gained momentum. In 1933, a controlling interest in the Cincinnati Reds was sold to Powel Crosley, who both manufactured radios and owned two radio stations, including the powerful WLW, which Crosley converted into the Reds' flagship station (Ohio History Central, n.d.). In 1935, MLB Commissioner Landis reached an agreement for exclusive national coverage of the World Series ("Today in World Series History," n.d.).

Essential legal protection for the sport broadcasting business model was provided by two important decisions in the late 1930s. In *Twentieth Century Sporting Club, Inc. v. Transradio Press Service, Inc.* (1937), a New York state court enforced an exclusive contract for play-by-play coverage of a boxing match. The following year, in *Pittsburgh Athletic Co. v. KQV Broadcasting Co.* (1938), a federal court in Pittsburgh ruled that the home team controls all commercial **broadcasting rights** to a sport event. The rationale for this landmark decision was that the team owner or event organizer, who invests in establishing the organization, training and paying the players, renting (or owning) a stadium or other venue, providing amenities to spectators, and engaging in the other activities required to conduct a sport competition, also has the legal right to control access to the venue by broadcasters and otherwise to commercially exploit the distribution of accounts and descriptions of the event. This holding remains a core principal in the sport industry to this day.

As important as the *Pittsburgh Athletic* legal case was in 1938, an even more important business milestone occurred that year—the first television sets were sold in the United States (Early Television Museum, n.d.). As had been the case with radio, the first telecasts were local in nature, and they included various sport events as well as news coverage and entertainment programming. However, the commercial television industry was put on hold during World War II. Production of radio and television equipment for consumers was banned during the war (Early Television Museum, n.d.). Radio remained the primary electronic medium for news, entertainment, and sports during World War II.

That changed dramatically when the war ended in 1945. At that time, less than one-half of one percent of U.S. homes had a television set. Fifteen years later, that number had grown to

86% ("Number of TV Households," 2001–2013). By 1960, the **Federal Communications Commission (FCC)** had licensed five times more commercial TV stations (515) than there had been in 1950 (96).

In the 1940s and 1950s, television's business model mirrored that of radio. Individual stations transmitted signals on government-regulated frequencies for viewing by receiving sets. Individual stations were owned by a variety of local and national interests, and were licensed and regulated by the FCC (Stephens, n.d.). Advertising revenue was the sole meaningful source of income for stations and networks (Meyers, 2011). Network telecasting became possible in the early 1950s with the completion of an infrastructure of coaxial cable and microwave relays (Early Television Museum, n.d.). Videotape playback technology was not perfected until 1956 (Ampex, n.d.), meaning that all of the value in the coverage of an event was vested in the live telecast.

With only three national television networks, most programming was intended to appeal to the broadest possible audience. During evening **primetime** hours, when the most people were at home, almost all network programming was entertainment in nature—comedies, dramas, movies, and variety shows. (Classic Television Database, n.d.). Sport programs appeared mostly on weekend afternoons, when fewer people were watching television (Keller, 1982). However, sport audiences have always been predominantly male. This **demographic** subset was an efficient way for advertisers of male-oriented products to target the audience most likely to be purchasers (MacDonald, 2009).

Inexorably during the 1950s, television replaced radio as the nation's primary mass medium. By 1960, television was generating twice as much advertising revenue as radio (Oracle, n.d.). Sport programming followed the migration of entertainment and news programming from radio to TV (MacDonald, 2009).

Television experienced explosive growth in the 1950s, but the industry truly came of age in the 1960s. Technology improved the quality of the product. After wrangling throughout the 1950s among the FCC, networks, and equipment manufacturers, color television went mainstream in the early 1960s (Television Obscurities, 2005, 2013). The first use of videotaped "instant replay" in a sport telecast was during the 1963 Army–Navy game on CBS (Gelston, 2008). "Solid state" transistor-based cameras and zoom lenses enhanced picture quality and mobility, making for increasingly compelling video images. The first Telstar communications satellite, allowing the transmission of live transcontinental programming, was launched in 1962 (Howell, 2013).

Network newscasts expanded from 15 to 30 minutes in 1963 (*Huntley-Brinkley Report*, n.d.). Variety shows such as the *Ed Sullivan Show* hosted then-controversial new performers such as The Beatles, whose 1964 American tour and the phenomenon of "Beatlemania" were major news events (Rauscher, n.d.).

This convergence of cultural forces and technology included sport, led by an upstart network. In 1960, ABC was still the weakest of the three domestic television networks. Its structure as a national network was not finalized until 1954, well after CBS and NBC had become entrenched (MacDonald, 2009). But three events occurred in the early 1960s that profoundly changed both ABC and sport television.

First, ABC purchased Sports Programs, Inc., an independent sport and production company, which became ABC Sports (Carter, 2002). The network named 29-year-old **Roone Arledge** as producer of its new weekly college football telecasts. In his new role, Arledge implemented a revolutionary vision of "taking sports fans to the game," including close-up shots of cheerleaders, the school bands, and the crowd and sideline images of players and coaches, instead of the traditional style of showing only play-by-play action (Meserole, 2002). Second, ABC acquired rights to the new American Football League (AFL), which started in 1960 (Loup, 2001). The AFL, which immediately became popular for its wide-open, high-scoring style of play, gave ABC its first coverage of a major professional sport. Third, an innovative anthology series, *ABC's Wide World of Sports*, debuted in 1961. Each program opened with the famous greeting, "Spanning the globe to bring you the constant variety of sport—The thrill of victory, and the agony of defeat." But the next line of the intro, although less well known, was more instructive about the essence of the programming: "The human drama of athletic competition." It was "up close and personal" stories of athletes, punctuated by compelling images that conveyed emotions as well as action, that personified Arledge's style of blending sport action with entertainment and pageantry.

Wide World of Sports covered everything from major events such as the Indianapolis 500 (which did not permit free live television coverage until 1986) and the FA Cup Soccer Finals to inane spectacles such as barrel jumping and cliff diving. It also provided riveting coverage of two politically charged track meets between the United States and the Soviet Union at the height of the Cold War (Shannon, 2010).

But the most important athlete to appear on *Wide World of Sports* was Muhammad Ali. No one personified the "modern" athlete more than Ali. He started the decade as Cassius Clay, a boxer who won a gold medal for the United States at the 1960 Olympics. But he soon became the most controversial athlete in the world. He broke the mold of the stereotypical humble athlete by brashly predicting that he would become heavyweight champion. When he backed up that boast, he changed his name to Muhammad Ali, converted to Islam, and

eventually refused to be enlisted into the U.S. Army. And it was on *Wide World of Sports*, hosted by Howard Cosell—himself a groundbreaking figure—where Ali received his most celebrated coverage (Kindred, 2006).

Cosell called the action during Ali's first six defenses of his heavyweight championship on *Wide World of Sports*. When Ali was stripped of his title for refusing to be drafted at the height of the Vietnam War, Cosell conducted numerous interviews with Ali and provided highly opinionated commentary about the controversy, which continued until 1971 when the U.S. Supreme Court overturned Ali's criminal conviction for draft evasion.

By 1960, the National Football League (NFL) was becoming a major force in the sport world. Its 1958 championship game, in which the Baltimore Colts defeated the New York Giants in sudden-death overtime, was already being called the greatest football game ever played (Maule, 1959). Although MLB was still regarded as America's "National Pastime," the NFL had become the nation's first truly national sport league in 1946 when the Cleveland Rams moved to Los Angeles (Pro Football Hall of Fame, n.d.), 12 years before the Dodgers and Giants became MLB's first teams on the West Coast ("May 28, 1957: Baseball Owners," n.d.). In 1950, the Rams had become the first team to televise all of its home and away games (NFL, n.d.). The team also hired a young public relations executive, **Pete Rozelle**, as its general manager in 1957. Three years later, Rozelle was elected NFL commissioner, and his media-savvy leadership transformed the league and the American sport landscape (Carter, n.d.).

Rozelle's first act as commissioner was to move the NFL headquarters to New York City, home to all of the television networks and major advertising agencies. He then convinced the league's owners to pool their television rights and equally share all television rights fees ("Economy in NFL History," n.d.). **Revenue-sharing** had a seismic impact on the league. It meant that the New York Giants, located in the largest media market in the country, received the same amount of national television revenue as the Green Bay Packers in the 70th-largest market. This promoted competitive balance among all teams, instead of large-market teams being able to dominate the NFL by having disproportionate financial resources. This, in turn, produced consistently close, exciting games, which made for a better television product. An unofficial slogan of the league was that, "On any given Sunday, any NFL team could beat any other team in the league." As the first U.S. professional sport league to have meaningful revenue-sharing, the NFL proved the importance of this economic structure. In the 1960s the Green Bay Packers, playing in the smallest market of any pro sport team in the country, were the best team in the NFL, winning five championships and the first two Super Bowls.

With the NFL's new business model in place, Rozelle then secured league-wide television agreements with CBS for the regular season and NBC for the NFL Championship Game. When a federal court held that these contracts violated antitrust law, Rozelle lobbied for and secured passage of the Sports Broadcasting Act of 1961, which provided an antitrust exemption for pooled media rights agreements by professional sport leagues (Davis, 2008).

In 1964, the fledgling AFL left ABC and signed a lucrative 5-year agreement with the more established NBC. "After I signed that contract," said AFL Commissioner Joe Foss, "people stopped asking me if we were going to make it. Everyone knew we were." (Gruver, 1997, p. 125). The following year, the AFL and NFL merged into one league (NFL, n.d.). The first Super Bowl was played on January 15, 1967, and was televised by both CBS and NBC (NFL, n.d.). By the mid-1960s, the NFL surpassed MLB as the most popular sport in the nation (Florio, 2009).

In 1968, the popularity of the NFL was demonstrated when NBC cut away from its New York Jets–Oakland Raiders game telecast to show the movie *Heidi* at its regularly scheduled time of 7:00 p.m. in the Eastern Time Zone. The resulting protest by football fans became a national news story (Davis, 2008). It also demonstrated that professional football fans wanted to watch their favorite sport at times other than Sunday afternoons.

Two years later, *Monday Night Football* became the first sport programming series in primetime. Arledge produced the games for ABC, using the same human-interest production techniques he pioneered on *Wide World of Sports*, and he included the bombastic Cosell on the announcing team. The series not only was a ratings success, it became a cultural phenomenon—up to 40% of the audience were women. (ABC Sports Online, 2003).

Television also played an important role in the growth of public interest in the Olympic Games during the 1960s. The Cold War rivalry between the United States and the Soviet Union translated into a sport-related propaganda war between the two countries and their allies, all covered by a television audience that was worldwide in scope due to the proliferation of telecommunications satellites. By 1968, ABC made itself into "The Network of the Olympics" (Chad & Reid, 1998). The Games involved ongoing controversies related to amateurism, political demonstrations, on-field issues, and, ultimately, in 1972, tragedy with the massacre of Israeli athletes by Arab terrorists. ABC turned all of it into compelling television (Guthrie, 2012).

The success of *Monday Night Football* prompted increased television coverage of sport at times traditionally reserved for entertainment programming. The final game of the NCAA men's basketball championship was first televised on Monday night in 1973. MLB began staging World Series games in primetime in 1971. Throughout the 1970s, virtually all major sports received coverage on network television. PGA Tour golf tournaments became weekly fixtures. The National Basketball Association (NBA) received regular national coverage, although the league's ratings were so low that playoff games were regularly shown on tape-delay. The first live flag-to-flag coverage of the Daytona 500 was in 1979. College football was a Saturday-afternoon staple in the fall. A new college basketball conference, the Big East, was formed in 1979 to take advantage of the large concentration of **television markets** in the Northeast.

Television occasionally was responsible for blurring the lines between sport and entertainment. "The Battle of the Sexes" was a tongue-in-cheek, made-for-TV extravaganza between Billie Jean King and Bobby Riggs in 1973. Riggs, who had won the 1939 Wimbledon men's singles championship, claimed that he could still beat King at a time when she was one of the top female tennis players in the world. The two played an exhibition match in the Houston Astrodome after Riggs was carted by a team of models onto the court in a rickshaw, and King was borne in Cleopatra-style by a team of muscular men. A worldwide television audience of nearly 50 million people watched King win in straight sets (Wertheim, 2012). Other made-for-TV shows, such as *The Superstars*, which debuted in 1973 and featured famous athletes competing against each other in a variety of sports other than the ones in which they were professionals, prompted the creation of a new word—**trashsports**—entertainment that purported to be sport but had no real sporting significance.

As secure as the over-air network business model seemed to be in the early 1970s, with the vast majority of television programming being delivered and received by free over-air signals, profound changes in the television industry began to occur. HBO became the first network

to continuously deliver its signal via telecommunications satellite when it telecast the *Thrilla In Manilla* boxing match between Ali and Joe Frazier in 1975 (Forsyth, 2002). In 1977, Ted Turner transformed a low-powered independent television station in Atlanta into a "superstation" by beaming its signal nationwide via satellite. In 1979, another cable network opened for business, based on the then-unimaginable notion that people would watch sports 24 hours a day—ESPN (Miller & Shales, 2011).

Cable television services had been available since the 1940s, when an appliance store owner in rural Pennsylvania got frustrated because the lack of clear broadcast signals meant that he could not sell TV sets. His solution was to build a **master antenna** on a nearby mountain and connect it by a cable to his showroom. When his customers saw a clear picture, they not only bought TVs, they paid fees for access to the master antenna. In the 1970s, the cable industry expanded to urban areas, offering enhanced picture quality plus access to additional networks other than the three networks and local independent stations (Eisenmann, 2000).

The growth of cable **penetration** of American households increased steadily in the 1980s (Grant & Meadows, 2013). By the end of the decade, nearly 60% of all U.S. homes were wired for cable, and there were 79 new cable networks distributing programming (National Cable and Telecommunications Association, n.d.). In the early 1990s, DIRECTV launched a competitive technology to cable, delivering programming to homes via **direct broadcast satellites (DBS)** (DIRECTV, n.d.).

The proliferation of networks had a major impact on sports, especially on the professional team sports that played games on a nearly daily basis—baseball, basketball, and hockey. Previously, their television coverage was limited either to over-the-air network stations willing to occasionally preempt network programming or independent stations having no network affiliations. Suddenly, there were new competitors for game-coverage rights, which increased rights fees to the clubs and increased the number of games on TV.

The willingness of consumers to pay for sport programming on cable was demonstrated in 1987, when ESPN signed its first agreement with the NFL. The only way the then-fledgling ESPN could afford the rights fee charged by the NFL was to levy a surcharge on its subscriber fees, which cable operators willingly paid (and passed along to their subscribers) (Miller & Shales, 2011).

By the mid-1980s, ESPN was emerging as a sport television force. It covered college football and basketball, the NBA, and the National Hockey League (NHL) and was the first network to extensively cover NASCAR. It provided the first "early round" coverage of professional golf tournaments simply by hiring the crews already on site to produce weekend coverage on the traditional over-air networks. ESPN also covered events that had never been televised before, such as the NFL draft. It also shrewdly associated itself with big events to which it was not a rightsholder, such as by sending its *College GameDay* pregame show to the sites of major college football games being covered by broadcast networks.

ESPN's *SportsCenter* program revolutionized sports journalism. Before *SportsCenter,* the only televised daily sports news was a 2- to 3-minute segment on late-night local news, usually limited to scores, highlights, and news related to local teams. *SportsCenter* offered a content-rich alternative, with scores, highlights, and news on a national scope, plus an entertaining blend of irreverence and humor. In 1987, ESPN introduced *NFL Primetime,* an hour-long show devoted entirely to NFL highlights, providing in-depth coverage that previously had not been possible on TV (Miller & Shales, 2011).

Until the 1980s, the NCAA strictly regulated all college football telecasts. Coverage of regular-season games was limited to one or two games on Saturdays on ABC (the NCAA's exclusive rightsholder). NCAA rules limited the best and most popular teams to two or three national appearances per season. ESPN and TBS secured "supplemental" cable rights in the early 1980s. Postseason bowl games were televised on various networks. But everything changed in 1981, when two NCAA members, the University of Oklahoma and the University of Georgia, filed an antitrust suit against the NCAA that resulted in a 1985 Supreme Court decision that NCAA control of college football television was an illegal restraint of trade (*NCAA v. Board of Regents of the University of Oklahoma,* 1984). As a result, the Big Ten and Pac-10 conferences aligned themselves with ABC and another group of conferences formed the College Football Association and made a deal with CBS. The CFA collapsed in the 1990s when Notre Dame signed a separate coverage agreement with NBC, leading to individual conferences signing their own deals with other networks. All of this resulted in a substantial increase in the number of games televised (Reed, 1991).

In 1993, the entire American television landscape changed profoundly, and it was sports that spurred the change. The Fox Broadcast Network, for years a loose confederation of independent stations, acquired telecast rights to the NFL, out-bidding the incumbent rightsholder CBS by 25%—roughly $400 million per year versus CBS's offer of $300 million. The deal established Fox as the nation's fourth broadcast network (Wulf, 1993).

Fox also acquired a number of regional sports networks during the 1990s. This provided additional financial resources for these relatively new niche cable networks. Fox unsuccessfully tried to amalgamate these regional networks into a national competitor to ESPN by producing a national news show to compete with *SportsCenter*, hosted by outspoken former *SportsCenter* anchor Keith Olberman (Olberman, 2011).

Other national media powers, such as Comcast, also invested in regional sports cable networks. This competition increased the rights fees paid to the teams whose games were covered on the networks, further solidifying the importance of television as a revenue stream to teams and leagues (Comcast, n.d.).

An even more significant cultural change occurred in the 1990s, when public usage of the Internet started growing at a rate of 100% per year (Internet World Stats, n.d.). The first mainstream "channel" of computer-delivered services was America Online, which grew from a startup with less than 150,000 subscribers in 1991 (McCracken, 2010) to a service with 20 million paying members by 2000 ("AOL: $2.5b," 2000). By 1994, AOL was offering **multimedia** content that included news, reference, entertainment, and educational material (McCracken, 2010). Two pioneering sport-only websites, ESPNET SportsZone (now ESPN.com) and SportsLine (now CBSSports.com), both launched in 1995. The Internet-connected personal computer became the first meaningful competitor to the TV set as an electronic appliance for delivering news, information, and entertainment.

In 1995, The Walt Disney Company purchased Capital Cities/ABC, Inc., the company that owned ESPN (Fabrikant, 1995). At that time, Disney was perceived as regarding ABC as the most valuable asset being acquired, but it soon became apparent that ESPN was the crown jewel of the transaction. Disney's deep financial pockets provided ESPN with additional working capital to fund its growth. ESPN also secured long-term **affiliate** agreements with cable and DBS companies with compounded annual subscriber fees, generating substantial

revenue that allowed ESPN to acquire rights to more events for higher rights fees, thus driving up the values of programming industry-wide (Miller & Shales, 2011).

In 1995, ESPN also staged the first Extreme Games, a collection of competitions in non-traditional "action sports," such as skateboard, bicycle, and motorcycle stunt competitions. Soon rebranded the X Games, it gave the network a television property it could own, instead of having to pay a rights fee for. The X Games also helped give a brand identity to ESPN2, which was marketed as the "hipper and hotter" version of ESPN when it was launched in 1993 (Pickert, 2009).

Technology developments continued to impact the television industry. After decades of work involving Congress, the FCC, television manufacturers, networks, and the emerging digital media industry, **high-definition television (HDTV)** established itself in the early 2000s as a force in the marketplace (Cianci, 2012). In 2003, ESPN became the first sports network to launch an HD channel (ESPN Media Zone, n.d.). The rest of the industry followed quickly (TVB, 2012). The enhanced picture quality and wider screen dramatically enhanced the experience of watching sports on TV.

The first **digital video recorder (DVR)** was introduced in 1999. (TiVo, n.d.). It allowed individuals to record TV programs. Like video cassette recorders (VCRs) that first popularized in-home recording of TV programming in the 1970s and 1980s, DVRs allowed people to **time-shift** their viewing of programs to after their live telecasts. Unlike VCRs, however, DVRs allowed viewers to skip commercials almost instantly, instead of having to fast-forward through videotape. The picture quality of digital recording, which was superior to that of analog videotape used in VCRs, combined with HDTV to make time-shifted programming an equivalent or even superior viewing experience in comparison to live television.

Another factor spurring this time-shifting phenomenon was the growing availability of high-speed **broadband** Internet connectivity. In the 1990s, most people connected to the Internet via relatively slow "dial-up" phone lines. New fiber-optic cable allowed video signals to be **streamed** without the need for traditional television networks (Hayes, 2013). High-speed broadband service became a lucrative new revenue source for cable companies, allowing them to further leverage the investments they already had made in installing high-speed wiring in most American homes for cable TV (NCTA, n.d.).

The easier it became to time-shift viewing of entertainment programming, the more valuable live sport programming became. By the end of the first decade of the 2000s, sport events became recognized as the only "DVR-proof" television programming. Because the inherent drama is based on the uncertain outcome of live games, and scores and information about games were readily available via the Internet, social media, and mobile devices, it was difficult to avoid learning a score or outcome before watching a recording of the event (Deninger, 2012).

During the 2011–2012 television season, the five most-watched programs were NFL games (topped by Super Bowl XlVI), and 22 of the 25 most-watched programs were sport related (TVB, 2012). As a result, sports rights fees paid by telecasters grew at unprecedented rates (Ourand, 2011). In 2011, the NFL renewed all of its network agreements for an average increase of 60% over previous deals. Each of the NFL's three broadcast rightsholders—Fox, NBC, and CBS—agreed to pay over $1 billion per year for 9 years (Hiestand, 2011). ESPN agreed to pay even more—$1.9 billion per year—for *Monday Night Football*, because the NFL was able to leverage the provision in ESPN's affiliation agreements requiring that its lucrative **subscriber fees** be reduced if the network were to lose NFL game coverage rights (Sandomir, 2011b).

Across the sport industry, other rights-holders also reaped major fee increases. For example, the growth in rights fees accelerated so drastically that in 2010 the Atlantic Coast Conference (ACC) more than doubled its previous rights fees and then tried to renegotiate the deal 4 months before it took effect because other conferences had signed even more lucrative agreements in the meantime (Ourand, 2011).

Sport programming has also affected the value of other sport-related assets. In 2012, the Los Angeles Dodgers sold for $2.15 billion. Not only was it the most money ever paid for a professional sport franchise in the world (Futterman, 2012), it meant that the Dodgers were worth almost six times as much as in 2004 when they were sold for $371 million (Gurnick, 2012). The new Dodgers owners then sold their cable rights for $8.5 billion over 25 years (Minami, 2013) to TimeWarner, which announced plans to make the Dodgers the centerpiece of a new regional sports network, SportsNet LA (Gurnick, 2013).

One of the reasons TimeWarner would pay so much for the Dodgers' rights was to incentivize the Dodgers not to form their own network. The model for the Dodgers to have done so was the New York Yankees, which launched the YES network in 2001. YES provides coverage of 125 Yankees games per season, plus extensive news and feature programming on the team and programming of other sports during the baseball offseason (including the New Jersey/Brooklyn Nets, which had an ownership interest in YES at the time it was founded) (YES, n.d.). By the time of the Dodgers–TimeWarner deal, YES was valued at more than $3 billion, an asset-value that had tripled in 11 years (Rovell, 2012).

The Yankees were not the only team to exploit their own TV rights. When the Boston Red Sox were sold in 2002, an essential element of the transaction was the new owners' acquisition of NESN, a cable network jointly owned by the Red Sox and the Boston Bruins (Boston

Red Sox, n.d.). Even the small-market Seattle Mariners acquired the network that televises its games, Root Sports, in 2013 (Thiel, 2013).

All the major professional sport leagues have launched their own networks—the NFL Network in 2003 (NFL, 2011), the MLB Network in 2009 (MLB, n.d.), NBA TV in late 1999 (NBA, n.d.), and the NHL Network in 2007 (Brady, 2007). The Big Ten became the first college conference to do so when it established the Big Ten Network in 2007 (Big Ten, 2007). It was followed by the Pac-12, which owns its own network (Facer, 2011), and the Southeastern Conference (SEC), which entered into an operating agreement with ESPN ("SEC Network to Broadcast 24/7," 2013). The University of Texas established the first network devoted to a single college athletic program when it formed the Longhorn Network in association with ESPN in 2011 (Staples, 2011). All such league/conference networks televise only a portion of their games while maintaining agreements with national networks.

In 2012, NBC rebranded the Versus network (acquired in the 2009 Comcast–NBC merger) as the NBC Sports Network, or NBCSN (Sandomir, 2011a). The following year News Corporation launched Fox Sports One ("Fox Announces Fox Sports1," 2013). National in scope and armed with famous brands and substantial corporate resources, they immediately began bidding for existing programming, further driving up the value of sports rights. In 2012 NBCSN acquired rights to the English Premiere League (EPL), previously televised on Fox and ESPN (Rische, 2012), and in 2013 it acquired NASCAR rights, previously held by ESPN (Badenhausen, 2013). The acquisition of the EPL demonstrates the emerging globalization of sports rights.

As the 2010s proceed, questions persist as to how long these increases in rights fees can continue and how many networks can be launched. Conventional wisdom dictates that growth cannot be perpetual, and the pendulum theory

of economic cycles suggests that the larger the arc of growth, the more severe the resulting correction could be. But in the midst of continuing, widespread growth, it is clear that broadcasting has never been a more substantial component of the sport industry (Boudway, 2013).

The Business of Sport Broadcasting

The standard sport broadcasting business model is for a telecaster to pay a rights fee to the organizer of a game or event, and then the telecaster produces the telecast, arranges for its distribution to the public, and recoups its fees and expenses by selling advertising in the game telecast and network distribution rights to cable and DBS operators.

Rights Fees

Negotiations

The legal presumption is that a home team controls the broadcasting rights to its games. When the team is a member of a league or conference, its television rights usually are ceded to the larger organization, which negotiates on behalf of all members. In most professional and college team sports, national television rights are controlled by the league or conference and individual teams retain radio rights and some local television rights. For individual sports, such as tennis tournaments and boxing matches, the event organizer controls the television rights.

The key business terms in a rights agreement include the amount of the rights fees, the territory in which the telecast can (or must) be distributed, the length of the deal, the process for selecting particular games for telecast, copyright ownership, sponsorship rights, the number of commercial units to be included in the telecast, procedures for preempting coverage in the event of inclement weather or other unforeseen circumstances, and whether the telecaster will have the first right to negotiate a renewal of the agreement before the rightsholder conducts competitive bidding for future rights on the open market.

Value

Broadcasters determine how much they are willing to pay in rights fees by calculating how much money they can make on the programming by selling advertising in the particular programming and whether the programming will make the network more attractive to cable/DBS companies. The NFL receives the largest rights fees of any American sport organization because NFL game telecasts are consistently the highest-rated sport programs.

NASCAR fans (according to studies conducted by market research companies) are especially likely to purchase the products advertised on NASCAR race telecasts, making advertisers willing to pay a premium for such loyalty. As a general rule, sport TV audiences are disproportionately male and young, in comparison to the general population, so sellers of products appealing to this demographic will pay a premium for their ads to run in programs watched by especially large numbers of their **target markets**.

The popularity of a network's programming also helps determine the subscription fees it can charge to cable and DBS operators. Since 1992, broadcast networks also are able to charge fees to cable and DBS systems for the appearance of the networks on those distribution systems, and the value of such **retransmission consent** fees depends in part on the quality of the network programming.

Revenue-Sharing

Rights fees paid to leagues or conferences usually are shared equally among all member teams. Because all NFL games are subject to league-wide contracts, all TV revenue is shared equally. However, in sports where teams receive television fees from both national and local rightsholders, revenue disparities can occur.

In MLB, the proceeds from its national "Game of the Week" series and postseason games are shared equally. However, most MLB games are not subject to the national agreements, leaving each team free to make its own television arrangements within its home market. Teams in large population areas earn larger rights fees for their local telecasts than teams do in smaller markets, and only 34% of those local rights fees are subject to revenue-sharing among all MLB teams. Similar disparities occur in the NBA and NHL, although each league has its own formulae for sharing portions of local TV revenue, in an effort to level the playing field economically for all member clubs.

The rights fees paid to organizers of individual events such as golf tournaments and boxing matches are a primary source of funding (along with ticket sales and sponsorship revenue) for the prize money paid to competitors in the event.

Production

In addition to paying a rights fee for a particular event or series, a broadcaster must pay the expenses necessary to produce the coverage. Typically, this involves setting up cameras at various locations within the playing venue, outfitting a booth in the venue press box for the announcers describing the action, and arranging for a **remote production facility**, frequently called the "production truck" because it is configured to travel to various events.

The truck houses most of the production crew, while additional personnel, such as camera operators, are located in the stadium/arena. All cameras and microphones are connected to the production truck. In the truck, the crew performs a vast array of tasks. Through an intercom system, they can speak directly to camera operators and announcers to request particular shots or provide them with information. The director decides which camera shots to include in the program feed, frequently making split-second decisions about the best camera angle and images of a particular play. Engineers constantly monitor the quality of the sound and pictures. Assistant producers and directors implement specific instructions they receive, such as incorporating replays into the telecast or creating graphics containing statistics or information about a team or player. The **clean feed** of the program is transmitted from the truck to a network studio, where commercial and promotional announcements are added. The finished program then is retransmitted to network affiliates (or, in the case of cable/DBS systems, to their local **head ends**, the master facilities where programs are received and then fed to individual subscribers).

The expenses of producing a game telecast usually are paid by the network. Rightsholders sometimes agree to reimburse the network for a portion of the production expenses. At times, a rightsholder may even agree to pay all of the production expenses or assume all responsibilities for producing the telecast, in which case the rightsholder then purchases time from a network—called a **time-buy**—at a price equivalent to the network's profit margin for producing, selling advertising for, and televising other programming at that time of day.

Advertising and Sponsorship

The advertising and promotional messages contained in a television program generate revenue to offset the costs of acquiring the programming rights and of producing the program.

Advertising

The traditional advertisement in a sport television program is a 30-second commercial message for a consumer product. These ads are shown during **commercial breaks** when there is no game action. Usually, multiple spots are grouped into a **pod** of commercials. The structure of certain sports is ideal for this format—baseball games have breaks between each half-inning, football games have time-outs

after a score or a change in possession, tennis matches have rest periods after every other game, and auto races require cars to run at low speeds and not pass each other during caution flags. Other sports, such as soccer and hockey, do not have such frequent breaks, making commercial formatting more challenging. But all sports alter their game-action format to some extent to accommodate commercials. For example, all NFL games are required to have five 2-minute commercial breaks per quarter. If you ever wondered why an NFL game shows commercials after a touchdown, then has a kickoff, followed by yet another commercial break, it is due to the need to get all five of those breaks in during every quarter.

These **commercial formats** contain advertising breaks for both national commercials, sold by the networks (or equivalent independent production company), and local advertisements, which are sold by local stations or cable systems. The operating agreements between networks and affiliates/distributors guarantee a certain amount of local advertising per hour.

The price of advertisements is calculated on the basis of the number of people watching the telecast. This is why **ratings**, which measure the size of the program audience, are vital to the economics of television. A program watched by 2.5 million people can charge 10 times more for ad units than one watched by 250,000 people, although the demographics of a particular program audience also affect prices. It is more efficient for companies selling products appealing primarily to men (such as shaving and grooming products, beer, and automobiles) to advertise on sport programs instead of on programs targeting a female audience. Advertising agencies invest heavily in audience research to determine where to run particular ads.

Ratings

The rating is the percentage of households having at least one television set that are tuned to a particular program. The Nielson Company, the leading audience-measurement company in the nation, estimates there were 115.6 million TV households in 2013. This means that an audience of 1.156 million for a particular show would equate to a 1.0 rating. A companion measurement to a program rating is its **share**, which is the percentage of television sets actually in use at a particular time that are tuned to a show (Nielsen Media Research, n.d.).

Sponsorship

Sponsorship is a form of financial support to an event or a telecast, either cash or in-kind goods or services, in exchange for public recognition that generates commercial exposure for the sponsor at times other than during a commercial unit. Sponsorships can be sold either by an event organizer or the broadcaster.

Event organizers can sell the naming rights to the event itself. Most of the golf tournaments on the PGA Tour, for example, are now named for "title sponsors." Other events retain their traditional name, but have a "presenting sponsor." Networks can insist that the sponsor purchase advertising units in the telecast as a condition of referring to the sponsor on the air. Depending on the terms of its contract with a rightsholder, a broadcaster also can sell sponsorships. *The Gillette Cavalcade of Sports* was a long-running series that personified a telecast title sponsorship (*The Gillette Cavalcade of Sports*, n.d.). "ESPN College GameDay—Built by The Home Depot" is a modern example of a telecast presenting sponsorship.

Some companies engage in **ambush marketing**, seeking television exposure for products or brands without paying any fees to the telecaster or event organizer. This frequently involves a company paying players to wear products bearing logos that compete with those of companies that sponsor an event, or by placing a billboard in a location within the range of cameras covering the game that cannot be controlled by the event organizer—for example, the Citgo energy company has long maintained a sign on the roof of a building near Fenway Park that is visible to spectators and television viewers every time a home run is hit over the "Green Monster" wall in leftfield.

Distribution

Broadcast Networks

Traditional broadcast television and radio networks are composed of various stations in cities throughout the nation. These affiliates are required to show all (or almost all) programming provided to them by their networks. These agreements, as well as rules established by the FCC, regulate the number of programming hours that can be provided by networks. At times when no network programming is provided, affiliates are free to televise whatever programming they choose.

Broadcast affiliates usually have limited rights not to "clear" a particular program; that is, not to show a network program in the local market. If the affiliate chooses not to show the program it is usually because the station does not believe it will generate good ratings, meaning that the station can make more money by acquiring independently produced programming and selling all advertising on a local basis. The contracts between networks and their affiliates require affiliates to clear a minimum percentage of network programming.

Syndication

Not all sport programming is distributed on networks. Independent producers can acquire rights, create programs, and **syndicate** them; that is, they can sell the programs to stations not affiliated with networks or to network affiliates for telecast at times when they are not obligated to show network programs.

Cable Networks

Until the 1970s, the signals of virtually all television stations were transmitted over public airwaves and received by people having their own antennae. Cable television networks have a "closed signal path" that can only be accessed by cable/DBS systems. Those systems have agreements with the cable networks to distribute their programming, for which they pay the networks monthly fees for each subscriber that has the right to receive each particular network, ranging from a few cents to over $5.00 for ESPN (the most expensive cable network). The cable/DBS companies also pay retransmission consent fees to broadcast networks for the right to show the networks' programming on their systems.

Cable/DBS systems, in turn, sell packages of television networks to the public. Various networks are divided into **tiers**, or groups of networks, that are marketed to customers at different fees. "Basic Service" or "Lifeline Service" usually includes the broadcast networks and a handful of local stations and is the lowest-priced package. Next in order is "Expanded Basic," which is composed of an array of highly rated cable networks, including channels specializing in entertainment, sports, news, and other popular programming genres. Additional tiers contain more specialized networks, such as a "sports tier," which includes various regional sports networks and networks devoted to specific sports, or "premium" services such as commercial-free movie networks. Although consumers can select which tiers to subscribe to, they cannot choose which networks to include in the various tiers. Cable/DBS companies decide which networks to include in particular tiers, although many cable networks make it a contractual requirement that they be included in a specific tier; Expanded Basic is where most networks want to be, because it usually is the most subscribed to tier.

Digital Networks

The emergence of broadband Internet as a means of distributing and viewing audio-video material now enables new networks to transmit programming without the need to be packaged on a tier by a cable/DBS systems. The ESPN3.com network pioneered this new genre of **digital networks**. ESPN3 allows viewers to select from a number of game-coverage telecasts, generally produced with fewer camera angles or enhanced production features. This provides an outlet for games not having mass-market appeal but still attracting market segments of fans and further diversifying the viewer's options. Because ESPN3 is delivered via the Internet, access to its signal is controlled by **Internet service providers (ISPs)** such as cable companies, which already do business with ESPN. The network is offered to subscribers as a part of a package of cable TV and Internet services. Operators of other digital networks have emulated the ESPN3 model.

Pay-Per-View

A limited number of sports programs, usually championship boxing matches and other fighting-oriented sports and exhibitions, are distributed on a **pay-per-view** basis. Instead of televising the event on commercial television and amortizing the costs by advertising sales, a pay-per-view program is distributed on a special channel on cable/DBS systems only accessible by consumers who pay a specified fee to watch the program. In this model, there is no advertising in the telecast and the sales revenue is shared by the cable/DBS operators, the event promoter, and, in the case of boxing matches, the fighters themselves.

Regionalization

Networks provide programming to their affiliates on either a national, regional, or local basis. For example, every NFL football game is televised into the home markets of the participating teams (except for home games when all stadium tickets are not sold, in which case there is a **blackout** of the game in the home market to encourage future ticket sales). Other sports, such as the NBA, authorize "split-national" telecasts, showing a game between two eastern teams to its audience in that half of the country and a different game between two western teams to its west coast audience, in order to maximize total viewership by taking advantage of regional and local fan interests. Coverage patterns are controlled by rightsholders in consultation with their telecasting partners.

Local telecasts, arranged for by individual teams, usually can only be shown in the participating teams' home territories. This limitation protects teams in weaker, smaller markets from having their local television revenue and exposure overwhelmed by bigger, more famous teams. The need for this protection is illustrated by the fact that, at the height of the Yankees–Red Sox rivalry in 2003–2004, game telecasts between those two teams received higher ratings in Los Angeles than games involving the Dodgers or Angels did in the Los Angeles area. Any fans of out-of-town teams now can pay a fee to acquire **out-of-market** coverage of game telecasts not available locally.

The Pac-12 Network has adopted an innovative regional coverage model. It has established a series of seven networks: one for a national audience, plus six regional networks focusing their programming on the geographic affinities of a region within the conference territory—in Arizona (the home of conference members University of Arizona and Arizona State), Oregon (Oregon and Oregon State), Northern California (California and Stanford), Rocky Mountains (Colorado and Utah), Southern California (USC and UCLA) and Washington (Washington and Washington State).

Radio

Most radio stations continue to operate on the traditional over-air model, although satellite-delivered radio has been available on a subscription basis since the early 2000s.

Highlights and Ancillary Rights

The conclusion of a game telecast does not mean an end to its commercial value. Game telecasts, like all television programs, are protected by copyright law. A **copyright** is literally the right to copy an original work that is in tangible form—songs, movies, books, webpages, video games, and game telecasts are examples of artistic works that cannot be used commercially without the permission of their creators. When a game ends, its results can be reported by anyone as news. However, video highlights can be included in a news report only with the permission of the owner of the game footage. Traditionally, permission has been limited to a handful of plays on newscasts during the 2 days following conclusion of the game.

Until the 1980s, ownership of game telecast copyrights was seldom a deal point in rights negotiations. Networks were the legal owners of the copyrights because they produced the game telecasts using their own equipment and personnel. But with the proliferation of programs such as *SportsCenter NFL Primetime*, *College GameDay*, and even entertainment programs such as *The ESPYs*, all of which rely heavily on highlights, plus emerging technology allowing on-demand highlight streaming on the Internet, the value of postgame footage rights has increased. Rightsholders now routinely insist on new rights agreements that own game telecast copyrights (permitted under the work-for-hire doctrine of copyright law). Those new agreements also frequently require networks to transfer copyright ownership of the game telecasts produced under prior agreements to leagues and conferences. Rightsholders such as NASCAR and the International Olympic Committee (IOC) were so intent on acquiring such copyrights that they made an assignment of those rights a prerequisite to negotiations with networks for new agreements.

By owning telecast copyrights and controlling highlight usage, rightsholders have created new opportunities to monetize those assets. This also allows them to more effectively control their images. As a condition of granting a license for use of highlights, a rightsholder can insist on having the right to approve the content of the program containing its footage. This is a powerful way to prevent an unflattering portrayal of a league, team, or player. For example, the 2004 World Series highlight video contains no references to a controversial play in the sixth game of the American League Championship Series, when Alex Rodriguez of the Yankees knocked the ball out of the glove of Red Sox pitcher Bronson Arroyo during a close play at first base. The play triggered a lengthy argument when Rodriguez was first called safe, and then out, ruining a potential series-altering rally by the Yankees. By exercising its right to keep footage of the play out of the video, MLB seems to have chosen to sanitize the controversy.

International Sport Coverage

As the world economy globalizes, American sport organizations and broadcasting companies are expanding their presence in foreign markets. Their international counterparts are doing the same in the United States.

International Sport Programming in the United States

American television networks regularly acquire rights to show international sport programming in the United States. The most valuable international property remains the Olympic Games. NBC has had the telecast rights since 1988. In 2011, NBC outbid its rivals with a $4.38 billion offer to cover the 2014, 2016, 2018, and 2020 Games. In 2014, following its success in Sochi, NBC forged a private deal with the IOC for $7.75 billion for the Olympic rights in 2022–2032 (Sandomir, 2014). Other international

sport events regularly shown on U.S. cable and broadcast networks include the Wimbledon, Australian Open, and French Open tennis tournaments; the British Open golf championship; the European Tour golf series; the Tour de France bicycle race; Formula One auto racing; and the world figure skating and gymnastics championships.

It is international soccer, however, that has made the biggest impact in recent years on the U.S. television market. As recently as 1978, the FIFA World Cup tournament received no American television coverage. In 1994, the event was held in the United States for the first time, with ABC and ESPN providing extensive coverage. Since then, the rights fees for the event have mushroomed. Fox and Telemundo agreed in 2011 to pay a reported $1 billion for the English- and Spanish-language rights to the 2018 and 2022 World Cups, more than twice what ESPN and Univision paid for the 2010 and 2014 tournaments ("FIFA Confirms Fox," 2011). As noted previously, the EPL has also recently received significantly increased rights fees in the United States from NBC.

New networks are using soccer as an entrée to establish a business presence in the United States. beIN Sport, owned by the Qatar-based Al Jazeera chain of networks, debuted in the United States in 2012. Its programming mix features rights to several well-regarded international soccer leagues, including La Liga (Spain), Ligue 1 (France), and Serie A (Italy) (Davis, 2012).

Commissioner Don Garber of Major League Soccer (MLS) expressed concern about a glut of soccer on American television (Peck, 2013). Garber's comments came amid public speculation about whether increased U.S. television coverage of foreign soccer would help or hurt MLS. The best future benchmark of this will be the amount of rights fees that MLS receives during its next round of negotiations for U.S. television rights (Smith, D., 2013).

International Broadcast of U.S. Sports

The telecasting of American sports internationally occurs by a variety of transactions. Many professional leagues and organizations, such as the NFL, the NBA, the Augusta National Golf Club (host of the Masters), and the United States Tennis Association (which operates the U.S. Open) negotiate rights agreements with networks on a country-by-country basis. Other rightsholders utilize agents to secure international television coverage. The agents negotiate rights fees on behalf of their clients and receive a percentage of the fees as payment for their services.

Foreign Language Sports Networks in the United States

To serve the growing Hispanic population in the United States, both ESPN and Fox operate domestic Spanish-language sports networks. Fox Sports en Espanol debuted in 1996 and was rebranded Fox Deportes in 2010. ESPN Deportes was launched in 2004. The programming of these channels is specifically targeted to Hispanic audiences, instead of merely being Spanish-language **simulcasts** of English-language stations.

The American Spanish-language broadcast networks Univision and Telemundo both include sports in their respective programming mixes. Univision owns the Univision Deportes network and Telemundo operates Telemundo Deportes in association with NBC Sports. In 2012, ESPN debuted the first-ever Spanish-language spot (featuring New York Yankees star Robinson Cano) in its famous "This Is *SportsCenter*" advertising campaign for telecast on the main ESPN channel.

Current Issues

Even at a time of unprecedented success, the sport broadcasting industry faces important challenges.

© jbk_photography/iStock/Thinkstock

Market "Bubble"?

Rights fees increased dramatically during the early 2000s. For example, the NFL's most recent TV deals with CBS, ESPN, Fox, and NBC in 2011 represented a 60% increase in fees over the previous deals (Hiestand, 2011). That same year, the Pac-12 tripled its national rights fees and the NHL secured nearly that same percentage increase (Ourand, 2011). This has raised questions about whether there is a growing **bubble** in sports media rights. A marketplace bubble occurs when prices rise steeply in a short time, followed by sudden decrease in value when the marketplace "corrects" itself. It is uncertain whether a crash in sports rights valuations is forthcoming, and what effect it could have on the television industry or the national economy.

Bundling

With sport programming now comprising as much as half of the total programming costs on television, there is increased public criticism about the impact of these costs on consumers' monthly cable bills (Thompson, 2013). One particularly vociferous critic has been U.S. Senator John McCain. In 2013, McCain introduced federal legislation to encourage cable operators to offer cable channels on an **a la carte** basis instead of **bundling** them into tiers and charging subscribers for an entire tier containing channels that subscribers never watched (Flint, 2013). Even one of the nation's largest cable operators has protested bundling. Cablevision filed a lawsuit in 2013 claiming it was an antitrust violation for Viacom, which owns multiple cable channels, to require Cablevision to distribute low-rated Viacom channels in order to get the better-rated networks (e.g., MTV, Comedy Central, Nickelodeon). Despite these criticisms, industry analysts have predicted that elimination of bundling and tiering could cost the industry $70 billion (Lazarus, 2013). This debate is likely to continue.

Technology

Technology is creating new pressures on the economic model for broadcast television. A new company, Aereo, was founded in 2012 based on a business plan of using antennae to receive broadcast TV signals and then storing them on computers and retransmitting them over the Internet to consumers for a small fee (as low as $8/month) without paying broadcasters the retransmission fees paid by cable/DBS systems. At the same time, the DBS company Dish Network began offering a device called "The Hopper" to let viewers automatically skip the commercials included in programming. Both companies have been subjected to multiple lawsuits that are expected to end up being decided by the U.S. Supreme Court (Carr, 2013).

Both Aereo and The Hopper involve recording live programming for replay at a later time. They could actually increase the relative value of live sport programming. Nevertheless, erosion

of the value of broadcast television could reduce the resources that broadcast networks have to operate, including their ability to bid on sport programming rights.

Cord-Cutting

Cord-cutting is the term for people who refuse to subscribe to cable TV and who instead watch television by using an over-air antenna for live viewing of broadcast networks and by subscribing to services such as Hulu and Netflix for cable-distributed and time-shifted programming (Flacy, 2013). Many industry analysts regard this as a genuine trend (Wallenstein, 2013).

If so, this would mean that two of the cable companies' three revenue streams are under pressure. The three services sold by cable companies are "landline" telephone, TV, and broadband internet. Wired telephone service is declining at the rate of 700,000 customers per month nationwide ("Cutting the Cord," 2009). TV service is being undermined by cord-cutting. Only the business of providing broadband Internet service is robust, although growth in that sector has slowed to 2.2% annually (IBIS World, n.d.).

Mobile Devices

The viewing of video content on mobile devices grew by 300% in 2012, and one of the largest telecommunications and technology companies in the world, Ericsson, predicts a 60% annual growth rate through 2018 (Marvin, 2013; Digital TV Europe, 2013). The entire TV industry, including sport broadcasting, is adapting to this trend by managing a convergence of interests and issues. Networks regard mobile devices as an extension of the receiving sets that can telecast their entire programming schedule. They are seeking to provide "TV Everywhere" service to allow their content to be viewed remotely, plus they are maximizing the volume of video highlights available on their websites. Distributors want to be compensated for this use of their mobile networks. Rightsholders want to be paid for the expansion of the revenue opportunities that mobile distribution represents and also to protect their existing out-of-market and highlight businesses.

As of mid-2013, the future of TV Everywhere was uncertain. Reasons cited for this include cumbersome authentication processes for mobile users to access TV Everywhere signals from distributors (who want to restrict access to their programming services to paid subscribers), the reluctance of advertisers to pay meaningful incremental fees for mobile distribution (due to the unreliability of audience-measuring techniques for mobile devices), and slow progress in negotiations between rightsholders and networks for the necessary additional rights (Ourand, 2013; Nakashima, 2013). Concerns also linger about the capacity of existing wireless transmission networks to handle the projected increases in usage (Fierce Wireless, n.d.).

Audience Fragmentation

The more choices available to people, the fewer people are likely to choose any one thing. This **fragmentation** is a seemingly endless trend in television. There are two forms of television audience fragmentation. One is the availability of more television networks, each catering to a specialized segment of the public. In 1979, for example, ESPN was considered a niche network because it only offered sport programming; now it is considered more of a general interest network in comparison to other channels specializing in such content as college sports (ESPNU), one particular sport (NFL Network, Golf Channel), one league (Big Ten Network, Pac-12 Network), and even one team (YES).

The second form of fragmentation is the availability of video games, social media, and on-demand entertainment programming services as alternatives to live television. Recent studies suggest that young people are watching less TV due to these alternatives (Marketing Charts staff, 2013). Sports television is considered to be one of the "winners" in the current fragmentation of the U.S. audience (Luckerson, 2012). Of the eight TV programs during the 2011–2012 TV season that attracted a rating of 20 or higher, six were sport telecasts (TVB, 2012). This means that big sport events have become the best programs on television for delivering a mass audience to advertisers, who are concerned about the diminishing **reach** of most TV ads (Smentek, 2011). The overall effect of fragmentation may be to force television advertisers to focus on targeted opportunities instead of the increasingly outdated mass-market strategies (Morgan, 2012).

Career Opportunities

Although sports media is heavily based on technology, it is a people-driven business that offers a wide array of career opportunities. There are two fundamental types of jobs at networks: business-related jobs and production-related jobs. Business-related jobs tend to be more strategic in nature. Programming jobs relate to the acquisition and exploitation of rights—identifying rightsholders, analyzing the value of rights and whether particular programming is compatible with the network's other content, negotiating with rightsholders, scheduling the network's programming, and administering the working relationship with rightsholders. Sales jobs involve the sale of advertising and sponsorship for particular programs or sports or the sale of network distribution rights to cable/DBS operators. Job titles for junior positions tend to be "associate," "assistant," and "coordinator," and then advance to "manager" and "director," with executive-level positions carrying the title of "vice president" or "senior vice president," or other modifiers. For example, an associate program planner would be a junior job for someone working on program scheduling. A research coordinator would gather statistics and other data related to ratings and demographics for use primarily in advertising sales. A director of finance would supervise personnel responsible for the accounting of costs and expenses related to a company's business operations. A vice president of programming would have management responsibilities for all or a significant part of the programming decisions made by a network.

© Ryan McVay/Photodisc/Thinkstock

Production-related jobs involve the creation of programs—producing and directing telecasts, operating cameras, recording highlights, mixing in music and other production elements, researching statistics, and transmitting program signals through the maze of satellites and fiber-optic cables that result in the program being available for viewing. A production assistant would be a junior position for someone responsible for a particular aspect of program production, such as operating a videotape machine or carrying a sideline microphone. A replay supervisor would oversee all available camera feeds for selection of the best views of a play for replaying highlights. An associate producer would oversee and troubleshoot designated elements of the event production, supervising various assistants while being subject to the control of the producer. A program engineer would be responsible for ensuring that the program feed is produced according to the

network's quality standards and transmitted from the production facility for "uplinking" to a satellite or to fiber-optic cable. The coordinating producer has overall control for planning and executing the creation of a program.

Most rightsholders employ staffs to manage their relationships with networks, ranging from negotiating rights agreements to regulating the access that production crews have to stadia to factoring TV-related considerations into the creation of playing schedules. Many individual teams also employ staff members to manage TV-related matters. Titles could range from a vice president of broadcasting to a media relations coordinator.

Sport programming is so important to cable companies and other content distributors that they employ staffs to analyze the industry and work directly with sports-related networks on matters of mutual interest. With sports playing an increasingly important role in the business of cable/DBS companies, job titles can be as lofty as senior vice president and general manager for oversight of all sport-related operations.

Advertising agencies employ specialists in sports media, who analyze program ratings, audience demographics and market trends to maximize the effectiveness of advertising and sponsorship in particular programming. Similarly, sport marketing companies seek opportunities for clients to engage in promotional programs and other strategic alignment with sport events and telecasts. Job titles can include "account executive" for a relatively junior position at an advertising agency working on the business of a particular client and "special events coordinator" for someone responsible for all travel and hospitality details of an agency for a trip to a big event such as the Super Bowl to entertain clients.

A portion of the business of sports-related consumer product companies, such as Nike, includes a media strategy for purchasing advertising, arranging for product placement to gain on-air exposure, and analyzing other marketing and promotional opportunities. A director of marketing would work on the management team responsible for implementing these objectives.

There are independent companies that work on everything from representing leagues in negotiating rights agreements to producing telecasts. These organizations vary in size from sole proprietorships to multinational corporations.

In an era when media rights can involve billion-dollar fees, there is a need for specialized lawyers, accountants, and financiers to properly structure a variety of transactions, ranging from writing and negotiating contracts to coordinating with a network's bank on how to structure payments of large rights fees.

Case Study 17-1   The Dominance of ESPN

ESPN is a dominant force in sport broadcasting. It has acquired programming rights to virtually all of the major sport properties in the United States, including the NFL, NBA, MLB, Big Ten, SEC, ACC, Pac-12, BCS Championship Series, The Masters, British Open, Wimbledon, U.S. Open Tennis, the FIFA World Cup, the Little League World Series, and more. *SportsCenter* is the premiere brand in sports news and information programming. ESPN also owns and operates the X Games, the best-known action sports competition in the world. Its *30 For 30* movie and documentary series has been acclaimed for high-quality content. Other assets include the ESPN2, ESPNEWS, ESPN Deportes, ESPNU, and ESPN Classic television networks, the ESPN3 digital network, the ESPN and ESPN Deportes Radio networks, *ESPN The Magazine*, ESPN.com (one of the nation's most heavily trafficked Internet sites), and several Latin American television networks.

ESPN earns enormous amounts of revenue for its business activities. In 2013, it expected to receive approximately $5.50 per month from cable/DBS companies for rights to distribute the ESPN network, which equates to $550 million per month from the 100 million households that receive ESPN's signal, or $6.6 billion per year. ESPN2 receives an additional $0.67 per month, and other ESPN channels receive lesser fees. ESPN also generates an estimated $3 billion annually in advertising revenue.

Despite all of its success, ESPN faces a number of challenges.

ESPN receives widespread criticism for its perceived role in the rising costs of cable/DBS television. ESPN's monthly subscription fee is five times higher than any other national cable network ("Four Sports Channels," 2012). Lawmakers and consumer advocacy groups view rising cable bills as a consumer-protection issue. Congress could enact legislation banning the current practice of bundling ESPN in a tier of programming services that virtually all consumers must subscribe to, even if they never watch sports television. Cable and DBS operators have a different concern—the higher their charges are to consumers, the more people are likely to become cord-cutters and stop paying for subscription TV services.

(continues)

Case Study 17-1   The Dominance of ESPN (Continued)

An additional concern arose when ESPN's ratings during the second quarter of 2013 declined 32% in comparison to the same time period the previous year. ESPN2 ratings also declined by 12% in primetime and 9% overall. Part of the decline was attributed to lackluster ratings for its NBA playoffs coverage, especially the Western Conference finals match-up between two small-market teams, the San Antonio Spurs and the Memphis Grizzlies. However, other more fundamental factors have been cited as reasons for long-term concern (Karp, 2013).

The recently launched Fox Sports 1 and NBCSN are national all-sports networks that now compete directly with ESPN. Both are backed by formidable corporate resources—Fox/News Corporation and NBC/Comcast. These competitors could further erode ESPN's audience and increase the already-robust competition for sports rights.

Rights fees have continued to escalate dramatically. Even though ESPN was reportedly generating $6.6 billion in affiliate fees in 2013, almost *one third* of it goes to the NFL to pay the $1.9 billion rights fee for *Monday Night Football* (Sandomir, 2011b). Negotiations for a new NBA deal must occur to replace the current NBA–ESPN agreement expiring at the end of the 2015–2016 season. Not only have rights fees increased, but the length of rights agreements have gotten significantly longer, with most contracts now extending well into the 2020s (Paulsen, 2013).

SportsCenter's status as the primary source for breaking sports news is under pressure from websites (available on computers as well as mobile devices) that can instantly stream the same video highlights that used to only appear on TV and from services such as Twitter that provide instant news. ESPN has responded to these dynamics by increasing the number of hours of *SportsCenter* programming and frequently interrupting game-coverage telecasts for *SportsCenter*–branded breaking news updates.

ESPN has been at the forefront of trying to stream its networks on mobile devices but its TV Everywhere initiative has struggled to gain widespread traction.

ESPN is far from the only network experiencing recent ratings declines. In the first quarter of 2013, ratings on the four broadcast networks declined by 17% among the most coveted audience demographic, those aged 18 to 49 (Stelter, 2013). This was only the latest development in a 50% ratings decline on broadcast TV from 2002 to 2011 (Edwards, 2013). At a time when television competes with electronic media ranging from video games and on-demand video content (such as Netflix and YouTube) to social media outlets (including Twitter and Facebook), electronic media–related consumer choices continue to expand.

In the summer of 2013, one of Wall Street's most prestigious firms, Goldman Sachs, downgraded its recommendation on the stock of Disney, ESPN's parent company ("Goldman Sachs Analysts," 2013). At the same time, ESPN reportedly laid off more than 400 employees—approximately 5% of its workforce (Smith, C., 2013). ESPN publicly stated that its business remained healthy and that it was not retrenching, citing new initiatives such as launching the SEC Network and opening a new digital production facility (Guthrie, 2013).

Questions for Discussion

1. Identify the risk factors confronting ESPN and rank how serious they are.

2. Identify one or more business activities that ESPN currently engages in that it should eliminate or modify.

3. Identify one or more business activities that ESPN currently is not engaged in that it should adopt.

4. How should ESPN argue against attempts by Congress to modify its pricing structure and bundling policies?

Resources

Because the sport broadcasting industry changes so rapidly, people who work in the industry—and those who want to—must keep abreast of the latest news and trends. Although many of the details of the broadcasting business are theoretically confidential, the trade press has cultivated sources in the industry that often are glad to share news about the latest contracts, advertising packages, and demographic trends.

The most widely read industry news publications are *Broadcasting & Cable, SportsBusiness Journal/SportsBusiness Daily, MediaWeek, AdWeek, Multichannel News, Variety,* and *Advertising Age.* As their titles suggest, each covers the industry from a different perspective. All are available online and many produce print editions. Many of these companies also produce annual directories and summaries. Virtually every media organization, ranging from networks to research firms such as Nielsen and SNL Kagan, maintain information-rich websites.

Network public relations offices are often helpful if contacted directly.

ABC Sports (See ESPN)
    c/o ESPN

beIN Sport
    7291 NW 74th Street
    Medley, FL 33166
    305-777-1900
    http://www.beinsport.tv

Big Ten Network
    600 W. Chicago Avenue
    Chicago, IL 60610
    312-665-0700
    http://www.btn.com

CBS Sports
    51 W. 52nd Street
    New York, NY 10019
    212-975-5100
    http://cbssports.com

ESPN (also ABC Sports)
    ESPN Plaza
    935 Middle Street
    Bristol, CT 06010
    860-766-2000
    http://www.espn.go.com
    http://sports.espn.go.com/nba/abcsports
    /television

Fox Sports
    10210 W. Pico Boulevard
    Los Angeles, CA 90035
    310-369-6000
    http://msn.foxsports.com

The Golf Channel
7580 Golf Channel Drive
Orlando, FL 32819
407-355-4653
http://www.golfchannel.com

HBO Sports
1 Time Warner Center
New York, NY 10019
212-512-1000
http://www.hbo.com/sports

MLB Network
1 MLB Network Plaza
Secaucus, NJ 07094
201-520-6400
http://mlbnetwork.mlb.com

NBC Sports/Comcast Sportsnet
1 Blachley Road
Stamford, CT 06902
203-356-7000
http://www.nbcsportsgrouppressbox.com

NBA TV
c/o Turner Sports
One CNN Center
Atlanta, GA 30303
404-827-1700
http://www.nba.us/nbatv/

New England Sports Network (NESN)
480 Arsenal Street, Building 1
Watertown, MA 02472
617-536-9233
http://www.nesn.com

NFL Network
10950 Washington Blvd.
Culver City, CA 90232
310-840-4635
http://www.nfl.com

NHL Network
c/o NBC Comcast
NBC Sports/Comcast Sportsnet
1 Blachley Road

Stamford, CT 06902
203-352-2806
http://www.nhl.com/ice/eventhome
.htm?location=/nhlnetwork

Pac-12 Networks
370 Third Street
San Francisco, CA 94107
415-580-4200
http://pac-12.com/networks

Root Sports/DIRECTV Sports Networks
601 Union Street, Suite 3020
Seattle, WA 98101
425-748-3400
http://www.rootsports.com

TBS Sports
One CNN Center
Atlanta, GA 30303
404-827-1700
http://www.tbs.com/sports/

Telemundo Deportes
2470 W. 8th Avenue
Hialeah, FL 33010
305-884-8200
http://www.telemundo.com

The Tennis Channel
2850 Ocean Park Boulevard, Suite 150
Santa Monica, CA 90405
310-314-9400
http://www.tennischannel.com

Univision Deportes
605 Third Avenue
New York, NY 10158
212-455-5200
http://deportes.univision.com/

Yankees Entertainment and Sports
Network (YES)
805 Third Avenue
New York, NY 10022
646-487-3600
http://www.yesnetwork.com

Key Terms

a la carte, affiliates, ambush marketing, Roone Arledge, blackout, broadband, broadcasting, broadcasting rights, bubble, bundling, clean feed, commercial breaks, commercial formats, copyright, cord-cutting, direct broadcast satellite (DBS), demographic, digital networks, digital video recorder (DVR), Federal Communications Commission (FCC), fragmentation, high-definition television (HDTV), head ends, Internet service provider (ISP), master antenna, multimedia, networks, out-of-market, pay-per-view, penetration, pod, primetime, ratings, reach, remote production facility, retransmission consent, revenue-sharing, rights fees, rightsholders, Pete Rozelle, share, simulcast, sponsor, sponsorship, streamed, subscriber fees, symbiotic relationship, syndicate, target market, television markets, tiers, time-buy, time-shift, trashsports

References

ABC Sports Online. (2003). History of ABC's *Monday Night Football*. Retrieved from http://espn.go.com/abcsports/mnf/s/2003/0115/1493105.html

Ampex. (n.d.). Ampex history. Retrieved from http://www.ampex.com/news/history.html?start=30

AOL: $2.5b in holiday sales. (2000, January 3). CNNfn. Retrieved from http://money.cnn.com/2000/01/03/technology/aol/.

Badenhausen, K. (2013, July 24). NBC nabs NASCAR TV rights for $4.4 billion. Retrieved from http://www.forbes.com/sites/kurtbadenhausen/2013/07/24/nbc-nabs-nascar-tv-rights-for-4-4-billion/

Barnouw, E. (1966–1970). *A history of broadcasting in the United States* (Vols. 1–3). New York: Oxford University Press.

Big Ten. (2007, July 20). Big Ten Network to officially launch August 30th. Retrieved from http://www.bigten.org/genrel/070207aaa.html

Boston Red Sox. (n.d.). Team history. Retrieved from http://boston.redsox.mlb.com/bos/fenwaypark100/own.jsp?year=2002_present

Boudway, I. (2013, August 8). Fox's new golf deal and the 'sports cable bubble.' Retrieved from http://www.businessweek.com/articles/2013-08-08/foxs-new-golf-deal-and-the-sports-cable-bubble

Brady, S. (2007). NHL Network launches in the U.S. Retrieved from http://www.cablefax.com/360AM/25974.html

Carr, D. (2013, July 29). VCR's past is guiding television's future. Retrieved from http://www.nytimes.com/2013/07/29/business/media/vcrs-past-is-guiding-televisions-future.html?ref=business&_r=0

Carter, B. (2002, December 7). Edgar Scherick, producer of television and movies. Retrieved from http://www.nytimes.com/2002/12/07/arts/edgar-scherick-78-producer-for-television-and-movies.html

Carter, B. (n.d.). Rozelle made NFL what it is today. Retrieved from http://espn.go.com/classic/biography/s/rozelle_pete.htm

Chad, N., & Reid, T. (1989, May 12). ABC, once the network of the Olympics, now the network of May. *Los Angeles Times*. Retrieved from http://articles.latimes.com/1989-03-12/sports/sp-1097_1_abc-sports-production

Cianci, P. J. (2012). *High definition television: The creation, development and implementation of HDTV technology.* Jefferson, NC: McFarland.

Classic Television Database. (n.d.). Retrieved from http://classic-tv.com.

Comcast. (n.d.). Comcast Sportsnet information. Retrieved from http://www.comcastsportsnet.com

Cutting the cord. (2009, August 13). *The Economist*. Retrieved from http://www.economist.com/node/14214847

Davis, J. (2008). *Rozelle*. New York: McGraw-Hill.

Davis, N. (2012, August 27). Al Jazeera's new sports network changes the soccer-watching landscape. Retrieved from http://www .grantland.com/blog/the-triangle/post /_/id/35493/al-jazeeras-new-sports-network -changes-the-soccer-watching-landscape

Deninger, D. (2012). *Sports on television: The how and why behind what you see.* London: Routlege.

Digital TV Europe. (2013, June 3). Ericsson predicts 60% annual mobile video growth. Retrieved from http://www.digitalveurope .net/61942/ericsson-predicts-60-annual -mobile-video-growth/

DIRECTV. (n.d.). DIRECTV history. Retrieved from http://www.directv.com/DTVAPP /content/about_us/company_profile

Dunning, J. (1998). *On the air: The encyclopedia of old-time radio.* Oxford: Oxford University Press.

Early Television Museum. (n.d.). Retrieved from http://www.earlytelevision.org

Economy in NFL history. (n.d.). Retrieved from http://www.shmoop.com/nfl-history /economy.html

Edwards, J. (2013, January 30). BRUTAL: 50% decline in TV viewership shows why your cable bill is so high. Retrieved from http:// www.businessinsider.com/brutal-50-decline -in-tv-viewership-shows-why-your-cable-bill -is-so-high-2013-1

Eisenmann, T. T. (2000). Cable TV: From community antennas to wired cities. Retrieved from http://hbswk.hbs.edu /item/1591.html

ESPN Media Zone. (n.d.). ESPN, Inc. fact sheet. Retrieved from http://espnmediazone.com /us/espn-inc-fact-sheet/

Evensen, B. J. (1996). *When Dempsey fought Tunney: Heroes, hokum, and storytelling in the Jazz Age.* Knoxville, TN: University of Tennessee Press.

Fabrikant, G. (1995, August 1). The media business: The merger; Walt Disney to acquire ABC in $19 billion deal to build a giant for entertainment. Retrieved from http:// www.nytimes.com/1995/08/01/business /media-business-merger-walt-disney -acquire-abc-19-billion-deal-build-giant-for .html?pagewanted=all&src=pm

Facer, D. (2011, July 28). Utah Utes football: Pac-12 creates its own TV network. Retrieved from http://www.deseretnews.com/article/700166468 /Utah-Utes-football-Pac-12-creates-its-own -TV-network.html

Fierce Wireless. (n.d.). Mobile video traffic: Alleviating the capacity crunch. Retrieved from http://www.fiercewireless.com/special -reports/mobile-video-traffic-alleviating -capacity-crunch

FIFA confirms Fox, Telemundo get U.S. World Cup rights. (2011, October 21). Associated Press. Retrieved from http://usatoday30 .usatoday.com/sports/soccer/worldcup /story/2011-10-21/fox-telemundo-us-tv -rights-2018-2022-world-cup/50856226/1

Flacy, M. (2013, January 2). Cord cutting 101: Four easy steps to cut the cord. Retrieved from http://www.digitaltrends.com/home-theater /cord-cutting-four-steps-to-cut-the-cord/

Flint, J. (2013, May 9). John McCain introduces Television Consumer Freedom Act of 2013. Retrieved from http://www.latimes.com /entertainment/envelope/cotown/la-et-ct -mccain-cable-20130509,0,2224732.story

Florio, M. (2009, May 16). The NFL declares its dominance over baseball. Retrieved from http://profootballtalk.nbcsports .com/2009/05/16/the-nfl-declares-its -dominance-over-baseball/

Forsyth, K. S. (2002). History of the Delta Launch Vehicle. Retrieved from http://kevinforsyth .net/delta/satcom.htm

Four sports channels among top 10 for cable net monthly subscriber fees. (2012, February 29). *SportsBusiness Daily*. Retrieved from http:// www.sportsbusinessdaily.com/Daily/Issues /2012/02/29/Research-and-Ratings/Sub-fees .aspx

Fox announces Fox Sports1 network. (2013, May 16). Fox Sports. Retrieved from http://msn .foxsports.com/other/story/FOX-Sports -announces-FOX-Sports-1-network-030513

Fullerton, H. S. (1915, October 19). Nothing but luck saved the Phillies. *New York Times.*

Futterman, M. (2012). $2 Billion Dodgers price tag shatters records. Retrieved from http://online .wsj.com/article/SB100014240527023034047 04577308483250633906.html

Gelston, D. (2008). Army–Navy, instant reply, Tony Verna, 45 years later. Retrieved from http://www.insidesocal.com/tomhoffarth /2008/12/05/army-navy-insta/

Gillette Cavalcade of Sports. (n.d.). Retrieved from http://www.imdb.com/title/tt0268788/

Goldman Sachs analysts downgrades Disney on rising sports rights, competition from Fox Sports 1. (2013). *Minneapolis Star Tribune.* Retrieved from http://www.startribune.com /lifestyle/212358091.html

Grant, A. E., & Meadows, J. H. (2013). *Communication technology update and fundamentals.* Boca Raton, FL: CRC Press.

Gruver, E. (1997). The *American Football League: A year-by-year history, 1960–1969.* Jefferson, NC: McFarland.

Gurnick, K. (2012, March 28). Dodgers sold to Magic Johnson's group. Retrieved from http:// losangeles.dodgers.mlb.com/news/article .jsp?ymd=20120327&content_id=27685944

Gurnick, K. (2013, January 28). Dodgers to launch network with Time Warner TV deal. Retrieved from http://mlb.mlb.com/news /article.jsp?ymd=20130128&content _id=41215548&c_id=l

Guthrie, M. (2012). CBS Sports' Sean McManus: How my dad covered the Munich Massacre. *Hollywood Reporter.* Retrieved from http:// www.hollywoodreporter.com/news /olympics-2012-cbs-sports-sean-mcmanus -munich-massacre-353669

Guthrie, M. (2013, June 26). ESPN's John Skipper on sports rights, layoffs, and Keith Olberman: "we don't have a policy here that you can never come back" (Q&A). Retrieved from http://www.hollywoodreporter.com/news /espn-john-skipper-keith-olbermann -574231?page=2

Hayes, D. (2013, January 14). Nielsen study reveals broadband growth, narrowband decline. Retrieved from http://www.cedmagazine .com/news/2003/01/nielsen-study-reveals -broadband-growth,-narrowband-decline

Head, S., Sterling, C., & Schofield, L. (1994). *Broadcasting in America* (7th ed.). Boston: Houghton Mifflin.

Hiestand, M. (2011, December 14). New NFL TV deals go up 60%. Retrieved from http:// content.usatoday.com/communities/gameon /post/2011/12/new-nfl-tv-deals-bonanza/1# .Uf_WoRblNcR

Howell, E. (2013). Telstar: Satellite beamed 1st TV signals across the sea. Retrieved from http:// www.space.com/19756-telstar.html

Huntley-Brinkley Report. (n.d.). Retrieved from http://www.imdb.com/title/tt0275133/

IBIS World. (2013). Global Internet Service Providers: Market research report. Retrieved from http://www.ibisworld.com/industry /global/global-internet-service-providers.html

Internet World Stats. (n.d.). Internet growth statistics. Retrieved from http://www .internetworldstats.com/emarketing.htm

Karp, A. (2013, July 9). ESPN Q2 viewership drops sharply, while NBC Sports Network sees audience gains. Retrieved from http://www .sportsbusinessdaily.com/Daily/Issues /2013/07/09/Research-and-Ratings/Q2 -viewership.aspx

KDKA. (2010). KDKA firsts. Retrieved at http:// pittsburgh.cbslocal.com/2010/04/01 /kdka-firsts/

Keller, R. (1982). Sport and television in the 1950s: A preliminary survey. Retrieved from: http:// library.la84.org/SportsLibrary/NASSH _Proceedings/NP1982/NP1982v.pdf

Kindred, D. (2006). *Sound and fury: Two powerful lives, one fateful friendship.* New York: Free Press.

Lazarus, D. (2013, July 18). How about a compromise on bundling cable TV channels? Retrieved from http://articles.latimes.com/2013/jul/18/business/la-fi-lazarus-20130719

Loup, R. (2001, January 22). The AFL: A Football Legacy. Retrieved from http://sportsillustrated.cnn.com/football/news/2001/01/22/afl_history_1/

Luckerson, V. (2012, October 4). The winners and losers of the new television landscape. Retrieved from http://business.time.com/2012/10/04/the-winners-and-losers-of-the-new-television-landscape/

MacDonald, J. F. (2009). Sports and television. Retrieved from http://www.jfredmacdonald.com/onutv/sportstv.htm

Marketing Charts staff. (2013). Are young people watching less TV? (Updated Q2 2013 Data). Retrieved from http://www.marketingcharts.com/wp/television/are-young-people-watching-less-tv-24817/

Marvin, G. (2013). Mobile video views surge 300%; tablets fuel growth and engagement. Marketing Land. Retrieved from http://marketingland.com/adobe-mobile-video-views-rise-300-tablets-see-fastest-growth-highest-completion-rate-39586

Maule, T. (1959). The greatest football game ever played. Retrieved at http://sportsillustrated.cnn.com/vault/article/magazine/MAG1133692/index.htm

May 28, 1957: Baseball owners allow Dodgers and Giants to move. (n.d.). History.com. Retrieved from http://www.history.com/this-day-in-history/baseball-owners-allow-dodgers-and-giants-to-move

McCracken, H. (2010). A history of AOL, as told in its own old press releases. Retrieved from http://technologizer.com/2010/05/24/aol-anniversary/

Meserole, M. (2002). Arledge created Monday Night Football. Retrieved from espn.go.com/classic/obit/arledgeobit.html

Meyers, C. B. (2011). The problems with sponsorship in U.S. broadcasting, 1930s–1950s: Perspectives from the advertising industry. *Historical Journal of Film, Radio, and Television, 31*(3), 355–372.

Miller, J. A., & Shales, T. (2011). *Those guys have all the fun.* Boston: Little, Brown Publishing

Minami, C. (2013). Dodgers, MLB reach tentative agreement on cable deal, per report. Retrieved from http://www.truebluela.com/2013/6/13/4429002/dodgers-mlb-reach-tentative-agreement-on-cable-deal

MLB. (n.d.). About MLB Network. Retrieved from http://mlb.mlb.com/network/about/

Morgan, D. (2012). TV audience fragmentation is an inescapable reality: Embrace it. Retrieved from http://www.mediapost.com/publications/article/182946/#axzz2b8Ut2qtl

Nakashima, R. (2013). Problems plague 'TV Everywhere.' Retrieved from http://www.buffalonews.com/20130612/problems_plague_x2018_tv_everywhere_x2019.html

NBA. (n.d.). NBA history. Retrieved from http://www.nba.com/history/

NCTA. (n.d.). Cable's ongoing evolution. Retrieved from http://www.ncta.com/who-we-are/our-story

NFL. (n.d.). History. Retrieved from http://www.nfl.com/history/chronology/1869-1910

NCAA v. Board of Regents of the University of Oklahoma, 468 U.S. 85 (1984).

Nielsen Media Research. (n.d.). Television audience measurement terms. Retrieved from http://www.nielsenmedia.ca/English/NMR_U_PDF/TV%20Terms.pdf

Number of TV households in America. (2001–2013). TVhistory.tv. Retrieved from http://www.tvhistory.tv/Annual_TV_Households_50-78.JPG

Ohio History Central. (n.d.). Powel Crosley, Jr. Retrieved from http://www.ohiohistorycentral.org/w/Powel_Crosley_Jr.

Olberman, K. (2011). How I was hired—and fired—by Rupert Murdoch. Retrieved from http://www.theguardian.com/commentisfree/cifamerica/2011/aug/01/rupert-murdoch-keith-olbermann

Oracle Education Foundation. (n.d.a.). Retrieved from http://library.thinkquest.org/27629 /themes/media/md60s.html.

Ourand, J. (2011, June 6). How high can rights fees go? Retrieved from http:// www.sportsbusinessdaily.com/Journal /Issues/2011/06/06/In-Depth/Rights-Fees .aspx

Ourand, J. (2013, May 6). Outside of big live events, is TV Everywhere going nowhere? Retrieved from http://www.sportsbusinessdaily.com /Journal/Issues/2013/05/06/Media/Sports -Media.aspx

Paulsen. (2013). An early look at NBA TV rights: Will anybody challenge ESPN? Retrieved from http://www.sportsmediawatch.com/2013/02 /an-early-look-at-nba-tv-rights-will-anybody -challenge-espn/

Peck, B. (2013). MLS commissioner thinks there's 'way too much soccer on television.' Retrieved from http://sports.yahoo.com/blogs/soccer -dirty-tackle/mls-commissioner-thinks-way -too-much-soccer-television-050024816.html

Pickert, K. (2009). A brief history of the X Games. Retrieved from http://content.time.com/time /nation/article/0,8599,1873166,00.html

Pittsburgh Athletic Co. v. KQV Broadcasting Co., 24 F. Supp. 490 (W.D. Pa. 1938).

Pro Football Hall of Fame. (n.d.). Rams team history. Retrieved from http:// www.profootballhof.com/history/team /st-louis-rams/

Rauscher, A. (n.d.). February 5, 1963. The Beatles in America: We loved them yeah, yeah, yeah. Retrieved from http://www.newseum.org /news/2009/02/the-beatles-in-america-we -loved-them--yeah--yeah--yeah.html

Reed, W. F. (1991). All shook up. Retrieved from http://sportsillustrated.cnn.com/vault/article /magazine/MAG1140740/1/index.htm

Rische, P. (2012, October 31). NBC Sports betting big on soccer with acquisition of Barclays English Premier League. Retrieved from http://www.forbes.com/sites/prishe/2012 /10/31/nbc-sports-betting-big-on-soccer -with-acquisition-of-barclays-english -premiere-league/

Rovell, D. (2012). News Corp acquires stake in YES. Retrieved from http://espn.go.com/new -york/mlb/story/_/id/8654665/news-corp -acquires-49-percent-stake-yes-network

Sandomir, R. (2011a, August 8). Versus renamed again. Retrieved from http://www.nytimes .com/2011/08/02/sports/versus-renamed -again.html

Sandomir, R. (2011b, September 9). ESPN extends deal with NFL for $15 billion. Retrieved from http://www.nytimes.com/2011/09/09/sports /football/espn-extends-deal-with-nfl-for-15 -billion.html

Sandomir, R. (2014, May 7). NBC extends Olympic deal into unknown. Retrieved from http:// mobile.nytimes.com/2014/05/08/sports /olympics/nbc-extends-olympic-tv-deal -through-2032.html?referrer=

Schexnayder, C. J. (2009, December 22). The 1927 Rose Bowl: Alabama vs. Stanford. Retrieved from http://www.rollbamaroll.com/2009/12 /22/1197979/the-1927-rose-bowl-alabama-vs

SEC Network to broadcast 24/7. (2013). ESPN .com. Retrieved from http://espn.go.com /espn/story/_/id/9235260/sec-espn-announce -sec-network-2014

Shannon, R. (2010). USA vs. USSR, 1962: The greatest track meet of all time. Retrieved from http://bleacherreport.com/articles/342578 -usa-vs-ussr-1962-the-greatest-track-meet-of -all-time

Smentek, S. (2011). Media experts say audience fragmentation is affecting advertiser reach and agency resources. Retrieved from http:// www.comcastspotlight.com/blog/take-five -fragmentation-webcast-recap

Smith, C. (1995). *The storytellers. From Mel Allen to Bob Costas: Sixty years of baseball tales from the broadcast booth.* New York: Macmillan

Smith, C. (2013, May 22). Meet the rights fees responsible for ESPN's layoffs. Retrieved from http://www.forbes.com/sites

/chrissmith/2013/05/22/meet-the-rights-fees
-responsible-for-espns-layoffs/

Smith, D. (2013). Will NBC's Premiere League
coverage hurt or help Major League Soccer?
Retrieved from http://theamericanpitch
.com/2013/04/16/will-nbcs-premier-league
-coverage-hurt-or-help-major-league-soccer/

Staples, A. (2011, Jul. 21). Texas' Longhorn
Network sparking another Big 12 Missile
Crisis. Retrieved from http://sportsillustrated
.cnn.com/2011/writers/andy_staples/07/21
/longhorn-network-big-12/index.html.

Stelter, B. (2013, May 13). As TV Ratings and
Profits Fall, Networks Face a Cliffhanger.
Retrieved at http://www.nytimes.com/2013
/05/13/business/media/tv-networks-face
-falling-ratings-and-new-rivals.html?
pagewanted=all

Stephens, M. (n.d.). History of television.
Retrieved from http://www.nyu.edu/classes
/stephens/History%20of%20Television%20
page.htm

Television Obscurities. (2005, February 15/2013,
February 17). Color adoption slow. Retrieved
from http://www.tvobscurities.com/articles
/color60s/

Thiel, A. (2013, April 16). Mariners buy Root
Sports; set for big $. Retrieved from http://
sportspressnw.com/2149666/2013/thiel
-mariners-buy-root-sports-set-for-big

Thompson, D. (2013). Mad about the cost of TV?
Blame sports. Retrieved from http://www
.theatlantic.com/business/archive/2013/04
/mad-about-the-cost-of-tv-blame-sports
/274575/

TiVo. (n.d.). TiVo history. Retrieved from http://
www3.tivo.com/jobs/questions/history-of
-tivo/index.html

Today in World Series history, Part 2. (n.d.).
Retrieved from http://www.todayinsport
.com/baseball/baseball-championships
/world-series?p=2

TVB. (2012). TV basics. Retrieved from http://
www.tvb.org/media/file/TV_Basics.pdf

*Twentieth Century Sporting Club, Inc. v.
Transradio Press Service, Inc.*, 300 N.Y.S. 159
(1937)

Wallenstein, A. (2013). Top Wall Street analyst:
Pay TV "cord-cutting is real." Retrieved from
http://variety.com/2013/digital/news/top
-wall-street-analyst-pay-tv-cord-cutting-is
-real-1200491763/

Wertheim, J. (2012). When Billy beat Bobby.
Retrieved from http://sportsillustrated.cnn
.com/vault/article/magazine/MAG1197984
/index.htm

Wulf, S. (1993). Out foxed. Retrieved from http://
sportsillustrated.cnn.com/vault/article
/magazine/MAG1138126/index.htm

YES. (n.d.). YES information. Retrieved from
http://web.yesnetwork.com/about/

Chapter 18

The Sporting Goods and Licensed Products Industries

Dan Covell

Learning Objectives

Upon completion of this chapter, students should be able to:

1. Estimate the size and scope of the sporting goods and licensed products industry.

2. Appraise the historical development of the sporting goods and licensed products industries with a particular emphasis on how leagues and players associations came to establish properties divisions and licensing programs.

3. Differentiate between licensed and branded products.

4. Assess the steps in the licensing process and the role licensing plays in generating revenue for licensors and licensees.

5. Identify the various career opportunities available in the sporting goods and licensed products industries and understand the skills needed to succeed in them.

6. Recognize the importance of innovation in producing and selling products.

7. Illustrate how the concept of expert usage, exhibited through product endorsements, helps overcome the risk factors that customers assess when making a purchase decision.

8. Analyze the role of global sourcing, particularly in the sport apparel and footwear industries, and explain how this practice may create an ethical dilemma for manufacturers.

9. Assess how the antitrust suit brought by American Needle against the NFL may affect the licensed product industry.

Introduction

This chapter presents information on two related segments of the sport industry: **sporting goods** and **licensed products**. According to Hardy (1997), an analysis of sport products reveals their triple commodity nature: the activity or game form, the service, and the goods. Hardy defines *sporting goods* as the physical objects necessary for the game form. The development and sale of such goods will serve as the focus of this chapter. The sporting goods industry has a long history and encompasses equipment, apparel, and footwear. Licensed products—clothing or products bearing the name or logo of a popular collegiate or professional sport team—have been around for a comparatively short period of time and comprise a specialized subset of the sporting goods industry. The following data outlines the scope of these industries in 2011:

- Total sales in the United States totaled $77.3 billion, up 4.2% from 2010.
- Sporting goods equipment sales rose 2.5%, increasing from $20.4 billion in 2010 to $20.9 billion in 2011. The largest categories of sporting goods were firearms/hunting ($2.9 billion), golf ($2.5 billion), fishing ($2 billion), camping ($1.8 billion), and optical goods ($1.3 billion).
- Wholesale sales of sports apparel were $31.4 billion, a 6.1% increase over 2010 ($29.6 billion). Branded activewear accounted for $14.4 billion of these sales.
- Sales in the athletic footwear category rose from $12.61 billion in 2010 to $13.18 billion, an increase of 4.5%. The top five athletic footwear categories are running/jogging ($3.89 billion), classics/originals ($1.88 billion), kids ($1.87 billion), basketball ($875 million), and skate/surf ($831 million). Licensed merchandise sales rose slightly—1.3%—to $7.385 billion (Sporting Goods Manufacturers Association, 2012).

So how do these issues impact sport organizations? Consider the case of Under Armour (UA). As the football team's special teams captain (and a business major) at the University of Maryland in 1995, Kevin Plank, the founder and CEO of UA, saw teammates suffer from heat stress during practice and wondered whether their sweat-soaked t-shirts contributed to their maladies. In response, Plank developed a performance undershirt that wicked moisture away from the skin. He initially financed the company with $20,000 of his own money, $40,000 spread on five credit cards, additional funds from family and friends, and a $250,000 loan from the Small Business Administration. Plank could not convince large manufacturers to back him, so he took to selling directly to team equipment managers out of the trunk of his car. In 1996, he booked $17,000 in sales and made a deal with an Ohio apparel manufacturer ("Call in your orders by noon," said plant owner Sal Fasciana, "and we'll make and ship the product by the end of the day"). Plank established official supplier agreements with Major League Baseball (MLB), Major League Soccer (MLS), the National Hockey League (NHL), USA Baseball, and the U.S. Ski team, much like Spalding had with MLB over a century before. The company now makes shirts, shorts, pants, socks, hats, and underwear and has launched a women's gear line, along with "LooseGear" and "Performance Grey" products (McCarthy, 2008).

Under Armour is the fastest-growing sport apparel and footwear brand in the world. The company's estimated worth is $1 billion, with revenues of $1.4 billion in 2011. As of 2011, it had 3% of the U.S. athletic apparel market (Oznian, 2011). Even as competitors such as Nike, Adidas, Champion, and Russell Athletic have tried to match UA, Michael May of the Sporting Goods Manufacturers Association says: "Under Armour is the dominant brand in the high-tech sports apparel industry . . . people love Under Armour" (Graham, 2004, p. 8). Even as competitors try to buy him out, Plank refuses, stating, "As foreign as it would be for you to go running in regular shoes, I want it to be just as foreign for you not to work out in your Under Armour" (Graham, 2004, p. 9).

In terms of brand strength, states writer Daniel Roberts (2011), the interlocking UA company logo "is becoming as recognizable as the Nike swoosh," and in contrast to Nike's "deification" of individual athletes, "UA's brand identity was always about the team" (p. 1). UA has apparel and footwear agreements with several National Collegiate Athletic Association (NCAA) Division I athletic programs, including Maryland (a 5-year deal signed in 2009 worth $17.5 million), Auburn, and Boston College. In fact, some dubbed the 2011 BCS national championship game (Auburn versus the University of Oregon, the pet athletic department of Nike founder Phil Knight) as UA versus Nike (Roberts, 2011). Recently, UA announced the most lucrative deal yet in college athletics, entering into a 10-year, reported $90 million contract with the University of Notre Dame (Rovell, 2014). The Irish had been outfitted by Adidas prior to signing with UA.

In 2011, UA built further on this team-based approach and used the opening of the college football season, along with its relationship with the University of Maryland, to introduce a brand new UA "Maryland Pride" uniform, the first of 32 combinations the team would wear over the season. The new look (including player footwear) was based on the yellow, black, red, and white design of the state flag, which in the opinion of one writer "made players look to some like chess pieces," whereas another suggested the design appeared like "a quilting bee enhanced by Jell-o shots" (Tanier, 2011, p. A1). Some other reactions were more pointed. A headline on Deadspin.com read "Maryland

football players will dress in whatever clown suit Under Armour tells them to." However, Maryland students approved of the uniforms, as explained by the school's student newspaper: "People have taken a real sense of pride in what the football team wore . . . What a lot of people don't understand is that the people who grow up in Maryland have a huge sense of pride in our state flag" ("New Uniforms," 2011, p. 7C). The look resonated with Maryland recruits as well. One local prospect had this to say: "I like that [the uniforms] represented Maryland, the state flag, the state, everything" ("New Uniforms," 2011, p. 7C). Team captains got to select the unique combinations for each week's game. A Maryland spokesperson justified the move, stating, "[UA is] trying to increase their visibility, and so are we" (Roberts, 2011, p. 1). In the immediate aftermath of the Maryland Pride rollout, UA's Plank lauded the move in an address to company workers, stating: "This company has got the world talking" (Tanier, 2011, p. B16).

But the uniform-as-fashion statement approach is neither new nor novel. Nike has been using Oregon teams as an incubator for new looks for several years (with nearly 400 different potential combinations for its football uniforms), and unveiled new looks for grid squads at the University of Georgia and Oklahoma State University the same weekend UA's Maryland duds were trotted out. Later in the year Adidas did the same for both teams in the University of Michigan versus Notre Dame game, choosing what one Adidas manager called "a retro-heritage look, which with these two programs makes all the sense in the world" (Tanier, 2011, p. B16).

These tactics by footwear and apparel manufacturers are examples of the market impact of sporting goods and licensed products. The remainder of the chapter examines the specifics of these related segments.

History of Sporting Goods and Apparel

Sporting Goods

The French economic philosopher J. B. Say (1964) coined the term **entrepreneur** to describe those who created ideas for better uses of existing technology. The early sporting goods industry in the United States is replete with entrepreneurial innovation. As early as 1811, George Tryon, a gunsmith, began to carve out a niche with people interested in sport. After expanding into the fishing tackle business, Tryon's company became a major wholesaler of sporting goods east of the Mississippi River. In the late 1840s and 1850s Michael Phelan and John Brunswick each had established production of billiards equipment. Brunswick, a Swiss immigrant, established billiard parlors across the country and by 1884 had merged with his two largest competitors, creating a $1.5 million operation that was larger than all of his competitors combined. The company moved into bowling in the 1890s. Hillerich and Bradsby began in 1859 as a wood-turning shop in Louisville and expanded to baseball bat production in 1884. Former professional baseball player George Wright, along with partner H. A. Ditson, operated Wright and Ditson in the late 1880s (the company was later bought by Albert G. Spalding [see below] but continued to operate under the original name). In 1888, Rawlings began operations in St. Louis, promoting itself as offering a "full-line emporium" of all sporting goods (Hardy, 1995; "The Great," 2003; Thorn, 2011).

But it was Albert G. Spalding who typified the early sporting goods entrepreneur. Spalding, a standout professional baseball pitcher in the late nineteenth century, parlayed his baseball reputation and a loan of $800 to create a sporting goods manufacturing giant based on selling to the expanding American middle class. While also owner of the Chicago White Stockings of the National League, Spalding adopted technological advances to manufacture bats, baseballs, gloves, uniforms, golf clubs, bicycles, hunting goods, and football equipment. Many other manufacturers also focused on the production of sporting goods, but Spalding understood that he had to create and foster the markets for these products as the newly affluent middle class sought to find uses for their leisure time. Spalding produced guides on how to play and exercise, promoted grassroots sport competitions, and gained credibility with consumers by claiming official supplier status with baseball's National League. Spalding also created a profitable distribution system in which the company sold directly to retailers at a set price with the guarantee that retailers would sell at a price that Spalding set. This technique created stable markets for Spalding goods and eliminated price cutting at the retail level (Levine, 1985). Spalding's connection with the National League helped establish the value of endorsements and licensing connections that would become industry staples.

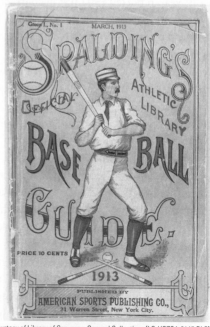

Courtesy of Library of Congress, General Collections [LC-USZC4-6145 DLC]

The twentieth century saw continued developments in the industry as consumer demand continued to grow. In 1903, Harvard football coach Bill Reid devoted many pages in his diary to his efforts in working with local merchants to design and manufacture pads to protect his players (Smith, 1994). The Sports and Fitness Industry Association (SFIA, formerly the Sporting Goods Manufacturers Association) was founded in 1906 as intercollegiate football leaders and athletic equipment manufacturers sought to make the sport safer and less violent. In the 1920s, a number of famous sport personalities began to endorse sporting goods products, including Knute Rockne, Honus Wagner, and Nap Lajoie. The 1940s saw a retrenchment in spending on sporting goods, but after the Korean War in the 1950s, as prosperity returned to the country, spending on sporting goods increased. Tennis greats Fred Perry and Jean Rene Lacoste (Izod) helped launch the fashion-sportswear segment in the 1950s. In the 1960s, imported products arrived in greater numbers in the U.S. market, especially Japanese baseball products. The 1970s also brought increased recognition of product liability and the injuries associated with sports equipment. This recognition engendered in teachers, coaches, and administrators increased concern for risk management. As the industry moved through the 1980s and 1990s, there was continuing growth as products and consumer demographics became more diverse (O'Brien, 2002).

In the middle of the twentieth century, German footwear and apparel manufacturer Adidas established a strong international presence. Founded in the 1920s by Adolph "Adi" Dassler (from whose name the company's would derive) from a family shoe business, the firm made strong inroads through the production of soccer cleats and track spikes. Dassler established his product, in part, by convincing U.S. track Olympian Jesse Owens to wear his spikes in the 1936 Berlin Summer Games. Adi's brother, Rudolf, would later go on to found Puma after a falling out between the two brothers. The two companies would compete for international market share for the remainder of the century, with Adidas ultimately prevailing, in part through its close partnership with Fédération Internationale de Football Association (FIFA, soccer's international governing body) (Smit, 2008).

In the 1980s and 1990s, the industry experienced the emergence of several industry giants, most notably Nike and Reebok. Nike, the brainchild of Phil Knight, began as an offshoot of Knight's original Blue Ribbon Sports. The Nike name came from one of Knight's colleagues in 1971. By 1980, Nike was pulling in $269 million a year and had replaced Adidas as the United States' top sneaker. Although Nike temporarily lost its top ranking to Reebok in 1986, the advent of the "Air Jordan" and "Bo Knows" marketing campaigns in the late 1980s propelled Nike back to the top, and Nike was a $2 billion company by 1990 (Katz, 1993). During the third quarter of fiscal year 2003, Nike claimed global revenues of $2.4 billion ($1.3 billion in the United States), with a net income of $125 million. By the end of 2009, net sales had reached $19.1 billion (although the period's severe global economic downturn forced the company to lay off 1,700 workers) (Horovitz, 2009). In 2012, Nike reported fiscal revenues of $24.1 billion (Nike, 2014). Adidas countered Nike's ascendance in 2005 when it purchased Reebok for $3.8 billion, in part to gain control over Reebok's licensing agreements with the National Football League (NFL) and the National Basketball Association (NBA) (Smit, 2008).

Licensed Products

Baseball historian Warren Goldstein (1989) noted that many early baseball teams (such as the Cincinnati Red Stockings in 1869) got their names from their distinctive apparel and that uniforms created a sense of apartness and defined who was a player and who was not. Davis (1992) commented that clothing styles are a transmitted code that can impart meanings of identity, gender, status, and sexuality. Licensed apparel communicates on each of these levels and is based on the notion that fans will purchase goods to draw them closer to their beloved organizations and athletes. Writer Bill Simmons (2004) described the early days of buying player-specific licensed products this way: "Fans bought them because they wanted to dress like players on the team. Not only were we supporting our guys, but the player we chose became an expression of sorts" (p. 12). The industry was slow to realize the financial potential of such connections. In 1924, sportswriter Francis Wallace observed displays and neckties in the colors of what he termed the aristocracy of the gridiron in the shops while walking down Fifth Avenue in Manhattan: Army, Harvard, Notre Dame, Princeton, and Yale. In 1947, University of Oregon Athletic Director Leo Harris and Walt Disney agreed to allow Oregon to use Disney's Donald Duck image for the university's mascot. Although these were some early steps toward the development of licensable properties, the University of California–Los Angeles (UCLA) is generally credited with being the first school to enter into a licensing agreement with a manufacturer when its school bookstore granted a license to a watch manufacturer in 1973. The NCAA formed its properties division to license championship merchandise in 1975, but it does not administer licensing programs for member schools. Significant revenue growth began in the late 1980s, when the University of Notre Dame, which began its licensing program in 1983, experienced growth of 375% from 1988 to 1989. Collegiate licensed product sales totaled $100 million in the early 1980s. In 1995, sales reached $2.5 billion. The peak for licensed sales for major college and professional licensed products was 1996, with

sales of $13.8 billion. That figure had slipped to $11.8 billion by 2001 (Hiestand, 2002; Nichols, 1995; Plata, 1996; Sperber, 1993).

© Christopher Penler/ShutterStock, Inc.

The licensing programs in professional sport leagues are administered by a for-profit branch of the league, generally referred to as a **properties division**. Properties divisions approve licensees, police trademark infringement, and distribute licensing revenues equally among league franchises. Properties divisions usually handle marketing and sponsorship efforts as well. The NFL was the first professional league to develop a properties component in 1963, under the leadership of then-commissioner Alvin "Pete" Rozelle. The first license was granted to Sport Specialties. David Warsaw, the founder of the company, had worked with Chicago Bears owner George Halas in the 1930s selling Bears merchandise and later developed licensing agreements with the Los Angeles Dodgers and the then-Los Angeles Rams ("Sports Merchandising," 1996). By the late 1970s, each NFL team's licensing share was believed to be nearly half a million dollars annually.

MLB followed with the creation of its properties division (MLB Properties) in 1966, although many teams that had strong local sales were reluctant to give up their licensing rights to the league. Indeed, some teams were loath to share their marks with licensees because of their perceptions that such actions would cheapen the product. George Weiss, general manager of the New York Yankees, recoiled at the notion of licensing agreements, saying, "Do you think I want every kid in this city walking around with a Yankees cap?" (Helyar, 1994, p. 70). NHL Enterprises began formal league-governed licensing in 1969, and NBA Properties initiated activities in 1982 (Lipsey, 1996).

Players unions also administer licensing programs. The Major League Baseball Players Association (MLBPA) was the first to enter into such an agreement in the late 1960s when then-Executive Director Marvin Miller entered into a 2-year, $120,000 pact with Coca-Cola to permit the beverage manufacturer to put players' likenesses on bottle caps. Such royalties helped fund the emerging union's organizing activities. Miller also negotiated a comprehensive agreement with trading card manufacturer Topps Company in 1968. Topps was permitted to continue manufacturing trading cards bearing player likenesses for double the player's previous yearly fees (from $125 to $250), and it paid the union 8% on annual sales up to $4 million and 10% on all subsequent sales. In the first year, the contract earned the MLBPA $320,000 (Helyar, 1994).

Industry Structure

Sporting Goods

The Sports and Fitness Industry Association (SFIA), the industry trade association for the sporting goods industry, defines the sporting goods industry as comprising the manufacturers of sporting goods equipment, athletic footwear, and sports apparel, as well as manufacturers of accessory items to the sport and recreation market (SFIA, 2013). **Sporting goods equipment** includes fitness products as well as sport-specific products for golf, soccer, tennis, in-line skating, and so on. In recent years, participation rates in sport and physical activities have remained constant, as have the

accompanying sales of sporting goods equipment. The second segment is **athletic footwear**. Athletic footwear is defined as branded and unbranded athletic shoes for casual wear or active usage, outdoor/hiking sports boots, and sports sandals. The third segment is **sports apparel**. Broadly defined, sports apparel encompasses garments that are designed for, or could be used in, active sports.

© Glenn Bloomquist/iStock/Thinkstock

Sporting Goods Trade Associations

Within the industry there are a number of **trade associations** for sporting goods professionals. One of these is the previously mentioned Sport and Fitness Industry Association (SFIA). The SFIA is the self-described "premier trade association for more than 750 sporting goods and fitness brands, manufacturers, retailers, and marketers in the industry" (SFIA, 2013, p. 1). SFIA's stated purpose is "to support our member companies and promote a healthy environment for the sporting goods industry by providing access to insight, information, influence and industry connections" (SFIA, 2013, p. 1). The industry employs more than 375,000 people and generates $77 billion in domestic revenue wholesale sales (SFIA, 2013).

Licensing

The manufacturers of licensed products, the **licensees**, include well-known sport-product companies such as Adidas, Reebok, and Nike; prominent electronics and video game manufacturers Electronic Arts and Sony; and smaller firms such as Artcarved (jewelry), Mead (stationery), and Topps (trading cards and memorabilia). Licensees pay teams and leagues, the **licensors**, for the right to manufacture products bearing team and school names, nicknames, mascots, colors, and logos. If these names and logos are registered with the U.S. Patent and Trademark Office, they are referred to as **trademarks**. A trademark is defined under the Federal Trademark Act of 1946, commonly referred to as the Lanham Act, as "any word, name, symbol, or device or combination thereof adopted and used by a manufacturer or merchant to identify his goods and distinguish them from those manufactured or sold by others" (Lanham Act, 15 U.S.C. § 1051–1127, 1946, p. 1). The law defines trademark infringement as the "reproduction, counterfeiting, copying, or imitation, in commerce of a registered mark and bars companies that do not pay for the right to use these trademarks from manufacturing products bearing those marks" (Lanham Act, 15 U.S.C. § 1051–1127, 1946, p. 1).

Licensing enables schools and teams to generate brand recognition and interest and increase revenues with very little financial risk. The licensees assume the risk by manufacturing the product, and then pay a fee to the licensor, called a **royalty**, for the use of specific trademarks on specific products. Royalty fees generally range from 4% (for toys and games) to 20% (for trading cards and video games) and are based on gross sales at wholesale costs. The royalty rates for teams and leagues vary, ranging from 8% to 20%, with the majority at around 12% ("Licensed Sports," 2012). Wholesale costs are those paid by the retailer, not the price paid by consumers. Licensees use the established images and popularity of sport teams to boost their sales.

Collegiate Sport

Some NCAA Division I schools administer their own licensing programs. The benefit of self-maintenance is that schools can retain a greater portion of sales revenues. The remainder of Division I Bowl Subdivision schools, like the smaller pro leagues and many Championship Subdivision schools, enlist the services of independent licensing companies to manage their programs. The Collegiate Licensing Company (CLC), formed in 1981, and recently purchased by sport marketing company IMG and now known as IMG College, articulates licensing agreements on behalf of approximately 200 colleges and universities, bowls, conferences, the Heisman Trophy, and the NCAA. Client colleges pay a portion of the royalties (usually 50%) to CLC for its efforts. According to Pat Battle, senior corporate vice president of IMG College, by 2008 the retail market for collegiate merchandise had grown to more than $3.5 billion in annual sales, with apparel accounting for 62%, and with less than 20% of those sales taking place on college campuses (Barr & Covell, 2010). Nonapparel, which continues to close the gap each year, is led by the college market's number one licensee, Electronic Arts (EA). The EA Sports NCAA Football video game has become the second best-selling sports game in North America, trailing only EA Sports' Madden franchise (Barr & Covell, 2010).

Career Opportunities

A number of career opportunities exist in these segments, ranging from entrepreneurs with an idea for a specific product (see below) to employment with firms such as Callaway, Russell, Under Armour, or New Balance. Sporting goods stores are another employment option, including locally owned single-unit stores; large chains, such as Champs Sports, Dick's, or Academy Sports; and niche retailers, such as Lids, which specializes in the sale of licensed and branded headwear. The potential career opportunities that exist in the licensing industry include employment with league licensing departments, collegiate licensing offices, and licensees, as well as with retail sales outlets and product manufacturers.

Within large companies, such as footwear and apparel manufacturer New Balance, there are divisions for each product line, such as basketball, tennis, cross-training/fitness, and children. New Balance has created a niche in the highly competitive footwear market by providing customers with footwear with extensive width sizing, and has done this, the company states, through a commitment to domestic manufacturing (the company employs over 4,000 workers and maintains manufacturing facilities in Massachusetts and Maine) and leadership in technological innovation. In 2004, the company acquired lacrosse equipment manufacturer Warrior, and by 2011 the company reported worldwide sales of $2 billion (Martin, 2012). New Balance has staff positions in manufacturing, research and development, sales and marketing, and promotions.

Sporting goods stores operate on many levels. Locally owned specialty retailers operate sporting goods stores in the traditional model of a family owned and operated store located for a number of years in the same town, offering a somewhat limited variety of sporting goods depending on the location. Some have more than one location. Consider the various specialty running shoe stores across the United States such as Metro Run & Walk (three stores in the Washington, D.C. area), soundRunner With No Boundaries (two stores in southern Connecticut), and Super Runners Shop in New York City and Long Island. According to industry surveys, there are about 700 specialty running stores in the United States, accounting for an estimated $700 million a year in sales (Spiegel, 2008). Gary Muhrcke of Super Runners says

his business survives in the face of competition from online running shoe retailers such as Road Runner Sports and larger chains such as Fleet Feet because of personal service. According to Muhrcke, "I can't see the shape of a person's foot over the phone. I can't look at a person's body structure or size or whether they're bowlegged over the Internet. The basic reason why we're still here—we're needed" (Spiegel, 2008, p. C6). Julie Francis of soundRunner notes that her stores survive because of running shoe sales (which account for 60% of all store sales); the fact that they can accommodate customer segments such as fitness walkers and runners, not just elite runners; and that these stores are more involved in the communities in which they are located, sponsoring races, clinics, medical referrals, and social networking. Manufacturers also like the specialty stores, because, according to Jim Weber of Brooks, which places 80% of its product in such stores, "It's introducing our brand to people a pair of feet at a time, and that usually happens in specialty stores . . . No one does it better than a specialty store" (Spiegel, 2008, p. C6).

The larger chain stores tend to offer a wider selection of products. Some of these stores, such as Champs or Lady Foot Locker, are usually located in malls, where people stop in if they go to the mall to shop. Others, such as Academy Sports and Dick's, are freestanding "big box" stores considered a final destination for shoppers. As opposed to the mall stores, where people stop in if they are shopping at the mall, people go to a Dick's with the intention of buying sporting goods and nothing else. Each of these stores needs sales staff, as well as managers who oversee the financial, marketing, and personnel aspects of the store. Larger chains need store managers as well as people to work on the corporate level. Depending on the size of a store, buyers may be needed to make decisions on what products to stock in the upcoming seasons.

Application of Key Principles

Management

As long as society, the economy, and technology remain somewhat stable or change only slowly, management has time to make the adjustments necessary to maintain and improve performance. However, rapid change is the rule in the sporting goods and licensed products industries, and industry managers face new challenges brought on by a changing environment. These include intense competition and new performance standards that every management team must now achieve. These standards include competition, quality, speed and flexibility, innovation, and sustainable growth (Covell & Walker, 2013).

Innovation is a key performance standard impacting sporting goods and licensed products, and according to industry experts it is a critical factor for survival, let alone success. As noted earlier in the chapter, entrepreneurs such as Albert Spalding and John Brunswick impacted these industries significantly through the creation of new products and services to meet the needs and wants of consumers. When combined with continual improvements in equipment and related products, one sees countless examples of entrepreneurial efforts throughout the history of sport management.

Consider sports cards. In 1951 the Topps Company started to use sports trading cards, specifically baseball cards, to sell bubble gum. Topps ruled the baseball card market until 1981, when a federal court antitrust decision broke its stranglehold, leading to an explosion of competition. By the late 1980s, new card companies such as Upper Deck and the production of greater card varieties developed a speculative market, with consumers flooding the market with cash seeking to buy cards as investments. The market bubble grew until 1991, when sports cards sales topped $1.2 billion, then burst,

settling to annual sales of $300 million by 2004, and to $200 million by 2008. Card shops closed at a rapid rate as well, from 5,000 in the early 1990s to 500 in 2009 ("Scorecard," 2003; Winn, 2009).

In response, card makers have struggled to regain market share with new products and sets, such as cards with pieces of bats or game-worn uniforms affixed to them. In 2003, four separate card companies released 87 separate sets of cards, and by 2005 brands such as Fleer, Pacific, and Sky Box had folded, and Topps concluded that the trading card market was going to shrink by 25% a year. According to one industry expert: "There was too much money going into competition and not enough into marketing, especially to younger kids" (Duerson, 2007, p. 30). Topps now has the exclusive MLB trading card licensing rights (Chozick, 2012; Winn, 2009).

Because today's sports trading card market is only 30% children, Topps is looking to the use of smartphone technology to continue to connect with more "techcentric" young consumers. With digital games such as Angry Birds vying for kids' attention, Topps recently released the iPhone and iPad app Topps Pennant, a data-based platform for the statistically infatuated, and Topps Bunt, an interactive game with properties similar to fantasy leagues. Topps hopes the new apps will be the beginning of an expansion into other digital and media offerings such as TV shows and movies. Topps CEO Michael Eisner, formerly of Disney, believes that Topps' brand is strong enough to make the tech transition. "In the world of beverages, there's Coke, but it's very hard to find companies that have the emotional brand of Topps" (Chozick, 2012, p. B4). Said a Topps product designer of the new offerings: "Our goal was to take that DNA and reconstitute them to new platforms" (Chozick, 2012, p. B4). The Pennant app (initially priced at $2.99, a little more than the price of a pack of cards) offers detailed interactive graphics on every player and every game played since 1952. Bunt (a free app) features rows of cards and rotates cards three-dimensionally to reveal biographical information. It also allows users to build teams, trade players, and compete with other users as in fantasy leagues. Both apps require iOS 4.3 to download and operate (Chozick, 2012).

The move is a good one, because, according to Evan Kaplan, vice president of licensing and business development for the MLBPA, "certain businesses could go away for us, but baseball cards will always be essential" (Chozick, 2012, p. B4). To keep something so essential for Topps, MLB, and its players, innovations such as these must continue to emerge.

Marketing

Endorsements

The heart of the sporting goods industry, as Albert Spalding first demonstrated, is the concept that expert usage helps overcome the risk factors customers assess when deciding on a purchase. Spalding sold consumers on the fact that his ball was the one used by the best baseball league in the world, conveying to buyers that if it's good enough for the best, it's good enough for them. The concept of endorsements in sport was born.

Today, this concept continues. Most athletic footwear companies spend huge amounts on star athletes. Consider the case of professional golfers and their selection of on-course apparel for competitions. For years, the looks sported by the golfers on the PGA Tour were dismissed by many as staid and boring. Recently, however, an increasing number of PGA pros are wearing more flamboyant ensembles, with designers such as Ralph Lauren pushing its players like Davis Love III and Webb Simpson to wear bright pink pants (actually termed "Bubblicious" by the maker), paired with pastel striped shirts. Clothing companies often script the outfits for their golfers at major tournaments.

"They tell me, 'Look, we sell more pink pants whenever you wear the pink pants,'" said Love (Macur, 2011, p. Y6). "Frankly, I'm not a fan of yellow or pink pants, but if they give them to me—and they do—I wear them. I figure they know better than me" (Macur, 2011, p. Y6). Dustin Johnson, however, draws the line at wearing orange. Why? "I don't like orange," he explained (Macur, 2011, p. Y6). When Rickie Fowler (outfitted by Puma), who made orange his signature color—an homage to his collegiate alma mater, Oklahoma State University—heard Johnson's remark, he said: "I've got to talk to him about that. Everybody needs some orange, man" (Macur, 2011, p. Y6). A writer for *Golf Digest* defends the approach this way: "People have to dress their personality . . . and there's nothing wrong with that" (Macur, 2011, p. Y6). British golfer Ian Poulter, who once wore pants with the Union Jack British flag design (channeling the same theme used by Under Armour at Maryland), summed up his sartorial choices this way: "I wanted to liven up golf . . . What I always say is, 'Look good, feel good, play good'" (Pennington, 2012, p. D7).

When Davis Love III modeled for his wife the look Ralph Lauren had proposed, her reaction was, "You've got to be kidding me" (Macur, 2011, p. Y6), but the issue of fashion seems to be less controversial on the LPGA Tour, as evidenced by "The 18 best-dressed ladies on the tour" list recently posted on the website Bleacher Report (number one, by the way, was Paula Creamer, who, ironically, often features pink in her on-course attire) (Burke, 2011). Writer Bill Pennington (2012) opined that "getting the right outfit on television for the final round of a women's major championship remains important to marketing" (p. D7). Colors and prints are not always the issue, however. Creamer explained that women's designers only recently began putting functional pockets on their shorts, skirts, and pants for storing tees and ball markers: "Thank goodness they've learned that you can hide the pockets and still be stylish," she said (Pennington, 2012, p. D7).

The Challenges of Creating a Brand

Throughout the chapter we have discussed some of the iconic sport figures who have influenced the sporting goods and licensed product industries. Most of the names are familiar to you and others across the globe. But what about Li-Ning? Doesn't ring a bell? Li-Ning is a male gymnast, described by writer Joe Nocera as "a Michael Jordanesque figure" in his home country of China, having won three gold medals in the 1984 Los Angeles Summer Olympic Games. Six years later, he used his image to found an eponymous athletic footwear company. In 2008, the company was generating $700 million a year in revenues. Nocera (2008) describes a visit to the company's headquarters this way:

> Almost everything about Li-Ning feels like your basic modern sneaker company: the airy, wide-open campus; the casually dressed young executives bustling about; the rows of basketball and tennis courts under construction; the huge posters of Chinese Olympians and other athletes who have endorsed Li-Ning shoes and clothing like the tennis player Ivan Ljubicic and, believe it or not, Shaquille O'Neal. (p. B1)

The company has even adopted a positioning statement (i.e., a slogan)—"Anything is possible"—which seems like a corrected Chinese translation of Adidas' grammatically off-kilter "Impossible is nothing," and a logo that, according to Nocera, looks like Nike's swoosh "except with a checkmark stuck at the front of it" (Nocera, 2008, p. B8). In addition, the Shaq figure stamped on his branded line of Li-Ning

shoes (costing $120) looked to Nocera (2008) "an awful lot like Nike's Air Jordan figure" (p. B8). Those who saw Shaq play before his retirement know that to believe the play of the two is equal would truly mean that "Anything is possible."

According to the company's chief operating officer, Guo Jianxin, by 2013 the company wants to achieve revenues of $2 billion, with 20% of that coming from international sales (in 2008, only 1% came from outside China). "But to get there," said Nocera (2008), "Li-Ning will have to become a brand like Nike or Adidas" (p. B8). But what does that mean? Note that a brand's image is defined as "the cumulative impact of all the associations with a particular brand" (Keller, 1998, p. 93), and is formed for sport organizations by a collection of elements that can include logos, players, traditions, facilities, rivalries, and ownership (Gladden, 2007). Li-Ning may have positive scores on all of these factors for Chinese consumers, but what about for Americans? Or Brazilians, Germans, or South Africans?

Even in China, "there is a powerful sense among Chinese consumers that domestic brands are inferior" (Nocera, 2008). This has been a problem for Li-Ning, because its domestic market share has dropped against Nike and Adidas since the late 1990s, when each was first allowed to sell products in China. So if Chinese companies such as Li-Ning have trouble connecting with their own consumers against established foreign brands, how will they compete against these brands in international markets? A branding consultant hired to help Li-Ning with its branding challenges notes, "I said to the Li-Ning executives, 'What does it mean to when you wear a Li-Ning shoe?'" (Nocera, 2008, p. B8), trying to show them that **branding** wasn't just about copying Nike, but to create a distinct identity. "They couldn't define it," the consultant said (Nocera, 2008, p. B8). For the time being, the company has put its international plans on hold, focusing instead on domestic markets in cities that Nike and Adidas have not penetrated with shoes that have a patriotic Chinese focus. One recent shoe is named for Lei Feng, a famous Chinese soldier glorified by the Chinese government after his death in 1962 (allegedly the soldier had kept a diary that showed how he had been inspired by Communist party head Mao Tse-Tung to do good deeds and to hate "class enemies") (Chang, 2006; Nocera, 2008). However, it won't be easy, because industry giant Nike is also setting its sights on the Chinese market, investing $1.5 billion in marketing there in 2009. Of these efforts, Nike CEO Mark Parker stated, "No matter how much you're investing (in China), it's not enough" (Horovitz, 2009, p. 2B).

As of late 2011, Li-Ning had experienced weak sales at its 900 domestic retail stores, and its stock price plunged, in part due to local competitors such as 361 Degrees. The company vowed to spend more on advertising and promotions to reverse the trend. The company has not given up on the U.S. market either. In 2012 the company announced an endorsement deal with NBA star Dwayne Wade, with shoes expected in stores in early 2013. "I am so proud to welcome Dwayne Wade to the Li-Ning family," said the company's founder. "I could not be more excited about developing a brand with him" (Sheridan, 2012, p. 1). The launch is planned for a collaborative footwear and apparel line called "WADE," which, according to writer Chris Sheridan, will serve as not only the company's foray into the United States, but also as "the centerpiece of the corporation's international basketball strategy" (Sheridan, 2012, p. 1).

Ethics

Manufacturer and Licensee Conduct

One of the most basic forms of global involvement occurs when a business turns to a foreign company to manufacture one or more of its products. This practice is called **global sourcing**, because the company turns to whatever manufacturer or source around the world will produce its products most cheaply. Companies that engage in global sourcing take advantage of manufacturing expertise or lower wage rates in foreign countries, and then sell their products either just in their home market or in markets around the world. Global sourcing is common in the clothing and footwear industries, for example, where companies in countries such as Mexico, China, and Malaysia have much lower production costs because workers are paid at much lower wage rates than workers in the United States. The foreign producer or source manufactures the product to a particular company's specifications and then attaches the company's label or logo to the product. Nike, Reebok, Benetton, and Banana Republic are examples of companies that do a great deal of global sourcing. Many sport apparel and shoe manufacturers have come under fire for paying unfairly low wages and having unsafe working conditions in their overseas operations, particularly in Asian nations. One consumer advocacy group sued Nike, saying that its claims of the fairness of its global sourcing practices were false, with the U.S. Supreme Court opting to have the case heard in California state court (Greenhouse, 2003).

Industry giants Adidas, Nike, and Puma have been universally and repeatedly criticized for paying low wages and treating workers poorly. The most recent case involved evidence of managers in Bangladeshi sweatshops verbally and physically abusing workers. At one supplier for Puma, two-thirds of workers claimed they had been beaten or slapped, and women working for Nike and Adidas reported sexual harassment incidents. Workers for all three companies also had to work illegally long hours for less than the established minimum wage (about $1.50 a day), with some working for as little as 12 cents an hour (Chamberlain, 2012).

All three companies dispute the claims or promise to address concerns. A Nike spokesperson told *The Guardian* that the company "takes working conditions in our factories very seriously. All Nike suppliers must adhere to our code of conduct . . . we will get back to you as soon as someone . . . has made an assessment" (Chamberlain, 2012, p. 1).

Finance

Returning to a Market

In 2012 the NFL chose to work with Nike to produce its uniforms and on-field apparel for the next 5 years. The NFL is likely looking to capitalize on Nike's position as a market leader to help promote its brand. The same is also true for Nike, because the NFL is the most popular professional sport league in the United States. However, the recent debut of the new NFL–Nike uniforms was met with a resounding yawn by experts and the media. Only the Seattle Seahawks look was significantly altered, but to many it looked a lot like the garb worn by the University of Oregon. Nike personnel instead chose to focus more on the technical improvements of the new uniforms, including four-way stretch hydroponic materials on the sleeves, stretch twill numbers, and "aircraft-grade aluminum" in the belts (Tanier, 2012, p. B16). The new gear, Nike claims, will be 5% drier, 8% lighter, and 22% cooler than its predecessors (McGrath, 2012; Tanier, 2012).

What do the players think? Pittsburgh Steelers quarterback Ben Roethlisberger told reporters at the introductory press conference that he loved it. "Super light and, uh, stylish? . . . I don't know," said Roethlisberger, who also said the one clothing item he wanted most as a kid was a pair of Jordan-brand shoes (McGrath, 2012, p. 42). Tampa Bay Buccaneers running back LaGarrett Blount was less enthused with the look his team retained. "I have to talk with the [owners]. I think we need to be kind of trendy, because we are one of the younger teams" (Tanier, 2012, p. B13).

Nike is also seeking to partner with the NFL so it can sell other products, such as coaches' and players' sideline apparel, as well as licensed apparel such as t-shirts and hats. This is where the relationship might be limiting for the NFL. On a recent visit to the Nike retail store in San Francisco, one could view a full range of new Nike-licensed apparel. All of the individual team products were nearly identical in design, save for team logos and colors, making it seem like the products were Nike-first and the NFL connection was an afterthought. In addition, the store heavily promoted products of those players who had endorsement deals with Nike, as well as former NFL players with Nike connections, such as Bo Jackson. With this deal, it seems reasonable to ask—just exactly who is working for whom? The NFL has 5 years to learn whether the Nike deal makes sense for its purposes.

Legal

Antitrust and Licensing Agreements

In 2000, the NFL signed a 10-year, $250 million deal with Reebok to be its exclusive provider of licensed apparel, ending deals with other companies. One of the companies spurned in the wake of the Reebok deal, American Needle (founded in 1918 and the first company to sell licensed headwear, and also was an official supplier to many MLB teams beginning in the 1940s), sued the NFL, arguing that based Section 1 of the Sherman Act, the NFL and Reebok were conspiring to stifle competition and inflate prices. American Needle argued that immediately after the Reebok deal was signed prices for NFL licensed products rose. In 2008, a unanimous three-judge panel of the U.S. Court of Appeals for the Seventh Circuit, in Chicago, ruled for the NFL on the grounds that the league is a single entity (Belson, 2010; Belson & Schwarz, 2010).

The properties divisions of the professional leagues have for decades negotiated such deals on behalf of all member franchises. These actions have been based on an exemption granted by the federal government that they can work as a single entity to negotiate broadcast deals. This "single-entity" approach is the concept American Needle sought to challenge in its suit, especially because its sales dropped 25% after the Reebok deal. Company president Robert Kronenberger (grandson of the company's founder who had convinced reluctant Chicago Cubs owner Philip Wrigley to let him sell Cubs caps at Wrigley Field on consignment), said of the suit: "For me, it's a principled thing. We just want to be competitive. I understand that it's probably a business decision. It's just black and white and this is wrong . . . It's not just headwear. It could be beyond that: television, concessions, food, beer. It's not just about me" (Belson, 2010, p. B15).

Kronenberger's comments were not merely the rhetoric of a jilted plaintiff. Industry experts believed that if the NFL was successful in defending its status in the case, and it was found exempt from Section 1 of the Sherman Act, it could extend its league-wide deals to stadium concessionaires, vendors, and parking operators, agreements currently managed by individual franchises. This could, potentially, drive up the cost of attending games. It could also mean that, according to legal experts, professional leagues could be empowered to unilaterally impose labor agreements when bargaining with players unions. But legal experts also believe if the case were decided in favor of American Needle, all professional leagues could lose their single-entity status exemption in negotiating labor agreements with players unions and broadcast agreements. However, one legal scholar did not think an NFL win would mean a future with $200 licensed fleece sweatshirts, because "people would just go buy a baseball sweatshirt instead" (Belson & Schwarz, 2010, p. B15).

In January 2010, after the NFL won at the trial and appeals court level, the U.S. Supreme Court heard arguments from both sides on the case. The NFL had actually joined with American Needle in asking for the review, an action taken, according to one legal expert, "because they think they can win" (King, 2010, p. 9). Some experts felt the NFL could count on four of the nine sitting justices at the time—Chief Justice John Roberts and Justices Samuel Alito, Antonin Scalia, and Clarence Thomas—and would not get two others—Justices John Paul Stevens and Ruth Bader Ginsberg—such that the league would only need to convert one of the remaining three (Justices Stephen Breyer, Anthony Kennedy, and Sonia Sotomayor). Justice Sotomayor, named to the High Court in 2009 by President Barack Obama, has the most direct contact with pro league sports concerns, having issued an injunction as an appeals court judge against MLB owners in 1995, ending the player lockout that led to the cancellation of the 1994 World Series. She was also part of a three-judge appeals court panel that upheld the NFL's draft eligibility rule, which had been challenged by former Ohio State University running back

Maurice Clarett (Broughton, 2010). American Needle drew support from the existing players unions and the NFL Coaches Association, whereas the NFL had support from the NCAA, the NBA, the NHL and video game manufacturer Electronic Arts, which expressed concerns about the difficulty in negotiating agreements with each individual team, a move it felt would result in higher costs to consumers (Kaplan, 2010). Writer Bill King (2010) noted that a reversal in favor of American Needle would be in line with 30 years of lower court rulings that found leagues to be joint ventures, even as most courts have upheld the single-entity structure in those instances where it is seen to have benefitted consumers. An unsigned op-ed piece in *The New York Times* the day of the hearing sided with American Needle, stating, "the league is actually a cooperative effort of 32 separately owned, profit-making teams. They compete in everything from hiring to ticket sales. They should have to comply with Section 1" ("Football," 2010, p. A26)

At the hearing, which lasted 1 hour and 11 minutes, eight justices chose to ask questions (Justice Thomas, who customarily remains silent, posed no questions). The justices sought to get each side to suggest, in the words of Justice Kennedy, "a zone where we are sure a rule of reason inquiry . . . would be inappropriate?" (King & Kaplan, 2010, p. 28).

Neither side was willing to set parameters on how the Court should act, and one observer remarked after the hearing, "Both sides have to walk away from that argument not knowing what's going to come out of it because the questions were . . . off the wall [and] unfocused . . . There are simply no principle standards for deciding when sports leagues should be allowed to cooperate and when they should be allowed to compete" (King & Kaplan, 2010, p. 28).

Indeed, Justice Sotomayor said to NFL lead attorney Gregg Levy, "I am very much swayed by your arguments, but I can very much see a counter argument that promoting t-shirts is only to make money. It doesn't really promote the game. It promotes the making of money. And once you fix prices for making money, that's a . . . violation" (King & Kaplan, 2010, p. 28).

On May 23, 2010, the Court unanimously found in favor of American Needle. "The league's decision to license independently owned trademarks collectively to a single vendor," Justice Stevens wrote for the Court, deprived the marketplace "of actual or potential competition.....Although NFL teams have common interests such as promoting the NFL brand," Stevens continued, "they are still separate, profit-maximizing entities . . . Each of the teams is a substantial, independently owned and independently managed business. The teams compete with one another, not only on the playing field, but to attract fans, for gate receipts and for contracts with managerial and playing personnel" (Liptak & Belson, 2010, p. 1). In addition, Stevens wrote that teams certainly compete in the market for intellectual property: "To a firm making hats, the [New Orleans] Saints and the [Indianapolis] Colts are two potentially competing suppliers of valuable trademarks" (Liptak & Belson, 2010, p. 1).

The ruling did not resolve the lawsuit. The Court said American Needle's claims were not barred at the outset but must rather be analyzed under a standard that antitrust lawyers call the "rule of reason" to determine whether the league's licensing practices harmed competition. The case will be returned to the lower courts. Robert Kronenberger said of the decision: "This is to protect competition and consumers and right a wrong. We hope to prevail, but we'll see what happens" (Liptak & Belson, 2010, p. 1).

Summary

This chapter considers two growing and expanding segments of the sport industry:

sporting goods and licensed products. Three product categories comprise the sporting goods industry segment: equipment, athletic footwear, and apparel. Several trade associations assist sporting goods professionals, the largest of which is the SFIA.

The licensed product industry continues to generate significant revenues. Teams and leagues earn a certain percentage of sales, called royalties, on items bearing logos. Leagues and players associations administer licensing programs on the professional level. Colleges may administer their own licensing programs

or may enlist the services of organizations such as IMG College. Individuals are needed to work in many capacities in both the sporting goods and licensed products industries. These areas cut across many other segments of the sport industry, including professional sport, intercollegiate athletics, recreational sport, and the health and fitness industry. Wherever there is a need for equipment to play a sport or a need for the right clothing to announce that a person is a fan of a particular team, the sporting goods industry and the licensed product industry become pivotal.

Case Study 18-1 Less Is More

New Balance (NB), the privately held footwear and apparel manufacturing company headquartered in Brighton, Massachusetts, has deliberately inched its way up in sales and growth in the last few years. NB benefited from the running boom of the 1970s, with sales growing from $200,000 annually to $80 million, and has found a niche with middle-aged and older consumers who were more concerned with performance than fashion. Consumers recognize NB as a leader in the athletic category and rate the company's products particularly high in comfort.

Following a few failed attempts at taking on Nike and becoming a flashy and "cool" brand to attract a bigger share of the market, NB chair and CEO Jim Davis said a lesson was learned: "If we try to be like everyone else, if we try to stress fashion over quality or marketing over performance, we won't be successful" (Reidy, 2005, p. E4). This sustainable approach to growth has allowed NB to retain its core market; however, because of its focus on quality, younger consumers are now discovering the brand and boosting sales. Even with this controlled focus, NB's domestic footwear sales reached 30 million pairs recently.

NB is not averse to innovation and responding to changes in the marketplace. One such example of this is in the running shoe market, where sales have increased over the past several months. This spurt is not from sales of traditional models, but rather from so-called "barefoot" or "minimal" shoes. You might own a pair or you might have seen someone wearing these minimal shoes, such as the FiveFingers model made by Vibram, which has articulated toes and thin, pliable soles. Sales for this new style of shoe, which is quite different from that of the traditional thick-soled and padded shoe, was prompted in part by *Born to Run*, the best-selling book by Christopher McDougal. The book describes how a tribe of Tarahumara Indians in Mexico run distances exceeding 100 miles wearing thin sandals and has encouraged many to try the new minimal shoes (Newman, 2011).

(continues)

Case Study 18-1   Less Is More (Continued)

Although only 29 years old, Bronwen Morrison is an industry veteran. When she first came out of her undergraduate sport management degree program, she took a job with the Liberty Sports Group, where she had interned while in college, and managed the launch of the "Beckster," a skateboarding shoe targeted toward the market's smaller grassroots users where companies such as Grenade tend to dominate. The shoe was a modest success, so much so that Morrison, when spotted wearing a throwback 1976 San Diego Padres jersey at the sporting goods Super Show in Atlanta, was asked to head the creation of a line of throwback-inspired urban fashion clothes for women by Trey Luce, creator and owner of Thugstaz. The line, which would be dubbed "Hugstaz," was also a solid market success and put the line in positive competition with similar products by Ecko and other urban fashion companies. Bronwen then went on to work at the apparel retail chain Lululemon Athletica (which describes its products as "yoga-inspired athletic apparel"), helping the company create a product line targeted toward men.

Her next professional challenge brought her back to the footwear market, specifically to NB, to increase sales for the company's "Minimus" line of minimal running shoes. Her new boss, Katherine Petrecca, manager of the Minimus line, has charged Bronwen with creating a plan for NB to increase sales of this new line. In a her first conversation with Bronwen, Katherine noted that competitor brands such as Vibram and TerraPlana sell minimal shoes only, whereas NB sells a wide range of running shoes. "We have to sell 'minimal' without hurting sales on the rest of our product line," said Katherine, and also warned Bronwen that she needed to "consider the trickiness of working with a supplier [Vibram outsoles] while technically competing against them in the market [Vibram FiveFingers]."

When Bronwen began to research the topic, and wondered why the Vibram shoe was not called "FiveToes" (rather than "FiveFingers"), she learned quickly that she faced another challenge: Not only was she looking to a shoe, but she also had to deal with the way the shoe impacted the runner. She came across an article by Gina Kolata (2012) of *The New York Times*, who wrote: "It's a topic of endless debate among runners. Is there a best way to run, so that you use the least energy and go the fastest? And does it help to run barefoot or in minimalist shoes?" (p. 1). Proponents of minimal shoes, wrote Kolata (2012), claim "barefoot running is more natural—humans evolved to run without shoes—and economical. When you lift a shod foot, you have to lift the weight of the shoe, and that requires energy. Added to that effort is the cushioning in shoes, which absorbs energy that should go into propelling you forward. If you must wear shoes, the argument goes, the next best thing to barefoot running is to strike the ground with the midfoot and not the heel" (p. 1).

Kolata (2012) then cited a study performed by a biomedical researcher who studied elite runners in conjunction with USA Track & Field, who noted that runners used any number of running styles: "Some landed on the midfoot. A few landed on the forefoot. Some twisted their feet inward as they struck the ground, while others kept their feet straight…That is good news in a way, because studies have repeatedly shown that when people try to change their natural running style, they tend to use more energy to cover the same distance" (p. 1).

"OK," thought Bronwen, "is there any data that support running with minimal shoes?" She then noted that Kolata examined the question of shoe weight and cushioning and referenced another study that found runners who wore very lightweight shoes were more efficient than those who ran barefoot. The study concluded that 10 millimeters of cushioning was best, which is about the amount in many lightweight running shoes (Kolata, 2012).

Although Bronwen felt she understood a bit more about minimal shoes, she still had to determine whom to target, and why they would want not just minimal shoes, but NB's version.

Questions for Discussion

1. How can Bronwen begin to identify a main target market group for NB's Minimus line?

2. How can NB utilize retailers to help sell this new type of shoe?

3. How can NB utilize social media to support this sales effort?

4. How can NB utilize endorsements to support this sales effort?

5. Are there any concerns about manufacturer conduct that NB can promote as a part of this sales effort?

Resources

New Balance Athletic Shoes, Inc.
Corporate Headquarters
20 Guest Street, Suite 1000
Brighton, MA 02135
617-783-4000
http://www.newbalance.com

Nike
World Headquarters
One Bowerman Drive
Beaverton, OR 97005
503-671-6453
http://nikeinc.com

Puma
U.S. Headquarters
1 Congress Street, Suite 110
Boston, MA 02114
617-488-2900
http://www.puma.com

Reebok International Ltd.
1895 JW Foster Blvd.
Canton, MA 02021
781-401-5000
http://www.reebok.com

Sport and Fitness Industry Association (SFIA)
8505 Fenton Street, Suite 211
Silver Spring, MD 20910
301-495-6321
http://www.sfia.com

Topps
One Whitehall Street
New York, NY 10004
212-376-0300
http://www.topps.com

Under Armour
1020 Hull Street
Baltimore, MD 21230
www.underarmour.com

References

Barr, C. A., & Covell, D. (2010). *Managing intercollegiate athletics*. Scottsdale, AZ: Holcomb Hathaway.

Belson, K. (2010, January 7). American Needle: From green celluloid visors to caps of all kinds. *The New York Times*, p. B15.

Belson, K., & Schwarz, A. (2010, January 7). Antitrust case has implications far beyond NFL. *The New York Times*, pp. B13, B15.

Broughton, D. (2010, January 4–10). Sports and this court: How the nine sitting justices have ruled on industry-related cases. *Street & Smith's SportsBusiness Journal*, p. 10.

Burke, J. (2011, August 22). The 18 best-dressed ladies on the tour. *Bleacher Report*. Retrieved from http://bleacherreport.com /articles/814894-lpga-the-18-best-dressed -ladies-on-the-tour#/articles/814894-lpga -the-18-best-dressed-ladies-on-the-tour /page/19

Chamberlain, G. (2012, March 3). Olympic brands caught up in abuse scandal. *The Guardian*. Retrieved from: http://www.guardian.co.uk /business/2012/mar/03/olympic-brands -abuse-scandal?INTCMP=SRCH

Chang, J., with Halliday, J. (2006). *Mao: The unknown story*. New York: Anchor Books.

Chozick, A. (2012, April 9). Apps take positions in the Topps baseball lineup. *The New York Times*, pp. B1, B4.

Covell, D., & Walker, S. (2013). *Managing sport organizations: Responsibility for performance* (3rd ed.). New York: Routledge.

Davis, F. (1992). *Fashion, culture and identity*. Chicago: University of Chicago Press.

Duerson, A. (2007, March 19). Back on Topps. *Sports Illustrated*, p. 30.

Football and antitrust. (2010, January 13). *The New York Times*, p. A26.

Gladden, J. M. (2007). Managing sport brands. In B. J. Mullin, S. Hardy, & W.A. Sutton (Eds.), *Sport marketing* (3rd ed.) (pp. 171–187). Champaign, IL: Human Kinetics.

Goldstein, W. (1989). *Playing for keeps: A history of early baseball*. Ithaca, NY: Cornell University Press.

Graham, S. (2004, January 19–25). Kevin Plank's drive makes Under Armour an industry overachiever. *Street & Smith's SportsBusiness Journal*, pp. 8–9.

Greenhouse, L. (2003, June 27). Nike free speech case is unexpectedly returned to California. *The New York Times*, p. A15.

Hardy, S. (1995). Adopted by all the leading clubs: Sporting goods and the shaping of leisure. In D. K. Wiggins (Ed.), *Sport in America* (pp. 133–150). Champaign, IL: Human Kinetics.

Hardy, S. H. (1997). Entrepreneurs, organizations, and the sports marketplace. In S. W. Pope (Ed.), *The new American sports history* (pp. 341–365). Champaign, IL: University of Illinois Press.

Helyar, J. (1994). *Lords of the realm*. New York: Random House.

Hiestand, M. (2002, August 19). Sports gear so out of style it's in style. *USA Today*, p. 3C.

Horovitz, B. (2009, December 7). Nike CEO knows how to just do it. *USA Today*, pp. 1B–2B.

Kaplan, D. (2010, January 4–10). All four unions, credit-card issuers among the 'friends of the court' filing briefs in the case. *Street & Smith's SportsBusiness Journal*, p. 9.

Katz, D. (1993, August 16). Triumph of the Swoosh. *Sports Illustrated*, pp. 54–73.

Keller, K.L. (1998). *Strategic brand management: Building, measuring and managing brand equity.* Upper Saddle River, NJ: Prentice Hall.

King, B. (2010, January 4–10). Supreme Court weighs a game changer. *Street & Smith's SportsBusiness Journal*, pp. 1, 8–11.

King, B., & Kaplan, D. (2010, January 18–24). NFL, Needle, get their High Court moment. *Street & Smith's SportsBusiness Journal*, pp. 1, 28.

Kolata, G. (2012, October 15). Myths of running: Forefoot, barefoot and otherwise. *The New York Times.* Retrieved from http://well.blogs .nytimes.com/2012/10/15/myths-of-running -forefoot-barefoot-and-otherwise

Lanham Act, 15 U.S.C. § 1051–1127 (1946).

Levine, P. (1985). *A. G. Spalding and the rise of baseball: The promise of American sport.* New York: Oxford University Press.

Licensed sports. (2012). Part 8: An insider's guide to the world of licensed sports products: Royalty rates—is 12% the norm and when 12% isn't enough. Retrieved from http:// license dsports.blogspot.com/2012/03 /insiders-guide-to-world-of- licensed_2802 .html

Lipsey, R. (Ed.). (1996). *Sports market place.* Princeton, NJ: Sportsguide.

Liptak, A., & Belson, K. (2010, May 24). N.F.L. fails in its request for antitrust immunity. *The New York Times.* Retrieved from http://www .nytimes.com/2010/05/25/sports/football /25needle.html

Macur, J. (2011, June 19). The fairway as runway. *The New York Times*, p. Y6.

Martin, E. (2012, May 3). New Balance wants its tariffs. Nike does not. *Bloomberg Businessweek.* Retrieved from http://www .businessweek.com/articles/2012-05-03/new -balance-wants-its-tariffs-dot-nike-doesnt

McCarthy, M. (2008, December 9). Under Armour is making a run at Nike. *USA Today*, p. 1C.

McGrath, B. (2012, April 16). On the runway: Inquisition. *The New Yorker*, pp. 40, 42.

New uniforms kick off debate. (2011, September 7). *USA Today*, p. 7C.

Newman, A. A. (2011, July 28). Appealing to runners, even the barefoot brigade. *The New York Times*, p. B3.

Nichols, M. A. (1995, April). A look at some of the issues affecting collegiate licensing. *Team Licensing Business*, 7(4), p. 18.

Nike. (2014). Nike, Inc. reports fiscal 2012 fourth quarter and full year results. Retrieved from http://nikeinc.com/earnings/news/nike-inc -reports-fiscal-2012-fourth-quarter-and-full -year-results

Nocera, J. (2008, April 12). China tries to solve its Brand X blues. *The New York Times*, pp. B1, B8.

O'Brien, G. (2002, June). Elements of style: A smashing shirt. *GQ*, p. 61.

Oznian, M. (2011, October 3). The Forbes Fab 40: The world's most valuable sports brands. *Forbes.* Retrieved from http://www.forbes .com/sites/mikeozanian/2011/10/03/the -forbes-fab-40-the-worlds-most-valuable -sports-brands-3

Pennington, B. (2012, July 9). Daring from tee to green: The clothes, not the shots. *The New York Times*, p. D7.

Plata, C. (1996). Ducks & dollars. *Team Licensing Business*, 8(6), 38.

Reidy, C. (2005, August 4). New Balance plots independent strategy. *The Boston Globe*, p. E4.

Roberts, D. (2011, October 26). Under Armour gets serious. *CNN Money.* Retrieved from http://management.fortune.cnn .com/2011/10/26/under-armour-kevin-plank

Rovell, D. (2014). Notre Dame Fighting Irish, Under Armour, agree to most valuable apparel contract in NCAA history. Retrieved from http://espn.go.com/college-football /story/_/id/10328133/notre-dame-fighting -irish-armour-agree-most-valuable-apparel -contract-ncaa-history

Say, J. B. (1964). *A treatise on political economy.* New York: Sentry Press.

Scorecard: Of a certain age. (2003, June 9). *Sports Illustrated*, p. 23.

Sheridan, C. (2012, October 10). D-Wade's new Li Ning shoes to available at a store near Yu. *Sheridan Hoops*. Retrieved from http://www.sheridanhoops.com/2012/10/10/d-wades-new-li-ning-shoes-to-be-available-at-a-store-near-yu/

Simmons, B. (2004, December 20). The sports guy. *ESPN Magazine*, p. 12.

Smit, B. (2008). *Sneaker wars: The enemy brothers who founded Adidas and Puma and the family feud that forever changed the business of sport.* New York: Ecco.

Smith, R. A. (Ed.). (1994). *Big-time football at Harvard, 1905: The diary of coach Bill Reid.* Champaign, IL: University of Illinois Press.

Sperber, M. (1993). *Shake down the thunder: The creation of Notre Dame football.* New York: Henry Holt.

Spiegel, J. E. (2008, February 7). Competition gaining on a niche market. *The New York Times*, p. C6.

Sport & Fitness Industry Association. (2013). About SFIA: Overview. Retrieved from http://www.sfia.org/about/overview

Sporting Goods Manufacturers Association. (2012, May 23). SGMA's wholesale study tallies $77 billion in sales. Retrieved from http://www.sfia.org/press/464_SGMA%27s-Wholesale-Study-Reports-$77%2B-Billion-In-Sales

Sports merchandising industry loses its creator, David Warsaw. (1996, July/August). *Team Licensing Business, 8*(5), 18.

Tanier, M. (2011, September 15). There's an exciting clash on the field. Oh, that's the uniform. *The New York Times*, pp. A1, B16.

Tanier, M. (2012, April 4). In Nike's rollout, flash everywhere but in the uniforms. *The New York Times*, p. B13.

The great American company: Brunswick. (2003, April). *FSB*, pp. 52–56.

Thorn, J. (2011). *Baseball in the Garden of Eden: The secret history of early games.* New York: Simon & Schuster.

Winn, L. (2009, August 24). The last iconic baseball card. *Sports Illustrated*, pp. 49–53.

Part V

Lifestyle Sports

Chapter 19 Golf and Club Management

Chapter 20 Recreational Sport

Chapter 19

Jo Williams

Golf and Club Management

Learning Objectives

Upon completion of this chapter, students should be able to:

1. Recognize the economic impact of golf courses and country clubs and the distinct imprint they leave on the landscape.

2. Illustrate the history of country clubs in the United States and understand the importance of golf in their development.

3. Distinguish between public and private clubs as well as private equity and non-equity clubs.

4. Describe the basic organizational structure of a club.

5. Analyze the market drivers that influence the demand for golf and country club services and understand the role that market segmentation plays in industry performance.

6. Identify the key skills needed to be an effective manager and leader in a golf and country club setting.

7. Recognize the career opportunities available in the golf and country club industry and the various educational programs designed to train professionals for the industry.

8. Discuss current issues of importance in the golf course and country club segment such as how to encourage participation by women and children, reducing the time needed to play a round of golf, the expense of joining a private club, sustainability and environmental concerns, and the impact of emerging technologies.

Introduction

Golf courses and country clubs operate as a significant international sport and business, attracting an estimated 80 million players on close to 40,000 golf courses throughout the world ("Golf's 2020 Vision," 2012). In the United States, approximately 26 million Americans play golf on nearly 16,000 courses (National Golf Foundation, 2013). Few sports leave as distinctive an imprint on the landscape as the golf course and the country club. In addition, it is one of the few sports where the playing field is not standardized, but differs from course to course and even from day to day. During the last quarter of the twentieth century, the number of golfers increased four times faster than the nation's population, from 10 million golfers to over 30 million (Napton & Laingen, 2008). Since then, golf courses and clubs have been challenged by economic and societal changes that have impacted demand and have forced the industry to reevaluate its management and marketing practices.

Golf courses and country clubs come in two major forms: public and private. This distinction is important. Private courses, especially country club facilities, outnumbered public courses until 1960. These private courses were popular because the game had evolved from being played solely by the American social elite who had brought it here from Scotland in the late 1800s. The evolution of the country club and the development of more public access courses and facilities created periods of rapid growth and a coming of age for the modern era of golf and club management. The game and its management for the general public at both private and public facilities are now considered to be in a mature phase of the game's life cycle (IBISWorld, 2013).

Golf courses throughout the United States have developed into business operations that require managers with a broad understanding of the golf industry. These managers must also recognize and understand the impact of a range of current issues. Declining demand, changes in lifestyles and family expectations, the need for sustainability, and technological advances have changed the industry. Declines in participation rates and closures of approximately 500 golf courses during the last decade have also forced managers and industry leaders to think differently about how these businesses are operated (Mona, Beditz, & Steranka, 2011). A number of programs have been initiated in an attempt to develop more golfers of all ages and ethnicities. Golf 2.0, The First Tee, Women's Golf Month, and Tee it Forward are examples of programs that aim to make golf more accessible and enjoyable.

History

The **country club** originated about 120 years ago and was conceived by affluent Americans, the overwhelming majority of whom were of Protestant and British ancestry. Today membership in exclusive private country clubs has spread to virtually every ethnic and religious group and to most other nations around the world (Gordon, 1990).

The American economic and political climate of the nineteenth century respected individualism and eschewed inherited nobility and the caste system of Europe. Many Americans had generated wealth and independence during the Industrial Revolution and from them rose a new entrepreneurial class. Rockefeller, Carnegie, Morgan, Vanderbilt, and others became the names of legend. By the 1880s, the United States had become the headquarters of the international banking system. This created a moneyed class of individuals who sought to spend time with people of their own kind, away from average citizens of modest means. This new economic elite was built on entrepreneurship and the principles of freedom and hard work. These wealthy businessmen began to emulate the behaviors of the formerly scorned privileged and noble classes of their British ancestors (Moss, 2001; Gordon, 1990; Miller, 1978).

Ironically, the American country club got its start because the economic elite lacked one of the central social institutions of the British aristocracy: the country house or estate. These estates were sources of wealth and privilege and also where they entertained other members of the British elite. In contrast, the American entrepreneurs and businessmen worked and lived in the city. They had no rural roots, but they yearned for a peaceful environment outside the hectic and polluted central city. Wealthy Americans began to seek destinations outside of the metropolitan areas and built private estates and summer homes in such places as Newport, Rhode Island, along the Hudson River north of New York City in the Catskill Mountains, and at the end of rail lines near urban areas. Thus, the time was now right for America's wealthy entrepreneurial class to enjoy the pleasures of its success. Opportunities and facilities were needed where they could express their wealth and engage in recreational activities, and the country club concept was born (Moss, 2001; Gordon, 1990; Miller, 1978).

Founded in 1882, The Country Club of Brookline, located near Boston, Massachusetts, is considered to be the first country club in the United States. It initially offered outdoor activities such as horseback riding. It built a small golf course in 1893 that was then expanded to 18 holes in 1899. Although the *country club movement* was a novel concept in the 1880s, members and guests of Brookline and other country clubs also sought another concept, that of *sportsmanship*. The rules of sportsmanship were established in the 1880s at Yale, but the concept was perfected and played out on the golf course. Country clubs met a need for a gentlemen's outlet where true sportsmanship

could be observed and played regularly and not limited to gifted athletes or hired professionals.

The country club became a highly successful concept that was copied in record numbers throughout the United States. The successful formula remains largely intact today. A *country club* is a place located in a country-like setting, with open areas and lots of green space, that also has a standard meeting facility—the clubhouse. Members go to the country club to enjoy sports and sportsmanship, engage in activities for the pursuit of happiness, develop friendships, and comingle with friends and like-minded others in peaceful surroundings. The Country Club of Brookline epitomized this formula for success. Its membership emphasized "true sport promoted and practiced by true sportsmen, true gentlemen and true friends" (Gordon, 1990; Miller, 1978). Today, The Country Club in Brookline is best known as the place where the game of golf was popularized in the United States. It has hosted a number of events, including the 1913, 1963, and 1988 U.S. Open Tournaments, a number of U.S. amateur events, and the 1999 Ryder Cup.

The Game of Golf and Golf Course and Club Development

The game of golf originated with the Scottish players and founders of the Royal and Ancient Golf Club of St. Andrews, Scotland. Construction of facilities for the sport of golf evolved quickly in the United States. Napton and Laingen (2008) document four major periods of golf course construction and development from 1878 through 2000. The game was first introduced to the U.S. market in Yonkers, New York, with the Apple Tree Gang, where the first small, three-hole course was built, also named St. Andrews. In 1895, the United States Golf Association (USGA) was formed and contributed greatly to the transformation of golf from a purely recreational game to a competitive sport. From 1878 to 1919, the growth of new golf courses and country clubs were concentrated primarily in *golf club villages* located on urban fringes. During this time, 962 courses were built, mostly private country clubs (Napton & Laingen, 2008). In 1914, the Club Managers Association of Boston was formed. At the same time in New York a similar organizational effort among club managers was taking place. These organizations ultimately formed the **Club Managers Association of America (CMAA)** and the **Professional Golfers Association (PGA)** (Morris, 2002). Today, more than 27,000 golf professionals are members of the PGA (PGALinks, 2013a).

Many new golf courses were built in the 1920s following World War I, but this growth spurt was slowed by World War II and the subsequent worldwide economic depression from 1929 to the early 1940s. Construction of the classic Augusta National golf course occurred in Georgia in 1932, setting a new standard in golf course design (Napton & Laingen, 2008). Golf was well positioned for a dramatic growth period corresponding with the increase in leisure time and affluence of the 1950s and 1960s. During these two decades, an upwardly mobile, wealthy growing population wanted to leave behind the Great Depression, war memories, and the polluted and decaying central cities in favor of open areas of land and the game of golf. During this period, 5,558 new golf courses were built (Napton & Laingen, 2008). The 1970s and 1980s saw a maturation and subsequent saturation of golf and the country club market and a slowdown in the number of new courses. Professional golf tours featuring popular players such as Jack Nicklaus and Arnold Palmer began to enjoy larger crowds.

The boom period of the 1990s saw additional growth that rivaled that of the 1960s. An important difference between the boom periods of the 1960s and the 1990s was the type of courses that were built. The courses built in the 1960s were generally affordable public courses, but those built in the 1990s were mostly courses with expensive daily fees or limited to those living in private gated communities. These differences had a negative impact on the growth rate of golf. From 2000 to 2008, many private clubs were converted to public facilities. A large number of these facilities were converted to a management contract, meaning that they were taken over by large golf management companies such as American Golf. From 2005 to 2010, 713 golf courses (18-hole equivalents) closed for business, and further decline is projected through 2020 (Mona et al., 2011).

Types of Clubs

The two major categories of clubs where recreational activities such as golf, tennis, or other sports are pursued are the public club and the private club. They differ in terms of access, membership, operation philosophy, profit motive, market orientation, and organizational structure.

A **public club** is like any typical business that is open to the public. Some of these clubs compete aggressively for members or business sponsorship in a public setting. Individuals and members are welcome to play or use the facilities if they can pay the required course fee. Some people are members, but the club is largely a public accommodation facility, welcoming participants from nearly all backgrounds to play golf and enjoy the club's offerings. Public golf facilities are typically just golf courses with very limited services. Some offer additional revenue-producing facilities, such as tennis or swimming, and a limited food and beverage outlet. A number of public facilities have banquet areas to support golf outings.

Public clubs that are privately owned for-profit enterprises also exist, with many providing high-end daily fee, resort, and destination experiences that are open to all socioeconomic classes to enjoy. In fact, until recently one of the fastest growing concepts in the golf sector was the high-end, daily fee public course. Public health clubs, day spas, and health spas, including many large hotel chains that have club concepts in their operations, now operate in this market. Luxury resorts, time share community club concepts, and hotels are replicating the *club experience* and compete aggressively for this business.

A **private club** restricts it membership and may either be a private for-profit entity or a private nonprofit entity. **Private exclusive clubs** go one step further by restricting membership to only those who are invited to join or become a member by a vote of the current existing membership. Although money may be an important factor in why a person joins a private country club, it is not the sole reason. Compatibility and like-mindedness with the membership are equally as important.

A private club can be defined as follows:

1. A place that is not open to the public.

2. A member or an individual must be accepted by the rest of the membership before he or she can join. Once accepted, the new member usually must pay an initiation fee and then continuing monthly membership dues. Some clubs also have minimum spending requirements for members (e.g., members must spend a certain amount of money each month or year in the club's food and beverage outlets).

3. It has a standard meeting place, typically a clubhouse, that is critical to its operation.

4. It is a place where comingling of social, recreational, or educational purposes occurs (Premier Club Services, 2010).

A *public accommodation club* or *private for-profit club*, in contrast, is open to the public, may have special membership plans, may advertise and compete readily for the public to use and enjoy its facilities, and typically does not restrict the number of potential users except for capacity issues. Private exclusive clubs are provided tax breaks and have restrictions on how they may compete in the public marketplace. For example, private exclusive clubs may not advertise (Premier Club Services, 2010).

People join private clubs for a variety of reasons. Some like the exclusive atmosphere of the club and see membership as a statement of social position or social class. Others join because of the recreational facilities, because the club is convenient for their types of interests, or because it is part of or close by their neighborhood. Others view club membership as a way to get ahead in business because people in their professions are also members or because their clubs give them an impressive place to entertain clients. Other people join clubs because their parents and grandparents were club members and club membership is a family tradition. These are typically called **legacy members**. Others simply enjoy the personal recognition and service they receive at a private club.

There are restrictions on what types of clubs can accept corporate memberships. Exclusively private, nonprofit clubs do not accept corporate memberships; they accept only individuals and families.

Private clubs are built for a variety of reasons. U.S. clubs that began in the nineteenth century or earlier were often started by a small group of individuals who decided to each put up a sum of money to buy a piece of land or an already-existing building and began the club for purely social reasons. Modern-day private clubs are built by developers (residential, resort, and freestanding facilities) as a way to help them sell homes, attract visitors, or target high-level playing communities. In such instances, the club and its golf course are the centerpiece of a housing development, and individuals who buy the homes surrounding it are either automatically members or have the option to become members. A resort type of course may be one of several centerpiece attractions to attract people to a vacation destination.

The unique environment of a signature-designed golf course and the historic sighting of the facility are all part of the major appeal for club members. Private clubs tend to have the best clubhouse furnishings in a state-of-the-art golf facility as well as impressive, well-kept grounds designed especially for playability. Most offer other recreational facilities as well. Furthermore, the goal of most private clubs is to provide a level of service that is rarely found elsewhere, which is created to keep the individual in a membership experience that will last a lifetime.

Today, all of a private club's facilities face competition from public and resort facilities. Clubs are also restricted in some of the services they can provide to their members due to tax regulations and other competitive advantages. Still, there is demand for the private club and the typical food service and recreation it offers. Competitors for a club's food and beverage outlets include high-end gourmet restaurants, corporate chain restaurants, sports bars, and even fast-food restaurants. Private clubs typically have multiple food outlets ranging from fine dining rooms to casual pubs or grill rooms, snack bars at the pool complex, and quick-service outlets on the golf course or in mobile units roaming the course.

Ownership Models

There are basically two types of ownership in the golf and club management industry: member-owned clubs called **equity clubs** and non-member-owned clubs called **non-equity clubs**. Equity clubs are owned by the members and typically have nonprofit status. This does not mean that such clubs are not profitable, rather it means that no individual or group of individuals or corporate entity may benefit from the income or profit from the club. The money earned must be reinvested back into the club. Most private exclusive clubs are **nonprofit 501(C)(7) clubs** as regulated by the U.S. Internal

Revenue Service (IRS). These are not open to the general public and are typically governed by a board of directors that is elected by the membership. Members are not only the customers and guests, they are also the owners or shareholders (i.e., they own equity in the club). Each member has a vote when deciding major club issues and admitting new members (unless the member has a type of membership that restricts voting privileges). Managers of these private exclusive clubs work directly for the members (Premier Club Services, 2010).

According to IRS regulations, nonprofit 501(c)(7) clubs are tax exempt from federal income tax liabilities, which provides substantial cost savings in taxes on an annual basis. For example, if a club earns $1 million in revenue after all expenses and is in the 46% corporate tax bracket, it would save 46%, or $460,000, in federal income taxes. In order to operate as a 501(c)(7) entity, the club must meet five criteria:

1. The club must be a club and organized for club purposes.

2. The club's purposes include being organized for pleasure, recreation, and other nonprofit purposes, and such purposes must be clearly stated in the articles of incorporation and in the club's bylaws.

3. Substantially all of the club's activities must be for pleasure, recreation, or other nonprofitable purposes (now called *the substantial rule,* replacing the exclusive rule in IRS standards).

4. There may be no inurnment, meaning no net earnings may benefit any one individual or group of shareholders.

5. The club's charter must not contain a provision that discriminates on the basis of race, color, or religion. Single-gender clubs (all male or all female) are permitted under the IRS rules (Premier Club Services, 2010; Part VII, Chapter 1, p. 2).

The regulations further require that a club files each year to retain and declare its 501(c)(7) status and must prove that its income is from member services. Failure to file or violation of these standards would require the club to pay back taxes on the previous 3 operating years at the prevailing rate, and the club would be taxed on full gross revenues, not the earnings after expenses and before taxes. Consequently, a 501(c)(7) private exclusive club is very highly regulated; detailed function sheets listing all members, nonmembers, and income must be maintained for each club event. Separate records for all member and nonmember income must be kept, and losses in event income may not be used to offset income or avoid taxes. If audited, the club must prove that each event held at the club was a member event (Premier Club Services, 2010).

When a 501(c)(7) private exclusive club hosts a major public event, such as a PGA Tour event or Ryder Cup Tournament, it is required to forego its 501(c)(7) status for the year and pay the appropriate taxes for the revenue realized during the income year. 501(c)(7) status must be documented and applied for each year, and being such a club one year does not automatically qualify that club to remain such forever (Premier Club Services, 2010).

Private for-profit equity clubs typically have a membership and are owned by an individual, group of individuals, partnership, or corporation and operated in such a manner as to earn a profit for the owners/investors. Members can sell their memberships for a profit or claim a loss should they leave the club during their lifetimes, but the income or loss is taxable. Non-equity clubs are owned by real-estate developers, corporations, individuals, or investment firms. These are taxed as a regular business according to their for-profit ownership type (Premier Club Services, 2010).

It is important to note that there are also a number of large corporations that own and operate hundreds of golf courses throughout the United States. These companies vary considerably in size and scope, with a few large corporations owning and operating hundreds of courses. Smaller companies may own and operate up to 20 courses, sometimes focusing on a specific region. There are also many stand-alone, single-course operations.

ClubCorp USA, Inc., Troon Golf, and American Golf Corporation are some of the larger corporations that operate within the golf market. ClubCorp USA is a private club operator that owns and operates 152 golf courses and country clubs. The company employs around 14,000 people and had estimated revenues of $541,700,000 in 2012. Troon Golf operates 180 courses worldwide, and American Golf Corporation owns/operates 95 courses, including public, private and resort courses. Many smaller companies manage everything from course design and construction to golf and dining operations (Business Insights Essentials, 2013).

Club Organizational Structure

A club's organizational structure depends, in part, on whether the club is an equity club, a private or nonprofit club, a private non-equity club, or a public club.

Management of Non-Equity and Public Course Clubs

The organizational structure of a non-equity club differs from an equity club's in that it is not owned by its members but is owned by an individual, group of investors, or a corporation. A non-equity club does not have a board of directors made up of club members. The club is managed and directed by the club's general manager, who follows the owner's policies rather than policies established by the club's members (Perdue, 2013).

Some non-equity clubs have an advisory board composed of club members (sometimes called a *board of governors*) and other member committees for the more important club areas (e.g., the clubhouse, golf course, and tennis facilities). However, these bodies typically have no policymaking authority, power, or direct authority. Depending on the scope of the advisory committee's recommendations, the management team and staff may act on the recommendations or simply pass them on to the owner(s) or ownership team for review. The general manager is usually given complete authority to operate the club and accept new members, subject to the owner's oversight and review.

Public golf courses and clubs operate in much the same way, with the general manager or management team typically reporting to a parks and recreation director who then reports to a government body entity that may be a board of selectmen, city manager, mayor, or county commissioner(s). Public courses may have an advisory board or committee that helps set policy, and these members may be appointed, elected, or serve on a volunteer basis.

Management of Equity Clubs

With equity private exclusive clubs, the club's members typically elect members from the membership to serve on the club's board of directors. The board of directors provides assistance and policy direction to the club's managers and carries out various other functions. These elected board members have various responsibilities, the most important of which is to establish club policy and hire the management team and general manager, who then will perform the day-to-day operational aspects of the club. The elected president appoints members to serve on the club's committees and calls and sets board meetings. The club's department managers, assistant management team, and professionals (i.e., the golf and tennis professionals and course superintendent) report directly to the general manager. The general manager then reports to the board. The

board reports directly to the members. At the top of the management hierarchy are the members. In the equity private exclusive club, the organizational structure is typically an inverted pyramid or hourglass shape, with the members at the top and the general manager at the midpoint of the hour glass, who then overseas a management team and staff (Perdue, 2013).

Board of Directors

Generally speaking, an equity club's **board of directors** (called a **board of governors** at some clubs) establishes club policies and governs the club. A club board is made up of directors (the number varies from club to club) and the club's officers, which include the president, vice president, secretary, and treasurer. The club's general manager attends board meetings but is not considered a board member and does not vote on policy. A board's specific duties and responsibilities are spelled out in each club's bylaws. Typical responsibilities include: establishing general operating policies; overseeing the financial stability of the club (which includes reviewing the club's financial statements, approving its operating budget, taking action if the budget is not being followed, and so on); voting on new member candidates; and handling member discipline problems, including voting on whether to suspend or expel members. Another very important responsibility of the board is to hire the club's general manager. The general manager works very closely with the board, making recommendations, helping to develop the agenda, keeping records, and orienting new members to the board and club. However, typically the general manager carries out the policies for the day-to-day operations of the club that have been set by the board members.

Executive Committee

If a club has an **executive committee**, it is usually composed of the club's officers. Sometimes the club's immediate past president is included, and the bylaws of some clubs permit the current president to appoint additional members if necessary. An executive committee usually has duties and responsibilities similar to those of the board of directors. It is essentially a "mini-board" that acts in lieu of the club's full board between board meetings and responds to issues that do not necessitate calling the whole board together (Perdue, 2013). The club's general manager typically participates in executive committee meetings as well as in meetings of the entire board, unless the committee is in executive session and/or reviewing the manager's or management team's performance(s).

Other Club Committees

In addition to these two major organizational structure components, a wide variety of other committees involve club members in decision making and implementing policy directives. These club committees exist to: (1) carry out the responsibilities assigned to them by the club's board or bylaws, (2) advise the board and help it carry out certain responsibilities and duties, (3) provide input and assistance to club managers, and (4) listen for suggestions and other feedback from members and act as liaisons between club members and the club's board and managers or management team (Perdue, 2013).

There are two types of club committees: standing and ad hoc. **Standing committees** are permanent committees that help the club conduct ongoing activities. **Ad hoc committees** are formed for a special purpose, such as assisting with a bigger-than-usual golf tournament, researching the club's history to prepare for a club's centennial celebration, or helping to plan and conduct a planning process for a major club renovation. Club committees can be very positive forces and provide an opportunity for the members to be more highly involved in the policy directives in the club and its operations. All club committee members should be provided orientations to the club's policies and

management team parameters to ensure the best possible working relationship between the committees, the board, and management. Some or all of these committees may or may not be found in a typical equity club, and there may be many other committees in larger, more complex, and diverse full-service clubs. The following standing committees are typically found in private exclusive clubs: strategic or long-range planning, finance, bylaws, nominating, membership, house, social, athletic, and golf course. Other ad hoc committees in a private exclusive club may include strategic planning, renovation, building, or a professional tour event committee. The ad hoc committees are formed for only short-term needs and for special reasons.

Golf and Country Club Industry Performance

Depending upon the source and method of data collection, the number of golf facilities in the United States varies. The latest statistics list 12,659 golf courses and country club facilities (establishments primarily engaged in operating golf courses, except miniature) in the United States (IBISWorld, 2013). They generate around $20 billion in annual revenues. The number of facilities in the United States has decreased each year from 2008–2013 and is projected to continue to do so at a rate of between 150 to 180 closures per year. In 2011, 157 courses were closed. In addition, the construction of new courses is at a historic low, with only 46 new courses being built in 2010 and 19 new courses in 2011 (Mona et al., 2011; "Course Closures," 2012) (see **Figure 19-1**). Golf participation in the United States was hit by the recession in the late 2000s and has now stabilized around 25.7 million golfers (National Golf Foundation, 2013).

Approximately 50% of all golfers are women, juniors, and minorities. Golf participation levels are also monitored for different types of players. In 2011, 14.4 million "core golfers" played

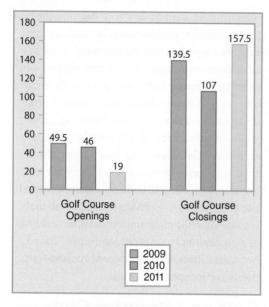

Figure 19-1 Golf Course Openings & Closings 2009–2011

Data from: GolfWeek (2012, March 19). Course closures. GolfWeek. Retrieved September 12, 2013, from http:// golfweek.com/news/2012/mar/19/ngf-course-closures -continue-market-correction/ and Mona, S., Beditz, J., & Steranka, J. (2011). The latest and greatest: Industry reports. Presented at the 2011 Golf20/20 Forum, May 10, 2011, St. Augustine, FL. Retrieved July 23, 2013, from http://www.golf2020.com/about-golf-2020/annual -forum/2011-conference.aspx

at least 8 rounds of golf a year, 11.3 million "occasional golfers" played one to seven rounds of golf a year, and 1.5 million "beginner golfers" played for the first time (Mona et al., 2011).

In 2011, the total number of golf rounds played decreased by 2.5%, falling from 475 million to 463 million (National Golf Foundation, 2013). However, the average number of rounds played per golfer increased from 16.8 in 2006 to 18.2 in 2010 (Mona et al., 2011). In 2012, almost every state experienced increases in rounds played, and PGA PerformanceTrak reported a 7% increase in playable days (days with favorable weather) nationwide. This increase in rounds played has been attributed to the rebound in the U.S. economy and growing consumer confidence (Mona et al., 2011).

Annual golf fee revenue per round is also considered to be a key factor in assessing the health of the game. When considering all facilities types, the average fee per round increased 1.9% from July 2012 to July 2013, averaging $26.10 (PGA PerformanceTrak, 2013).

Market Drivers

Market demand in the golf and country club industry is influenced by a number of factors, or *market drivers*, including:

- Participation and access to playing partners
- Number of courses and types of courses available to the playing public and private club members
- Condition of the course and the playing experience
- Demand for quality experiences and services
- Price to play a round of golf
- Available time to play a full 18-hole round of golf
- Seasonal play and weather patterns

Golf participation is a key driving factor in the demand for golf. As more people play, more facilities and services are needed, more equipment is purchased, and more soft goods (balls, shoe, clothing, etc.) are consumed. The growth in recent years of junior, women, and minority golfers also cannot be overlooked, because these trends may influence current and future demand for the game and facilities. The social nature of golf and the need for access to playing partners is an important element for many players. Clubs that promote leagues and socially focused programs can assist players in finding appropriate playing partners (Hatami, 2013).

The number and type of golf courses and country clubs available for participation also influences demand. Differing demographics, geographic location, and income levels impact the choices made by golfers in selecting courses to play. The overall condition of golf courses will also affect how regularly people play. As competition for the consumer has increased, clubs are striving to provide quality conditions and services to gain a competitive edge. This has directly led to golf course condition improvements and the demand from the golfing public for course beauty and action similar to what they have observed on televised PGA tournaments. New golf course maintenance technology improvements have enhanced the overall course design, layout, and playing conditions. These factors have contributed to a general demand for high-quality courses over the past few decades, which has challenged superintendents who are managing the costs of golf course maintenance (Williams, 2012).

The ability to afford and be associated with a high-quality or unique, long-standing exclusive club also influences membership demand. With this type of demand comes the status of being associated with a country club, especially a prestigious club with a waiting list. This status will influence overall demand for membership and, although membership in a country club may include both negative and positive connotations, the demand for these private exclusive, unique golf services, courses, and experiences has increased strongly over the past two decades. The long-standing tradition of a country club membership that drove the evolution of the country club cannot be underestimated (Perdue, 2013).

The cost of participation in a typical round of golf also affects demand. If fee increases are too rapid or too high, people may reduce or withhold paying for the increased costs, reduce their playing volume, trade down to lower cost alternatives, and/or simply seek different recreational pursuits. The impact of the economic downturn in the late 2000s was significant to the golf industry and led many courses to offer discounts to entice more people to play. This was seen as an unusual practice at that time but

as competition among clubs has increased more discount offers and packages can be found.

Other factors affecting demand include the popularity of other sports, including tennis and exercise activities; the availability of fitness centers at country clubs and more full-service facilities; the amount of leisure time available to people who play golf and other activities; the impact of weather on participation; the latent demand factor, or desire, to increase sport participation and fitness levels; and the success of U.S. golfers on the professional golf circuit (i.e., the "win on Sunday, play on Monday" syndrome) (Mona et al., 2011).

The seasonal use of clubs and the opportunity to play throughout the year varies substantially across various regions of the United States. Generally, usage of country club and golf facilities declines during the first (January to March) and fourth (October to December) quarters of the year in the northern climates, when colder temperatures and shorter days reduce the demand for golf. Usage may also decline in southern climates when temperatures become too hot to play, due to extremely high heat indices, humidity, threat of thunderstorms, and overall heat stress conditions. Typically, country clubs generate a greater share of their yearly revenues in the third and fourth quarters, which includes end-of-the-year tournaments, the holidays, and the year-end party season. As a result, firms usually generate a disproportionate share of revenues and cash flows in the second, third, and fourth quarters of each year and have lower revenues and profits in the first quarter (Perdue, 2013).

Golf demand may also be affected by nonseasonal and severe weather patterns. Periods of extremely hot, cold, or rainy weather in a given region can be expected to reduce golf-related revenue. Droughts and extended periods of low or reduced rainfall may affect the availability and cost of water needed to irrigate golf courses and to keep fairways, tee boxes, and especially greens in optimal playing conditions. Optimal playing conditions require turf grass to remain at a stable growing cycle to retain color and speed to carry the golf ball across playing surfaces. This requires significant amounts of water, fertilization, and maintenance. Conversely, too much rain, floods, and high winds or violent storms may reduce or interrupt golfing opportunities.

Market Segmentation

The golf industry considers many characteristics when analyzing the golf market. To fully understand golf consumers, their behaviors, and their needs and wants, it is necessary to identify meaningful market segments. A variety of demographic and psychographic data are used to develop segmentation models. Marketers use a variety of data, such as gender, ethnicity, education level, family status, spending on golf-related purchases, and household income, to gain a better understanding of each segment. The average golfer in the United States is approximately 41 years old with a household income of $85,000 and plays 18 rounds annually. The industry is dominated by male golfers, but the number of women who play is increasing ("Golf's 2020 Vision," 2012).

Frequency of play is a key factor in developing market segmentation models. The National Golf Course Owners Association (NGCOA), Golf 20/20 Executive Board, and other leading golf associations in the United States identify and define different segments of golfers based on rounds played per year. According to NGCOA (2013a), *avid golfers* play more than 25 rounds per year, *core golfers* play 8 to 24 rounds per year, *occasional golfers* play 1 to 7 rounds per year, and *beginning golfers* play for the first time. *Junior golfers* (children and teens ages 5 to 17 who play at least one round per year) are also identified as a distinct segment, recognizing the importance of cultivating

future golfers. Understanding these segments is important in developing marketing strategies that are designed to meet the needs of each particular group.

Market Segmentation Product Types

Public golfers are responsible for approximately 75% of rounds played and dollars spent on golf in the United States each year (Beditz & Kass, 2008). These golfers have access to 11,683 public courses of which approximately 75% are daily fee, privately owned courses and 25% are municipal courses owned by a city or county. Interestingly, nearly one third of public courses are nine-hole courses. There are also 3,936 private courses (National Golf Foundation, 2013). Even though fewer golfers play in private clubs, they are considered an attractive group due to their spending potential. Private club golfers tend to be older, have higher incomes, and spend more annually on golf-related purchases. The number of women golfers playing regularly is higher in private clubs than on public courses.

Both public and private organizations have experienced challenges over the last 10 years due to the economic downturn. Both areas have seen closures, and managers have been challenged to find new ways to do business in order to survive. Private clubs have attempted to respond to members needs for value and variety by creating new membership options, making capital improvements to facilities, and offering new programs. The public golf market offers plenty of options that are good for golfers but not as positive for the facilities themselves as demand is diluted. Public courses have responded by focusing on customer service, developing new players, improving the overall experience, and increasing potential revenue sources. They have also taken a more focused and strategic approach to planning and marketing (O'Neal, 2008).

The location of a golf course and access to the population of golfers in the area can have a significant impact on its viability. Regional differences also exist in the golf market within the United States. Florida and California have the highest number of courses on a statewide basis (1,050 and 920, respectively) (National Golf Foundation, 2013). States such as Florida and California can also expand their potential target markets by focusing on tourists.

Managing and Leading in a Course Club Setting

The traditional model of management within golf club settings involves the general manager (GM) acting as the chief operating officer (COO) and being accountable for all aspects of a club's operation (Perdue, 2013). In this model the GM/COO acts as a liaison to the board of directors while managing the intricacies and day-to-day details of 10 essential competencies identified by the Club Managers Association of America (CMAA, 2013a) (see Table 19-1).

As clubs continue to develop into more diverse enterprises with changing needs, the CMAA has expanded its professional development program and embraced an adapted model, the "Management to Leadership Model" (CMAA, 2013a). This expanded model recognizes the role and responsibilities of general managers in three major areas (see Figure 19-2): operations, assets and investments, and club culture.

Table 19-1 CMAA Competency Areas

Competency Area	Skills
Club governance	Membership types, bylaws, policy formation, board relations, committees
Food and beverage management	Trends, service, menu development, catering operations, dining room design, equipment, wine and beverage operations, personnel, training
Accounting and financial management	Accounting and financial issues, budgeting, cash-flow and forecasting, long-range planning
Human and professional resources	Employee relations, communication, time management, recruiting and hiring, training and development, labor issues, performance evaluation
Leadership	Motivation and team building, coaching and developing others, diversity, conflict management, professional image and dress, negotiation
Membership and marketing	Membership strategies & planning, satisfaction surveys, marketing, media, newsletters, membership technology
Golf, sports, and recreation management	Golf operations and etiquette, rules, course maintenance, role of superintendent, turf and grasses, tournament operations, future trends in golf, environmental issues, tennis/pool/fitness center management
External and governmental influences	Legislative influences, privacy, club law, liquor liability, labor laws, Internal Revenue Service, current legal issues, disaster preparedness
Facilities management	Preventative maintenance, housekeeping, security, insurance and risk management, clubhouse renovation, lodging, energy and water management, sustainability and conservation
Interpersonal skills	Active listening skills, writing skills, oral and written presentations, seeking feedback, promoting communication, developing positive working relationships, role modeling

Courtesy of Club Managers Association of America (CMAA) (2013). Retrieved from http://www.cmaa.org/template.aspx?id=6376

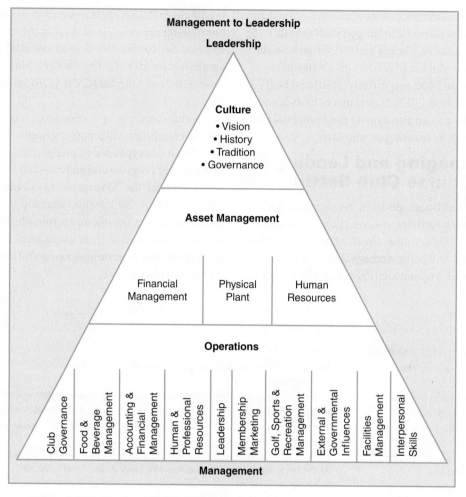

Figure 19-2 CMAA Management to Leadership Model
Courtesy of Club Managers Association of America

The foundation of this model is the successful management of club operations as identified in the CMAA competency areas. It also recognizes that a true leader must go beyond operational concerns and also focus on the equally important areas of asset management and club culture (Perdue, 2013). The second tier of the CMAA model addresses the need for additional competencies, such as managing the club's financial health, club staff, and physical property. The top tier of the pyramid identifies the general manager's responsibilities in maintaining the club's culture, vision, history and traditions, and governance structure. Sport management students interested in pursuing a career in golf and club management should pay particular attention to these competencies and take advantage of coursework and co-curricular opportunities where they can learn about and improve their skill set in these areas.

Financial Management and Benchmarking

Club managers must understand the financial issues that impact the success of the organization. Golf club revenues include membership dues and initiation fees (private clubs), food and beverage revenues, room rentals, golf operations, and tournaments. Operating expenses include costs related to golf course maintenance, such as equipment and fertilizer; golf operations; food and beverage service; labor; and capital costs (Schmidgall, 2013). Clubs with additional sport programs, such as tennis or aquatics, may have revenues and expenses associated with these areas. Nonprofit clubs with 501(c)(7) status seeking to breakeven will reinvest any profits.

Performance tracking metrics are relatively new in the golf industry, in part, because of the diverse nature of the industry and the different types of courses and clubs. Identifying key data that can be used to monitor performance over time is now recognized as an important element of successful planning and management of facilities. The PGA and NCGOA have partnered to provide a financial data and benchmarking service known as PGA PerformanceTrak. This service provides data in four different categories: private clubs, daily fee/semi-private clubs, municipal courses, and resort courses. The database includes information on rounds played per day open and days open for play. In addition, four key performance indicators (KPIs) are measured: golf fee revenue, merchandise revenue, food and beverage revenue, and total facility revenue (includes golf fee, merchandise, and food and beverage revenue, as well as any other facility revenues, including membership fees). Comparative reports are available on a national level, at the PGA section level, and also in over 70 local markets, providing managers with valuable insight on revenue comparisons and performance metrics (PGALinks.com, 2013b).

Competition in the Marketplace

The success of a golf or country club operation depends on its ability to attract new members; retain existing members; sell the club's amenities and golf-outing business for tournaments, charitable events, and special events; and maintain or increase the level of club usage by both members and guests. Golf operations experience strong competition from comparable and noncomparable rivals. Establishments compete primarily on the basis of the management and professionals' expertise, their reputation, featured facilities, quality and breadth of services, golfing and recreational and entertainment options, and price.

For potential patrons and members, the geographic location of the facility may be a major influence when choosing a golf course to play. This factor alone can be particularly influential when one is deciding to join a club, considering the substantial monetary outlay for the initiation and ongoing membership fees. The level of competition among facilities varies from region to region and locale to locale and is subject to change as existing facilities are renovated or new facilities are developed. For business and corporate usage, facilities such as conference rooms, business facilities, reciprocal rights, restaurants, bars, cafes, other complimentary sports facilities, and unique features can influence the choice of venue (Perdue, 2013).

Competition among courses can also be based on the skill level of particular players. A golfer with either a high handicap or low playing ability is less likely to regularly play on a very expensive golf course. Similarly, a golf course that is particularly challenging to play is less likely to attract low-skilled players. Courses that provide high-quality playing experiences tend to attract higher demand, and if the course is perceived to be a good value for the quality and is priced reasonably then demand should increase. Golfers are reluctant to play on a high-priced golf course that is not maintained to a superior standard or is overly difficult to play. Players with high skills or low handicaps are more likely to pay to play on a high-quality golf course. The median cost to play 9 holes is $26 and $44 for 18 holes (National Golf Foundation, 2013). At the best courses, fees are upwards of $80 to $100 for an 18-hole round. Value pricing and packaging of meals/dinner, cart rental, and lessons with a round of golf are now much more commonplace. Resorts are packaging golf experiences into their vacation plans as well.

Professional Staff Positions in a Private Golf Club

The management team of a golf club is made up of a group of highly skilled and trained professionals. This was not always the case. In the past, members of the club often tried to manage and operate the club or course on their own. However, due to the size of the clubs and lack of volunteers, more clubs have hired staff and given the day-to-day operations over to professional management teams, who are specialists in a variety of skill areas. The following describes the types of positions available in golf course and country club operations.

Management Team

Private equity clubs, because the members own them, can operate as the members desire, but many of these clubs, along with non-equity clubs and public clubs, now typically involve professional managers and industry specialists. The preferred organizational management structure employs a management team endorsed by the CMAA that is composed of club professionals; department heads; certified professionals in food and beverage management (including chefs, cooks, and bartenders); sport-related professionals (golf, tennis, and aquatics professionals); grounds and golf course superintendents; building and engineering technicians/specialists, and other specialty staff members who report to a general manager (Perdue, 2013; CMAA, 2013b).

General Manager

The official executive management position in the club is the general manager. This person's title may vary from club to club; he or she can be referred to as an executive director, director of club operations, or COO, but most refer to the lead executive of the management team as simply the general manager. The general manager is hired by the club's board of directors or owners and is responsible to the entire board but usually reports directly to the club president or owner(s). It is the general manager's duty to carry out the policies set by the board (Perdue, 2013).

Club Professionals

Professionals commonly found at country or city clubs are golf, tennis, and fitness club/center professionals. In recent years, many clubs have added spa professionals as they have expanded their member services. A club's golf course superintendent is not considered a club professional, though, but instead a professional in turf, agronomy, or plant and soil sciences. The golf course or grounds superintendent position works very closely with golf professionals and is considered to be at a similar organizational level. Because of its sport-related nature, an aquatic director's position may or may not be considered a club professional. However, the aquatic director is the head of a typical administrative function area overseeing a sport facility, which in this case is the swimming center, pool area(s), or beach, and sport-related staff, including lifeguards and water safety instructors (Perdue, 2013).

Golf Professional

A club's golf professional, also referred to as a *golf pro* or *director of golf*, is in charge of all activities related to the club's golf program, such as working with the general manager to prepare the golf budget; teaching golf to members; supervising other teaching pros on staff; conducting club golf tournaments; overseeing the club's handicap system and tee-time reservation system; maintaining the locker room operations; supervising the use and maintenance of the club's golf cars, equipment rentals, and repairs; and running the golf pro shop. The golf pro may or may not own the pro shop merchandise, depending on the club and whether the golf pro is considered to be club staff or a professional. The golf pro may also act in a service role as an independent contractor. Golf professionals are certified through the PGA and are likely graduates of a professional golf management school or program. These professionals are typically trained in all aspects of golf instruction and golf business techniques, and most often begin their careers as interns, progressing to assistant golf professionals before rising to the level of golf professional in positions of increasing responsibility. Some eventually become the director of golf in single large or multiple club operations. In seasonal clubs, assistant golf professionals may split their time between seasonal clubs in northern and southern climates (Perdue, 2013; PGALinks, 2013c).

Tennis Professional

A club's tennis professional manages the tennis program and provides individual lessons to members, establishes clinics, and oversees the maintenance of the tennis courts. The tennis professional also works with the club's tennis committee and the general manager to prepare a budget for the program. Some tennis professionals work *swing jobs*, where their season is split between two different locations, such as a New England club during the summer and a Florida club in the winter. Tennis professionals are certified through the U.S. Tennis Association (USTA) and most likely played

tennis competitively. Upon completion of their competitive careers, these tennis professionals moved into teaching and management responsibilities, first as interns and then later as a teaching assistant professionals before promotion to head tennis professional positions (Perdue, 2013).

Golf Course Superintendent

A club's golf course superintendent is in charge of maintaining the course's green environment and playing areas in an ideal playing condition. The golf course superintendent's expertise is basically in the business of keeping the grass green, free of disease, and in top playing condition. A superintendent typically has a degree in turf grass management or agronomy and works to mold the natural elements of grass, trees, hills, streams, and ponds, or, in a dry climate, rock formations, native plants, and topography, into a beautiful golf course that works with the existing landscape. The superintendent must constantly monitor the environment to protect the course, including carefully tracking the weather conditions. The superintendent and his or her staff develop integrated pest and disease management programs to aid against plant disease, insects, pests, adverse weather conditions, and other environmental factors that threaten the prime playing and turf conditions. The golf course superintendent also works with the club's general manager and golf course committee to develop the golf course budget. Many golf course superintendents begin their careers as a grounds staff member and then acquire an assistant golf course superintendent position before advancing to a head golf course superintendent position. The Golf Course Superintendents Association of America (GCSAA) offers golf course superintendents a professional certification program, enabling them to be recognized for their achievements in golf course management. The professional designation Certified Golf Course

Superintendent (CGCS) is bestowed upon those who meet the association's stringent certification requirements. This designation is the most widely recognized in the golf industry and is the highest level of recognition to be achieved in grounds and turf management.

Aquatics Director

A club's aquatics director, also known as the head swim professional in some clubs, is an important water safety professional. An aquatic director's responsibility is substantial and life preserving, because he or she is constantly dealing with members in situations where bad judgment or lack of skill might end in tragedy. Aquatics directors typically begin their careers as lifeguards, water safety instructors, and then assistant aquatics directors before eventually becoming aquatics directors (Perdue, 2013).

Spa Directors

With the addition of new spa complexes to private clubs and country clubs, spa management and staff positions are becoming more prominent. The rapid development of new day, resort, and club spas has been a fast-evolving trend in recent years. As traditionally occurs in emerging growth industries, a corresponding demand for qualified employees to occupy key management and support positions within the facilities that were built to capture a hot market has intensified. Spa directors should be certified and able to identify and hire qualified massage therapists to be able to meet the needs of clientele who may not be entirely familiar with the various massage techniques. The spa professional must also be able to balance the competing needs of the club's management staff, therapists, and members. The National Certification Board certifies spa directors and therapists for Massage and Bodywork (NCBMB).

Department Managers

The number and type of department managers a club has depends on the type and size of the club. For example, a very small city club might have only an executive chef and a catering or banquet manager in addition to the general manager. At the other extreme, a very large country club might have a food and beverage director, an executive chef, banquet manager, beverage manager, clubhouse manager, director of security, executive housekeeper, controller, membership director, director of human resources, spa and/or fitness director, an events and communications director, and a director of purchasing in the main clubhouse in addition to the sport professionals and administrators of the sport facilities (Perdue, 2013).

Clubhouse Manager

The clubhouse manager is usually the general manager's second in command. He or she is in charge of managing the clubhouse and its personnel and enforcing clubhouse policies and operating procedures. An assistant manager, in some clubs, might assume the second-in-command role and have more extensive duties, and the clubhouse manager may report to this manager (Perdue, 2013).

Controller

A club's controller develops and oversees policies to control and coordinate accounting, auditing, budgeting, and related duties; prepares or oversees the preparation of the club's financial statements; and analyzes and forecasts financial information for the club's managers, board of directors, and committees. This person is typically a certified public accountant (CPA) or a degreed accountant (Perdue, 2013).

Executive Chef

The executive chef is responsible for all food preparation in a club's food and beverage outlets. Executive chefs create menus, develop food purchase specifications and recipes, supervise food-production staff members, and generate budget reports to monitor food and labor costs for the department. He or she is also responsible for maintaining the highest food quality and sanitation standards. The executive chef is typically trained as a culinary chef and usually requires a formal culinary education (Perdue, 2013).

Banquet or Event Manager

A club's banquet manager promotes the club's dining facilities for private banquets, business and social meetings, and other activities. This person oversees all administrative and operational aspects of preparing and serving food at banquets, and works with the executive chef to put together banquet menus. This person typically has a formal education in hospitality and food service management with a concentration in food, restaurant, or event management. Some event management professionals may have education training in sport event management if the club is heavily involved in outings and tournaments (Perdue, 2013).

Membership Director

A membership director may work closely with the membership committee in a private equity club to help identify, close and/or introduce, and oversee club membership categories and the club's waitlist. In a private non-equity for-profit club, the membership director may have a highly active role in membership recruitment and retention. There may also be incentives and a commission paid to the individual in recruiting new members. This person may help manage and coordinate member guest events and invitations and assist the event manager and the banquet manager on special membership events. This person typically has a sales management or marketing background and/or education and must promote the facility through direct personal contact and one-to-one sales and membership meetings. The membership director may hold a degree in marketing, sport management, or hospitality management.

Strategies for Entering Golf Management and Club Operations

The club management field provides opportunities for career development and advancement for those who choose to pursue the club management career path. This is largely achieved by following the strategy to become a certified club manager (CCM).

Students may begin their career path by accumulating certification points while still in school. Students may seek work or summer internships with independent, stand-alone, private nonprofit clubs as one entry path into club management. On the sport professional side, students who have a passion for such sports as golf, tennis, racquetball, and others may pursue positions as assistant professionals who teach and direct these sports for the membership. The PGA (golf), USTA (tennis), and American Red Cross (swimming) offer career paths for those who love these sports and would like to teach them as part of their career. Those wanting to work outdoors may pursue a career as a golf course superintendent. Students may find an internship involving turf and course grounds and recreational facilities maintenance; certification would be through the GCSAA (discussed previously).

Educational preparation for careers in club management is derived from college and professional associations. Because success in this field requires an understanding of business and club management skills and sport professional concepts, degree programs in club management in a hospitality program, sport management, and exercise science or professional golf management are particularly relevant. These areas of study may be viewed as complementary, and colleges that offer courses in each of these professional areas offer the best opportunity for the widest choices and preparation for the club management field.

Courses in turf management, plant and soil sciences, pest management, and grounds maintenance are essential for those destined for a career in golf course turf management. Those seeking entry through the clubhouse side of the industry must take management courses in club, events, food and beverage, and banquet management, plus related hospitality management courses. A background in business and club management can prepare a person to face the myriad of management, legal, marketing, accounting, and financial issues involved in the successful operation of a golf or country club.

Beyond earning a college degree in the above-named fields, a person on the club management career track can connect with the CMAA, the PGA, or the USTA for advanced educational opportunities and certification programs. CMAA offers the appropriate education training for entry-level managers to advance in a club management career as well as the Certified Club Manager (CCM) program.

Students wishing to pursue a career in the golf side of the business as a golf professional may pursue a golf management degree at one of the 20 Professional Golf Management (PGM) programs located at various universities across the country. The PGA Golf Management University Program is a 4.5- to 5-year college curriculum for aspiring PGA professionals that requires 600 hours of work experience. Four specifically designed golf internships are offered. Existing college students may also become PGA professional members by becoming registered apprentices and going through the PGA Professional Golf Management (PGA PGM) program. This program provides the opportunity to acquire the knowledge and skills necessary for success in the golf industry through extensive classroom studies and internship experiences. The PGA claims a 100% job placement rate for those who complete the PGA PGM University Program (PGALinks, 2013d).

Students seeking a career in the turf management side of the business can gain a turf management degree by completing courses in agronomy, plant science, soil science, and turf management at an agricultural college or university. A list of schools offering turf management degrees is available on the PGALinks website (www.pgalinks.com). To be a golf course superintendent, a student must master agronomy and turf grass management practices; possess a working knowledge of golf facility construction principles, practices, and methods; and have a thorough understanding of the rules and strategies of the game of golf.

Other positions in the golf course maintenance operations include assistant golf course superintendent, equipment manager, and assistant equipment manager. Students interested in learning more about the golf maintenance side of the industry should become involved with the GCSAA by visiting the association's website (www.gcsaa.org) or becoming involved with a local university student chapter.

Current and Future Issues for Golf and Club Management

Since 2000, the golf industry has faced a number of challenges as it deals with the impact of the economic downturn and an oversupply of golf courses brought about by the building boom of the 1990s. Even with course closures, the supply of golf courses exceeds demand, which is positive for golfers but rather problematic for the golf industry. The golf industry must also respond to changes in social structure and lifestyles, including an increased focus on families, that have had an impact on the demand for golf. More women golfers, increased diversity, and a focus on health-related benefits of sport must also be considered. Golfers have less time, more choices, and different priorities, therefore the challenge for the industry is to address these issues and find ways to increase participation in golf ("Golf's 2020 Vision," 2012).

Changing the Format of the Product

The goal of increasing participation across all groups of golfers requires the industry to look differently at how it operates. The traditional format of playing 18 holes of golf is time consuming and often costly. Today's golfers seek experiences that allow them to maintain strong family relationships and, as such, spending a full day at the club or out on the course is no longer considered a viable option for many. Golf clubs and courses must change to accommodate these needs. Family friendly facilities are likely to replace traditional club house formats with formal lounges and bars. Changes in facilities provide a platform for golf to develop as a family oriented game, with greater attention being paid to women and children. Cafes and family rooms as well as more family friendly course layouts are potential options for future facilities ("Golf's 2020 Vision," 2012).

The golf industry is also recognizing the importance of women golfers as drivers of new business. Women golfers are likely to have different needs and expectations that, if addressed in a proactive manner, can contribute to increased participation levels and revenue. According to the "The Right Invitation: 2011 Women's Golf Longitudinal Research," a study conducted by the Sports and Leisure Research Group, women who play golf at facilities tailored to them play more and have a more positive experience, increasing revenues for course operators. The research highlighted eight best practices that resonate with women golfers and lead to increases in play and merchandise and food and beverage spending. Courses hoping to attract women should consider implementing these best practices (Sports and Leisure Research Group, 2011):

1. Provide four or more sets of tees, with the forward-most set of tees ideally under 4,500 yards, which allows all golfers to reach greens in regulation.

2. The golf shop should have a solid selection of well-displayed women's clothing and equipment and a dedicated women's department.

3. The golf shop should employ both male and female staff.

4. The golf course should have abundant directional signage.

5. Greeters should be present at the facility entry/starting area.

6. Ample drinking water should be available, ideally at a minimum of three tees per nine holes.

7. Male and female staff should be available for golf instruction.

8. Childcare should be made available.

The image of golf as a time-consuming, expensive activity that is difficult to learn creates significant barriers for many potential golfers (Mona et al., 2011). Aging baby boomers, the lifestyle needs of generations X and Y, consumer confidence in the economy, and a focus on families all impact the availability of time and money to participate in golf on a regular basis. The industry has begun to respond by offering alternative formats that meet golfers' needs and offer a different experience than the traditional 18-hole outing. Building alternative facilities is one strategy that can be used to meet the needs of today's golfers. Short courses, learning facilities, and holes that are designed to accommodate younger and less experienced golfers are becoming more common and acceptable alternatives. Monarch Dunes Golf Course in Nipoma, California, is one example of a new design of golf course that is designed to appeal to a wide range of golf abilities. The course features a 12-hole layout of par 3 holes ranging from 65 to 205 yards. The design allows players to hit a variety of clubs and includes large, undulating greens some with elevation changes of 3 to 4 feet. The course can be divided into shorter three- to four-hole challenges to accommodate fun competitions. Osgood Golf Course in Fargo, North Dakota, provides a similar experience on a par 33, nine-hole course. Golfers challenged for time can play a three-hole loop for just $5.

The traditional price structure is also changing as courses attempt to be competitive in the marketplace and recognize individual financial constraints. Courses are collaborating on joint membership packages that allow golfers to experience multiple facilities for one membership fee. In a new recruiting strategy, private equity clubs are beginning to offer reciprocal access packages to their members, providing them with access to more facilities and increased flexibility (Tengberg, 2011). Heritage Hunt Golf and Country Club in Gainesville, Virginia, offers members reciprocity at eight clubs in the area. This allows golfers to play a variety of courses at a minimal fee. The Greater Portland Golf Association in Maine was formed to provide access to four public golf courses. Players can participate as a single-round member, multiplay member, or as an existing member of one of the four clubs. Nine- and 18-hole passes are available along with access to scramble format tournaments. Grow the Game of Golf is an international collaboration of influential golf associations, including the European Tour, the PGA of Europe, and the PGA of Australia, that promotes a family golf program known as "Pay per Hole." The program is designed to eliminate time and cost barriers and allows families to play as few holes as they choose and pay only for the number that they play (Grow the Game of Golf, 2013).

An issue discussed at the 2011 Golf 20/20 Forum was how to improve the image of golf and participation levels by making it more fun. Suggestions such as "It is ok not to keep score," "play from the shortest tees," and "give yourself a better lie when you are learning" were presented as ideas that could make golf more attractive and less rigid for the average golfer. Other ideas included allowing players to throw a ball out of a bunker after the first try, playing a four-, five-, or six-hole round, or skipping a hole, with the idea of encouraging enthusiasm and fun (Mona et al., 2011).

Golf 2.0 & Player Development

In 2012 the PGA of America began to promote a comprehensive, industry-wide initiative, **Golf 2.0**, that focuses on player development and boosting golf participation by targeting specific groups with tailored programs. The program is seen as a long-term plan that will build participation levels toward a goal of 40 million golf players by 2020 and will be based on three key strategies (see **Figure 19-3**):

1. Retain and strengthen the golfing core.

2. Engage the lapsed.

3. Drive new players.

In retaining and strengthening the core, the program encourages PGA professionals to get to know their customers better, recognizing what is important to them and nurturing these customers to make sure they keep coming back. Lapsed golfers, particularly women, families, and seniors, are seen as high-value market segments that should be the focus of targeted programs designed to reengage them as frequent participants. Attention to new golfers and programs designed to reach the "other 84%"— those who do not currently play golf—are also highlighted as part of this initiative. Additional underlying elements of Golf 2.0 are based on the need to provide increased professional development, education, and training to PGA professionals so that they can improve their skills in marketing and managing relevant facilities and programs that highlight the value of golf in today's world (Golf 2.0, 2013).

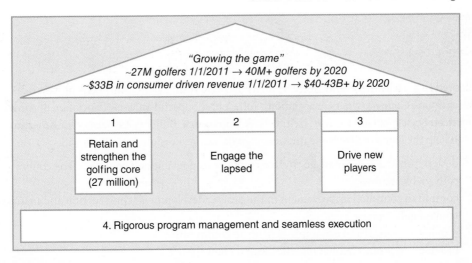

"Growing the game"
~27M golfers 1/1/2011 → 40M+ golfers by 2020
~$33B in consumer driven revenue 1/1/2011 → $40-43B+ by 2020

1	2	3
Retain and strengthen the golfing core (27 million)	Engage the lapsed	Drive new players

4. Rigorous program management and seamless execution

Figure 19-3 Golf 2.0 Three Core Strategies
Courtesy of Golf 2.0

Numerous programs have been developed in an attempt to attract the next generation of golfers. The First Tee program has over 200 chapters around the United States that are focused on introducing children to golf. Get Golf Ready is an adult-oriented player development program that provides a five-lesson package designed to get new people into the game. Tee It Forward is another industry initiative that encourages golfers to play from the tee that is most suited to their ability. This approach makes the game more fun for the average golfer and speeds up the pace of play. "Take Your Daughter to the Course Week" and "Women's Golf Month" are additional programs that are designed to bring more girls and women to the game of golf (NCGOA, 2013). SNAG is an international golf development program that utilizes modified equipment so that the basic skills can be learned in a fun environment (Barrow, Last, & Anton, 2011). Golfers and potential golfers under the age of 35 have also received attention from golf industry professionals who would like to strengthen participation rates among this group, often referred to as the "next generation." Lifestyle and cultural values are important when marketing to this group; they expect personalized experiences and respond well to flexible programs that offer a more varied golf experience, such as "Play and Pay by the Hour" or "Fast Golf" (Barrow et al., 2011).

Sustainability and the Environment

Sustainability and environmental stewardship are important issues for many businesses. The golf industry has been considering these issues when building and managing new courses for many years now. Management of existing courses within the context of supporting a sustainable environment requires modification of existing practices in many areas. Developers of new courses must be aware of federal guidelines designed to protect the environment from the very beginning of the design process. Today's courses are adopting policies to conserve and protect water resources, reduce pollution, conserve energy, and protect the natural habitat. In 2012, the International Golf Federation published a statement on sustainability that was subsequently adopted by allied golf associations from 150 countries around the world, including the United States (see **Box 19-1**). The statement

Box 19-1   Shared Principles on Sustainability

Adopted in 2012 by the World Golf Foundation, PGA Tour, LPGA Tour, PGA of America, National Golf Course Owners Association, Golf Course Superintendents Association of America, American Society of Golf Course Architects, & Golf Course Builders Association of America.
  To help the game realize these important goals, our professional members will:

* design, construct and manage environmentally responsible golf courses in an economically viable manner
* commit to continual improvement in the design, development, construction and management of golf courses
* provide ecological and economic benefits to communities
* provide and protect habitat for wildlife and plant species
* recognize that every golf course must be developed and managed with consideration for the unique conditions of the ecosystem of which it is a part
* provide important green space benefits
* use natural resources efficiently
* respect adjacent land use when planning, constructing, maintaining and operating golf courses
* create desirable playing conditions through practices that preserve environmental quality
* support ongoing research to scientifically establish new and better ways to design, construct and manage golf courses in harmony with the environment
* document outstanding development and management practices to promote more widespread implementation of environmentally sound golf
* educate golfers and developers about the principles of environmental responsibility and promote the value of environmentally sound golf courses.

Courtesy of wearegolf.org. Retrieved July 20, 2013, from http://wearegolf.org/news/shared-principles-sustainability.

clarifies essential principles and practices of sustainability in the context of the golf industry in the United States.

Audubon International offers the Audubon Cooperative Sanctuary Program that recognizes the efforts of individual golf clubs/courses in managing their properties in an environmentally responsible manner. Courses that meet specific criteria related to wildlife and habitat management, water conservation, environmental planning, and chemical reduction can be designated as Certified Audubon Cooperative

Sanctuaries. The program began in 1991 and has steadily grown to include 2,300 courses in the United States and 36 countries worldwide. Complete details of the program can be found on the Audubon International website (www.auduboninternational.org).

The Impact of Technology

Advances in technology have impacted every business, and golf is no different. Golf professionals have a variety of technologies and tools available to them to help improve the experience for golfers. The growth of the Internet and social media have created new communication channels for golf organizations. Many of today's golfers are connected to smartphones and tablets and expect to use these tools in their golf activities. The *Golf 2.0 Player Development Playbook* (PGAlinks, 2013c) promotes the use of social media to reach golfers in the environments that they frequently use. Promotions, discount offers, or special events can easily be communicated to large groups of current and potential customers. Tools such as Facebook and Twitter can be used to offer instant updates and announcements.

Technological advances have also improved golf equipment, leading to changes in the way the game is played at the higher levels. Today's state-of-the-art golf clubs allow even amateur golfers to hit the ball further. Technologies for teaching golf, such as tools used for swing analysis and simulation, are now more affordable and easier to use. Golf professionals can incorporate the use of these tools to enhance the teaching experience for golfers who are trying to improve their skills. Golf-related smartphone apps are also widely available and can enhance the golf experience in many ways. Golfers can use GPS apps to help them read the golf course and the Ping Putting app for putting stroke analysis. The USGA offers an app that provides the rules of the game. Swing analysis is also available by uploading video to an app, and shopping apps allow golfers to purchase the equipment and apparel needed to play ("Nine Best Golf Apps," 2013). As technology continues to develop, golf managers must stay ahead of what is new in their field so that they can use these tools to build the business and enhance the experience of their customers.

Summary

Golf courses and country clubs are significant business enterprises operating throughout the United States that provide diverse experiences and opportunities for golfers of all ages. The industry is expected to rebound from recent declines in participation, and new initiatives are currently being implemented in order to make the game more appealing and accessible to a diverse golfing population. Managers in the industry must recognize that the traditional structure of the golf enterprise is now evolving into a new model that provides flexibility, is more relaxed, and meets the needs of a changing demographic. Families, women, and minorities are expected to become more active and will drive the demand for facilities and programs that address their expectations.

Future golf professionals must prepare for the complexities of this environment by developing the skills needed to be successful. It is not enough to be an active and/or strong golfer; business skills are needed as well as specific knowledge of specialty aspects of the field. The recently implemented Golf 2.0 program highlights the professional development of existing professionals, especially in areas related to management and marketing. In a competitive marketplace these skills are as important as understanding how to run a member tournament or staff the driving range.

Golf industry professionals must also ensure that they are involved in professional organizations and continue to stay ahead of changes that may impact their business. Current lifestyle changes and trends may challenge existing practices or provide opportunities to expand into new areas. In 2016, golf will be an Olympic sport for the first time in over 100 years. How will this contribute to new business opportunities? How can a club take advantage of the attention the sport will receive before and during the Olympic Games? This is just one example of how external events may impact golf business operations and provide new and exciting opportunities if golf managers are prepared.

Case Study 19-1 To Host or Not to Host?

Casco Bay Country Club (CBCC) is considered one of the premier golf clubs in Maine. It features a scenic golf course; a sophisticated, state-of-the-art clubhouse; and a beautiful swimming pool complex and tennis facilities. The golf course is a nationally renowned 18-hole Donald Ross course in a scenic oceanside setting. The course is also the first in Maine to become a Certified Audubon Cooperative Sanctuary, highlighting the club's commitment to the environment. The club is a private 501(c)(7) organization that was established in 1890 and currently has 300 members. The club hosts numerous events for its members, including member tournaments and guest events, as well as weddings, banquets, family gatherings, and corporate meetings.

The board of directors and the golf planning committee are considering a proposal to bid on hosting the USGA US Senior Amateur Men's Championship in 2019. This event brings together 156 qualifying golfers from across the country for a weeklong tournament that begins with two rounds of match play and culminates with the top 64 golfers advancing to match play. Qualifying tournaments are held nationwide, and in 2013 more than 2,000 amateur golfers participated. Hosting a USGA event requires clubs to meet basic golf facility requirements with regards to course length/yardage, the driving range, club house capabilities, parking capacity, and so on. It also requires the host club to provide a host hotel with special rates, accommodations for USGA officials, a welcome dinner, and other events during the week.

CBCC General Manager Charlie Lowton and Head Golf Professional Nancy Canning both support the proposal based on the potential benefits and exposure that the club can expect to receive. Charlie and Nancy feel that this event will bring additional prestige and recognition to the club. This would be the first USGA event to be hosted in the state since 1976, and only 13 events are held around the United States each year. Hosting the event is also likely to have a positive impact on the demand for membership at the club.

The club will incur some costs that need to be fully assessed. Costs of hosting the event will be incurred in the following categories (unless sponsors are secured): housing of officials, the welcome dinner, a champions reception, transportation for officials, meals for golfers, gift packets, and any necessary course and/or facility improvements that are needed.

The board of directors agrees that this is a prestigious event and the opportunity to host it would further enhance the club's image. The board does, however, have other concerns that need to be considered before a final decision is made. First, the club's membership is already at capacity, and a waiting list for new members exists, which may diminish the value of hosting the event in terms of its impact on membership recruitment. Second, the golf course will also be out of commission to members for the week of the tournament and for 2 additional days prior to the event. Third, because the event will be held in September, members would lose access to potential tee times during some of the best playing times in the Maine golf season. Finally, members would also have to vacate the locker rooms during this time and have limited access to certain areas of the clubhouse.

Charlie and Nancy plan to get feedback from the members prior to the board meeting and are hopeful that the board will see this as an exciting opportunity for the Casco Bay Country Club. They are also preparing a presentation to inform the board of the details of this undertaking. The board will need to make a decision quickly and also send a formal invitation to the USGA declaring the club's interest in hosting this prestigious event.

Questions for Discussion

1. What information should be gathered from the membership prior to the meeting with the board of directors?

2. If you were preparing this presentation for the board, what five key points would you make to open your remarks?

3. What are the most significant benefits to the club in hosting this event?

4. What areas are likely to be most costly and time consuming in managing the USGA event?

5. How would you manage the additional work that will come with the event?

6. How would you measure success after the event has been completed?

Resources

American Golf Corporation
6080 Center Drive, Suite 500
Los Angeles, CA 90045
http://www.americangolf.com

Club Managers Association of America
(CMAA)
1733 King Street
Alexandria, VA 22314
703-739-9500
https://www.cmaa.org

ClubCorp USA, Inc.
3030 Lyndon B. Johnson Freeway, Suite 600
Dallas, TX 75234
972-243-6191
http://www.clubcorp.com

Ladies Professional Golf Association
(LPGA)
100 International Golf Drive
Daytona Beach, FL 32124
386-274-6200
http://www.lpga.com

National Golf Course Owners Association (NGCOA)

> 291 Seven Farms Drive, Suite 2
> Daniel Island, SC 29492
> 843-881-9956
> http://www.ngcoa.org

National Golf Foundation (NGF)

> 1150 S. US Highway One, Suite 401
> Jupiter, FL 33477
> 561-744-6006
> http://www.ngf.org

Professional Golfers Association (PGA)

> 100 Avenue of the Champions
> Palm Beach Gardens, FL 33418
> 561-624-8400
> http://www.pga.com

United States Golf Association (USGA)

> P.O. Box 708
> Far Hills, NJ 07931
> 908-234-2300
> http://www.usga.org

Troon Golf

> 15044 N. Scottsdale Road, Suite 300
> Scottsdale, AZ 85254
> 480-606-1000
> http://www.troongolf.com

World Golf Foundation

> 1 World Golf Place
> St. Augustine, FL 32092
> 904-940-4000
> http://www.worldgolffoundation.org

References

Barrow, J., Last, J., & Anton, T. (2011). The next generation. Paper presented at the 2011 Golf 20/20 Forum, May 10, St. Augustine, Florida. Retrieved from http://www.golf2020.com /about-golf-2020/annual-forum/2011 -conference.aspx

Beditz, J., & Kass J. B. (2008). The future of private golf courses in America. Retrieved from http://media.naplesnews.com/media/static /Private_Club_Report_final.pdf

Business Insights Essentials. (2013). Retrieved from http://bi.galegroup.com.ursus-proxy-1 .ursus.maine.edu/essentials/?u=maine_usm

Club Managers Association of America. (2013a). *Ten Competency Areas.* Alexandria, VA: Author.

Club Managers Association of America. (2013b). CMAA—Who we are. Retrieved from http:// www.cmaa.org/template.aspx?id=216

Course closures continue market correction. (2012, March 19). *GolfWeek.* Retrieved from http://golfweek.com/news/2012/mar/19/ngf -course-closures-continue-market-correction/

Golf 2.0. (2013). PGA. Retrieved from http://met .pga.com/gui/metropolitan13/uploadedfiles /dups/HTMLpages/2.0.pdf

Golf's 2020 Vision: The HSBC report. (2012). Retrieved from http://thefuturescompany .com/wp-content/uploads/2012/09/The _Future_of_Golf.pdf

Gordon, J. S. (1990). The country club. *American Heritage, 41*(6), 75–84.

Grow the Game of Golf. (2013). Pay per hole. Retrieved from http://www .growthegameofgolf.org/payperhole/

Hatami, D. (2013). Thoughts from the industry golf show. *HVS Global Hospitality Report.* Retrieved from http://www.hvs.com /article/6272/thoughts-from-the-golf -industry-show-part-1-of-3/

IBISWorld. (2013, September). *IBIS World Industry Report 71391: Golf Courses and Country Clubs in the U.S.* (SIC 71391). Retrieved from http://www.ibisworld.com /industry/default.aspx?indid=1652

Miller, D. (1978). The saga of the American country club. *Town & Country, 132*, 41.

Mona, S., Beditz, J., & Steranka, J. (2011). The latest and greatest: Industry reports. Paper presented at the 2011 Golf 20/20 Forum, May 10, St. Augustine Florida. Retrieved from http://www.golf2020.com/about-golf-2020/annual-forum/2011-conference.aspx

Morris, R. R. (2002). In Martin J. (Ed.), *Club Managers Association of America: Celebrating seventy-five years of service, 1927–2002.* (English Trans.). (1st ed.). Virginia Beach, VA: Donning Company Publishers.

Moss, R. J. (2001). *Golf and the American country club.* Urbana, IL: University of Illinois Press.

Napton, D. E., & Laingen, C. R. (2008). Expansion of golf courses in the United States. *Geographical Review, 98*(1), 24–41.

National Golf Course Owners Association. (2013a). Golf industry definitions. Retrieved from http://www.ngcoa.org/pageview.asp?doc=511

National Golf Course Owners Association. (2013b). NGCOA Player Development. Retrieved from http://www.ngcoa.org/pageview.asp?doc=312

National Golf Foundation. (2013). FAQ. Retrieved from http://secure.ngf.org/cgi/faqa.asp#6

Nine best golf apps for iPhone or android. (2013). Back Nine Network. Retrieved from http://back9network.com/article/nine-best-golf-apps-for-iphone-or-android/

O'Neal, K. (2008). Successfully market your golf course. Charleston, SC: National Golf Course Owners Association.

Perdue, J. (2013). *Contemporary club management* (3rd ed.). Upper Saddle River, NJ: Pearson Education.

PGA PerformanceTrak. (2013, July). Performance Trak news. Retrieved from http://images.pgalinks.com/vmc/pressReleases/PerformanceTrakNews_July2013.pdf

PGALinks. (2013a). *The Official Member Site of the PGA of America.* Retrieved from http://www.pgalinks.com/

PGALinks. (2013b). PerformanceTrak. Retrieved from http://www.pgalinks.com/index.cfm?ctc=1778

PGALinks. (2013c). *Golf 2.0 Player Development Playbook.* Retrieved from http://pdf.pgalinks.com/golf20/Golf2.0_PlayerDev_Playbook.pdf

PGALinks. (2013d). *PGA PGM University Program.* Retrieved from http://pgajobfinder.pgalinks.com/helpwanted/empcenter/pgaandyou/pro.cfm?ctc=5729

Premier Club Services. (2010). Your club and the law. Club Managers Association of America. Retrieved from http://www.cmaa.org/uploadedFiles/PCS/Governance/ycltoc.pdf

Schmidgall, R. S. (2013). Club financial management. In Perdue, J. (Ed.), *Contemporary club management* (3rd ed.). Upper Saddle River, NJ: Pearson Education.

Sports and Leisure Research Group. (2011). The right invitation: 2011 women's golf longitudinal research. Retrieved from http://www.golfwithwomen.com/wp-content/uploads/2012/02/2011-Women-Golfers-Longitudinal-Study.pdf

Tengberg, V. A. (2011). A new world order for private clubs. Golf Course Industry. Retrieved from http://www.golfcourseindustry.com/gci-080811-private-clubs-new-world-order.aspx

We Are Golf. (2012, October 9). Shared principles on sustainability. Retrieved from http://wearegolf.org/news/shared-principles-sustainability

Williams, B. (2012). How do you measure up? Golf Course Industry. Retrieved from http://www.golfcourseindustry.com/gci0212-state-of-industry-report.aspx

Chapter 20

Tara Q. Mahoney

Recreational Sport

Learning Objectives

Upon completion of this chapter, students should be able to:

1. Recognize that although the recreation industry is extensive and diverse, all organizations strive to provide activities that offer personal and social benefits to individuals during their leisure time.

2. Differentiate between activities which involve active performance (direct participation) and those in which the consumer is primarily a spectator (indirect participation).

3. Appraise the history of recreation and leisure activities in the United States.

4. Assess the trends in recreation participation in the United States and identify some of the reasons for those trends.

5. Identify the six segments of the recreation industry: Community-based, public, military, outdoor, campus, and therapeutic recreation.

6. Assess the career opportunities available in the recreation industry and understand the skills and professional preparation necessary to succeed in each of them.

7. Debate current issues of importance in the recreation industry, such as increased government regulation, growing environmental and cultural awareness, the challenges of complying with the American with Disabilities Act, and the need for recreation organizations to have a high quality risk management agenda.

Introduction

An interest in recreation is integral to the lives of most people in the United States from childhood through adulthood. Whether the arena is indoors or outdoors, people seek to be involved directly or indirectly with recreational activities for a variety of reasons, including fun, excitement, relaxation, social interaction, physical or mental challenge, and lifestyle enhancement.

The roots of involvement with organized recreation may begin in childhood with Little League baseball or softball. It can be nurtured through involvement in Young Men's Christian Association (YMCA) aquatics programs and summer camp experiences. In adulthood, people explore enjoyable activities such as the thrill of whitewater kayaking and summer vacations with families in state or national parks. Through retirement a person can embrace a range of "masters" activities, such as "70-plus" ski clubs, that encourage lifelong participation in an activity.

The recreation industry in the United States is extensive and diverse, although the various segments usually share a common mission. Organizations strive to provide activities that

offer personal and social benefits to individuals during their leisure time. A characteristic of recreation that sets it apart from other segments of the sport industry is that there is often **direct participation** by people through active performance in an activity, such as sea kayaking classes, mountain bike racing, or fishing with a certified guide. However, **indirect participation** by spectators may also occur in recreation and also contributes to the economic base, a strategy effective in the tourism industry, which seeks to promote recreation-based events such as triathlons that draw spectators to a particular region.

History

In the nineteenth century, leisure time emerged as a result of the urbanization and industrialization of U.S. society. Technological innovations in factories made work more monotonous and prompted citizens to seek diversions. The recreation movement sought to address social issues affecting a population faced with a 66-hour workweek (6 days a week, 11 hours a day). Public attitudes toward work and leisure changed from a more Puritan ethic, which valued work over play, to a perception of recreation as important to the growth and health of the individual and as a means to improve community well-being.

By mid-century, a number of developments helped expand and formalize recreation. In reaction to accelerating urban development, the **parks movement** prompted the establishment of public lands, such as Central Park in New York City, that were open free of charge to all people. Boston's famous Emerald Necklace of parkways began to surround and provide an escape from its urban center. Technology also brought innovations, such as the bicycle and golf ball, and the moderate price of sporting goods such as canoes and rowboats opened these activities to all economic classes. Social and religious institutions

© Fuse/Thinkstock

such as the YMCA and YWCA, as well as the Young Men's and Young Women's Hebrew Associations, were organized in many cities.

An increasing fascination with the wilderness in the United States prompted an interest in outdoor travel and construction of the famous mountain houses and wilderness camps of the Northeast, mostly popular in the Adirondacks of New York. Only the most daring ventured to the uncivilized West, yet in 1872 President Ulysses S. Grant was able to convince the federal government to establish Yellowstone as the world's first national park. This act established the U.S. commitment to preserving public lands, a unique philosophy later exported to European countries. The creation of the National Park Service (NPS) in 1916 by Theodore Roosevelt escalated the preservation of extraordinary geologic and cultural sites, including national seashores, historic battlefields and monuments, and wildlife areas. In 2012, the NPS recorded nearly 283 million recreational visits to the national parks, yielding evidence of their importance to individuals for recreation purposes (NPS, 2013). In addition, recent studies have shown that these recreational visitors generate almost $13 billion through spending on lodging, meals, entertainment, and retail purchases, providing economic benefits to the surrounding communities as well (Cui, Mahoney, & Herbowicz, 2013).

By the end of the nineteenth century, the recreation movement had created formal organizations in the form of local clubs and national associations devoted to recreation and committed to developing standards for activities. Organizations such as the American Canoe Association, established in 1880, began to shape not only recreational participation through the development of instructional guidelines but also competition rules for races and regattas. Early in the twentieth century, interest in recreation continued to accelerate with the establishment

of well-known organizations such as the Boy Scouts in 1910 and the Girl Scouts in 1912.

A phenomenon unique to the United States also emerged during this time when organized summer camps for children began to proliferate. In the nineteenth century, the camping movement often focused on gatherings of a religious nature for adults. Concerned about the effect of urbanization on children, advocates developed the first fresh air camps in the latter half of the 1800s to allow urban children to travel to the country. By the early 1900s, the camping movement had gained momentum in attracting children to these popular outdoor experiences. Today, specialty camps for sports and recreational activities have been added to the mix. The American Camping Association (ACA) reported in 2011 that an estimated 12,000 camps existed nationwide, serving 11 million children and adults and employing 1.5 million adults (ACA, 2013). Since 2002, the number of day camps has increased by 69% (American Camping Association, 2013).

Following World War II, an expanding U.S. economy broadened the scope of the recreation industry. This economic growth led to the creation of local parks and recreation departments, the establishment of armed forces recreation to improve the morale of soldiers and their families, and the emergence of commercial recreation enterprises such as the ski industry. The federal government also approved legislation that created the National Wilderness Preservation System, the National Wild and Scenic Rivers System, the National Trails System, a system of National Recreation Areas, and the Land and Water Conservation Fund, which provides matching grants to state and local governments for acquiring and developing public outdoor recreation areas. Today in the United States, growing numbers of people are participating in outdoor recreation, especially women and older adults. Walking is the most popular activity, with 62% of people in the United States walking for recreation in 2012, compared to 56% in 2005 (Centers for Disease Control and Prevention, 2012).

Technological improvements continue to drive the development of new sporting goods, generating growing interest in other activities such as snowboarding, artificial wall climbing, kayaking, and wake boarding. As other emerging technologies, such as electronic entertainment, have sought to capture more of the public's leisure time in the twenty-first century, President Barack Obama established America's Great Outdoors Initiative in 2010 to reconnect people in the United States, particularly children, to the nation's natural and cultural heritage. He directed a consortium of federal agencies to promote community-based recreation and conservation, create job and volunteer opportunities related to conservation and outdoor recreation, and support existing programs and projects that educate people in the United States about the country's history, culture, and natural resources (U.S. Department of the Interior, 2013).

Trends in Participation

An appreciation of the outdoors is central to the American lifestyle, and recent trends in participation support the enduring value of outdoor recreation. The total number of people who participated in one or more outdoor activities grew by approximately 7.5% from an estimated 208 million in 2000 to 224 million in 2009. At the same time, the total number of participation days in all activities increased from 61 billion to 81 billion, representing growth of approximately 32% (Cordell, 2012).

The 2010 National Survey on Recreation and the Environment, conducted by the USDA Forest Service, shows the top outdoor recreation activities for people aged 16 years and older (Table 20-1). Walking for pleasure remains

Table 20-1 Top 10 Outdoor Recreation Activities, 2005–2009

Activity	Number (in millions)
Walk for pleasure	200
Family gathering	174.2
Gardening/landscaping for pleasure	157.9
View/photograph natural scenery	149.8
Visit nature centers, etc.	133.3
Sightseeing	123.9
Picnicking	121.6
View wildflowers/trees	121.3
Driving for pleasure	120.5
View wildlife besides birds and fish	118.1

Reproduced from: National Survey on Recreation and the Environment, USDA Forest Service, Southern Research Station, Athens, GA (H. Ken Cordell, Project Leader).

the top outdoor recreation activity, along with family centered outdoor activities, gardening, viewing natural scenery, sightseeing, and swimming (Cordell, 2012). Interest in extreme sports continues to grow among a variety of ages (Figure 20-1), along with some long-lasting favorites, such as skateboarding, and newer activities, such as paintball. Over the past 5 years, the recreational activities with the greatest growth rate among individuals have been adventure racing and triathlons. Adventure racing has grown by 211%, off-road triathlons by 199%, and traditional triathlons by 174% (Outdoor Industry Association, 2013).

In addition, researchers have assessed trends and made predictions for the future of recreation participation. Camping, geocaching, and wildlife festivals are three rapidly growing outdoor activities (Cordell, 2012). Accessibility to amenities such as water, electricity, hot showers, and cell phone reception are important to campers and influence individuals' and families' decisions to go camping. As many public

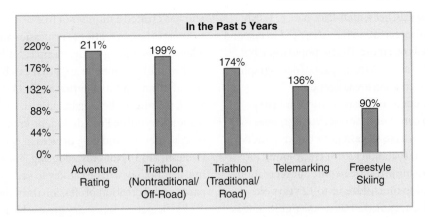

Figure 20-1 Trends in Outdoor Participation: Top Five Biggest Participation Increases in Outdoor Activities (2008–2013)

Reproduced from: Outdoor Industry Association (2013). Outdoor Participation Report. Retrieved from https://www.outdoorindustry.org/research/participation.php?action=detail&research_id=193

and private campgrounds have embraced these comforts and conveniences, participation rates have continued to increase. Geocaching is part treasure hunt, part orienteering, where individuals search for a 'cache,' or hidden container, by following GPS coordinates. The increased availability of GPS technology spurred the creation of this recreational activity and trends indicate that it will continue to be popular in the future. Lastly, wildlife festivals have grown from 10 in 1992 to 240 in 2002. Tourists tend to be attracted to events that combine nature with education (Cordell, 2012).

As the U.S. population ages and the 76 million baby boomers approach retirement, the recreation industry can capitalize on this generation's optimism about their retirement and their popularizing of the fitness movement in the 1960s (Sporting Goods Manufacturers Association, 2010a). Baby boomers are redefining expectations of aging and retirement and likely will not settle for a typical sedentary lifestyle (Jayson, 2013). According to the American Association of Retired Persons (AARP, 2004),

approximately 68% of baby boomers say they expect to participate in recreational activities during retirement. Short-term experiences that are available relatively close to home at a low cost are gaining in popularity (Sporting Goods Manufacturers Association, 2010b). The age distribution among the United States population is shifting from younger to older. By 2030, approximately one in five U.S. citizens will be 65 or older (U.S. Department of Commerce, 2010). The largest segment of the country's population will be middle-aged or older, most likely with diverse interests and a range of fitness levels. Recreation professionals will need to respond to the needs of these participants. Increased racial and ethnic diversity is anticipated with related growth in urban areas.

Between 2000 and 2050, the U.S. population is expected to increase from 310 million to 439 million (U.S. Department of Commerce, 2010). The Hispanic population was responsible for 32% of the nation's population growth from 1990 to 2000 and 39% from 2000 to 2010. It is expected to contribute 45% from 2010 to 2030 and 60% from

2030 to 2050 (Cheeseman-Day, n.d., p. 1). Not only will the recreation industry need to respond to the needs of a more diverse population, but it must also address the impact of demographic shifts on recreation areas near cities.

A challenge for the recreation industry will be to continue to attract younger ages to activities so as to sustain growth. An Outdoor Industry Association (2013) study found an overall downward slide in outdoor recreation participation for children 6 to 12 years old, although the decrease was not as significant as in past studies. Children are also changing their relationship to recreation, as "pick-up" or casual play in team sports continues to decline. One reason organized/sanctioned play dominates is because more young athletes specialize in one sport at an earlier age. Researchers have found that introducing children to outdoor recreation and physical activities at an early age impacts their recreational decisions in adulthood. Among adults who currently participate in outdoor recreation activities, 75% had physical education classes and 42% enjoyed outdoor activities in elementary school.

The emergence of technology-based entertainment is another trend that has affected the recreation industry. Technology is a part of our daily lives and is often unavoidable. Adult recreation preferences often are formed during childhood. A National Recreation and Parks Association (NRPA) study found that 78% of youth ages 12 to 17 have a cell phone; of those, two in five have a smartphone (Dolesh, 2013). If we want to attract youth to the outdoors, technology may be the ticket. Instead of resisting technology in the outdoors, many recreation professionals have embraced technology as a communication platform to raise awareness about the benefits of recreation as well as incorporating technology into recreation. The National Environmental Education Foundation (NEEF) is one of the leading supporters of technological acceptance within recreation

and has created a number of free resources to assist other recreational professionals in adopting technology. For example, NEEF has created multiple mobile apps that can be used in conjunction with its Environmental Education Week website. Other organizations, such as the National Wildlife Foundation, promote the use of smartphones and GPS devices in geocaching (Dolesh, 2013). Not only adopting, but embracing, technology will be the key to success for parks and recreation professionals in the future.

Participation rates vary greatly by activity, and a newcomer to the recreation field would be wise to examine demographic trends in each area. As national demographics shift both with regards to age and ethnicity, managers will be faced with the difficult task of changing recreation facilities and programs to meet participants' needs. Overall, participants will be more likely to be women, older, more racially and ethnically diverse, and come from urban areas. These factors will shape the industry in the coming years as recreation managers modify strategies for designing facilities, marketing programs, and hiring staff to deliver recreational opportunities responsive to this changing population.

Segments of the Recreation Industry

The recreation industry offers people a wealth of opportunities for participation across its many segments. Consumers can find many intriguing activities to suit their needs. Competent recreation professionals are needed to staff the industry, and those interested in this field would be wise to explore the variety of options in what has become a very competitive job market. The industry is so diverse that it can appear fragmented because it is divided into a myriad of professional associations specific to certain activities. The categories presented in the next few sections are meant to explore the major segments, and the prospective employee should realize that a particular recreation field may fit into two or three of the basic segments.

Community-Based Recreation

The term **community-based recreation** implies that participants are united by a common interest in recreation at the local level. Local parks and recreation departments and community agencies such as the YMCA, YWCA, Jewish Community Centers, Girls and Boys Clubs, and Scouts offer general community recreation services. Some agencies may target specific ages through youth centers and senior centers. Parks and recreation departments are supported through a mix of local property tax monies and user fees from participants. Many of these programs are no longer free to the public, given the increased competition for budgetary support among all municipal services (e.g., fire and police departments). As a result, recreation managers are becoming increasingly creative in soliciting private sponsorships from local companies to sponsor special programs to keep program costs low for the public. To support their programs, agencies such as the YMCA, Jewish Community Centers, and Boys and Girls Clubs often rely on a greater mix of funding sources, including user fees and memberships, private donations (such as United Way), grant programs from public and private sources, and in-house fund-raising events.

Public Recreation

Public recreation reaches beyond the local level to those programs supported by state and federal agencies. State forest and parks departments, the National Park Service (a division of the U.S. Department of the Interior), and the National Forest Service (a division of the U.S. Department of Agriculture [USDA]) manage recreational opportunities on public lands. Interest in national forests and parks remains high, and the number of visits to the 390

areas in the national park system and the 155 national forests has exploded in recent years. The National Park Service recorded 283 million visits to national parks, seashores, monuments, and historic sites in 2012, an increase of 4 million from the previous year (National Park Service, 2013). This high use continues to affect a system beleaguered by federal budget constraints. The National Park Service also is grappling with policy issues concerning vehicle congestion, recreational vehicle access, a deteriorating infrastructure, and control of visitor volume and duration, and has identified the need to conduct a comprehensive study of public use of the park system (Lee, 2003).

The National Forest Service employs more than 30,000 permanent employees to manage the nation's 193 million acres of forest lands (USDA Forest Service, 2013). Traditionally, available positions focused on resource management, but the agency has added recreation employees to its field offices and examines forest recreation through its research and development teams. Its Job Corps program employs 900 people at 18 centers on forest lands. The program trains 9,000 enrollees annually in vocational and social skills as well as basic educational training that leads to college or the military (USDA Forest Service, 2013). Additionally, the National Forest Service recruits new talent and cultivates new leadership for the organization through its Presidential Management Fellows program.

© Photos.com

Military Recreation

The U.S. Department of Defense maintains extensive **military recreation** programs through branches of the armed services. Although an overriding mission is the fitness and military readiness of personnel, the armed services also seek to provide an array of recreational opportunities for families on bases in the United States and abroad as a means of improving overall morale and a sense of community. Facilities include, but are not limited to, ski areas, marinas, recreation centers, fitness centers, youth centers, golf courses, and bowling centers. The military is also creating new programs for enlisted personnel and veterans with disabilities who have returned from the country's recent wars, such as the Wounded Warriors Project at Fort Carson, Colorado. Since 1948, the armed services have also supported the training of athletes for the Olympic Games and other major international competitions, and more than 400 active-duty personnel have achieved Olympic status as a result (Quigley, 2004). Seventeen American veterans with disabilities represented the United States at the 2012 Summer Paralympic Games in London (U.S. Department of Veterans Affairs, 2013). The Sochi 2014 Winter Paralympic Games gold medal winning US Sledge Hockey team featured four Wounded Warriors, military veterans from the conflicts in Iraq and Afghanistan (Heika, 2014)

Military recreation organizations face the same challenges as other government-funded recreation programs. Recent decreases in appropriated funds have challenged the armed services to maintain program quality and improve their economic performance. The majority of recreation employees at military facilities are civilians rather than military personnel, which creates job opportunities for trained people from the local communities.

Outdoor Recreation

Outdoor recreation attracts those who enjoy natural environments in different seasons, and people's increasing passion for the outdoors continues to expand this already large segment of the industry. The Outdoor Industry Association (2012) reported that the active outdoor recreation economy is a $646 billion business, with more than 140 million people in the United States participating annually. Spending on outdoor recreation falls primarily in two categories: outdoor recreation product sales (e.g., gear, apparel, footwear) and trips and travel-related spending (e.g., accommodations, transportation, and entertainment). This booming industry has created more than 6.1 million jobs and sustains economic growth in many rural economies. Running, jogging, and trail running top the list of popular activities, with 53 million participants (Outdoor Industry Association, 2013).

The outdoor industry is highly diverse, with a mix of for-profit and nonprofit ventures in each subcategory. Activities include, but are not limited to, skiing and snowboarding, boating (e.g., rafting, canoeing, kayaking, and sailing), golf, summer camps, backpacking and camping, natural resource management, and tourist travel. Adventurous programs modeled after Outward Bound are also popular among people seeking challenging outdoor experiences.

Campus Recreation

Campus recreation includes any recreational activity provided by colleges or universities, ranging from exercise facilities and fitness programming to club and intramural sports and coordinated outdoor recreation activities. With the goal of inspiring wellness through collegiate recreation, the National Intramural-Recreation Sports Association (NIRSA) includes over 4,000 recreation professionals providing recreational opportunities for over 7.7 million students

(NIRSA, 2013). Three out of four college students participate in some form of campus recreation. Interestingly, smaller colleges and universities with fewer than 5,000 students have even higher student participation rates, with upwards of 87% participating in campus recreation (Youseey-Elsner, 2012).

Additionally NIRSA offers excellent resources for students, including a student leadership team, a mentoring program, and beneficial career resources (NIRSA, 2013). The goal of many campus recreation programs is to teach students about the benefits of recreation and encourage participation in a variety of contexts with the hopes they will continue to participate into adulthood. Organizations such as NIRSA and the Association for Experiential Education (AEE) aim to provide educational trainings and host activities to develop prospective leaders in the recreation field or otherwise.

Therapeutic Recreation

The **therapeutic recreation** field uses recreational activities as a means to improve a participant's physical, emotional, and mental health. The activities can be offered as part of an overall treatment or rehabilitation program that may have evolved from medical care at a hospital, psychiatric facility, or nursing home. Therapeutic recreation services are also offered through park and recreation departments, independent living centers, schools, community mental health agencies, specialty recreation organizations, and social service agencies. Such services may also include programs for individuals who may be at risk of entering or are already in the judicial system. The programs vary widely, from hospital-based cardiac rehabilitation, for which recreation is used to improve physical fitness, to a wilderness camp sponsored by a state division of youth services that seeks to change the behaviors of court-referred youth.

Therapeutic recreation organizations often seek personnel with experience in recreation, counseling, or social work. Most important, they need employees whose specific skills and experience match the needs of a specific population, such as trained chemical dependency counselors. Therapists who do not have specialized training in recreational activities such as ropes/challenge courses or water sports work in conjunction with other recreation professionals who can offer that leadership. As the U.S. population continues to age, prospective employees should explore the opportunities available in adult day care, outpatient programs, psychiatric rehabilitation, and physical rehabilitation, especially services for people with disabilities.

Career Opportunities

The recreation field offers individuals excellent opportunities to work indoors and outdoors in pleasant surroundings, enjoy a healthy lifestyle, and introduce others to the benefits of participation at any age and any ability level. A number of common positions exist at recreation organizations, whether public or private, for-profit, or nonprofit (Table 20-2). Recreation consumers, particularly those ready to pay a fee for participation, are increasingly savvy customers who expect a high degree of professional service in instruction and overall service delivery. From the moment they contact an organization to inquire about recreation programs and services, customers often seek to be reassured that they will obtain an educational, enjoyable, and safe experience. Some recreational activities can be very exciting, offering higher degrees of risk than other activities. After all, the challenging nature of outdoor sports such as whitewater kayaking or rock climbing is the very element that intrigues participants. Recreation professionals have a responsibility to deliver these programs with a high degree of skill and manage them with an eye to providing acceptable degrees of risk.

Table 20-2 Typical Recreation Positions

Activity director (cruise ships, senior centers)
Aquatics director
Aquatics specialist (town summer programs, YMCAs, YWCAs)
Armed forces recreation leader
Camp counselor
Camp director
Facilities manager (bowling, marinas, rafting)
Guide (river, fishing, hunting)
Instructor (skiing, swimming, canoeing, kayaking, scuba diving, wilderness)
Naturalist
Outdoor travel/tour leader
Park ranger
Park superintendent
"Pro" (golf, tennis)
Program director
Recreation director (town, community center)
Recreation therapist
Retail manager
Youth coordinator

Job Search Strategies

Recreation managers are always seeking effective instructors, leaders, or guides who can create and execute programs, deliver excellent instruction tailored to the participants' needs, and provide leadership in challenging situations. A recreation manager wants people-oriented employees who know how to communicate well with the public, who work well with a diverse population of customers and staff, and who are responsible individuals committed to delivering quality programs and services. A recreation agency is often a small, lean operation that also needs employees who bring business skills to the workplace. As recreation professionals move into managerial positions, they may need to supervise programs and staff, monitor risk management concerns in programs, create innovative marketing campaigns, develop and administer budgets, act as a liaison with public and private agencies, and develop alternative sources of funding beyond user fees.

Finding a recreation job requires a general understanding of all segments of the industry and a sense of where expansion in this highly competitive industry is occurring or is likely to occur. A prospective employee should analyze the specialized instructional and managerial skills necessary in specific areas of interest. A multifaceted approach should be adopted to successfully obtain a recreation position:

1. *Participate in a variety of activities.* Explore both popular and relatively uncommon activities (such as backpacking, scuba diving, sailing, or rock climbing). Share your interests and hobbies during interviews, whether they include music, travel, or other useful experiences. Employers and clients want to see staff with active experience in a variety of interesting undertakings.

2. *Develop general instructional and programming skills.* Working with a wide variety of ages, genders, abilities, and types of programming is helpful, particularly for those who aspire to an administrative position as a coordinator or director. Recreation managers seek employees with tangible skills, and a useful strategy is to obtain training and hands-on experience through internships, cooperative education, summer employment, and volunteer opportunities.

3. *Refine skills in several specific programming areas.* Recreation is becoming increasingly specialized, and prospective employers may want an employee with a set of skills unique to a specific activity. Obtaining specific training and certification from a designated national governing body such as the Professional Ski Instructors of America, the American Red Cross, or the American Canoe Association is necessary. First aid and emergency preparedness skills are essential parts of this training.

4. *Consider associated skills that can strengthen a resume.* A versatile candidate also offers a base of knowledge and skills useful to a business office, including marketing, accounting, public relations, business computer applications, writing, knowledge of legal issues, and computer-aided promotional design. Academic programs enable a prospective candidate to develop this more extensive background.

Professional Preparation

Two approaches to professional preparation exist in the recreation field. The recreation skills approach provides shorter, more intensive preparation in a particular area, often resulting in certification. The other approach is to select an academic program of 1, 2, or 4 years' duration at a college or university, which provides a broader knowledge base. It is important to realize that not every prospective employee has a recreation or outdoor recreation degree. Other related useful degrees include sport management, environmental science and forestry, social work, business, early childhood education, criminal justice, environmental education, and public administration.

The skills approach enables a person to obtain training and experience through organizations such as the National Outdoor Leadership School (NOLS) or Outward Bound, two of the largest outdoor organizations that provide specialized leadership development. A person might also participate in the certification processes offered by national governing bodies such as the American Canoe Association or Professional Ski Instructors of America. Other nationally recognized agencies also provide training. Project Adventure, for example, teaches people to use structured activities on challenge/obstacle courses in environments ranging from summer camps to corporate training and development. Project Adventure provides

a short-term, focused program at a lower cost (than other training avenues) that develops an individual's instructional and leadership skills in one specific activity.

Academic programs at colleges and universities offer a broader base of knowledge through expanded curricula for bachelor's and master's degrees. Individuals who seek to advance to managerial positions in program development or general administration would be wise to seek a master's degree. These programs vary in their alignments within the institution, and such alignments may flavor the curriculum. For instance, they may be housed in schools of health, physical education, recreation, or education as well as departments of sport management, forestry and natural resources, regional planning, or travel and tourism.

Interested students would be wise to establish a foundation of knowledge through general courses and select a focus in a particular segment that provides deeper knowledge and skills. Table 20-3 provides an overview of some basic courses that can be useful in the recreation field. Because industry segments overlap, it is difficult to strictly divide academic courses into the various segments. A blend of courses from those listed for specific segments is useful preparation for the field.

Current Issues

The traditional roots of the recreation industry continue to shape the modern profession. The value of recreation programming is still judged in terms of its ability to improve health and well-being. Managers will need to monitor shifting demographic trends to adequately handle the impact of continuing financial constraints facing the recreation industry.

A fundamental shift in financing recreation has occurred as federal, state, and local governments have reduced their proportionate shares of recreation budgets. Public recreation

Table 20-3 Academic Course Preparation for the Recreation Industry

General Recreation Courses Useful for Any Industry Segment
Introduction to Recreation and Leisure Services
History of Recreation
Recreation and Society
Program Planning and Organization
Group Leadership and Supervision
Risk Management in Recreation
Recreation Facilities Planning and Design
Internship/Cooperative Education Placement
General Business Courses Useful for Any Industry Segment
Financial Accounting
Introduction to Marketing
Fundamentals of Finance
Management Principles
Personnel Management
Public Relations
Computer Business Applications
Courses for Public Recreation
Park and Recreation Administration
Public Administration
Recreation Resource Management
Conservation Law and Enforcement
Courses for Outdoor Recreation
Introduction to Outdoor Recreation
Commercial Recreation
Travel and Tourism
Environmental Education and Interpretation
Courses for Therapeutic Recreation
Introduction to Therapeutic Recreation
Recreation and Rehabilitation
Special Populations in Therapeutic Recreation

now competes for funding in an economic climate shadowed by a rising federal deficit, the emergence of state tax reform initiatives, and constrained local budgets. The recreation professional is often faced with the task of finding alternatives to government funding or user fees to support recreation services.

Park and recreation officials at local, state, and federal levels face challenges that include deteriorating park and recreation infrastructures, increasing crime, and declining federal, state, and local tax resources. Professionals must determine creative methods for capital development while simultaneously controlling operating expenses and establishing spending priorities in light of increasingly reduced budgets. Recreation managers must also strategize how to make parks and recreation areas safe from vandalism, crime, gangs, and substance abuse so they do not have an image that prevents citizens from enjoying them. They must advocate for the essential role that public recreation plays in promoting individual and community health and well-being (National Recreation and Park Association, 2010).

Public and Private Sectors

Gone are the days when a recreation programmer could simply take a group onto public lands with little understanding of pertinent regulatory agencies. The **public sector**, or government, owns or manages the trails, beaches, information centers, and wildlife that attract individuals and enhance community life. The **private sector**, or nongovernment arena, often provides the jobs and services that enable people to enjoy their experience while they are there. The relationship can be very complex and often requires an understanding of land management plans, regulatory processes, permit requirements, and natural heritage constraints, such as protection of endangered species. Interactions may be quite formal, as when the government contracts with concessionaires to provide food services or run hotels in national parks or when ski areas use national forest land for their operations. The effects of this interaction can be far-reaching. For instance, proposals by ski areas to expand their snowmaking capacity on federal lands require review by a host of government agencies, including federal, state, and local environmental protection divisions. To be successful, a commercial operator must have knowledge of public laws, policies, and practices.

Many private or nonprofit businesses not related to recreation also use public lands, as in the case of ranchers who graze cattle on public lands or logging companies that cut timber in national forests. Effective government coordination is needed among all interested parties to promote a viable recreation and tourism industry. Although an awareness of public policy is essential at every government level, it is particularly crucial for managers grappling with controversial issues. Proposed resource management plans—particularly changes in forest practices—often attract the attention of diverse groups, including logging interests, recreational users, and environmental or conservation agencies. Today's park managers need to be politically savvy to balance a variety of constituents' interests in public lands and handle the public scrutiny inherent in their positions.

Commercial outdoor recreation organizations grapple with continuing challenges in achieving financial security. As segments of the industry expand rapidly, they may face a shakedown similar to that occurring in the maturing ski industry. Snowsports Industries America (SIA) reported skier/snowboarder visits totaled 56.6 million in 2012–2013, a decline from 60.5 million 2 years prior. The ski industry is also experiencing an aging skier population and the flattening of expansion in snowboarding (Snowsports Industries America, 2013). Anticipating and planning for the adverse effects of unfavorable weather is necessary in outdoor recreation and affects financial stability. For instance, snow-making costs at ski areas have increased to cover fluctuations in snow conditions, and increased insurance premiums have also contributed to rising costs in the industry.

As the number of visitors to public lands increases, recreation professionals have a responsibility to monitor and control use of those areas to prevent destruction of natural resources and enhance participant safety. Improved **environmental awareness** is necessary as instructors, guides, and managers need to abide by the increasingly strict regulations that control public use and educate their participants about those guidelines. Users must understand recommended environmental practices for minimizing impact on trails, rivers, and camping areas, particularly in high-traffic areas, and must abide by the restrictions in group numbers levied by federal and state agencies. Leaders need to minimize conflicts between diverse users, such as hikers and mountain bikers, skiers, snowshoers, snowmobilers, and users of personal watercraft and off-road vehicles. They also need to conduct activities in accordance with recognized safe practices in the activity to minimize accidents and rescues. Although client safety itself is an issue, cost is a concern as well. The public cannot afford to underwrite the costs of rescues, which increase as the total number of visitors in the outdoors escalates. Managers need to consider how sustainable or "green" practices for facilities can promote ethical use of natural resources, such as the National Ski Areas Association's Sustainable Slopes project, which has been endorsed by almost 200 ski areas (National Ski Areas Association, 2012).

Beyond increased environmental awareness, recreation professionals need to develop **cultural awareness** in an industry that has become more global. Travel companies now attract customers to trekking in Nepal, sea kayaking in New Zealand, bird watching in Central America, and skiing in Scandinavia, among many other opportunities. For recreational professionals who do their work abroad, understanding local customs, laws, and the environment is important in providing successful experiences. For instance, Norway has a heritage of land use for recreation that allows a visitor to camp on private lands as long as the camping is unobtrusive, but this practice would not be advisable in a place such as the province of Quebec, where certain rivers are strictly regulated and reserved for private salmon fishing and guiding.

Americans with Disabilities Act

Access to recreational facilities and services is being reexamined in light of the **Americans with Disabilities Act (ADA)** of 1990, which creates a unique set of challenges and opportunities for the industry. Recreation programmers need to adapt their programs to meet a variety of needs as people with physical disabilities grow more interested in enhancing their lifestyle with physical activity. For instance, water sports offer freedom of movement to people who use wheelchairs, enabling them to access the outdoors more easily. However, rugged terrain, remote wilderness environments, and necessary safety equipment inherent in some outdoor activities require a manager to be creative and practical in developing programs accessible to people with disabilities. The USDA Forest Service noted that early federal ADA task forces addressed the high level of modifications necessary in urban areas but did not take into consideration how those standards in an outdoor recreation area could change the setting and the experience for all people (USDA Forest Service, 2006). As a result, its Outdoor Recreation Accessibility Guidelines (2006) strive to protect unique characteristics of natural settings while integrating universal designs in facilities and programs to maximize accessibility.

The Forest Service guidelines address outdoor recreation access routes, beach access routes, camping and picnicking areas, and other constructed features. A separate section outlines guidelines for pedestrian hiking trails. The document addresses issues beyond the Forest Service's 1993 *Universal Access to Outdoor Recreation: A Design Guide*, which means it

may apply in situations such as primitive areas that the *Design Guide* would have exempted. Rapid advances in technology are enabling use of outdoor resources by those with disabilities, and interested participants with disabilities are becoming increasingly savvy about accessible opportunities.

Park managers, recreation programmers, outdoor outfitters, and guides must keep abreast of developments in this area as they create frameworks for improved access to programs and activities such as rafting, canoeing, hiking, and horseback riding. They must be aware of unique issues that can affect programming, such as how to accommodate assistive devices (including service animals) and how to review regulations and policies for inadvertent discrimination against people with disabilities, such as group size restrictions. More specific resources are now available for programmers, such as the American Canoe Association's *Teaching Paddling to People with Disabilities.*

A good example of an organization that is doing great work in promoting recreational activities for people with disabilities is the National Ability Center in Park City, Utah. It offers a broad range of activities, including skiing, snowboarding, horseback riding, swimming, cycling, sled hockey, and quad rugby. In 2013 the National Ability Center served over 18,000 people with disabilities through its various sport programs and activities (National Ability Center, 2013).

Therapeutic recreation professionals need to study the economic restructuring of the healthcare system and understand how a shift from institutional care to home-based care will affect delivery of services. As the population of the United States ages and the number of people with disabilities increases, the demand for services is likely to increase as well. The therapeutic recreation professional may be asked to integrate recreation services as a part of a comprehensive home healthcare plan. He or she might also explore respite care, wherein caregivers provide for older citizens at a central facility during the day, providing stimulating programs to involve and challenge participants.

In therapeutic recreation, staff may also need specialized training to effectively meet the needs of a particular population. A professional may need to understand substance abuse; eating disorders; attention deficit and hyperactivity disorders; mental health issues, such as depression and post-traumatic stress syndrome; and physical health issues, such as cardiac problems and disability challenges. Understanding the range of medications and their side effects in combination with exercise and environment effects is also important. Developing an accurate and positive portrait of each participant's capability is necessary, and recreation staff must work with agency personnel prior to establishing programs to develop program goals that meet participants' needs.

Risk Management

Understanding the role of **risk management** in recreation is integral to all segments of the industry. Employees have a responsibility to develop enjoyable programming at appropriate sites and conduct it prudently without eliminating the challenge and excitement that originally attracted people to the activity. Administrators and staff who understand the laws affecting recreation and are familiar with the elements of risk management can mitigate the increase in lawsuits against recreational professionals and settlements by the courts and insurance companies.

Recreation programs need written, well-defined risk management plans to establish guidelines for equipment and facility use, program development and operation, management of changing environmental conditions, and emergency preparedness. An organization's recommended practices should be reflected in its risk management plan, and an ongoing review of the plan is necessary to ensure that employees abide by the guidelines and that the guidelines are still appropriate in light of current standards in the field. Many programs have designated risk management committees to review procedures and accident reports and use outside evaluators to help target areas for improvement. Smaller businesses conduct internal reviews among staff and administrators to improve their practices. Many use advisory boards comprised of industry experts to review new programs and general operations.

Elements of a risk management program include, but are not limited to, the following:

- Participant health screening prior to participation to determine the appropriate level of involvement, if any
- Preprogram information to inform participants about an activity
- Equipment and facility safety checks
- Criteria for staff hiring, including necessary activity certifications or experience and first aid credentials
- Continuing education and training for staff
- Recommended progressions of activities that meet current national standards
- Adequate staff–student ratios and protocols for general and specific supervision of groups
- Emergency response protocols, including first aid response, evacuation, and search and rescue
- Critical accident protocols, including those covering interaction with families and the press.

Informed participant consent is an important legal issue in recreation programming. Participants must be made aware of the potential risks inherent in activities before they begin so they can make informed decisions about the nature of their participation. Organizations often provide preprogram activity information, recommended clothing and equipment lists, and an assumption-of-risk/waiver-of-liability form in an effort to inform people about the upcoming experience. Safety education is an integral part of a program plan, and individual and group responses and rescues in emergency situations are often practiced in recreational activities as a part of a participant's education. As the popularity of adventurous activities increases, professionals have a responsibility to train participants in rescue so that they do not have to rely on agencies to execute rescues on their behalf.

Greater degrees of risk are inherent in some recreational activities, which make them exciting, but organizations have a responsibility to use this element wisely. Leaders have a legal responsibility to develop programs that do not involve unreasonable risks, and they should only ask participants to perform activities with a clear benefit.

Summary

The complexity of modern life is likely to promote a continuing need for enjoyable, safe, and challenging recreational activities as a diversion for the public and as a partial solution to social problems in our society. Just as lifestyles have become more complex in the United States, so has the nature of the recreation profession. Industry professionals face numerous challenges as they seek to provide quality recreational experiences for diverse participants.

Technological changes in equipment and communications require employees to understand the impact of these changes on the recreation industry. Such things as cellular and satellite phones on wilderness trips and marketing through Internet websites and social media have changed the face of the industry. The ease of international travel and the emergence of popular eco-vacations overseas have prompted professionals to gain an understanding of different cultures and physical environments. Increasing government regulation, particularly in the area of safety, means professionals must be aware of and comply with new laws, policies, and procedures. As specific industry segments mature, employees will be held to higher and higher standards of training and performance. These challenges require employees to bring a broad range of skills to their positions and continue their education to deliver quality experiences that meet current standards in the field. The reward is involvement in enriching experiences that enhance the recreation employee's life and can effect social change.

Case Study 20-1 Collegiate University Embracing Technology

Collegiate University recently finished construction of a $56 million student recreation center in 2012. Prior to construction of the facility, the director of campus recreation, Aaron Burgoon, surveyed the student population to better understand their wants and needs for the facility. The administration aimed to take everyone's opinion into consideration and design a facility that would become the epicenter of campus life and fulfill the recreational needs of the student population. Although the benefits of the recreation center would reach faculty, staff, alumni, and the greater community, student participation was the major goal of the facility.

Highlights of the 8,000 square-foot state-of-the-art facility include:

- 3 pools
- 8 racquetball courts
- A 6-court gymnasium
- A quarter-mile elevated track
- A 40-foot rock-climbing wall
- 3 multipurpose rooms
- 200 pieces of cardiovascular equipment
- 100 weight machines
- Over 20,000 pounds of free weights

Student membership fees for the facility are incorporated into the student activity fee and are included in tuition. Faculty, staff, alumni, and community members pay approximately $50 per month.

Collegiate University was excited to unveil the new facility at the beginning of the 2012–2013 school year. Considering that the primary goal for the facility was to engage the student population in recreation participation, the director of campus recreation, Burgoon, collected baseline participation data for the facility and programs throughout the first year. Burgoon knew that the national average for participation in recreational opportunities on campus was approximately 75% (NIRSA, 2013) and was very disappointed to see that after the first academic year of operation only 40% of students at Collegiate University had used the recreational facility and programming.

To address this problem and make changes for the 2013–2014 year, Burgoon held a focus group meeting at the end of the school year with 50 of his student employees. The student employees provided very insightful feedback to Director Burgoon. They made statements such as, "Everyone knows the facility is here, but no one really understands what we have to offer," "Many students do not read their university e-mail," and "A lot of people are afraid to participate alone." Burgoon assessed the information he gained through the focus groups along with the initial survey data he had from the facility.

Through his analysis, he realized that one of the major factors associated with student participation had to do with communication. The facility itself met all of the needs of the student population, yet if students do not know what is offered and when, they will not attend. After doing more research, Burgoon realized a vast majority of students were on some, if not many, social media platforms. He realized that embracing social media may be a cost-effective and efficient way to reach his target student population. Considering that Burgoon is nearing retirement and has yet to embrace technology and social media into his lifestyle, he once again sought the assistance of his student employees.

Put yourself in the shoes of one of the student employees hired by the Burgoon and answer the following questions.

(*continues*)

Case Study 20-1   Collegiate University Embracing Technology (Continued)

Questions for Discussion

1. How can the recreation center use technology and social media to better communicate with the student population? What platforms would you use? What types of messages would you send through each platform? Why? Identify specific messages that you could potentially use.

2. In addition to raising awareness about the recreation center, how else could the facility use social media? What else could the recreation center do to embrace technology (in addition to the social media platforms previously addressed)? Explain.

3. Create an event that the recreation center could organize that would both embrace technology and aid in the goal of increasing student participation.

4. What are your recommendations to Director Burgoon on how to assess the recreation center's use of technology? How could you tell if your social media efforts were in fact helping to increase student participation rates?

Resources

American Camp Association (ACA)
5000 State Road 67 North
Martinsville, IN 46151
765-342-8456
http://www.acacamps.org

American Recreation Coalition (ARC)
1225 New York Avenue NW, Suite 450
Washington, DC 20005
202-682-9530
http://www.funoutdoors.com/arc

Association for Experiential Education (AEE)
3775 Iris Avenue, Suite 4
Boulder, CO 80301
303-440-8844
http://www.aee.org

Disabled Sports USA
451 Hungerford Drive, Suite 100
Rockville, MD 20850
301-217-0960
http://www.dsusa.org

Jewish Community Centers of North America
520 Eighth Avenue
New York, NY 10018
212-532-4949
http://www.jcca.org/index.lasso

National Golf Foundation (NGF)
1150 S. US Highway One, Suite 401
Jupiter, FL 33477
561-744-6006
http://www.ngf.org

National Intramural-Recreation Sport Association (NIRSA)
4185 SW Research Way
Corvallis, Oregon 97333
541-766-8211
http://www.nirsa.org

National Park Service (NPS)
  1849 C Street, NW
  Washington, DC 20240
  202-208-6834
  General information: http://www.nps.gov
  Job information: http://www.nps.gov
  /gettinginvolved/employment/index.htm

National Recreation and Park Association
(NRPA)
  22377 Belmont Ridge Road
  Ashburn, VA 20148
  703-858-0784
  http://www.nrpa.org

Resort and Commercial Recreation
Association (RCRA)
  P.O. Box 1564
  Dubuque, IA 52004
  http://www.rcra.org

Shape America
(formerly American Alliance for Health,
Physical Education, Recreation and
Dance—AAHPERD)
  1900 Association Drive
  Reston, VA 22191

  800-213-7193
  http://www.shapeamerica.org

USDA Forest Service
  1400 Independence Avenue, SW
  Washington, DC 20250
  202-205-8333
  http://www.fs.fed.us

Young Men's Christian Association
(YMCA) of the USA
  101 N. Wacker Drive
  Chicago, IL 60606
  800-872-9622
  http://www.ymca.net

Young Women's Christian Association
(YWCA) of the USA
  1015 18th Street NW, Suite 1100
  Washington, DC 20036
  202-467-0801
  http://www.ywca.org

Key Terms

Americans with Disabilities Act (ADA), campus recreation, community-based recreation, cultural awareness, direct participation, environmental awareness, indirect participation, informed participant consent, military recreation, outdoor recreation, parks movement, private sector, public recreation, public sector, risk management, therapeutic recreation

References

American Association for Retired Persons. (2004). *Baby boomers envision retirement II: Survey of baby boomers' expectations for retirement.* Washington, DC: Author.

American Camping Association. (2013). Facts and trends. Retrieved from http://www.acacamps.org/media/aca-facts-trends

Centers for Disease Control and Prevention. (2012). CDC vital signs. Retrieved from http://www.cdc.gov/vitalsigns/Walking/index.html

Cheeseman-Day, J. (n.d.). *Population profile of the United States.* Washington, DC: U.S. Census Bureau.

Cordell, H. K. (2012). Outdoor recreation trends and futures: A technical document supporting the Forest Service 2010 RPA

Assessment. Retrieved from http://www.srs
.fs.usda.gov/pubs/40453#sthash.6PT33UFT
.dpuf

Cui, Y., Mahoney, E., & Herbowicz, T. (2013).
Economic benefits to local communities
from national park visitation, 2011. Natural
Resource Report NPS/NRSS/EQD/NRTR—
2013/631. Fort Collins, CO: National Park
Service.

Dolesh, R. J. (2013, May 1). Really? We want
kids to use technology now? *Parks &
Recreation*. Retrieved from http://www
.parksandrecreation.org/2013/May/Really--
We-Want-Kids-to-Use-Technology-Now-/

Heika, M. (2014). PBS to air behind the scenes look
at USA sled hockey team. Retrieved from
http://starsblog.dallasnews.com/2014/02
/pbs-to-air-behind-the-scenes-look-at-usa
-sled-hockey-team-featuring-planos-taylor
-lipsett-beginning-monday.html/

Jayson, S. (2013, May 28). AARP to coach aging
Boomers 'reimagining' their lives. *USA Today*.
Retrieved from http://www.usatoday.com
/story/news/nation/2013/05/28/aarp
-boomers-jobs-coaching/2358551/

Lee, R. F. (2003). *Public use of the national park
system 1872–2000*. Washington, DC: National
Park Service.

National Ability Center. (2013). Our story.
Retrieved from http://www.discovernac.org
/about/our-story/

National Intramural-Recreation Sports
Association. (2013). NIRSA Services
Corporation. Retrieved from http://www
.nirsa.org/wcm/About_Us/NIRSA_Services
/wcm/About_Us/NIRSA_Services
_Corporation/NIRSA_Services_Corporation
.aspx?hkey=bff8f04b-264a-4394-b5cf
-710e8975c4ff

National Park Service. (2013). Annual summary
report. Retrieved from https://irma.nps.gov
/Stats/SSRSReports/System%20Wide%20

Reports/Annual%20Summary%20Report%20
%28One%20Year%29

National Recreation and Park Association. (2010).
*Why parks and recreation are essential public
services*. Retrieved from http://www.nrpa.org
/uploadedFiles/nrpa.org/Advocacy/Resources
/Parks-Recreation-Essential-Public-Services
-January-2010.pdf

National Ski Areas Association. (2010). *NSAA
sustainable slopes annual report 2012*.
Lakewood, CO: Author.

Outdoor Industry Association. (2012). The
outdoor recreation economy. Retrieved from
http://www.outdoorindustry.org/pdf/OIA
_OutdoorRecEconomyReport2012.pdf

Outdoor Industry Association. (2013). Outdoor
recreation participation report. Retrieved
from https://www.outdoorindustry.org
/research/participation.php?action=detail
&research_id=19

Quigley, S. (2004). Military athletes have proud
Olympic history. Retrieved from http://www
.defense.gov/news/newsarticle.aspx?id=25521

Snowsports Industries America. (2013). 2013
SIA snowsports fact sheet. Retrieved
from http://www.snowsports.org
/SuppliersServiceProviders/ResearchSurveys
/SnowSportsFactSheet

Sporting Goods Manufacturers Association.
(2010a). SGMA's 2010 state of the industry
report released. Retrieved from http://www
.sgma.com/press/224_SGMA's-2010-State
-of-the-Industry-Report-Released

Sporting Goods Manufacturers Association.
(2010b). SGMA study identifies active
segments of U.S. population. Retrieved from
http://www.sgma.com/press/237_SGMA
-Study-Identifies-Active-Segments-of-U.S.
-Population

U.S. Department of Commerce. (2010). *The next
four decades: The older population in the
United States 2010–2050*. Washington, DC:
Author.

U.S. Department of the Interior. (2013). What is AGO? Retrieved from http://www.doi.gov/americasgreatoutdoors/index.cfm

U.S. Department of Veterans Affairs. (2013). In the spotlight. Retrieved from https://www.myhealth.va.gov/mhv-portal-web/anonymous.portal?_nfpb=true&_nfto=false&_pageLabel=spotlightArchive&contentPage=spotlight/September2012/spotlight_sep2012_paralympics.html

USDA Forest Service. (2006). Accessibility guidebook for outdoor recreation and trails. Retrieved from http://www.fs.fed.us/recreation/programs/accessibility/htmlpubs/htm06232801/toc.htm

USDA Forest Service. (2013). Jobs. Retrieved from http://www.fs.fed.us/fsjobs/

Yousey-Elsener, K. (2012, October 29). National benchmarking spotlight: National trends in participation in campus recreation. Retrieved from http://www.campuslabs.com/2012/10/national-benchmarking-spotlight-national-trends-in-participation-in-campus-recreation/

Part VI

Career Preparation

Chapter 21 Strategies for Career Success

Chapter

21

Mary A. Hums and
Virginia R. Goldsbury

Strategies for Career Success

© Hemera/Thinkstock

Learning Objectives

Upon completion of this chapter, students should be able to:

1. Assess the realities of employment opportunities in the sport industry.

2. Recognize the importance of internships and volunteering for gaining valuable sport industry experience.

3. Design a personal job search plan.

4. Evaluate the role of informational interviewing and develop a professional network as part of an overall career development program.

5. Compose an effective resume, reference list, and cover letter.

6. Develop an effective "elevator speech."

7. Take the steps necessary to prepare for a successful job interview.

8. Identify the factors that make for a successful job candidate.

9. Recognize that landing a job in the sport industry is often the result of being more prepared than the other candidates.

Introduction

What is your dream job in sport management? General manager of the Miami Heat? Director of stadium operations at Yankee Stadium? Athletic director at the University of Oregon? Marketing director for the U.S. Olympic Committee? Director of social media for the NFL? How do you begin to climb the sport industry ladder? What are the realities of trying to break into the sport industry? This chapter deals with these questions and gives you suggestions on how to market your most valuable resource—you!

Myths About Careers in Sport Management: A Reality Check

People are drawn to the sport management profession for a great number of reasons. The most common reason is a love of sport. To be very honest, many people love sport, but a love of sport is simply not enough to land a job in the industry. As a matter of fact, if you gave that as your answer to a prospective sport employer in an interview, it would be a very short interview! Prospective employers look for people who want to work in the business of sport. An often used expression is, "It's nice that you love sports, but can you put people in seats?" In other words, sport employers look for people who are businesspeople first and sport enthusiasts second.

People seeking careers in the sport industry often have misperceptions about what working in the industry will be like, resulting in a number of common myths about working in the sport industry. This section is not meant to discourage students from going into the industry but rather is intended to present a realistic picture of what the job market is like for people trying to break in.

Myth 1: A Sport Management Degree Is a Ticket to Success

The number of sport management programs in the country is growing, with more than 300 colleges and universities currently offering sport management as a major at either the undergraduate or graduate level. All of these graduates are seeking employment in the sport industry. In addition, some students graduating with degrees in management, marketing, public relations, communications, or exercise science, as well as many from MBA programs and law schools, are vying to land jobs in the field. People currently working in industries outside of sport, such as advertising, banking, law, or financial services, are increasingly considering career changes into the sport industry, showcasing the transferable skills, such as sales or merchandising, they acquired in those other industries.

A couple of examples illustrate the demand for jobs in the industry. On average, 450 to 550 job openings are posted each year at the Professional Baseball Employment Opportunities (PBEO) Job Fair that is held in conjunction with the Winter Baseball Meetings (PBEO, 2013). When the New Orleans Hornets had an opening for a community relations position with an annual salary of $25,000, the opening drew 1,000 applications in 1 week (Helyar, 2006). Positions with the organizing committee for the Chicago 2016 Olympic and Paralympic bid drew thousands of applications, and once the bid was awarded to Rio de Janeiro, those working for the bid committee found themselves unemployed (Chicago Press Release Services, 2009). The large volume of job applicants has caused a number of sport organizations to incorporate electronic databases and websites to gather job applicant information. Obviously, competition for jobs is intense, and a sport management degree does not guarantee a job in the industry.

It is important to note, however, that the sport industry is broader than just professional sport. A myriad of employment opportunities exist in health and fitness, facility management, higher education, recreational sport, sport for people with disabilities, youth sports, nonprofit agencies, and other areas. Also, the more willing a person is to relocate, the better the chance he or she has of finding employment.

What, then, are the advantages to earning a degree in sport management? First, one learns about the application of business principles to the sport industry. Taking a marketing class, for example, provides groundwork in basic marketing concepts. Sport marketing is inherently different from traditional marketing because the sport product is unpredictable and perishable, and the sport marketer has very little, if any, control over the core product. A sport management major will have a solid understanding of this difference. A sport management degree also gives a student working knowledge of the industry. Because classes are geared specifically toward sport, students are immersed in industry happenings in the classroom, constantly learning about current issues and current events. Students read publications such as *Street & Smith's SportsBusiness Journal* and *Athletic Business*.

Many sport management degree programs allow initial access to the industry via **internship** opportunities with sport organizations. These hands-on learning experiences give students the chance to live the sport industry firsthand, gaining valuable work experience. Beyond this, the internship allows students to meet people working in the industry and begin establishing a professional **network**. In addition, a good number of sport management academic programs have professors who have come to academia after working in the industry and who actively maintain industry ties, giving students another way to access a network of sport industry professionals. The importance of networking is discussed later in this chapter. Finally, when working on a sport management degree, students learn about opportunities to build their resumes. What will make your resume stand out from all the others? Being involved in as many sport management–related opportunities as possible! Sport management programs often stage campus or community events such as 3-on-3 basketball tournaments, golf tournaments, and road races. Sport management programs routinely receive requests from sport organizations such as their university's athletic department or local sport commission for event volunteers. Students are wise to take advantage of these opportunities and get involved. Having these experiences on a resume makes a difference because they indicate one's commitment to the industry. People who do not major in sport management do not necessarily have access to these resume-building opportunities.

Myth 2: It's Not Who You Know, It's What You Know

The truth is, "It's not what you know, it's who you know." Actually, we could take this a step further and say, "It's not who you know, it's who knows you." Having a degree is simply not enough. In the sport industry, as much or perhaps more than in just about any other industry, people hire someone because of a personal recommendation from someone else. The importance of networking cannot be overstated.

Sport managers have to actively work to expand their networks to include all kinds of people. It is easy and comfortable for people to build networks with others like themselves, but for the sport industry to continue to thrive and to serve all constituents, sport managers must diversify their networks so that opportunities will be available to all. Diversity in the workforce is the key to success for innovative organizations and having as diverse a network as possible strengthens one's opportunities and experiences.

Myth 3: Most Employment Opportunities Are in Professional Sport or NCAA Division I Athletic Departments

When people hear the term *sport management*, the jobs that most often come to mind are in professional sport or National Collegiate Athletic Association (NCAA) Division I college athletics. To the question, "What do you want to do with your sport management degree?" a common answer is, "I want to be the general manager of the (name of the nearest major professional sport franchise)" or "I want to be the athletic director at (name of the school that won the most recent national football or basketball championship)." The fact is that the number of jobs in professional sport is limited. For example, at present, there are only 30 Major League Baseball (MLB) general manager jobs. The same is true for the other major league professional sports. Professional sport front offices tend to be relatively small compared with other employers. Minor league offices employ minimal staff as full-time employees. A minor league baseball franchise at the A level may have as few as 10 to 12 full-time employees, whereas a AAA franchise may have 20 to 25. Also, there tends to be a relatively low turnover rate in these positions. People who get jobs in professional sport tend to stay in their jobs. In addition, people already in the industry tend to get "recycled" when positions come open. If the owner of a ball club is looking for a new general manager, for example, he or she will look to former general managers or current assistant general managers to fill the position.

Many colleges and universities are currently dealing with economic setbacks or concerns unrelated to sport that, in turn, affect the amount of money spent on athletic programs. If funding is not available to athletic departments, those departments will be unable to hire staff. State universities are especially susceptible to this problem, because state lawmakers make decisions about where limited state funding will go. If the state legislature cuts the amount of dollars available to a university, the cutbacks will be felt throughout all areas of the institution, including athletics. This makes it difficult for college and university athletic departments to create new positions. To make up for this shortfall in personnel, however, a number of college and university athletic departments are offering more graduate assistantships and internships. These positions offer opportunities for those trying to enter the field to gain experience.

Someone entering the sport industry needs to look beyond professional and college sport for job opportunities. The multibillion-dollar segments of the industry include sporting goods and apparel, recreational sport, and the health and fitness area, to name a few. The purpose of this text is to help students broaden their horizons to see the vast opportunities that lie in front of them in all different segments of the industry.

Myth 4: Sport Management Jobs Are Glamorous and Exciting

Many people have the impression that working in the sport industry is glamorous and exciting. They have visions of "hanging out" with famous athletes, driving around in chauffeured limousines, and being in the glare of the spotlight. However, when it comes to working in the sport industry, nothing could be further from the truth. No one goes to a University of Alabama football game to watch the ticket manager do his or her job. People do not go to a Lakers game in the Staples Center to watch the event coordinator organize the operational details of the game. The bottom line is that sport managers labor in the background so that others can enjoy the spotlight. A typical work schedule for an event coordinator is 60 to 70 hours per week, including lots of late nights and long weekends. When other people are going out to be entertained they are coming to the place where the sport manager is hard at work. Although it is exciting to work at games or events, a sport manager very seldom—if ever—gets to see any of the action of the game or event itself. There are too many behind-the-scenes details to take care of to be a fan.

To a large degree, the work of sport managers is similar to jobs in the corporate world, but they are unique in that they require industry-specific knowledge. Someone who is an accountant for the St. Louis Cardinals, for example, is doing the same job as someone who is an accountant for any large business, but the sport accountant needs to understand player salary concerns such as deferred compensation. A sport lawyer works with the same legal issues as a nonsport lawyer, such as contracts or licensing agreements, but the sport lawyer has to understand salary caps and luxury taxes. General business knowledge is important, but specific knowledge of the sport industry is essential. Another distinction is the affiliation with a team or league. People just feel differently about working in sport. It is more fun to say, "I work in sales for the San Francisco 49ers" than it is to say, "I work in the business office for Artisan Steel Fabrication." There is just something special about going to your office when your office is in a ballpark or an arena.

Myth 5: Sport Management Jobs Pay Well

The expression "You have to pay your dues" is as true in the sport industry as in other parts of the business world. In general, salaries—especially starting salaries—tend to be low in the sport industry. Because of the high number of applicants for these jobs, salaries can stay low and people are thankful for the opportunities when they do get jobs. Demand for the jobs far outstrips the supply. How many times have you heard someone say something like, "I'd work for the Atlanta Braves for free!" The starting

salaries tend to be rather low, although there is potential for increased earnings as you move up in the industry. According to Belson (2012), be prepared for salaries around $35,000, although some jobs will pay even less.

Now that you are aware of some of the barriers you may encounter on the way to finding your place in the sport industry, how do you go about starting down the road to your sport management career? How do you begin undertaking a successful job search? The remainder of this chapter gives you some tools to work with—tools such as informational interviews, job interview skills, and resume writing. Good luck!

Finding a Job

Finding a job, any job, is a difficult, time-consuming, and challenging process. At this time, you are dealing with building a career; therefore, your first job in the sport industry is just that—your first job, the first step in what it is hoped will be a satisfying career. To prepare yourself, you need to begin early in your collegiate experience, as early as your first year!

You need to have a plan when seeking a job. **Figure 21-1** shows you the various phases of this process. The following section provides details that will help guide you along the way.

Steps to Finding the Best First Job

1. Know Yourself

Analyze your skills, abilities, interests, and preferred workplace environment. Before you know anything else, you must know yourself. Your goal is to find a job utilizing your strengths, challenging yourself where you want/need to be challenged, and minimizing your frustrations. A variety of instruments can help you with this exercise. Although many are online, do not use such assessments in a vacuum. Use your college's career office. Think of yourself as a brand—how would you describe yourself and sell your strengths and abilities?

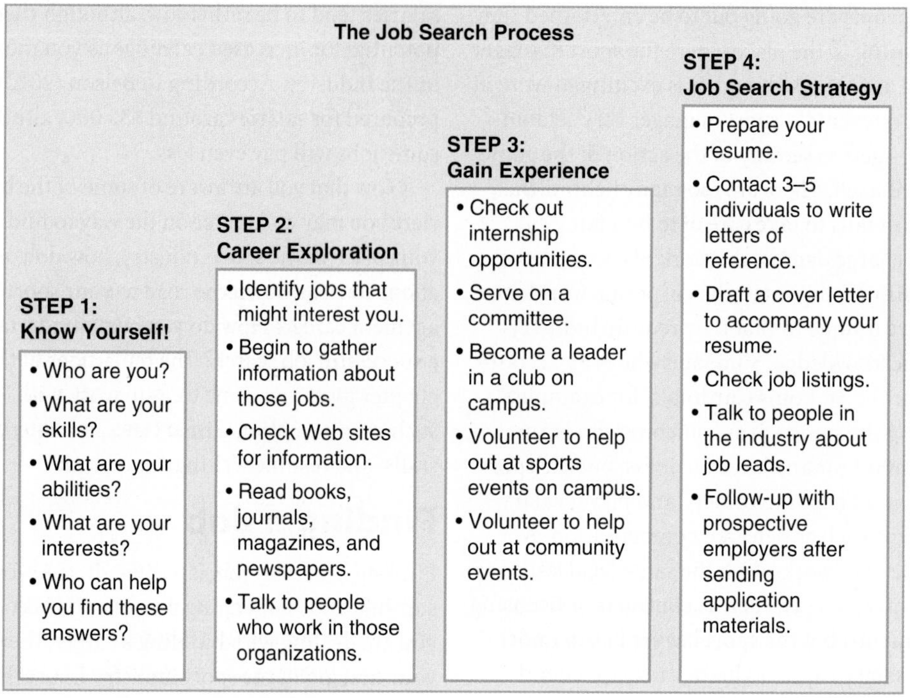

The Job Search Process

STEP 1:
Know Yourself!

- Who are you?
- What are your skills?
- What are your abilities?
- What are your interests?
- Who can help you find these answers?

STEP 2:
Career Exploration

- Identify jobs that might interest you.
- Begin to gather information about those jobs.
- Check Web sites for information.
- Read books, journals, magazines, and newspapers.
- Talk to people who work in those organizations.

STEP 3:
Gain Experience

- Check out internship opportunities.
- Serve on a committee.
- Become a leader in a club on campus.
- Volunteer to help out at sports events on campus.
- Volunteer to help out at community events.

STEP 4:
Job Search Strategy

- Prepare your resume.
- Contact 3–5 individuals to write letters of reference.
- Draft a cover letter to accompany your resume.
- Check job listings.
- Talk to people in the industry about job leads.
- Follow-up with prospective employers after sending application materials.

Figure 21-1 The Job Search Process

2. Career Exploration

Exploring careers and jobs, although time consuming, can prove to be interesting and valuable. Explore all aspects of the sport industry and then select those most interesting to you and begin your research. The more informed you are, the better prepared you will be to make a decision about your own career. The first step is to learn as much as you can about each area. Read professional journals, magazines, newspapers, online resources, and books. Follow leading sport managers on Twitter. Once you can speak intelligently regarding your field of interest, begin informational interviewing. Talk to people who work in positions or organizations that interest you. This is a wonderful way to utilize and expand your network while gaining valuable insight into a variety of career paths. Informational interviewing will be discussed in detail later in the chapter.

3. Gain Experience

It is a well-known fact that with experience comes marketability. What do employers mean when they ask if you have experience? What kind of experience are they expecting? One way to begin to answer these questions is to learn what makes a candidate valuable for employment. Ask yourself - what you would expect from someone you were going to pay? How do you gain this valuable experience? As a student, you have numerous opportunities to experiment with different segments of the sport industry, gain new skills, and improve the skills you have. You have access to people in all segments of the sport industry as well as volunteer opportunities. In many cases you can earn college credit while experiencing a portion of the industry or a particular department within the area and making valuable connections. Professional sport franchises, marketing agencies, health clubs, facilities, sports commissions, sporting goods companies, and your college or university athletic department all offer internships. The work is demanding and the pay often nonexistent, but you will gain valuable experience. An internship can occasionally lead to permanent employment, but even if it does not, you will be increasing your marketability. Remember—no matter the pay—an internship is an investment in yourself.

In addition to an organized internship, take advantage of as many opportunities to expand your horizons as you can. Organizations such as the Professional Golfers Association (PGA), the Ladies Professional Golfers Association (LPGA), the United States Tennis Association (USTA), the Special Olympics, the National Wheelchair Basketball Association, and local sports commissions need hoards of volunteers for their events. Take the initiative and create your own volunteer opportunities if none currently exist. Remember, on-campus organizations also offer leadership opportunities. Student government associations, fraternities or sororities, and other student-run organizations always need people. You can gain valuable—and transferable—leadership skills working with these groups. Each experience will help define your long-term goals and in the process make you more interesting to potential employers. Get involved early and often!

4. Job Search Strategy

Finding a job requires time, energy, and thoughtful preparation. Now that you have a clearer picture of your skills, abilities, and goals, you are in a position to begin writing an effective resume and accompanying cover letter. These documents should reflect the energy you have expended preparing for a management career and demonstrate a professional attitude. You may have heard the comment that "Looking for a job is a full-time job." This certainly can be true. However, you may not be able to spend 40 hours per week on your job search, so make sure to set up a schedule that works for you and stick to it. Decide to make a certain number of phone calls, send a certain number of e-mails, mail or e-mail a certain number of applications, and/or research particular organizations each week. Keep a well-documented journal of your job search activities. Follow up each application with a phone call a week or two later. There is a fine line between being persistent and being aggressive, but you want your prospective employers to know you are interested in working with them (without being perceived as a stalker!).

Where should you look for job openings in the sport industry? As a sport management student, your college or university sport management program is a good place to start. Sport organizations routinely send information about job and internship openings to these programs. Check with your departmental faculty; they may have connections in the industry and may know of some openings that are not publicly advertised. Also check the websites for teams and sport organizations. For example, *NCAA News*, which lists openings in intercollegiate athletics, is available online. Organizations such as Nike, the United States Olympic Committee, and the International Paralympic Committee also list job and internship opportunities online. Traditional job websites such as Monster.com or Jobs.com may also have a selection of sport jobs. Although a number of websites and Twitter accounts provide information specifically about job opportunities in the sport industry, remember that these are often not free services, and there will be a cost associated with using them. Some sport-related job websites include Team-Work Online (www.teamworkonline.com), JobsInSports.com, or SportsRecruitment.com. You can also find out about jobs by attending a career fair sponsored by a local sport organization. For example, Pacers Sports and Entertainment hosts an annual career fair that includes more than 25 employers (Pacers Sports and Entertainment, 2012), and the Atlanta Braves host an annual Sports Industry Career Fair featuring opportunities in the Southeastern region of the United States (Atlanta Braves, 2013). Finally, your university's career services office also may have a jobs database where employers who list employment opportunities may be particularly interested in students from your school.

© Jaimie Duplass/ShutterStock, Inc.

Informational Interviewing

One effective means of expanding your understanding of an industry, an organization, or a particular job or department is to speak to someone who is already there. The information you glean from **informational interviewing** serves as a foundation for making your own career decisions, while simultaneously building a valuable network of professional connections. You may choose to interview relatives, friends, acquaintances, alumni of your university, or someone you have never met but has a position of interest to you. Alumni are sometimes an overlooked resource; however, they are often very willing to help students from their school. Check with your career center or the alumni relations office, which may maintain a database of alumni who have offered their services for just this purpose. Your academic department or specific faculty may also be able to supply you with a list of helpful alumni.

Once you have decided to do an informational interview, how should you proceed? First, you need to schedule an appointment for a phone interview, Skype call, or in-person meeting. Have your questions prepared before you call in case the person you are trying to reach is available immediately. You want to present yourself as an aspiring professional, so have your questions written down. You have 20 minutes to talk to the person who has a job you may like to have and who you may want to work with/for some day. What is it you really want to know? If you feel you need more time, excuse yourself and ask if you might talk to him or her again if you have additional questions. You might also ask for suggestions of someone else to contact.

What Do I Ask?

Only you can decide what is truly important to you. Some suggestions to consider are as follows:

- Please briefly describe what you do. What tasks take most of your time? How would you describe your working conditions, including hours, pressure, pace, and so on? How does your position relate to the rest of the organization?
- What particular character and personality traits would you suggest one needs to be successful in your position in this industry?
- What experiences, education, and other training would prepare me to enter this field?
- What kind of lifestyle choices have you had to make because of your job and how do you feel about them?
- What about your job do you find most satisfying? What is the most challenging or frustrating?
- I know that the sport industry is very difficult to break into. What two pieces of career advice would you offer to help me successfully enter this world?

- During the course of your career, did you have a mentor? If so, who was it and how did that person help you?
- Can you recommend two or three other people who would be worthwhile for me to speak with? May I use your name when writing or calling them?

Additional Hints About the Informational Interviewing Process

- Conduct your interview at the interviewee's place of business, if possible.
- Dress appropriately. This is a business meeting, so wear business attire.
- Be professional and articulate in your presentation.
- Observe the setting, the overall culture of the organization, and the relationships among the employees.
- Bring copies of your resume and business cards (if you have them—and you should have them).
- While there, ask yourself if you would be comfortable working in this environment.
- Get business cards from each person you meet.
- Send a personally written thank-you note immediately afterward. It can be hand-written if your handwriting is legible; otherwise, it should be typed. E-mail is also acceptable if you have been communicating that way. Remember: appropriate grammar is expected in an e-mail, not text messaging, tweets, or chat abbreviations!
- Keep accurate notes of your interviews, as you may need to refer to them later.

Other Sources of Information

Professional journals, websites, relevant books, and industry publications are valuable sources of career information. They provide current trends and plans for the future. Many of these have been discussed in previous chapters, such as *Street & Smith's SportsBusiness Journal*,

which is required reading for any sport management student and professional. Know the sources for your particular segment of interest, whether it is college athletics, professional sport, event management, facility management, marketing, health and fitness, or recreation. Most industry segments have an association that provides support for the profession. For example, the National Intramural-Recreational Sports Association (NIRSA) is the professional organization for campus recreation. The National Association of Collegiate Directors of Athletics (NACDA) serves this purpose in intercollegiate athletics. The National Federation of State High School Associations (NFSHSA) provides information for people working in scholastic sport. These associations provide valuable connections, current relevant information, and sometimes job postings. Some have student memberships, which is a convenient way to begin your professional affiliations.

Marketing Yourself

Writing an Effective Resume

Before you begin to write your **resume**, make a list of your previous jobs and extracurricular activities. Evaluate your activities relative to your career goals. You will need to discuss each experience with prospective employers, demonstrating its significance to you as well as the organization for which you worked. Present yourself as a potential colleague, not "just" a student.

Tips to Effectively Interpret and Present Your Experiences

- Your experience counts! Acknowledge your accomplishments in activities, internships, and jobs.
- Use the language of the industry when appropriate. This is not to be confused with slang. Each industry has vocabulary, including acronyms, that may be specific to it. Using these terms demonstrates your knowledge of the industry.

- Present your experiences through the lens of your career goal. Draw connections between your work and your field of interest.
- Convey your learning as well as your duties. Did you attend marketing strategy meetings, brainstorming sessions, or other relevant meetings? Demonstrate insights gained and information acquired.
- Quantify whenever appropriate. That means monetary amounts, percentages, and numbers. How many participants were part of the event you organized? How many additional corporate sponsors participated this year because of your efforts? How much money was raised? Figures give the reader a clearer picture of the depth and breadth of your experience.
- Demonstrate the value you brought to the environment: the job, internship, volunteer, or extracurricular activity.
- Be prepared with "talking points" demonstrating the valuable personal attributes you bring to the workplace, such as time management, conflict resolution, decision making, adaptability, and leadership.
- Assemble a portfolio of projects and documents showcasing your skills and talents related to your career goals.

Resume Outline

1. *Heading: Name, address, telephone number, e-mail address.* Remember, you want to be easy to reach while presenting a professional image. Therefore, provide a phone number where you will get messages if you are not available and an e-mail address that you regularly check. Be sure to set up a professional-sounding e-mail address. What professional image do you convey to a potential employer if your e-mail address is partygirl@myschool.edu or partyboy@school.com?

If you have your own website or an account on a social network such as Facebook, Twitter, Foursquare, or Pinterest, make sure the information you have on it presents an image that you want a prospective employer to see. There is no way to be sure exactly who is looking at your online profile. You may think if you allow only your "friends" to have access, your information is secure. However, there are always cracks. For example, government agencies can access your profile under the auspices of the Patriot Act. Consider using LinkedIn for your professional networking.

Understand the ramifications of posting questionable material. Even if the material is intended for friends, it can be viewed by anyone with Internet access. What is funny or cute to friends may have a very different (and negative) impact on potential employers. If you are in a photo that someone else posts with your name on it, you will come up in a search! According to a recent poll conducted by Harris Interactive, 37% of hiring mangers use social networking sites to screen applicants and an additional 11% said they intended to start doing so. The majority of employers said they were looking to see if the candidates presented themselves professionally. Potential red flags to employers included provocative photos, discussions of alcohol/drug use, complaints about former employers, and poor writing ("37 Percent of Employers," 2013). There is only one way to ensure that no one has access to potentially damaging information or photographs online: Don't put them online in the first place!

2. *Objective: Your resume needs a focus.* This section is optional, but if you choose to include a written objective on your resume, then it must be well thought out and

constructed. Be specific, but not limiting. You may write a summary statement that includes your long-term goals.

3. *Education.* Include the college or university you are attending or have graduated from and your degree, major, and minor. Do not include high school information. If your university grade point average (GPA) is a 3.00 or better, you should include it. Employers may think it is less than that if they do not see it on the resume.

   Include any national or international student-exchange experience. Students sometimes list honors with education; some have a separate section. In either case, they should be listed. Honors include scholarships, dean's list, honor societies, and academic awards. Students sometimes include a selection of the courses they have taken that may not be obvious to the reader but are related to the position for which they are applying.

4. *Experience.* When writing about your experiences, think in terms of your accomplishments, what you brought to the organization, and any positive changes resulting from your work there. Use impact statements. Begin each statement with an action verb or skill. Never just restate the job description.

   Experiences can be grouped to ensure the employer focuses on those most relevant to your career goals, such as "Sport Experience" and "Other Experience." By using this format, you can highlight all the sport activities in which you have participated (excluding varsity and intramural athletics). Be sure to list experiences in reverse chronological order, listing your most recent experiences first.

5. *Accomplishments.* Include major accomplishments demonstrating the qualities an employer looks for in a potential employee (e.g., self-financed 100% of my educational expenses; salesperson of the month 3 consecutive months; hiked the entire Appalachian Trail, Spring 2013). This should include at least two entries. The placement of this section depends on the types of accomplishments listed.

6. *Skills.* In this section you may include foreign languages you speak, including a level of understanding: fluent, intermediate, or basic. You may include specific computer packages and systems (e.g., desktop publishing, Web design, ticketing systems), particularly if you have advanced skills.

7. *Activities.* These are activities organized by the school, the local area, or region (athletics, student government, band member) independent of the things you do by yourself (reading, playing music, fitness), which should not be on your resume.

Final Resume Tips

- Organize information logically.
- Use a simple, easy-to-read font.
- Tailor the information to the job you are seeking.
- Pay attention to spelling, punctuation, and grammar. Making even one spelling error means the employer will not consider you any further.
- Have several people proofread your document.
- Consult the professionals in your campus career services office.
- Typically, a resume for someone just graduating with an undergraduate degree is one page. A resume can be two pages, but the information on the second page must be important enough for the reader to turn the page. Therefore, one-page-only resumes are encouraged.

- If you are mailing your resume, use good-quality white or off-white paper, and be sure to mail it in a large, flat envelope so you do not have to fold your resume.
- E-mailed resumes: Copy and paste your document into the body of the e-mail. Never submit your resume as an attachment unless specifically requested to do so. Not all e-mail programs can read all attachments. The same is true for the cover letter. Resumes submitted as Word documents are easier for employers to access but also may be modified by others. If you choose to submit your application materials in PDF format, they will have a higher level of security, but may present a barrier to being read.

Remember, the goal of your resume is to get an interview. The goal of the interview is to get the job.

As an example, a typical one-page resume is presented in **Figure 21-2**. This document is a good example of how the information in this chapter can be utilized to create a winning resume. You can also visit websites such as Monster.com or Forbes.com to find additional examples and suggestions for resumes.

The "Elevator Speech"

In the course of looking for employment in the sport industry, there will be times when you will meet potential employers or influential people in an informal setting. When they find out you are a job seeker and ask you about yourself, you had better be prepared with an answer that is professional, focused, and projects positivity about you and your experiences. This 30-second to 1-minute conversation is sometimes referred to as an "elevator speech" or "elevator pitch"—in reference to the amount of time you might ride in an elevator with someone between floors. Collamer (2013) offers the following nine steps for developing a successful elevator speech:

1. Clarify your job target.
2. Put it on paper.
3. Format it.
4. Tailor the pitch to them, not you.
5. Eliminate industry jargon.
6. Read your pitch out loud.
7. Practice, practice, practice (then solicit feedback).
8. Prepare a few variations.
9. Nail it with confidence.

Having this description of yourself prepared in advance will help with those potentially awkward meetings with people. You will always be prepared and professional!

References

Assume that employers will want to check your **references** before they make you a job offer. Who should you ask to serve as a reference? How many references do you need?

Most employers will want to speak to at least three references; therefore, your list should include four to five people. Include their titles and contact information. Your references should be able to speak articulately and comfortably about you. If someone seems uncomfortable with the idea of a verbal interview, give them an "out" by suggesting that perhaps they would prefer to write a letter instead. It is not just what your references say, but how they say it that makes the difference.

As an undergraduate, your references should include faculty, coaches, and previous/current employers. Unless they specify otherwise, potential employers are not interested in personal references. Choose people who know

JEFFREY CHARLES WILSON
416 Someplace Road
Highland Park, IL 60035
246-234-5678
hpgiants55@aol.com

EDUCATION

Pennsylvania State University
B.S. Sport Management, May 2013 G.P.A. 3.48

HIGHLIGHTS

Studied in Sydney, Australia, from January 2012 through April 2012.
Accepted into New Balance Haigis Hoopla Event Management class.
Made $56,170 for the athletic ticket office of Northwestern University.
Dean's List, four semesters.
Inducted into the National Society of Collegiate Scholars.
Inducted into the Golden Key International Honour Society.

EXPERIENCE

U.S. Soccer Federation, Chicago, IL   *Summer 2013*
Intern
Assisted in all aspects of U.S. Open Cup Tournament.
Contributed to other event operation projects, including media coordination and signage setup.

Pennsylvania State University Athletic Department, State College, PA   *September 2013*
Intern
Managed ticket call booth and supervised two other interns at two home football games.

Northwestern University Athletic Department, Evanston, IL   *Summer 2012*
Intern
Generated $7,500 in season ticket sales through telephone solicitation.
Sold individual game tickets for football, men's and women's basketball.
Promoted Northwestern University's football program throughout the community.

Chicago Rush, Rosemont, IL   *June 2012*
Game Day Staff Volunteer
Implemented game-day promotions at eight home games.
Monitored pregame festivities.

Chicago Wolves, Glenview, IL   *Summer 2011*
Intern
Contacted customers to encourage season ticket purchases.
Represented the Wolves at 12 charity events.
Contributed game promotional ideas, which were subsequently used.

ACTIVITIES

Vice President of Recruitment, Inter Fraternity Council.
Alumni Co-chairperson, Epsilon Psi Chapter of Beta Alpha Fraternity.
Volunteer, New Balance Haigis Hoopla; student-run three-on-three basketball tournament involving
450 teams, 20,000 spectators, and 15 vendors.

Figure 21-2 Sample Resume

you well enough to address your true abilities to perform the job successfully.

You want to have conversations with all the people who will serve as your references, so make an appointment to see them or speak to them on the phone. You want your references to have a good idea of the work you are seeking and why you are qualified for the position. They should also have a sense of your personality, your goals, and your strengths and weaknesses as they apply to the job.

Make sure your references have a copy of your current resume and keep them informed of your career progress. They should have an expectation that someone will be calling about you—the employer's contact should not come as a surprise. It is also important that you tell your references whether you receive an offer and if you accept it.

Employers check references only if they are seriously considering making an offer. References do have an influence on the outcome, so choose yours wisely. Also remember that the sport industry really is not that large and many sport managers know each other, even if they work in different industry segments. Do not be surprised if potential employers go "off-the-list" to talk to someone they know whom you did not include on your reference list.

The Cover Letter

Each resume must be accompanied by a **cover letter**. This document must also be professional and informative without being identical to your resume. There is no one model for a particular job application. Each letter should address the specific concerns of the organization to which you are applying. Consequently, you should expect to thoroughly research each organization and, after careful analysis, write a letter that demonstrates your value to the prospective employer.

Structure your letters of application with three or four paragraphs:

- Why are you writing? How did you learn of the position? Why is it of interest to you? Demonstrate your knowledge of the organization. By including a reference to the company, you form a positive connection from the start.
- Discuss your strongest qualifications that match the position as you understand it. Provide concrete evidence of your experience as it relates to what the job posting is asking for.
- Reinforce qualifications presented in your resume, but do not repeat them exactly. Show your strong writing skills.
- Request an interview. Mention that you will call within a specific period of time to discuss an appointment, and follow up accordingly.

Always generate your own unique job search correspondence. This is an opportunity to demonstrate your value to the employer, your professionalism, and your strong writing abilities. Be sure to address the letter to a specific individual with his or her appropriate business title and address. Some job opening postings will ask you to send your materials to the human resources office, and there will be no specific person's name listed. If this is the case, when you send your materials you should address the person as "Dear Hiring Manager" or "Dear Internship Director" and avoid using "Dear Sir" or "To Whom It May Concern." Adapt your letter for each situation and always be able to offer specific examples to confirm the main points of your experiences. Finally, always produce error-free copy. As with your resume, one spelling mistake in a cover letter can mean that the employer will no longer consider your application.

Use the cover letter to enhance your resume, not restate it. If the job search is a marketing campaign, then this letter is an integral part of it. You are the product, and, unlike the sport product, you want to be positively predictable. You do have total control over the product. Show this in your application package by making it professional and confident.

The Job Interview

The job **interview** is your opportunity to demonstrate to a prospective employer that you are the best candidate for the position. It is also a chance to learn more about the organization, the position, and opportunities for advancement—in short, to determine if you are interested in continuing to pursue employment with the organization. The keys to an effective interview are threefold: preparation, the interview itself, and follow-up.

Preparation

The interview preparation phase is critical and should be given the same respect the actual interview receives. It will take more energy and time than either of the other two phases. To be effective in the interview, you must be very well prepared. A football team practices for hours each day of the week for Saturday's 3-hour game. The harder and more efficiently the players practice, the better and more successful they will be in the game and the greater the chance of a win. The same principle is true for the interview. The more time you spend in preparation, the more comfortable you will be in the interview; consequently, the greater your opportunity for a successful interaction.

To present a clear picture of who you are and what you have to offer, you must take time to assess yourself. Be honest with yourself. Evaluate the person you are, not the person you would like to be. Assess your strengths and weaknesses. We all have them. You should be able to discuss your strengths with confidence and your weaknesses with a plan for improvement. In assessing the appropriate industry,

organizations, and job, ask yourself questions such as the following:

- Do I prefer working independently or with a group?
- How do I deal with stress and frustration?
- What kind of supervision works best for me?
- Do I like to write? Am I good at it?
- Am I energetic and good-humored?
- Am I happy in competitive, fast-paced situations?
- Am I persuasive and able to motivate others?
- Is salary a top priority for me?
- Am I flexible, able to work long hours or on changeable projects?

The interviewer will assume you know something about his or her organization. Do not disappoint him or her; learn as much as you can. Here are some potential information sources:

- Make use of the Internet, which is a prime information source for almost every industry. Most sport organizations have their own home page. It is also possible to use the Internet to gather valuable information regarding the competition.
- Call the public relations office of the sport organization and request written information, such as media guides.
- Read newspapers and professional journals.
- Follow the organization and/or its executives on Twitter.
- Talk to someone who currently works for the organization. Perhaps that person had the job for which you are applying or worked with the person who did.
- Speak to clients, customers, and competitors.

The Interview

Behavior is the foundation of the interview process. The best predictor of future performance is past performance in a similar situation. Interviewers are looking not just for particular skills, but also for personal attributes of a successful professional. What is it an employer wants to know about a candidate that is relative to the job? Characteristics of a successful employee include oral and written communication skills, adaptability, ability to learn, analysis, critical thinking, initiative, creativity and innovation, integrity, interpersonal skills, ability to work with diverse populations, decisiveness, leadership, planning and organizing, sensitivity, time management, stress tolerance, tenacity, and high standards of performance.

Interviews are limited in time; therefore, it is important to begin appropriately. Remember the old cliché: "You only get one chance to make a first impression." As in any new relationship, the first goal is to establish rapport.

- Dress appropriately. Appropriate attire for an interview is a suit. The sport industry may seem like a casual industry, but it is a business.
- Be early—it is better to be 10 minutes early than 1 minute late!
- Shake hands firmly and smile, making eye contact with the person.
- Engage in conversation, but do not talk incessantly (which sometimes happens if you are nervous).
- Be friendly, warm, and interested.

One common interview method is known as behavioral interviewing. During a behavioral interview, the interviewer will ask questions probing for examples of specific, relevant behaviors. Questions may be phrased to extract the most telling response from the interviewee. Here are some sample questions from a behavioral interview:

- We've all experienced times when we felt over our heads in a class or a project. Tell me about a time when that happened to you. How did you handle the situation?
- What would you identify as the biggest achievement of your college career? What did you do to contribute to that achievement?

- Have you ever had trouble getting along with a classmate or teacher? How did you deal with the situation so you could continue to work with that person?

In each of these examples, the interviewer is asking the interviewee to describe a specific situation or task, the action that took place, and the outcome or consequence of that action. Quality responses are not feelings or opinions but factual statements about what your actual behavior was in the situation being presented. They are not plans for the future, nor are they vague statements. If you spend some time identifying situations representing each of the characteristics mentioned earlier, you should be prepared for any type of question. If the employer asks a theoretical question such as "Describe your strengths and weaknesses," you can still respond with a situation demonstrating the strengths you want to showcase or how you make accommodations for your weaknesses.

In addition to questions you can answer using the behavioral format, be ready for some of the old standards: "Tell me about yourself." "How would your friends describe you?" Be honest. When answering interview questions, honesty is the best policy. An interviewer can always tell when a candidate is being less than honest. It is not only what you say that impresses an interviewer but also how you conduct yourself. The recruiter is trying to find out how well you know yourself and how comfortable you are with who you are.

© Dmitriy Shironosov/ShutterStock, Inc.

Again, the best predictor of future performance is past performance in a similar situation. Be prepared with anecdotes demonstrating your behaviors in a positive light.

Once the actual interview begins, concentrate on communicating effectively:

- Listen attentively. Restate the question if you are unsure what the interviewer is actually asking.
- Answer questions directly, providing examples.
- Make good eye contact with the interviewer.
- Talk openly about yourself, your accomplishments, and your goals.
- Maintain a positive, interested demeanor.
- Ask appropriate questions. Demonstrate interest in, and knowledge of, the organization.
- Make certain you have a clear idea of the position for which you are interviewing.
- Always get a business card or a means of connecting with the interviewer later.

Illegal Questions

The law prevents employers from asking certain questions in interview situations. Interviewers must limit themselves to gathering information that will help them decide whether a person can perform the functions of a particular job. Therefore, questions seeking more personal information—for example, marital status, sexual orientation, national origin or citizenship, age, disability, or arrest record—do not have to be answered. The decision to answer or not is the interviewee's. Although most interviewers will not ask these questions, you should think about how you will respond if the situation arises. If you feel particularly uncomfortable, discuss this issue with a career counselor on your campus or one of your sport management faculty members before your first interview.

Follow-Up

The follow-up to an interview is an indication of your interest and maturity. As part of the follow-up, do the following:

- Assess the interview. Were all your questions answered? Was there anything you could have presented more clearly?
- Write a thank-you note immediately, reinforcing your interest and qualifications for the position.
- Call the interviewer if you have something to add or if you have additional questions. This shows you are enthusiastic, persistent, and interested.
- Call the sport organization if you have not heard from someone there in the designated time.

If you are well prepared, aware of your competencies and areas requiring development, understand the type of work environment you would prefer, and believe you have the necessary skills and abilities, you will be successful. When qualifications of competing candidates are relatively equal, interviewers are inclined to hire people who have been honest and straightforward. Be yourself.

What Makes a Successful Candidate?

A successful candidate exhibits certain traits and skills. Some of these include the following:

- *Preparation:* Knowledge of and interest in the employer and the specific job opening
- *Personal or soft skills:* Confidence, adaptability, flexibility, maturity, energy, drive, enthusiasm, initiative, and empathy
- *Goal orientation:* Ability to set short- and long-term goals
- *Communication skills:* Written and oral, including listening and nonverbal communication skills
- *Organizational skills:* Teamwork, leadership, problem identification and solving, critical thinking, and time management

- *Experience:* Ability to articulate the relevance of previous experience to the position for which you are interviewing.
- *Professional appearance:* Business suits for men and women alike. Remember, some people have allergic reactions to perfumes and colognes, so it is best not to use them prior to your interview. Tatoos? Have them show at your own risk. They may not matter to some people, but they will to others.
- *Cross-cultural awareness:* Multiple languages, international or intercultural experience
- *Computer skills:* Website development, statistical packages, word processing, spreadsheets, and desktop publishing

Summary

Finding a job in the sport industry is an arduous task, but the results can be rewarding. This chapter presents information about the realities of looking for a job in the sport industry. Make no mistake—this is a difficult industry to break into. This chapter, while informing you about some of the barriers you will face, also gives you some tools to use to help you along the way. Incorporating the techniques included in this chapter, such as networking, informational interviewing, resume and cover letter writing, and interviewing skills, will help increase your marketability in the sport industry.

Key Terms

cover letter, informational interviewing, internship, interview, network, references, resume

References

Atlanta Braves. (2013). 2013 career fair. Retrieved from http://atlanta.braves.mlb.com/atl/ticketing/career_fair.jsp

Belson, K. (2012, February 29). Studying to release your inner George Costanza. *New York Times*. Retrieved from http://www.nytimes.com/2012/03/01/education/learning-sports-management-in-graduate-school.html

Chicago Press Release Services. (2009). Chicago 2016 Olympic bid team now unemployed, in search of new jobs. Retrieved from http://chicagopressrelease.com/news/chicago-2016-olympic-bid-team-now-unemployed-in-search-of-new-jobs

Collamer, N. (2013, February 4). The perfect elevator pitch to land a job. *Forbes*. Retrieved from http://www.forbes.com/sites/nextavenue/2013/02/04/the-perfect-elevator-pitch-to-land-a-job/

Helyar, J. (2006, September 16). Are universities' sport management programs a ticket to a great job? Not likely. Retrieved from http://www.gamefacesportsjobs.com/breaking_in/WSJ/prwsjflngeffrt.htm

Pacers Sports and Entertainment. (2012). Pacers to host career fair. Retrieved from http://www.insideindianabusiness.com/newsitem.asp?ID=52920#middle

Professional Baseball Employment Opportunities. (2013). Get started in Nashville and launch your baseball career at the 19th annual PBEO Job Fair. Retrieved from http://www.pbeo.com/12_job_fair.aspx

37 percent of employers use Facebook to pre-screen applicants, new study says. (2013, April 20). *Huffington Post*. Retrieved from http://www.huffingtonpost.com/2012/04/20/employers-use-facebook-to-pre-screen-applicants_n_1441289.html

Glossary

a la carte   To select options individually.

absolutism   The belief that moral precepts are universal, that is, applicable to all circumstances.

activation   The commitment of financial resources in support of a company's sponsorship through promotion and advertising that thematically includes the sport property's imagery.

ad hoc committees   Type of committee formed for a special purpose, usually focused on a single problem or issue, that remains in existence until that problem or issue is resolved. The club's board dissolves an ad hoc committee once its purpose is served.

administrative law   The body of law created by rules, regulations, orders, and decisions of administrative bodies.

affiliate   A local or regional broadcaster or station that carries some or all of the programming of the network.

aftermarketing   Customer retention activities that take place after a purchase has been made; the process of providing continued satisfaction and reinforcement to individuals or organizations who are past or current customers.

Age Discrimination in Employment Act (ADEA)   A 1967 law that prohibits employment discrimination on the basis of age.

agency   A relationship in which one party (the agent) agrees to act for and under the direction of another (the principal).

agent   A party acting for and under the direction of another (the principal).

ambush marketing   A strategy that involves placement of marketing material and promotions at an event that attracts consumer and media attention, without becoming an official sponsor of that event.

Americans with Disabilities Act (ADA)   A 1990 law that has as its intent the prevention of discrimination against people with disabilities in employment, public services, transportation, public accommodations, and telecommunications services; it protects employees with disabilities at all stages of the employment relationship.

ancillary revenue   Occurs from the sale of food and beverage, merchandise, parking charges, ticket fees, and sponsorships.

antitrust law   The body of state and federal law designed to protect trade and commerce from unlawful restraint, monopolies, price fixing, and price discrimination.

apps   Term used to define mobile applications that allow the customer to have access to websites, social media sites, and real-time information feeds, including live game tracking.

arenas   Indoor facilities that host sporting and entertainment events; they are usually built to accommodate one or more prime sports tenants.

Arledge, Roone   An executive at ABC TV who was responsible for the development of sport broadcasting so that it appealed as entertainment to an audience beyond hard-core fans.

assets   Things that an organization owns that can be used to generate future revenues, such as equipment, stadiums, and league memberships.

Association for Intercollegiate Athletics for Women (AIAW)   A governance organization for women's athletics, established in 1971, that emphasized the educational needs of students and rejected the commercialized men's athletics model. It became effectively defunct in 1982.

athletic footwear   Branded and unbranded athletic shoes for casual wear or active usage, outdoor/hiking sports boots, and sport sandals.

balance sheet   A financial statement that shows the assets, liabilities, and owners' equity of an organization.

barnstorming tours   The travel and appearances at events of star athletes and teams to promote the popularity of a particular sport.

beat reporter   A writer or media personality from a local media outlet who is specifically assigned to cover a sport organization, its games, and its practices; also known as a *beat writer*.

beat writer   See *beat reporter*.

benefit selling   A sales approach that involves the promotion and creation of new benefits or the promotion and enhancement of existing benefits to offset existing perceptions or assumed negatives related to the sport product or service.

Big Ten Conference   An athletic conference formed in 1895 by college and university faculty representatives (under the name Intercollegiate Conference of Faculty Representatives) to create student eligibility rules for football. The athletic conference has a 100-year tradition of shared practices and policies that enforce the priority of academics and emphasize the values of integrity, fairness, and competitiveness in all aspects of its student-athletes' lives.

blackout   A sporting contest is not televised in the home market if the game itself is not a sellout. This practice is used to encourage future ticket sales.

blog   A personal website featuring a series of chronological entries by an author.

board of directors   Also called a board of governors at some clubs, this select group of people establishes club policies and governs the club.

board of governors   See *board of directors*.

bona fide occupational qualification (BFOQ)   An employment qualification that, although it may discriminate against a protected class (i.e., sex, religion, or national origin), relates to an essential job duty and is considered reasonably necessary for the normal operation of a business or organization and therefore not illegal.

bonds   Financial instruments typically issued by large corporate entities or governments that allow the borrower to borrow large dollar amounts, usually for a relatively long period of time.

booking director   A person responsible for scheduling events for a facility.

Boras, Scott   Founder of the Scott Boras Corporation and an innovator in baseball representation. He is known for his free-market philosophy, the use of data in negotiations, his level of preparation, and his knowledge of the game and rules.

box office director   A person responsible for the sale of all tickets to events as well as the collection of all ticket revenue.

branding   The cumulative view, beliefs, and associations of consumers and others about a brand. It evokes the idea that a consumer is not just purchasing a product or a service, but also the impression of that product or service.

breach   The breaking of a promise in a contract.

broadband   High-speed Internet connectivity that is supported by fiber-optic cable.

broadcasting   To transmit through signals by way of radio or television.

broadcasting rights   The property interest possessed under law that allows an entity to broadcast sound and/or images of an event.

b-roll   A film, DVD, or videotape of raw footage chosen by the organization to accompany a written news release; it is not a finished segment ready for broadcast.

bubble   Occurs when prices rise steeply in a short time, followed by a sudden decrease in value when the marketplace "corrects" itself.

budgeting   The process of developing a written plan of revenues and expenses for a particular accounting cycle; the budget specifies available funds among the many purposes of an organization to control spending and achieve organizational goals.

bundling   Packaging various options together so the customer pays one price for all of the options, as in cable companies bundling TV, Internet, and phone services.

business development   A business function focused on strategy, creating strategic partnerships, and relationships with suppliers and customers. The business development function focuses on strategic deal-making with a goal of increasing sales, attracting new clients, and expanding a company's long-term business success or scope.

call-to-action ad   An advertisement that aims to encourage consumers to do something, such as buy a ticket to a sport event.

campus recreation   Includes any recreational activity provided by colleges and universities, ranging from exercise facilities and fitness programming to club and intramural sports and coordinated outdoor recreation activities.

capacity   The ability to understand the nature and effects of one's actions; generally, individuals over the age of 18 possess capacity.

Carnegie Reports of 1929   Documents by the Carnegie Foundation that examined intercollegiate athletics and identified many academic abuses, recruiting abuses, payments to student-athletes, and commercialization of athletics. These reports pressured the NCAA to evolve from a group that developed rules for competition into an organization for overseeing all aspects of intercollegiate athletics.

cash-flow budgeting   Accounting for the receipt and timing of all sources and expenditures of money.

cause-related marketing effort   An event sponsored by a corporation for the purpose of generating money for a particular cause.

clean feed   A video signal that does not have added graphics and text.

club   Sport management structures composed of a limited number of members who organize events, standardize rules, and settle disputes.

Club Managers Association of America (CMAA)   Organization composed of club professionals, department heads, and certified professionals in food and beverage management (including chefs, cooks, and bartenders); sport management professionals (golf, tennis, and aquatics professionals); grounds and golf course superintendents; building and engineering technicians/specialists; and other specialty staff members who report to a club's general manager.

coaches   People who instruct or train players in the fundamentals of a sport and directs team strategy.

code of conduct   Statements of a company, business, organization, or profession that explicitly outline and explain the principles under which it operates and provide guidelines for employee behavior; also called code of ethics.

code of ethics   See *code of conduct*.

collective bargaining agreement (CBA)   A legal agreement between an employer and a labor union that regulates the hours, wages, and terms and conditions of employment.

commercial breaks   Breaks in play during a sport contest to allow for commercial advertising (e.g., all NFL games are required to have five 2-minute commercial breaks per quarter).

commercial formats   Advertising breaks provided for national commercials, sold by the networks, and local advertisements, sold by local stations or cable systems.

Commission on Sport Management Accreditation (COSMA)   A specialized accrediting body launched by NASSM and NASPE that promotes and recognizes excellence in sport management education in colleges and universities at the baccalaureate and graduate levels.

Commission on Intercollegiate Athletics for Women (CIAW)   A governance organization for women's athletics created in 1966; forerunner of the Association for Intercollegiate Athletics for Women (AIAW).

commissioner   The administrative head of a professional sport league.

communications   All methods used by an organization to proactively deliver its key messages to a diverse universe of constituencies.

communication skills   Oral and written skills for presenting facts and information in an organized, courteous fashion.

community-based recreation   Recreational activities at the local level, such as those offered by community agencies and local parks and recreation departments.

community relations   Activities and programs that have the objective of having a positive impact on the community and thereby improving an organization's public image.

competitive balance   The notion that the outcome of a competition is uncertain, and thus provides greater entertainment value for spectators.

compliance   Adherence to NCAA and conference rules and regulations. The compliance coordinator in an athletic department is responsible for educating coaches and student-athletes about the rules and regulations, overseeing the initial and continuing eligibility of student-athletes, and preventing or investigating any violations that occur.

concerts   Musical events.

conference call   A method of communication that allows an arranged call by telephone or Internet connection between multiple parties.

conference realignment   A school wanting to join a conference or change conference affiliation. An issue that occurs periodically, effectively changing the landscape of college athletics.

conference rules   Standards set forth by particular conferences that require member institutions to abide by, in addition to NCAA regulation.

conflicts of interest   Situations in which one's own interests may be furthered over those of the principal to whom one owes a fiduciary duty (e.g., the athlete being represented by the agent).

consideration   The inducement to a contract represented by something of value, such as money, property, or an intangible quality.

constitutional law   The body of law developed from precedents established by courts applying the language of the U.S. Constitution and state constitutions to the actions and policies of governmental entities.

contests   Competitions that award prizes based on contestants' skills and abilities; a purchase may be required as a condition of entering the contest.

contract   A written or oral agreement between two or more parties that creates a legal obligation to fulfill the promises made by the agreement.

convention centers   Facilities built and owned by a public entity and used to lure conventions and business meetings to a particular municipality.

convocations   An assembly of people for a specific purpose (i.e., graduation, speaking engagement).

copyright   The right to copy an original work that is in tangible form, such as songs, movies, books, webpages, video games, and sports game telecasts.

Corcoran, Fred   The architect of the professional golf tournament.

cord-cutting   When people refuse to subscribe to cable TV and instead watch television by using an over-air antenna for live viewing of broadcast networks and by subscribing to services such as Hulu and Netflix for cable-distributed programming.

corporate governance model   A model of league leadership in which owners act as the board of directors, and the commissioner acts as the chief executive officer.

corporate ownership   The ownership of a team by a corporation.

country club   An exclusive private facility to socialize, network, and participate in leisure activities.

coupons   Certificates that generally offer a reduction in price for a product or service.

cover letter   A document accompanying a resume that introduces yourself and demonstrates your value to the prospective employer.

crisis plan   A strategy for handling a crisis; it should include a system to notify key members of the organization as soon as possible of a crisis situation and should identify roles and responsibilities for members of the organization.

crisis team   A group of key organizational individuals who will be responsible for managing any crises.

cross-ownership   Ownership of more than one sport franchise.

cross-promotion   A joining together of two or more companies to capitalize on a sponsorship or expand its scope.

crowd management plan   A document that assesses the type of event, surrounding facilities and/or environment, team or school rivalries, threats of violence, and details emergency contingencies, taking crowd size and seating configuration, and the use of security personnel and ushers into consideration.

cultural awareness   Understanding of local customs, laws, and the environment.

cultural differences   Differences between the customs, values, and traditions of cultures.

Curt Flood Act   This act granted Major League Baseball players, but not minor leaguers, the legal right to sue their employers under the Sherman Act. It confirmed that baseball's exemption from federal antitrust laws applies to business areas including the minor leagues; the minor league player reserve clause; the amateur draft; franchise expansion, location or relocation; franchise ownership issues; marketing and sales of the entertainment product of baseball; and licensed properties.

customer relationship management (CRM)   The implementation of relationship marketing practices that involves creating a database usually of demographic and psychographic information of current and prospective customers.

debt   An amount of money that an organization borrows.

decision making   A process of gathering and analyzing information so as to make a choice on how to pursue an opportunity or solve a problem.

de Coubertin, Pierre   Founder of the modern Olympics.

default   Occurs when a borrower is unable to repay a debt.

defendant   The person or organization against whom a lawsuit is brought.

delegation   Assigning responsibility and accountability for results to employees.

demographic   Related to the statistical characteristics of a group of people (i.e., age, income, gender, social class, or educational background).

digital networks   The transmission of programming via broadband Internet without the need to be packaged on a tier by cable/DBS systems.

digital video recorder (DVR)   Consumer electronics device or application software that records digital video to a storage device so that it can be replayed at a later time.

direct broadcast satellite (DBS)   Satellite television broadcasts intended for home reception.

direct mail   A type of marketing solicitation sent via the U.S. Mail to targeted lists of current or potential clients.

direct marketing   A method of communication that uses material sent directly to a specific target audience either via mail or e-mail.

direct participation   Active performance of an activity.

disaffirm   To opt out of a contract.

diversity   Any differences between individuals, including age, race, gender, sexual orientation, disability, education, and social and economic background, that affect how people perform and interact with each other.

Division I   A subgroup of NCAA institutions that, in general, supports the philosophy of competitiveness, generating revenue through athletics, and national success; these institutions offer athletic scholarships.

Division II   A subgroup of NCAA institutions that, in general, attracts student-athletes from the local or in-state area, who may receive some athletic scholarship money but usually not a full amount.

Division III   A subgroup of NCAA institutions that does not allow athletic scholarships, and that encourages participation in athletics by maximizing the number and variety of opportunities available to students; the emphasis is on the participants' experience rather than that of spectators.

due process   The right to notice and a hearing before life, liberty, or property may be taken away.

duty of care   A legal obligation that a person acts toward another as a reasonable person would in the circumstances. This duty arises from one's relationship to another, a voluntary assumption of the duty of care, or from a duty mandated by law.

eduselling   An evolutionary form of selling that combines needs assessment, relationship building, customer education, and aftermarketing in a process that originates at the prospect-targeting stage and progresses to an ongoing partnership agreement.

electronic newsletters   A newsletter sent via e-mail rather than by being printed and mailed to subscribers.

emotional intelligence   The ability of workers to identify and acknowledge people's emotions and, instead of having an immediate emotional response, to take a step back and allow rational thought to influence their actions.

empowerment   The encouragement of employees to use their initiative and make decisions within their areas of operations, and the provision of resources to enable them to do so.

enforcement   An area within the NCAA administrative structure, created in 1952, that deals with enforcing the NCAA's rules and regulations.

entrepreneur   A person who creates an idea for a better use of existing technology.

environmental awareness   Knowledge of the regulations that control public use of lands, and the responsibility to monitor and control human relationships with natural environment use to prevent destruction of natural resources.

Equal Pay Act (EPA)   A 1963 law that prohibits an employer from paying one employee less than another on the basis of sex when the two are performing jobs of equal skill, effort, and responsibility and are working under similar conditions.

equal protection   The Fourteenth Amendment guarantee that no person or class of persons shall be denied the protection of the laws that is enjoyed by other persons or other classes in like circumstances in their enjoyment of personal rights and the prevention and redress of wrongs.

equity club   Clubs owned by the members; typically hold a private nonprofit status.

ethical decision making   Requires decision makers to consider how their actions will affect different groups of people and individuals.

ethical dilemma   A practical conflict involving more or less equally compelling values or social obligations.

ethical reasoning   The process of making a fair and correct decision; it depends on one's values or the values of the organization for which one works.

ethics   The systematic study of the values guiding decision making.

ethnic marketing   Advertising that targets an ethnic group, such as Hispanics or African Americans.

evaluating   A functional area of management that measures and ensures progress toward organizational objectives by establishing reporting systems, developing performance standards, observing employee performance, and designing reward systems to acknowledge successful work on the part of employees.

event director   A person involved in planning, organizing, and executing projects, celebrations, sporting contests, etc. Management of the show from start to finish may involve dealing with ushers, security, and medical personnel, show promoters, patrons, and coping with crises that may occur.

event marketing   The process of promoting and selling a sport or special event; it encompasses nine areas: sales of corporate sponsorship, advertising efforts, public relations activities, hospitality, ticket sales, broadcasting, website development and management, licensing/merchandising, and fund-raising.

executive committee   A group that usually has duties and responsibilities similar to those of the board of directors, but it acts as a "mini-board" between board meetings by responding to issues that do not necessitate bringing the entire board together.

expenses   The costs incurred by an organization in an effort to generate revenues.

faculty athletics representative (FAR)   A member of an institution's faculty or administrative staff who is designated to represent the institution and its faculty in the institution's relationships with the NCAA and its conference.

family events   Products geared toward the toddler and through the "tween" markets. Often these are acts produced from television or movie programs that are run on mainstream television or theaters, such as Sesame Street Live or Disney On Ice.

fan identification   The personal commitment and emotional involvement that customers have with a sport organization.

Federal Communications Commission (FCC)   Federal agency that regulates interstate and international communications by radio, television, wire, satellite, and cable.

fiduciary duties   Obligation to act in the best interest of another party.

Football Bowl Subdivision (FBS)   A category of Division I institutions that are large football-playing schools; they must meet minimum attendance requirements for football. Formerly known as Division I-A.

Football Championship Subdivision (FCS)   A category of Division I institutions that play football at a level below that of Division I-A; they are not held to any attendance requirements. Formerly known as Division I-AA.

fragmentation   With the emergence of more TV networks and other outlets for entertainment programming, fewer people are likely to choose any one thing, thus leading to audience fragmentation.

franchise free agency   A strategy in which team owners move their teams to cities that provide them newer facilities with better lease arrangements and more revenues.

franchise rights The privileges afforded to owners of a sport franchise.

freestanding inserts Separately printed advertising or coupon sections that are inserted into a newspaper.

freestanding sport management firm A full-service sport management firm providing a wide range of services to the athlete, including contract negotiations, marketing, and financial planning.

full-service agencies Sport management/marketing agencies that perform a complete set of agency functions.

fund development An area of responsibility within a collegiate athletic department that seeks new ways to increase revenues, oversees alumni donations to the athletic department, and oversees fundraising events.

gate receipts Revenue from ticket sales.

global sourcing The use of whatever manufacturer or source around the world that will most efficiently produce a company's products.

global strategy A corporate strategy of creating products that have the same appeal and generate the same demand worldwide.

Golf 2.0 A comprehensive, industry-wide initiative that focuses on player development and increased golf participation by targeting specific groups with tailored programs.

governing bodies Groups that create and maintain rules and guidelines and handle overall administrative tasks.

government relations Activities conducted to influence public officials toward a desired action; also known as *lobbying*.

grassroots efforts Programs and activities undertaken to increase sport participation and interest in a particular region.

grassroots programs Activities and events that target individuals at the most basic level of involvement, sport participation.

gross negligence Occurs when a defendant acts recklessly, when a person knows that the act is harmful but fails to realize it will produce the extreme harm that results.

head ends In broadcasting, the master facilities where programs are received and then fed to individual subscribers.

high-definition TV (HDTV) Television broadcast that has a resolution substantially higher than standard-definition television.

hospitality Providing a satisfying experience for all stakeholders in an event (participants, spectators, media, and sponsors).

Hulbert, William The "Czar of Baseball"; he developed the National League of Professional Baseball Players.

human relations movement Management theory focusing on the behavior and motivations of people in the workplace.

image ad An advertisement created to reinforce an organization's brand imagery in the minds of consumers.

impasse A breakdown in negotiations.

income The difference between revenues and expenses, also called *profit*.

income mismanagement A form of unethical behavior by a sports agent that consists of mishandling a client's money, whether by incompetence or criminal intent.

income statement A summary of the revenues, expenses, and profits of an organization over a given time period.

independent contractor A worker who is not under the employer's supervision and control.

indirect participation Participating in an activity as a spectator.

informational interviewing   Asking questions of someone employed in a particular career or organization in an effort to expand one's understanding of that industry, organization, or career.

informed participant consent   Making participants aware of the potential risks inherent in activities before they begin so they can make informed decisions about the nature of their participation.

in-house agencies   Separate departments or divisions within a major corporation that deal with event management.

initiative   Going beyond one's formal job description to help the organization.

injunction   An order from a court to do or not to do a particular action.

in-kind sponsorship   Benefits given to a newspaper, magazine, radio station, or television station in exchange for a specified number of free advertising spots or space, rather than money.

integrated marketing   Long-term strategic planning for managing functions in a consistent manner.

integrated marketing communications (IMC)   The symbiosis of advertising, marketing, and public relations.

intellectual property   Refers to creations of the mind.

intercept interviews   See *pass-by interviews*.

Intercollegiate Athletic Association of the United States (IAAUS)   The forerunner of the National Collegiate Athletic Association (NCAA); formed in 1905 by 62 colleges and universities to formulate rules making football safer and more exciting to play.

Intercollegiate Conference of Faculty Representatives   See *Big Ten Conference*.

Intercollegiate Football Association   An athletic association formed in 1876 and made up of students from Harvard, Yale, Princeton, and Columbia who agreed on consistent playing and eligibility rules for football.

interest   Money that is paid for the use of money lent, or principal, according to a set percentage (rate).

internal communications   Communication with and to an organization's staff.

International Association of Venue Managers (IAVM)   The professional trade association for the facility management field.

international federations (IFs)   Organizations responsible for managing and monitoring the everyday running of the world's various sports disciplines, including the organization of events during the Olympic Games, and the supervision of the development of athletes practicing these sports at every level. Each IF governs its sport at world level and ensures its promotion and development.

International Olympic Committee (IOC)   A nongovernmental, nonprofit organization that is the legal and business entity; entrusted with the control, development, and operation of the modern Olympic Games.

Internet Service Provider (ISP)   Organization that provides services for accessing the Internet.

internship   A job position in which students or graduates gain supervised practical experience.

interview   A formal meeting between an employer and a prospective employee to evaluate the latter's qualifications for a job.

invasion of privacy   An unjustified intrusion into one's personal activity or an unjustified exploitation of one's personality.

inverted pyramid   A style of writing used for press releases, in which the most important facts are presented in the lead paragraph and then the remaining paragraphs are arranged in a descending order of importance.

Jockey Club   A group established in Newmarket, England, around 1850 to settle disputes, establish rules, determine eligibility, designate officials, regulate breeding, and punish unscrupulous participants in the sport of thoroughbred racing.

judges   See *officials.*

judicial review   Evaluation by a court that occurs when a plaintiff challenges a rule, regulation, or decision.

key messages   The messages that an organization wants to convey to the media during an interview or press conference.

Knight Commission   A commission created in 1989 by the Trustees of the Knight Foundation, composed of university presidents, CEOs and presidents of corporations, and a congressional representative, to propose a reform agenda for intercollegiate athletics.

labor exemption   An exception that states that terms agreed to in a collective bargaining agreement are immune from antitrust scrutiny during the term of the agreement.

Lanham Act   A federal law that governs trademarks and service marks and gives protection to the owner of a name or logo.

law practice only   A type of sport management firm that deals only with the legal aspects of an athlete's career, such as contract negotiation, dispute resolution, legal representation in arbitration or other proceedings, and the preparation of tax forms.

leading   A functional area of management that is the "action" part of the management process; it involves a variety of activities, including delegating, managing differences, managing change, and motivating employees.

league   A profit-oriented legal and business entity organized so that teams can compete against each other, but also operate together in areas such as rule making, broadcasting, licensing, and marketing.

"league think"   A term coined by NFL Commissioner Pete Rozelle to describe the need for owners to think about what was best for the NFL as a whole rather than what was best for their individual franchises.

LEED certification   A gold standard for facilities that helps operators identify green building design, construction, operation, and maintenance. LEED stands for Leadership in Energy and Environmental Design.

legacy members   People who join clubs because their parents and grandparents were club members and club membership is a family tradition.

legality   Concept that the subject matter of a contract cannot violate laws or public policy.

legislation and governance   An area within the NCAA administrative structure that deals with interpreting NCAA legislation.

legitimate interest   Refers to a reason for upholding the use of separate-gender teams.

liabilities   The sum of debts that an organization owes.

licensed merchandise   See *licensed products.*

licensed products   Items bearing the logo or trademark of a sport organization; their sale generates a *royalty* (percentage of the net or wholesale selling price) for the sport organization.

licensees   The manufacturers of licensed products.

licensors   Teams and leagues that own the rights to logos, names, and so forth.

local/civic venues   Typically located in towns or small cities, these locations offer small capacity.

luxury tax   A fee that a team incurs when it exceeds a set payroll threshold.

managing change   Effectively implementing change in the workplace and being aware of employees' natural resistance to change.

managing technology   Being familiar with technology and using it to one's advantage.

marketing director   A person involved with analyzing and purchasing media (e.g., TV, radio, print, billboards), coordinating promotions, and designing marketing materials (e.g., brochures, flyers).

marketing fund   A pool of money that is set aside from the profits of other shows. The concessionaire and the venue director each agree to a certain share of the percentage of sold goods, and they use the pool to help invest in future programs.

marketing mix   The controllable variables a company puts together to satisfy a target market group, including product, price, place, and promotion.

Mason, James G.   Co-inventor, with Walter O'Malley, of the idea of a sport management curriculum.

master antenna   The emergence of cable television services in the 1940s through the selling of access to an appliance store owner's master antenna which provided a clearer picture on their TVs.

McCormack, Mark   Founder of IMG (International Management Group) who invented the modern sports agency. He built IMG from one client in 1960 to a global sports, entertainment, and media company with 2,200 employees in 70 offices in 30 countries at the time of his death in 2003. IMG at the time billed itself as the world's largest, most diverse, truly global company dedicated to the marketing and management of sport and leisure lifestyle.

media buyer   A person who purchases advertising for clients.

media guide   An annual publication containing all of the information a reporter will need to know about an organization, including staff directories; biographies of all coaches, players, owners, and front office staff; and team and individual records and statistics.

media list   A list of members of the media, such as beat writers, editors, columnists, and news directors.

media notes   A packet of information for the press containing all the statistical information and biographical information on the teams competing in a game, from both an individual and a team perspective.

media planning   Choosing the correct medium in which to place advertising in an effort to reach the most people fitting the target audience's demographic profile.

media training   Education of players, coaches, athletic directors, and so forth about interview techniques, handling hostile interviewers, and shaping messages into sound bites.

member conferences   Groupings of institutions within the NCAA that provide many benefits and services to their members. Conferences have legislative power over their member institutions in the running of championship events and the formulation of conference rules and regulations. Member conferences must have a minimum of six member institutions within a single division to be recognized as a voting member conference of the NCAA.

metropolitan facilities   Venues located in large cities with very large capacities, such as Madison Square Garden in New York, The Wells Fargo Center complex in Philadelphia, and the Staples Center in Los Angeles.

military recreation   Recreational programs offered by the armed services for military personnel and their families on bases in the United States and abroad.

modern Olympic Games   An international athletic event, started in 1896, based on ancient Greek athletic games.

monopoly   A business or organization that faces no direct competition for its products or services, and as a result possesses high bargaining power.

morality   Concerned with the values guiding behavior; a specific type of ethical issue.

moral principles   Virtues or moral precepts.

morals The fundamental baseline values dictating appropriate behavior within a society.

motivation The reasons why individuals strive to achieve organizational and personal goals and objectives.

multibox A device that allows multiple cameramen and radio reporters to plug into an audio feed without having to place too many microphones on the podium.

multimedia Content that includes various programming including news, entertainment, educational material, etc.

mutual assent A requirement by a valid contract involving an offer by one party and an acceptance by another.

National Association of Intercollegiate Athletics (NAIA) An athletic governance organization for small colleges and universities, founded in 1940.

National Association of Professional Baseball Players (NAPBP) A group of professional baseball teams formed in 1871; any ball club that was willing to pay its elite players could join.

National Collegiate Athletic Association (NCAA) A voluntary association that is the primary rule-making body for college athletics in the United States. It oversees academic standards for student-athletes, monitors recruiting activities of coaches and administrators, and establishes principles governing amateurism.

National Federation of State High School Associations (NFHS) A nonprofit organization that serves as the national coordinator for high school sports as well as activities such as music, debate, theater, and student council.

national governing bodies (NGBs) Organizations that administer a specific sport in a given country, operating within the guidelines set forth by their respective international federations; also known as *national federations (NFs)*.

nationalism A feeling of pride in one's nation.

National Junior College Athletic Association (NJCAA) An athletic association founded in 1937 to promote and supervise a national program of junior college sports and activities.

National Labor Relations Act (NLRA) A 1935 law that establishes the procedures for union certification and decertification and sets forth the rights and obligations of union and management once a union is in place.

National League of Professional Baseball Players (NLPBP) The successor to the National Association of Professional Baseball Players; formed in 1876, it was a stronger body in which authority for the management of baseball rested.

National Olympic Committees (NOCs) The organizations responsible for the development and protection of the Olympic Movement in their respective countries.

national youth league organizations Organizations that promote participation in a particular sport among children and are not affiliated with schools.

NCAA National Office The main office of the National Collegiate Athletic Association, located in Indianapolis, Indiana; it enforces the rules the NCAA membership passes and provides administrative services to all NCAA committees, member institutions, and conferences.

negligence An unintentional tort that occurs when a person or organization commits an act or omission that causes injury to a person to whom he, she, or it owes a duty of care.

network People who know you and can serve as a reference for you during the job search process.

networks The predominant national organizations where most programming occurs (e.g., the traditional Big Three included ABC, CBS, and NBC although more national and regional networks have emerged).

new media The emergence of digital, computerized, or networked information and communication technologies in the later part of the twentieth century.

new media industry An industry that combines elements of computing, technology, telecommunications, and content to create products and services that can be used interactively by consumers and business users.

news release See *press release*.

niche sports Sports that are unique and appealing to a distinct segment of the market, whether defined by age demographics, such as the Millennial Generation or Generation Y (the teenagers and 20-somethings of today), or socioeconomic class, as is seen with sailing and polo's appeal to those with higher incomes.

non-equity clubs Nonmember owned clubs.

nonprofit 501(c)(7) clubs Private exclusive social and recreational clubs not open to the general public and typically governed by a board of directors who are elected by the membership. Members are not only the customers and guests, they are also the owners or shareholders (i.e., they own equity in the club).

nonschool agencies Organizations that are not affiliated with a school system.

North American Society for Sport Management (NASSM) An organization that promotes, stimulates, and encourages study, research, scholarly writing, and professional development in the area of sport management, in both its theoretical and applied aspects.

not-for-profit A classification of an event or organization; most often, not-for-profit events focus on raising money for a charitable enterprise.

officials Individual contractors employed by schools or leagues to supervise athletic competitions.

off the record Remarks made to the media that are not meant to be published or broadcast.

Ohio University The first university to establish a master's program in sport management, in 1966.

Olympism The philosophy behind the Olympic Games, which seeks "to create a way of life based on the joy found in effort, the educational value of good example and respect for universal fundamental ethical principles."

O'Malley, Walter Co-inventor, with James G. Mason, of the idea of a sport management curriculum. Also owner of the Brooklyn and Los Angeles Dodgers from 1943 until his death in 1979.

one-school/one-vote A structure of organization in the NCAA from 1973 to 1997 in which each member school and conference had one vote at the NCAA's annual convention, which was assigned to the institution's president or CEO.

operations director A person who supervises facility preparation for all types of events, and coordinates, schedules, and supervises the numerous changeovers that take place as one event moves in and another moves out.

organizational behavior A field involved with the study and application of the human side of management and organizations.

organizational politics The use of power or other resources outside of the formal definition of a person's job to achieve a preferred outcome in the workplace.

organizing A functional area of management that focuses on putting plans into action by determining which types of jobs need to be performed and who will be responsible for doing these jobs.

organizing committees for the Olympic Games (OCOGs) The organizations primarily responsible for the operational aspects of the Olympic Games; such an organization is formed once a city has been awarded the Games.

outdoor recreation   Type of activities that take place in natural environments (e.g., camping, canoeing, golfing, etc.).

out-of-market   Fans of out-of-town teams now can pay a fee to acquire out-of-market coverage of game telecasts not available locally.

overly aggressive client recruitment   A form of unethical behavior by sports agents that includes such behaviors as paying athletes to encourage them to sign with agents early and promising athletes things that may not be achievable.

owners' equity   The amount of their own money that owners have invested in the firm.

parks movement   A political movement in the nineteenth century to permanently set aside lands for preservation, conservation, multi-use, and/or public use in the United States. The concept of preserving wilderness, important geomorphological formations, wildlife habitat and fragile ecosystems, and/or areas of great beauty or scientific interest as well as land dedicated towards public recreation and tourism has spread worldwide.

participative decision making   Involving employees or members of an organization in the decision-making process.

pass-by interviews   On-site interviews in heavy-traffic areas (such as malls) that utilize visual aids and assess the interviewee's reaction to the visual aids.

pay-per-view   A program that is distributed on a special channel on cable/DBS systems and only accessible by consumers who pay a specified fee to watch the program.

penetration   Describes the number/percentage of people or households receiving a particular product or service.

people skills   Knowing how to treat all people fairly, ethically, and with respect.

personal selling   Face-to-face, in-person selling.

physical therapists   See *trainers*.

plaintiff   The person or organization that initiates a lawsuit.

planning   A functional area of management that includes defining organizational goals and determining the appropriate means by which to achieve those desired goals.

pod   A grouping of multiple TV commercial spots. Pods fit well with many sports due to their natural commercial breaks between innings, periods, halftimes, quarters, etc.

podcast   A series of digital audio files that can be downloaded through online syndication.

point-of-sale/point-of-purchase marketing   Display materials used by marketers to attract consumers' attention to their product or service and their promotional campaign at the retail level.

premium seating   Personal seat licenses, luxury suites, and club seating.

premiums   Merchandise offered free or at a reduced price as an inducement to buy a different item or items.

press conference   A formal invitation for the press to gather at a specific location to hear an announcement and ask questions concerning it.

press release   A written announcement sent to editors and reporters to let people know what an organization is doing and to stimulate stories about the organization; also known as a *news release*.

primetime   During hours of the day, evening hours, when most people are at home and can watch TV.

principal   (1) The original amount that an organization borrows. (2) One who authorizes another to act on his or her behalf as an agent.

private club   A place where people hold a common bond of special interests, experiences, backgrounds, professions, and desires for coming together in a standard meeting place to gather for social and recreational purposes; not open to the public.

private exclusive clubs   A specific type of private club restricting membership to only those who are invited to join or become a member by a vote of the current existing membership.

private schools   Institutions that do not receive government assistance. In the United States, they were the first schools to provide athletic participation opportunities.

private sector   Nongovernment population.

Professional Golfers Association (PGA)   An organization comprised of more than 28,000 golf professionals who work at golf courses and country clubs.

professional tournaments   Sporting events that are sponsored by community groups, corporations, or charities; players earn their income through prize money and endorsements.

profits   The difference between an organization's revenues and expenses.

Progressive movement   An early twentieth-century social and political movement that believed in social improvement by governmental action and advocated economic, political, and social reforms.

properties division   A for-profit branch of a league that administers the league's licensing program; such divisions approve licensees, police trademark infringement, and distribute licensing revenues.

psychographic   Related to the preferences, beliefs, values, attitudes, personalities, and behavior of an individual or group.

public club   A public accommodation facility welcoming participants from nearly all types of backgrounds to play golf and enjoy the offerings of the club.

public ownership   By stockholders via shares that can be freely traded on the open market.

public policy   Pertains to a service important to the public.

public recreation   Recreational activities or opportunities offered at the state and federal level, such as state and federal forest and parks departments.

public relations (PR) or communications director   A person who works with the media, including TV and radio news directors, newspaper editors, and reporters, to establish or promote a person, corporation/manufacturer, or product.

public school   A free tax-supported school controlled by a local governmental authority.

public sector   Government.

rating   The percentage of television households in the survey universe that is tuned in to a particular program.

rational basis   Lowest standard of review in a discrimination case and focuses on any basis other than race, religion, national origin, or gender. Examples include economic or social background, sexual orientation, physical or mental disability, or athletic team membership.

reach   To capture or gain the attention of.

references   People who know you well enough to speak on your behalf.

registration system   A system for registering participants in events and collecting and disseminating the appropriate information.

relationship marketing   Aims to build mutually satisfying long-term relations with key parties (e.g., customers, suppliers, and distributors) in an attempt to earn and retain their business.

relativism   The belief that what is moral depends on the specific situation.

release of liability   Contract that parties sign after an injury occurs, by which a party gives up the right to sue later (usually in return for a financial settlement).

religious events   Encompass mass worship.

remote production facility   Houses most of the production crew and frequently called the "production truck."

reserve clause   A clause in a player's standard contract that gives a team the option to renew the player for the following season.

reserve list   A list of reserved players that was sent to each team in Major League Baseball; the teams had a gentleman's agreement not to offer contracts to any player on this list, thus keeping players bound to their teams.

reserve system   A restrictive system used to limit a free and open market so that owners retain the rights to players and control salary expenditures.

resume   A short summary of one's career and qualifications prepared by an applicant for a position.

retainer   A fee paid monthly to an agency or individual to retain their services.

retransmission consent   Broadcast networks charge fees to cable and DBS systems for the appearance of the networks on those distribution systems.

return on investment (ROI)   (1) The expected dollar-value return on the financial cost of an investment, usually stated as a percentage. (2) The achievement of specific marketing and sales objectives from a sport sponsorship.

revenues   The funds that flow into an organization and constitute its income.

revenue sharing   A system in which each team receives a percentage of various league-wide revenues.

rights fee   A type of rights arrangement in which the network pays the rightsholder a fee, and is responsible for all costs and expenses associated with producing the game(s) or event(s) for television, sells all of the advertising time itself, and retains all the revenue.

rightsholder   The person or entity that owns or controls the rights to an event.

risk   The uncertainty of the future benefits of an investment made today.

risk management   Protecting a business or organization from anything that could possibly go wrong and lead to a loss of revenues or customers; developing a management strategy to prevent legal disputes from arising and to deal with them if they do occur.

rival leagues   Compete directly with established leagues.

Rooney Rule   NFL rule named for Steelers owner Dan Rooney that requires teams with coaching openings to interview minority coaches during the search process.

roster management   Capping the roster sizes for men's teams in an effort to comply with Title IX gender equity provisions.

royalty   A fee paid to the licensor for the use of specific trademarks on specific products.

Rozelle, Alvin "Pete"   A commissioner of the National Football League (NFL) and shrewd promoter of the league who is largely credited with building the NFL into the model professional sport league. While commissioner, Rozelle increased shared broadcasting and marketing revenues, restructured the revenue sharing system, and negotiated the merger of the American Football League into the NFL.

sabermetrics   The empirical, analytical study of baseball.

salary cap   A financial mechanism that limits team payroll to a percentage of league revenues, thereby preventing large market teams from exploiting their financial advantage to buy the best teams.

sales inventory   The products available to the sales staff to market, promote, and sell through a range of sales methodologies.

sales promotion   A short-term promotional activity that is designed to stimulate immediate product demand.

sampling   Giving away free samples of a product to induce consumers to try it.

school athletic director   An administrator of a school athletic program whose responsibilities include risk management, researching and purchasing insurance, handling employment issues, ensuring gender equity, and fund-raising.

scientific management   The idea that there is one best way to perform a job most efficiently that can be discovered through scientific studies of the tasks that make up a job, and the belief that managers can get workers to perform the job in this best way by enticing them with economic rewards. Also known as *Taylorism*.

script   A specific, detailed, minute-by-minute schedule of activities throughout an event's day, including information on (a) the time of day and the activities taking place then, (b) the operational needs (equipment and setup) surrounding each activity, and (c) the event person or persons in charge of the various activities.

seasonal events   Take place during a specific time frame.

secondary meaning   Refers to the protection afforded geographic or descriptive terms in a product that a producer has used through advertising and media to lead the public to identify the producer or that product with the trade or service mark, thus permitting the user to protect an otherwise unprotectable mark.

segmentation   Identifying subgroups of the overall marketplace based on a variety of factors, such as age, income level, ethnicity, geography, and lifestyle.

self-governance   System in which leagues organize themselves (opposite of corporate governance).

senior women's administrator (SWA)   The highest-ranking female administrator involved with the conduct of an NCAA member institution's intercollegiate athletics program.

share   The percentage of all television households watching television at the time that are tuned into a particular program.

simulcast   The broadcast of programs or events across more than one medium.

single entity   Meaning one person, place, thing, business, and so on.

single-entity structure   A model of league ownership in which the league is considered as a single entity to avoid antitrust liability and to create some centralized fiscal control.

soccer-specific stadium (SSS)   Facilities built solely for soccer teams. SSS has become the legacy of soccer investor, Lamar Hunt, owner of the Columbus Crew, whose soccer specific stadium in Columbus, Ohio, was the first venue of its size to be built in the United States and has fueled SSS growth.

specialized agency   A sport management/marketing agency that limits the scope of services performed or the type of clients serviced.

speculation   A guess or answer to a hypothetical question or situation.

sponsor   A person or organization that provides funding or support for an event or broadcast in exchange for commercial exposure or financial gain.

sponsorship   The acquisition of rights to affiliate or directly associate with a product or event for the purpose of deriving benefits related to that affiliation.

sport events   Games or tournaments in facilities that typically take place on a seasonal basis and can be scheduled up to 8 months in advance.

sporting goods   The physical objects necessary to play a sport.

sporting goods equipment   Fitness products and sport-specific products.

sport law   The application of existing laws to the sport setting.

sport management firm affiliated with a law firm   A type of arrangement in which a freestanding sport management has a working relationship with a law firm so that each entity can fill a void by providing the services the other does not offer.

sport management/marketing agencies   A business that acts on behalf of a sport property (i.e., a person, company, event, team, or place).

sport management structures   Help managers organize and run sports; they are conceived and evolve in response to broad social changes or to address specific issues within a segment of the sport industry.

sport property   An athlete, company, event, team, or place.

sports agent   A person who acts as a representative of an athlete or coach to further the client's interests.

sports apparel   Garments that are designed for, or could be used in, active sports.

sports event managers   Personnel who administer, promote, and operate any type of events related to sport.

sports information director (SID)   Person in a college athletic department responsible for communications involving sport teams, coaches, athletes, and outcome of contests.

sports marketing representative   A person who coordinates all of the marketing and sponsorship activities for sport properties, which include sporting events run by the agency firm and the athletes represented by the firm.

stadiums   Outdoor or domed facilities that provide sites for sports teams and other nonsport events, such as outdoor concerts.

stakeholders   Groups and individuals who have a direct or indirect interest in an organization.

standard or uniform player contract   An individual contract used by a league for its professional athlete employees in which all terms are standardized except for the time period and salary.

standing committees   Permanent committees that help a club to conduct ongoing activities.

state actor   A private entity that is so enmeshed with a public entity that the private entity is considered a governmental one for purposes of subjecting the private entity to the rights protected by the U.S. and state constitutions.

state associations   Nonprofit groups that have a direct role in organizing state championships and competitions in athletics and activities and are the final authority in determining athlete eligibility.

statutes   Legislatively created laws codified in an act or a body of acts collected and arranged according to a particular theme or session of a legislature.

streamed   Broadcasting of video signals through usage of fiber-optic cable without the need for traditional television networks.

strict scrutiny   First standard of review in a discrimination case. Applies where one discriminates on the basis of race, religion, or national origin.

student-athlete services   An area of responsibility within a collegiate athletic department that addresses the academic concerns and welfare of student-athletes, overseeing such areas as academic advising, tutoring, and counseling.

subscriber fees   Additional revenue that cable networks earn from the money individuals pay to receive cable television in their homes.

sweepstakes   A game of chance or luck in which everyone has an equal chance to win; purchase may be required to enter a sweepstakes.

symbiotic relationship   A relationship that is mutually beneficial such as the sports industry and the broadcast media business relationship that produces valuable, compelling programming content that has become an essential element of the worldwide sports industry.

syndicate   The selling of programs by independent producers to stations not affiliated with networks or to network affiliates for telecast.

target market   A group of consumers to whom a product is marketed.

telecast rights   Includes broadcast (cable) and narrowcast (all other developing distribution media) rights.

telemarketing   Sales efforts conducted over the phone.

television markets   Group of counties or cities geographically identified as consisting of a large number of television households.

territorial rights   Rules that limit a competitor franchise from moving into another team's territory without league permission or without providing compensation.

theaters   Public assembly facilities that are primarily used for the presentation of live artistic entertainment; they are usually constructed by universities, public entities, and private (usually nonprofit) groups.

The Olympic Partner Program (TOP)   A sponsorship program established by the International Olympic Committee in which corporations pay millions of dollars for status as an official Olympic sponsor for a 4-year period and are granted exclusivity in a sponsorship category.

therapeutic recreation   Recreational activities that are offered as a means to improve a participant's physical, emotional, and mental health.

ticket rebate   Part of the surcharge that the consumer must pay when they purchase a ticket to an event. This is an additional fee that is structured based on the ticket price and returned to the facility or venue as a result of the sale.

tiers   Groups of networks that are marketed to customers at different fees.

time-buy   A type of rights arrangement in which the organizer buys time on the network and, subject to the network's quality control, is responsible for production of the event and handling sales.

time-shift   The ability, provided through DVR, to watch programs after their live telecasts.

Title VII of the Civil Rights Act   A statute that specifically prohibits any employment decision, practice, or policy that treats individuals unequally due to race, color, national origin, sex, or religion; it covers employers with 15 or more employees.

Title IX   A comprehensive statute aimed at eliminating sex discrimination in any educational program or activity that receives federal funding.

tort   An injury or wrong suffered as the result of another's improper conduct.

tournament operations   Pre-event, actual event, and postevent activities for staging an event.

trade associations   Organizations dedicated to promoting the interests of and assisting the members of a particular industry.

trade shows   Multiple-day events held annually in the same location.

trademark   A word, name, or symbol used by a manufacturer or merchant to identify and distinguish its goods from those manufactured and sold by others.

trainers   Individuals who treat the ailments and injuries of the members of an athletic team.

trashsports   Entertainment that advertises itself as sport but that has no real sporting significance.

universal design   A new concept which extends the Americans with Disabilities Act and makes facilities more accessible for all people.

university venues   Consist of stadiums, arenas, and theaters. The market for university and college venues is generally dictated by the student population.

unreasonable searches and seizures   Searches and seizures conducted without probable cause or other considerations that would make them legally permissible.

up-selling   Persuading an existing customer to move up to the next more expensive sales level.

value-added   The difference between the total sales revenue of an industry and the total cost of components, materials or services purchased from other firms (and therefore outside the industry).

variable pricing   Charging a premium price for tickets to events or games in greater demand.

vicarious liability   Provides a plaintiff with a cause of action to sue a superior for the negligent acts of a subordinate.

video news release (VNR)   A preproduced video piece that is edited for broadcast and includes a written story summary or press release.

volunteer management   The supervision of volunteers involved with an event; it involves two areas: (1) working with event organizers and staff to determine the areas in which volunteers are needed and the quantity needed and (2) soliciting, training, and managing the volunteers.

waivers   A contract in which parties agree to give up their right to sue for negligence before participating in the activity for which they are waiving the right to sue.

Web conferencing   The real-time exchange of audio, video, and text-based messages via the Internet.

website   A public relations outlet on the Internet that allows an organization to get its message out in an unfiltered manner and to interact with stakeholders.

youth league director   A supervisor of a youth league, whose responsibilities may include hiring, supervising, and evaluating coaches; coordinating nearly all facets of contest management, including the hiring and paying of officials and event staff; setting league training and disciplinary policies; determining league budgets; overseeing all associated fund-raising; determining and verifying game scheduling and athlete eligibility; transmitting relevant publicity; and handling public relations.

zero-base budgeting   Reviewing all activities and related costs as if the event were being produced or occurring for the first time; previous budgets and actual revenues and expenses are ignored.

About the Authors

Editors

Lisa P. Masteralexis, JD

Lisa P. Masteralexis is the Department Head and an Associate Professor in the Department of Sport Management at the University of Massachusetts Amherst. She holds a JD from Suffolk University School of Law and a BS in Sport Management from the University of Massachusetts. She teaches courses in Sport Agencies, Sport Law, and Labor Relations in Professional Sport. Her primary research interests are in legal issues and labor relations in the sport industry.

Professor Masteralexis is the lead editor of *Principles and Practice of Sport*, now in its fifth edition. She has contributed numerous book chapters to that textbook and others on sport management and sport law. Her scholarly work also includes contributions to the *Journal of the Legal Aspects of Sport*, *Journal of College and University Law*, *Jeffrey S. Moorad Sports Law Journal* (Villanova), *Marquette Sports Law Review*, *New England Law Review*, *Journal of Sport Management*, *Journal of Sport and Social Issues*, and *European Journal for Sport Management*. Professor Masteralexis has made over 60 presentations in the United States and abroad before the American Bar Association, the Sport and Recreation Law Association, the North American Society for Sport Management, the European Association for Sport Management, Women in Sports and Events, and numerous law schools and business schools.

In 2000, Professor Masteralexis coauthored an amicus brief to the U.S. Supreme Court on behalf of disabled athletes and in support of professional golfer Casey Martin. She is a member of the Massachusetts and U.S. Supreme Court Bars.

Professor Masteralexis has received the College Outstanding Teacher Award three times and has been nominated for the University Distinguished Teaching Award. She has received the Harold J. VanderZwaag Distinguished Alumnus Award from the Mark H. McCormack Department of Sport Management. She has served on the Board of the National Sports Law Institute and was part of the Women's Sports Foundation. Professor Masteralexis is also one of the few women certified as an agent with the Major League Baseball Players Association and is a consultant with DiaMMond Management Group, a professional athlete management firm.

Carol A. Barr, PhD

Carol A. Barr currently serves as Vice Provost for Undergraduate and Continuing Education at the University of Massachusetts Amherst. In this role, she provides overall leadership for undergraduate and continuing education programs on campus. She works closely with the campus leadership to develop a comprehensive plan for undergraduate education reflecting best practices related to teaching and learning, promotion of undergraduate academic success, and campus initiatives impacting student learning and student success. Dr. Barr holds a BS in Athletic Administration from the University of Iowa (4-year letter winner in field hockey) and an MS and PhD in Sport Management from the University of Massachusetts Amherst. She joined the UMass Amherst faculty in 1991 and is a tenured faculty member in the Mark H. McCormack Department of Sport Management.

Dr. Barr's research interests lie in the areas of management issues and gender equity within collegiate athletics. She has published articles in the *Journal of Sport Management, Sport Marketing Quarterly, Journal of Higher Education, Journal of Business Ethics, Sex Roles,* and the *International Sports Journal.* Dr. Barr has published more than 40 articles for sport practitioners in publications such as *Athletic Business* and *Street & Smith's SportsBusiness Journal.* Dr. Barr is also the coauthor of *Managing Intercollegiate Athletics,* a textbook that provides unique, relevant course material on intercollegiate athletic management. She has performed consulting work for the National Collegiate Athletic Association and has been involved in legal research surrounding gender equity, concentrating on its application to the collegiate athletic arena.

Within her academic association, Dr. Barr has served on the Executive Council of the North American Society for Sport Management (NASSM), serving as President in 2006–2007. She was a 2011 recipient of the North American Society for Sport Management Garth Paton Distinguished Service Award. She has also served on the editorial board of the *Journal of Sport Management.*

Mary A. Hums, PhD

Mary A. Hums is a Professor in the Sport Administration Program at the University of Louisville, where she coordinates the PhD program. She holds a PhD in Sport Management from Ohio State University, an MA in Athletic Administration and an MBA from the University of Iowa, and a BBA in Management from the University of Notre Dame. In addition

to being a past President of the Society for the Study of Legal Aspects of Sport and Physical Activity (SSLASPA; now Sport and Recreation Law Society [SRLA]), Dr. Hums is an active member of the North American Society for Sport Management (NASSM); the European Association of Sport Management (EASM); and the International Olympic Academy Participants Association (IOAPA).

Prior to coming to the University of Louisville, Dr. Hums served on the Sport Management faculty at the University of Massachusetts Amherst; directed the Sport Management Program at Kennesaw State University in Atlanta; and was Athletic Director at St. Mary-of-the-Woods College in Terre Haute, Indiana. She worked as a volunteer for the 1996 Summer Paralympic Games in Atlanta, the 2002 Winter Paralympic Games in Salt Lake City, and the 2010 Winter Paralympic Games in Vancouver. In 2004, she lived in Athens, Greece, for 5 months, working at both the Olympic (softball) and Paralympic (goalball) Games.

A past Editor of the *Sport Management Education Journal,* her scholarly contributions also include publications in the *Journal of Sport Management, European Sport Management Quarterly, Journal of Business Ethics, Journal of Sport and Social Issues, Sport Management Review, Journal of Legal Aspects of Sport, International Journal of Sport Management,* and *Advancing Women in Leadership.* She has made over 180 scholarly presentations in the United States and abroad.

In 2006, Hums was selected by the United States Olympic Committee to represent the United States at the International Olympic Academy's Educators' Session. In 2008, Dr. Hums was an Erasmus Mundus International Research Fellow at the Katholieke Universiteit of Leuven, Belgium. She is currently a Research Fellow with the Institute for Human Centered Design, which is based in Boston.

In 2009, she was named the Earle F. Zeigler Lecturer by NASSM. In 2014, she received the NASSM Diversity Award and also the Southern Sport Management Association Scholar Achievement Award. She is an inductee into the Indiana ASA Softball Hall of Fame and also the Marian High School (Mishawaka, Indiana) Athletic Hall of Fame.

Contributors

Nola Agha, PhD

Nola Agha is an Assistant Professor in the Sport Management Program at the University of San Francisco. She holds a BS from Indiana University Bloomington, an MA in Sport Management from the University of San Francisco, and a PhD in Management from the Mark H. McCormack Department of Sport Management at the University of Massachusetts Amherst.

Dr. Agha's primary research focuses on the economic impacts of teams and stadiums, the efficiency and equity outcomes of stadium subsidies, and a variety of issues related to minor league baseball. She brings a multidisciplinary approach to her research, combining her training in both economics and management. She has published sport-related articles in journals such as the *Journal of Sports Economics* and the *Sport Management Review*. Dr. Agha worked in international business operations for several years and has also consulted to the sport and fitness industry by conducting economic impact studies, competitive analyses, and feasibility studies for clients in MLB, the NBA, and minor league hockey.

Gregory Bouris

Gregory Bouris is the Director of Communications for the Major League Baseball Players Association (MLBPA), where he is responsible for developing and managing all internal and external communications activities. His responsibilities include media relations, marketing communications, website development and oversight, advertising, publications, and promotional and cause-related marketing. Bouris holds a BS in Sport Management from the University of Massachusetts. In his 30-year professional career, he has established himself as one of the industry's most experienced public relations and communications professionals, witnessing the growth of the sport industry from the inside. When the New York Islanders named him publicity director in 1986, he became the youngest such director in professional sports. Since then, he has acquired experience dealing with many of the top issues that face the industry, including expansion, franchise development, ownership transfers, arena construction, collective bargaining, licensing, cause-related marketing initiatives, the Internet, digital and social media, and broadcasting. Prior to joining the MLBPA in 1999, Bouris held similar roles at 1-800-FLOWERS .com, Sports Channel New York, the Florida Panthers, and the New York Islanders. Upon graduating from UMass, he spent a season as an intern with the NHL's marketing and public relations department and worked game nights for the communications department of the New York Knicks.

Bouris also teaches part time at Adelphi University in Garden City, New York and has served on the board of the Nassau County Sports Commission.

John S. Clark, PhD

John S. Clark is a Professor of Sport Management and Director of the MBA Program in the Robert Morris University School of Business. He received his MS and PhD in Sport Management from the University of Massachusetts Amherst and a BA in English Literature from the University of Wisconsin-Eau Claire. Dr. Clark's research has been published in both sport management and business journals, and focuses on sponsorship, cause-related marketing, and sport consumer behavior.

Dan Covell, PhD

Dan Covell is a Professor of Sport Management in the College of Business at Western New England University. He earned his undergraduate degree in Studio Art from Bowdoin College in 1986 (where he also lettered in football).

After working in public and private secondary education as a coach, teacher, and athletic administrator, Covell earned his MS in Sport Management from the University of Massachusetts Amherst (UMass) in 1995. After a 1-year administrative internship in Harvard University's athletic department, Covell then earned his PhD from UMass in 1999.

His primary research interests are management issues in intercollegiate and secondary school athletics, with a recent track toward historical perspectives on these issues.

Todd W. Crosset, PhD

Todd W. Crosset is an Associate Professor and the Director of the Undergraduate Program in the Mark H. McCormack Department of Sport Management in the Isenberg School of Management at the University of Massachusetts Amherst. He holds an MA and PhD in Sociology from Brandeis University, as well as a BA from the University of Texas Austin where he was an All-American swimmer and a member of a national championship team. Prior to arriving at the University of Massachusetts, he held positions as Head Coach of Swimming at Northeastern University and Assistant Athletic Director at Dartmouth College. Dr. Crosset's academic interests include gender and racism in sport management and sexual assault in sport. His book, *Outsiders in the Clubhouse*, which is about life on the LPGA golf tour, won the North American Society for Sport Sociology Book of the Year Award in 1995. Dr. Crosset may be best known for his work on the issue of athlete sexual assault on college campuses. Dr. Crosset was one of the first scholars to identify and name coach–athlete abuse as a problem. In this area of study his focus is on prevention. Currently, Dr. Crosset is consulting on legal issues exploring the intersection between athlete sexual assault and Title IX.

Neil Longley, PhD

Neil Longley is a Professor in the Mark H. McCormack Department of Sport Management in the Isenberg School of Management at the University of Massachusetts Amherst. Dr. Longley holds a bachelor's degree in Administration and an MA in Economics from the University of Regina, an MBA from the University of Manitoba, and a PhD in Economics from Washington State University. Dr. Longley's primary academic interests are in the areas of sport economics and sport finance. His research on discrimination in the NHL has been particularly influential. His article "Salary Discrimination in the National Hockey League: The Effects of Team Location," originally published in the journal *Canadian Public Policy*, was reprinted in *International Library of Critical Writings in Economics: The Economics of Sport*—a book that reprints the most important articles in the field of sport economics over the past 50 years. During his career, Dr. Longley has also done considerable consulting work—particularly in the areas of market impact studies and cost-benefit analyses—for clients in both the private and public sectors.

Tara Q. Mahoney, PhD

Tara Q. Mahoney is an Assistant Professor in the Sport Management Department at the State University of New York College at Cortland. She earned her PhD in Educational Leadership and Organizational Development with a concentration in Sport Administration at the University of Louisville. She also earned an MBA from West Virginia Wesleyan College and a BA from Nazareth College of Rochester, where she played volleyball.

Prior to pursuing a career in academia, Dr. Mahoney worked in various sectors of the recreation industry including municipal, campus, and outdoor recreation. Dr. Mahoney's research interests are in the areas of charity sport participation and the use of social media to facilitate sport participation.

Stephen McKelvey, JD

Stephen McKelvey is an Associate Professor in the Mark H. McCormack Department of Sport Management at the University of Massachusetts Amherst. Professor McKelvey holds a BA from Amherst College, an MS in Sport Management from the University of Massachusetts Amherst, and a JD from Seton Hall School of Law. He brings a unique perspective to the department, combining his sport industry experience in marketing, sales, and the law to provide students with valuable insights. His research focuses primarily on the legal and practical application of intellectual property issues to the sports marketing industry. He has authored articles on sport marketing, sponsorship, and the law for a number of publications, including the *Virginia Entertainment and Sport Law Review*, *The Journal of Legal Aspects of Sport*, *Journal of Sport Management*, *Sport Management Review*, *International Journal of Sport Marketing and Management*, *Seton Hall Journal of Sport Law*, *Entertainment and Sports Lawyer*, and *Sports Business Journal*, among others. A noted authority on the topic of "ambush marketing," Professor McKelvey has over 15 years of industry experience, both on the sport property and the agency side. From 1986–1991, he worked in the Corporate Sponsorship department of Major League Baseball, and later was responsible for building an in-house sports sponsorship consulting agency within PSP Sports, a New York City–based sports publishing company. In 1999, McKelvey conceived, sold, and managed two of the year's most innovative sport marketing programs: Century 21's "Turn Ahead the Clock" promotion (baseball's first-ever league-wide series of futuristic-themed baseball games, featuring games with players outfitted in futuristic-styled uniforms) and the first-ever promotion allowing consumers to vote for the Heisman Trophy Award winner (the linchpin of Suzuki's Heisman Trophy sponsorship).

Jim Noel, JD

Jim Noel oversees all legal operations for DIRECTV Sports in Seattle, WA. He is former Vice President, Business Affairs for ESPN, where he was the lead contract negotiator for all content-acquisition transactions. He also was Associate General Counsel at ESPN, where he was responsible for programming and affiliation transactions, creating the legal framework for ESPN.com, and providing editorial counseling for the SportsCenter and Outside The Lines programs. He also has been Assistant Counsel to the Commissioner of the NFL, Director of Legal Affairs of NFL Properties, and Chief Legal Officer of the United States Golf Association. He also practiced at the Seattle-based law firm of Davis Wright Tremaine. He is a graduate of the University of Alabama School of Law and the University of Oregon School of Journalism.

Per G. Svensson, MS

Per G. Svensson is a Doctoral Fellow at the University of Louisville in the Department of Health and Sport Sciences. His research interests are organizational capacity in sport-for-development and the role of sport as a tool for promoting social change. Per has a diverse background in sport, including experiences with the PGA TOUR, the PGA of America, the Special Olympics, and the 2010 Alltech FEI World Equestrian Games. He holds an MS degree in Sport Administration from the University of Louisville and a BS degree in Sport Management from Slippery Rock

University. Per also holds a professional certificate in Sports Philanthropy from The George Washington University.

Jo Williams, PhD

Jo Williams is an Associate Professor of Sport Management in the School of Business at the University of Southern Maine. She holds masters' and doctoral degrees in Sport Management from Springfield College, Massachusetts. In addition, she holds a bachelor's degree in Physical Education from West London Institute of Higher Education. Prior to working in higher education, Dr. Williams worked in event management with professional golf and tennis events, including work as the Tournament Director of the McCalls LPGA Classic at Stratton Mountain, Vermont. This position involved a focus on golf event operations and marketing. Dr. Williams has been actively involved in the Commission on Sport Management Accreditation, serving as a Commissioner and member of the Board of Directors. Her research interests are focused on sport marketing, including the use of social media in the sports industry. She has also conducted research in sport management accreditation and pedagogy.

Glenn Wong, JD

Glenn Wong is a Professor in the Mark H. McCormack Department of Sport Management in the Isenberg School of Management at the University of Massachusetts Amherst. He received a BA in Economics and Sociology from Brandeis University and a JD from Boston College Law School. While at the University of Massachusetts, he served as the Sport Management Department Head, Interim Director of Athletics, Acting Dean of the School of Physical Education, and Faculty Athletics Representative for the university to the National Collegiate Athletic Association. A lawyer, he is author of *The Essentials of Sports Law,* Fourth Edition (2010) and *The Comprehensive Guide to Careers in Sports,* Second Edition (2012). Wong has published over 100 articles. He has worked extensively in salary arbitration in Major League Baseball as both an arbitrator and as outside counsel to the Boston Red Sox and Baltimore Orioles. He is currently President of the Sports Lawyers Association, of which he has been a member of the Board of Directors since 2000. Wong received both the University Distinguished Teaching Award as well as the College Outstanding Teaching Award, along with two Chancellor's Medals of Honor.

Index

Note: Page numbers followed by *f* and *t* indicate material in figures and tables, respectively.

A

AAHPERD. *See* Alliance for Health, Physical Education, Recreation and Dance
AARP. *See* American Association of Retired Persons
absolutism, 141
ACA. *See* American Camping Association
ACC. *See* Atlantic Coast Conference
access for persons with disabilities, 330–331
activation, 384
ADA. *See* Americans with Disabilities Act
ADEA. *See* Age Discrimination in Employment Act
ad hoc committees, 499
administrative law, 98
advertising, event management, 347–348
advertising inventory, 370
advertising salesperson, facility management, 327–328
affiliate, 444
AFL. *See* American Football League
aftermarketing, 366–367
Age Discrimination in Employment Act (ADEA), 118
agency, defined, 104
agency law, 104–105
agents, 104
  professional sport, 253
"aggressive accounting" techniques, 143
AHL. *See* American Hockey League
AIAW. *See* Association for Intercollegiate Athletics for Women
a la carte, 454
Alliance of Action Sports, 339
amateurism rules, NCAA, 124
Amateur Sports Act of 1978, 212
ambush marketing, 53, 123, 124, 449
  licensing, 395
American Alliance for Health, Physical Education, Recreation and Dance (AAHPERD), 159
American Association of Retired Persons (AARP), 525
American Camping Association (ACA), 523

American Football
  collegiate, safety concerns, 154
  franchise values, 87, 87*t*
  revenues, 87–88, 87*t*
American Football League (AFL), 440
American Hockey League (AHL), 233
American Sport Education Program (ASEP), 169
Americans with Disabilities Act (ADA), 118–119, 534–535
  facility management, 330
  reasonable accommodation, 119
ancillary revenue, 322
annuity value, 376
antitrust law, 112–115, 247
  and college athletics, 114–115
  Curt Flood Act, 113–114
  exemptions, 113
  and professional sport, 112–113
  Sports Broadcasting Act of 1961, 114
apps, 421
arenas, 312–313
  financing, 316–319
    mechanisms, 317–319
    private methods, 318
  modern construction, 310–311
Arledge, Roone, 51, 439
ASEP. *See* American Sport Education Program
assets, 77
assisted-listening systems, 331
Association for Intercollegiate Athletics for Women (AIAW), 178
athlete representative, sports agent, 267–269
athlete sponsorship, 395
athletic department, organizational chart, 31*f*
athletic director
  collegiate sport, 184–185
  role of, 191–192
athletic footwear, 473
Atlantic Coast Conference (ACC), 445
audience audit, 55
audience research, broadcasting, 448

B

balance sheet, 80
barnstorming tours, 338
baseball
　gambling and, 13
　history, 11–15
　league structure, 11–15
basketball, history, 310
BCS. *See* Bowl Championship Series
beat reporter, 414
behavioral interview, 560
benefit selling, 365
BFOQ. *See* bona fide occupational qualification
Big Ten Conference, 174, 176
blackout, 450
Black Sox scandal, 237–238
bloggers, 421
blogs, 411
board of directors, 498
board of governors, 498
bona fide occupational qualification (BFOQ), 118
bonds, 79–80, 316
booking director, facility management, 326
Boras, Scott, 279
Boston Marathon, 352
Bowl Championship Series (BCS), 401
box office director, facility management, 328
branding, 479
BrandMatch, 287
breach, contract, 106
broadband, 445
broadcasting, 435–459, 437
　audience research, 448
　as business, 446–452
　　advertising, 448
　　broadcast networks, 449
　　cable networks, 449–450
　　digital networks, 450
　　highlights and ancillary rights, 451–452
　　pay-per-view, 450
　　production, 447–448
　　radio, 451
　　ratings, 448–449
　　regionalization, 450–451
　　rights fees, 446–447
　　sponsorship, 449
　　syndication, 449
　career opportunities, 455–457
　current issues, 453–455
　　audience fragmentation, 455
　　bundling, 453–454
　　cord-cutting, 454

　　market bubble, 453
　　mobile devices, 454–455
　　technology, 454
　electronic media, 436, 437
　event management, 349–350
　evolution, 51–52
　history, 436–446
　　cable television services, 442
　　DVRs, 444
　　FCC, 439
　　NFL, 440–441, 443
　　radio, 437–438
　　telegraph machines, 436
　　telephone, 436–437
　importance to sport industry, 436
　international sport, 452–453
　rating, 448
　resources, 459–460
　revenues, 88
　rights, 436
　rights holder, 436
　rights-only agreement, 446
　share, 449
　Sports Broadcasting Act of 1961, 114, 441
　subscriber, 445
　　fees, 445
　symbiotic relationship, 436
　time buy, 448
broadcasting rights, 438
bubble, 453
Buckley Amendment. *See* Family Educational Rights and Privacy Act
budgeting
　defined, 76
　event management, 342
　process, 76
bundling, 454
business development, 351

C

CAA sports. *See* Creative Artists Agency sports
cable television, 442, 450
call-to-action ads, 426
campus recreation, 528–529
capacity, contract, 105–106
career, 545–562
　informational interviews, 552–553
　job search, 549–552
　marketing yourself, 553–562
career opportunities, event management, 351–352
career planning, sports agent, 290–291
Carnegie Reports of 1929, 176

Casco Bay Country Club (CBCC), 516
cash-flow budgeting, event management, 342
cause-related marketing efforts, 350–351
CBA. *See* collective bargaining agreement
center for visitors bureau (CVB), 321
CFL Players Association (CFLPA), 269
change
    managing, 40–41
    reasons for resistance, 40
charities, event management, 351
charity event, professional golf, 17
chief operating officer (COO), 503
CIAW. *See* Commission on Intercollegiate Athletics
        for Women
Civil Rights Act, Title VII, 117–118
CLC. *See* Collegiate Licensing Company
clean feed, 448
club management, 491–518
    ad hoc committee, 499
    board of directors, 498
    board of governors, 498
    country club, 492
    course club setting, managing and leading in
        financial management and benchmarking, 505
        marketplace, competition in, 505–506
    current and future issues, 510–515
        facilities, changes in, 511
        Golf 2.0, 512–513
        player development, 512–513
        sustainability and environment, 513–514
        technology, impact of, 514–515
    executive committee, 498–499
    general manager, 506
    history, 492–494
    industry performance, 499–503
        market drivers, 500–502
        market segmentation, 502
        market segmentation product types, 502–503
    legacy member, 495
    non-equity club, 496, 497–498
    non-profit 501c7 club, 496
    organizational structure, 497–499
    ownership and types of clubs, 496–497
        equity club, 496, 498–499
    private club, 495
    private exclusive club, 495
    public club, 494
    staff positions, 506–509
        aquatics director, 508
        banquet/event manager, 509
        clubhouse manager, 508
        controller, 508
        department managers, 508
        executive chef, 508–509
        general manager, 506
        golf course superintendent, 507–508
        golf professional, 506–507
        management team, 506
        membership director, 509
        spa directors, 508
        tennis professional, 507
    standing committee, 499
    strategies for entering, 509–510
Club Managers Association of America (CMAA), 494
club system, 4, 5–11
    American culture, 10–11
    English system, 5–8
    Jockey club, 7
    modern Olympics, 7–8
    thoroughbred racing, 5–7
    today, 9–10
cluttered marketplace, 64–67
coach
    high school/youth sport, 158
        fundraising, 158
        supervision, 160
    National Collegiate Athletic Association, 184–185
    as predators, 163–164
code of conduct, 136–138
code of ethics, 136–138
collective bargaining agreement (CBA), 90, 110, 241
    labor exemption, 113
collective bargaining process, 114, 116
College Sports Information Directors of America
        (CoSIDA), 429
Collegiate Licensing Company (CLC), 474
collegiate sport, 174
    athletic director, 184–185
    career opportunities, 183–186
    compliance, 185
    conference rules, 183
    current issues, 186–191
    enforcement, 181
    faculty athletics representative (FAR), 185
    Football Bowl Subdivision, 182
    Football Championship Subdivision, 182
    foreign student-athletes, 221
    fund development, 185
    gender equity, 188–190
    governing body, 180
    hiring practices, 190
    history, 174–179
    licensing, 474
    member conferences, 182–183

collegiate sport (*Cont.*)
  NCAA, 180
  organizational structure, 179–183
  resources, 193
  roster management, 189
  senior women's administrator (SWA), 185
  student-athlete services, 185
  Title IX, 188–190
collegiate, sport management, 124–125
Collins, Jim, 43
commercial breaks, 448
commercial formats, 448
commercial moral rules, 141
commissioner, professional sport, 237–239, 249
Commission on Intercollegiate Athletics for Women
      (CIAW), 178
Commission on Sport Management Accreditation
      (COSMA), 21
communications, 411
  advertising, 426
  awareness, 425
  career opportunities, 427–430
  current issues, 430–431
  direct marketing, 427
  government relations, 430–431
  history of, 412–413
  integrated marketing communications, 426–427
  media planning, 426–427
  media training, 425
  off-the-record comments, 425
  outside agencies, 430
  resources, 432
  speculations, 425
communication skills, 34–35
community-based recreation, 527
competing leagues, development of, 272
competitive balance, 91
compliance, collegiate sport, 185
concerts, 315
conference calls, 417–418
conference realignment, 183, 186
conference rules, 183
conflicts of interest, 104, 293
consideration, 105
constitutional law, 107–110
contests, 387
contract, 104
  breach, 106
  consideration, 105
  defined, 105
  disafirm, 106
  legality, 106

mutual assent, 105
  release of liability, 106
  waivers, 106
contract law, 105–107, 105*f*
contract negotiation, sports agent
  athlete's contract, 283–284
  coach's contract, 284–285
convention center, 313
convocations, 316
Cooke, Lenny, 289
"cookie-cutter stadiums," 311
co-promotional agreements, 321
co-promotional model, 321
copyright, 451
cord-cutting, 454
corporate governance model, 234
corporate ownership, 237
corporate sponsorship, 52–54
  event management, 346–347
  sport management/marketing agency, 339
corporate sponsors, Olympics, 219
corporation
  global strategy, 202
  international sport, 198–200
corruption, 142–144
  and Enron, 143
  and PEDs, 143
  and Rosie Ruiz, 142
CoSIDA. *See* College Sports Information Directors
      of America
COSMA. *See* Commission on Sport
      Management Accreditation
country club, 492
coupons, 388
cover letter, 558–559
Creative Artists Agency (CAA) sports, 274
cricket, 7
crisis plan, 423
crisis team, 424
CRM. *See* customer relationship management
cross-ownership, 237
cross-promotion, 389
crowd management plan, 329
cultural awareness, 220–221, 533
cultural differences, 220
Curt Flood Act, 113–114
customer relationship management (CRM), 62, 363
Czar of Baseball, 12

D
database marketing, 64
DBC. *See* Deutsche Bank Classic

DBS. *See* direct broadcast satellites
debt, 79
decision making, 38–39
   ethical, 132
   participative, 38
decision-making process, 145, 146
de Coubertain, Pierre, 8
default, 83
defendant, 100
delegation, 32
demographic, 55, 60, 439
Deutsche Bank Classic (DBC), 242
digital networks, 450
digital video recorder (DVR), 444
D.I.M. process, 100
direct broadcast satellites (DBS), 442
direct mail, 636
direct marketing, 427
direct participation, 522
disaffirm, contract, 106
discipline, ethical issues, 147
discrimination, 108
dispute resolution, sports agency, 284, 291
diversity in workforce, 547
diversity management, 35–37
   defined, 35
   minorities, 36
   people with disabilities, 36
   professional sport, 248–249
   women, 36
doping, 222–223
drug testing, professional sport, 254–255
drug testing program, 121, 122*b*
due process, 108
duty of care, 102
DVR. *See* digital video recorder

E

EASM. *See* European Association of Sport
      Management
East Coast Hockey League (ECHL), 233
ECHL. *See* East Coast Hockey League
Educational Amendments of 1972, 110–112
eduselling, 365–366, 366
Eighth International Sports Event Management
      Conference, 339
electronic media, 436, 437
electronic newsletters, 420
"elevator speech," 556
emergency medical technician (EMT), 102
emotional intelligence, 43
employment laws, 115–119

empowerment, 43
EMT. *See* emergency medical technician
endorsement contract, sports agent, 287–288
English club system, 5–8
entertainment, options, 67
entrepreneur, 470
environmental awareness, 533
EPA. *See* Equal Pay Act
Equal Pay Act (EPA), 116–117
equal protection, 108–109
   standard of review, 108–109
equity clubs, 496
ESPN, 51–52, 453
   dominance of, 457–458
ethical considerations, 133–138
ethical decision making, 132, 134
ethical dilemma, 132
   self-examination, 145–146
ethical issues, 131–147
   code of conduct, 136–138
   consequences, 146–147
   ensuring morality in the workplace, 145–146
   forum for moral discourse, 146
   key skills, 144–147
   morality, 138–144
      absolutism, 141
      and the changing nature of work, 144
      and corruption, 142–144
      moral principles, 139
      and multiple roles, 142
      relativism, 141
      vs. the law, 140
      in the workplace, 140–142
   regulation, 295–297
   self-examinations, 145–146
   sports agency, 292–295
ethical reasoning, 132
ethics, defined, 132
ethnic marketing, 398–399
European Association of Sport Management
      (EASM), 22
evaluating, 33
event director, facility management, 325–326
event management, 337–356
   advertising, 347–348
   broadcasting, 349–350
   budgeting, 342
   business development, 351
   career opportunities, 351–352
   cash-flow budgeting, 342
   corporate sponsorship, 346–347
   critical functions, 341–351

event management (*Cont.*)
  current issues, 352–353
  event marketing, 346
  fundraising, 350–351
    not-for-profit, 350
  history, 338–339
  hospitality, 348
  in-kind sponsorship, 348
  insurance, 343
  key skills, 351–352
  licensing, 350
  marketing, 346–351
    cause-related marketing efforts, 350–351
    integrated marketing approach, 346–351
  merchandising, 350
  niche sports, 353
  planning stages, 343–344
  post event stage, 344
  public relations, 348
  registration, 344–345
  resources, 355–356
  risk management, 342–343
  sport management/marketing agency
    functions, 339–341
    types of, 341
  ticket sales, 348–349
  tournament operations, 343–344
    script, 344
  volunteer management, 345–346
  waiver and release of liability form, 342, 343
  website development, 350
  zero-base budgeting, 342
event marketing
  advertising, 347–348
  broadcasting, 349–350
  corporate sponsorship, 346–347
  fundraising, 350–351
  hospitality, 348
  licensing/merchandising, 350
  public relations, 348
  ticket sales, 348–349
  website development and management, 350
event security, 352
event sponsorship, 396
events, types of, 314–315
  concerts, 315
  convocations, 316
  family events, 315
  religious events, 316
  seasonal events, 316
  sport events, 315
  trade shows, 315–316

executive committee, 498
expenses, 77

F
facility expenses, financing, 322–324
facility management, 309–333
  access for persons with disabilities, 330–331
  advertising salesperson, 327–328
  Americans with Disabilities Act, 330
  booking director, 326
  box office director, 328
  career opportunities, 324
  city subsidies, 319–320
  concerts, 315
  convocations, 316
  crowd management plan, 329
  current issues, 328
  event director, 325–326
  family events, 315
  financing, 316–319
    mechanisms, 317–319
  group ticket salesperson, 328
  history, 310–311
  local/civic venue, 314
  marketing, 320–328
  marketing director, 324
  marketing fund, 323
  metropolitan facilities, 314
  operations director, 327
  private management, 320
  public relations director, 324–325
  religious events, 316
  resources, 333
  seasonal events, 316
  security, 328–329
  signage salesperson, 327–328
  sponsorship salesperson, 327–328
  sports events, 315
  sustainability, 329–330
  ticket rebate, 322
  trade shows, 315–316
  universal design, 331–332
  university venues, 313–314
facility marketing, 320–321
  advertising, sponsorship, and signage salesperson, 327–328
  booking director, 326
  box office director, 328
  event director, 325–326
  group ticket salesperson, 328
  marketing director, 324
  operations director, 327

promoting, 321–322
public relations/communications director,
    324–325
revenues and expenses, 322–324
facility ownership and management staff, 320
facility revenue, financing, 322–324
facility sponsorship, 396
faculty athletics representative (FAR), 185
    collegiate sport, 180
Family Educational Rights and Privacy Act
    (FERPA), 418
family events, 314, 315
fan identification, 61
FAR. *See* faculty athletics representative
FCC. *See* Federal Communications Commission
Federal Communications Commission (FCC), 439
Fédération Internationale de Football Association
    (FIFA), 268–269
Fenway Sports Group (FSG), 245
FERPA. *See* Family Educational Rights and
    Privacy Act
fiduciary duties, 104
FIFA. *See* Fédération Internationale de
    Football Association
finance, 76–77
    event management, 342
financial planning, sports agency, 272, 289–290
financial principles, 73–93
    current issues, 86–93
    key skills, 86
    principal, 79
financing
    arena, 316–319
        mechanisms, 317–319
    convention center, 316
    facility management, 316–319
        mechanisms, 317–319
    stadium, 316–319
        mechanisms, 317–319
    taxes, 317–318
financing decisions, 82–83
Football
    American
        collegiate, safety concerns, 154
        franchise ownership, 235–236
        franchise values, 87, 87t
        revenues, 87–88, 87t
    Australian Rules, 224
Forest Service, USDA, 527, 534
Fourteenth Amendment, equal protection,
    108, 109
    standard of review, 108, 109

Fourth Amendment, unreasonable search and
    seizure, 109
fragmentation, 455
franchise free agency, 244
franchise ownership, professional sport league,
    235–236
    revenue sharing, 92
franchise rights, 237
franchise values and revenue generation, 244–246
Fred, Corcoran, professional tournament, 16–18
freestanding inserts (FSIs), 388
freestanding sport management firm, 278
FSG. *See* Fenway Sports Group
FSIs. *See* freestanding inserts
full-service agencies, 341
fund development, collegiate sport, 185
fundraising
    event management, 350–351
    high school and youth sport, 158

G
gambling
    horse racing, 6–7
    sponsorship, 400
gate receipts, 88, 232
gender equity, 124
    collegiate sport, 188–190
    high school sport, 164–165
gender, professional sport, 247–249
general manager, 250
globalization, professional sport, 253–254
global sourcing, 479
global strategy, 202
Goleman, Daniel, 43
Golf 2.0, 512–513
governance, high school and youth sport, 156–158
governing bodies, 156
governing body sponsorship, 393
governmental scrutiny toward sport, 125
government relations, 430–431
grassroots efforts, 204
grassroots programs, 340
gross negligence, 102
group ticket salesperson, facility management, 328

H
harness racing, 10–11
HDTV. *See* high-definition television
head ends, 448
Heraea Games, 19
HGH. *See* human growth hormone
high-definition television (HDTV), 444

high school athletic director, 158–159
   fundraising, 158
   gender equity, 164–165
   management, 159–160
high school league director
   fundraising, 158
   gender equity, 164–165
high school sport, 151–170
   career opportunities, 158–159
   coach, 158
   ethics, 163–165
   gender equity, 164–165
   governance, 156–158
   history, 153–156
   judge, 159
   legal, 165
   marketing, 162–163
   nineteenth century, 153–154
   official, 159
   physical therapist, 158
   private school, 153
   public school, 154
   resources, 169–170
   sex discrimination, 164
   trainer, 158
   twentieth century, 154–155
Hispanic population, 525
horse racing, 5–7, 10–11
   gambling, 6–7
hospitality, event management, 348
   inventory, 369–370
Hulbert, William, 11–15
human growth hormone (HGH), professional sport,
   254–255
human relations movement, 29

I

IAAF. *See* International Amateur Athletics
   Federation
IAAUS. *See* Intercollegiate Athletic Association of
   the United States
IAVM. *See* International Association of Venue
   Managers
IDSDP. *See* International Day of Sport for
   Development and Peace
IEG Sponsorship Report, 339
IFs. *See* international federations
image, 67–68
image ads, 426
IMC. *See* integrated marketing communications
IMG. *See* International Management Group
immoral behavior, 142

impasse, 241
income, 77
income mismanagement, 292
income statement, 77
independent contractor, 104
indirect participation, 522
individual professional sport, history, 15–18
individual professional sports, 241–243
informational interviewing, 552–553
informed participant consent, 535
in-house agency, 341
initiative, 41
injunction, 101
in-kind sponsorship, 348
Institute for Human Centered Design, 331
insurance, event management, 343
integrated marketing approach, 346
integrated marketing communications (IMC),
   426–427
intellectual property (IP), 119
intellectual property law, 119–120
intercept interviews, 56
Intercollegiate Athletic Association of the United
   States (IAAUS), 176
Intercollegiate Conference of Faculty
   Representatives, 175–176
Intercollegiate Football Association, 175
interest, 79
internal communications, 425–426
International Amateur Athletics Federation
   (IAAF), 210
International Association of Venue Managers
   (IAVM), 310
International Day of Sport for Development and
   Peace (IDSDP), 209
International Federation, Olympics, 210, 213–214,
   215*t*, 216*t*
international federations, 213–214, 215*t*, 216*t*
International Health, Racquet and Sportsclub
   Association, 139*f*
International Management Group (IMG), 266–267,
   270, 338
International Olympic Committee (IOC), 203,
   209–211, 347
   career opportunities, 217–220
International Paralympic Committee (IPC), 20,
   217, 220
international sport, 197–224
   broadcasting, 204–205, 221
   collegiate sport, foreign student athletes, 221
   competitions, 218
   corporate sponsorship, 203–204, 220

current issues, 220–223
for development and peace, 207–209
globalization of sport, 202–207
history, 200–201
licensing, 205
marketing foreign athletes, 205–206
merchandising, 205
professional sports league, 201
exhibition and regular-season games, 205
resources, 225–226
international sport management, 42–43
Internet, new media and, 419–422
Internet service providers (ISPs), 450
internship, job search, 547
interview, 559
preparing for, 422–427
invasion of privacy, 109–110
inverted pyramid, 415
IOC. *See* International Olympic Committee
IP. *See* intellectual property
IPC. *See* International Paralympic Committee
ISPs. *See* Internet service providers

J
job interview, 559–562
follow-up, 561
illegal questions, 561
preparation, 559
professional qualities, 561–562
job search, 549–552
career exploration, 550
gaining experience, 550–551
internship, 547
personal inventory, 549
process, 549, 550*f*
professional qualities, 561–562
self-analysis, 549
steps, 549–552
strategy, 541–542
Jockey club, 7
Josephson's Six Pillars of Character, 136, 136*t*
judges
high school sport, 159
youth sport, 159
judicial review, 100–101

K
key messages, 422
Knight Commission, 177
Kraft's promotion, 388–389
KSM. *See* King Sport Management

L
labor exemption, 113
labor laws, 115–119
labor relations, 116, 239–241
Ladies Professional Golf Association (LPGA), 15
Landis, Kenesaw Mountain, 238
Lanham Act, 120
LAV. *See* lifetime asset value
law, moral values, contrasted, 140
law practice only, 278
leadership role, 29
leading, 32–33
league office personnel, 249–250
league revenues, 244
league structure, 4, 11–15
league think philosophy, 239
LEED certification, 330
legacy members, 495
legal counseling, sports agency, 291
legal issues, 98–125
current issues, 123–125
high school and youth sports, 165
history, 98–99
key concepts, 99–120
key skills, 121–123
legal duty of care, 102
legality, 106
legitimate interest, 108
Levine, Matt, 55
liabilities, 79
licensed merchandise, 350
licensed products, 467–485, 468
career opportunities, 474–475
collegiate sport, 474
defined, 468
ethics, 479–480
finance, 480
history, 470–473
key principles, 476–482
legal, 480–482
MLB properties, 472
NBA properties, 473
NFL properties, 472
resources, 485
royalty, 474
trademark, 474
licensee, 473
licensors, 474
lifetime asset value (LAV), 376
lifetime value (LTV), 366
loan pools, 80

local/civic venue, 314
LOCOG. *See* London Organizing Committee for the
    Olympic Games
"London Olympics association right," 124
London organizers, 330
London Organizing Committee for the Olympic
    Games (LOCOG), 213
LPGA. *See* Ladies Professional Golf Association
LTV. *See* lifetime value
luxury tax, 93

M

Major League Baseball (MLB), 246
Major League Baseball Players Association
    (MLBPA), 239, 267, 281, 294, 473
Major League Soccer (MLS), 234–235, 385
management, 28–44
    bottom line, beyond, 43
    current issues, 41–43
    functional areas, 30–33
    history, 28–30
    key skills, 34–41
management staff, facility ownership and, 320
managing change, 40–41
marketing, 50–69
    current issues, 63–68
    history, 50–56
    key concepts, 56–62
marketing director, facility management, 324
marketing fund, 323
marketing mix
    defined, 56
    five Ps, 56–58
Mason, James G., 21
master antenna, 442
Mathare Youth Sports Association (MYSA), 207
Mayo, Elton, 29
McCormack, Mark, 50, 266, 270
media buyer, 426
media channel sponsorship, 396
media notes, 415
media planning, 426–427
media relations, 413–415
    conference calls, 417–418
    media guides, 415–416
    photography, 416
    press conferences, 415
    press releases, 415
    videography, 416–417
media revenues, 88
media training, 425
member conferences, 182

merchandising
    event management, 350
    international sport, 205
metropolitan facilities, 314
Miami Heat front office, 250–251, 251*f*
military recreation, 528
Miller, Marvin, 239–240
minority issues, diversity management, 36
MLB. *See* Major League Baseball
MLBPA. *See* Major League Baseball
    Players Association
MLB properties, 472
    licensing, 472
MLS. *See* Major League Soccer
modern Olympic Games, 7
Monday Night Football, 51, 441
monopoly, 84
moral discourse, forum for, 146
morality, 132
    absolutism, 141
    and the changing nature of work, 144
    and corruption, 142–144
    moral principles, 139
    and multiple roles, 142
    relativism, 141
    in the workplace, 140–142
moral principles, 140–141
moral reasoning, 144
moral rules, 141
morals, 132
    and work, 141
moral values, 140
motivation, 41
M-ticketing, 38
multibox, 415
multimedia, 444
MYSA. *See* Mathare Youth Sports Association

N

NAIA. *See* National Association of
    Intercollegiate Athletics
naming rights, 370–371
NASCAR. *See* National Association for Stock Car
    Auto Racing
NASL. *See* North American Soccer League
NASSM. *See* North American Society for Sport
    Management
National Ability Center, 534
National Association for Stock Car Auto Racing
    (NASCAR), 385
National Association of Intercollegiate Athletics
    (NAIA), 179

National Association of Professional Baseball Players, 12
National Basketball Association (NBA), 385, 442
National Basketball Players Association (NBPA), 240, 281
National Center for Spectator Sports Safety and Security, 329
National Collegiate Athletic Association (NCAA), 99, 176, 289, 295, 469
    career opportunities, 185–186, 548
    Division I, 178, 181–182
    Division I-A, 182
    Division I-AA, 182
    Division II, 181–182
    Division III, 181–182
    governance, 179–183
    one-school/one-vote, 179
    organizational structure, 179–183
    philosophy statement, 182
    restructuring, 179
National Environmental Education Foundation (NEEF), 526
National Federation of State High School Associations (NFSHSA), 152, 152t, 156–157, 553
National Football League (NFL), 235, 385, 440
    franchise ownership, 235–236
    ownership, 236t, 237
    players, 240
    properties, 239
National Football League Players Association (NFLPA), 281, 295
National Forest Service, 527
National Golf Course Owners Association (NGCOA), 502
national governing bodies (NGBs), 210
National Hockey League (NHL), 385, 443
    professional sport, 240, 247
National Hockey League Players Association (NHLPA), 281
National Intramural-Recreation Sports Association (NIRSA), 528–529
nationalism, 200
National Junior College Athletic Association (NJCAA), 182
National Labor Relations Act (NLRA), 115–116
National Labor Relations Board (NLRB), 115
National League, history, 11–15
National Olympic Committees (NOCs), 210, 212
    career opportunities, 220
    sponsorship programs, 222
National Park Service (NPS), recreational sport, 523, 527

National Recreation and Parks Association (NRPA), 526
national sport confederations, 219
national youth league organizations, 157–158
NB. See New Balance
NBA. See National Basketball Association
NBA league office/team front office, 249–250
NBA Properties, licensing, 473
NBPA. See National Basketball Players Association
NCAA. See National Collegiate Athletic Association
NCAA Crisis Management Team, 135
NCAA Division I college. See National Collegiate Athletic Association Division I college
NEEF. See National Environmental Education Foundation
negligence, 100, 102, 103
networking, 547
    defined, 547
networks, 437
New Balance (NB), 483
new media, 420
new media industry, 419
news releases, 415
NFL. See National Football League
NFLPA. See National Football League Players Association
NFSHSA. See National Federation of State High School Associations
NGBs. See national governing bodies
NGCOA. See National Golf Course Owners Association
NHL. See National Hockey League
NHLPA. See National Hockey League Players Association
niche sports, 353
Nike, 53
NIRSA. See National Intramural-Recreation Sports Association
NJCAA. See National Junior College Athletic Association
NLRA. See National Labor Relations Act
NLRB. See National Labor Relations Board
NOCs. See National Olympic Committees
noncommercial moral rules, 141
non-equity clubs, 496
nonprofit 501c7 clubs, 496
nonschool agencies, 155
nonschool youth sport organizations, 155–156
North American professional sports league
    exhibition and regular season games, 205
    international sport, 201, 204
    marketing foreign athletes, 205–206

North American Soccer League (NASL), 202
North American Society for Sport Management (NASSM), 21
not-for-profit, 350
NPS. *See* National Park Service
NRPA. *See* National Recreation and Parks Association

O

OCOGs. *See* Organizing Committee for the Olympic Games
Octagon, 267
officials
    high school sport, 159
    youth sport, 159
off the record, 425
Ohio University, 21
Olympic Movement Anti-Doping Code, 213
Olympics, 123–124
    broadcasting, 204–205, 221
    corporate sponsorship, 203–204, 220
    current issues, 220–223
    for development and peace, 207–209
    international federations, 213–214, 215*t*, 216*t*
    licensing, 205
    marketing foreign athletes, 205–206
    merchandising, 205
    NGBs, 214–216
    NOCs, 212
    The Olympic Partner (TOP) Programme, 210
    Paralympic Games, 216–217
    resources, 225–226
    in Russia, 352–353
    USOC, 212
    web addresses, 216*t*
The Olympic Partner (TOP) Programme, 210, 222
Olympism, 209
O'Malley, Walter, 21
one-school/one-vote, NCAA, 179
operations director, facility management, 327
oral communication, 62
oral presentation, 34–35
organizational behavior, 29
organizational chart
    athletic department, 32
    executive, 252*f*
    professional team example, 250, 252
organizational politics
    defined, 39
    tactics, 39
organizing, 31–32

Organizing Committee for the Olympic Games (OCOGs), 210, 213
    career opportunities, 219–220
    sponsorship programs, 222
orientation, 32
Outdoor Industry Association, 528
outdoor recreation, 528
    activities, 524*t*
out-of-market, 451
overly aggressive client recruitment, 294
owners' equity, 78

P

PACMail, 38
Palmer, Arnold, 270
Paralympic Games, 201, 206, 212, 216–217
parks movement, 522
participative decision making, 38
PASPA. *See* Professional and Amateur Sports Protection Act
pass-by interviews, 56
pay-per-view, 450
PED. *See* performance-enhancing drug
penetration, 442
people skills, 34
people with disabilities, diversity management, 36
percentage cap, 281
performance-enhancing drug (PED), 143
performance evaluation, high school, 160
personal care, sports agency, 291
personal inventory, job search, 549
personal selling, 364
person-centered branding, 277
PGA. *See* Professional Golfers' Association
PHPA. *See* Professional Hockey Players Association
physical therapists, high school and youth sport, 158
place, 58–59
    price, 58
    product, 56–58
    promotion, 58–59
plaintiff, 100
planning, 30–31
player development, 512–513
players association, 239–241
    sports agency and, 271
players league, 239
POCOG. *See* PyeongChang 2018 Organizing Committee
pod, 448
podcasts, 421
point-of-sale/point-of-purchase marketing, 388

postcareer planning, sports agent, 290–291
potential revenue streams, 340
pre-event tournament operations, 343
premiums, 387
premium seating, 232
price, 58
   place, 58–59
   product, 56–58
   promotion, 59–60
primetime, 439
principal, agency, 104
private club, 495
private exclusive clubs, 495
private sector, 532–534
product, 56–58
   place, 56–58
   price, 58
   promotion, 59–60
product endorsement, growth of, 272–273
product extension, 54–55
Professional and Amateur Sports Protection Act
      (PASPA), 125
professional golf, 15–18, 241–243
   charity event, 16–18
   corporate sponsorship, 17
Professional Golfers' Association (PGA), 15, 119,
      241–243, 494
Professional Hockey Players Association (PHPA), 240
professional sport, 125, 231–263
   agents, 253
   analytics, 255
   career opportunities, 249–253
   commissioner, 237–239, 249
   concussion litigation, 254
   current issues, 253–255
   drug testing, 254–255
   franchise ownership, 235–236
   franchise values and revenue generation, 244–246
   general manager, 250
   globalization, 253–254
   HGH, 254–255
   history, 234–243
   individual professional sports, 241–243
   labor relations, 239–241
   league revenues, 244
   leagues, 234–235
   legal issues, 246–247
   office personnel, 249–252
   organizational charts, 250f–252f
   ownership rules, 236–237
   race and gender, 247–249
   resources, 258–260

salary caps, 253
teams in North America, 232t
tour, 241–243
tour personnel, 252
professional sport league, 218, 234–235
   revenue sharing, 92
   salary caps, 85, 93
professional tournament, 4, 15–18, 242–243
   Corcoran, Fred, 16–18
   today, 18
profits, 77
progressive movement, sport history, 154
promotion, 59–60
   place, 59–60
   price, 58
   product, 56–58
   sales, 371
properties division, 472
psychographic, 55
public assembly facility, 316
   Americans with Disabilities Act, 330
   growing cost of, 316–319
   history, 312–314
   types, 312–314
public club, 494
publicly traded sport companies, 79, 79t
public ownership, 237
public policy, 106
public recreation, 527
public relations, 418
   event management, 348
public relations director, facility management,
      324–325
public school, sport history, 154
public sector, 532–534
punitive damages, 102
PyeongChang 2018 Organizing Committee
      (POCOG), 213

Q
Q-School tournament, 243

R
race
   collegiate sport, 190
   professional sport, 247–249
radio, history, 436, 437
ratings, 448
rational basis, 109
reach, 455
reasonable accommodation, 118, 119

recreational sport, 521–539
  academic course preparation, 532*t*
  career opportunities, 529–530
    job search strategies, 530–531
    professional preparation, 531
  current issues, 531–532
    ADA, 534–535
    public and private sectors, 532–534
    risk management, 535–536
  history, 522–524
  participation trends, 524–526, 525*f*
  positions, 530*t*
  resources, 538–539
  segments
    campus recreation, 528–529
    community-based recreation, 527
    military recreation, 528
    outdoor recreation, 528
    public recreation, 527
    therapeutic recreation, 529
references, 556–558
registration system, event management, 344–345
relationship marketing, 50, 61–62
relativism, 141
release of liability, 106
religious events, 316
remote production facility, 447
research, sport marketing, purposes, 55–56
reserve clause, 271
reserve list, 271
reserve system, 271
resume, 553–556
  effective, 553–556
  sample, 557*f*
retainer, 430
retransmission consent, 447
return on investment (ROI), 81, 384
revenue generation, franchise values and, 244–246
revenues, 77
  media, 88
  median generated, 90, 90*t*
revenue sharing, 85, 92, 93, 237, 441
rights fees, 436, 448–447
rightsholders, 436
risk, 82
risk management, 100, 535
  event management, 342–343
  recreational sport, rival leagues, 84
ROI. *See* return on investment
Rooney Rule, 248
roster management, 189
royalty, 474

Rozelle, Alvin "Pete, 440
Rozelle, Pete, 440
Russia, Olympic games in, 352–353

S
sabermetrics, 255
salary caps, 85, 92, 93, 253
sales inventory, 369
sales promotion, 385
sales promotion, sport sponsorship
  cross-promotion, emergence of, 389–390
  in-store promotions
    contests and sweepstakes, 387–388
    coupons, 388
    point-of-sale/point-of-purchase marketing, 388
    premiums, 387
    sampling, 388
  in-venue promotions, 386–387
  Kraft's promotion, 388–389
sampling, 388
saturated markets, 321
school athletic directors, 158
scientific management, 29
script, 344
seasonal events, 316
SEC. *See* Southeastern Conference
secondary meaning, 120
security, facility management, 328–329
segmentation, 60
  demographic, 60
  ethnic marketing, 60
  generational marketing, 60
  geographic, 60
  psychographic, 60
  usage, 60
self-examinations, ethical issues, 145–146
self-governance, 234
senior women's administrator, collegiate sport, 185
service marks, 120
sex discrimination, high and youth school sport, 164–165
SFX sports, 273–274
share, 449
Sherman Act, 112, 113
SIA. *See* Snowsports Industries America
SID. *See* sports information director
signage inventory, 370
signage salesperson, facility management, 327–328
simulcasts, 453
single entity, legal, 113
single-entity structure, 235
Sixteen Women, 19

SMAANZ. *See* Sport Management Association of
  Australia and New Zealand
SMARTS. *See* Sport Management Arts and
  Science Society
Snowsports Industries America (SIA), 533
soccer-specific stadiums (SSS), 311
Southeastern Conference (SEC), 384
Spalding, Albert G., 52, 470
SPARTA. *See* Sports Agent Responsibility and
  Trust Act
specialized agencies, 341
speculation, 425
sponsor, 438
sponsorship, 50, 51, 52–54, 323, 372–373, 449
  agencies, 398
  Olympics, 222
  packages, 390–392
  sport sponsorship platforms
    athlete sponsorship, 395
    event sponsorship, 396
    facility sponsorship, 396
    governing body sponsorship, 393
    media sponsorship, 395–396
    sport-specific sponsorship, 396
    team sponsorship, 393, 395
Sponsorship Research International (SRi), 397
sponsorship sales, 221–222
sponsorship salesperson, facility management,
  327–328
sport broadcasting, 435–459. *See also* broadcasting
sport economics, 83–85
sport event management, 337–356. *See also* event
  management
sport event manager, 342
sport events, 315
Sport for All Movement, 206–207
sport franchises, owned by corporations, 78, 79*t*
sport industry
  economic magnitude, 74–76
  financial challenges, 89–93
  governmental scrutiny, 125
sporting goods, 468
sporting goods companies, 219
sporting goods equipment, 473
sporting goods industry, 467–485
  brand's image, 478
  career opportunities, 474–475
  challenges, brand, 478–479
  defined, 468
  endorsements, 477–478
  entrepreneur, 470
  ethics, 479–480

finance, 480
global sourcing, 479
history, 470–473
industry structure, 473
key principles, 476–482
legal issues, 480–482
management, 476–477
marketing, 477–478
resources, 485
sporting goods trade association, 473
sport law, 98
sport management
  as academic field
    history, 20–22
    management principles, 28–44. *See also* marketing
    marketing principles, 50–69. *See also* marketing
  ethical issues. *See* ethical issues
  financial and economic principles, 73–93. *See also*
    financial principles
  history, 4–22
  legal issues, 98–125
  myths, 546–549
  pay level, 549
  reality check, 546–549
Sport Management Arts and Science Society
  (SMARTS), 21
Sport Management Association of Australia and
  New Zealand (SMAANZ), 22
sport management degree
  advantages, 546–547
  value of, 546–547
sport management firm affiliated with a law firm, 279
sport management/marketing agency, 338–341, 351
  full-service agency, 341
  grassroots program, 340
  in-house agency, 341
  specialized agencies, 341
  Sport Sponsor FactBook, 340
  types, 341
sport management programs, 547
sport management structure, 4, 9
sport marketing, 50–69, 547. *See also* marketing
  current issues, 63–68
  defined, 50
  historical development, 50–56
  key skills, 62
  mix, 56–60
  products, 56–58
  research, purposes, 55–56
  segmentation, 60
  social media's role in, 65b–66b
  vs. traditional marketing, 57*t*

sport organizations
  financial flows in, 77–83
  global strategy, 202
sport property, defined, 338
sports account executive, 283
sports agency, 265–300
  career opportunities, 282–292
  current issues, 292–297
  development of competing leagues and, 272
  ethical issues, 292–295
  evolution of agencies, 273–275
  fees, 280–282
  financial planning and, 272
  firms, 278–282
  growth of industry, 271–275
  history, 269–278
  key skills, 291–292
  marketing, 285–287
  players association, 271
  product endorsement opportunities and, 272–273
  regulation, 295–297
  representing coaches and managers, 277–278
  representing individual athletes, 275–277
  reserve system, 271
  resources, 300–302
sports agent, 267
  career and post-career planning, 290–291
  contract negotiation
    athlete's contract, 283–284
    coach's contract, 284–285
  defined, 283
  dispute resolution, 291
  endorsement contract, 287–288
  financial planning, 289–290
  marketing, 285–287
  personal care, 291
Sports Agent Responsibility and Trust Act
      (SPARTA), 296
sport sales, 359–379
  advertising inventory, 370
  after marketing, 366–367
  benefit selling, 365
  community programs, 371–372
  direct mail, 363
  eduselling, 365–366
  flex book, 365
  history, 360–361
  hospitality inventory, 369–370
  key skills, 368–369
  methods, 362–368
  miscellaneous inventory, 372

naming rights, 370–371
online inventory, 371
personal selling, 364–365
promotions inventory, 371
sales function, 361
sales inventory, 369–373
signage inventory, 370
sport setting, 362
sport sponsorship, 372–373
strategies, 362–368
telemarketing, 364
ticket inventory, 369–370
upselling, 365
sports apparel, 473
Sports Broadcasting Act of 1961, 114, 441
sports event managers, 282
sports events, 310
sports information director (SID), 412
sports marketing representative, 282–283
Sports Marketing Surveys, 340
sport sponsorship, 372–373, 381–406
  activation, 384
  agencies, 398
  athlete sponsorship, 395
  contests, 387–388
  corporate partners
    MLB, 390, 394t
    NBA, 390, 392t
    NFL, 390, 393t
    NHL, 390, 391t
    Olympics, 390, 394t
  coupons, 388
  cross promotion, 389–390
  current issues, 398–401, 404
  ethnic marketing, 398–399
  evaluating, 397–398
  event sponsorship, 396
  facility sponsorship, 396
  free standing inserts, 388
  governing body sponsorship, 393
  history, 382–385
  Kraft's promotion, 388–389
  marriage with gambling, 400–401, 404
  media sponsorship, 395–396
  overcommercialization, 400
  platforms, 392–396
  point of purchase, 388
  point of sale, 388
  premiums, 387
  resources, 405–406
  return on investment (ROI), 384

sales promotion, 385–390
    in store promotion, 387–388
    in venue promotion, 386–387
sampling, 388
sponsorship packages, 390–392
sport specific sponsorship, 396
sweepstakes, 387–388
team sponsorship, 393–395
top U.S. sponsors, 383, 383*t*
sport tourism, 206
SRi. *See* Sponsorship Research International
SSS. *See* soccer-specific stadiums
stadium, 310, 313
    financing, 316–319
        mechanisms, 317–319
    history, 313
    modern construction, 310–311
    single-purpose, 311
    soccer-specific, 311
stakeholders, 411
standard/uniform player contract, 271
standing committees, 499
state action, 107–108
state actor, 107
state associations, high school and youth sport, 157
statutes, 98
Stop the Seventy Tour Committee (STST), 201
streamed, 445
strict scrutiny, 108
STST. *See* Stop the Seventy Tour Committee
student-athlete services, collegiate sport, 185
subscriber fees, 445
sustainability, facility management, 329–330
SWA. *See* senior women's administrator
sweepstakes, 387
symbiotic relationship, 436
syndicate, 449

T
target markets, 447
    defined, 50
    products, 54–55
taxes, financing, 317–318
Taylor, Frederick, 28–29
team front-office
    general manager, 250
    organizational chart, 251*f*
    personnel, 250–252
team sponsorship, 393–395
technology management, 37–38, 42
telemarketing, 364

television
    broadcasting, 445
    event management, 349
    international sport, 204–206, 211
television markets, 442
territorial rights, 237
theaters, 315
therapeutic recreation, 529
thoroughbred racing, 5–7
ticket rebate, 322
ticket sales
    event management, 348–349
    outsourcing of, 374–377
    price comparisons, 63
    sales inventory, 369–370
tiers, 450
time-buy, 448
timeshift, 444
Title IX, 110–112
    collegiate sport, 188–190
    high school sport, 164–165
Title VII, 117–118
tort, defined, 102
tort liability, 102–103
tournament operations, event management, 343–344
    script, 344
trade associations, 473
trademark, 474
    defined, 119
trade shows, 315–316
traditional branding *vs.* person-centered
        branding, 287*t*
trainers, high school and youth sport, 158
training, 32
trashsports, 442

U
UA. *See* Under Armour
UAAA. *See* Uniform Athlete Agent Act
UCLA. *See* University of California–Los Angeles
uncertainty of outcome concept, 91
Under Armour (UA), 468
Uniform Athlete Agent Act (UAAA), 296
uniform player contract, 271
United States
    foreign language sports networks in, 453
    international broadcast of, 453
    international sport programming in, 452
United States Australian Football League
        (USAFL), 224
United States Olympic Committee (USOC), 212

universal design, 331–332
University of California–Los Angeles (UCLA), 472
university sport management program
    growth, 21
    history, 20–22
    Ohio University, 21
university venues, 313–314
unreasonable search and seizure, 109
upselling, 365
USAFL. *See* United States Australian Football League
USDA. *See* U.S. Department of Agriculture
U.S. Department of Agriculture (USDA), 527, 534
USOC. *See* United States Olympic Committee
U.S. Olympic Committee (USOC), 124

V
value added concept, 75
Veeck, Bill, 54–55
vicarious liability, 103–104
vice-president in charge of broadcasting, 456
videography, media relations, 416–417
volunteer management, event management, 345–346

W
WADA. *See* World Anti-Doping Agency
waiver and release of liability form, event
        management, 342, 343
waivers, 106
Wasserman Media Group (WMG), 274, 275
web conferencing, 430
website, 419
website development, event management, 350
WFSGI. *See* World Federation of Sporting
        Goods Industry
William Morris Endeavor (WME), 274
WME. *See* William Morris Endeavor
WMG. *See* Wasserman Media Group
WNBA. *See* Women's NBA
women
    collegiate sport, 190
    diversity management, 36
    gender equity, 164–165, 189
    high school sport, 164–165

    in intercollegiate athletics, 177–179
    in sport management, 18–20
Women's NBA (WNBA), 235
workforce, diversity in, 547
workplace, morality in, 140–142
    consequences, 146–147
    forum for moral discourse, 146
    self-examination, 145–146
Works Progress Administration (WPA), 156
World Anti-Doping Agency (WADA), 222
World Federation of Sporting Goods Industry
        (WFSGI), 219
World Sports Entertainment (WSE), 294
WPA. *See* Works Progress Administration
written communication, 62
WSE. *See* World Sports Entertainment

Y
Young Men's Christian Association (YMCA), 155,
        522, 523, 527
youth league directors, 158–159
youth sport, 151–170. *See also* high school sport
    career opportunities, 158–159
    coach, 158
    ethics, 163–165
    gender equity, 164–165
    governance, 156–158
    high school sport, 164–165
    history, 153–156
    judge, 159
    marketing, 162–163
    national youth league organization, 157–158
    nineteenth century, 153–154
    nonschool agencies, 155
    official, 159
    physical therapist, 158
    sex discrimination, 164–165
    state association, 157
    trainer, 158
    twentieth century, 154–155

Z
zero-base budgeting, event management, 342